London

timeout.com/london

Published by Time Out Guides Ltd, a wholly owned subsidiary of Time Out Group Ltd.
Time Out and the Time Out logo are trademarks of Time Out Group Ltd.

10 9 8 7 6 5 4 3 2 1

This edition first published in Great Britain in 2005 by Ebury
Ebury is a division of The Random House Group Ltd,
20 Vauxhall Bridge Road, London SW1V 2SA

Random House Australia Pty Limited, 20 Alfred Street, Milsons Point, Sydney, New South Wales 2061, Australia
Random House New Zealand Limited, 18 Poland Road, Glenfield, Auckland 10, New Zealand
Random House South Africa (Pty) Limited, Endulini, 5A Jubilee Road, Parktown 2193, South Africa

Random House UK Limited Reg. No. 954009

Distributed in USA by Publishers Group West
1700 Fourth Street, Berkeley, California 94710

Distributed in Canada by Penguin Canada Ltd
10 Alcorn Avenue, Toronto, Ontario, Canada M4V 3B2

For further distribution details, see www.timeout.com

ISBN 1-904978-29-0

A CIP catalogue record for this book is available from the British Library

Colour reprographics by Icon, Crowne House, 56-58 Southwark Street, London SE1 1UN

Printed and bound by Cayfosa-Quebecor, Ctra. De Caldes, KM 3 08 130 Sta, Perpètua de Mogoda, Barcelona, Spain

Time Out Guides Limited
Universal House
251 Tottenham Court Road
London W1T 7AB
Tel + 44 (0)20 7813 3000
Fax + 44 (0)20 7813 6001
Email guides@timeout.com
www.timeout.com

Editorial
Editor Ruth Jarvis
Deputy Editor Sam Le Quesne
Copy Editors Edoardo Albert, Simon Coppock
Listings Checkers Rob Norman, Cathy Limb, Jill Emeny
Proofreaders Tamsin Shelton, Angela Jameson
Indexer Jonathan Cox

Editorial/Managing Director Peter Fiennes
Series Editor Ruth Jarvis
Deputy Series Editor Lesley McCave
Business Manager Gareth Garner
Guides Co-ordinator Holly Pick
Accountant Sarah Bostock

Design
Art Director Mandy Martin
Deputy Art Director Scott Moore
Senior Designer Tracey Ridgewell
Designer Oliver Knight
Junior Designer Chrissy Mouncey
Digital Imaging Dan Conway
Ad Make-up Charlotte Blythe

Picture Desk
Picture Editor Jael Marschner
Deputy Picture Editor Tracey Kerrigan
Picture Researcher Ivy Lahon, Monica Roche

Advertising
Sales Director Mark Phillips
Sales Manager Alison Gray
Advertising Sales Michael MacDonald, Jason Trotman, Matthew Salandy
Advertising Assistant Lucy Butler
Copy Controller Amy Nelson

Marketing
Marketing Director Mandy Martinez
US Publicity & Marketing Associate Rosella Albanese

Production
Production Director Mark Lamond
Production Controller Samantha Furniss

Time Out Group
Chairman Tony Elliott
Managing Director Mike Hardwick
Group Financial Director Richard Waterlow
Group Commercial Director Lesley Gill
Group General Manager Nichola Coulthard
Group Circulation Director Jim Heinemann
Group Art Director John Oakey
Online Managing Director David Pepper
Group Production Director Steve Proctor
Group IT Director Simon Chappell

Contributors
Introduction Ruth Jarvis. **History** *Cockneys – or Mockneys?, The Great Stink, Gimme Shelter* Juliet Gardiner. **London Today** Rebecca Taylor. **Architecture** David Littlefield. **Where to Stay** Hugh Graham. **Sightseeing Introduction** Ruth Jarvis. **The South Bank & Bankside** Charlie Godfrey-Faussett (*My kind of town* Joseph Bindloss). **The City** John Watson (*The London Stone* Zoë Strimple). **Holborn & Clerkenwell** Adam Barnes (*Walk this way* John Nicholson). **Bloomsbury & Fitzrovia** Sam Le Quesne, Zoë Strimple (*Cross purposes* Rebecca Taylor). **Marylebone** Lisa Ritchie. **Mayfair & St James's** Adam Barnes (*Fantastic voyagers* Ruth Jarvis). **Soho** Will Fulford-Jones (*Go-go gone* Joseph Bindloss). **Covent Garden & St Giles's** Edoardo Albert (*Don't go there* Ruth Jarvis). **Westminster** Charlie Godfrey-Faussett (*Watermarks* Adam Barnes). **South Kensington & Knightsbridge** Adam Barnes (*Water palaver* Ronnie Haydon). **Chelsea** Adam Barnes (*Chelsea Pensioners* Ronnie Haydon). **North London** Dominic Wells. **East London** Joseph Bindloss (*London Muslim Centre, Rich Mix* Rebecca Taylor). **South-east London** Ronnie Haydon (*My kind of town* Joseph Bindloss). **South-west London** Hugh Graham (**Watermarks** Rhodri Marsden). **West London** Mary Helen Trent (*A load of hot [dry] air* Malcolm Shifrin, *Literature with attitude* Lily Dunn. **Restaurants & Cafés** Sam Le Quesne and contributors to *Time Out London Eating & Drinking* (*RIP, classic caffs* Bob Stanley). **Pubs & Bars** Natalie Whittle and contributors to *Time Out Pubs & Bars*. Shops & Services Jan Fuscoe and contributors to *Time Out Shopping* (*Quality street* Stephanie King, *Bargain abasement* Charlotte Williamson, *Let us eat cake!* Guy Dimond, Lily Dunn, Dan Leppard, *Mushroom for manoeuvre* Sebastian Burford. **Festivals & Events** Kathryn Miller. **Children** Ronnie Haydon. **Comedy** Sharon Lougher. **Dance** Allen Robertson (*Super troupers* Sam Le Quesne). **Film** Nick Bradshaw. **Galleries** Rebecca Geldard (**Space invaders** Kelley Knox). Gay & Lesbian Hugh Graham (*Walk this way* Ottilie Godfrey). Music Peter Watts (*Asian explosion, Grime time* John Lewis). **Nightlife** Simon Baird. **Sport & Fitness** Sam Le Quesne, Natalie Whittle (*The rise of the Roman empire* Andrew Shields, *The icing on the wall* Cyrus Shahrad). **Theatre** Natalie Whittle. **Trips Out of Town** Lily Dunn. **Getting around** Cathy Limb. **Resources A-Z** Ruth Jarvis, Cathy Limb. **Further Reference** *Blog jam* Alice Fordham.

Maps JS Graphics (john@jsgraphics.co.uk).

Photography by Andrew Brackenbury and Jonathan Perugia, except: pages 10, 39 Topham; page 13 AKG; page 14 Heritage Images; page 17 Bridgeman Art Library; page 22 Getty Images; page 26 Johnson Banks; page 40 PA Photos; page 96 Kelly Burwitz; pages 111, 204, 248, 249, 253 Rob Greig; page 117 The Royal Collection © 2004, Her Majesty Queen Elizabeth II,by Derry Moore; page 147 Rex Features; page 168 Corbis; page 174 Pierce Allerdyce; pages 181, 317 Hadley Kincade; pages 186, 192, 241, 251, 252, 315, 357 Heloise Bergman; page 191, 215 Britta Jaschinski; page 195 Ming Tang-Evans; pages 197, 221,222, 225, 229 Thomas Skovsende; pages 201, 208, 209, 231, 246, 249 Tricia De Courcy Ling; pages 216, 330, 341, 342, 347, 348 Alys Tomlinson; page 226 Matt Carr; pages 262, 265 Britain on View; page 281 Cillian Murphy; page 291 Elisabeth Blanchet; page 294 Paul Mattsson; pages 297, 298, 299 Pierce Allerdyce; page 303 Grant Smith; page 308 Dean Chalkley; page 312 Will Fenning; pages 317, 318, 323, 324 David Swindells; page 326 Empics; page 329 Janie Airey; page 339 Hugo Glendinning; page 351 Paul Carter. The Following images were provided by the featured establishment/artist: pages 37, 54, 87, 157, 189, 242, 258, 260, 278, 307

The Editor would like to thank Dave Calhoun, Kerry Collins, Sarah Guy, Will Fulford-Jones, Andrew Shields, Chris Salmon, Samir Savant and previous *Time Out London* contributors, on whose work parts of this book are based.

Contents

South-west London 174
West London 182

Eat, Drink, Shop 191

Restaurants & Cafés 192
Pubs & Bars 220
Shops & Services 233

Arts & Entertainment 259

Festivals & Events 260
Children 268
Comedy 275
Dance 278
Film 281
Galleries 287
Gay & Lesbian 294
Music 301
Nightlife 315
Sport & Fitness 325
Theatre 332
  Map: Theatreland 333

Trips Out of Town 341

Getting there 342
  Map: Trips Out of Town 343
Bath 345
Brighton 347
Cambridge 349
Canterbury 350
Oxford 351
Stratford-upon-Avon 353
Winchester 353
Seaside towns 357

Directory 359

Getting Around 360
Resources A-Z 366
Further Reference 379
Index 381
Advertisers' Index 390

Maps 391

London Overview 392
Street Maps 394
Street Index 406
Central London by Area 412
London Underground 414

Introduction 6

In Context 9

History 10
London Today 26
Architecture 31
Gangland London 39

Where to Stay 43

Where to Stay 45

Sightseeing 71

Introduction 72
The South Bank & Bankside 75
The City 88
Holborn & Clerkenwell 101
Bloomsbury & Fitzrovia 106
Marylebone 112
Mayfair & St James's 115
Soho 121
Covent Garden & St Giles's 126
Westminster 132
South Kensington & Knightsbridge 140
Chelsea 145
North London 148
East London 157
South-east London 167

Introduction

Introduction

London is a bewildering place to those who visit for the first time. And the second, and the third. Who could so swiftly decipher the arcane language of postcodes, the beautiful but skewed tube map or the random street patterns, or fully absorb the sheer size of the place, along with the impossibility of getting from point A to point B, especially not *fast*? This is a city where it is no shame to be seen with your nose buried in the *A-Z*, for only locals who never leave their neighbourhood could ever know where they are all the time, and never leaving your neighbourhood is not something to be admired.

London has always been chaotic. For most of its life it has been by far the biggest city in the UK (and for centuries in the world), and a centre not just of government but of finance, trade, opportunism, empire and dirty industry. Human traffic has surged through it for a millennium, from and to the rest of the country and the globe. More than other capitals it has been scourged by disease, disaster and alcohol – and sometimes even by its own inhabitants.

Enjoying London to its fullest extent is partly about submitting to its chaos. Throughout history people from all over the world have, like you, been lost on its confusing streets. Take comfort from the fact that nobody cares or judges you, and that at least people are on the streets. In a city where a private car is usually a liability, London's residents mix on the tube and on the roads. It might be our way not to acknowledge anyone else's presence, but we're certainly aware of the thousands of varied others who share our trajectories.

Somehow, in an era when every square foot of the city is recorded on security camera and endless websites offer up people's urban experiences, London remains unknowable and mysterious. Yet still people find their wave on its open sea. Scenes spark into life, the right people meet, an idea takes fire. Life goes off.

So use this book to master the city's geography, learn its transport tricks and experience the best it has to offer – and it's in a purple patch at the moment for restaurants and bars, art and architecture. Appreciate the fact that our writers, all die-hard Londoners, have taken you to their own private corners of the city. But also put it in your pocket every now and again, and see where the current takes you. Should you find you need it, we have included a street index with our maps for instant reorientation. It starts on page 406. And if anyone looks at you funny, pity the buggers.

ABOUT TIME OUT GUIDES

This is the 13th edition of the *Time Out London Guide*, one of the expanding series of *Time Out* guides produced by the people behind London and New York's successful listings magazines. Our guides are written and updated by resident experts who have striven to provide you with all the most up-to-date information you'll need to explore the city or read up on its background, whether you're a local or a first-time visitor.

THE LIE OF THE LAND

Thanks to the chaotic street plan – or, rather, the lack of one – London is one of the most complicated of all major world cities to find your way around. To make it a little easier, we've included an area designation for every venue in this guide. Our area divisions are based on local usage and are clearly shown on the colour-coded map on page 394. Each entry also has a grid references that points to our street maps at the back of the book (starting on page 394).

ESSENTIAL INFORMATION

For all the practical information you might need for visiting the area – including visa and customs information, details of local transport, a listing of emergency numbers and a directory of useful websites – turn to the Directory chapter at the back of this guide. It starts on page 360.

THE LOWDOWN ON THE LISTINGS

We have tried to make this book as easy to use and practically useful as possible. Addresses, phone numbers, transport information, opening times and admission prices are all included. However, owners and managers can change their arrangements at any time. Before you go out of your way, we'd advise you to phone ahead to check opening times and other particulars. While every effort and care has been made to ensure the accuracy of the information contained in this guide, the publishers cannot accept responsibility for any errors it may contain.

PRICES AND PAYMENT

In the listings, we have noted which of the
following credit cards are accepted: American
Express (AmEx), Diners Club (DC), MasterCard
(MC) and Visa (V). Some venues will also accept
other cards, such as Delta, Switch or JCB. Some
of the major sights, designated 'LP', offer
discounts to London Pass holders, and some to
members of English Heritage (EH) and the
National Trust (NT). For details, *see p73*.

The prices we've listed in this guide should be
treated as guidelines, not gospel. If prices vary
wildly from those we've quoted, ask whether
there's a good reason. We aim to give the best
and most up-to-date advice, so please let us
know if you've been badly treated or
overcharged.

TELEPHONE NUMBERS

The area code for London is 020; regular
numbers have eight digits in two groups of four.

The 020 code is not used internally and is not
given in our listings. From abroad, dial your
country's exit code (01 in the United States),
followed by 44 (the international code for the
UK), then 20 for London (dropping the first
zero of the area code) and the eight-digit
number. Mobile phone numbers have a
five-digit code, usually starting 07, then a
six-digit number. Freephone numbers start
0800, national-rate numbers 0870 and local-
rate numbers 0845.

MAPS

The map section at the back of this book
includes a trips out of town map, orientation
and neighbourhood maps of the London area,
and street maps of most of central London,
with a comprehensive street index. The maps
start on page 392.

LET US KNOW WHAT YOU THINK

We hope you enjoy *Time Out London*, and we'd
like to know what you think of it. We welcome
your tips for places to include in future editions
and take note of your criticism of our choices.
There's a reader's reply card at the back of this
book for your feedback, or you can email us at
guides@timeout.com.

There is an online version of this book,
along with guides to over 45 other
international cities, at **www.timeout.com**.

Discover Apsley House - The Duke of Wellington's London Town House.

An aristocratic house with a great past and full of English history.

See where the Duke of Wellington displayed his remarkable trophies and outstanding art collection including works by Velazquez, Goya, Rubens and Van Dyck.

149 Piccadilly, Hyde Park Corner, London W1J 7N

Tel: 020 7499 5676   Open: Tuesdays - Sundays

www.english-heritage.org.uk/apsleyhouse

ENGLISH HERITAGE

In Context

History   **10**
London Today   **26**
Architecture   **31**
Gangland London   **39**

Features

Cockneys – or Mockneys?   15
The Great Stink   18
Gimme shelter   22
Key events   25
No butts?   29
Cloud capp'd towers   37

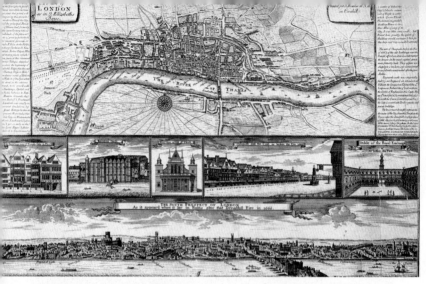

The City of London, 1560, population approximately 120,000.

History

From Londinium to dominion.

The 12th-century chronicler Geoffrey of Monmouth would have it that London was founded by the Trojan prince Brutus and run by a race of heroic giants descended from the Celtic King Lud. The truth is rather more prosaic. Though Celtic tribes lived in scattered communities along the banks of the Thames prior to the arrival of the Romans in Britain, there's no evidence to suggest that there was a settlement on the site of the future metropolis before the invasion of the Emperor Claudius' legions in AD 43. During the Romans' conquest of the country, they forded the Thames at its shallowest point and, later, built a timber bridge here (near the site of today's London Bridge). Over the following decade, a settlement developed on the north side of this crossing.

During the first two centuries AD, the Romans built roads, towns and forts in the area, and trade flourished. Progress was brought to a halt in AD 61 when Boudicca, the widow of an East Anglian chieftain, rebelled against the Imperial forces who had seized her land, flogged her and raped her daughters. She led the Iceni in a savage revolt, destroying the Roman colony at Colchester and then marching on London. The inhabitants were massacred and the settlement burned to the ground.

After order was restored, the town was rebuilt and, around AD 200, a two-mile long, 18-foot (six-metre) high wall constructed around it. Chunks of the wall survive today, and the names of the original gates – Ludgate, Newgate, Bishopsgate and Aldgate – are preserved on the map of the city. The street known as London Wall traces part of its original course.

By the fourth century, racked by barbarian invasions and internal strife, the Empire was in decline. In 410 the last troops were withdrawn and London became a ghost town. The Roman way of life vanished, their only enduring legacies being roads and early Christianity.

INTO THE DARK AGES

During the fifth and sixth centuries, history gives way to legend. The Saxons crossed the North Sea and settled in eastern and southern England, apparently avoiding the ruins of London; they built farmsteads and trading posts outside the walls.

Pope Gregory sent Augustine to convert the English to Christianity in 596. Ethelbert, Saxon King of Kent, proved a willing convert, and consequently Augustine was appointed the first Archbishop of Canterbury. Since then, the Kentish city has remained the centre of the English Christian Church. London's first Bishop, though, was Mellitus: one of Augustine's missionaries, he converted the East Saxon King Sebert and, in 604, founded a wooden cathedral dedicated to St Paul inside the old city walls. On Sebert's death, his fickle followers gave up the faith and reverted to paganism, but later generations of Christians rebuilt what is now St Paul's Cathedral.

London, meanwhile, continued to expand. The Venerable Bede, writing in 731, described 'Lundenwic' as 'the mart of many nations resorting to it by land and sea'. This probably refers to a settlement west of the Roman city in the area of today's Aldwych (Old English for 'old settlement'). During the ninth century the city faced a new danger from across the North Sea: the Vikings. The city was sacked in 841 and, in 851, the Danish raiders returned with 350 ships, leaving London in ruins. It was not until 886 that King Alfred of Wessex – aka Alfred the Great – regained the city, soon re-establishing London as a major trading centre with a merchant navy and new wharfs at Billingsgate and Queenhithe.

Throughout the tenth century the Saxon city prospered. Churches were built, parishes established and markets set up. However, the 11th century brought more harassment from the warlike Vikings, and the English were even forced to accept a Danish king, Cnut (Canute, 1016-40), during whose reign London replaced Winchester as the capital of England.

In 1042 the throne reverted to an Englishman, Edward the Confessor, who devoted himself to building the grandest church in England two miles west of the City at Thorney ('the isle of brambles'). He replaced the timber church of St Peter's with a huge abbey, 'the West Minster' (Westminster Abbey; consecrated in December 1065), and moved his court to the new Palace of Westminster. A week after the consecration, Edward died and was buried in his new church. London now grew around two hubs: Westminster, as the centre for the royal court, government and law, and the City of London, as the commercial centre.

1066 AND ALL THAT

On Edward's death, there was a succession dispute. William, Duke of Normandy, claimed that the Confessor, his cousin, had promised him the English Crown, but the English instead chose Edward's brother-in-law Harold. Piqued, William gathered an army and invaded; on 14 October 1066 he defeated Harold at the Battle of Hastings in Sussex and marched on London. City elders had little option but to offer William the throne, and the conqueror was crowned in Westminster Abbey on Christmas Day, 1066.

Recognising the need to win over the prosperous City merchants by negotiation rather than force, William granted the Bishop and burgesses of London a charter – still kept at Guildhall – that acknowledged their rights and independence in return for taxes. But, 'against the fickleness of the vast and fierce population', he also ordered strongholds to be built alongside the city wall, including the White Tower (the tallest building in the Tower of London) and the now-lost Baynard's Castle at Blackfriars. The earliest surviving written account of contemporary London was written 40 years later by a monk, William Fitz Stephen, who conjured up the walled city and the pastures and woodland outside the perimeter.

POWER PLAYS

In the growing city of London, much of the politics of the Middle Ages – the late 12th to the late 15th centuries – revolved around a constant three-way struggle for power between the king and the aristocracy, the Church, and the Lord Mayor and city guilds.

'Relations between the monarch and the City were never easy.'

The king and his court frequently travelled to other parts of the kingdom and abroad in the early Middle Ages. However, during the 14th and 15th centuries, the Palace of Westminster became the seat of law and government. The noblemen and bishops who attended court built themselves palatial houses along the Strand from the City to Westminster, with gardens stretching to the river.

The Model Parliament, which agreed the principles of government, was held in Westminster Hall in 1295, presided over by Edward I and attended by barons, clergy and representatives of knights and burgesses. The first step towards establishing personal rights and political liberty – not to mention curbing the power of the king – had already been taken in 1215 with the signing of the Magna Carta by King John. Later, in the 14th century, subsequent assemblies gave rise to the House of Lords (which met at the Palace of Westminster) and the House of Commons (which met in the Chapter House at Westminster Abbey).

Relations between the monarch and the City were never easy. Londoners guarded their privileges with self-righteous intransigence, and resisted all attempts by successive kings to squeeze money out of them to finance wars and building projects. Subsequent kings were forced to turn to Jewish and Lombard moneylenders,

but the City merchants were as intolerant of foreigners as of the royals. Rioting, persecution and the occasional lynching and pogrom were all commonplace in medieval London.

The privileges granted to the City merchants under Norman kings, allowing independence and self-regulation, were extended by the monarchs who followed, in return for financial favours. In 1191, during the reign of Richard I, the City of London was formally recognised as a commune – a self-governing community – and in 1197 it won control of the Thames, which included lucrative fishing rights that the City retained until 1857. In 1215 King John confirmed the city's right 'to elect every year a mayor', a position of great authority with power over the Sheriff and the Bishop of London. A month later, the Mayor had joined the rebel barons in signing the Magna Carta.

Over the next two centuries, the power and influence of the trade and craft guilds – later known as the City Livery Companies – increased as trade with Europe grew, and the wharfs by London Bridge were crowded with imports such as fine cloth, furs, wine, spices and precious metals. Port dues and taxes were paid to Customs officials including part-time poet Geoffrey Chaucer, whose *Canterbury Tales* were the first published work of English literature.

Alfred the Great merchant. *See p11.*

> **'These appalling conditions provided a breeding ground for the greatest catastrophe of the Middle Ages.'**

The City's markets, already established, drew produce from miles around: livestock at Smithfield, fish at Billingsgate and poultry at Leadenhall. The street markets, or 'cheaps', around Westcheap (now Cheapside) and Eastcheap were crammed with a variety of goods. As commerce increased, foreign traders and craftsmen settled around the port; the population within the city wall grew from about 18,000 in 1100 to well over 50,000 in the 1340s.

DISEASE AND DISORDER

Perhaps unsurprisingly, lack of hygiene became a serious problem in the City. Water was provided in cisterns at Cheapside and elsewhere, but the supply, which came more or less direct from the Thames, was limited and polluted. The street called Houndsditch was so named because Londoners threw their dead animals into the furrow that formed the City's eastern boundary. There was no proper sewerage system; in the streets around Smithfield (the Shambles), butchers dumped the entrails of slaughtered animals.

These appalling conditions provided the breeding ground for the greatest catastrophe of the Middle Ages: the Black Death of 1348 and 1349, which killed about 30 per cent of England's population. The plague came to London from Europe, carried by rats on ships. Although the epidemic abated, it recurred in London several times during the next three centuries, each time devastating the population.

The outbreaks of disease left the labour market short-handed, causing unrest among the overworked peasants. The imposition of a poll tax of a shilling a head proved the final straw, leading to the Peasants' Revolt of 1381. Thousands marched on London, led by Jack Straw from Essex and Wat Tyler from Kent. In the rioting and looting that followed, the Savoy Palace on the Strand was destroyed, the Archbishop of Canterbury was murdered and hundreds of prisoners were set free. When the 14-year-old Richard II rode out to Smithfield to face the rioters, Wat Tyler was fatally stabbed by Lord Mayor William Walworth. The other ringleaders were subsequently rounded up and hanged. But no more poll taxes were imposed.

THE TUDORS AND STUARTS

Under the Tudor monarchs (who reigned from 1485 until 1603) and spurred by the discovery of America and the ocean routes to Africa and the

M. WILLIAM

SHAKESPEARES

COMEDIES,
HISTORIES, and
TRAGEDIES.

Publifhed according to the True Originall Copies.

Drama, and the Bard, flowered in the 1500s.

Orient, London became one of Europe's largest cities. Henry VII brought to an end the Wars of the Roses by defeating Richard III at the Battle of Bosworth and marrying Elizabeth of York. Henry VII's other great achievements included the building of a merchant navy, and the Henry VII Chapel in Westminster Abbey, the eventual resting place for him and his queen.

Henry VII was succeeded in 1509 by arch wife-collector (and dispatcher) Henry VIII. Henry's first marriage to Catherine of Aragon failed to produce an heir, so the King, in 1527, determined that the union should be annulled. As the Pope refused to co-operate, Henry defied the Catholic Church, demanding that he himself be recognised as Supreme Head of the Church in England and ordering the execution of anyone who refused to go along with the plan (including his chancellor Sir Thomas More). Thus England began the transition to Protestantism. The subsequent dissolution of the monasteries transformed the face of the medieval city with the confiscation and redevelopment of all property owned by the Catholic Church.

On a more positive note, Henry found time to develop a professional navy, founding the Royal Dockyards at Woolwich in 1512 and at Deptford the following year. He also established palaces at Hampton Court and Whitehall, and built a residence at St James's Palace. Much of the land he annexed for hunting became the Royal Parks, including Hyde, Regent's, Greenwich and Richmond parks.

Post-Henry, there was a brief Catholic revival under Queen Mary (1553-8), though her marriage to Philip II of Spain met with much opposition in London. She had 300 Protestants burned at the stake at Smithfield, earning her the nickname 'Bloody Mary'.

VIRGIN QUEEN, BURGEONING CITY

Elizabeth I's reign (1558-1603) saw a flowering of English commerce and arts. The founding of the Royal Exchange by Sir Thomas Gresham in 1566 gave London its first trading centre, allowing it to emerge as Europe's leading commercial centre. The merchant venturers and the first joint-stock companies (Russia Company and Levant Company) established new trading enterprises, and Drake, Raleigh and Hawkins sailed to the New World and beyond. In 1580 Elizabeth knighted Sir Francis Drake on his return from a three-year circumnavigation; eight years later, Drake and Howard defeated the Spanish Armada.

As trade grew, so did London. It was home to some 200,000 people in 1600, many living in dirty, overcrowded conditions; plague and fire were constant, day-to-day hazards. The most complete picture of Tudor London is given in John Stow's *Survey of London* (1598), a fascinating first-hand account by a diligent Londoner whose monument stands in the City church of St Andrew Undershaft.

The glory of the Elizabethan era was the development of English drama, popular with all social classes but treated with disdain by the Corporation of London, which went as far as to ban theatres from the City in 1575. Two theatres, the Rose (1587) and the Globe (1599), were erected on the south bank of the Thames at Bankside, and provided homes for the works of Marlowe and Shakespeare. (The Globe is now restored.) Bankside, deemed 'a naughty place' by royal proclamation, was the Soho of its time: home not just to the theatre, but to bear-baiting, cock-fighting, taverns and 'stewes' (brothels).

The Tudor dynasty ended with Elizabeth's death in 1603. Her successor, the Stuart King James I, narrowly escaped assassination on 5 November 1605, when Guy Fawkes and his gunpowder were discovered underneath the Palace of Westminster. The Gunpowder Plot had been hatched in protest at the failure to improve conditions for the persecuted Catholics, but only resulted in an intensification of anti-papist feelings in ever-intolerant London. To this day, 5 November is commemorated with fireworks as Bonfire Night.

Cockneys – or Mockneys?

Just who exactly are these loveable East End rogues?

Cockney folklore is the nation's folklore. We all know the drill. True cockneys are born within hearing distance of Bow bells; they're costermongers with their own language, an endearing slang developed as secret code to fox the police. Cockney rhymes 'plates of meat' with feet and 'Brahms and Liszt' with pissed (drunk) in a mixture of pig Latin, backspeak, Romany and Yiddish that drops aitches, loves glo(tt)al stops, exchanges vs for ws and vice versa à la Charles Dickens's Sam Weller ('weal and winegar wery well') and puts f in place of th ('fings ain't what they used to be'). Cockney traditions encompass pearly kings and queens, knees-ups in pubs, 'doing the Lambeth Walk', bank holiday Mondays on Hampstead Heath (sorry, 'ampstead 'eath), regular consumption of eels and mash and a cheeky, rough and ready, salt-of-the-earth humour that saw East Enders come up smiling through the Blitz.

It's not quite that straightforward, though. For a start, where are Bow bells? St Mary's in Bow is in prime present-day East End residential territory, but, in fact, the bells in question are those at St Mary-Le-Bow in Cheapside, bang in the centre of the City. But how far away can they be heard? If, as was supposed, it was the bells of Bow that urged Dick Whittington to 'turn again' and become Lord Mayor of London, they must have been heard in Highgate a good six miles away. In 1991 a scientist, Dr Malcolm Hough, researched this knotty problem and concluded that the catchment area could have never extended this far and that today, with the volume of motorised traffic, a true cockney by that definition could live no further east than Aldgate.

Even the origin of the word 'cockney' is somewhat obscure, and its meaning disputed. John Minsheu's lexicon *Ductor in Linguas* (1617) relates the story of a town-bred child who, on hearing a horse neigh, asked if 'a cock neighed too', while others say it derives from the 'Cockaigne', a Utopia that featured in medieval tales (though this is now thought to refer to Ireland). But Sir James Murray at the end of the 19th century nailed 'cockney' as describing a small, or misshapen egg sometimes laid by young hens. It was also used to describe a child who had been 'overlong nursed by its mother, hence to a simpleton or milksop', according to the definitive 1911 edition of the *Encyclopaedia Britannica*.

It wasn't until the beginning of the 17th century that 'cockney' appears to have been confined to Londoners. Until then it meant any town-bred person ignorant of country ways and with dandified airs – not a producer like those on the land or in the industrial regions, but a trader making a living selling goods from a horse and cart or market stall. And that is what the notion of 'cockney' remained, flagging both the urban/rural divide and a divide within London itself, between the vulgar East Enders whose horizons and knowledge of the wider world were much narrower than those of their genteel rulers, the 'toffs up west'.

However old the etymological roots of cockney might be, the cockney figure of popular stereotype is a 'tradition' dating only from around the 1890s that can be laid at the door of music hall star Albert Chevalier and his songs such as 'Knocked 'em in the Old Kent Road' and 'My Old Dutch'. The cockney caught on, and was soon everywhere from Sickert's paintings to Shaw's *Pygmalion* to Kipling's ordinary soldier 'Tommy Atkins' and Phil May's drawings for *Punch*. It was timely. The 1867 Reform Act had begun the process of giving the vote to the urban working class, and the threat that might pose to the existing order was one that exercised the middle classes. And now here was a friendly cockney sparrer, a rough diamond, maybe, but no threat to the status quo with his (and her) pearly-suited 'royalty' (probably an invention of the music hall), his own language and a seeming acceptance of his place as a quaint and colourful 'other' within the metropolis.

With tower blocks having replaced court-yarded tenements, and television and cinema having killed the music hall, Hoxton as London's Tribeca, and a new rap-style slang on the street, the cockney has been consigned to Tourist Board leaflets for several decades now. Today London is a multiracial, supposedly classless city that no longer feels the need for an enclave of predominantly white cockney 'characters' to reassure itself about its identity.

wagamama

positive eating + positive living

bloomsbury WC1A
4 streatham st
tube | tottenham court rd

soho W1R 3HS
10 lexington st
tube | piccadilly circus

west end W1H 9LA
101 wigmore st
tube | bond st /
marble arch

camden NW1 7BW
11 jamestown rd
tube | camden town

kensington W8 4PF
26 kensington high st
tube | high st kensington

knightsbridge SW1X 7RJ
harvey nichols
lower ground floor
tube | knightsbridge

covent garden
WC2E 7PG
1 tavistock st
tube | covent garden

kingston KT1 1EY
16-18 high st

leicester square
WC2H 7AF
14 irving st
tube | leicester square

haymarket SW1Y 4RJ
8 norris st
tube | piccadilly circus

moorgate EC2V 0HR
1 ropemaker st
tube | moorgate

fleet street EC4A 2AB
109 fleet st
tube | st pauls

st albans AL3 5DQ
christopher place

islington N1 0PS
N1 centre parkfield st
tube | angel

old broad street
EC2N 1HQ
(by tower 42)
22 old broad st
tube | liverpool st

guildford GU1 3DY
25-29 high st

canary wharf E14 5NY
jubilee place
tube | canary wharf

tower hill EC3N 4EB
tower place
(off lower thames st)
tube | tower hill

mansion house
EC4V 2BH
4 great st thomas
apostle (off garlick hill)
tube | mansion house
/ cannon st

brent cross NW3
shopping centre

richmond TW9 1SX
3 hill st
tube | richmond

tunbridge wells
TN1 1RB
mount pleasant road

putney SW15 1SQ
50-54 high street
tube | east putney

for menu visit: www.wagamama.com
uk | dublin | amsterdam | sydney | dubai

But aside from his unwitting part in the Gunpowder Plot, James I merits remembering for other, more important reasons. For it was he who hired Inigo Jones to design court masques, and what ended up as the first – beautiful and hugely influential – examples of classical Renaissance style in London, the Queen's House in Greenwich, south-east London (1616), and the Banqueting House in Westminster (1619).

CIVIL WAR

Charles I succeeded his father in 1625, but gradually fell out with the City of London (from whose citizens he tried to extort taxes) and an increasingly independent-minded and antagonistic Parliament. The last straw finally came in 1642 when he intruded on the Houses of Parliament in an attempt to arrest five MPs. The country soon slid into a civil war (1642-9) between the supporters of Parliament (led by Puritan Oliver Cromwell) and those of the King.

Both sides knew that control of the country's major city and port was vital for victory. London's sympathies were firmly with the Parliamentarians and, in 1642, 24,000 citizens assembled at Turnham Green, west of the City, to face Charles's army. Fatally, the King lost his nerve and withdrew. He was never to seriously threaten the capital again; eventually, the Royalists were defeated. Charles was tried for treason and, though he denied the legitimacy of the court, he was declared guilty. He was then taken to the Banqueting House in Whitehall on 30 January 1649, and, declaring himself to be a 'martyr of the people', beheaded.

For the next 11 years the country was ruled as a Commonwealth by Cromwell. However, the closing of the theatres and the banning of the supposedly Catholic superstition of Christmas, along with other Puritan strictures on the wickedness of any sort of fun, meant that the restoration of the exiled Charles II in 1660 was greeted with relief and rejoicing by the populace.

PLAGUE, FIRE AND REVOLUTION

However, two major catastrophes marred the first decade of Charles's reign in the capital. In 1665 the most serious outbreak of bubonic plague since the Black Death killed many of the capital's population. By the time the winter cold had put paid to the epidemic, nearly 100,000 Londoners had died. On 2 September 1666 a second disaster struck. The fire that spread from a carelessly tended oven in Farriner's Baking Shop on Pudding Lane was to rage for three days and consume four-fifths of the City, including 89 churches, 44 livery company halls and more than 13,000 houses.

The **Great Fire** at least allowed planners the chance to rebuild London as a rationally planned modern city. Many blueprints were considered, but, in the end, Londoners were so impatient to get on with business that the City was reconstructed largely on its medieval street

The **Great Fire of London**.

The Great Stink

In the dismal summer of 2004, heavy rain and flash floods in London forced 600,000 tons of raw sewage into the Thames. Thousands of fish were killed and public health concerns raised, causing commentators to recall the 'Great Stink' experienced by the capital nearly 150 years ago in what was then the hottest summer on record. That stink so got up the noses of MPs that Benjamin Disraeli, the Conservative Chancellor of the Exchequer, was able to rush a bill through the Commons in just 18 days allocating some £3 million to construct a massive new sewerage scheme for London.

It was hardly before time. The population of London had nearly tripled in the first half of the century and, like the rest of Britain's large towns and cities, it was a desperately unhealthy place. Residents of the inner city had a life expectancy of around half that of their rural cousins; in London cholera and typhoid carried by polluted water had become endemic with mortality rates in London at a level not seen since the Black Death.

The causes were various, but one stood out. Since the early 19th century those who could afford it had installed water closets in their homes in place of privies and cesspits, and sewers, originally designed to carry rainwater into the Thames, now pumped raw sewage into the river – the same river that provided Londoners with their drinking water. In the dry hot summer of 1858 the

back-up of sewage became intolerable. In Parliament 'our legislators were driven from those portions of the buildings which overlook the river', while the few who ventured to investigate further 'were instantly driven to retreat, each man with a handkerchief to his nose' as *The Times* put it. Curtains were soaked in chlorine of lime, and there was even talk of the House decamping to Henley-upon-Thames, since overlaying the MPs' olfactory sensitivity was fear: the 'miasma' theory, that fevers and infections were caused by exhalations from decaying matter that poisoned the air, still held sway.

Step forward the unlikely hero Joseph Bazalgette (forefather of Peter Bazalgette who served up *Big Brother*). Chief engineer to the Metropolitan Board of Works, Bazalgette had already come up with an ambitious plan for a sewage disposal system for the capital that involved building some 82 miles of huge brick tunnels that would carry waste away from the centre to outfalls into the Thames at Barking Creek in the north and Plumstead in the south, past the tidal segment of the river. Now funding was forthcoming and the massive project could begin. Bazalgette's complicated sewage network, an engineering feat to rate alongside the best of the era, was officially opened by the Prince of Wales (the future Edward VII) on 4 April 1865. And today, when Londoners flush their loos, they can reflect that their poo will be traversing those self-same sewers that were built as a response to the 'Great Stink' of 1858.

Except the ones that get away. As Bazalgette's system reaches capacity, up to 20 million tons of raw sewage are flushed into the Thames every year. A £1.5 billion tunnel under the Thames is generally accepted as the preferred solution but will take ten years to build – and probably as long again to dicker about the financing.

plan, albeit in brick and stone rather than wood. The towering figure of the period turned out to be the prolific Sir Christopher Wren, who oversaw work on 51 of the 54 churches rebuilt. Among them was his masterpiece, the new St Paul's, completed in 1711 and, effectively, the world's first Protestant cathedral.

After the Great Fire, many well-to-do former City residents moved to new residential developments in the West End. In the City, the Royal Exchange was rebuilt, but merchants increasingly used the new coffee houses to exchange news. With the expansion of the joint-stock companies and the chance to invest capital, the City was emerging as a centre not of manufacturing, but of finance.

Anti-Catholic feeling still ran high. The accession of Catholic James II in 1685 aroused fears of a return to the Pope, and resulted in a Dutch Protestant, William of Orange, being invited to take the throne with his wife, Mary Stuart (James's daughter). James fled to France in 1688 in what became known – by its beneficiaries – as the 'Glorious Revolution'. One development during William III's reign was the founding of the Bank of England in 1694, initially to finance the King's wars with France.

THE GEORGE METTLE

After the death of Queen Anne, according to the Act of Settlement (1701), the throne passed to George, great-grandson of James I, who had been born and raised in Hanover, Germany. Thus, a German-speaking king – who never learned English – became the first of four long-reigning Georges in the Hanoverian line.

During his reign (1714-27), and for several years afterwards, Sir Robert Walpole's Whig party monopolised Parliament. Their opponents, the Tories, supported the Stuarts and had opposed the exclusion of the Catholic James II. On the King's behalf, Walpole chaired a group of ministers (the forerunner of today's Cabinet), becoming, in effect, Britain's first prime minister. Walpole was presented with 10 Downing Street (constructed by Sir George Downing) as a residence; it remains the official home of all serving prime ministers.

During the 18th century London grew with astonishing speed, in terms of both population and construction. New squares and many streets of terraced houses spread across Soho, Bloomsbury, Mayfair and Marylebone, as wealthy landowners and speculative developers who didn't mind taking a risk given the size of the potential rewards cashed in on the demand for leasehold properties. South London, too, became more accessible with the opening of the first new bridges for centuries, Westminster Bridge (1750) and Blackfriars Bridge (1763).

Until then, London Bridge had been the only bridge over the Thames. The old city gates, most of the Roman Wall and the remaining houses on Old London Bridge were demolished, allowing access to the City for traffic.

THE RUINED POOR VS THE IDLE RICH

In the older districts, however, people were still living in terrible squalor and poverty, far worse than the infamous conditions of Victorian times. Some of the mostΩ or with organised trips to Bedlam to mock the mental patients. On a similar level, public executions at Tyburn – near today's Marble Arch – were among the most popular events in the social calendar.

The outrageous imbalance in the distribution of wealth encouraged crime, and there were daring daytime robberies in the West End. Reformers were few, though there were exceptions. Henry Fielding, author of the picaresque novel *Tom Jones*, was also an enlightened magistrate at Bow Street Court. In 1751 he and his blind half-brother John set up a volunteer force of 'thief-takers' to back up the often ineffective efforts of the parish constables and watchmen who were the only law-keepers in the city. This crime-busting group of early cops, known as the Bow Street Runners, were the forerunners of today's Metropolitan Police (established in 1829).

Disaffection was also evident in the activities of the London mob during this period. Riots were a regular reaction to middlemen charging extortionate prices, or merchants adulterating their food. In June 1780 London was hit by the anti-Catholic Gordon Riots, named after ringleader George Gordon; the worst in the city's violent history, they left 300 people dead.

Some attempts were made to alleviate the grosser ills of poverty with the setting up of five major new hospitals by private philanthropists. St Thomas's and St Bartholomew's were already long established as monastic institutions for the care of the sick, but Westminster (1720), Guy's (1725), St George's (1734), London (1740) and the Middlesex (1745) went on to become world-famous teaching hospitals. Thomas Coram's Foundling Hospital for abandoned children was another remarkable achievement of the time.

THE VICTORIAN METROPOLIS

It wasn't just the indigenous population of London that was on the rise. Country people, who had lost their land because of enclosures and were faced with starvation wages or unemployment, drifted into the towns in large numbers. The East End became the focus for poor immigrant labourers with the building of the docks towards the end of the century. London's population had grown to almost a million by 1801, the largest of any city in

Europe. And by 1837, when Queen Victoria came to the throne, five more bridges and the capital's first passenger railway (from Greenwich to London Bridge) gave hints that a major expansion might be around the corner.

'The first underground line proved an instant success, attracting more than 30,000 travellers on the first day.'

As well as being the administrative and financial capital of the British Empire, which spanned a fifth of the globe, London was also its chief port and the world's largest manufacturing centre, with breweries, distilleries, tanneries, shipyards, engineering works and many other grimy industries lining the south bank of the Thames. On the one hand, London boasted splendid buildings, fine shops, theatres and museums; on the other, it was a city of poverty, disease and prostitution. The residential areas were becoming polarised into districts with fine terraces maintained by squads of servants, and overcrowded, insanitary, disease-ridden slums.

The growth of the metropolis in the century before Victoria came to the throne had been spectacular enough, but during her reign, which lasted until 1901, thousands more acres were covered with housing, roads and railway lines. Today, if you pick any street within five miles of central London, chances are that its houses will be mostly Victorian. By the end of the 19th century, the city's population had swelled to in excess of six million.

Despite social problems – memorably depicted in the writings of Charles Dickens – major steps were being taken to improve conditions for the majority of Londoners by the turn of the century. The Metropolitan Board of Works installed an efficient sewerage system (*see p18* **The Great Stink**), street lighting and better roads. The worst slums were replaced by low-cost building schemes funded by philanthropists such as the American George Peabody, who established the Peabody Donation Fund, which continues to this day to provide subsidised housing to the working classes. The London County Council (created in 1888) also helped to house the poor.

The Victorian expansion would not have been possible without an efficient public transport network with which to speed workers into and out of the city from the new suburbs. The horse-drawn bus appeared on London's streets in 1829, but it was the opening of the first passenger railway seven years later that heralded the commuters of the future.

The first underground line, which ran between Paddington and Farringdon Road, opened in 1863 and proved an instant success, attracting more than 30,000 travellers on the first day. Soon after, the world's first electric track in a deep tunnel – the 'tube' – opened in 1890 between the City and Stockwell, later becoming part of the Northern line.

ALBERT'S PRIDE

The Great Exhibition of 1851 captured the zeitgeist: confidence and pride, discovery and invention. Prince Albert, the Queen's Consort, helped organise this triumphant event, for which the Crystal Palace, a giant building of iron and glass – designed not by a professional architect but by the Duke of Devonshire's gardener, Joseph Paxton – was erected in Hyde Park. During the five months it was open, the Exhibition drew six million visitors from Great Britain and abroad, and the profits inspired the Prince Consort to establish a permanent centre for the study of the applied arts and sciences: the result is the South Kensington museums and Imperial College. After the Exhibition, the Palace was moved to Sydenham and used as an exhibition centre until it burned down in 1936.

When the Victorians were not colonising the world by force, they combined their conquests with scientific developments. The Royal Geographical Society sent navigators to chart unknown waters, botanists to bring back new species, and geologists to study the earth. Many of their specimens ended up at the Royal Botanic Gardens at Kew.

TURN-OF-THE-CENTURY JOIE DE VIVRE

During the brief reign of Edward VII (1901-10), London regained some of the gaiety and glamour it lacked in the dour last years of Victoria's reign. A touch of Parisian chic came to London with the opening of the Ritz Hotel in Piccadilly; the Café Royal hit the heights of its popularity as a meeting place for artists and writers; and 'luxury catering for the little man' was provided at the Lyons Tea Shops and new Lyons Corner Houses (the Coventry Street branch, which opened in 1907, could accommodate an incredible 4,500 people). Meanwhile, the first department store, Selfridges, opened on Oxford Street in 1909.

Road transport, too, was revolutionised. Motor cars put-putted around the city's streets, before the first motor bus was introduced in 1904. Double-decked electric trams had started running in 1901 (though not through the West End or the City), and continued doing so for 51 years. In fact, by 1911 the use of horse-drawn buses had been abandoned. A few years later, London suffered its first devastating air raids in World War I. The first bomb over the city was dropped from a Zeppelin near Guildhall in September 1915, and was followed by many gruelling nightly raids on the capital; bomb attacks from planes began in July 1917. In all, around 650 people lost their lives as a result of Zeppelin raids.

ROARING BETWEEN THE WARS

Political change happened quickly after World War I. Lloyd George's government averted revolution in 1918-19 by promising (but not delivering) 'homes for heroes' for the embittered returning soldiers. But the Liberal Party's days in power were numbered, and by 1924 the Labour Party, led by Ramsay MacDonald, had enough MPs to form its first government.

After the trauma of World War I, a 'live for today' attitude prevailed in the Roaring '20s among the young upper classes, who flitted from parties in Mayfair to dances at the Ritz. But this meant little to the mass of Londoners, who were suffering greatly in the post-war slump. Civil disturbances, brought on by the high cost of living and rising unemployment, resulted in the nationwide General Strike of 1926, when the working classes downed tools in support of the striking miners. Prime Minister Baldwin encouraged volunteers to take over the public services and the streets teemed with army-escorted food convoys, aristocrats running soup kitchens and students driving buses. After nine days of chaos, the strike was called off by the Trades Union Congress (TUC).

The economic situation only worsened in the early 1930s following the New York Stock Exchange crash of 1929; by 1931 more than three million Britons were jobless. During these years, the London County Council began to have a greater impact on the city's life, undertaking programmes of slum clearance and new housing, creating more parks and taking under its wing education, transport, hospitals, libraries and the fire service.

London's population increased dramatically between the wars, too, peaking at nearly 8.7 million in 1939. To accommodate the influx, the suburbs expanded quickly, particularly to the north-west with the extension of the Metropolitan line to an area that became known as Metroland. Identical gabled, double-fronted houses sprang up in their hundreds of thousands, from Golders Green to Surbiton.

All these new Londoners were entertained by the new media of film, radio and TV. London's first radio broadcast was beamed from the roof of Marconi House in the Strand in 1922, and families were soon gathering around enormous Bakelite wireless sets to hear the British Broadcasting Company (the BBC; from 1927 called the British Broadcasting Corporation). Television broadcasts

The **Albert Memorial**, a gift from Victoria.

started on 26 August 1936, when the first telecast went out live from Alexandra Palace.

WORLD WAR II (1939-45)

Neville Chamberlain's policy of appeasement towards Hitler's increasingly aggressive Germany during the 1930s collapsed when the Germans invaded Poland, and on 3 September 1939 Britain declared war. The government implemented precautionary measures against the threat of air raids – including the evacuation of 600,000 children and pregnant mothers – but the expected bombing raids did not happen during the autumn and winter of 1939-40, a period that became known as the Phoney War. In July 1940, though, Germany began preparations for an invasion of Britain with three months of aerial attack that came to be known as the Battle of Britain.

For Londoners, the Phoney War came to an abrupt end in September 1940, when hundreds of German bombers dumped their loads of high explosives on east London and the docks. Entire streets were destroyed; despite precautions (*see p22* **Gimme shelter**) the dead and injured numbered more than 2,000. The Blitz had begun. The raids on London continued for 57 consecutive nights, then intermittently for a further six months. Londoners reacted with tremendous bravery and stoicism, a period still nostalgically referred to as 'Britain's finest hour'. After a final massive raid on 10 May 1941, the Germans focused their attention elsewhere, but by the end of the war, a third of the City and the East End was in ruins.

Gimme shelter

Juliet Gardiner examines civilian protection in World War II London.

'Go in, stay in, tune in', the government instructed householders in the booklet *Preparing for Emergencies*, which plopped through every UK letterbox in summer 2004 – though exactly what the 'emergency' might be was not made clear. In 1939 every British household received rather more precise information in another government leaflet, *Some Things You Should Know if War Should Come*, which alerted Londoners to the likelihood of air raids and gas attacks. The government calculated that within the first 24 hours of war breaking out 1,700 people would be killed and 3,300 wounded by bombs on London, and every subsequent 24 hours would bring 850 dead and 1,650 wounded – carnage on a level that was thankfully never realised.

Householders were advised to equip their basement or cellar, if they had one, as an air raid shelter, and local authorities instructed to submit plans for how they intended to shelter their citizens. There was the usual wrangling about who would foot the bill, and some of the more pacifist-inclined boroughs such as Stepney were reluctant to comply, regarding taking any steps to protect its citizens against air raids as tantamount to warmongering.

Anderson shelters (named after the then Home Secretary Sir John Anderson), corrugated steel structures provided free of charge to those with an annual income of less than £250 a year, were of no use to those living in inner London in tenements and back-to-back terraces with no gardens. And it was on them that the bombs were most likely to fall since their houses clustered round docks, factories and goods yards, prime targets for the German Luftwaffe. Ignoring calls for deep shelters on grounds of cost and the fear of 'deep shelter mentality', which

was supposed to turn Londoners into panic-stricken troglodytes who would refuse to emerge, the basements of public buildings and commercial premises were requisitioned; trenches were dug in public parks; and brick shelters were built – most with neither seating nor sanitation since it was imagined that air raids would be of short duration. Unfortunately, many of these were made on

From 1942 onwards, the tide of the war began to turn, but Londoners still had a new terror to face: the V1, or 'doodlebug'. Dozens of these deadly, explosives-packed pilotless planes descended on the city in 1944, causing widespread destruction. Later in the year, the more powerful V2 rocket was launched and, over the winter, 500 of them dropped on London, mostly in the East End. The last fell on 27 March 1945 in Orpington, Kent, around six weeks before Victory in Europe (VE Day) was declared on 8 May 1945.

RECOVERY AND RECONSTRUCTION

World War II left Britain almost as shattered as it left Germany. Soon after VE Day, a general election was held and Churchill was heavily defeated by the Labour Party under Clement Attlee. The new government established the National Health Service in 1948, and began a massive nationalisation programme that included public transport, electricity, gas, postal and telephone services. But for all the new schemes, life in London for most people remained regimented and austere.

the cheap with insufficient mortar in the cement, and when the bombs began to fall several collapsed crushing or trapping their occupants and earning the grim sobriquet 'Morrison sandwiches' after the newly appointed Home Secretary.

But one local authority with ambitious plans was the small borough of Finsbury (now part of Islington), which gave the task to the avant-garde architect Bertold Lubetkin, working again with engineer Ove Arup (the pair were responsible for the famous concrete spiral for the Penguin Pool at London Zoo). Lubetkin came up with an ambitious scheme intended to shelter every one of Finsbury's 59,000 citizens. This went against the government policy of dispersal and furthermore the Penguin-Pool like ramps were the only way in (or out) of the vast underground concrete shelters, each designed to shelter 12,000 citizens: with a seven-minute air raid warning, there would be a potentially lethal scrum of Londoners anxious to take shelter. The scheme was turned down.

In the event, when the Blitz started on 8 September 1940, thousands of Londoners disobeyed government orders and stormed down into tube stations, spending night after night on the platforms, where part of the attraction was that they couldn't hear the bombs dropping overhead – unlike those sheltering in their own Anderson shelter who reported feeling nightly that it felt as if 'a coal scuttle was being emptied on the roof'.

● Historian Juliet Gardiner is the author of *Wartime: Britain 1939-1945* (Headline, 2004).

In war-ravaged London, the most immediate problem faced by both residents and the local authorities was a critical shortage of housing. Prefabricated bungalows provided a temporary solution for some (though many of these buildings were still occupied 40 years later), but the huge new high-rise housing estates that the planners devised were often badly built and proved to be unpopular with their residents.

However, there were bright spots during this dreary time. London hosted the Olympics in 1948; three years later came the Festival of Britain (100 years after the Great Exhibition), a celebration of British technology and design. The exhibitions that took over land on the south bank of the Thames for the Festival provided the incentive to build the South Bank Centre.

As the 1950s progressed, life and prosperity gradually returned to London, leading Prime Minister Harold Macmillan in 1957 to famously proclaim that 'most of our people have never had it so good'. The coronation of Queen Elizabeth II in 1953 had been the biggest television broadcast in history, and there was the feeling of a new age dawning.

However, many Londoners were moving out of the city. The population dropped by half a million in the late 1950s, causing a labour shortage that prompted huge recruitment drives in Britain's former colonies. London Transport and the National Health Service were particularly active in encouraging West Indians to emigrate to Britain. Unfortunately, as the Notting Hill race riots of 1958 illustrated, the welcome these new immigrants received was rarely friendly. Yet there were several areas of tolerance: among them was Soho, which, during the 1950s, became famed for its smoky, seedy, bohemian pubs, clubs and jazz joints, such as the still-jumping Ronnie Scott's.

THE SWINGING '60S

By the mid '60s, London had started to swing. The innovative fashions of Mary Quant and others broke Paris's stranglehold on couture: boutiques blossomed along King's Road, while Biba set the pace in Kensington. Carnaby Street became a byword for hipness as the city basked in its new-found reputation as the music and fashion capital of the world. The year of student unrest in Europe, 1968, saw the first issue of *Time Out* (a fold-up sheet for 5p) hit the streets in August. The decade ended with the Beatles naming their final album *Abbey Road* after their studios in London, NW8, and the Rolling Stones playing a free gig in Hyde Park that drew around 500,000 people.

The bubble, though, had to burst – and burst it did. Many Londoners remember the 1970s as a decade of economic strife: inflation, the oil crisis and international debt caused chaos, and the IRA began its bombing campaign on mainland Britain. The explosion of punk in the second half of the decade, sartorially inspired by the idiosyncratic genius of Vivienne Westwood, provided some nihilistic colour.

LIFE UNDER THE IRON LADY

Historians will regard the 1980s as the decade of Thatcherism. When the Conservatives won the general election in 1979, Britain's first woman prime minister, a monetarist economic

Symbols of power old and new: Tower Bridge and **City Hall**, the GLA's HQ.

policy and cuts in public services widened the divide between rich and poor. In London, riots in Brixton (1981) and Tottenham (1985) were linked to unemployment and heavy-handed policing. The Greater London Council (GLC), led by Ken Livingstone, mounted spirited opposition to the government with a series of populist measures, the most famous being a fare-cutting policy on public transport. So effective was the GLC, in fact, that Thatcher decided to abolish it in 1986.

The replacement of Margaret Thatcher by John Major in October 1990 signalled a shortlived upsurge of hope among Londoners. A riot in Trafalgar Square had helped to see off both Maggie and her inequitable Poll Tax. Yet the early 1990s were scarred by continuing recession and homelessness in London, and IRA terrorist attacks punctuated the decade.

EXIT MAGGIE, ENTER KEN

In May 1997 the British people ousted the tired Tories and Tony Blair's Labour Party swept to the first of two General Election victories. However, initial enthusiasm from a public delighted to see fresh faces in office didn't last. The government hoped the Millennium Dome, built on a patch of Greenwich wasteland, would be a 21st-century rival to the 1851 Great Exhibition. It wasn't. Badly mismanaged, the Dome ate nearly £1 billion of public money and become a national joke along the way. It's now slated to become a gambling complex.

The government's plans for Iraq in 2003 generated the largest public demonstration in London's history; more than two million participated – to no avail. This wasn't the first time the government had ignored the people's wishes. The new millennium saw Ken Livingstone, charismatic former leader of the

'Ken's popularity was no flash in the pan.'

GLC and general thorn in the Labour Party's flesh, become London's first directly elected mayor. Despite evidence that most London voters wanted to see Livingstone as the Labour candidate, Blair imposed his own candidate on the party. Livingstone quit Labour in disgust and ran in the election as an independent, winning in a landslide to head the new Greater London Assembly (GLA). After a second victory in 2004 – having been welcomed back into the Labour Party fold – it became clear that Ken's popularity was no flash in the pan. The legacies of his first term are now firmly established: the congestion charge, which forces drivers to pay a fiver to enter the city centre, has shown what the mayor can do, and his Totally London Campaign, launched in 2003, to get visitors back into the city following the tourist slump of 2001-2, has proved to be a success, with visitor numbers back to pre-9/11 levels. Add to that a competitive bid for the 2012 Olympics and the ambitious Crossrail project, which aims to provide a rail link between London's most outlying destinations, and this city's future is looking bright.

Key events

AD 43	The Romans invade; a bridge is built on the Thames; Londinium is founded.	**1803**	The first horse-drawn railway opens.
61	Boudicca burns Londinium; the city is rebuilt and made the provincial capital.	**1812**	Spencer Perceval PM assassinated.
		1820	Regent's Canal opens.
122	Emperor Hadrian visits Londinium.	**1824**	The National Gallery is founded.
200	A city wall is built; Londinium becomes capital of Britannia Superior.	**1827**	Regent's Park Zoo opens.
		1829	London's first horse-drawn bus runs; the Metropolitan Police Act is passed.
410	Roman troops evacuate Britain.	**1833**	The London Fire Brigade is set up.
c600	Saxon London is built to the west.	**1835**	Madame Tussaud's opens.
604	St Paul's is built by King Ethelbert.	**1836**	The first passenger railway opens.
841	The Norse raid for the first time.	**1837**	Parliament is rebuilt after a fire.
c871	The Danes occupy London.	**1843**	Trafalgar Square is laid out.
886	King Alfred of Wessex takes London.	**1848-9**	Cholera epidemic sweeps London.
1013	The Danes take London back.	**1851**	The Great Exhibition takes place.
1042	Edward the Confessor builds a palace and 'West Minster' upstream.	**1853**	Harrods opens its doors.
		1858	The Great Stink: pollution in the Thames reaches hideous levels.
1066	William I is crowned in Westminster Abbey; London is granted a charter.	**1863**	The Metropolitan line, the world's first underground railway, opens.
1067	The Tower of London begun.	**1864**	The Peabody buildings, cheap housing for the poor, are built in Spitalfields.
1123	St Bartholomew's Hospital founded.		
1197	Henry Fitzalwin is the first mayor.	**1866**	London's last major cholera outbreak; the Sanitation Act is passed.
1213	St Thomas's Hospital is founded.		
1215	The Mayor signs the Magna Carta.	**1868**	The last public execution is held at Newgate Prison.
1240	First Parliament sits at Westminster.		
1290	Jews are expelled from London.	**1884**	Greenwich Mean Time established.
1348-9	The Black Death.	**1888**	Jack the Ripper prowls the East End; London County Council is created.
1381	The Peasants' Revolt.	a	
1388	Tyburn becomes place of execution.	**1890**	The Housing Act enables the LCC to clear the slums; the first electric underground railway opens.
1397	Richard Whittington is Lord Mayor.		
1476	William Caxton sets up the first ever printing press at Westminster.		
		1897	Motorised buses introduced.
1512-3	Royal Dockyards at Woolwich and Deptford founded by Henry VIII.	**1915-8**	Zeppelins bomb London.
		1940-1	The Blitz devastates much of the city.
1534	Henry VIII cuts off Catholic Church.	**1948**	The Olympic Games are held.
1554	200 martyrs burned at Smithfield.	**1951**	The Festival of Britain takes place.
1566	Gresham opens the Royal Exchange.	**1952**	The last London 'pea-souper' smog
1572	First known map of London printed.	**1953**	Queen Elizabeth II is crowned.
1599	The Globe Theatre opens.	**1966**	England win World Cup at Wembley.
1605	Guy Fawkes fails to blow up James I.	**1975**	Work begins on the Thames barrier
1642	The start of the Civil War.	**1981**	Riots in Brixton.
1649	Charles I is executed; Cromwell establishes Commonwealth.	**1982**	The last of London's docks close.
		1986	The GLC is abolished.
1664-5	The Great Plague.	**1990**	Poll Tax protesters riot.
1666	The Great Fire.	**1992**	Canary Wharf opens; an IRA bomb hits the Baltic Exchange in the City.
1675	Building starts on the new St Paul's.		
1686	The first May Fair takes place.	**1997**	Diana, Princess of Wales dies.
1694	The Bank of England is established.	**2000**	Ken Livingstone is elected mayor; Tate Modern and the London Eye open.
1711	St Paul's is completed.		
1750	Westminster Bridge is built.	**2001**	The Labour government re-elected.
1766	The city wall is demolished.	**2002**	Queen mother dies aged 101.
1769	Blackfriars Bridge opens.	**2003**	London's biggest ever public demonstration – against the war on Iraq.
1780	The Gordon Riots take place.		
1784	The first balloon flight over London	**2004**	Ken Livingstone is re-elected.
1802	The Stock Exchange is founded.		

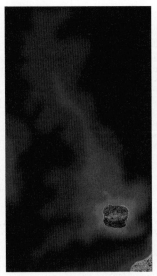

London Today

The ever-expanding capital tries to cure its growing pains.

On 4 June 2004 Ken Livingstone romped home for a second term as London's Mayor. Ken was back, in a position which is fast becoming synonymous with a man who both infuriates and delights Londoners in equal measure. Although this time he wore the crown of Tony Blair's Labour Party, not an independent, Londoners still gave him a hearty endorsement. In his brief speech of thanks, he pledged to 'leave London more beautiful' than he found it. While architecture and street planning undoubtedly have a huge impact on the lives of any city's residents, Livingstone undoubtedly had more on his mind than putting a few flowerpots on the street corners. If you asked the average Londoner for a list of things that need beautifying in their city, there's a fair chance that transport, crime and housing would feature right at the top.

HOW DO YOU GET THERE FROM HERE?
If you want to break the ice with any Londoner, a surefire winner is to ask them about London transport. Every Londoner has an opinion on the overcrowded, and often unreliable behemoth of a system – and expect some expletives. The main bone of contention is the Underground network (the tube), which is already stretched beyond capacity and the subject of constant delays, engineering works and occasional derailments. According to a recent report by Transport for London (TfL), the future for London Underground looks grim. It stated that unless there is a substantial injection of funds into the system the whole network will face meltdown, companies will fail to invest in the capital and tourists will disappear. TfL claims that, for each year from 2005 to 2010, it needs up to £250 million just to ensure that the system runs smoothly – and that's without repairs and improvements.

So who is going to cough up the readies? Although the Underground is under the jurisdiction of the Mayor (in 2004 he was also given authority over the capital's overground trains), it ultimately falls to the government to pay the hefty pricetag – something that successive governments have failed to take on over the years. But in 2003, after fighting a noble but ultimately doomed battle, the Mayor was forced to accept a ruling that meant that future funding for the Underground would partly come from private companies (Private-Public Partnership), a move that he and many other Londoners regard as compromising the safety and efficiency of the system. Now the Mayor has entered an uneasy relationship with the private companies who have 30-year leases over the infrastructure of the tube network. The jury is still out on whether this alliance will bring any real benefits to the ailing tube. But already fares have been substantially increased, purportedly to invest in improvements.

'This state-of-the-art railway will transport 160,000 rush-hour passengers.'

If you are caught in one of those interminable periods during a tube journey while the train waits ten minutes for a signal to change/a train passing in the other direction/the driver to finish his lunch, you could while away the time by playing join-the-dots with the tube map. In May 2004 the Mayor published a radically redrawn transport map of London to show how the city would be joined up by the construction of ten new tube, rail and tram projects to cope with a predicted surge in the city's population by 2016. Among the new proposals were long-delayed projects such as Crossrail and the East London Line extension, which have been awaiting government funding for a decade or more. Crossrail is potentially the most exciting development – if it goes ahead and funding is still uncertain, this state-of-the-art rail system will provide 24 trains an hour, capable of transporting 160,000 morning rush-hour passengers across London.

The other topic currently causing waves in the capital is the congestion charge. Introduced in 2003, this requires car drivers to pay £5 if they bring their cars into central London. Loved by some, hated by others, the charge has undoubtedly bought down the number of cars clogging the capital's streets: since its introduction in February 2003, traffic has been cut by 18 per cent and delays reduced by 30 per cent within the central zone. Never shy of controversy, Livingstone has now announced an extension to the zone westwards that will take in Knightsbridge, Paddington and the fringes of Earl's Court and Shepherd's Bush, incorporating a swathe of affluent Kensington and Chelsea neighbourhoods. Despite vehement opposition from local residents, retailers, politicians and motoring organisations, who maintain that the extension is unnecessary and potentially damaging to businesses, it should

come into effect by late 2006. Some suspect that this area was excluded from the original zone precisely because it had clout; congestion charging had to be proved viable first.

IS IT A CRIME?

The buzzword of 2004 was 'anti-social behaviour'. New government legislation gave the 33 boroughs and Metropolitan Police new powers to get tough on anyone they deemed to be behaving in a disorderly fashion on the streets or otherwise disturbing the peace. And get tough they did. ASBOs (anti-social behaviour orders), which involve a fine, or possibly prison, were slapped on the most unlikely subjects. For example, Camden council slammed ASBOs on the Sony and BMG music labels for illegal flyposting, while Westminster handed them to graffiti artists, leading critics of the legislation to declare that some boroughs were becoming ASBO trigger happy. Other measures to keep the streets of London clean and crime free included establishing 'bad behaviour zones' (Camden, again), whereby those found involved in dubious activities on the streets around Camden Town could be banned from the area for 24 hours. Meanwhile, Islington council brought in a US-style three-strikes-and-you're out system to curb begging in the borough.

'Government evacuation plans have been condemned as 'outdated and incoherent.'

Ken's latest big idea is the Six Steps Safer Neighbourhoods scheme, whereby teams of six officers are deployed to every ward in London. The approach, part of an attempt to get back to a more personalised 'bobby on the beat' style of policing, takes its cue from policing in New York under Mayor Rudolph Giuliani. Six months after the new scheme was introduced here, statistics showed that crime had been halved in parts of the capital.

TERRORISM

The round-up of terror suspects and the arrest of radical Muslim cleric Abu Hamza (who was based at the north London mosque in Finsbury Park) in 2004 have kept terrorism at the forefront of the public consciousness. It has also led to increased tensions between the police and the Asian community, who claim they are being unfairly targeted in the 'war against terrorism': It was found that in 2002/3, out of 17,845 people stopped and searched in London under the Terrorism Act, only nine were arrested in connection with terrorist activities – and most of these were Asians. Alarmingly, government

plans to evacuate up to 300,000 Londoners if terrorists launch an attack on the capital have been condemned as 'outdated and incoherent' by the Metropolitan Police.

SAFE AS HOUSES?

When we're not worrying about the morning commute to work or terrorist bombs, the next best dinner table topic is house prices. The staggering rise in prices (which saw the average house in London go for £262,000 in 2003) has placed most property far out of reach of the city's first-time buyers. Although the market is undoubtedly cooling, affordable housing is one of the most pressing issues the capital faces. Livingstone has stipulated that all new developments must ensure that 50 per cent of the properties are 'affordable' but there is a lack of clarity about how this will work in practice. The capital is facing another problem: it is growing at an exponential rate – the population is expected to grow by 800,000 by 2016. Where on earth is everyone to live? In order to address the problem, the city is in the throes of several enormous regeneration programmes, including Thames Gateway, which aims to provide up to 160,000 homes in the swathe of undeveloped land to the east of the city and along the Thames estuary, and the Lea Valley, which has been earmarked for development as part of the

No butts?

A ban on smoking has long been mooted for the capital, but things got suddenly more serious towards the end of 2004 when the Association of Local Governments (ALG) approached London's boroughs with the aim of putting together a no-smoking bill aimed specifically at the capital. Whether such a bill would be a blanket ban, following in the footsteps of New York and Dublin, or whether you'd see people in, say, Islington puffing merrily away while down the road in Camden smokers could face a fine remains to be seen but there are indications that a ban of some sort is definitely on the cards.

Smokers won't go without a fight, says Simon Clarke, director of Forest, the pro-smoking group. 'London tends to be seen as a cosmopolitan, liberal place and therefore politicians are unlikely to want to put their heads on the block to bring in somewhat draconian legislation. Attempts to bring in a ban here would be met by one hell of a fight.' Ken Livingstone, who has no direct powers regarding smoking, said, 'Support

for (a ban) varies, with backing for smoke-free restaurants and offices much higher than in relation to pubs and bars'. Jonathan Downey, who runs the members club Milk & Honey and Soho bar the Player recently introduced no-smoking areas after he canvassed members on the issue. He was surprised that 'a very vocal percentage of non-smokers were against forbidding smoking because they didn't want to belong to a club where they would have to tell their guests they couldn't smoke'.

Not to be left out, pro-dope campaigners are vocally opposing a smoking ban, which Dave Crane, from Hempire, the cannabis legalisation campaign, says will cause more tension between police and dope smokers. He said, 'A smoking ban would be disastrous for cannabis smokers. We need – and deserve – to be able to come out of the living rooms where we have been hiding.' If London becomes non-smoking, whip out the air freshener because those living rooms will be crowded and smoggy.

The new **East London Muslim Centre** demonstrates London's changing demographics.

London 2012 Olympic bid. Regardless of the outcome of the bid there are big plans for this area: long-term regeneration could create 40,000 jobs and 30,000 homes; work is already going ahead on an enormous aquatic centre with 50-metre pool. And in central London, every bit of spare land is being reconsidered for development, with large-scale regeneration schemes planned for the railway hinterlands of Paddington and King's Cross (*see p111* **Cross purposes**).

> ## 'Most people who overstay their visas are Australians and white South Africans.'

It's not just houses that are pricey in the capital. According to the annual Mercer Report for 2004, which measures the cost of living in the world's cities, London is now the second most expensive, after Tokyo (a statistic that will come as no surprise to residents). And it's unlikely to become any cheaper in the immediate future. Although people are increasingly leaving London in large numbers, either cashing in on property values or trading down for a quiet life, for everyone who has left, someone has come in from overseas or elsewhere in Britain. Despite the high costs, many people stay in the city because they believe there are enough positive things to compensate.

RICH MIX

One of London's most attractive qualities is its ethnic – and therefore cultural – diversity. Over 300 languages are spoken and more than one in three residents are from minority groups. In ten years' time, the figure will be 40 per cent. As in other European cities there is a threat from the far right in the form of the anti-immigration British National Party. In the 2004 mayoral elections the BNP increased its share of the vote – but it remains a tiny minority. London is still one of Europe's most tolerant cities. And the BNP might do well to remember that most people who overstay their visas in London are Australians and white South Africans.

Most Londoners consider that cultural diversity is one of the great benefits of living here – whether you want to boogie to bhangra at a Bollywood club night, attend a black poetry jam at a café in Brixton or listen to Iranian comedians perform at a West End pub. The Mayor's annual cultural events run the gamut from Asian Melas (festivals), Chinese New Year celebrations and St Patrick's Day festivities – and, of course, there's the Notting Hill carnival, which celebrated its 40th birthday in 2004, attracting crowds of over 1.5 million.

It might be noisy and dirty at times, overcrowded and getting bigger, but if beauty means belonging to one of the most exciting, vibrant, cosmopolitan and entertaining cities in the world, then maybe Mayor Livingstone is halfway towards his goal already.

Swiss Re tower.
See p32.

Architecture

Controversy, fire and the odd post-millennial wobble…
London's buildings have risen to many a challenge.

Hassle, hassle, hassle. With few exceptions, London's architectural renewal seems to be accompanied by design dispute, cost overruns, contextual debates and political dithering. Take, for example, Crossrail – the long-overdue, east–west transport link. It was first mooted more than a decade ago and it's still just a signature away from delivery. Latest estimates are that Crossrail will happen, but not until 2013 – unhelpfully, a year after the Olympics that London is pressing so hard to host.

Meanwhile, a planning enquiry is raging about whether or not to build eight residential towers on Potters Fields, that slab of empty land opposite the Tower of London where David Blaine starved himself in 2003. Further north in Hackney, the new £30 million Clissold Leisure Centre seems to be permanently shut due to alleged design faults. Over in Battersea, engineers have found dangerous chemicals in the chimneys of the iconic Battersea Power Station, further delaying its redevelopment. Oh, and the design and technology teacher at

Capital City Academy in Brent, a new school designed by British architecture supremo Norman Foster, has resigned after complaining that he doesn't like the place.

Actually, this is nothing new. The architects of Buckingham Palace, St Pancras Chambers and the Royal Courts of Justice all had a hellish time realising their plans, one way or another. Criticism seems to go with the territory and one of the skills of an architect is to shrug and get on with it. Remember the Wobbly Bridge? The wobble goes down as a footnote in history and the perfectly safe and stable bridge is one of the capital's must-see destinations.

That's architecture for you. The truth is that architects are often the last people who should be blamed when things go wrong. Planners, developers, banks, politicians, building firms – they all stick their oar in and manage to make the construction industry a messy business. It's a wonder that anything gets built at all. The redevelopment of the **South Bank Centre** is a case in point: there has been no shortage of design solutions for this difficult site, but planning and finance problems have never been overcome. Indeed, all discussion of the South Bank seems to have faded away. So the next time you read of a bold new scheme to regenerate the South Bank arts complex, don't get too excited – three imaginative proposals have bitten the dust since the late 1980s.

Somehow, though, things get done and London can boast a number of world-class contemporary buildings, such as the **Swiss Re** ('Gherkin') tower at 30 St Mary Axe, the **Laban** dance centre in Deptford, some stations on the new Jubilee line, the newly remodelled **Peter Jones** department store and a handful of Millennium projects. And there is much to look forward to, including a rejuvenated St Pancras Station, due to open in 2007, the completion of Wembley Stadium around the same time, and possibly even the conversion of the ultimate white elephant, the **Dome**, into a 20,000-seat indoor arena. King's Cross Station is also due for a major makeover, if architect John McAslan gets his way (*see p109* **Cross purposes**). Richard Rogers, the man behind the Lloyd's building, insists that London architecture has never had it so good. 'London hasn't had such a fantastic skyline since Wren,' he said recently.

Thankfully, the controversial **Paternoster Square** is now complete. Like the South Bank site, this project had a tortured history, largely because of its proximity to the revered St Paul's Cathedral and the unwanted attentions of Prince Charles and the heritage lobby. After more than ten years in the making, the result is a fairly restrained development that has tried terribly hard to please everyone and delights almost no one. Architect Robert Adam calls it 'insipid classicism and dull modernist orthodoxy'. Ironic, since at the time of its construction, St Paul's itself was hugely controversial, which should have been an eloquent reminder that in architecture boldness is a prerequisite for long-lasting success. The best bit is the sundial that projects from the side of a south-facing office block, designed by a computer programmed to generate structurally efficient objects. The programme, devised by an engineer from Cambridge University, ran out half a dozen alternatives – all the design team had to do was choose the one they preferred.

Importantly (and thankfully), not all of London's new architecture is of the grand variety. There's plenty of smaller-scale stuff elbowing its way into the capital's crowded cityscape. Take the **Cross**, for example, a small office development on King's Cross Road – an angular, metal-clad, four-storey scheme that gleams between its missable neighbours.

Similarly, there's the steel and glass box that architect William Russell has built for himself a stone's throw from Brick Lane (he also designed the superb new Alexander McQueen store on Bond Street). And then there's the new ferry pier outside Tate Britain, an eye-catching, assymetrical steel and timber construction designed by the team behind the London Eye.

These little gems will eventually play a part in changing the character of this elderly city. Which is typical. Unlike many major cities, London has never been planned. It is a hotch-potch, a gradual accumulation of towns and villages, adapted, renewed and disfigured by the changing needs of its populace. The tide of history has given London no distinctive architectural style, leaving it at once imperial, industrial, medieval and experimental.

'Nothing cheers a builder like a natural disaster.'

LONDON'S BURNING

Any number of events have left their imprint on the buildings of the city, but the Great Fire of 1666 is a useful marker: it signals the end of medieval London and the start of the city we know today. Commemorated by Christopher Wren's 202-foot (62-metre) **Monument**, the fire destroyed five-sixths of the city, burning 13,200 houses and 89 churches.

London was asking for it. It was a densely populated place built of wood, where rubbish would go uncollected and fire control was primitive. It was only after the three-day inferno that the authorities felt they could insist on a few basic building regulations. From now on, brick and stone would be the construction materials of choice, and key streets widened to act as firebreaks. Most of what can now be seen is a testament to the talents of Wren, the architect of its remodelling, and his successors.

In a sense, though, the city of the Plague did not entirely disappear. In spite of grand proposals from architects hoping to reconceive the city along classical lines, London reshaped itself around its historic street pattern, with buildings that had survived the Fire standing as monuments to earlier ages. One of these was the 13th-century **St Ethelburga-the-Virgin** (68-70 Bishopsgate, The City, EC2), noteworthy as the city's smallest chapel. Sadly, where fire failed, the IRA succeeded, destroying two-thirds of this building in a 1993 bomb attack. The church has now been reconstructed as a peace and reconciliation centre.

The Norman **Tower of London**, begun soon after William's 1066 conquest and extended over the next 300 years, remains the country's most perfect example of a medieval fortress. This is thanks to the Navy, which cheated the advancing flames of the Great Fire by blowing up the surrounding houses before the inferno could get to them. The Tower is now better than ever thanks to a handsome new entrance that helps pedestrians negotiate the complex road system more effectively.

And then there is **Westminster Abbey**, begun in 1245 when the site lay far outside London's walls and completed in 1745 when Nicholas Hawksmoor added the west towers. (That said, cathedrals are never really finished: the statues over the main entrance, with Martin Luther King centre stage, were added just a few years ago.) Though the abbey is the most

French of England's Gothic churches, deriving its geometry, flying buttresses and rose windows from across the Channel, the chapel, added by Henry VII and completed in 1512, is pure Tudor. 'Stone seems, by the winning labour of the chisel, to have been robbed of its weight and density, suspended aloft, as if by magic,' gushed Washington Irving centuries later.

The Renaissance came late to Britain, making its London debut with Inigo Jones's 1622 **Banqueting House**. The addition of a sumptuously decorated ceiling by Rubens in 1635, celebrating the benefits of wise rule, made the building a key piece of London's architecture. The following decade, King Charles I provided the public with an even greater spectacle as he was led from the

Paternoster Square, *qui es in caelis*, or at least near St Paul's. *See p32.*

building and beheaded. Tourists also have Jones to thank for **Covent Garden** and the **Queen's House** at Greenwich, but these are not his only legacies. By the 1600s Italian architecture, rooted in the forms and geometries of the Roman era, was all the rage. So, as a dedicated follower of fashion, Inigo Jones became proficient in the art of piazzas, porticos and pillasters, changing British architecture forever. His work not only influenced the careers of succeeding generations of architects, but also introduced a habit of venerating the past that would take 300 years to kick. Even today, London has a knack for glueing classical extras over the doors of cheap kit buildings in the hope that it will lend them dignity.

RELIGIOUS ICONS

Nothing cheers a builder like a natural disaster, and one can only guess at the relish with which Christopher Wren and co began rebuilding after the Fire. Taking their cue from Jones, they brandished classicism like a new broom: the pointed arches of English Gothic were rounded off, Corinthian columns made an appearance and church spires became as multi-layered and complex as a baroque wedding cake. (In fact, the spire of Wren's **St Bride**, Fleet Street, is said to have inspired the now-traditional form of the wedding cake.)

The **Tower of London**'s new approach (*p32*).

Wren blazed the trail with daring plans for **St Paul's Cathedral**, spending an astonishing £500 on the oak model of his proposal. But the scheme, incorporating a Catholic dome rather than Protestant steeple, was too Roman for the reformist tastes of the establishment and the design was rejected. To his credit, the undaunted architect did what any wounded ego would do. He quickly produced a redesign and gained planning permission by incorporating the much-loved spire, only to set about a series of mischievous U-turns once work had commenced, giving us the building – domed and heavily suggestive of an ancient temple – that has survived to this day.

So prolific was the building of churches that Londoners turned a blind eye to the odd synagogue. Allowed back into England by Oliver Cromwell in 1657, the city's Sephardic community from Spain and Portugal later commissioned a Quaker to build them a simple and elegant home in a quiet enclave. **Bevis Marks Synagogue** (2 Heneage Lane, The City, EC3), the UK's oldest, was completed in 1701 and gives little of its Semitic purpose away from the outside... and very little internally. It is a tribute to the pride lavished on the building that the extraordinary chandeliers that festoon the interior have yet to be electrified.

Wren's architectural baton was to be picked up by Nicholas Hawksmoor and James Gibbs, who were to benefit from worries over London's ungodly population when, in 1711, it was decreed that 50 extra churches should be built. Gibbs became busy in and around Trafalgar Square, building the steepled Roman temple that is **St Martin-in-the-Fields**, the baroque **St Mary-le-Strand** (Strand, WC2; now set against the monstrous lump of King's College) and the tower of **St Clement Danes**. A £34 million programme will see St Martin-in-the-Fields restored to its original state and its grounds upgraded by 2007.

All in all, Gibbs's work was well received, but the more prolific and experimental Hawksmoor had a rougher ride. His imposing **St Anne's** (Commercial Road, Limehouse, E14) proved so costly that the parish was left with insufficient funds to pay for a vicar, and **St George's** in Bloomsbury cost three times its £10,000 budget and took 15 years to build. Recent cracking in the pale blue interior suggests the authorities again need to dig deep.

Later to be dismissed as the 'most pretentious and ugliest edifice in the metropolis' (in 1876 by an anonymous critic), St George's aims to evoke the spirit of the ancients. Rather than a spire, there is a pyramid topped by a statue of George I decked out in a toga, while the interior boasts all the Corinthian columns, round arches and gilding you'd expect from a man steeped in antiquity. Many of these features are repeated in Hawksmoor's rocket-like **Christ Church Spitalfields**, just completing a much-needed and successful restoration. Strangely, this classical dedication never extended to seeing the ancient sights at first hand; Hawksmoor never left the country.

'Regent Street began as a device to separate the toffs from the riff-raff.'

THE ADAM FAMILY AND BEYOND

Robert Adam was quite the traveller. One of a large family of Scottish architects, Adam found himself at the forefront of a movement that came to see Italian baroque as a corruption of the real thing. Architectural exuberance was eventually dropped in favour of a simpler interpetation of the ancient forms.

The best surviving work of Adam and his brothers James, John and William can be found in London's great suburban houses **Osterley Park**, **Syon House** and **Kenwood House**, but the project for which they are most famous no longer stands. In 1768 they embarked on the cripplingly expensive Adelphi housing estate (after the Greek for 'brothers') off the Strand. Most of the complex was pulled down in the 1930s and replaced by an office block of the same name. Part of the original development survives in what is now the **Royal Society for the Arts** (8 John Adam Street, Covent Garden, WC2), a good example of how the family relieved the simplicity of brick with elegant plasterwork.

Just as the first residents were moving into the Adelphi, a young unknown called John Soane was embarking on a tour of his own. In Rome, Soane met the wealthy Bishop of Derry who persuaded the 25-year-old to abandon his travels and accompany him to Ireland in order to build a house. But the project came to nothing and Soane dealt with the setback by working hard and marrying into money.

His loss is our gain, however, as he went on to build the Bank of England and the recently remodelled **Dulwich Picture Gallery**. Sadly, the Bank was demolished between the wars, leaving nothing but the perimeter walls and depriving London of what is said to have been Soane's masterpiece. But a hint of what these ignorant bankers might have enjoyed can be gleaned from a visit to Soane's house, now the **Sir John Soane Museum**, a collection of exquisite architectural experiments with mirrors, coloured glass and folding walls.

A near-contemporary of Soane's, John Nash was arguably a less talented architect, but his contributions to the fabric of London have proved greater than those of anyone else. Among his buildings are **Buckingham Palace**, the **Haymarket Theatre** (Haymarket, St James's, W1) and **Regent Street** (W1). The latter began as a proposal to link the West End to the planned park further north, as well as a device to separate the toffs of Mayfair from the Soho riff-raff. In Nash's words, the intention was 'complete separation between the Streets occupied by the Nobility and Gentry, and the narrow Streets and meaner houses occupied by mechanics and the trading part of the community'.

THE 19TH CENTURY

By the 1830s the classical form had been established for 200 years, and a handful of upstarts began pressing for change. In 1834 the **Houses of Parliament** burned down, leading to the construction of Charles Barry's Gothic masterpiece. This was the beginning of the Gothic Revival, a move by the new romantics to replace what they considered to be foreign and pagan with a style that was not only native but Christian. The architectural profession was divided, but the argument was never resolved, merely made irrelevant by the advent of modernism a century later.

Barry would have preferred a classical design, but the brief was unambiguous and Gothic was to prevail. He needed help, and sought out a designer whose name alone makes him worthy of a mention, Augustus Welby Northmore Pugin. The result of Pugin's labours was a Victorian fantasy that, while a fine example of the perpendicular form, shows how the Middle Ages had become distorted in the minds of 19th-century architects. New buildings were constructed as a riot of turrets, towers and winding staircases that would today be condemned as the Disneyfication of history.

Even in renovating ancient buildings, architects would often decide that they weren't Gothic enough; as with the 15th-century **Guildhall**, which gained its corner turrets and central spire in 1862. Bombed by the Luftwaffe, the Guildhall was rebuilt largely as the Victorians had left it, apart from the interior statues of Gog and Magog, the protagonists in a legendary battle between ancient Britain and Troy. In the post-war reconstruction of this stately building, these two ugly bastards got even uglier. There's also a good statue of Churchill, looking stereotypically grumpy.

The argument between classicists and goths erupted in 1857, when the government commissioned Sir George Gilbert Scott, a leading light of the Gothic movement, to design a new HQ for the Foreign Office. Scott's design incensed anti-goth Lord Palmerstone, then prime minister, whose diktats prevailed. But Scott exacted his revenge by building an office in which everyone hated working, and by going on to construct Gothic edifices all over town, among them the **Albert Memorial** and **St Pancras Chambers**, the station frontage housing the Midland Grand Hotel.

St Pancras was completed in 1873, after the Midland Railway commissioned Scott to build a London terminus that would dwarf that of its rivals next door at King's Cross. Using the project as an opportunity to show his mastery of the Gothic form, Scott built an asymmetrical castle that obliterated views of the train shed behind, itself an engineering marvel completed earlier by William Barlow. This 'incongruous medievalism' did not go unnoticed by critics, prompting one to write that company directors should go the whole hog and dress their staff in period costume. 'Their porters might be dressed as javelin men, their guards as beefeaters.'

Still, the Gothic style was to dominate until the 20th century, leaving London littered with charming and imposing buildings such as the **Royal Courts of Justice**, the **Natural History Museum**, **Liberty** and **Tower Bridge**. World War I and the coming of modernism led to a spirit of tentative renewal. **Freemason's Hall** (Great Queen Street, WC2) and the BBC's **Broadcasting House** (Portland Place, Marylebone, W1) are good examples of the pared-down style of the '20s and '30s.

THIS IS THE MODERN WORLD

It must be evidence of the British love of animals that perhaps the finest example of between-the-wars modernism can be found at **London Zoo**. Built by Russian émigré Bertold Lubetkin and the Tecton group, the spiral ramps of the Penguin Pool (no longer used by penguins) were a showcase for the possibilities of concrete, which was also put to good use on the Underground: it enabled the quick and cheap building of large, cavernous spaces with the sleek lines and curves associated with speed. The Piccadilly line was a particular beneficiary: its 1930s expansion yielded the likes of Charles Holden's **Arnos Grove station**, the first of many circular station buildings and the model for the new Canada Water station on the Jubilee line.

There was nothing quick or cheap about the art deco **Daily Express building** (Fleet Street, The City, EC4). A black glass and chrome structure built in 1931, it is an early example of 'curtain wall' construction where the façade is literally hung on to an internal frame.

The building has been recently refurbished and extended for a new occupant, but the deco detailing of the original building – crazy flooring, snake handrails and funky lighting – remain intact. Public access is not guaranteed, but it's worth sticking your head around the door of what the *Architects' Journal* has called a 'defining monument of 1930s London'.

WHAT IS IT GOOD FOR?

World War II left large areas of London ruined, providing another opportunity for builders to cash in. Lamentably, the city was little improved by the rebuild, and, in many cases, was left worse off. The destruction left the capital with a dire housing shortage, giving architects a chance to demonstrate the speed and efficiency with which they could house large numbers of families in tower blocks. Many were not a success, partly because of poor build quality and partly because of a lack of imagination about the social consequences of high-rises. The architectural profession did great damage to its reputation and its chances of getting anything radical up without going through endless hoops of planning permission.

There were post-war successes, however, including the **Royal Festival Hall** on the South Bank. The sole survivor of the 1951 Festival of Britain, the RFH was built to celebrate the war's end and the centenary of the Great Exhibition. In spite of its size, the Festival Hall can be a crowded and awkward space, but refurbishment work is restoring what little grandeur the builders of post-war Britain managed to impart. It's now a much-loved piece of London's fabric – unlike the neighbouring **Hayward Gallery** and **Queen Elizabeth Hall**, concrete exemplars of the 1960s vogue for brutalist experimentation.

But brutalism couldn't last forever. The '70s and '80s offered up a pair of architectural replacements: post-modernism and high tech. The former is represented by Cesar Pelli's **Canary Wharf** tower (Isle of Dogs, E14) an over-sized obelisk that has become the archetypal expression of 1980s architecture and holds an ambiguous place in the city's affections. Its splendid isolation lent it an element of star quality, but the current building boom has provided this giant beacon with equally large neighbours, opening up another part of the city's traditionally low-rise skyline to high-rise clutter.

Richard Rogers's **Lloyd's Building** (Lime Street, The City, EC3) is London's best-known example of high tech, in which commercial and industrial aesthetics cleverly combine to produce what is arguably one of the most significant British buildings since the war.

Cloud capp'd towers

Traditionally, London has been a city dominated by church spires, godly needles that pointed elegantly upwards from the rooftops. But these days, this horizon has been eclipsed by tower blocks forming not the smartly uniform wall of a New York skyline but a snaggle-toothed smile riddled with gaps, from Centre Point to the Barbican to the NatWest Tower and Canary Wharf.

Things are beginning to change. Planners now talk about creating 'clusters' of towers across the city, designating areas where towers are allowed (and even encouraged) and others where low-rise will remain the norm. The number of towers in the City is set to grow, and the Canary Wharf complex will get more of the things. You can also expect to see less of the sky around Paddington Basin, Elephant & Castle, Croydon and (maybe) Victoria.

Indeed, the move in London is generally upwards, and some of the proposed buildings, while remaining tiddlers by international standards, promise to be exceptional designs. Take the new project from Nicholas Grimshaw & Partners, the architects behind Waterloo's Eurostar terminal and Cornwall's Eden Project, who have received planning permission for what promises to be a stunning new tower near Algdate tube station. This sleek, sharp-edged, 700-foot (217-metre) structure will tower over its neighbours and provide a public restaurant on its 49th floor when completed in around 2007. A special 'double-skin' façade will allow **Minerva**'s occupants to open the windows, almost unheard of in a new tower building.

Down the road, the Richard Rogers Partnership is planning an equally dramatic 735-foot-high (224-metre) wedge of a building, while across the river, preparation will soon start on the mighty London Bridge Tower, a gigantic spike that will almost certainly dwarf everything else for years – at nearly 1,000 feet high (300 metres), this 'shard' will rank about 25th in the world. It was undoubtedly the quality of the design that allowed it to make it through the planning process after three costly years of legal wrangling. The talents of Italian architect Renzo Piano were never in question, but the sheer scale of the thing made a public enquiry inevitable, with property developer Sellar and Southwark council fighting it out

with English Heritage over concerns that views of St Paul's might be spoiled.

Nonetheless, Deputy Prime Minister John Prescott, who has the final word on such matters, is convinced of the overall quality of the proposal – as is Ken Livingstone, who just likes the idea of tall buildings in London full stop. London Bridge Tower is just what a 'vibrant, populous and cutting-edge city like London needs', he says.

When completed (in around 2009), this £350 million beacon will reach a staggering 66 storeys. The bottom half is to be reserved for office use, with most of the rest being kitted out as apartments and hotels. A three-storey public gallery will be located halfway up, giving views comparable to those seen from the top of the London Eye.

Minerva's projected appearance.

Mocked upon completion in 1986, the building still manages to outclass newer projects, a fact not lost on Channel 4 when it commissioned Rogers to design its HQ in Horseferry Road, SW1 in the early 1990s.

Future Systems' NatWest Media Centre at **Lord's Cricket Ground**, built from aluminium in a boatyard and perched high above the pitch like a giant bar of soap, is arguably London's most daring construction to date, especially given its traditional, old world setting. And Will Alsop's multicoloured **Peckham Library** (171 Peckham Hill Street, Peckham, SE15) redefined community architecture so comprehensively that it walked away with the £20,000 Stirling Prize in 2000.

The problem with being innovative, though, is that things can go wrong. And there's no better example of this than the **Millennium Bridge** that links St Paul's with Tate Modern, designed by Foster and engineers Arup. Designed as an elegantly thin suspension structure, the bridge began to sway noticeably as soon as the public were allowed to cross it in mid 2000, and it was closed a few days later. After a long-running battle over who would pay for the repairs, this steel and aluminium structure now offers a wobble-free crossing to pedestrians and skateboarders, and there's now talk of slinging a similar bridge between Chelsea and Battersea.

THE SHOCK OF THE OLD

London's architecture is also marked by the 'green belt', a slice of protected countryside that prevents the city from bursting its banks and spilling into the rest of south-east England. Effectively a perimeter fence limiting sprawl, the green belt forces architects to work with what's there rather than building out. Done well, the new is grafted on to the old in a way that is often invisible from street level; visitors will be surprised by the way contemporary interiors have been inserted into old buildings.

Fortunately, the best examples of this can be found in the public museums and art galleries, many of which underwent millennial make-overs and expansion programmes. The **National Portrait Gallery**, the **Royal Opera House** and **Tate Britain** are good examples of architects adding modern signatures to old buildings, while the **British Museum**, the **National Maritime Museum** and the **Wallace Collection** have all gone one better. With the help of large lottery grants and glass roofs, these last three added to their facilities by invading what were once external courtyards. Foster's exercise in complexity at the British Museum, where the £100 million Great Court created the most spectacular and largest covered square in Europe, is without doubt the most impressive – every one of its 3,300 triangular glass panels is unique.

The more complete conversion of Sir Giles Gilbert Scott's power station into premier league art venue **Tate Modern** made a mockery of the architectural mantra 'form follows function'. This imposing edifice was dragged from obscurity by Swiss architects Herzog and de Meuron, who managed to preserve much of the original building while installing seven new floors of exhibition space.

The **National Gallery** is next in line for this treatment, with Dixon Jones, the architects responsible for redeveloping the National Portrait Gallery and the Royal Opera House, slotting new galleries and public spaces into neglected courtyards. Building work was already advanced as this book went to press and a grand new entrance, leading directly off Trafalgar Square, had just opened. The new light-filled East Wing entry point will do much to ease the pressure on the over-congested main entrance. Stage Two of this project (to restore the main entrance to its Victorian grandeur) hit the buffers when the Heritage Lottery Fund refused to stump up the cash.

Around the corner is the newly restored **Coliseum**, home of the English National Opera, where the wrappers have now come off a £40 million redevelopment (*see p303* **London Coliseum**). The results are first class. In the auditorium, look up at the golds, coppers and bronzes and remember that the roof was completely blacked out in the 1960s.

Transport infrastructure and the mixed developments that surround it look like being the story of the next few years. Richard Rogers's plans for a **Terminal 5** at Heathrow the size of a whole new airport are now well under way. There is also talk of extending the East London line into Hackney and the DLR is almost certainly going to reach to City airport and beyond. One respected architectural practice suggests constructing a monorail along Euston Road, while another has drawn up detailed plans for a similar system, costing £1.7 billion, to link Liverpool Street, Canary Wharf and the Lea Valley. It's not a bad idea, as tunnelling for the Crossrail scheme involves dodging all manner of existing tunnels and foundations (if it's ever finished, Crossrail will be a bit of a rollercoaster). As they say, desperate problems require radical solutions.

> ► Where no location is given in the text, buildings are listed elsewhere in this book; for details consult the index.

Under fire on **Sidney Street**. *See p41.*

Gangland London

Observer crime reporter Tony Thompson sends
back dispatches from history.

Your London villain is an archetype
recognised throughout the world. This
despite the fact that he's neither suave nor,
usually, particularly successful. Unlike his
American counterparts, he craves the limelight
– despite not being aesthetically cut out for it,
often thanks to his past as an ex-boxer. And the
limelight likes him right back. His hits are often
vicious, amateurish and played out publicly.
He has a self-aggrandising sense of humour
and a coterie of friends and family to whom
he is unfailingly loyal, despite a jarring lack of
sentiment towards the rest of the human race.
So ripe is this stereotype for lionisation that it
has spawned an entire sub-genre of film. And,
for once, it comes quite close to historical reality
– at least until the notorious Kray twins proved
that too much visibility was bad for business.

WALK ON THE WILD SIDE
The mould was made back in the early 18th
century. To the public he was a hero: a man
who caught criminals, returned stolen goods
and made the streets of the capital just that
little bit safer. But in reality Jonathan Wild was

a cunning pioneer in the world of organised
crime and London's first true gangster. Born
around 1682, the young Wild worked as a
servant but ended up in debtor's gaol after
being fired from his job. A model prisoner,
he soon earned enough trust to be allowed
out at night to help with the arrest of thieves
(an early form of community service) and met
prostitute Mary Milliner. She introduced Wild
to the ways of the underworld and invited him
to join her gang of thieves. Within a few months
Wild had made enough money to buy his way
out of prison and set himself up as a fence.

In the London of Wild's time, the vast gulf
between rich and poor fuelled crime rates, and
fear of crime obsessed the rich. The fact that
newspapers regularly regaled their readers with
sensational stories about highwaymen, thieves
and murderers did little to help. In a bid to
reduce spiralling crime rates in the capital, the
government began to offer substantial rewards
for those helping to bring criminals to justice.
Wealthy victims of crime also began to offer
rewards for the return of their goods.

The notorious **Blind Beggar**. See p42.

It didn't take long for Wild to see an easy way to make a killing. He established his own gang of thieves who carried out robberies on his behalf. Rather than risking selling the stolen goods he simply returned them to the owners and claimed the reward, splitting it with the thieves. At the same time he used his underworld contacts to get rid of rival gangs, informing on their activities and claiming government rewards in the process.

By 1718 Wild's testimony had sent more than 60 men to the gallows and he declared himself 'Thief Taker General of Great Britain and Ireland'. His influence was so great that the government even consulted him on methods of controlling crime. His chief recommendation? That the size of the rewards for apprehending thieves be substantially increased. And once the proposal had been accepted, Wild's income soon trebled and he moved into plush offices close to the Old Bailey.

> **'A record crowd went to the gallows to watch the man who was both poacher and gamekeepr swing.'**

Suspicions about his success grew and an Act of Parliament was passed making receivers of stolen property accessories to theft. Wild's so-called 'lost property office' had very little difficulty in evading the new law, and became so prosperous that two branch offices were opened. Those criminals who refused to work with him found themselves framed for robberies and thefts and ultimately arrested, including the charismatic highwayman and

housebreaker Jack Sheppard, whose exploits were lovingly recorded in the newspapers of the day. After four prison escapes, Sheppard was placed in the centre of Newgate Prison, loaded down with 300 pounds of iron chains and kept under constant observation. Such was his fame that gaolers charged high-society visitors a hefty fee to come into the prison and look at him. The notorious Sheppard was finally hanged on 16 November 1724.

Soon afterwards Wild's own misdeeds came to light. Members of his gang turned against him and he was arrested, tried and sentenced to hang. A record crowd went to the gallows to watch the man who was both poacher and gamekeeper swing.

TWO SMOKING BARRELS

Wild's case exposed the shortcomings of the thief-taker system and led to calls for the establishment of a proper police force. At the time, all law enforcement was carried out by householders appointed to the voluntary role of parish constable. They were required to apprehend anyone accused of a crime and bring them before a justice of the peace. With a few exceptions, this lack of a decent opposition meant that London's gangsters were able to operate with only a minimal amount of sophistication. But after the Metropolitan Police Force came into being in 1829 the chances of getting caught increased – and so did the stakes played for. Take, for example, the case of James Saward, a successful barrister who also worked as a forger, emptying the Bank of England of more than £100,000. Saward was also believed to have had a hand in the 1855 bullion robbery in which £12,000 worth of gold was stolen from a train travelling from London to Paris.

a few miles per hour because they had forgotten to take the brakes off. The police were closing in fast, and the two men ran along a path by Chingford Brook until they reached a high fence. Lepidus scrambled over but Hefeld was exhausted. As police closed in he shot himself in the head and died three weeks later. Lepidus used his last bullet to kill himself in a nearby cottage. The stolen wages bag was never found.

In all, Lepidus and Hefeld had fired more than 400 shots at their pursuers, showing that they had come fully prepared for a massive shoot-out. The 'Tottenham Outrage', as it came to be known, led to a massive shift in both police and public perception of immigrants and their role in London's criminal underworld.

ENTER THE MEDIA

These perceptions were reinforced the following year when a second gang of Latvian burglars killed three policemen and injured two others while fighting their way out of a robbery in a Houndsditch jewellery store. A few days later, in January 1911, two of the gang were tracked down to a flat in Sidney Street, Whitechapel.

Several officers went to knock on the door. Receiving no answer they threw pebbles at the window, from which there immediately came a volley of pistol shots, one of which found its mark. The police made a hasty retreat. Their revolvers and shotguns had such a limited range that it was impossible to get close enough to the flat to fire without being shot first. Totally outgunned, the police were forced to call in the Army. The then Home Secretary, none other than Winston Churchill, authorised the deployment of troops before going himself to Sidney Street to take command. The soldiers and the gangsters exchanged shots for over four hours before the building burst into flames. The fire brigade arrived quickly but Churchill told them to let the building burn. Two bodies were later discovered inside the house. A third gang member is believed to have somehow got away.

The Sidney Street Siege coincided with the early days of the cinema newsreel:footage both fanned and documented the fervent public interest that characterises London's relationship with violent crime. Thousands of people turned out to quietly watch the events unfold; selling their wares in the trade press, the newsreel companies headlined their advertisements with siege footage, vaunting their individual scoops.

YOU'RE (NOT) NICKED

Gangsters continued to flourish during the two world wars, profiting from the black market, but it is the characters who emerged at the end of this period who still have a lasting impact on London's underworld today.

As the police became more organised, so the tactics of the criminals changed. One of the most notable early robberies took place in January 1909, bringing the gun battle into the folklore in an extraordinary and violent chase caper. Latvian immigrants Jacob Lepidus and Paul Hefeld stole the wages from Schnurrman's rubber factory on the corner of Tottenham High Road, firing several shots at the driver of the wages car in the process. The sound of gunfire brought constables William Tyler and Albert Newman running out of the nearby police station with others following on foot and bicycle. Newman jumped in the wages car and urged the driver to run down the gunmen. In response Lepidus and Hefeld shot and injured both Newman and the driver. Ten-year-old Ralph Joscelyne was caught in the crossfire and fatally wounded.

The chase continued with the gunmen racing towards Tottenham Marshes where they were confronted by PC Tyler who'd found a short cut. 'Come on, give in. The game's up,' he told Hefeld, whose response was to shoot Tyler in the face at point blank range, killing him instantly.

By now more police had joined the chase, many of them armed. Members of the public, including a group of duck hunters and part of a football team, also joined in, throwing potatoes or whatever else came to hand at the villains. The gunmen commandeered a tram to make their escape; the police commandeered another tram going in the opposite direction and made the driver reverse after the robbers. Shots were liberally exchanged.

The gunmen ran out of the tram and jumped into a parked milk van but wrecked it by cornering too fast. They transferred to a horse-drawn greengrocer's van but could only manage

Few men typify this more than Joey Pyle. A promising professional boxer, Pyle carried out his first robbery at the age of 14 and made the mistake of bringing his bounty home in a canvas bag. 'My mum was furious – she didn't mind me doing the robbery, she just didn't want the police finding the money.' Pyle went on to become part of a gang of safe blowers, soon graduating to the status of armed robber specialising in cash in transit vans. In 1960 he was accused of being involved with a murder at the Pen Club where well-known underworld figure Selwyn Cooney had been shot dead. With hanging still in force Pyle spent months on death row before he and three others were cleared of all but the most minor charges. The acquittal led one newspaper to note that, so far as the law was concerned, 'Cooney just happened to lean on a passing bullet'.

'While the Krays courted publicity, Pyle remained in the background.'

During the 1960s Pyle was a close associate of the Kray twins, Ronnie and Reggie, and offered to help them to hide after Ronnie murdered George Cornell in the Blind Beggar pub in Whitechapel (see p158). It was the Krays who become iconic, the subject both of tabloid fascination and more serious analysis, but influencing fashion shoots is hardly a measure of gangster success. While the Krays courted publicity, Pyle remained in the background – and while the Krays were sent to prison for life, Pyle remained at liberty, to amass a great deal of money. He was arrested more than 50 times on charges ranging from robbery to murder, but was always acquitted, much to the chagrin of the police. He developed a close association with the New York mafia and spent a great deal of time in the States.

Then, like many gangsters of his generation, he became involved in drug trafficking – by far the fastest way to make money illegally. Pyle was caught and eventually sentenced to eight years in 1995 for his involvement with a heroin deal. Pyle has few regrets. 'Not only does crime pay,' he notes, 'but the hours are good.'

WANNA BE IN MY GANG?

Today all crime in the capital revolves almost entirely around the drug trade. And although indigenous Londoners make up the majority of the underworld workforce, they are increasingly working alongside other gangsters whose allegiance can be traced along ethnic lines, something entirely in keeping with the multicultural nature of the city. In the Green

Lanes area to the north, members of the Turkish mafia control the trade in heroin for most of the country. Of late, this dominance has been increasingly challenged by various Bangladeshi and Pakistani gangs based in the East End. Areas with a high proportion of Afro-Caribbean residents, including Hackney and Harlesden, have proved the ideal hiding place for members of so-called Yardie gangs. Originally from Jamaica, these gangs have cornered the capital's highly lucrative market in crack cocaine.

Colombian gangs based in Edgware control much of the cocaine market, while Albanian gangs now run much of London's vast vice trade. Around eight out of ten women working in off-street prostitution in Soho hail from that part of the world.

London's sizeable Chinese community has long been victimised and exploited by Triad gangsters. Their involvement in extortion and illegal gambling is well documented but in recent years people-smuggling has become their chief source of income. Only occasionally – such as with the deaths of 58 Chinese migrants at Dover in June 2000 or with the shooting of a Chinese businessman in Gerrard Street in June 2003 – do their exploits become public.

Regardless of background, the best and most successful of today's gangsters have learned from the Kray era that it is better to keep as low a profile as possible. In Southall the so-called Fiat Bravo gang drove nondescript cars to avoid police attention despite running a multi-million pound heroin business. The drug baron known as Father Fowl lived and dressed modestly despite being one of the capital's most prolific drug barons.

Meanwhile, one of London's most successful villains, a vicious killer and gang leader so seemingly lily-white that he cannot be named, has lived for years in a tiny council flat. Unable to move out for fear of drawing excessive police attention, he has instead lavished his millions on converting the place into a palace. From the outside it appears to be just another tower block. Inside, there are marble floors, gold taps in the bathroom and a chandelier that could have come straight out of the ballroom at the Savoy (not, of course, that we're saying it did).

No one gang or gangster has overall control. Even the infamous Krays never truly controlled London. (In fact, despite their notoriety, the twins made a great deal more money from merchandising, books and film rights while they were in prison than they ever did when they were on the outside.) None of this is cause for complacency, though. As one wry police officer notes, 'There are no Mr Bigs, but there are plenty of Mr Big-Enoughs.'

Where to Stay

Where to Stay 45

Features

The best Hotels 47
Daylight robbery 51
A room with a view 54

Where to Stay

Forty winks have never been this much fun.

Pavilion. *See p69.*

London may be one of the world's top tourist destinations, but its hotels get a consistently bad rap. The litany of criticisms is long: they're overpriced; you couldn't swing a cat in the rooms; the chintz is blinding; and the service is straight out of Fawlty Towers. In the late 1990s the scene got a burst of energy with the arrival of a slew of sleek designer hotels – St Martin's Lane, the Metropolitan et al – but they provided no relief to the long-suffering budget brigade. However, it seems that good things come to those who wait – or complain. People have started to demand value for money – a novel concept in London. And after 2003's *annus horribilis*, when occupancy rates dropped to record lows, the capital's hoteliers were forced to oblige. The snooty luxury hotels have started offering special deals; the budget hotels are making an effort to smarten up their decor; and the proliferation of discount hotel websites means it's a buyer's market.

But the most encouraging trend is the crop of new designer hotels, which have taken the Schrager hotel template and slashed the prices. The cream of the new crop are the **Zetter** and **Malmaison** (for both, *see p49*) and **Guesthouse West** (*see p66*).

The other welcome trend is the emergence of bona fide budget hotels in central London. At the new **Travelodge Covent Garden** (10 Drury Lane, WC2B 5RE, 7208 9988, www.travelodge.co.uk), you can book a room online for as little as £25 per night. And the new **easyhotel** (Lexham Gardens, W8, www.easyhotel.com), due to open in late 2004, takes the budget hotel concept to the extreme. Depending on demand, and how early you book, easyhotels will offer rooms in Kensington for as little as £5. And we mean just that: a room. No TV, no phone, no towels, no pictures, and in some cases, no windows (they will have bathrooms). Modelled on the Japanese capsule hotels, the shoebox rooms will be prefabricated plastic jobs. Frankly, sleeping on a park bench sounds more romantic. But we applaud the easygroup's rationale: making London affordable for ordinary mortals.

INFORMATION AND BOOKING

Many of London's swankier hotels are in **Mayfair**. **Bloomsbury** is good for mid-priced hotels. For cheap ones, try Ebury Street near **Victoria** (SW1), Gower Street in **Bloomsbury** (WC1) and **Earl's Court** (SW5). Other areas

The Zetter Restaurant & Rooms. *See p49.*

that are worth exploring for budget hotels include **Bayswater**, **Paddington** (W2) and **South Kensington** (SW7).

If you haven't booked ahead, the obliging staff at **Visit London** (08701 566366, www.visitlondon.com) will look for a place within your selected area and price range for a £5 fee. You can also check availability and reserve rooms either on its website or by going in person to its Piccadilly office.

PRICES AND CLASSIFICATION

We don't list official star ratings, which tend to reflect facilities rather than quality; instead, we've classified hotels, within their various area headings, according to the price of the cheapest double room per night.

Many high-end hotels sneakily quote room prices exclusive of VAT. Always check. We've included this 17.5 per cent tax in rates listed here; however, room rates change frequently, so do call and verify rates before you book.

Hotels are constantly offering special deals, particularly for weekends; check websites or ask for a special rate when booking. Also check discount hotel websites for prices that can fall well below the rack rates listed here.

FACILITIES AND ACCESSIBILITY

We've listed the main services offered by each hotel; note that concierges can arrange far more than are listed here. Some hotels in the Cheap category indicate which hotels offer rooms adapted for the needs of disabled guests, but check when booking. **Holiday Care** (0845 124 9971/www.holidaycare.org.uk) has details of wheelchair accessible places.

The South Bank & Bankside

Cheap

London County Hall Travel Inn Capital

County Hall, Belvedere Road, SE1 7PB (0870 238 3300/fax 7902 1619/www.travelinn.co.uk). Waterloo tube/rail. **Rates** £84.95-£86.95 double. **Credit** AmEx, DC, MC, V. **Map** p401 M9.

You know that design hotels have become positively mainstream when the Travel Inn chain starts imitating the Metropolitan. Since last year, this busy branch has banished its bland, hospital-esque lobby. Style gurus have brought in purple carpets, funky photographs and a postmodern clock without any numbers. The bedrooms have been spruced up, too, even if they aren't quite *Wallpaper** material. Some things haven't changed, though: the fantastic prices – children can often stay for free (phone ahead to check) – and the prime location, on the Thames near tourist attractions such as the London Eye and Big Ben. Other locations include Tower Bridge (Tower

Bridge Road, SE1, 0870 238 3303), Euston (1 Dukes Road, WC1H 9PJ, 0870 238 3301) and Kensington (11 Knaresborough Place, SW5 0TJ, 0870 238 3304). **Hotel services** *Bar. Disabled-adapted rooms. No-smoking rooms. Internet (dataport). Restaurant. TV.*

Mad Hatter

3-7 Stamford Street, SE1 9NY (7401 9222/fax 7401 7111/www.fullershotels.com). Southwark tube/Waterloo tube/rail. **Rates** £85-£105 double. **Credit** AmEx, DC, MC, V. **Map** p404 N8.
Owned by the Fuller's pub chain, the Mad Hatter doesn't exactly ooze authenticity. However, it successfully fuses 'Ye Olde England' pastiche with a bit of corporate comfort, efficient staff, and large and pleasant rooms. Tate Modern is nearby; the attached Fuller's pub offers a decent selection of English ales.
Hotel services *Bar. Concierge. Disabled-adapted rooms. No-smoking rooms. Internet (dataport). Restaurant. TV.*

The City

Deluxe

Great Eastern Hotel

40 Liverpool Street, EC2M 7QN (7618 5000/fax 7618 5001/www.great-eastern-hotel.co.uk). Liverpool Street tube/rail. **Rates** £266 single; £335-£394 double; £470-£675 suite. **Credit** AmEx, DC, MC, V. **Map** p405 Q6.
Once a faded railway hotel, the Great Eastern has been reborn. Thanks to a £70m overhaul by Sir Terence Conran, it's now a mammoth, urban style mecca, though one whose design is well thought out and sympathetic to its glorious Victorian building. Close to the City and the hipster districts of Shoreditch and Hoxton, the hotel attracts a mixture of suits and style mavens; in the lobby, copies of the *Financial Times* sit alongside avant-garde art. The six-storey atrium, overlooking a Zen rock garden lounge, is a show stopper. The bedrooms wear the regulation style mag uniform: Eames chairs, chocolate shagpile rugs and white Frette linens. And you'll never go hungry or thirsty here. The hotel has four bars, including a swanky new champagne bar and the atmospheric George, a faux-Elizabethan pub. Restaurants include the mandatory Japanese joint, a fish restaurant and the lovely Aurora, with its elegant stained-glass dome.
Hotel services *Bars (4). Business centre. Concierge. Disabled-adapted rooms. Gym. No-smoking floors. Internet (dataport, high-speed). Parking (valet). Restaurants (5). Room service. Spa. TV (pay movies/music/DVD).*

Expensive

Saint Gregory

100 Shoreditch High Street, E1 6JQ (7613 9800/www.saintgregory-hotel.com). Shoreditch tube/Old Street or Liverpool Street tube/rail. **Rates** £168-£195 double. **Credit** AmEx, MC, V. **Map** p403 R4.

The Saint Gregory has got all the ingredients to be fashionable: trendy Shoreditch location, modern building, bold interior design. But for all that, it feels a bit like a Holiday Inn masquerading as a style hotel. Yet that's no bad thing. The rates, particularly special weekend deals, are reasonable. The staff are chipper. And the bedrooms – decorated in a game attempt at retro chic, right down to the brown and orange colour schemes – are spacious and comfortable. On the top floor, the airy Globe Bar and Restaurant boasts mesmerising views of the City.
Hotel services *Bars (3). Concierge. Disabled-adapted rooms. Gym. No-smoking rooms/floors. Internet (web TV). Parking (£20/day). Restaurant. Room service. TV (pay movies/music).*

Holborn & Clerkenwell

Deluxe

Rookery

12 Peter's Lane, Cowcross Street, EC1M 6DS (7336 0931/fax 7336 0932/www.rookeryhotel.com). Farringdon tube/rail. **Rates** £252-£264 single; £287-£323 double; £581 suite. **Credit** AmEx, DC, MC, V. **Map** p402 O5.
Squirrelled away down a suitably Dickensian lane in Clerkenwell, the Rookery is an irresistible period piece. In a row of converted 18th-century houses, it's crammed full of glorious antiques: Gothic oak beds, plaster busts and clawfoot bathtubs. But don't worry, it's also equipped with modern creature

The best Hotels

For budget with beauty
The **Vancouver Studios**, the **Mayflower** and the **Rushmore** (for all three, *see p69*).

For Clerkenwell hipsters
The **Zetter** (*see p49*).

For colonial fantasies
Blakes (*see p61*), the **Portobello Hotel** and **Twenty Nevern Square** (for both, *see p68*).

For country living
The **Riverside Hotel** (*see p66*) and **Windmill on the Common** (*see p65*).

For cyber luxury
The **Dorchester** (*see p55*).

For family holidays
London County Hall Travel Inn Capital (*see p46*).

For flashy fashionistas
The **Baglioni** (*see p59*).

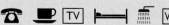
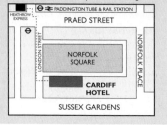

comforts: Egyptian cotton sheets and plush towels draped over heated towel racks. The public rooms, covered in dark wood panelling, resemble a decadent gentleman's club; by contrast, the staff are young and relaxed. Though it's got a garden, the hotel's relentless cosiness – try curling up by the fire in the library – makes it a particularly appealing place during the winter months.

Hotel services *Bar. Concierge. Disabled-adapted rooms. No-smoking rooms/floors. Internet (dataport). Room service. TV.*

Moderate

Malmaison

Charterhouse Square, EC1M 6AH (7012 3700/www.malmaison.com). Farringdon tube/rail. **Rates** £99-£165 double; £165-£194 superior double. **Credit** AmEx, DC, MC, V. **Map** p402 O5.

When the first Malmaison opened in Edinburgh ten years ago, it managed to make other hotels look like they'd lost their way. Despite providing the kind of facilities that the market craved – handsome, thoughtfully specced rooms, non-institutional public areas and restaurants that weren't just for guests who didn't have the initiative to go out – the 'Mal' nevertheless charged rates that seemed entirely reasonable. Now a small chain, Malmaison has brought the formula to a former nurses' home in Clerkenwell. In general, it works well. You don't get ego-sopping luxuries bumping up your room rates, but stuff you need: 24-hour room service, CD players, ubiquitous free broadband access, enjoyable decor (with lovely London photos). A couple of notes ring hollow in the capital, particularly the packed-lunch style breakfast with its jokey franglais packaging and sachet coffee – but we're assured they're working on that. *Bar. Disabled-adapted rooms. Gym. No-smoking floors. Internet (free broadband). Restaurant. Room service. TV.*

Zetter Restaurant & Rooms

86-88 Clerkenwell Road, EC1M 5RJ (7324 4444/fax 7324 4445/www.thezetter.com). Farringdon tube/rail. **Rates** £153-£211 double; £282-£305 suites. **Credit** AmEx, MC, V. **Map** p 402 O4.

It was only a matter of time before trendy Clerkenwell got a hip hotel. And the Zetter pushes all the right buttons: its snazzy Italian restaurant is buzzing; the lobby is decked out in a chic retro style; the popular Match Bar is just across the road. In true Clerkenwell style, the hotel is housed in a converted warehouse, complete with a dazzling atrium. The bedrooms, done up in creams and greys, are small but stylish. Their ecological credentials are impeccable: if you open a window, the air-con goes off; water comes from the hotel's own well. Instead of minibars, posh vending machines in the corridors dispense gin and tonics, champagne and cappuccinos. The rooftop suites have fantastic wooden decks (and, of course, the best views in the house). Not quite the Sanderson, then, but almost as easy on the eye – and much easier on the wallet.

Hotel services *Bar. Concierge. Disabled-adapted rooms. No-smoking rooms/floors. Internet (dataport, high-speed, web TV, wireless). Restaurant. Room service. TV (pay movies/music/DVD).*

Bloomsbury & Fitzrovia

Deluxe

Sanderson

50 Berners Street, W1T 3NG (7300 1400/fax 7300 1401/www.morganshotelgroup.com). Oxford Circus tube. **Rates** £400-£458 double; £658 loft studio. **Credit** AmEx, DC, MC, V. **Map** p398 J5.

London may be drowning in design hotels, but this Schrager and Stark creation still thrills. The theatrical lobby resembles a surreal film set, with its sheer flowing curtains, Salvador Dali red-lip sofa and ornately framed portraits of chihuahuas. Next door, the silvery Long Bar is similarly ethereal; the glamorous Purple Bar – open to residents only – is dark and discreet. Spoon, the acclaimed Alain Ducasse restaurant, offers a playful fusion menu. Upstairs, the minimalist bedrooms continue the dreamy theme, with landscape paintings on the ceilings and more filmy curtains. But the hotel's real showpiece is the spa, a maze of shimmering curtains, romantic lighting and beautiful bodies.

Hotel services *Bars (2). Business services. Concierge. Disabled-adapted rooms. Gym. Internet (dataport, wireless). No-smoking rooms/floors. Restaurant. Room service. TV (DVD).*

Expensive

Charlotte Street Hotel

15-17 Charlotte Street, W1T 1RJ (7806 2000/ fax 7806 2002/www.firmdalehotel.com). Goodge Street, Oxford Circus, Tottenham Court Road or Warren Street tube. **Rates** £230 single; £241-£335 double; £388 suite. **Credit** AmEx, MC, V. **Map** p399 J5.

Designer Kit Kemp, the doyenne of London boutique hotels, pioneered the 'modern English' decorative style currently sweeping London. This stunning boutique hotel – one of six in Kemp's exclusive Firmdale mini chain – fuses traditional English furnishings with avant-garde art and glossy American luxury. The public rooms are adorned with Bloomsbury paintings, including works by Duncan Grant and Vanessa Bell, mixed with abstract art. The bedrooms merge English understatement with bold flourishes; soft beiges and greys spiced up with brazen plaid-floral combinations. The glossy granite and oak bathrooms, with their mini TVs, make you feel like a star. So does the luxury screening room, which shows cinematic classics every Sunday. And the beautiful Oscar restaurant and bar is filled with plenty of beautiful people.

Hotel services *Bar. Concierge. Disabled-adapted room. Gym. Internet (high-speed, wireless). No-smoking rooms. Restaurant. Room service. TV (DVD).*

Montague on the Gardens

15 Montague Street, WC1B 5BJ (7637 1001/fax 7637 2516/www.redcarnationhotels.com). Holborn or Russell Square tube. **Rates** *£212 single; £247 double; £406-£517 suite.* **Credit** *AmEx, DC, MC, V.* **Map** *p399 L5.*

The Montague is a flamboyant tribute to Victorian England. The doormen are dressed in top hats and tails, and the sitting room is decked out like a Christmas tree, with crystal chandeliers, crimson walls and riotous floral upholstery; just the ticket for glamorous grannies. The floral motif extends to the summery conservatory bar, which overlooks the Duke of Bedford's garden, and to the luxurious bedrooms, where flora covers the curtains, bedspreads and wallpaper. Despite the period glitz, the rooms are thoroughly modern, kitted out with business technology and entertainment; the gym is similarly well equipped. Not quite the Ritz, but a reasonable and reasonably priced facsimile.

Hotel services *Bar. Business services. Concierge. Disabled-adapted room. Gym. No-smoking floors/rooms. Internet (dataport). Parking (valet). Restaurants (3). Room service. TV (pay movies).*

myhotel bloomsbury

11-13 Bayley Street, WC1B 3HD (7667 6000/fax 7667 6001/www.myhotels.co.uk). Goodge Street or Tottenham Court Road tube. **Rates** *£190 single; £223-£258 double; £293-£423 studio.* **Credit** AmEx, DC, MC, V. **Map** p399 K5.

Back in 1999 this sleek Conran-designed hotel introduced London to Asian fusion decor and feng shui principles. But with the backlash against minimalism, the hotel is getting a facelift – and a splash of colour. In the bedrooms, the stark white walls are being repainted in warmer shades, from beige to fuchsia. Single rooms, meanwhile, are being redone with foldaway day beds to increase work space; all rooms are now equipped with flat-screen TVs and DVDs. Elsewhere, the hotel ticks over as before: the aquarium, scented candles and floral arrangements lend the lobby a bit of Zen; the airy, buzzy bar still teems with groovers and shakers; and the adjoining Yo! Sushi restaurant ensures the hotel's East meets West theme endures.

Hotel services *Bar. Business services. Concierge. Gym. Internet (dataport, wireless). No-smoking rooms/floors. Restaurant. Room service. Spa. TV (DVD, pay movies).*

Moderate

Academy Hotel

21 Gower Street, WC1E 6HG (7631 4115/fax 7636 3442/www.theetoncollection.com). Goodge Street tube. **Rates** *£164 single; £137-£192 double; £182-£256 suite.* **Credit** AmEx, DC, MC, V. **Map** p399 K5.

If Laura Ashley opened a townhouse hotel, it might look a bit like the Academy. But the traditional country house decor is not oppressive: the look is soft, floral and summery. The library, for example, opens on to a fragrant walled garden, and the hotel's colour

scheme consists of soft pastel greens and yellows. The rooms are decked out with luxurious upholstery, thick carpets and antique furniture. Yet the old-fashioned Englishness comes with a sheen of modernity: the windows, for instance, are double-glazed to keep out the noise.

Hotel services *Bar. Disabled-adapted rooms. No-smoking rooms. Internet (dataport, wireless broadband). Room service. TV.*

Harlingford Hotel

61-63 Cartwright Gardens, WC1H 9EL (7387 1551/fax 7387 4616/www.harlingfordhotel.com). Russell Square tube/Euston tube/rail. **Rates** *£75 single; £95 double; £105 triple; £110 quad.* **Credit** AmEx, MC, V. **Map** p399 L3.

Formerly a dowdy London B&B, the Harlingford got the mother of all makeovers last year. Down came the flock wallpaper, up went the white paint; out went the chintz, in came the bright and breezy fabrics. Now the grungy old bathrooms have been replaced with smart modern affairs. Sometimes it tries a bit too hard: in an attempt to appear cutting edge, the owners have scattered issues of *Wallpaper** in the lounge. Still, they should be commended for injecting some flair into the budget hotel formula. And the location, on one of Bloomsbury's Georgian crescents, is lovely: the adjacent garden and tennis court are available to guests.

Hotel services *Restaurant. TV.*

Jenkins Hotel

45 Cartwright Gardens, WC1H 9EH (7387 2067/fax 7383 3139/www.jenkinshotel.demon.co.uk). Russell Square tube/Euston tube/rail. **Rates** *£72 single; £85 double; £105 triple.* **Credit** MC, V. **Map** p399 L3.

On the same sweeping crescent as the Harlingford, the Jenkins is a more traditionally English B&B: an episode of Poirot was filmed here. Nevertheless, this Georgian townhouse has a pleasingly informal feel: the check-in desk is located in the owner's kitchen and guests are welcome to browse through the bookshelf of travel guides. The rooms are painted in soft pastel hues – light yellows, blues and creams – and are relatively tasteful (for the price range). Guests have access to the garden and tennis court out front.

Hotel services *No-smoking throughout. TV.*

Morgan Hotel

24 Bloomsbury Street, WC1B 3QJ (7636 3735/fax 7636 3045). Tottenham Court Road tube. **Rates** *£75 single; £95 double; £140 triple. Flat £90 1 person; £120 2 people; £160 3 people.* **Credit** MC, V. **Map** p399 K5.

Imagine *EastEnders* transplanted to Bloomsbury: this cheap and cheerful family-run hotel could easily stand in for the Queen Vic. Its owners are chirpy old-school Londoners, who've been running the place for 27 years. Last year, the Morgan received a long-overdue renovation: the rooms got new carpets and mattresses and a fresh coat of paint. The rooms won't be gracing the pages of any style mags, but they're comfy and air-conditioned. And the cosy, panelled breakfast room – with its framed London memora-

Daylight robbery

Thou shalt not steal. That's what it says in the Bible. Which, funnily enough, is routinely pilfered from hotel rooms. Along with towels and bed linen (30 per cent of guests steal these, according to an industry survey), bathrobes, toilet rolls and light bulbs. Rounding out the top ten are pillows, hairdryers, kettles, ashtrays and ironing boards. We may consider ourselves law-abiding citizens, but it seems as soon as we enter a hotel room we're transformed into raving kleptomaniacs: 66 per cent of Britons admit to stuffing 'extras' into their suitcases.

And according to the new industry exposé, *Hotel Babylon*, by Imogen Edwards-Jones and 'Anyonymous', we're getting more devious: cheapskate guests routinely polish off minibar vodka bottles and refill them with water; whisky, meanwhile, is replaced with tea. Unsurprisingly, luxury hotels are the biggest targets: with the rise of bling-bling culture, people want logos. That's why fluffy monogrammed bathrobes routinely go missing from the Dorchester, the Ritz and the Savoy – and end up being auctioned on ebay.

This label larceny also extends to toiletries. Here's the designer dish on bath-product booty: Bulgari (the Ritz), Floris (the Savoy, Claridge's), Ren (Great Eastern), Molton Brown (No.5 Maddox Street), Aveda (myhotel) and Penhaligon's (the Bentley).

But this five-star filching is getting out of hand. In the hotel industry, they used to say, 'If it's not screwed down, they'll take it.' These days, guests bring screwdrivers. In a recent survey by *Caterer & Hotelkeeper*, a UK trade mag, hoteliers revealed a bizarre array of stolen items: toilet seats (two wooden Victorian ones were nicked from the Savoy), bathroom sinks, door hinges, a spy hole and, in one case, the hotel owner's dog.

Art thieves are finding rich pickings, too: in the past, chi-chi Blakes has lost valuable paintings and antique furniture. One exclusive hotel lost the grand piano from its lobby: thieves dressed as maintenance men brazenly wheeled it out of the front door. But the most breathtaking steal occurred at myhotel chelsea last year. A thief cheekily sent the concierge to Harrods to buy a pair of computer bags. Then he proceeded to fill said bags with a pair of £5,000 flat-screen TVs from his room – and checked out using a stolen credit card.

Psychologists say that, as hotels become more corporate and less personal, guests feel entitled to a few extras. Others blame a new design trend: decorating your home to resemble a chic hotel. At the Sanderson and St Martin's Lane, Philippe Starck objects were disappearing so frequently that the hotels started selling every item in the bedrooms: Philippe Starck dumbbells (£525), throw rug (£210), cherrywood tray (£105), pillow (£63), plastic bin (£52), clothes hanger (£16). Even the Savoy has got in on the act: it now sells its trademark watering-can showerheads (£171).

But no matter what spoils you spirit away, there's no such thing as a free lunch – or Ritz bathrobe. We all pay the price in the end: hotels now factor thievery into the room rates; roughly ten per cent of the cost. So the more we pinch, the more we'll pay.

bilia – is quintessentially English. Also, the hotel's annexe of spacious flats – one of London's best deals – is due to be revamped in 2005.
Hotel services *No-smoking rooms/floors. TV.*

Cheap

Arosfa

83 Gower Street, WC1E 6HJ (tel/fax 7636 2115).
Goodge Street tube. **Rates** £45 single; £66 double;
£79 triple. **Credit** MC, V. **Map** p399 K4.
Arosfa means 'place to stay' in Welsh. And, until recently, that about summed this place up: a bed, a roof over your head, and there's your money. But, in these sophisticated times, spartan doesn't cut it anymore: in 2003 this townhouse hotel was extensively refurbished. The rooms have been given paint jobs, new furniture and carpets, and, most importantly, bathrooms (admittedly, they're the size of airplane lavatories). It's always had a great location – in the heart of Bloomsbury, opposite a huge Waterstone's – and a pleasing walled garden. At press time, the hotel was up for sale. Let's hope the new owners don't change its best asset: the prices.
Hotel services *No-smoking throughout. TV.*

Ashlee House

261-265 Gray's Inn Road, WC1X 8QT (7833 9400/fax 7833 9677/www.ashleehouse.co.uk). King's Cross tube/rail. **Rates** (per person) £34-£36 single; £22-£24 twin; £20-£22 triple; £13-£16 dorm. **Credit** MC, V. **Map** p399 M3.
Ashlee House is a rare beast: a youth hostel with a bit of style. The funky lobby is decorated with London Underground wallpaper and sheepskin-covered sofas. Some of the bedrooms have brave colour schemes – shocking pink or olive green – and boldly striped duvets (red, orange and fuchsia). It's also got all the handy hostel stuff – internet stations, a kitchen, luggage room, laundry – plus entertainment (TV room, table football). Unlike its rival, Generator (*see below*), the partying doesn't seem quite so relentless – its oldest guest was 86 – which is probably due to the fact that there's no curfew.
Hotel services *No-smoking throughout.*

Generator

37 Tavistock Place, WC1H 9SE (7388 7666/fax 7388 7644/www.generatorhostels.com). Russell Square tube. **Rates** (per person) £42 single; £26.50 twin/double; £22.50 multi; £15-£17 dormitory.
Credit MC, V. **Map** p399 K4.
In the cafeteria of the Generator, there are posters advertising drinking contests, breakfast menus entitled 'the Big Hangover Cure' and, on the noticeboard, Polaroids of people mooning. Like a London version of a Club 18-30 holiday, this place is party central for the backpacker brigade. It's got that popular MTV industrial look: steel, exposed pipes, neon signs and coloured lighting. The massive bar hosts karaoke nights and happy hours galore. There's also a games room and a movie lounge. When you've sobered up, there's practical stuff: a travel agent, a shop, an i

nternet room and staff who can party in several languages. Oh, we almost forgot: there are beds, too, 857 of them, should you ever want to get some sleep.
Hotel services *Bar. No-smoking throughout. Restaurant.*

St Margaret's Hotel

26 Bedford Place, WC1B 5JL (7636 4277/fax 7323 3066). Holborn or Russell Square tube. **Rates** £51.50-£78 single; £63.50-£99.50 double; £89.50-£121.50 triple. **Credit** MC, V. **Map** p399 L5.
This bustling townhouse hotel is enormous – there are 64 rooms – but it retains a homely ambience. The friendly feel is down to the Marazzi family, who have run the place for 52 years. The rooms are simple, comfy and relatively spacious; all have reading lights and fans in the summer. The huge triple rooms are especially good for families. Bathrooms are shared, but they're spotless; the watering-can showerheads are another plus. Rooms at the back have views of two gardens: the Duke of Bedford's formal affair and the hotel's own little green patch. Guess which one you can go in.
Hotel services *Disabled-adapted floors. No-smoking rooms/floors. TV.*

Marylebone

Moderate

Sherlock Holmes Hotel

108 Baker Street, W1U 6LJ (7486 6161/fax 7958 5211/www.sherlockholmeshotel.com). Baker Street tube. **Rates** (breakfast incl weekends) £128-£264 double; £199-£317 suite. **Credit** AmEx, DC, MC, V. **Map** p398 G5.
How do you transform a dreary, chintz-filled Hilton into a hip boutique hotel? It's elementary: hype up the Baker Street address; banish the bland chain decor; and create a gorgeous lobby bar that gives the place a buzz. That's what the Sherlock Holmes did a couple of years ago and it hasn't looked back. The bar is the epitome of casual chic: wood floors, cream walls and brown leather furniture. The rooms, meanwhile, resemble hip bachelor pads: beige and brown colour scheme, leather headboards, pinstripe sheets and spiffy bathrooms. There's a good gym with sauna, and you can eat at Sherlock's Grill.
Hotel services *Bar. Business services. Concierge. Disabled-adapted rooms. Gym. Internet (dataport). No-smoking rooms. Restaurant. Room service. Spa. TV (pay movies).*

Mayfair & St James's

Deluxe

Claridge's

55 Brook Street, W1A 2JQ (7629 8860/fax 7950 5481/www.claridges.co.uk). Bond Street tube. **Rates** £234-£406 single; £246-£450 double; £375-£4,524 suite. **Credit** AmEx, DC, MC, V. **Map** p400 H6.

A room with a view

For a view to a thrill, London hotel rooms generally offer three choices: river, park or city. And though *Time Out* is reluctant to promote the big, bland chains, nor would we want to churlishly overlook them. Therefore, the blue ribbon for best view surely goes to the **London Marriott County Hall** (Westminster Bridge Road, SE1 7PB, 7928 5200, www.marriott.co.uk). Its riverfront rooms (from £264) are the stuff of postcards: half overlook Big Ben, the other half face the London Eye. For a view both ways, splash out on a spectacular balcony suite.

For classic London scenes, the **Savoy** (*see p58*) comes a very close second. Monet painted his famous London watercolours from the river suites (from £581), which take in the same landmarks as the Marriott, but from the other bank. Ask (and, of course, pay) for a room from the fourth floor or higher; one river room, No.817, has a balcony.

Hyde Park is another pleasing London prospect. At the **Metropolitan** (*see p55*), in west-facing rooms above the fourth floor, the park is laid out before you like a lush green carpet. The penthouse suite (£2,100) has a shower with a view – so you can lather up while looking out. For a royal view, at a royal price, the suites at the **Milestone** (*see p61*) – the Viscount and the Regency (from £646)

– look on to Kensington Palace and Gardens. For a hint of Hollywood romance, hire an apartment at the **Hempel** (*see p66*); its flats overlook the private garden that featured in the love scene in *Notting Hill* (from £528). Garden scenes at **Dolphin Square** (*see p63*; from £109) are even better: the three acres of lush, landscaped gardens resemble a tropical resort.

As the name suggests, the **Trafalgar** overlooks one of London's most iconic landmarks, Trafalgar Square. As usual, the corporate bigwigs get the best perspective: the corner boardroom has full-on, floor-to-ceiling views of the square. But bedrooms 203, 207, 303, 307 and 309 (from £246) all overlook the square too.

City slickers might prefer the grittier view from the **Zetter** (*see p49*): its rooftop studios have decks that face south – taking in the City and the Gherkin – or west (BT Tower, sunset). The breathtaking rooftop Globe Bar and Restaurant at the **Saint Gregory** (*see p47*) boasts panoramic views of the City, both from its balcony and tables. And the **City Inn Westminster** (*see p63*) features a striking urban outlook from its 13th floor Thames Suite (from £1,116): this encompasses the MI6 building, the Tate and Battersea Power Station.

'When I die,' Spencer Tracy once said, 'I don't want to go to heaven; I want to go to Claridge's.' Perhaps he was an art deco fan: the hotel's 1930s interior is so convincing you could skip the Victoria & Albert museum. The rooms are subtle and classy: soft mauves, olive greens and dainty antiques, with the odd flamboyant twist. The rooftop gym is almost too beautiful to get sweaty in – and the spa is so classy you expect to bump into Audrey Hepburn (this was her favourite hotel). In the swish bar, customers get through an average of 90 bottles of champagne per night. Then there's Gordon Ramsay's famous restaurant (see p206). Despite the chef's recent foray into reality TV, it's lost no cachet: there's still a three-month queue to get a table.

Hotel services Bar. Business services. Concierge. Gym. Internet (dataport, high-speed). No-smoking rooms. Restaurants (2). Room service. Spa. TV (pay movies).

Dorchester

53 Park Lane, W1A 2HJ (7629 8888/fax 7409 0114/www.dorchesterhotel.com). Hyde Park Corner tube. **Rates** £358 single; £452-£546 double; £646-£1,469 suite. **Credit** AmEx, DC, MC, V. **Map** p400 G7.

Sister to the Beverly Hills Hotel, the Dorchester is the height of old-fashioned glamour: it's got the most opulent lobby in London, Prince Philip had his stag night here and Elizabeth Taylor and Richard Burton honeymooned in the ostentatious Oliver Meissel suite (which comes with gold-leaf toilet seats and a fake bookshelf that hides a bar). Liberace's piano, meanwhile, sits gaudily in the bar. Less snooty than the Ritz, the Dorchester is just as luxurious: the four-poster beds are draped in sumptuous floral upholstery and mountains of plump cushions. And the technology is staggering: to help you navigate the sophisticated web TVs, the hotel's e-butlers – computer geeks in tails – are at your beck and call.

Hotel services Bar. Concierge. Disabled-adapted rooms. Gym. Internet (dataport, high-speed, web TV). No-smoking rooms/floors. Parking. Restaurants (3). Room service. Spa. TV (pay movies/music/DVD).

Ritz

150 Piccadilly, W1J 9BR (7493 8181/fax 7493 2687/www.theritzlondon.com). Green Park tube. **Rates** £353 single; £429-£506 double; £588-£917 suite. **Credit** AmEx, DC, MC, V. **Map** p400 J8.

This is one London hotel that needs no introduction: it is, quite simply, the Ritz. Let's face it, Irving Berlin wrote a song about it, and endorsements don't come much better than that. Also, it's the only London hotel whose name has spawned an adjective: 'ostentatiously luxurious and glamorous', according to the dictionary. No kidding. Decorated in a Louis XVI theme, the hotel is an orgy of ornate chandeliers, rococo mirrors and marble columns. The bedrooms are Versailles in miniature: plush peaches and cream upholstery and real gold paint. What's more, the hotel has finally entered the 21st century and installed wireless internet. Another addition, the Rivoli bar, is a fine art deco pastiche. If you can't

afford to stay here, splash out on tea in the lavish Palm Court, but book ahead: there's a two-month waiting list. And a £32 price tag for a few cuppas and cucumber sandwiches. Not to mention supercilious staff. Still, it's the Ritz.

Hotel services Bar. Business services. Concierge. Gym. Internet (dataport, high-speed, wireless). No-smoking rooms and floors. Restaurant. Room service. TV (VCR).

Expensive

Metropolitan

19 Old Park Lane, W1K 1LB (7447 1000/fax 7447 1100/www.metropolitan.co.uk). Green Park, Hyde Park Corner or Piccadilly Circus tube. **Rates** £225-£405 double; £405-£2,820 suite. **Credit** AmEx, DC, MC, V. **Map** p400 G8.

The Metropolitan has become better known as the site of bust-ups and quickies than as a hotel. But with those episodes in the past, it is today the preferred choice of moneyed travellers with an eye for design. While the Met has aged better than some of its newer rivals, it's not as cool as it likes to think it is – the insipid beige carpets and black marble in the small bathrooms aren't exactly the height of style, but crisp white sheets, huge beds, CD players and wide-screen TVs with plenty of channels go some way to compensate. And should you need some proper pampering, massages are available in the elaborately named COMO Shambhala Spa (really just two treatment rooms, nice as they are). As for the rates, they range from not-bad-for-London to frankly shocking – from £605 for suites, which, on the lower floors, miss out on those great park views and have the added annoyance of loud traffic. Staff are suitably chic in their black Armani outfits but some could do with a humour injection.

Hotel services Bar. Business centre. Concierge. Disabled-adapted rooms. Gym. No-smoking rooms/floors. Parking. Restaurant. Room service. Spa. TV (cable/pay movies/DVD).

No.5 Maddox Street

5 Maddox Street, W1S 2QD (7647 0200/fax 7647 0300/www.living-rooms.co.uk). Oxford Circus tube. **Rates** £200-£288 double suite; £529 2-bedroom suite; £705 3-bedroom suite. **Credit** AmEx, DC, MC, V. **Map** p398 J6.

For a hip pad in the heart of swinging London, this discreet boutique hotel is just the ticket. It doesn't look like a hotel: blink and you'll miss the unassuming entrance. The smart lobby, with its huge aquarium, resembles a chic bank. And the rooms themselves are actually trendy flats. The theme is East meets West: bamboo floors and Far Eastern furniture mixed with fake fur throws and the obligatory crisp white sheets. There's no bar, but Soho is nearby. And the kitchens are stocked with organic treats (room service will shop for you too). So you could whip up dinner and throw your own party.

Hotel services Concierge. Internet (dataport, high-speed). No-smoking rooms. Room service. TV (DVD).

Trafalgar

2 Spring Gardens, SW1A 2TS (7870 2900/fax 7870 2911/www.hilton.co.uk/trafalgar). Charing Cross tube/rail. **Rates** £169-£189 double; £339-£480 studio. **Credit** AmEx, DC, MC, V. **Map** p401 K7.

Part of the Hilton group, this property is a welcome break from the norm in central London – cheaper than the big boys but a step up from the chintz and florals you tend to get elsewhere for the same price. Decor-wise, rooms are minimalist but with dull colour schemes, though some have nice touches in the form of leather sofas and chairs. A lack of mod cons doesn't help – sure, there are robes, slippers and an iron, but very few TV channels. The location is the hotel's biggest draw – corner rooms overlook the square and the surprisingly intimate rooftop bar has views of the city – though it's not always open. Ironically, while the double glazing drowns out the traffic noise, the award-winning Rockwell bar in the lobby is prone to booming out into the night (ask for a room on an upper floor if you're a light sleeper). However, our main niggle is the pricing of extras: the room service menu includes a bowl of soup for £11.50 plus service charge plus a £5 room tray.
Hotel services *Bar. Concierge. Disabled-adapted rooms. Internet (dataport). No-smoking floors. Parking. Restaurant. Room service. TV (pay movies).*

Soho & Chinatown

Expensive

Hazlitt's

6 Frith Street, W1D 3JA (7434 1771/fax 7439 1524/www.hazlittshotel.com). Tottenham Court Road tube. **Rates** £205 single; £240 double; £350 suite. **Credit** AmEx, DC, MC, V. **Map** p399 K6.

Hazlitt's, a rustic Georgian townhouse hotel, has an impressive literary pedigree: it's named after William Hazlitt, a famous 18th-century essayist; Jonathan Swift once slept here (there's a room named after him); and, more recently, it was immortalised in Bill Bryson's *Notes from a Small Island*. What's more, famous authors stay here whenever they're in town (in the library there are signed first editions from the likes of Ted Hughes and JK Rowling). It's no wonder writers love the place: it oozes historical charm. The floors are lopsided, the walls are warped and the antiques are the real deal: massive oak beds, clawfoot bathtubs and rich Persian rugs. But don't worry: Hazlitt's brims with 21st-century comforts too, such as air-conditioning, web TV and triple-glazed windows to keep out the sounds of Soho.
Hotel services *Business services. Concierge. Internet (dataport, web TV). No-smoking floors. Room service. TV (pay movies/DVD).*

Soho Hotel

4 Richmond Mews (off Dean Street), W1D 3DH (7559 3000/fax 7559 3003/www.sohohotel.com). Tottenham Court Road tube. **Rates** £235-£295 double; £395-£2,500 suite; £1,400-£5,950 apartment (weekly). **Credit** AmEx, MC, V. **Map** p399 K6.

It's official: Kit Kemp is taking over London. The capital's resident hotel queen has just unveiled her sixth property. And the Soho Hotel, her attempt at urban hip, is her most edgy creation yet. Critics say Kemp brings the country house to the city. But the aesthetic at the Soho Hotel is a very long way indeed from the shires. The new red-brick structure resembles a converted loft building. Some of the public rooms feature groovy colours: shocking pink or acid green, for example. Refuel, the loungey bar and restaurant, has an open kitchen and a car-themed mural. And though the bedrooms are classic Kemp – soft neutrals, bold pinstripes and traditional florals – they've got a contemporary edge: modern furniture, retro lighting and industrial-style windows. They're also huge. Downstairs, there are two screening rooms for Hollywood types and treatment rooms for stressed executives.
Hotel services *Bar. Business services. Concierge. Disabled-adapted rooms. Gym. Internet (high-speed, dataport). No-smoking rooms. Room service. TV (wide-screen/DVD).*

Cheap

Piccadilly Backpackers

12 Sherwood Street, W1F 7BR (7434 9009/ fax 7434 9010/www.piccadillybackpackers.com). Piccadilly Circus tube. **Rates** (per person) £34 single; £24 double; £16 multi; £12 dorms. **Credit** AmEx, MC, V. **Map** p400 J7.

Let's cut to the chase. Piccadilly Backpackers has two things going for it: rates – from £12 per night – and location. But there's an aesthetic price to pay for such a great bargain. Whereas the Generator hostel (*see p53*) incorporates industrial-style decor as a fashion statement, Piccadilly Backpackers resembles a boiler room out of sheer cheapness. On a positive note, the bedrooms are relatively spacious; there's a friendly buzz throughout; and the walls are thick, which means you shouldn't hear the pandemonium in the halls. Should you get bored of sightseeing, slob out in the common room where you can surf 100 channels on the wide-screen TV or get online. There's handy stuff, too, such as luggage storage, a bar, a travel shop and discount theatre tickets. Luckily, the hostel has no curfew, which means you can make the most of your cheap digs – by getting out on the town.
Hotel services *Disabled-adapted rooms. No-smoking throughout.*

Covent Garden & St Giles's

Deluxe

Covent Garden Hotel

10 Monmouth Street, WC2H 9HB (7806 1000/fax 7806 1100/www.firmdalehotels.com). Covent Garden or Leicester Square tube. **Rates** £247 single; £300-£358 double; £412-£1,052 suite. **Credit** AmEx, MC, V. **Map** p399 L6.

The achingly fashionable **Baglioni**.

In Kit Kemp's mini empire of design hotels, the Covent Garden is the most showbiz in both look and atmosphere. For one thing, it's in the heart of theatreland. Film stars and Hollywood executives attend screenings in the basement cinema (which also shows classics for guests every Saturday night – you can call ahead to get a programme of upcoming movies). And the decor, too, is much more flamboyant. Kemp's distinctive modern English style is a bold mix: traditional stuff – pinstriped wallpaper, floral upholstery – with a contemporary twist. The comfy bedrooms have two Kemp trademarks: upholstered mannequins and shiny granite and oak bathrooms. The restaurant is unremarkable, but the clubby library, with its pink plaid couches, is striking. Snuggle up by the fire with a drink and – if you're lucky – a Hollywood heart-throb.
Hotel services *Bar. Business services. Concierge. Disabled-adapted rooms. Gym. Internet (dataport). No-smoking rooms. Parking (valet). Restaurant. Room service. TV (DVD).*

St Martin's Lane Hotel

45 St Martin's Lane, WC2N 4HX (reservations 0800 634 5500/7300 5500/fax 7300 5501/www.morgans hotelgroup.com). Covent Garden tube. **Rates** £235-£323 single; £259-£347 double; £323-£405 penthouse. **Credit** AmEx, DC, MC, V. **Map** p401 L7.
Back when it opened in 2000 as a Schrager hotel, this was the toast of the town. The flamboyant lobby was always buzzing; the Light Bar was filled with celebrities, and guests giggled at Philippe Starck's playful decor. Five years later, the novelty is starting to wear off. Sure, the 'theatrical minimalist' decor is still striking. And Asia de Cuba remains a good restaurant. But Starck objects – such as the gold

tooth stools in the lobby – have become positively mainstream, and there have been complaints about service. Admittedly, the place still induces a smile.
Hotel services *Bar. Business services. Concierge. Disabled-adapted rooms. Gym. Internet (dataport, high-speed). No-smoking rooms. Parking (£42/day). Restaurant. Room service. TV (pay-movies, DVD).*

Savoy

Strand, WC2R 0EU (7836 4343/fax 7240 6040/www.savoygroup.com). Covent Garden or Embankment tube/Charing Cross tube/rail. **Rates** £341-£410 single; £405-£499 double; £546-£1,821 suite. **Credit** AmEx, DC, MC, V. **Map** p401 L7.
Built in 1889, the Savoy is London's original grande dame. And what a legacy. Monet painted the views from the River Suites; Noel Coward played in the Thames Foyer; and Vivien Leigh met Laurence Olivier in the Savoy Grill. More importantly, a bartender invented the Martini at the chic American Bar. So you know this place is glamorous. But where the Ritz is ostentatious, the Savoy's grandeur is more dignified. Its aesthetic is mixed: neo-classical, art deco and gentlemen's club. Bedrooms are luxurious but restrained: most people remember the watering-can showerheads and – in certain rooms – the Thames views. The rooftop gym, with a small pool, is another forte. The legendary Savoy Grill has had a revamp: chef Marcus Wareing updated the menu and Californian designer Barbara Barry jazzed up the decor. A new casual restaurant, Banquette, is a chi-chi homage to a 1950s American diner.
Hotel services *Bars (3). Business centre. Concierge. Disabled-adapted rooms. Gym. Internet (dataport). No-smoking rooms. Pool. Restaurants (3). Spa. TV (pay movies, DVD).*

Expensive

One Aldwych

1 Aldwych, WC2B 4RH (7300 1000/fax 7300 1001/ www.onealdwych.com). Covent Garden or Temple tube/Charing Cross tube/rail. **Rates** *£210-£370 single; £210-£394 double; £380-£1,170 suite.* **Credit** AmEx, DC, MC, V. **Map** p401 M7.

A great deal has been written about this hotel, and once you set foot inside the lobby, with its wonderful sculpture of a hunched oarsman and its colourful sprays of flowers, you'll see why. One Aldwych is a modern classic. An appealing mix of traditional and trendy, it's a good emblem for 21st-century London. It's got the attentive service of the Ritz, but staff are more cosmopolitan (and less pompous); it's housed in an Edwardian bank building but rooms come equipped with up-to-date gadgetry – TVs in the bathroom, say, or ecologically friendly toilets. Londoners come here for drinks in the elegant Lobby Bar, which boasts full-length arched windows, modern art and flamboyant floral displays. The bedrooms, meanwhile, have a streamlined, minimalist appeal (with original artworks in every room). The restaurants are fine, the gym is well equipped and there's even a private cinema with specially designed seats (made in Italy – where else?) providing even more padding for those executive derrieres. But the pièce de résistance is the shimmering underground swimming pool, complete with subtle lighting and classical music piped into the water.

Hotel services *Bars (3). Concierge. Disabled-adapted rooms. Gym. Internet (dataport, wireless). No-smoking floors. Parking (valet). Pool. Restaurants (2). Room service. TV (pay movies, DVD).*

South Kensington & Knightsbridge

Deluxe

Baglioni

60 Hyde Park Gate, SW7 5BB (7368 5700/www. baglionihotellondon.com). High Street Kensington/ South Kensington tube. **Rates** *£300-£390 single/ double; £500-£1,900 suite.* **Credit** AmEx, MC, V. **Map** p396 C9.

Attention, fashionistas. The Baglioni, part of an exclusive Italian group, has made a flamboyant foray into London. In a bold move, it has nixed the tired minimalist aesthetic and upped the glam. The fantastic lobby bar is part baroque, part Donatella Versace: spidery black chandeliers, burnished gold ceilings and gigantic vases filled with roses. The chic bedrooms are more masculine: dark wood floors, black lacquered tables and taupe walls, enlivened by brash, clashing, striped sofas. In the swanky black bathrooms, the flattering lighting would make even Norma Desmond look young. Downstairs, the flashy Brunello restaurant serves expensive Italian food to ladies in sparkly tops. Ostentatious, yes. And about time, too: when you're spending this kind of money, you want a good show. The Baglioni has brought a welcome touch of bling to the boutique market.

Hotel services *Bar. Business centre. Concierge. Disabled-adapted rooms. Gym. No-smoking rooms. Internet (dataport, high-speed, web TV, wireless). Parking £40/day. Restaurant. Room service. Spa. TV (pay movies/music).*

Blakes

33 Roland Gardens, SW7 3PF (7370 6701/fax 7373 0442/www.blakeshotels.com). South Kensington tube. **Rates** £176-£199 single; £287-£325 double; £611-£663 suite. **Credit** AmEx, DC, MC, V. **Map** p397 D11.
Back when Ian Schrager was partying at Studio 54, Anouska Hempel brought the first boutique hotel to London. Opened in 1983, Blakes has stood the test of time. In a welcome respite from the ubiquitous minimalist look, the bedrooms here are done up in rich colours: blacks, golds and crimsons. The rooms evoke the romance of colonial travel, with influences from India, Turkey and China. Exotic antiques – black lacquered cabinets, Chinese birdcages – are everywhere. Downstairs is a chic Thai restaurant, once described as resembling 'an opium den run by Coco Chanel'. In a bid to stay current, Blakes has opened a gym and installed wireless internet.
Hotel services *Bar. Business services. Concierge. Gym. Internet (dataport, wireless). No-smoking rooms. Parking (valet). Restaurant. Room service. TV (pay movies/DVD).*

Milestone Hotel & Apartments

1 Kensington Court, W8 5DL (7917 1000/fax 7917 1010/www.milestonehotel.com). High Street Kensington tube/9, 10, 52 bus. **Rates** £340-£405 double; £530-£950 suite; £3,000 apartment/wk. **Credit** AmEx, DC, MC, V. **Map** p395 B9.
Overlooking Kensington Gardens, this quietly charming luxury hotel has won a slew of industry awards. The rooms are the stuff of romance: themes include English rose, Venetian and Ascot; best is the Safari suite, adorned with ostrich eggs and leopard-print upholstery. In the basement, builders are digging what looks like London's smallest swimming pool. You can also get wet in the hotel's elegant bars: the Stable, with its tartan sofas and hunting prints, is pleasingly rugged; the jazzy black and white Conservatory is pure panache. The inspired decor is the work of South African owner Beatrice Tillman.
Hotel services *Bar. Business services. Concierge. Disabled-adapted rooms. Gym. Internet (dataport, wireless). No-smoking rooms. Pool. Restaurant. Room service. TV (pay movies).*

Expensive

Bentley

Harrington Gardens, SW7 4JX (7244 5555/fax 7244 5566/www.thebentley-hotel.com). Gloucester Road tube. **Rates** £250-£425 double; £575-£4,000 suite. **Credit** AmEx, DC, MC, V. **Map** p396 C10.
In a backlash against minimalism, chandeliers are back in fashion. And there are plenty to swing from at the Bentley, London's most opulent new boutique hotel. They sparkle in the lobby; they glitter in the bedrooms; hell, you can even shave under one in the luxurious bathrooms. Over the top? You bet. Like a miniature version of the Dorchester, the Bentley's decorative template is Versailles: hence the Louis XV-style furniture, the gilt mirrors and gleaming marble – 600 tons of it, imported from Greece and

Italy. The bedrooms are pure *Dynasty*: thick carpets, gold satin bedspreads and jacuzzi tubs. And the spa features gold-laced mosaics and a Turkish hammam. Next to the glitzy restaurant 1880, the Malachite Bar is a dim, decadent hideaway. But the real showpiece is the lobby's sweeping circular staircase – perfect for making a grand entrance.
Hotel services *Bar. Business centre. Concierge. Disabled-adapted rooms. Gym. No-smoking rooms/floors. Internet (dataport, high speed). Restaurants (2). Room service. Spa. TV (pay movies/music/DVD).*

Gore

189 Queen's Gate, SW7 5EX (7584 6601/fax 7589 8127/www.gorehotel.com). South Kensington tube. **Rates** £155 single; £190 double; £295 deluxe.
Credit AmEx, DC, MC, V. **Map** p397 D9.
Like its sister hotels Hazlitt's (*see p57*) and the Rookery (*see p47*), the Gore is a classy, creaky period piece. Housed in a couple of Victorian townhouses, it's crammed with old paintings – 4,500 of them – and evocative antique furniture. The bedrooms have fantastic 18th-century oak beds and Persian rugs; the bathrooms feature Victorian clawfoot tubs and cast-iron toilets. The public rooms – the Tudor bar, the shabby-chic lounge – are deliciously cosy. For a treat, splash out on a suite: the Tudor Room has a 16th-century four-poster, a minstrels' gallery and a wooden Thomas Crapper; tragedy queens should plump for the Venus room for a chance to sleep in Judy Garland's old bed.
Hotel services *Bar. Business services. Concierge. Internet (dataport). No-smoking rooms/floor. Restaurant. Room service. TV.*

myhotel chelsea

35 Ixworth Place, SW3 3QX (7225 7500/fax 7225 7555/www.myhotels.com). South Kensington tube. **Rates** £175-£190 single; £205-£220 double; £360 suite. **Credit** AmEx, DC, MC, V. **Map** p397 E11.
This trendy boutique hotel is a softer, gentler version of its flashier alter ego, myhotel bloomsbury. It, too has lots of feng shui touches: an aquarium in the lobby, crystals and candles scattered just so. But the designers have toned down the oriental look and concocted what they call 'traditional English meets *Sex and the City*'. Presumably, this is due to the Chelsea location: female shopaholics will appreciate the feminine colours – dusty pinks and purples – and lush fabrics, which include cashmere throws and velvet cushions. Rooms come with New Agey accessories – herbal wellness/hangover kits, say – and wireless internet access. Chill-out places include the Cape Cod-influenced bar and conservatory-style lounge.
Hotel services *Bar. Business services. Concierge. Gym. No-smoking rooms. Internet (dataport, wireless). Restaurant. Room service. Spa. TV (pay movies/DVD).*

Number Sixteen

16 Sumner Place, SW7 3EG (7589 5232/fax 7584 8615/www.firmdalehotels.com). South Kensington tube. **Rates** £112 single; £200 double. £294 suite. **Credit** AmEx, MC, V. **Map** p397 D11.

Finally, chic designer Kit Kemp has created a slightly more affordable hotel. The lower room rates at this gorgeous B&B are presumably down to the lack of bar/restaurant or big hotel perks. Which leaves Kemp to get on with what she does best: create beautiful rooms. The whole place has a garden-fresh appeal: the drawing room is decorated with bird paintings and fresh flowers; the bedrooms have a summery look, with tasteful floral patterns and muted creams, greens and mauves. Breakfast is served in a conservatory overlooking a garden.
Hotel services *Bar. Business centre. Concierge. Internet (dataport, wireless). No-smoking rooms. Parking (valet). Room service. TV.*

Moderate

Aster House

3 Sumner Place, SW7 3EE (7581 5888/fax 7584 4925/www.asterhouse.com). South Kensington tube. **Rates** £105 single; £150 double; £188 deluxe. **Credit** AmEx, MC, V. **Map** p397 D11.

Aster House bravely attempts to live up to its upmarket address. In reality, the lobby – with its pink faux-marble and gold chandeliers – is more kitsch than glam, but the effect is still charming. So is the lush garden, with its pond and wandering ducks. Even lovelier is the palm-filled conservatory, where guests eat breakfast. The bedrooms are comfortable, with traditional floral upholstery, air-conditioning and smart marble bathrooms – ask for one with a power shower. The hotel now lends its guests mobile phones during their stay, and the rooms all have wireless internet connection. The museums and big-name shops are all close at hand. All in all, then, a good and affordable option.
Hotel services *Business services. Internet (dataport, wireless). No-smoking throughout. TV.*

Five Sumner Place

5 Sumner Place, SW7 3EE (7584 7586/fax 7823 9962/www.sumnerplace.com). South Kensington tube. **Rates** £100 single; £153 double. **Credit** AmEx, MC, V. **Map** p397 D11.

Housed in a row of white Victorian townhouses, Five Sumner Place is a smart address, and a convenient one, too. The decor, the usual faux-period English, is pleasant enough; and the rooms are clean and comfortable. They're also technologically advanced for the price category: all rooms now have free broadband wireless access and voicemail. Breakfast is served in a conservatory; the lift will save you dragging your suitcases up the stairs; and the manager is friendly.
Hotel services *Internet (dataport, wireless). No-smoking rooms/floors. TV.*

Hotel 167

167 Old Brompton Road, SW5 0AN (7373 0672/fax 7373 3360/www.hotel167.com). Gloucester Road or South Kensington tube. **Rates** £72-£86 single; £90-£99 double; £115 triple. **Credit** AmEx, DC, MC, V. **Map** p397 D11.

It may be located in a Victorian townhouse, but this funky little hotel is no period clone. On the contrary, its decor is positively quirky. The lobby makes a bold statement, with its black and white tiled floor and striking abstract art. Upstairs, the bedrooms are an eclectic mix of traditional and arty: the odd antique piece or Victorian painting, with contemporary touches (Mexican bedspreads, Klee prints). The whole place has a whiff of bohemia (not to mention pot pourri), and its shambolic charm has inspired artists: it's been the subject of a song (an unreleased track by the Manic Street Preachers) and a novel (*Hotel 167* by Jane Solomons).
Room services *No-smoking rooms. Internet (dataport). TV.*

Swiss House Hotel

171 Old Brompton Road, SW5 0AN (7373 2769/fax 7373 4983/www.swiss-hh.demon.co.uk). Gloucester Road tube. **Rates** £56-£78 single; £97-£114 double; £132 triple; £147 quad. **Credit** AmEx, DC, MC, V. **Map** p397 D11.

Don't expect an Alpine-themed hotel: this Victorian townhouse used to be a private residence for SwissAir crews, hence the name. Still, the whole place has a country fresh appeal and tasteful decor, from the attractive pine furniture to the dark wooden beams in the breakfast room. The bedrooms have a crisp, clean aesthetic, with white walls and classic navy bed linens – a welcome change from the chintz nightmare that is most budget hotels. Pretty good value, for the location.
Hotel services *Room service. TV.*

Cheap

Vicarage Hotel

10 Vicarage Gate, W8 4AG (7229 4030/fax 7792 5989/www.londonvicaragehotel.com). High Street Kensington/Notting Hill Gate tube. **Rates** £46-£75 single; £78-£102 double; £95-£130 triple; £102-£140 quad. **No credit cards. Map** p394 B8.

This Victorian townhouse hotel has a split personality: the lobby is glitzy, with red and gold wall paper and ornate mirrors. The rooms, by contrast, are tasteful: they're painted in pastels and furnished with faux antiques, comfy beds and subtle floral fabrics. And the summery TV lounge is actually pleasant: you might even consider sitting in it. Another bonus: nine of the 17 rooms now have bathrooms.
Hotel services *TV.*

Belgravia & Pimlico

Deluxe

Lanesborough

Hyde Park Corner, SW1X 7TA (7259 5599/fax 7259 5606/www.lanesborough.com). Hyde Park Corner tube. **Rates** £335-£393 single; £464-£558 double; £699-£881 suite. **Credit** AmEx, DC, MC, V. **Map** p400 G8.

It may not be a household name, but the Lanesborough matches the Ritz for sheer unbridled luxury. It's got plenty of period grandeur: magnificent Regency architecture, a marble neo-classical lobby, and the domed Conservatory restaurant, a swish tribute to the Brighton Pavilion. But it's the decadence that boggles the mind: the Library Bar serves vintage cognac for £750 a swill; the Royal Suite (£5,000) comes with a chauffeur-driven Bentley and round-the-clock security guards. The regular bedrooms are a lavish combination of mahogany, period furniture and cutting-edge technology; butlers are available at your beck and call (they once filled Michael Jackson's bathtub with 28 bottles of Evian). New this year is a spa and gym, complete with plasma-screen TVs on each piece of equipment. If you've got money to burn, the Lanesborough will spoil you rotten.

Hotel services *Bar. Business centre. Concierge. Disabled-adapted rooms. Gym. Internet (dataport). No-smoking rooms. Parking (£30/night). Restaurant. Room service. Spa. TV (DVD).*

Expensive

City Inn Westminster

30 John Islip Street, SW1P 4DD (7630 1000/fax 7233 7575/www.cityinn.com). Pimlico tube. **Rates** £264-£311 double; £646-£1,116 suite. **Credit** AmEx, MC, V. **Map** p401 K10.

City Inn Westminster.

The City Inn opened to a great fanfare in 2003: it's London's largest new hotel in 40 years and its modern design has won several awards. But, apart from the blue, Lego-like exterior, don't expect anything flashy. The airy lobby has a clean, contemporary look, adorned with the odd piece of modern art. The bedrooms incorporate the usual minimalist schtick – white sheets, neutral colours – but they're not stark. There's an emphasis on natural light – some rooms have floor-to-ceiling windows – and comfort: beds boast a selection of different pillows; walls are 18 in thick so you can't hear the neighbours whooping it up. The Millbank Bar, with its glam red sofas and dim lighting, recalls the Met Bar, but without the attitude – an apt summary of the hotel itself.

Hotel services *Bar. Business centre. Concierge. Disabled-adapted rooms. Gym. No-smoking floors/ rooms. Internet (dataport, high-speed). Restaurant. Room service. TV (music/pay movies/DVD).*

Dolphin Square Hotel

Dolphin Square, Chichester Street, SW1V 3LX (7798 8890/fax 7798 8896/www.dolphinsquarehotel.co.uk). Pimlico tube. **Rates** £175 studio; £195-£225 1 bedroom; £260-£330 2 bedrooms; £450 3 bedrooms. **Credit** AmEx, DC, MC, V. **Map** p401 M8.

Dolphin Square is a London legend. This massive 1930s mansion block is built like a fortress and survived bombing during the war. Its posh flats are home to politicians, barristers and civil servants. And one wing of the building is devoted to an attractive hotel. The decor mixes a nautical theme – the lobby feels a bit like a cruise ship – with art deco.

Hampstead Village Guesthouse.

The rooms are large and contemporary; all come with kitchenettes. Allium, the smart navy restaurant, run by former Savoy chef Anton Edelmann, is complemented by a glam '30s cocktail bar: both overlook the 18m indoor pool. Other highlights are the lush gardens and great, old-fashioned arcade.
Hotel services *Bar. Business centre. Concierge. Disabled-adapted rooms. Gym. No-smoking rooms/floors. Internet (dataport). Pool. Restaurants (2). Room service. Spa. TV.*

Windermere Hotel

142-144 Warwick Way, SW1V 4JE (7834 5163/ fax 7630 8831/www.windermere-hotel.co.uk). Victoria tube/rail. **Rates** £64-£96 single; £89-£139 double; £139-£149 family. **Credit** AmEx, MC, V. **Map** p400 H11.
The Windermere has a proud legacy: London's first B&B opened on this site in 1881. Surprise, surprise, the rooms are done up in English chintz, but it's all in good taste. Classy decorative touches – mother-of-pearl trays, chrome fans, the odd coronet bed – lend character. The bathrooms are clean and modern, with power showers. It's unusual to find a B&B with extras such as room service, modem points and satellite TV. And the rustic Pimlico restaurant – another rarity for a budget hotel – has a sophisticated, reasonably priced menu.
Hotel services *Bar. Business services. Internet (dataport). No-smoking rooms/floors. Restaurant. Room service. TV.*

Cheap

Morgan House

120 Ebury Street, SW1W 9QQ (7730 2384/fax 7730 8442/www.morganhouse.co.uk). Pimlico tube/ Victoria tube/rail. **Rates** £46-£74 single; £66-£86 double; £86-£110 triple; £122 quad. **Credit** MC, V. **Map** p400 H10.
The Morgan is a quintessential, small English B&B. The passages are narrow and the rooms cosy – a polite way of saying tiny. But the contemporary decor is pleasing, with its pastel hues of blues, yellows and pale mauves. And it's constantly being refurbished: some rooms have orthopaedic mattresses. Children will appreciate the bunk beds and stuffed animals in the family rooms. Husband and wife owners Rachel Joplin and Ian Berry lend the place a friendly feel, from the cheery breakfast room – where the delicious home-made muesli is served – to the patio garden, where guests can chill out on a summer's evening with a bottle of wine.
Hotel services *No-smoking throughout. TV.*

North London

Cheap

Hampstead Village Guesthouse

2 Kemplay Road, NW3 1SY (7435 8679/fax 7794 0254/www.hampsteadguesthouse.com). Hampstead tube/Hampstead Heath rail. **Rates** £48-£66 single; £72-£84 double; £90-£150 studio. **Credit** AmEx, MC, V.
This comfy B&B, in a characterful Victorian pile, is right on the doorstep of Hampstead Heath, but the decor is more bohemian than *Country Life*: it's filled with an eccentric mix of books, rag dolls, Delft earthenware and other curios. Whether you think it's cluttered or charming, it definitely feels like a home – owner Annemarie van der Meer lives on site. Breakfast is served in the garden, weather permitting; there's also a garden studio, which sleeps five. Take note, though: there's a five per cent surcharge if you pay by credit card.
Hotel services *No-smoking throughout. TV.*

South-west London

Moderate

Windmill on the Common

Clapham Common Southside, Clapham, SW4 9DE (8673 4578/www.youngs.co.uk). Clapham Common or Clapham South tube. **Rates** £85-£99 single; £95-£115 double. **Credit** AmEx, DC, MC, V.
Perched on the edge of Clapham Common, one of London's loveliest green spaces, the Windmill pub is a pleasant neighbourhood watering hole. But it also boasts one of London's most reasonably priced hotels. In terms of comfort and decor, the bedrooms – decked out in typical chain period finery – are far

superior to most of London's dowdy B&Bs. Central London is a short tube journey away, and Clapham is brimming with bars and restaurants.

Hotel services. *Bar. Disabled-adapted room. No-smoking rooms. Internet (dataport). Parking (free). Restaurant. Room service. TV (movies).*

Cheap

Riverside Hotel

23 Petersham Road, Richmond-upon-Thames, Surrey TW10 6UH (8940 1339/www.riverside richmond.co.uk). Richmond tube/rail. **Rates** £60-£65 single; £80-£95 double; £115-£125 suite. **Credit** AmEx, DC, MC, V.

A little slice of the country, 20 minutes from Waterloo, Richmond is a welcome respite from urban grime. This hotel, perched on the edge of the Thames, is good for the soul: it's got its own waterfront garden; some rooms have views of the river. It's also near Richmond Park, Kew Gardens and stately homes such as Marble Hill House and Ham House. The pleasing rooms are decorated in a traditional English style, but the hotel's best feature is its proximity to the tranquil Thames Footpath.

Hotel services *Internet (dataport, wireless). No-smoking rooms. Parking (free). Room service. TV.*

West London

Deluxe

The Hempel

31-35 Craven Hill Gardens, Bayswater, W2 3EA (7298 9000/fax 7402 4666/www.the-hempel.co.uk). Lancaster Gate or Queensway tube/Paddington tube/rail. **Rates** £275 single; £322 double; £440-£990 suite. **Credit** AmEx, DC, MC, V. **Map** p394 C6.

As the minimalist backlash gathers pace, the Hempel – the most clinical design hotel of the bunch – has been forced to change with the times. Last year, in a move that sent shockwaves through the hotel industry, designers introduced colour to the hotel's stark, white lobby. Diehard minimalists can relax though: the pristine, Japanesey bedrooms are still feng shui at its finest; one of the dreamy suites has a bed that hangs from the ceiling, and the garden is still Zen-like. Trendy I-Thai restaurant fuses Italian and Asian cuisines.

Hotel services *Bar. Business services. Concierge. Disabled-adapted rooms. Internet (dataport, high-speed, wireless). No-smoking rooms. Restaurant. Room service. TV (DVD, pay movies/music).*

Expensive

Miller's Residence

111A Westbourne Grove, Notting Hill, W2 4UW (7243 1024/fax 7243 1064/www.millersuk.com). Notting Hill Gate or Westbourne Park tube. **Rates** £176-£217 double; £270 suite. **Credit** AmEx, MC, V. **Map** p394 B6.

Nobody's heard of Miller's Residence. And we're almost sorry to spill the beans. But the truth is, this discreet little B&B is possibly London's most romantic hotel. The unmarked red door off Westbourne Grove doesn't look promising. But the interior is a glittering Aladdin's Cave: the rooms are dripping in gilt, chandeliers and ornate mirrors; the 18th-century furniture is straight out of a period drama; and the shiny candelabra, baubles and gewgaws add a bit of sparkle. Despite the antique treasures, it's not stuffy: there's a casual, bohemian feel, with well-worn, comfy sofas, old Persian rugs and relaxed staff. In the salon, help yourself to whisky and curl up by the massive oak fireplace. Ordinary name, extraordinary place.

Hotel services *Internet (dataport). TV.*

Moderate

Colonnade Town House

2 Warrington Crescent, Little Venice, W9 1ER (7286 1052/fax 7286 1057/www.theeton collection.com). Warwick Avenue tube. **Rates** £114-£148 single; £119-£173 double; £179-£288 suite. **Credit** AmEx, DC, MC, V.

Little Venice is one of London's prettiest neighbourhoods. It's off the beaten track, though, which is why this dignified townhouse hotel is cheaper than its luxury competitors. Still, it's handy for Paddington and the Heathrow Express. And the stately bedrooms are wonderfully plush: the old-fashioned beds are draped in Egyptian cotton sheets and velvet bedspreads. What's more, the hotel oozes history: the JFK suite has an enormous four-poster bed built for the president's 1962 state visit; Sigmund Freud, another former guest, has a suite named after him; and Alan Turing, who cracked the Enigma code, was born here.

Hotel services *Bar. Concierge. Internet (dataport, wireless). No-smoking rooms. Parking. Restaurant. Room service. TV.*

Guesthouse West

163-165 Westbourne Grove, Notting Hill, W11 2RS (7792 9800/fax 7792 9797/www.guesthouse west.com). Notting Hill tube. **Rates** £153-£182 double. **Credit** AmEx, MC, V. **Map** p394 B6.

Formerly the Westbourne Hotel, Guesthouse West looks the same as its trendy predecessor: groovy retro lobby bar, minimalist bedrooms, arty black and white photographs. The difference is, the owners have cut back on the frills – no room service, for example – and slashed the prices. The target market is young hipsters who can't afford the Sanderson. So naturally, the rooms have wireless internet access, air-conditioning and flat-screen TVs. They're also small. No matter: movers and shakers will spend most of their time schmoozing in nearby Notting Hill or the lobby bar. Or having liquid lunches on the front terrace, though it's only licensed to serve until 8pm. The hotel's relaunch has been funded in part by a ground-breaking buy-to-let scheme:

Miller's Residence.
See p66.

Guesthouse West. *See p66.*

punters can purchase a hotel room for £235,000, use it for 52 nights of the year, and, when they're not there, split the rental income with the hotel. So if you've always fantasised about living in a hotel, here's your big chance.

Hotel services *Bar. No-smoking rooms. Internet (high-speed, wireless). Restaurant. TV (pay movies/music/DVD).*

Pembridge Court

34 Pembridge Gardens, Notting Hill, W2 4DX (7229 9977/fax 7727 4982/www.pemct.co.uk). Notting Hill Gate tube. **Rates** £125-£165 single; £160-£195 double. **Credit** AmEx, DC, MC, V. **Map** p394 A7.

Not your typical townhouse hotel, the Pembridge Court has brought a bit of showbiz flair to the old English formula. The comfy bedrooms, done up in standard English chintz, are jazzed up by framed costumes on the wall: feather boas, Victorian fans, 1940s cigarette cases and glam vintage handbags. Theatrical touches attract theatrical people: rock stars like Iggy Pop regularly stay here. To cater for the musos, copies of *Billboard* magazine are scattered in the homely sitting room, where you can surf the internet or cuddle up to Churchill, the hotel's resident ginger cat. Portobello Road is at the back door.

Hotel services *Bar. Business services. Internet (dataport). Parking (limited). Room service. TV (VCR).*

Portobello Hotel

22 Stanley Gardens, Notting Hill, W11 2NG (7727 2777/fax 7792 9641/www.portobello-hotel.co.uk). Holland Park or Notting Hill Gate tube. **Rates** £120 single; £160-£275 double. **Credit** AmEx, MC, V. **Map** p394 A6.

Bohemian chic reigns supreme at the Portobello. Like the set of *The English Patient*, the elegant rooms ooze colonial romance: potted palms, ceiling fans, wooden shutters and oriental antiques. Some are poky, some are spectacular: Room 16, for instance, has a circular bed and a clawfoot bathtub in the middle of the room – Johnny Depp allegedly filled it with champagne for Kate Moss. After a day of shopping on Portobello, you can soothe aching muscles in one of the hotel's many jacuzzi tubs.

Hotel services *Bar. Internet (dataport). No-smoking rooms. Restaurant. Room service. TV.*

Twenty Nevern Square

20 Nevern Square, Earl's Court, SW5 9PD (7565 9555/fax 7565 9444/www.twentynevernsquare.co. uk). Earl's Court tube. **Rates** £99-£150 double; £250 suite. **Credit** AmEx, DC, MC, V. **Map** p396 A11.

The words 'stylish' and 'Earl's Court' don't usually appear in the same sentence. But times are changing. Like its sister hotel, the Mayflower (*see below*), this townhouse hotel has been refurbished in exotic colonial style into a budget version of Blakes. Rooms boast carved oriental furniture, silk curtains and sleek marble bathrooms; the Far East feel extends to the lounge and the airy conservatory breakfast room, done up in wicker furniture and greenery.

Hotel services *Bar. Internet (dataport). No-smoking rooms/floors. Parking. Room service. TV.*

Vancouver Studios

30 Prince's Square, Bayswater, W2 4NJ (7243 1270/fax 7221 8678/www.vancouverstudios.co.uk). Bayswater or Queensway tube. **Rates** *£65 single; £85-£95 double; £120 triple.* **Credit** *AmEx, DC, MC, V.* **Map** *p394 B6.*

Vancouver Studios is almost a contradiction in terms: a good-looking budget hotel. The countrified sitting room is cosy and funky, with Mexican upholstery, cacti and an old-fashioned gramophone. It opens on to a lush, walled garden with a gurgling fountain. Studio rooms come equipped with kitchenettes. For the price, the bedrooms are surprisingly stylish. Being refurbished as we go to press (check the website or call for details of when the work is due to be completed), Vancouver Studios' proposed new aesthetics will include nautical, country fresh gingham and Far Eastern chic. Staff are friendly and so is the resident cat. A great deal.

Hotel services *Concierge. Internet (dataport, shared terminal). TV.*

Cheap

Garden Court Hotel

30-31 Kensington Gardens Square, Bayswater, W2 4BG (7229 2553/fax 7727 2749/www.gardencourthotel.co.uk). Bayswater or Queensway tube. **Rates** *£39-£58 single; £58-£88 double; £72-£99 triple; £82-£120 quad.* **Credit** *MC, V.* **Map** *p394 B6.*

The Garden Court, a charming townhouse hotel, has been run by the same family for 50 years. But it's not resting on its laurels. The lobby, decorated with a giant Beefeater statue, marble busts and bonsai trees, has real flair. At press time, the cheery bedrooms were being refurbished. And a lift was being installed – always a godsend in townhouse hotels. As the name suggests, the hotel has a small walled garden; guests have access to the private square, too (a rare privilege in London!).

Hotel services *Business services. No-smoking hotel. TV.*

Mayflower Hotel

26-28 Trebovir Road, Earl's Court, SW5 9NJ (7370 0991/fax 7370 0994/www.mayflowerhotel.co.uk). Earl's Court tube. **Rates** *£59-£79 single; £69-£109 double; £99-£129 triple; £110-£150 quad.* **Credit** *AmEx, MC, V.* **Map** *p396 B11.*

The Mayflower has given Earl's Court – once a rather boring and far from glamourous budget wasteland – a kick up the backside. Following a spectacular makeover, the hotel has transformed itself from cheap and mediocre to cheap and chic. Decorated in a minimalist theme, the rooms have wooden floors and hand-carved beds from the Far East. Ceiling fans add a tropical feel, and the marble bathrooms, CD players and dataports lend an air of modern luxury. Downstairs, the lobby is dominated by a gorgeous teak arch from Jaipur. It's got a trendy juice bar, too.

Hotel services *Bar. Business services. Internet (dataport). No-smoking rooms. Parking. TV.*

Pavilion

34-36 Sussex Gardens, Bayswater, W2 1UL (7262 0905/fax 7262 1324/www.pavilionhoteluk.com). Edgware Road/Marylebone or Paddington tube/rail. **Rates** *£60 single; £85-£100 double; £120 triple.* **Credit** *AmEx, DC, MC, V.* **Map** *p395 E5.*

In a row of dowdy hotels, the Pavilion is a shining star. Or more like a disco ball. When it comes to decor, this hilariously kitsch B&B has tongue firmly planted in cheek. The themed rooms are a riot: the Highland Fling is a tartan theme park, with plaid bedspreads and stag antlers; Better Red Than Dead is a glam extravaganza of crimson, vermilion and burgundy. Rock stars love the place: a favourite shag pad is Honky Tonk Afro, with its mirror ball, fuzzy dice and heart-shaped mirrored headboards. OK, so the location's not exactly rocking and the bathrooms are small. But there's more personality in this humble budget hotel than in many of the capital's big-name boutiques.

Hotel services *Parking. Room service. TV.*

Rushmore Hotel

11 Trebovir Road, Earl's Court, SW5 9LS (7370 3839/fax 7370 0274/www.rushmore-hotel.co.uk). Earl's Court tube. **Rates** *from £59 single; from £79 double; from £99 quad.* **Credit** *AmEx, DC, MC, V.* **Map** *p396 B11.*

The Rushmore is living proof that, with a bit of imagination, a budget hotel can be beautiful. The hotel's biggest talking point is the trompe l'oeil paintings that adorn the walls, depicting everything from pastoral Tuscany to tranquil ocean scenes. In some rooms, curtains are draped sensuously over the beds; shoestring travellers need glamour too. The Italianate breakfast room, with its granite surfaces and glass tables, also achieves the impossible: bringing elegance to Earl's Court.

Hotel services *Business services. Internet (dataport). No-smoking rooms. TV.*

Apartment rental

The companies we have listed below specialise in holiday lets, although some have minimum stay requirements (making this an affordable option only if you're planning a relatively protracted visit to the city). Typical daily rates on a reasonably central property are around £70-£90 for a studio or one-bed, up to £100 for a two-bed, though, as with any aspect of staying in London, the sky's the limit if you want to pay it. **Accommodation Outlet** (7287 4244, www.outlet4holidays.com) is a lesbian and gay agency. Recommended all-rounders include **Astons Apartments** (7590 6000, fax 7590 6060/www.astons-apartments.com), **Holiday Serviced Apartments** (0845 060 4477, www.holiday apartments.co.uk), **Palace Court Holiday Apartments** (7727 3467) and **Perfect Places** (8748 6095, www.perfectplaceslondon.co.uk).

Camping & caravanning

If the thought of putting yourself at the mercy of the English weather in some far-flung suburban field doesn't put you off, the transport links into central London just might. Nevertheless, these campsites will undoubtedly offer a singular view of the city, and they are all conveniently cheap.

Crystal Palace Caravan Club *Crystal Palace Parade, SE19 1UF (8778 7155/fax 8676 0980). Crystal Palace rail/3 bus.* **Open** *Mar-Oct* Mon-Thur, Sat, Sun 8.30am-6pm; Fri 8.30am-8pm. *Nov-Feb* Mon-Thur, Sat, Sun 9am-6pm; Fri 9am-8pm. **Rates** £4.50-£8 caravan pitch; £3.80-£5 adults; £1.10-£1.80 children. **Credit** MC, V.

Lee Valley Campsite *Sewardstone Road, Chingford, E4 7RA (8529 5689/fax 8559 4070/www.leevalleypark.com). Walthamstow Central tube/rail, then 215 bus.* **Open** *Apr-Oct* 8am-9pm daily. Closed Nov-Mar. **Rates** £5.95; £2.65 under-16s. **Credit** AmEx, MC, V.

Lee Valley Leisure Centre Camping & Caravan Park *Meridian Way, Edmonton, N9 0AS (8803 6900/fax 8884 4975/www.leevalleypark. com). Edmonton Green rail/W8 bus.* **Open** 8am-10pm daily. **Rates** £6; £2.50 5-16s; free under-5s. **Credit** MC, V.

Staying with the locals

Several agencies can arrange for individuals and families to stay in Londoners' homes. Prices range from around £20 to £85 single and £45 to £105 double, including breakfast, depending on the location and degree of comfort. They include **At Home in London** (8748 1943, www.athomeinlondon.co.uk), **Bulldog Club** (7371 3202, www.bulldogclub), **Host & Guest Service** (7385 9922, www.host-guest.co.uk), **London Bed & Breakfast Agency** (7586 2768, www.londonbb.com) and **London Homestead Services** (7286 5115, www.lhs london.com). There may be a minimum stay.

University residences

During university vacations much of London's dedicated student accommodation is open to visitors, providing basic but cheap digs.

Goldsmid House *36 North Row, Mayfair, W1R 1DH (7493 6097/fax 7495 6451/uclgoldsmid@ studygroup.com). Bond Street or Marble Arch tube.* **Rates** *July, Aug* from £30 single; £20 (per person) twin; *June, Sept* from £25 single; £15 (per person) twin. **Available** 13 June-19 Sept 2005. **Map** p398 G6.

International Students House *229 Great Portland Street, Marylebone, W1W 5PN (7631 8300/fax 7631 8315/www.ish.org.uk). Great Portland Street tube.* **Rates** (per person) £12-£18.50 dormitory; £33.50 single; £25.50 twin. **Available** all year. **Map** p398 H5.

King's College Conference & Vacation Bureau *Strand Bridge House, 138-142 Strand, Covent Garden, WC2R 1HH (7848 1700/fax 7848 1717/www.kcl.ac.uk/kcvb). Temple tube.* **Rates** £17-£34 single; £39.50-£49 twin. **Available** 16 June-14 Sept 2005. **Map** p404 N8.

Walter Sickert Hall *29 Graham Street, Islington, N1 8LA (7040 8822/fax 7040 8825/www.city.ac. uk/ems). Angel tube.* **Rates** £30-£40 single; £50-£60 twin. **Available** 10 June-11 Sept 2005 (executive rooms available throughout the year). **Map** p402 P3.

Youth hostels

Hostel beds are either in twin rooms or dorms. If you're not a member of the International Youth Hostel Federation (IYHF), you'll pay an extra £2 a night (after six nights you automatically become a member). Alternatively, join the IYHF for £13 (£6.50 for under-18s) at any hostel, or through www.yha.org.uk. Prices include breakfast.

City of London *36-38 Carter Lane, EC4V 5AB (7236 4965/fax 7236 7681). St Paul's tube/ Blackfriars tube/rail.* **Reception open** 7am-11pm daily; 24hr access. **Rates** £15-£30; £15-£24 under-18s. **Map** p404 O6.

Earl's Court *38 Bolton Gardens, SW5 0AQ (7373 7083/fax 7835 2034). Earl's Court tube.* **Reception open** 7am-11pm daily; 24hr access. **Rates** £19.20-£21.50; £17.20 under-18s. **Map** p396 B11.

Holland House *Holland Walk, W8 7QU (7937 0748/fax 7376 0667). High Street Kensington tube.* **Reception open** 7am-11pm daily; 24hr access. **Rates** £21; £19.30 under-18s. **Map** p394 A8.

Oxford Street *14 Noel Street, W1F 8GJ (7734 1618/fax 7734 1657). Oxford Circus tube.* **Reception open** 7am-11pm daily; 24hr access. **Rates** £22.60-£24.60; £18.20 under-18s. **Map** p398 J6.

St Pancras *79-81 Euston Road, NW1 2QS (7388 9998/fax 7388 6766). King's Cross tube/rail.* **Reception open** 7am-11pm daily; 24hr access. **Rates** £24.60; £20.50 under-18s. **Map** p399 L3.

YMCAs

You may need to book months ahead; this Christian organisation is mainly concerned with housing homeless young people across the world. A few of the larger London hostels open to all are listed below (all are unisex), but you can get a full list from the National Council for YMCAs (8520 5599/www.ymca.org.uk). Prices are around £25-£30 per night for a single room and £40-£45 for a double.

Barbican *YMCA 2 Fann Street, EC2Y 8BR (7628 0697/fax 7638 2420). Barbican tube.* **Map** p402 P5.

London City *YMCA 8 Errol Street, EC1Y 8SE (7628 8832/fax 7628 4080). Barbican/Old Street tube/rail.* **Map** p402 F4.

Wimbledon *YMCA 200 The Broadway, SW19 1RY (8542 9055/fax 8542 1086). South Wimbledon tube/Wimbledon tube/rail.*

Sightseeing

Introduction	72
The South Bank & Bankside	75
The City	88
Holborn & Clerkenwell	101
Bloomsbury & Fitzrovia	106
Marylebone	112
Mayfair & St James's	115
Soho	121
Covent Garden & St Giles's	126
Westminster	132
South Kensington & Knightsbridge	140
Chelsea	145
North London	148
East London	157
South-east London	167
South-west London	174
West London	182

Features

The best Sights	73
My kind of town Ken Livingstone	87
The London Stone	94
My kind of town Tracey Emin	96
Walk this way Life's a stage	104
Cross purposes	109
Fantastic voyagers	118
Go-go gone	122
Don't go there	130
Watermarks What lies beneath	136
Water palaver	143
Chelsea Pensioners	147
Watermarks Regent's Canal	152
London Muslim Centre	158
Age of Empire	162
Rich Mix	165
My kind of town 'Mad' Frankie Fraser	168
Watermarks Wandling free	176
A load of hot (dry) air	183
Literature with attitude	189

Introduction

How to get the most interest out of your capital.

Taken as a glorious whole, London can't fail to satisfy. However, undercutting the thrill of experiencing an iconic sight or a random, only-in-London moment will be the little disappointments: among them the difficulty of getting around such a large and incoherent area, the dirt and litter, and the occasional unfriendliness of residents. There's little we can do about the latter two points, but the former can be greatly ameliorated with an understanding of London's geography and transport.

GETTING AROUND

The tube is the most straightforward way to get around, popping you up within a ten-minute walk of your destination pretty much everywhere in the central area. Services are frequent and, outside rush hours, you'll usually get a seat. But mix and match your tube journeys with bus rides: though the classic open-back Routemasters are disappearing from the streets in 2005 (see p118), buses not only allow you to see the territory you pass through but also to get a handle on London's topography. Some good routes for stringing the sights and major streets together in various directions are the 7, 8, 11 and 12, all double-decker, and the RV1, a single-decker plying the river circuit. We recommend that you free yourself to explore by purchasing a Travelcard (see p361), which covers bus, rail and tube. It would also be clever to add river services to your transport portfolio (see p363). And while the higgledy-piggledy nature of London's streets makes them hard to navigate, it also makes them a pleasure to walk.

For more information on all methods of transport, see p360.

DECODING THE MAP

London is huge; central London alone would fit over most small towns. The Congestion Charge Zone alone is five miles across. Are these great distances linked by a stately, well-planned road network? No: the map looks more like a piece of kindergarten crochet, thanks to a long and pragmatic evolution (the City, for example, was razed to the ground in the 17th century, but complications of land ownership meant the street plan was largely reinstated).

London, very loosely, developed east to west. First the City, then Westminster, then the bits in the middle, where lots of the service and entertainment industries took root, and then

beyond. The wealth followed. So anywhere with a W or SW postcode is likely to be a bit more salubrious than your Es or your SEs (for a full explanation of postcodes, see p366).

A BRIEF TOUR

In the ever-fascinating **City** (see p88), towers monumentalising today's financial industry jostle with reminders of London's ancient and historic past. The areas north and east of here, the old industrial hinterlands of **Shoreditch** and **Hoxton** (for both, see p159), are now known for their nightlife scenes. Heading west across the City, **Clerkenwell** (see p103) has a fascinating history of doing the dirty work for the medieval city it bordered, and now has some of London's best restaurants and gastropubs, while **Holborn** (see p101) is the legal quarter. Where High Holborn crosses Tottenham Court Road/Charing Cross Road, it becomes Oxford Street, running east to west. Dominated by the distinctive 1980s Centrepoint skyscraper, this junction is a handy reference point. In the north-east quadrant is literary land **Bloomsbury** (see p106), home to the British Museum; **Fitzrovia** (see p110) and its boho rebel past and media industry present are across Tottenham Court Road to the north-east. South-east is **Covent Garden** (see p126), with its theatres and opera houses, diverting streets and pleasant if touristy Piazza, then comes London's spiciest square mile, **Soho** (see p121), to the south-west.

Further west, after the intersection with Regent Street at Oxford Circus, Oxford Street becomes the divider betwen affluent, appealing **Marylebone** (see p112) to the north and affluent, important **Mayfair** (see p115) to the south. From Oxford Circus, elegant Regent Street leads south to another landmark Circus, Piccadilly, marking the convergence of the southern extremes of Soho and Covent Garden with the start of more stately London: to the east, Piccadilly – which runs east to west south of and more or less parallel to Oxford Street – is the southern border of Mayfair, and the northern edge of **St James's** (see p118), and royal London. Trafalgar Square is a short hop away from Piccadilly Circus. As well as being the home of the National and National Portrait Galleries and a worthy destination in its own right, it is the gateway (literally, via Admiralty Arch) to the politics and pomp of **Westminster** (see p132).

The best Sights

For bookish types
Dickens' House (*see p109*); Dr Johnson's House (*see p89*); Keats House (*see p154*).

For blood and gore
London Dungeon (*see p85*); the Chamber of Horrors in Madame Tussaud's (*see p114*); Old Operating Theatre, Museum & Herb Garret (*see p85*).

For drama kings and queens
Shakespeare's Globe (*see p82*); Theatre Museum and St Paul's Covent Garden (for both, *see p127*).

For flâneurs
The Bloomsbury squares (*see p92*); the villagey streets of Hampstead (*see p151*); Marylebone High Street (*see p113*); the Spitalfields area at the weekend (*see p159*).

For homely pleasures
Dennis Severs' House (*see p159*); Geffrye Museum (*see p160*); the Secret Life of the Home in the Science Museum (*see p141*); the William Morris Gallery (*see p164*).

For palatial splendour
Buckingham Palace (*see p117*); Hampton Court Palace (*see p180*); Kensington Palace (*see p142*).

For pilgrims
Abbey Road (*see p150*); Bloomsbury Group HQ (*see p106*); Diana, Princess of Wales Memorial Playground (*see p274*); Karl

Marx's grave at Highgate Cemetery (*see p155*); St Pancras Gardens, where Shelley proposed to Mary Godwin; the tombs of Wren, Wellington and Nelson in St Paul's Cathedral (*see p92*).

For sporting heroes
Lord's Tour & MCC Museum (*see p150*); Rugby Museum/Twickenham Stadium (*see p181*); Wimbledon Lawn Tennis Museum (*see p179*).

For a trip back in time
Bevis Marks Synagogue (*see p98*); the Foundling Museum (*see p220*); 19 Princelet Street (*see p159*).

For views of the city
Alexandra Park & Palace (*see p156*); British Airways London Eye (*see p77*); Monument (*see p98*); Primrose Hill (*see p149*); Tower Bridge Exhibition (*see p99*); Waterloo Bridge (*see p79*).

For young artists
Camden Arts Centre (*see p151*); Saatchi Gallery (*see p78*); Tate Modern (*see p83*); Whitechapel Art Gallery (*see p158*).

Worth the suburban jaunt
Osterley House (*see p190*); Syon House (*see p188*); Red House, Eltham Palace (for both, *see p173*); Royal Air Force Museum Hendon (*see p156*); Royal Botanic Gardens (*see p177*).

To the west, Oxford Street and Piccadilly end at the easily identifiable landmarks of Marble Arch and Wellington Arch respectively, which are linked by Park Lane. To its west are Hyde Park and Kensington Gardens. After Wellington Arch, Piccadilly becomes **Knightsbridge** (home of Harrods and much designer shopping), south of which are the salubrious SWs, including 1960s survivor **Chelsea** (*see p145*) and **South Kensington** (*see p140*), location of the great Victorian museums.

London's areas are clearly delineated on the colour-coded map on page 412.

PRACTICALITIES
Don't overestimate your capacity. Of the places we list in the following pages – the British Museum springs immediately to mind – take days to fully appreciate. To avoid queues and

overcrowding follow the tips given in the text, and try to avoid weekends, when you'll find yourself competing with the locals.

It's gratifying that so many attractions are free to enter. If you're on a budget and time is on your side, you can tick off large numbers of places on your 'must see' list for the price of a bus pass. If you want to extend your sightseeing options to more expensive places, such as London Zoo and the Tower of London, a **London Pass** (0870 242 9988, www.londonpass.com) may be of interest. This gives you pre-paid access to more than 50 sights and attractions and costs from £23 daily per adult, or £27 with a Travelcard thrown in.

If we have included the initials 'LP' before the admission price of a certain place, it means your London Pass will allow free admission, tours or free entry to exhibitions. The initials

'EH' mean the sight is an **English Heritage** (www.english-heritage.co.uk, 7973 3000) property, so members of that organisation can get in free. 'NT' means that **National Trust** (www.nationaltrust.org.uk, 0870 458 4000) members can expect free admission.

See the sights

By balloon

Adventure Balloons *Winchfield Park, London Road, Hartley Wintney, Hampshire RG27 8HY (01252 844 222/www.adventureballoons.co.uk).* **Flights** *London* May-Aug 5am Tue, Wed, Thur. **Fares** *London* £165 per person. **Credit** MC, V.
Balloon flights over London leave from either Vauxhall Bridge or Tower Hill, very early in the morning. Flights must be booked well ahead and are dependent on the weather. There's champagne or juice all round on landing.

By boat

City Cruises (*7740 0400/www.citycruises.com*). The river's biggest pleasure cruise operator, City Cruises' Rail and River Rover (£9 adults; £4.50 children), a collaboration with Docklands Light Railway, combines a cruise with unlimited DLR travel.

By bus

Big Bus Company *48 Buckingham Palace Road, Westminster, SW1W 0RN (07233 7797/www.bigbustours.com).* **Open-top bus tours** 3 routes, 2hrs; with commentary (recorded on Blue route, live on Red and Green). Tickets include river cruise and walking tours. **Departures** every 10-15mins from Green Park, Victoria & Marble Arch. *Summer* 8.30am-6pm daily. *Winter* 8.30am-4.30pm daily. **Pick-up** Green Park (near the Ritz); Marble Arch (Speakers' Corner); Victoria (outside Thistle Victoria Hotel, 48 Buckingham Palace Road). **Fares** £18 (£16 if booked online); £8 5-15s; free under-5s. Tickets valid for 24hrs, interchangeable between routes. **Credit** AmEx, DC, MC, V.

Original London Sightseeing Tour
8877 1722/8877 2120/www.theoriginaltour. com. **Departures** *Summer* 9am-7pm daily. *Winter* 9am-5.30pm daily. **Pick-up** Grosvenor Gardens; Marble Arch (Speakers' Corner); Baker Street tube (forecourt); Coventry Street; Embankment station; Trafalgar Square. **Fares** £16; £10 5-15s; free under-5s (£1 discount if booked online or by phone). **Credit** MC, V.

By duck

London Duck Tours *55 York Road, Waterloo, SE1 7NJ (7928 3132/www.londonducktours.co.uk).* **Tours** *Feb-Dec* daily (ring for departure times). **Pick-up** Chicheley Street (behind the London Eye). **Fares** £16.50; £11 under-12s; £49 family ticket. **Credit** MC, V.
City of Westminster tours in a DUKW (amphibious vehicle developed during World War II) comprise a 75-minute road and river trip starting at the London Eye and going in the Thames at Vauxhall.

By helicopter

Cabair Helicopters *Elstree Aerodrome, Borehamwood, Hertfordshire WD6 3AW (8953 4411/www.cabairhelicopters.com).* Edgware tube/Elstree rail. **Flights** from 9.45am Sun. **Fares** £129 (age 7s and above only). **Credit** MC, V.

By pedal power

London Pedicabs *07866 628462/www. londonpedicabs.com.* **Fares** £2-£5/mile/person.
Pedicabs (where someone cycles you to your destination in a rickshaw-style bike) are based around Covent Garden, Soho and Leicester Square.

London Bicycle Tour Company *Gabriel's Wharf, 56 Upper Ground, Waterloo, SE1 9PP (7928 6838/www.londonbicycle.com).* **Open** 10am-6pm daily. **Tours** 2pm Sat, Sun; 3½ hours (including pub stop). **Fares** *Bike hire* £2.50 per hour; £14 per day; £7 subsequent days; £40 per week; *Bike tours* £15/person.

Metrobike *08450801952/www.promobikes.co.uk.* **Fares** from £2-£5 for a short trip; £40/hr private hire. **No credit cards.**
These futuristic bike taxis, which originated in Germany, can take two people on short trips around town, or longer sightseeing tours. Metrobikes are based around Regent Street.

By taxi

Black Taxi Tours of London *7935 9363/ www.blacktaxitours.co.uk.* **Cost** £75 day tours; £85 evening tours. **No credit cards.**
A tailored two-hour tour for up to five people.

On foot

Arguably the best company organising walks around London is **Original London Walks** (7624 9255, www.walks.com), which encompasses sorties on everything from the shadowy London of Sherlock Holmes to picturesque riverside pubs, and plenty of Jack the Ripper.

Other walks companies worth noting include Citisights (8806 4325), **Historical Tours** (8668 4019, www.historicalwalksoflondon. com) and **Pied Piper Walks** (7435 4782), along with **Performing London** (*see p104*) and **Silvercan Tours** (*see p296*). Good self-guided walks are listed in *Time Out London Walks* volumes 1 and 2 (£9.99 and £11.99).

With the specialists

Open House Architecture *Unit C1, 39-51 Highgate Road, NW5 1RS (7267 7644/ www.londonopenhouse.org).* Call for tour details. **Departures** 10.05am Sat. **Meeting point** in front of Royal Academy of Arts, Piccadilly (Piccadilly Circus tube). **Duration** 3hrs (& occasional 1-day tours). **Tickets** £18.50; £13 students; advance booking advisable. **Credit** MC, V.
Tour Guides *7495 5504/www.tourguides.co.uk.* Tailor-made tours with Blue Badge guides for individuals or groups, on foot, by car, coach or boat.
Premium Tours *7278 5300/www.premium tours.co.uk.*
Private tours of specific sites and attractions in London and the south of England.

The South Bank & Bankside

The Cinderella side of the river is having a ball.

British Airways London Eye. *See p77.*

Sightseeing

With its massive observation wheel, converted government offices, concrete concert halls, national theatres, cinemas and contemporary art galleries, the south side of the river has become the arts and entertainment showpiece of the capital, as was its manifest destiny. The South Bank and Bankside are the places that Londoners have always come to be entertained. The only change is in the level of refinement. Art, music, theatre, film and food today; books and buskers too. Bears, bards and prostitutes a millennium ago. This is an area that has long lived on the margins: not just of the river, but of the City and society itself.

The transformation of this stretch of river over the last 50 years or so has been steady but laborious. The Festival of Britain in 1951 opened the way for the building of the blockish South Bank Centre, whose brutalist design is now considered one of the acmes of that movement's achievement. The biggest and most expensive party, however, was the one

to celebrate the turn of the century. Eight years earlier, Marks Barfield architects had taken part in a competition to come up with a structure to celebrate the millennium. Their amazing big wheel, the **British Airways London Eye**, came second. No one can remember what won. The 'blade of light' shooting across the river to St Paul's Cathedral is the **Millennium Bridge**, which has done wonders for visitor numbers, and the equally lovely **Hungerford** footbridges, linking the South Bank to Embankment on the north side, are another reason to start a walking tour here.

With its riverside walkways, frequent festivals, outdoor cafés and fine views, the South Bank is eminently strollable. The South Bank Marketing Group has an ordering line (7202 6900) for its free Walk This Way leaflets, but you can't really go wrong just wandering. Another way to explore is to hop on the RV1 bus, which links all the riverside attractions between Covent Garden and Tower Gateway.

YOU'LL FIND US AT LONDON AQUARIUM

Have fun finding the real clown fish, not to mention several different species of sharks, including the Sand Tiger pictured. London Aquarium is full of surprises with over 350 unique underwater species to discover.

Located in County Hall and right next to the London Eye, London Aquarium is only a short walk from Waterloo Station and just over Westminster Bridge from Big Ben and the Houses of Parliament.

So don't plan time out in London without visiting London's only aquarium!
Open every day from 10am to 6pm.

For further details call **020 7967 8000**
or log on to www.londonaquarium.co.uk

LONDON
AQUARIUM

The South Bank

Lambeth Bridge to Hungerford Bridge

Map p11 M8-M10

Embankment or Westminster tube/Waterloo tube/rail.

The Lambeth Bridge is adorned by carved pineapples as a tribute to the father of British gardening (John Tradescant, whose plant-hunting habit brought the exotic fruit here in the 16th century). On its southern side, **Lambeth Palace**, official residence of the Archbishops of Canterbury since the 12th century, opens to the public on high days and holidays, notably during Open House London (*see p266*). The church next door, St Mary-at-Lambeth, was deconsecrated in 1972 to become the **Museum of Garden History** (*see p78*).

Walking west along the Albert Embankment and under **Westminster Bridge** you come to London's major tourist zone. The **British Airways London Eye** (*see below*) packs in the crowds, while the various establishments in the grand **County Hall** (once the residence of the London government) get them as they come off the wheel: the **London Aquarium** (*see below*) bags the family market and the surreal works of Salvador Dali (**Dalí Universe**, *see below*) vie for the arts crowd with Damien Hirst's sharks in the **Saatchi Gallery** (*see below*), which specialises in modern British art.

British Airways London Eye

Riverside Building, next to County Hall, Westminster Bridge Road, SE1 7PB (0870 500 0600/customer services 0870 990 8883/www.ba-londoneye.com). Westminster tube/Waterloo tube/rail. **Open** *Oct-Apr* 9.30am-8pm Mon, Wed-Sun; 10.30am-8pm Tue. *May-Sept* 9.30am-10pm daily. **Admission** £11.50; £9 concessions (only applicable Sept-June, Mon-Fri); £5.75 5-15s; free under-5s. **Credit** AmEx, MC, V. **Map** p401 M8.

Such is its impact on the London skyline, it's hard to believe that this giant wheel was originally intended to turn majestically over the Thames for only five years after the Millennium. Celebrating that anniversary in 2005, it's proved so popular that no one wants it to come down, and it's now scheduled to keep spinning for another 20 years. The 450ft (137m) monster, whose 32 glass capsules each hold 25 people, commands superb views over the heart of London and beyond. A 'flight' (as a turn is called) takes half an hour, which gives you plenty of time to have an argument about which hill is which in south London, ogle the Queen's back garden and follow the silver snake of the Thames. You can buy a guide to the landmarks for £2. Some people book in advance (although they take a gamble with the weather), but it is possible to turn up and queue for

a ticket on the day, though there can be long queues in summer. Night flights offer a more twinkly experience, with the bridges all lit up and lovely.

Dalí Universe

County Hall Gallery, County Hall Riverside Building, Queen's Walk, SE1 7PB (7620 2720/www.dali universe.com). Waterloo tube/rail. **Open** 10am-5.30pm daily. **Admission** *Oct-May* £8.50; £7 concessions; £5.50 8-16s; £3.50 4-7s; £23 family. *June-Sept* £9; £5.50 8-16s; £3.50 4-7s; £24 family. **Credit** AmEx, DC, MC, V. **Map** p401 M8.

Here's the place to get as close as you dare to the work of the Great Masturbator. Trademark attractions such as the 'Mae West Lips' sofa and the *Spellbound* painting enhance the main exhibition, curated by long-term Dali friend Benjamin Levi, which leaves you in no doubt as to the Spanish artist's eccentricity. The wall-mounted quotes by, and (silent) videos and photographs of, Dali give an insight into his life. There are sculptures, watercolours (including his flamboyant tarot cards), rare etchings and lithographs, all exploring his favourite themes such as the hyper-surreal 'Dreams and Fantasy', the exotic and indulgent 'Femininity and Sensuality', and 'Religion and Mythology'. Check out the interesting series of Bible scenes by the Catholic-turned-atheist-turned-Catholic again. The gallery also shows works by new artists.

Florence Nightingale Museum

St Thomas's Hospital, 2 Lambeth Palace Road, SE1 7EW (7620 0374/www.florence-nightingale.co.uk). Westminster tube/Waterloo tube/rail. **Open** 10am-5pm Mon-Fri (last entry 4pm); 10am-4.30pm Sat, Sun (last entry 3.30pm). **Admission** £5.80; £4.20 5-18s, concessions; £13 family; free under-5s. **Credit** AmEx, MC, V. **Map** p401 M9.

The nursing skills and campaigning zeal that made Florence Nightingale's Crimean War work the stuff of legend are honoured here with a chronological tour through her remarkable life, illustrated along the way by her pronouncements. On returning from the battlefields of Scutari she opened the Nightingale Nursing School here in St Thomas's Hospital. Displays of period mementoes, clothing, furniture, books, letters and portraits now include her stuffed pet owl, Athena. In 2005, the museum celebrates the 200th anniversary of the birth of another Crimean war hero, Mary Seacole. A nurse of Jamaican and Scottish extraction, she was recently voted the greatest black Briton. Free children's activities, such as art workshops, take place every other weekend.

London Aquarium

County Hall, Riverside Building, Westminster Bridge Road, SE1 7PB (7967 8000/tours 7967 8007/www. londonaquarium.co.uk). Westminster tube/Waterloo tube/rail. **Open** *Term time* 10am-6pm daily (last entry 5pm). *School holidays* 10am-7pm (last entry 6pm). **Admission** (LP) £8.75; £6.50 concessions; £5.25 3-14s; £6.50 disabled; free under-3s; £25 family. (All prices £1 more during school holidays) **Credit** AmEx, MC, V. **Map** p401 M9.

Millennium...

... and **Hungerford** bridges. *See p75.*

The aquarium, one of Europe's largest, displays its habitants according to geographical origin, so there are tanks of bright fish from the coral reefs and the Indian Ocean, temperate freshwater fish from the rivers of Europe and North America, and crustaceans and rockpool plants from shorelines. Rays glide swiftly around touch pools, coming up to the surface frequently. There are tanks devoted to jellyfish, octopuses, sharks and piranhas. Information is liberally posted around. The shop is a vast and garish provider of cuddly crabs and plastic sharks.

Museum of Garden History

Lambeth Palace Road, SE1 7LB (7401 8865/ www.museumgardenhistory.org). Waterloo tube/rail/C10, 507 bus. **Open** *Feb-mid Dec* 10.30am-5pm daily. **Admission** free. Suggested donation £3; £2.50 concessions. **Credit** AmEx, MC, V. **Map** p401 L10.

Intrepid plant hunter and gardener to Charles I, John Tradescant is buried here at the world's first museum of horticulture. A replica of a 17th-century knot garden has been created in his honour. The garden uses geometric shapes based on squares and circles that incorporate the letter 'T' (for Tradescant). Topiary and box hedging, old roses, herbaceous perennials and bulbs give all-year interest. A sarcophagus in the graveyard garden contains the remains of Captain Bligh, the breadfruit transplanter famous for being abandoned in the Pacific by the mutinous crew of HMS *Bounty*. Inside are displays of ancient tools, exhibitions about horticulture through the ages, a shop and café. A little green gem.

Saatchi Gallery

County Hall, Riverside Building, Westminster Bridge Road, SE1 7PB (7823 2363/www.saatchi-gallery. co.uk). Westminster tube/Waterloo tube/rail. **Open** 10am-8pm Mon-Thur, Sun; 10am-10pm Fri, Sat. **Admission** £8.75; £6.75 concessions, 5-16s; £26 family. **Credit** MC, V. **Map** p401 M9.

Advertising impresario Charles Saatchi has long made it his business to back emerging talent. That's what he did with young Damien Hirst, Tracey Emin and Marc Quinn, whose most famous pieces, *The Physical Impossibility of Death in the Mind of Someone Living*, *My Bed* and *Self*, respectively, are central to the permanent collection in the rotunda meeting room of County Hall (previously headquarters of the Greater London Council). The austere panelled Edwardian offices contrast oddly with the pickled sharks, unmade beds and frozen heads full of blood. Then again, maybe they don't. The advent of Saatchi in this wonderful space has given the public a chance not only to judge for themselves the value of these pieces, but to admire the architecture too.

Hungerford Bridge to Blackfriars Bridge

Maps p11 M7-8 & p404 N7

Embankment or Temple tube/Blackfriars or Waterloo tube/rail.

When riverside warehouses were cleared to make way for the **South Bank Centre** in the 1960s, the big concrete complex containing the

Royal Festival Hall, Purcell Room and Queen Elizabeth Hall was hailed as a daring testament to modern architecture. Together with the Royal National Theatre and the Hayward Gallery, it comprises one of the largest and most popular arts centres in the world. The centrepiece, Sir Leslie Martin's **Royal Festival Hall** – built for the Festival of Britain – is currently being given a £90-million overhaul: the improvement of its river frontage should be complete by mid 2005. The main auditorium will have its acoustics enhanced, closing from summer of 2005 to early 2007.

The **Hayward Gallery** (see below) next door is a landmark of brutalist architecture and also undergoing renovations. Its new pavilion was designed in collaboration with light artist Dan Graham. The gallery's trademark neon-lit tower, designed in 1970 by Phillip Vaughan and Roger Dainton, is a kinetic light sculpture of yellow, red, green and blue tubes controlled by the direction and speed of the wind.

Another player, supposedly, in the proposed masterplan is the useful **National Film Theatre** (see 285), squatting underneath Waterloo Bridge. No one yet knows whether a proposed five-screen film centre will finally materialise, but we can all hope. The second-hand book stalls and semi-official skate park add to the atmosphere here.

The **Royal National Theatre** (see p335) has emerged from its own renovation scheme with a Theatre Square (an interesting space for free open-air performances), restyled Lyttelton Theatre and plenty of praise heaped upon its new 100-seat Loft space.

Beyond the heavy concrete blocks of the South Bank Centre, the mellow red bricks of **Oxo Tower Wharf** come as light relief. The warehouse building's deco tower incorporates covert advertising for the stock cube company that bought it. Earmarked for demolition in the 1970s, it was saved by the Coin Street Community Builders, and now provides affordable housing, interesting designer shops and galleries, and a rooftop restaurant, bar and bistro with wonderful views (see p195). The bustling cafés and shops of **Gabriel's Wharf** nearby are another Coin Street enterprise.

Hayward Gallery

Belvedere Road, SE1 8XX (box office 0870/ www.hayward.org.uk). Embankment tube/Charing Cross or Waterloo tube/rail. **Open** *During exhibitions* 10am-6pm Mon, Thur, Sun; 10am-8pm Tue, Wed; 10am-9pm Fri. **Admission** £9 but can vary. **Credit** AmEx, MC, V. **Map** p401 M8.
In the new foyer extension and mirrored, elliptical glass pavilion/artwork, Waterloo Sunset at the Hayward Gallery, casual visitors can watch cartoons on touch screens as they sip their Starbucks.

Art lovers dismayed by the latter nonetheless enjoy the pavilion and the excellent exhibition programme. In 2005 that includes a show of German installation artist Rebecca Horn, and also 'Intimate Relations': a look at sex and sexuality in art, culture and science. In 2006, look out for a major celebration of the work of Georges Bataille and 'Oceania', art from the Pacific.

Around Waterloo

Map p401 M8
Waterloo tube/rail.
Redevelopment of the Belvedere Road area has improved access to **Waterloo Station**, where Nicholas Grimshaw's glass-roofed terminus for Eurostar trains provides an elegant departure point for travellers bound for Brussels and Paris. Outside, the jury's still out on the stonking great £20-million BFIIMAX cinema (see p285) that was plonked down in the middle of the roundabout a few years ago at the expense of its homeless occupants.

Another place of interest around the station is the street market on **Lower Marsh** (the name originates from the rural village known as Lambeth Marsh until the 18th century). On the corner of Waterloo Road and the street known as the Cut is the restored Victorian façade of the **Old Vic Theatre**. Known in Victorian times as the 'Bucket of Blood' for its penchant for melodrama, it is now in the hands of Hollywood actor Kevin Spacey. Further down the Cut is the functional exterior of a hotbed of youthful theatrical talent, the **Young Vic** (see p340), currently undergoing redevelopment and due to reopen in 2006.

Walking down Lower Marsh in the other direction takes you to Westminster Bridge Road, where at No.121 is what's left of the **London Necropolis Station**, founded in 1854 and used purely for train transport of the city's dead to an overflow cemetery in Surrey. The ground floor was redeveloped after bombing in 1941, but much of the original façade remains.

Bankside

Map p404 O8-P8
Borough or Southwark tube/London Bridge tube/rail.
The area around the river between London Bridge and Blackfriars Bridge known as **Bankside** was the epicentre of bawdy Southwark in Shakespeare's day. As well as playhouses such as the Globe and the Rose stirring up all sorts of trouble among the groundlings, there were the famous 'stewes' (brothels), seedy inns and other dens of iniquity where decent folk could be led astray. Presiding over all this depravity were the Bishops of

Sightseeing

Conceived and designed by Marks Barfield Archite

Experience the world's
tallest observation wheel

Phone +44(0) 870 5000 600 to book, or just turn up.
Nearest tube stations ⊖ : Waterloo and Westminster

ba-londoneye.com

BRITISH AIRWAYS
London ey

Museum of Garden History. *See p78*.

Winchester, who made a tidy income from the fines they levied on prostitutes (or 'Winchester Geese' as they were known at the height of the Bishops' power) and other lost souls. All that's left of the grand Palace of Winchester, home of successive bishops, is the rose window of the Great Hall on Clink Street, a short walk from the river, next to the site of the Clink prison (now the **Clink Prison Museum**; *see below*).

The parish church at this time was St Saviour's, formerly the monastic church of St Mary Overie and now (since 1905) the Anglican **Southwark Cathedral** (*see p82*). Shakespeare's brother Edmund was buried in the graveyard here and there's a monument to the playwright inside. You have to walk back down Clink Street, past **Vinopolis**, the wine attraction (*see p83*), to reach **Shakespeare's Globe** (*see p82*). Built on the site of the original, this reproduction in wattle and daub is separated from its neighbour, **Tate Modern** (*see p83*), by a wonky terrace of houses, where Sir Christopher Wren stayed when building St Paul's across the water. The Tate's repository of modern art was a power station designed by Sir Giles Gilbert Scott in a defining moment of utility architecture. The crowds that pass through its massive portals prove that it's culture vultures, rather than the clients of Winchester Geese, who seek their pleasures in Bankside now.

Bankside Gallery

48 Hopton Street, SE1 9JH (7928 7521/ www.banksidegallery.com). Blackfriars tube/rail/ Southwark tube. **Open** 10am-6pm daily. **Admission** free (optional donations). **Credit** DC, MC, V.
Crouching beside the Tate, this little gallery is the home of the Royal Watercolour Society and the Royal Society of Painter-Printmakers. Its changing exhibitions reflect established and experimental practices. In May 2005, the gallery explores the relationship between artists and BBC Radio 4. The shop has books and art materials, alongside prints and watercolours by members of both societies.

Bramah Museum of Tea & Coffee

40 Southwark Street, SE1 1UN (7403 5650/www. bramahmuseum.co.uk). London Bridge tube/rail. **Open** 10am-6pm daily. **Admission** £4; £3.50 concessions. **Credit** AmEx, DC, MC, V. **Map** p405 S9.
As a nation we get through 100,000 tons of teabags a year, a fact that no doubt appals tea purist Edward Bramah, a former tea taster who set up this museum in the early 1990s. Bramah's collection displays pots, maps, caddies and ancient coffee makers. They work as visual aids to the history of the beverages and the role they have had to play in the refreshing (and near destruction) of nations. The exhibition doesn't take long to work round, but it's tempting to linger in the naturally well-stocked café.

Clink Prison Museum

1 Clink Street, SE1 9DG (7403 0900/www. clink.co.uk). London Bridge tube/rail. **Open** June-Sept 10am-9pm daily. Oct-May 10am-6pm daily. **Admission** £5; £3.50 concessions, 5-15s; £12 family. **Credit** MC, V. **Map** p404 P8.
A small, grisly exhibition looks behind the bars of the hellish prison 'The Clink', owned by the Bishops of Winchester from the 12th to the 18th centuries. Thieves, prostitutes and debtors served their sentences within its walls during an era when boiling in oil was legal. On display for the 'hands-on' experience are torture devices and the fetters whose clanking gave the prison its name.

Golden Hinde

St Mary Overie Dock, Cathedral Street, SE1 9DE (0870 011 8700/www.goldenhinde.co.uk). Monument tube/London Bridge tube/rail. **Open** daily, times vary. **Admission** £3.50; £3 concessions; £2.50 4-13s; free under-4s; £10 family. **Credit** MC, V. **Map** p404 P8.
Weekends see this reconstruction of Sir Francis Drake's 16th-century flagship swarming with children dressed up as pirates for birthday dos. When it hasn't been taken over by cutlass-wielding youths, the meticulously recreated ship is fascinating to explore. It has even reprised Drake's circumnavigatory voyage. 'Living History Experiences' (some overnight), in which participants dress in period clothes, eat Tudor fare and learn the skills of the Elizabethan seafarer, are a huge hit with the young, as is the eye-patch and parrot-selling shop.

Saatchi Gallery. *See p78.*

HMS Belfast

Morgan's Lane, Tooley Street, SE1 2JH (7940 6300/
www.iwm.org.uk). London Bridge tube/rail. **Open**
Mar-Oct 10am-6pm daily (last entry 5.15pm). *Nov-*
Feb 10am-5pm daily (last entry 4.15pm). **Admission**
£7; £5 concessions; free under-16s (must be
accompanied by adult). **Credit** MC, V. **Map** p405 R8.
This 11,500-ton battlecruiser is a floating museum
and an unlikely playground for children, who tear
around its nine decks, boiler, engine rooms and
gun turrets. Belfast was built in 1938 and played
a leading role in the Normandy Landings. She
supported UN forces in Korea before being decom-
missioned in 1965; a special exhibition looks at
that 'forgotten war'. The ship will also be getting
involved in 2005's Year of the Sea. Guided tours
take in living quarters and explain what life was
like on board. The Walrus Café is on the ship, the
souvenir shop on dry land.

Rose Theatre

56 Park Street, SE1 9AR (7902 1500/www.rose
theatre.org.uk). London Bridge tube/rail. **Open** *May-*
Sept (by appointment) for groups of 15+ as part of
summer tour with Shakespeare's Globe. **Credit**
AmEx, MC, V. **Map** p404 P8.
The Rose – built by Philip Henslowe and opera-
tional from 1587 until 1606 – was the first playhouse to be built at Bankside. It's currently being
looked after by the folks at Shakespeare's Globe
(*see below*) while funds are being sought for new
excavation work in search of as yet uncovered portions of the old theatre that could restore its original ground plan.

Shakespeare's Globe

21 New Globe Walk, Bankside, SE1 9DT (7902
1500/www.shakespeares-globe.org). Mansion
House or Southwark tube/London Bridge tube/rail.
Open *Tours & exhibitions* Oct-Apr 10am-5pm
daily. May-Sept 9am-noon daily. **Admission**
(LP) £8.50; £7 concessions; £6 5-15s. **Credit** MC,
V, AmEx. **Map** p404 O7.
The original Globe Theatre, where many of
William Shakespeare's plays were first staged and
which he co-owned, burned down in 1613 during
a performance of *Henry VIII*. Nearly 400 years
later, it was rebuilt not far from its original site
under the auspices of actor Sam Wanamaker (who,
sadly, didn't live to see it up and running), using
construction methods and materials as close to the
originals as possible. You can tour the theatre outside the May to September performance season,
when historically authentic (and frequently very
good) performances are staged (*see p335*). A fine
exhibition based on famous productions of
Shakespeare's plays is open year round. Expect
celebrations in 2005 of the tenth anniversary of
actor Mark Rylance's inspired directorship.

Southwark Cathedral

London Bridge, SE1 9DA (7367 6700/tours 7367
6734/www.dswark.org/cathedral). London Bridge
tube/rail. **Open** 8am-6pm daily (closing times vary
on religious holidays). *Services* 8am, 8.15am,
12.30pm, 12.45pm, 5.30pm Mon-Fri; 9am, 9.15am,
4pm Sat; 8.45am, 9am, 11am, 3pm, 6.30pm Sun.
Choral Evensong 5.30pm Tue (boys & men), Fri (men
only); 5.30pm Mon, Thur (girls). **Admission** *Audio*
Tours £2.50. **Credit** AmEx, MC, V. **Map** p404 P8.

The oldest bits of this building are more than 800 years old. The retro-choir was where the trials of several Protestant martyrs took place during the reign of Mary Tudor. After the Reformation, the church fell into disrepair and parts of it became a bakery and a pigsty. In 1905 it became a cathedral: centenary celebrations this year include celebrity organ recitals and a big beanfeast on 3 July in conjunction with Borough Market. An interactive museum called the Long View of London, a refectory and a lovely garden are some of the millennial improvements that make Southwark look so ship-shape these days. There are memorials to Shakespeare, John Harvard (benefactor of the US university), Sam Wanamaker (the force behind Shakespeare's Globe) and stained-glass windows with images of Chaucer and John Bunyan.

Tate Modern

Bankside, SE1 9TG (7401 5120/www.tate.org.uk). Blackfriars tube/rail. **Open** 10am-6pm Mon-Thur, Sun; 10am-10pm Fri, Sat. *Tours* 11am, noon, 2pm, 3pm daily. **Admission** free. *Temporary exhibitions* prices vary. **Map** p401 O7.

A powerhouse of modern art, Tate Modern's imposing form is awe-inspiring even before you embark on a tour of the collection, moved here in 2000 from the original Tate (now called Tate Britain; *see p138*). Also impressive is the sheer number of visitors tramping through the vast Turbine Hall installation space and wandering through galleries with titles like History/Memory/Society and Still Life/Object/Real Life. Arranging the works according to themes like this was considered by some critics to be a touch obtuse, but the innovation has gone down well with most visitors. The artists are listed on the doorway of each gallery, so it's pretty easy to find the one you want. If you don't know where to start in all the hugeness, take a guided tour (ask at the information desk). Leave time for the cafés and the shop.

From February-2 May 2005, the gallery mounts a thorough assessment of the work of Joseph Beuys, followed by a major exhibition of the paintings, photographs and drawings of Mexican artist Frida Kahlo (June-2 October). The Unilever Series of super-size works will continue in the Turbine Hall from autumn through spring 2006. Look out too for a warming winter exhibition in 2005 of Henri 'Le Douanier' Rousseau's jungle paintings.

The Tate to Tate boat service – decor courtesy of Damien Hirst – links Tates Britain and Modern and runs every 20 minutes, stopping along the way at the London Eye. Tickets are available from ticket desks at the Tates, on board the boat, online or by phone (7887 8888). Prices are £5 for an adult (£3.40 if you have a travelcard) and £2.50 for children.

Vinopolis, City of Wine

1 Bank End, SE1 9BU (0870 241 4040/www. vinopolis.co.uk). London Bridge tube/rail. **Open** noon-9pm Mon, Fri, Sat; noon-6pm Tue-Thur, Sun (last entry 2hrs before closing). **Admission** £12.50; £11.50 concessions; under-16s free. **Credit** MC, V. **Map** p404 P8.

This wine experience is more for amateurs than for oenophiles, but you do need to have some interest to get a kick out of this glossy experience. Participants are furnished with a wine glass and an audio guide. Exhibits are set out by country, with five opportunities to taste wine or champagne from different regions. Gin crashes the party courtesy of Bombay Sapphire (you get to sample a Bombay Sapphire cocktail – Ginopolis?). It will soon be joined by whisky and a microbrewery. Highlights include a virtual voyage through Chianti on a Vespa and a virtual flight to the wine-producing regions of Australia. The wine shop has some interesting offers for dedicated tipplers and the restaurant Cantina Vinopolis is very smart. The complex also contains a tourist information centre.

Borough

Map p405 Q8-Q9

Borough or Southwark tube/London Bridge tube/rail.
Hard by Southwark Cathedral is lovely **Borough Market** (*see p256*), a busy food market dating back to the 13th century. For years this historic area has been under threat from the Thameslink rail extension, but campaigners now think that a large part of the market, currently being renovated, will be safe for another 250 years.

The area rings literary bells, especially where Charles Dickens is concerned. Few of the landmarks he wrote about survive today. Marshalsea Prison, where his father was imprisoned for debt, which once stood north of **St George-the-Martyr church** (on the corner of Borough High Street and Long Lane), is long gone, but one of his drinking haunts, the George pub (77 Borough High Street), remains, London's only surviving galleried inn.

The area around **Borough High Street** was lively, especially until 1750, because nearby London Bridge was the only dry crossing point on the river. Nowadays bridges are plentiful on this stretch, but that hasn't stopped the powers that be from planning yet another, about two minutes away from London Bridge. It'll be called Jubilee Bridge and if it goes ahead will be the only covered bridge across the Thames.

Around London Bridge Station tourist attractions clamour for attention. The one that attracts the biggest queues at weekends is the **London Dungeon** (*see p85*). Blood-curdling shrieks emanate from the entrance, while next door the dulcet tones of Vera Lynn attempt to lure travellers to **Winston Churchill's Britain at War Experience** (*see p86*). Across Tooley Street from these pleasures stands a spookily empty mall called **Hay's Galleria**, once an enclosed dock, now dominated by a peculiar sculpture called *The Navigators* (by David Kemp). Here the twinkling

A new outdoor space humanises the **Royal National Theatre**. *See p79.*

Christmas Shop (7378 1998) remains doggedly festive, and half-hearted craft stalls await custom. Exiting on the river side, past the great grey hulk of **HMS Belfast**, you can walk east toward Tower Bridge and City Hall.

London Dungeon

28-34 Tooley Street, SE1 2SZ (7403 7221/ www.thedungeons.com). London Bridge tube/rail. **Open** *Sept-June* 10am-5.30pm daily. *July, Aug* 9.30am-7.30pm daily. **Admission** £13.95; £11.25 concessions; £9.95 5-16s. **Credit** AmEx, MC, V. **Map** p405 Q8.

Join the queue for this disturbing world of torture, death and disease under the Victorian railway arches of London Bridge, and you are led through a dry-ice fog past gravestones and hideously rotting corpses. Screeches and horror-movie soundtracks add to the experience. Don't inflict it on very young children or anyone liable to be offended by fibreglass stonework, squeaking rats or spilled guts.

There is plenty to offend. White-faced visitors experience nasty symptoms from the Great Plague exhibition: an actor-led medley of corpses, boils, projectile vomiting, worm-filled skulls and scuttling rats. Then there are the Wicked Women, the big, bad, brutal lady leaders such as Boudicca, Anne Boleyn, Queen Elizabeth I. A television presenter called Anne Robinson also gets a mention. Other hysterical revisions of horrible London history include the Great Fire and the Judgement Day Barge, where visitors play the part of condemned prisoners (death sentence guaranteed). A 'seriously, folks' type notice on the wall at the exit remarks that torture is still widespread in many parts of the world.

London Fire Brigade

94A Southwark Bridge Road, SE1 0EG (7587 2894/www.london-fire.gov.uk). Borough tube. **Open** *Shop* 9am-5pm Mon-Fri. *Tours* 10.30am, 2pm Mon-Fri by appointment only. **Admission** £3; £2 7-14s, concessions; free under-7s. **Credit** MC, V. **Map** p404 O9.

Visitors must book in advance to explore this small eight-room museum, which traces the history of fire-fighting from the Great Fire of London in 1666 to the present. Tours last an hour and take in the appliance bay, where pumps dating back to 1708 stand in tribute to conflagrations of the past. Exhibits include uniforms, medals, equipment and paintings by firemen-artists of their Blitz experiences.

Old Operating Theatre, Museum & Herb Garret

9A St Thomas's Street, SE1 9RY (7955 4791/ www.thegarret.org.uk). London Bridge tube/rail. **Open** 10.30am-5pm daily (last entry 4.45pm). **Admission** £4.75; £3.75 concessions; £2.75 6-16s; free under-6s; £13 family (2 adults and up to 4 children). **No credit cards**. **Map** p405 Q8.

The tower that houses this curiosity used to be part of the chapel of St Thomas's Hospital, founded on this site in the 12th century. When the hospital was moved to Lambeth in the 1860s most of the buildings were torn down to make way for London Bridge station. The chapel was preserved, and in 1956 the atmospheric old herb garret was discovered. Visitors enter via a vertiginous wooden spiral staircase (sadly, there's no disabled access) to view the medicinal herbs on display. Further in is the centrepiece: a Victorian operating theatre with tiered viewing seats for students. Even more horrifying are the displays of operating equipment that look like implements of torture. Other display cases hold strangulated hernias, leech jars and amputation knives. A life-size anatomical figure with removable organs dating from the 18th century was recently installed in celebration of the place's 300th anniversary. Check the website for events (such as Victorian Surgery demonstrations) and lectures.

Winston Churchill's Britain at War Experience

64-6 Tooley Street, SE1 2TF (7403 3171/ www.britainatwar.co.uk). London Bridge tube/rail. **Open** *Apr-Sept* 10am-5.30pm (last entry 5pm) daily. *Oct-Mar* 10am-4.30pm daily (last entry 4pm). **Admission** £8.50; £5.50 concessions; £4.50 5-16s; free under-5s; £18 family. **Credit** AmEx, MC, V. **Map** p405 Q8.

An authentically drab and dusty exhibition calls to mind the privations endured by the British people during the Second World War. There's plenty about London during the Blitz, including real bombs, rare documents and photos. The displays on rationing, food production and Land Girls are fascinating, and the huge set-piece bombsite (you enter just after a bomb has dropped on the street, and witness pyjamaed legs sticking out of the rubble – children love it) is quite disturbing. It's a funny old place, but it conjures up wartime austerity pretty well.

Tower Bridge & Bermondsey

Map p405 R8-R9

Bermondsey tube/London Bridge tube/rail.
Walking riverside from London Bridge to Tower Bridge, you pass the pristine environs (no skateboards, thank-you!) of **City Hall**, the rented home of the current London government. Designed by Norman Foster (who also did the Millennium Bridge; *see p75*), the rotund glass structure leans squiffily away from the river (to prevent it casting shade on the walkers below). It uses just a quarter of the energy of a normal office building because of its simple water cooling system (there's no air-conditioning). The building has an exhibition blowing the Mayor's trumpet on the ground floor, a café on the lower ground floor and a pleasant outdoor amphitheatre for lunch breaks and sunbathing.

Just near **Tower Bridge** a noticeboard announces when the bridge is next due to open (which it does about 500 times a year for tall ships to pass through). The bridge is one of the lowest crossings over the Thames, which is why the twin lifting sections (bascules) were designed by architect Horace Jones and engineer John Wolfe Barry. The original steam-driven hydraulic machinery can still be seen if you visit the **Tower Bridge Exhibition** (*see p99*), although the lifting gear has been run by electricity since 1976.

Further east, upscale riverside dining is mainly what **Butler's Wharf** is about, with its series of Sir Terence Conran restaurants. Shad Thames is the main thoroughfare behind the wharves, where in days long gone dockworkers unloaded tea, coffee and spices into huge warehouses (now pricey apartments and offices, and the **Design Museum**; *see p86*). Shad Thames comes from the area's original name St John at Thames, as it was called when Knights Templar ran the area.

Up past the Design Museum across Jamaica Road and down Tanner Street is historic Bermondsey Street, site of Zandra Rhodes's labour of love, the **Fashion & Textile Museum** (*see p87*). It's just one symptom of the area's booming popularity with artists and designers. On the way, take a peek at **St Saviour's Dock**, originally the mouth of the lost River Neckinger, whose name comes from 'Devol's Neckenger', a reference to this spot's popularity as a place of execution for pirates. The Neckinger was also responsible for the slime-filled tidal ditches that surrounded a deeply unwholesome part of Bermondsey once known as Jacob's Island. Charles Dickens was so appalled by the conditions here that he chose it as a suitably pestilential place for Bill Sykes to meet his end in *Oliver Twist*. Further south, around Bermondsey Square, it's all Starbucks and delis, new cobbles and hanging baskets. The Friday antiques market (4am-2pm) here is lovely, though it's well picked over by dealers by the time most of us have had breakfast.

Design Museum

28 Shad Thames, SE1 2YD (7403 6933/www. designmuseum.org). Tower Hill tube/London Bridge tube/rail/42, 47, 78, 100, 188 bus. **Open** 10am-5.45pm daily (last entry 5.15pm). **Admission** £6; £4 concessions, 5-15s; free under-5s; £16 family. **Credit** AmEx, MC, V. **Map** p405 S9.

This white, 1930s-style building was once a warehouse but is now a fine container for exhibitions devoted to design in all its forms. Outside the main building, the Design Museum Tank is a little outdoor gallery of constantly changing installations by leading contemporary designers; it also offers a taster of exhibitions within the museum. Once inside this shrine to design, it's hard to ignore the shop's glossy design books and chic household accessories, but remember you're here for the exhibitions. The Design Museum has recently become a lightning rod for criticism of the popularisation of culture, with its many fashion-oriented exhibitions. However, the 2005 programme has a broad remit, covering the history of information design from tube maps and motorway signage to the latest computer imagery in 'You Are Here', (until 15 May); the late architect Cedric Price (1 July-9 October; and 20th-century maverick autodidact Eileen Gray (24 September-8 January 2006), as well as Designer of the Year (5

March-19 June) – most recently iPod designer Jonathan Ive – a celebration of the diversity of UK design talent. The Blueprint Café (a smart restaurant) has a balcony overlooking the Thames; the café downstairs is run by the estimable Konditor & Cook.

Fashion & Textile Museum

83 Bermondsey Street, SE1 3XF (7407 8664/ www.ftmlondon.org). London Bridge tube/rail. **Open** 11am-5.45pm (last entry 5.15pm) Tue-Sun. **Admission** £5; £3 concessions, students, 5-16s; free under-5s; £13 family. **Credit** MC, V. **Map** p405 Q9.

Like the flamboyantly coiffed fashion designer who dreamed it up, this pink and orange museum stands out like a beacon among the grey streets of south London. The grand pink foyer, with its jewel-inlaid floor, leads to a long gallery and exhibition hall. The core collection comprises 3,000 garments donated by Zandra Rhodes, along with her archive collection of paper designs and sketchbooks, silk screens, finished textiles, completed garments and show videos. At least two temporary exhibitions are staged each year: check the website for details.

My kind of town Ken Livingstone

Maverick, outspoken and red as the Kremlin, Ken Livingstone is one of British socialism's most enduring figures. He's also Mayor of London. In political terms, Ken Livingstone is the dinosaur who roared. His style of socialism went out with the GLC, yet he beat all comers as an independent candidate in the 2000 mayoral elections and repeated the trick for Labour in 2004. The mayor's lefty leanings may get under the skin of the Labour Party, but he still manages to hit a sweet note with Londoners. Where else could a politician charge drivers £5 a day to use their cars and walk comfortably into a second term as mayor?

Where would you take visitors to London?
London Zoo (*see p114*) because it's a great institution that's moved with the times. The setting of Regent's Park must be one of the most relaxing green spaces in any city centre

in the world. Plus Trafalgar Square now that it's pedestrianised. The concerts and events we've been able to hold there have made it much more of a focal point, not just a glorified bus stop.
Where do you like to go for peace and quiet?
My garden. I do my best thinking when I'm gardening.
What place for you is quintessentially London?
If I was forced I would say a great rail terminus like Paddington or Waterloo – they're full of Londoners coming in and out of the city, streaming in and out of the tube, going out for the night or heading home to the suburbs.
Where would you go to feel a sense of history?
County Hall, for obvious reasons. It was home to the great shining high point of human civilisation, the GLC (Greater London Council) of 1981 to 86.
What is your favourite building or landmark in London?
At the moment I'd have to say City Hall, the home of the new shining high point in human civilisation. It is really uplifting to be able to come to work in such a remarkable location. It's also ideal for me because it's on the Jubilee Line.
What is you favourite quirky feature of London?
Why doesn't Barons Court underground have an apostrophe whereas Earl's Court does? People ask me about it, but I have absolutely no idea what to say.
Where would you go for an ideal London night out?
To be honest, I think I'd do something very relaxing, just a meal with friends or family in one of my favourite restaurants, possibly Vasco & Piero's Pavilion (15 Poland Street, 7437 8774), an Italian restaurant that I've been going to for years.

The City

The engine room of London past, present and future.

'... and then we just lop their heads off.' **Tower of London**. *See p99.*

The Square Mile is the economic heart of London and, indeed, of the country as a whole. And it certainly feels that way when you see the phalanxes of besuited business people striding purposefully along (a hectic pace best witnessed at the end of the business day as commuters stream down Walbrook to Cannon Street station with zero patience for ambling tourists). But visit again at the weekend and the contrast couldn't be more marked: it's as if some disaster has decimated the population, leaving a ghost town where even the usual cafés and sandwich bars are shut up tight.

The City of London was built nearly 2,000 years ago as an outpost of the Roman Empire. The first locals of what was then called Londinium built a fort, a temple to Diana and a 6,000-seat amphitheatre where, respectively, the Barbican (*see p333*), St Paul's Cathedral (*see p92*) and the Guildhall (*see p96*) now stand. In around AD 200, the Romans built a defensive wall arcing north from the riverbank between the present-day Tower Bridge and Blackfriars Bridge; the area enclosed by it, roughly 300 acres (121 hectares), is the bulk of what, today,

is known as the City. Parts of this wall still stand; a series of plaques mark a walking route of the remains (*see p100*).

The Romans stayed for four centuries, but when they left, no one really moved in. Anglo-Saxons and poorly organised tribespeople inhabited some of the ruins, but they mostly feared what they called 'the City of Giants', living outside it but occasionally pilfering it for building materials. The Anglo-Saxons' reticence let in the French, who quickly moved into the ready-made capital after the Norman invasion and marked their arrival by building the Tower of London (*see p99*).

The medieval period saw the coming and going three times of Dick Whittington, who, as a boy, believed the streets to be paved with gold. Metaphorically, they were; by the time Whittington was elected first Mayor in 1397, the merchants had grown more prosperous than ever, and have maintained their wealth ever since. The Plague of 1665 and the Great Fire of 1666 (*see p19*) halted progress, but only briefly. Indeed, the destruction wrought by the latter provided an opportunity to rebuild

Sightseeing

London in brick and stone as the most modern city in the world (albeit sticking to its medieval street plan). Despite serious damage caused by World War II bombings, many of these 17th-century buildings remain, as do other landmarks erected in the 18th century: the Mansion House, the façade of the Guildhall, and St Paul's Cathedral, completed in 1711.

Gradually, as sea travel declined and London ceased to handle stocks of material goods, the merchants turned to the money markets – with great success. The modern-day City has grown into one of the world's leading financial centres. This shift in priorities hasn't been the only change, however. Over 13,000 houses were burned down in the Great Fire of 1666; today, barely half that number of people live in the City. Yet the area remains a world apart from its neighbours. Its ruling body, the arcane and fiercely independent Corporation of London, is arguably the most powerful local council in the country, and certainly the richest.

Although people tend to see the City as a vast temple to money, there's no shortage of spiritual retreats. There are 40-odd churches (Christopher Wren is responsible for the varied and beautiful designs of most of them) and another ten church towers dotted about the city. Pop into any of them for details of opening times (usually Mon-Fri only), services, concerts and a map of all the churches. Most have a pleasant garden or yard with benches for a quiet moment of reflection (or a picnic lunch).

City Information Centre

St Paul's Churchyard, EC4M 8BX (7332 1456). St Paul's tube. **Open** *Easter-Sept* 9.30am-5pm daily. *Oct-Easter* 9.30am-5pm Mon-Fri; 9.30am-12.30pm Sat.* **No credit cards. Map** p404 O6.
Come here for information on sights, events, walks and talks in the Square Mile.

Along Fleet Street

Map p404 N6

Chancery Lane tube/Blackfriars tube/rail.
Fleet Street takes its name from the largest of London's lost rivers. In its heyday, the Fleet was a major inlet for trade in London; flowing into the Thames at Blackfriars Bridge, it was flanked by docks that received ships bearing coal, spices and fabrics. However, pollution of the river at its upper reaches – it rises up in Hampstead – ended its usefulness, and the river was covered over in stages during the 19th century. It now flows entirely beneath ground.

One of the arterial roads linking Buckingham Palace to the City (and the monarch to the money), Fleet Street is still famous as the home of the country's press, even though most have long since moved elsewhere. 'Media' is the

perfect word to describe the industry that was first undertaken here centuries ago, back when reporters mediated between Westminster's policies and the City's economic schemes. The proximity of the law courts proved handy for settling disputes that got a little too fiery.

The journalistic tradition has its roots in Wynkyn de Worde, who set up a printing press beside the River Fleet in 1500 at **St Bride's** church. Its late 17th-century successor is still referred to as 'the printers' and journalists' church', and is topped by a beautiful Wren-designed spire – his tallest – which inspired the tiered wedding cake.

Only Reuters, the press agency that began in 1850 with a basket of carrier pigeons, remains; the rest of the newspapers have moved, mostly east to Wapping or Canary Wharf. However, traces of the industry remain: in the buildings that housed the Daily Telegraph (No.135) and the Daily Express (Nos.121-8, known as the Lubianka building after the architect who gave it a glass face and sleek art deco interior), and in the pubs and bars that once hosted endless liquid lunches for the bibulous hacks, including El Vino (No.47) and the Punch Tavern (No.99, where satirical magazine Punch was founded in 1841). Other writers left their mark, too; you can still sit in Samuel Johnson's seat in Ye Olde Cheshire Cheese (*see p221*).

Dr Johnson's House

17 Gough Square, off Fleet Street, EC4A 3DE (7353 3745/www.drjohnsonshouse.org). Chancery Lane or Temple tube/Blackfriars tube/rail. **Open** *May-Sept* 11am-5.30pm Mon-Sat. *Oct-Apr* 11am-5pm Mon-Sat. *Tours* by arrangement; groups of 10 or more only. **Admission** £4.50; £3.50 concessions; £1.50 5-14s; free under-5s; £10 family. *Tours* free. *Evening tours* free with admission. **No credit cards. Map** p404 N6.
The writer Samuel Johnson (1704-84) lived in this typical Georgian townhouse while working on his Dictionary of the English Language, published in 1755. The museum, which celebrates the book's 250th anniversary in 2005 (call for details of special events), is lent a tremendous atmosphere by its creaky floorboards, Queen Anne furniture and authentic sash windows; indeed, you can almost feel the old wit's presence. Johnson, though, didn't always love his job: 'To make dictionaries is dull work,' he wrote in his definition of the word 'dull'.

Around St Paul's

Map p404 O6

St Paul's tube.
Is there a finer sight in London than **St Paul's Cathedral** (*see p92*), rising majestically above the mainly undistinguished office blocks that currently pass for a City skyline? Unlikely. Its dome, familiar from a million postcards, is a

Sightseeing

serene curve in a concrete jungle of angles. At night, when it's floodlit, there really isn't anything in London to touch it.

There has been a cathedral dedicated to St Paul on this site for 14 centuries. After one incarnation was destroyed in the Great Fire of 1666, Sir Christopher Wren designed the present structure, and though he had to fight hard to get it built as he wanted, build it he did; in just 35 years too – next to no time in cathedral terms. If you're passing at lunchtime, listen for the 17-ton 'Great Paul' bell, which tolls daily at 1pm from one of the baroque towers.

North of the cathedral sits **Paternoster Square**, reopened to the public in September 2003 following a long and contentious development programme. A sterile plaza centred on a 75ft-high (23m) Corinthian column that's oddly topped by a ball of fire that echoes the Monument, it's surrounded by buildings with postmodern touches like vaulting that is actually suspended from the ceilings of the colonnades. They're joined by the oft-moved **Temple Bar**, the 1672 gateway to the City from the Strand, installed here in 2004 with the original statues reinstated. A rather more successful public space is the zigzag steps of **Peter's Hill**, sloping south of St Paul's to the Millennium Bridge.

To the east, **Bow Lane** is a cosy alleyway that offers a quaint little row of shops, bistros and champagne bars. It's bookended by **St Mary-le-Bow**, whose peals once defined a true Cockney, and **St Mary Aldermary**, an attempt by Wren to hark back to the pre-Great Fire perpendicular style. Inside the latter is a little display containing oyster shells; a step up from the usual communion wafer, you might think, but in fact Thames oysters were a staple part of workmen's diets in the 17th and 18th centuries. Once the oysters were eaten, the shells were used in the walls of the buildings they were erecting. Over Queen Victoria Street, meanwhile, is **Garlick Hill**, its medieval name proving false the supposed antipathy between the English and the pungent bulb. And at the bottom of the street is Wren's **St James Garlickhythe**, which, after St Paul's has the highest ceiling in the City.

Back to the west of St Paul's, on Ludgate Hill, stands **St Martin-within-Ludgate**, its lead spire still visible over the surrounding buildings as Wren intended. Around the corner is the most famous court in the land, the **Old Bailey** (*see below*). However, we'd recommend a detour down the delightful tangle of winding alleys that lead from St Paul's Cathedral to Blackfriars station following medieval street plans; though some modern offices sit uneasily, the lanes conceal shops, pubs and Wren's dour

Tower Bridge. *See p99.*

St Andrew-by-the-Wardrobe. Built between 1685 and 1695, the church's curious name dates from 1361, when the king's official wardrobe was moved to the adjoining building.

Nearby sit two more Wren creations, **St Benet Welsh Church** and **St Nicholas Cole Abbey**, though they're usually closed. Facing the former across scruffy Queen Victoria Street is the neat, red-brick, 17th-century **College of Arms** (*see p92*), where 'heralds' examine the pedigrees of those to whom such things matter. And just north of Blackfriars station is the **Apothecaries' Hall**, one of several livery halls.

Central Criminal Court (Old Bailey)

Corner of Newgate Street & Old Bailey, EC4M 7EH (7248 3277). St Paul's tube/4, 8, 11, 22, 23, 25, 26, 56 bus. **Open** *Public gallery* 10.30am-1pm, 2-4.30pm Mon-Fri. **Admission** free. No under-14s; 14-16s accompanied by adults only. **Map** p404 O6.

It is a mark of success in the criminal world to be tried at the Central Criminal Court, commonly known as the Old Bailey after the street on which it sits. The courthouse, famous for its copper dome and golden statue representing justice, was built by Edward Mountford in 1907 on the site of the infamous Newgate Prison and its execution grounds; part of London's old Roman wall is preserved behind glass in the basement (group visits only).

A dome we can be proud of: **St Paul's Cathedral**. *See p89*.

The public is welcome to visit the courts and watch British justice in action; a notice by the front door provides details of the trials taking place on any given day. High-profile cases take place in Courts 1 to 4, for which the entrance is in Newgate Street; the others are entered from Warwick Passage. Join the queue but note that you will not be allowed in with food, large bags, cameras or mobile phones. Note: there are no facilities for leaving items – try nearby shops or pubs (which may charge).

College of Arms

Queen Victoria Street, EC4V 4BT (7248 2762/www. college-of-arms.gov.uk). St Pauls tube/Blackfriars tube/rail. **Open** 10am-4pm Mon-Fri. *Tours* by arrangement 6.30pm Mon-Fri; prices vary.
Admission free. **No credit cards. Map** p404 O7.

In medieval times, heralds' main role in society was to organise tournaments. The knights who took part were recognised by the arms on their shields and the crests on their helmets. The heralds got to be such experts at recognising the symbols that they became responsible for recording arms, and, eventually, for controlling their use. The practice continues within the venerable college, the present building dating from the 1670s. Only the original wood-panelled Earl Marshal's Court is accessible to the public, although tours can be booked to view the Record Room and the artists working on the intricate certificates.

St Paul's Cathedral

Ludgate Hill, EC4M 8AD (7236 4128/www.stpauls. co.uk). St Paul's tube. **Open** 8.30am-4pm Mon-Sat. *Galleries, crypt & ambulatory* 9.30am-4pm Mon-Sat.

Hours may change; special events may cause closure; check before visiting; . *Tours* 11am, 11.30am, 1.30pm, 2pm Mon-Sat. **Admission** *Cathedral, crypt & gallery* £8; £3.50 6-16s; £7 concessions; free under-6s; £19.50 family. **Audio guide** £3.50; £3 concessions. **Credit** *Shop* AmEx, MC, V. **Map** p404 O6.

Sir Christopher Wren had to fight to get his plans for this most famous of cathedrals approved, and the building process was by no means simple. However, be glad he persisted – St Paul's is an impressive sight, both during the day and, illuminated, at night. With the most comprehensive refurbishment programme in its 300-year history largely completed, St Paul's fairly glows with renewed health – the Portland stone interior is luminous and the detail on the garlanding and Corinthian pilasters stands out crisply. In the pendentives below the dome, the golden Byzantine mosaics fight for attention with the trompe l'oeil effects restored to the Whispering Gallery (open throughout renovations, due to finish summer 2005). And while the photogenic west portico is freshly scrubbed, the south façade, exposed to pollution from the coal-fired power station that now houses Tate Modern, will be under scaffolding for another few years.

Of the millions who visit each year, many come as much for the views as anything: it's a 530-step, 280ft (85m) climb to the open-air Golden Gallery. Walk around it, taking in London in all its magnificence. En route, you'll pass the Whispering Gallery (259 steps up), which runs around the dome's interior and takes its name from the acoustically implausible but absolutely true fact that if you whisper along the

Though it was gutted in 1941, Dykes Bower restored it in 1962; of the dozen churches that once stood in the immediate vicinity, it's the sole survivor. Fans claim its delicately phased tower is the prettiest in town; certainly, it contrasts beautifully with the elaborate steeple of St Mary-le-Bow down the road (*see p91*).

Between Foster Lane and St Bartholomew's Hospital lies the delightful **Postman's Park**. The green space is pretty enough, but its most famous feature is the Heroes Wall, an expanse of ceramic plaques inscribed in florid Victorian style. 'William Donald of Bayswater, aged 19, Railway Clerk,' begins one typical thumbnail drama, 'Was drowned in the Lea trying to save a lad from a dangerous entanglement of weed (July 16, 1876).'

St Bartholomew's Hospital has the Augustinian pilgrim Rahere to thank for its existence; he had a hospital built here in the 12th century. **St Bartholomew's Hospital Museum** (7601 8152, open 10am-4pm Tue-Fri) charts the hospital's history and contains epic biblical murals by William Hogarth, who was baptised in nearby **St Bartholomew-the-Great** (*see below*), the oldest parish church in the capital. Between the two, a memorial to William Wallace marks the spot of his nearby execution on 23 August 1305.

Today's Londoners know **Smithfield** as the city's meat market. It opened for business in 1868, and trades today. Or, rather, tonight: trucks begin to pull into the market from around midnight, with the buying and selling commencing around 3am. It may not be around for long, though; Horace Jones's General Market at the west end is slated for redevelopment and there are also worries about the future of his colourful Meat Market.

Night owls have long flocked here for a fix of greasy food, as the nocturnal nature of the business means there are a number of all-night caffs here. But since the addition of **Fabric** (*see p318*), the area's become fashionable among the clubbing fraternity, with other cool bars and restaurants opened nearby. The **Fox & Anchor** at 115 Charterhouse Street (7253 5075) is one of a handful of longer-established pubs, traditional in all but its hours: it serves beers and breakfasts from 7am (but closes early).

dome's wall, someone at the other side of the gallery can hear you perfectly. Less well-known is the Triforium tour (pre-book on 7246 8357, £12 including admission), which takes in the geometric staircase, cathedral library, a view from the west end gallery and the Great Model of Wren's Greek-cross design for the cathedral.

There's plenty to see in this vast building; buying a guidebook (£4) is imperative if you want to make the most of it. That said, some of the monuments are easily explained, such as the one to the Americans who died in Great Britain during World War II, and the one to poet John Donne (1572-1631) in the south aisle, the only monument in the building to have survived the Great Fire. The two most eye-catching tombs in the crypt are of the Duke of Wellington and Horatio Nelson, though among the notable figures from the arts buried here are Henry Moore, JMW Turner, Joshua Reynolds, Max Beerbohm, Arthur Sullivan and Wren himself, whose inscription, 'Reader, if you seek his monument look around you,' applies as much to the City as St Paul's.

North to Smithfield

Maps p404 O6 to p402 E5

Barbican or St Paul's tube.

From St Paul's, a short walk north across Cheapside takes you to Foster Lane, and another Wren church, **St Vedast-alias-Foster** (7606 3998, open 7am-6pm Mon-Fri). Wren built it in 1673, using the remnants of an earlier church destroyed in the Great Fire.

St Bartholomew-the-Great

West Smithfield, EC1A 7JQ (7606 5171/www. greatstbarts.com). Barbican tube/Farringdon tube/rail. **Open** *Mid Feb-mid Nov* 8.30am-5pm Tue-Fri; 10.30am-1.30pm Sat; 8.30am-1pm, 2.30-8pm Sun. *Mid Nov-mid Feb* 8.30am-4pm Tue-Fri; 10.30am-1.30pm Sat; 8.30am-1pm, 2.30-8pm Sun. **Services** Sun 9am, 11am & 6.30pm; Tue 12.30pm; Thur 8.30am. **Admission** free; donations welcome. **Map** p402 O5.

Sightseeing

The London Stone

Every day hordes of City workers rush past a stone lodged in the side of the Chinese Overseas Bank in Cannon Street with no inkling that it is one of the oldest, most mysterious and possibly most historic relics in London. Supposedly once marking the centre point of London, in 1742 it was deemed an obstacle to traffic on Cannon Street and relocated to the wall of St Swithin's Church across the road. It was the sole relic to survive – perhaps a sign of its mystical powers – after the German bombing of the church in 1941.

Shrouded in legend and attributed with mystical, religious and judicial powers, the stone has been thought to date back as much as 3,000 years, possibly even to the Druids. One story is that one Brutus of Troy conquered London a millennium before the AD 43 invasion and brought the stone from his home town to use as an altar in a temple to Diana on the site of St Paul's. However, it is most commonly believed to be Roman, installed in around AD 50 during the creation of the walled city that is now London. For all the numerous theories about the stone's provenance, the first known reference to it appears in a book belonging to Athelstone, King of the West Saxons, in the early tenth century. By 1198 it was a well-known milestone, medieval London's ground zero.

Dubbed 'Lonenstane', the stone's symbolic power made it a favoured spot for staging rebellions. Famously in 1450 a Kentish Irishman called John Mortimer (renamed

Jack Cade) initiated an uprising in reaction to Henry IV's ludicrously high taxes. He and his troop made for the stone where he gave it a good, traditional whack and pronounced himself Lord Mayor. The stone was also an attractive site for such peculiar rituals as the breaking of sub-standard spectacles by the Worshipful Company of Spectacle Makers. Unsurprisingly – just look at *Harry Potter and the Sorcerer's Stone* – it drew the attentions of occultists as well as oculists, including Queen Elizabeth's 'Merlin', John Dee.

Writers from Shakespeare to Blake to Dickens have venerated the stone and the 17th-century poet Fabyan heralded it as so pure 'that though some have it threat... Yet hurte had none', as quoted in Peter Ackroyd's London biography. These days, though, the stone is unnoticed by the public and scorned by museums. Brushed off as an impenetrable mystery, the British Museum says there is no reason to suspect that it is Roman and no way to date it before its first record. Medieval and Roman specialists also denounce the mythology woven around it and the Museum of London scathingly calls it 'an uninteresting lump of stone'. Ostensibly, it is just a mini fridge-sized piece of limestone; blank but for a pair of grooves on top. But the London Stone couldn't have fallen out of the sky. Despite its marginal treatment at the hands of academics, it has been an icon for a millennium. Its earlier past, then, is all the more alluring, even if only for speculation that continues to surround it.

This historic church is a remnant of a 12th-century monastic priory, built by a former courtier of Henry I as a thanksgiving for his delivery from malaria. Its nave was demolished during Henry VIII's monastic purge; the gateway across the yard used to be the front door. Despite restoration in the 19th century, the dark and gloomy interior still evokes a much earlier time with its eroded and much-patched masonry, stumpy columns and heavy Romanesque arches. This is also where Benjamin Franklin completed his training as a printer in 1724.

Around Bank

Map p404 Q6
Mansion House tube/Bank tube/DLR.
A triumvirate of buildings – the Bank of England, the Royal Exchange and Mansion House – stake their claim to being, if not the geographical centre of the Square Mile, then its symbolic heart. These imposing buildings, made from the best Portland stone, are only let down by the postmodern monstrosity at nearby **Number 1 Poultry**, which resembles the prow of a ship.

The **Bank of England** was founded in 1694 to fund William III's war against the French. Most of what you see today was the work of Sir Herbert Baker in the 1920s; Sir John Soane's original building was demolished to make room for it, though a reproduction of his Stock Office was built a few years ago and now houses the **Bank of England Museum** (*see below*).

The Lord Mayor of London's official residence, **Mansion House** (7626 2500, group visits only, by written application to the Diary Office, Mansion House, Walbrook, EC4N 8BH, at least two months in advance), was designed by George Dance and completed in 1753. It's the only private residence in the UK to have its own court of justice, complete with 11 prison cells. The building's pediment, by Robert Taylor, depicts London defeating envy and bringing plenty through exploitation of its empire.

The current **Royal Exchange**, the third on the site, was opened by Queen Victoria in 1844. The only trading that takes place now is in the high-class shops set in the arcades around the vast central court. Off to the west is the centre of the City's civic life: the **Guildhall**, the base of the Corporation of London and home to a library, the **Clockmakers' Museum** (for both *see below*), the church of **St Lawrence Jewry** and the **Guildhall Art Gallery** (*see p96*).

Next to Mansion House stands one of the City's finest churches, St Stephen Walbrook. Wren's coffered dome (purported to be a trial run for St Paul's, although the construction here is markedly different) and delightfully proportioned cross-in-square plan focus attention

on the modern altar – a huge rounded block of travertine sculpted by Henry Moore. Nearby is a heap of stones that once were part of the Roman Temple of Mithras (*see p97*). Other churches in the area include Hawksmoor's St Mary Woolnoth on Lombard Street and Wren's exquisite St Mary Abchurch, off Abchurch Lane.

To the east is one of the City's loveliest places. 'Foreigners' (anyone from outside London) were allowed to sell poultry (and cheese and butter) at **Leadenhall Market** from the 14th century. The arcaded buildings, painted in green, maroon and cream with wonderful decorative detail, are the work of Horace Jones, who built Smithfield Market. Today, a mix of shops competes for trade: alongside high-street standbys sit florists and fruiterers, butchers and fishmongers, a shoeshine stall and a number of pubs and bars spilling over with City workers. It backs on to Richard Rogers's high-tech **Lloyd's of London Building**, wearing its mechanical services (ductwork, stairwells and even loos) on the exterior. It's a marked contrast to rival architect Norman Foster's sleek, banded Swiss Re tower facing off against it at 30 St Mary Axe, known by all as the **Gherkin** (for reasons obvious once you see it).

Bank of England Museum
Entrance on Bartholomew Lane, EC2R 8AH (7601 5491/cinema bookings 7601 3985/www.bankof england.co.uk/museum). Bank tube/DLR. **Open** 10am-5pm Mon-Fri. *Tours by arrangement.* **Admission** free. *Audio guide £1. Tours free.* **Map** p405 Q6.
The life story of the national bank unfolds quite amusingly in these elegant rooms, a gleaming replica of Soane's Stock Office. As well as coin and banknote galleries and wall adornments, display cases contain Roman vases and drawing/writing instruments, including a sovereign-weighing machine dating back to 1845. Those with strong forearms can lift a real gold bar worth around £92,000 (depending on the bullion market rate). Entry costs nothing, though unfortunately there are no free samples.

Clockmakers' Museum
Guildhall Library, Aldermanbury, EC2P 2EJ (Guildhall Library 7332 1868/1870/www. clockmakers.org). Mansion House or St Paul's tube/Bank tube/DLR/Moorgate tube/rail. **Open** 9.30am-4.45pm Mon-Sat (closed bank holidays). **Admission** free. **Map** p404 P6.
All types of clocks, from 6ft (1.8m) grandfathers to delicate pocket watches, tick merrily as you pass the time with a potted history of horology. A collection of the creations of 17th-century clockmaker Thomas Tompion includes curious, possibly priceless, timepieces. There's plenty to fascinate here, should you want to devote 30 minutes to watching the clocks in this neatly ordered room.

Guildhall

Gresham Street, EC2P 2EJ (7606 3030/tours ext 1463/www.corpoflondon.gov.uk). Bank/St. Pauls tube/DLR. **Open** *May-Sept 9.30am-5pm daily. Oct-Apr 9.30am-5pm Mon-Sat. Last entry 4.30pm. Closes for functions, call ahead. Tours by arrangement; groups of 10 or more people only.* **Admission** *free.* **Map** p404 P6.

The centre of the City's government for more than 800 years, the Guildhall has had its share of tribulations. The cathedral-like Great Hall was damaged by the Great Fire and the Blitz, but has been restored.

Banners and shields of the 100 livery companies adorn the walls, and every Lord Mayor since 1189 gets a namecheck on the windows. Meetings of the Court of Common Council (the governing body for the Corporation of London, presided over by the Lord Mayor) take place monthly, though the Guildhall is mostly used for banquets and ceremonial events.

Guildhall Art Gallery

Guildhall Yard, off Gresham Street, EC2P 2EJ (7332 3700/www.guildhall-art-gallery.org.uk). Mansion House or St Paul's tube/Bank tube/DLR/Moorgate

My kind of town Tracey Emin

She may have a thing or two to learn about making the bed, but Tracey Emin has never been shy about putting her private life on display. Her 'living autobiography' style of art has been causing a stir in London since 1995, when she famously stitched the names of all her past lovers into the side of a tent at the South London Gallery. Although she grew up in Margate, most people associate Emin with London's East End, where she now lives and works. You can see the fruits of her labour on display all over the capital: try the Tate Modern (*see p83*), the Saatchi Gallery (*p78*) or the White Cube (*p292*).

Where would you take visitors to London?
Spitalfields Market (*see p256*). It's my local market and they have great organic vegetables on a Sunday. Then I'd take them to the Golden Heart pub (110 Commercial Street, 7247 2158). It has the best landlady in London and a brilliant jukebox. And at the end of the evening we all end up dancing on the tables.

Where do you like to go for peace and quiet?
There aren't many parks around where I live, but I went to St James's Park the other Sunday and just walked around really slowly, soaking up the atmosphere. Otherwise, I like to swim at my health club in Broadgate.

What place for you is quintessentially London?
I think the East End is so London. The cultural variety here is so fantastic. I don't think there's anywhere else like it in the world.

Where would you go to feel a sense of history?
The Tower of London. I've never been, which is crazy as I only live a ten-minute walk away. That or a cruise along the Thames from Tower Bridge to Hampton Court.

What is your favourite building or landmark in London?
I really like the Norman Foster gherkin. I see it every day from my studio. I also like the Dome as a structure. I get really excited whenever I fly over it.

What is you favourite quirky London feature?
The old doormen at restaurants who have been there for years. There's one old guy on Liverpool Street who always has a kind word for everyone. I love that kind of human contact in London.

Where would you go for an ideal London night out?
I'm quite a home girl, really. I'd start with dinner at St John Bread & Wine on Commercial Street (*see p196*). Then I'd go to the Golden Heart for a drink and take a taxi to Sketch and dance till two in the morning.

tube/rail. **Open** 10am-5pm Mon-Sat (last entry 4.30pm); noon-4pm Sun (last entry 3.45pm). **Admission** £2.50; £1 concessions; free under-16s. Free to all after 3.30pm daily, all day Fri. **Credit** (over £5) MC, V. **Map** p404 P6.

The newest exhibit at the Guildhall Art Gallery is not a work of art at all, but the ruins of London's Roman amphitheatre in the basement, which date from about AD 200; archaeologists discovered them as late as 1988. The full extent of the oval arena is marked with a black line on the surface of Guildhall Square above; all that remains below is the gladiators' entrance, a drainage gutter and a section of wall, though the ruins are beautifully presented. The amphitheatre seated around 6,000 people, about a quarter of the population at the time. Entertainment included the ritual slaughter of slaves.

The gallery contains works of mixed quality. The Pre-Raphaelites in the basement are exquisite, the Egyptian scenes hot and exotic, the bust of Clytie positively sensuous. Yet hanging between the ground and first floors, and surrounded by a mishmash of contemporary works, John Copley's *Siege of Gibraltar*, more congratulatory than great. This is true also of the official paintings on the top floor. From May 2005, the group of conceptual artists known as Art & Language will be producing interventions throughout the gallery, questioning how we perceive the paintings. Following on in the autumn of 2005 will be another conceptual piece, *City Line* by Jon Fawcett, and a show on how contemporary artists have interpreted London.

Temple of Mithras
On raised courtyard in front of Sumitomo Bank, Legal & General Building, Temple Court, 11 Queen Victoria Street. For further information contact the Museum of London. Mansion House tube. **Open** 24hrs daily. **Admission** free. **Map** p404 P6.

In the third century AD, the rival cults of Mithraism and Christianity were battling for supremacy. The Persian god Mithras appealed to Roman soldiers, and the troops on the British frontier built a small temple to their champion near this spot (AD 240-50). The reconstructed foundations aren't much to look at, but they do show the Roman influence on the later design of churches: that is, a rounded apse, a central nave and side aisles. Most of the artefacts that were found at the site are now on display at the Museum of London (*see p100*).

Around the Tower of London

Map p405 R7
Tower Hill tube/Tower Gateway DLR.
Most visitors head straight for the Tower (and wisely so – it's best to get there early, ahead of the crowds), but although this isn't an obviously attractive area there's plenty more to see if you know where to look. Few notice the bronze statue of the Emperor Trajan en route

The Monument. *See p98.*

from the tube station or wonder as to the antiquity of the wall behind him (its lower half is part of the original Roman wall that ringed the city); fewer still wander to the **Trinity Square** memorial gardens, where the names of the tens of thousands of merchant seamen who died in both World Wars are etched in stone, and where executions once took place. Hard to miss, though, is the bombastic former **Port of London Authority** HQ that looms over it, dominated by a statue of Father Thames.

The City's most famous chronicler, Samuel Pepys, lived and died close by in Seething Lane. There's a bust of him in **Seething Lane Gardens**, though he's actually buried in nearby **St Olave Hart Street** (nicknamed by Dickens 'St Ghastly Grim' after the leering skulls at the entrance). Pepys watched London burn in 1666 from **All Hallows by the Tower** (*see p98*).

Along the river, between Tower and London Bridges, stand two reminders of London's great days as a port. David Lang built the **Custom House** in 1817, but the most appealing part of the building, its riverfront façade, was added by Robert Smirke a decade later. Next door is **Billingsgate Market**, for years London's fish market; trading ceased in 1982. The lanes behind the waterfront are packed with churches – St Magnus-the-Martyr, St Mary-at-Hill, St Margaret Pattens and St Dunstan-in-the-East, the latter with lovely gardens in and around the remains of the church walls and an ethereal 'floating' steeple – presided over by the **Monument** (*see below*).

Between the Tower and Liverpool Street rail station to the north sit many more churches, including **St Helen Bishopsgate**, **St Botolph-without-Aldgate** (for both *see below*) and **St Katharine Cree** on Leadenhall Street, the latter an extraordinary hybrid of classical and Gothic styles. Nearby, in a courtyard off Bevis Marks, is the oldest synagogue in the country, the superbly preserved **Bevis Marks Synagogue**, built in 1701 by Sephardic Jews who had escaped from the Inquisition in Portugal and Spain.

This area suffered considerable damage from IRA bombs in 1992 and 1993, and the tiny pre-fire church of **St Ethelburga-the-Virgin** (built 1390) was devastated. A great deal of restoration work has been undertaken, however, and the church has risen from the ashes as a peace and reconciliation centre.

All Hallows by the Tower

Byward Street, EC3R 5BJ (7481 2928/www.all hallowsbythetower.org.uk). Tower Hill tube. **Open** *Church* 9am-5.45pm Mon-Fri; 10am-5pm Sat, Sun. *Service* 11am Sun. **Admission** free; donations appreciated. **Audio tour** £3 (suggested donation). **Map** p405 R7.

Though just the walls and a 17th-century brick tower were left standing after World War II attacks, post-war rebuilding at All Hallows has created a pleasingly light interior. A Saxon arch testifies to the church's seventh-century roots. Other notable relics include Saxon crosses and a superb carved limewood font cover (1682) by Grinling Gibbons. Ask to visit the crypt, where the original Roman tessellated pavement and archaeological finds share space with a Knights Templar altar brought back during the Crusades.

Fishmongers' Hall

London Bridge, EC4R 9EL (7626 3531/www.fish hall.co.uk). London Bridge/Monument tube/rail. **Open** tours only, by arrangement. **Admission** price on application. **Map** p405 Q7.

The most interesting of the remaining City guilds or livery companies (the union HQ of once-powerful trades), this 19th-century hall displays, amid a jumble of other precious loot, the dagger used by fishmonger and mayor William Walworth to stab the revolting peasant Wat Tyler in the back, thereby putting down the Peasants' Revolt of 1381.

The Monument

Monument Street, EC3R 8AH (7626 2717/ www.towerbridge.org.uk). Monument tube. **Open** 9.30am-5.30pm daily. **Admission** £2; £1 5-15s; free under-5s. **No credit cards. Map** p405 Q7.

The Monument, built between 1671 and 1677 by Sir Christopher Wren and his friend Robert Hooke to commemorate the Great Fire of 1666, is little more than a 311-step spiral staircase enclosed within a 202ft (65m) Doric column; its height is the distance from here to Farriner's bakery in Pudding Lane, where the fire began. In its day, the Monument was the tallest object for miles, as Wren had not yet started St Paul's; the golden ball of flame at the top shone in the sun, a salutary reminder of the vanity of man and the awesome power of nature. It still impresses, even against a skyline inconceivable to its architects. Look out for the reliefs carved on the pedestal by one Caius Cibber, who'd done time in a debtors' prison. His revenge was to perch King Charles II's finger on the nipple of a woman's exposed breast. The views from the top are well worth the climb.

St Botolph-Without-Aldgate

St Botolph's Church, Aldgate High Street, EC3 1AD (7283 1670). Aldgate tube. **Open** 9.30am-3pm Mon-Fri; services only Sun. *Eucharist* 1.05pm Mon, Thur; *prayers* 1.05pm Tue, Wed. **Admission** free; donations appreciated. **Map** p405 R6.

The oldest of three surviving churches of St Botolph, built at the gates of Roman London as homage to the patron saint of travellers. The present building was largely reconstructed by George Dance in 1744 and is noted for its beautiful ceiling decorated by John Francis Bentley in 1884. Daniel Defoe married here in 1683. Today a homeless support service works from the crypt.

St Ethelburga Centre for Reconciliation & Peace

78 Bishopsgate, EC2N 4AG (7496 1610/www.centre ethelburgas.org). Bank tube/DLR/Liverpool Street tube/rail. **Open** 11am-3pm Wed; 8.45am Mon for prayers; noon-2.30pm 1st Fri of mth. **Admission** free; donations appreciated. **Map** p405 R6.

In 1994, the poet John Betjeman wrote of the tiny church of St Ethelburga, destroyed by an IRA bomb. Ten years on, it has risen from the ashes. A new east window has been created using broken stained glass from the original, an altar made from the ancient beams and a cross formed from scattered nails. Despite these ecclesiastical features, the building is no longer a church but a conference centre dedicated to world peace.

St Helen's Bishopsgate

Great St Helen's, off Bishopsgate, EC3A 6AT (7283 2231/www.st-helens.org.uk). Bank tube/DLR/ Liverpool Street tube/rail. **Open** 9am-12.30pm Mon-Fri. *Lunchtime meetings* 1-2pm Tue, Thur. *Services* 10.15am, 7pm Sun. **Admission** free. **Map** p405 R6.

Because of the huge number of monuments and memorials within, St Helen's is known as the City's version of Westminster Abbey. It owes its unusual

shape to the fact that it is really two medieval churches knocked into one. After surviving the Great Fire and the Blitz, it was damaged by terrorist bombs in the 1990s.

Tower Bridge Exhibition

Tower Bridge, SE1 2UP (7403 3761/www.tower bridge.org.uk). Tower Hill tube. **Open** *May-Sept* 10am-6.30pm daily (last entry 5.30pm). *Oct-Apr* 9.30am-6pm daily (last entry 5pm). **Admission** £5.50; £4.25 concessions; £3 5-15s; free under-5s; £14 family. **Credit** AmEx, MC, V. **Map** p405 R8.
You're paying mainly for the views 140 feet (43 metres) above the Thames here – and they are fabulous, especially from the west walkway – though there are also short films, photo displays and touch screens to fill you in on the design, construction and trivia, like why the bridge wasn't bombed by the Luftwaffe (they used it as a navigational aid). In its day, the drawbridge idea was hugely ambitious, its construction a triumph of Victorian technology and city architect Horace Jones's perseverance. Visitors ascend in the north tower, cross at the upper level, and descend the south tower, from where you can carry on to the engine rooms to see the steam-driven heavy machinery that was used to lift the bridge.

Tower of London

Tower Hill, EC3N 4AB (0870 756 6060/www.hrp. org.uk). Tower Hill tube/Fenchurch Street rail. **Open** *Mar-Oct* 10am-6pm Mon, Sun; 9am-6pm Tue-Sat (last entry 5pm). *Nov-Feb* 10am-5pm Mon, Sun; 9am-5pm Tue-Sat (last entry 4pm). **Admission** £13.50; £10.50 concessions; £9 5-15s; free under 5s; £37.50 family. **Credit** AmEx, MC, V. **Map** p405 R7.

One of London's essential visitor destinations, the history-saturated Tower, which has served as a fortress, a palace, a prison and a royal execution site over its 900-year history, doesn't disappoint. In 2004 its entrance area was much improved and a Welcome Centre added to better reflect and cater for its landmark status.

The best way to see the Tower is on a free hour-long tour led by one of the 40 Yeoman Warders (Beefeaters), cheery red-coated ex-soldiers resident within the grounds. The tales they tell are fascinating: of imprisonment, of treason, of torture and of execution; if the crowd's a bit much, the £3 audio tours are a less colourful alternative.

Of permanent haunting fascination is Traitor's Gate, the traditional river entrance to the Tower reserved for enemies of the state, and the chopping block on Tower Green, the traditional exit. The Crown Jewels are in the Jewel House; you'll glide past them on airport-style travelators. The Armoury, meanwhile, is in the White Tower; here you can admire Henry VIII's enormous codpiece. And wherever you are in the Tower, you're never far from a jolly costumed presentation, especially in summer.

New interactive audio-visual displays in the Bloody and Beauchamp Towers focus on the myths and realities of the Tower's famous prisoners. To celebrate the 400th anniversary of the Gunpowder Plot, a Guy Fawkes-related exhibition and costume events will take place from May 2005. Book ahead for the Christmas, half-term and summer events for families. Although disabled access has been improved, much remains inaccessible, though staff will help where they can (call for details).

North of London Wall

Map p402 P5

Barbican tube/Moorgate tube/rail.

Running close to the attractively redeveloped Liverpool Street Station and the rather bland Broadgate Centre next to it, **London Wall** follows the northerly course of the old Roman fortifications to the **Museum of London** (*see below*). Running roughly along the same route is a signposted 1.75-mile (2.8-kilometre) walk, with interpretive panels (some in poor shape) pointing out the highlights. The best bits are just north of the Tower of London (near the tube entrance) and to the east of the Museum of London: the Bastion Highwalk overlooks the remains of one of the gates into the Cripplegate Roman fort, alongside the Barber-Surgeons Herb Garden; continue east along the walkway and straight through a modern office building, before veering left across the raised plaza to reach St Alphage Gardens (off Fore Street), sunk behind a large stretch of wall, and a pleasant picnicking place.

The area just to the north of here was levelled during the Blitz. Rather than encourage office developments, the City of London and London County Council purchased a large site in 1958 to build 'a genuine residential neighbourhood, with schools, shops, open spaces and amenities'. We ended up with the **Barbican**, a vast concrete estate of 2,000 flats and an arts complex that exudes little warmth or sense of community (other than that of fellow visitors lost in the maze of 'highwalks'). Those who live there or regularly use the wonderful (once inside) Barbican art gallery (*see below*), library, cinema, theatre and concert hall (reviewed in the appropriate chapters) defend it passionately, arguing for the convenience of its location and the design standards of its interiors. But to the outsider, it's a strangely unknowable place.

Marooned amid the towering blocks is the only pre-war building in the vicinity: the heavily restored 16th-century church of **St Giles Cripplegate**, where Oliver Cromwell was married and John Milton buried. Further north-east, **Bunhill Fields** was set aside as a cemetery during the Great Plague, though it wasn't used for that purpose. Instead, apparently because the ground was never consecrated, the area became popular for Nonconformist burials, gaining the name of 'the cemetery of Puritan England'. Much of the graveyard is cordoned off these days (ask the attendant or call 7374 4127 for access), but it's still possible to stroll beneath the plane trees and look at the monuments to John Bunyan, Daniel Defoe and William Blake. Opposite

Bunhill Fields on City Road is the **Museum of Methodism and John Wesley's House** (*see below*) where, in 1951, the late Denis Thatcher married Margaret Hilda Roberts.

Barbican Art Gallery

Level 3, Barbican Centre, Silk Street, EC2Y 8DS (box office 7638 8891/www.barbican.org.uk). Barbican tube/Farringdon or Moorgate tube/rail. **Open** 11am-8pm Mon, Wed, Fri-Sat; 11am-6pm Tue, Thur, Sun. **Admission** £8, £6 concessions. **Credit** AmEx, MC, V. **Map** p402 P5.

The recently refurbished Barbican Art Gallery has no permanent collection on display. Fixtures for 2005 will include solo exhibitions by American photographer Tina Barney and artist Christian Marclay, whose works seek to highlight the gap between aural and visual stimuli, running consecutively until 2 May.

Museum of London

150 London Wall, EC2Y 5HN (0870 444 3852/ www.museumoflondon.org.uk). Barbican or St Paul's tube. **Open** 10am-5.50pm Mon-Sat; noon-5.50pm Sun. **Admission** free. **Credit** Shop AmEx, MC, V. **Map** p402 P5.

Don't let the forbidding entrance – via a dark brick bastion in the middle of a roundabout – put you off this excellent museum tracing all aspects of the history of London. Better circulation means that you can now go straight to the gallery that interests you, but if you're not in a hurry, it's rewarding to walk the detailed, engaging displays in chronological order, beginning with 300,000-year-old flint tools found near Piccadilly. Among the highlights: the Great Fire Experience, one for the kids; the walk-through Victorian street scene, like stepping into the pages of a Dickens novel; the red and gold fairytale Lord Mayor's coach, a rococo extravaganza; and the central garden, which presents a curious botanical history of the City. There's a decent shop, and a café with outdoor tables overlooking a working Roman water-pumping device. Temporary exhibitions include The London Look – Fashion from Street to Catwalk, which runs until 8 May 2005, followed later in the year by Black Photographer Archives.

Museum of Methodism & John Wesley's House

Wesley's Chapel, 49 City Road, EC1Y 1AU (7253 2262/www.wesleyschapel.org.uk). Moorgate or Old Street (exit 4) tube/rail. **Open** 10am-4pm Mon-Sat. *Tours* arrangements on arrival; groups of 10 or more must telephone ahead. **Admission** free; donations requested. **Credit** Shop MC, V. **Map** p403 Q4.

John Wesley (1703-91), the father of Methodism, built this chapel beside his house in 1778. The museum in the crypt contains letters, Bibles, manuscripts and other ecclesiastical items. Wesley's house, meanwhile, contains a number of his personal effects including his nightcap, preaching gown and his personal experimental electric shock machine.

Holborn & Clerkenwell

Legal eagles and high-flyers.

Holborn

Maps p399 & p401
Holborn tube.
The Saxons chose Holborn as their London home, and where they led, the lawyers have followed. The area became the heart of the British justice system and, unlike Fleet Street vis-à-vis journalists, it has remained so. The four **Inns of Court**, where English common law first developed during the Middle Ages, still provide working space for myriad barristers and their acolytes. The Inns – Lincoln's Inn, Gray's Inn, Inner Temple and Middle Temple – were founded in medieval times (none has exact dates) and were originally public houses where barristers gathered to do business, lodge and eat – hence 'inns'. They eventually became formal institutions where barristers could be trained. Every barrister is aligned to one of them. Today their narrow alleys, courtyards and lawns are wonderful, archaic places to wander.

Other administrative offices and related institutions grew up in the area – a short schlepp in medieval times via the river from both the City and Westminster.

Aldwych

Map p399/p401 M6
Temple tube.
Wandering away from the City along the Strand takes you past some historic churches, including **St Clement Danes** (*see p102*) and **St Mary-le-Strand** (James Gibbs's first public building; 1714-17). Before reaching Waterloo Bridge you pass King's College, its 1960s buildings sitting uneasily with Robert Smirke's 1829 originals, and the rather more regal **Somerset House** (*see p102*). Just to the north, on the Aldwych crescent, is a trio of imperial buildings: India House, Australia House and Bush House (home to the BBC's World Service).

One of a handful of functioning cabmen's shelters sits on **Temple Place** above the Embankment. These green sheds, which were not allowed to take up more space than a horse and cab, are a legacy of the Cabmen's Shelter Fund, set up in 1874 to give cabbies an alternative to pubs. Nearby, on sinister Strand Lane is the so-called 'Roman' bath, reached via

Surrey Street, where Dickens took many a cold plunge. It can be viewed through a window – there is a light-switch – if you miss its limited opening times (2-4pm Wed, by appointment only, 7641 5264). Back near King's College, on the Strand and on Surrey Street, are entrances to one of London's ghost tube stations, Aldwych (although the signs say 'Strand', the station's earlier name). Today it's hired out for special events and movie shoots.

Further south, opposite the **Royal Courts of Justice** (*see p102*), are **Middle Temple** (Middle Temple Lane, 7427 4800) and **Inner Temple** (Inner Temple Treasury Office, 7797 8241, tours £10 per person). The name derives from the Knights Templar, who owned the site for 150 years. Built around a maze of courtyards, these Inns have a villagey feel and are especially atmospheric when gas-lit after dark. The **Middle Temple Hall**, built in 1573, has a huge table made from a single oak tree donated by Queen Elizabeth I, and a smaller table made from the hatch of Drake's ship the *Golden Hinde*. The Inner Temple has several fine buildings, and its lawns are a beautiful spot for picnics. Of particular note is **Temple Church** (King's Bench Walk, 7353 8559, www.templechurch.com); consecrated in 1185, it is London's only surviving round church. Part of Dan Brown's *The Da Vinci Code* is set here.

North of Middle Temple, on the Strand, is **Temple Bar**, the monument dividing Westminster from the City of London. In the Middle Ages, it was a barrier to the City, past which the monarch could not stray without the approval of the Lord Mayor. On formal occasions, the Queen still pauses here to seek that permission. A Wren-designed archway stood on the site but was replaced in 1878 by a fearsome bronze griffin.

Prince Henry's Room

17 Fleet Street, EC4Y 1AA (7936 4004). Temple tube (closed Sun). **Open** 11am-2pm Mon-Sat. **Admission** free; donations appreciated. **Map** p404 N6.
One of the oldest houses in the City, dating from the early 17th century, this oak-panelled space with its fine Jacobean plaster ceiling is among few survivors of the 1666 Great Fire. It is believed to have been used by the lawyers of Prince Henry, the hugely popular eldest son of King James I. The rest of the building was once a tavern, a favourite haunt of Samuel Pepys, memorabilia of whom is on display.

Sightseeing

Royal Courts of Justice

Strand, WC2A 2LL (7947 6000/www.courtservice. gov.uk). Temple tube (closed Sun). **Open** 9am-5pm Mon-Fri. **Admission** free. **Map** p399 M6.

If you want to see British justice in action, then pay a visit to these splendid Gothic buildings. Anyone is free to take a pew in one of these 76 courts, where the High Court presides over the most serious civil trials in the country. Cameras and children under 14 years of age are not permitted. Note that there are few trials in August and September.

St Clement Danes

Strand, WC2R 1DH (7242 8282). Temple tube (closed Sun). **Open** 9am-4pm Mon-Fri; 9am-3pm Sat, Sun. *Services* 11am Sun. **Admission** free; donations appreciated. **Map** p399 M6.

Tradition holds that the first church here was built in the ninth century by, you've guessed it, the Danes. Another church (St Clement Eastcheap) gave rise to the nursery rhyme *Oranges and Lemons*, but the vicar of this Wren-designed church made a theme song of it in 1920 and now the bells ring out the tune at 9am, noon, 3pm and 6pm Monday to Saturday. Destroyed by a 1941 air raid, the church was restored in the 1950s as a memorial to Allied airmen. These days it's the central church of the RAF.

St Dunstan in the West

186A Fleet Street, EC4A 2HR (7405 1929/www.st dunstaninthewest.org). Chancery Lane or Temple tube (closed Sun). **Open** 11am-3pm Tue. **Admission** free. **Map** p404 N6.

The first St Dunstan was built on this site some time before 1070, but the present building dates from 1831-3. John Donne was rector here (1624-31) and Izaak Walton (whose *Compleat Angler* was published in the churchyard in 1653) held the posts of 'scavenger, questman and sidesman' (1629-44). Sweeney Todd, the demon barber of Fleet Street, shaved and murdered next door at No.186, before selling the bodies to a local pie shop.

Somerset House

Strand, WC2R 1LA (7845 4600/www.somerset-house.org.uk). Aldwych or Temple tube (closed Sun). **Open** 10am-6pm daily (last entry 5.15pm); extended hours for courtyard & terrace. *Tours* phone for details. **Admission** *Courtyard & terrace* free; £5/£4 concessions for exhibitions. **Credit** *Shop* MC, V. **Map** p401 M7.

Walking into the courtyard of this magnificent Georgian building for the first time is one of London's great pleasures. It was closed to the public for almost a century, but following a millennial makeover – inspired by Arthur Gilbert's massive donation – it is now one of London's cultural foci. Originally, there was a Tudor palace here, built in 1547 by the first Duke of Somerset. In 1775 George III ordered Sir William Chambers to rebuild the crumbling palace in neo-classical style to house various societies and government offices. The Navy Office took the largest part, in due course replaced by mundane offices such as the Inland Revenue.

Today the taxmen remain, but the rest of the building is open to the public. It houses the **Courtauld Gallery**, **Gilbert Collection** and **Hermitage Rooms** (for all of which, *see below*) around the beautiful fountain court, which becomes an ice rink in winter. There's also a little café, a posh and excellent restaurant (the Admiralty, *see p210*) and a pleasant river terrace, which gives views to Westminster and St Paul's.

Somerset House museums

Strand, WC2R 0RN. Aldwych or Temple tube (closed Sun). **Open** 10am-6pm daily (last entry 5.15pm). **Admission** 1 collection £5; £4 concessions. 2 collections £8; £7 concessions. 3 collections £12; £11 concessions. Free students, under-18s; Courtauld Gallery free to all 10am-2pm Mon. *Tours* phone for details. **No credit cards**.

Courtauld Gallery *(7848 2526/www. courtauld.ac.uk/gallery).*

The eclectic collection at the Courtauld offers an introduction to a range of painting styles and eras, on a very manageable scale. For those daunted by the likes of the National Gallery, it's perfect. Early Florentine art downstairs leads to Impressionists, post-Impressionists and others higher up. Famous works include Manet's *A Bar at the Folies Bergère*, Van Gogh's *Self-Portrait with a Bandaged Ear* and Degas's *Two Dancers on the Stage*. The 20th-century collection has also been expanded with pieces by Kandinsky, Matisse and Barbara Hepworth. Exhibitions for 2005 include 'Drawings of London' by John Virtue, one of Britain's leading contemporary artists, from 9 March to 5 June.

Gilbert Collection *(7420 9400/www. gilbert-collection.org.uk).*

You might want to keep your sunglasses on, because this collection is not short on glitz. British-born real-estate magnate Arthur Gilbert donated a huge range of silver, mosaics, baubles and knick-knacks – some of it once owned by the likes of Napoleon and Louis XV – to the UK in 1996. The treasures are deliciously OTT, with highlights including 18th-century snuff boxes, adorned with gold, diamonds, rubies and emeralds; gilt candelabras that are fit for Liberace's piano; Florentine cabinets from the 17th century, inlaid with mosaics of agates, amethysts, jasper and lapis; and a dazzling silver collection. The temporary exhibition 'Masterpieces of American Jewellery' runs from 1 February to 26 May 2005.

Hermitage Rooms *(7845 4630/www. hermitagerooms.co.uk).*

The Hermitage Rooms host rotating exhibitions of items from their doughty Russian counterpart in St Petersburg and are decorated in the same imperial style as the rooms at the Winter Palace. New exhibitions arrive twice a year, with everything from paintings and drawings to decorative art and fine jewellery. For each ticket sold, £1 goes to the State Hermitage. A display of 'Avant-garde Porcelain from Revolutionary Russia' will be on show until the end of July 2005.

Sir John Soane's Museum.

Lincoln's Inn & Gray's Inn

Map p399 M5-M6

Chancery Lane or Holborn tube.
Of the four Inns of Court, **Lincoln's Inn** (Lincoln's Inn Fields, 7405 1393) is the most spectacular. On a tour, you can relive scenes from *Bleak House*, Dickens's ferocious attack on the legal system, as virtually nothing has changed in hundreds of years. Its Old Hall dates from 1422, and its buildings – a mixture of Gothic, Tudor and Palladian styles – all survived bombing during the war. **Gray's Inn** (Gray's Inn Road, 7458 7800) was not so lucky: it was devastated by the Luftwaffe, and rather uninspiringly rebuilt.

Lincoln's Inn Fields is London's largest garden square and the focal point of Holborn life. On its north side sits the splendid **Sir John Soane's Museum** (*see below*), and on the south side the **Royal College of Surgeons** (7869 6560) hosts the Hunterian Museum, which reopens in February 2005. North of here, on the other side of High Holborn, **Red Lion Square** has one building of note, **Conway Hall**, which is the headquarters of the Ethical Society (7242 8037) and hosts a variety of events.

Chancery Lane, running up from the Strand to High Holborn, is home to the Public Records Office and the Law Society. More than 30 shops occupy the subterranean depths of the **London** **Silver Vaults** (7242 3844, www.thesilver vaults.com) at the street's northern end. East toward Holborn Circus, the half-timbered **Staple Inn** (which features in *Bleak House*) is a fine example of Tudor architecture.

Sir John Soane's Museum

13 Lincoln's Inn Fields, WC2A 3BP (7405 2107/ www.soane.org). Holborn tube. **Open** 10am-5pm Tue-Sat; 10am-5pm, 6-9pm 1st Tue of mth. *Tours* 2.30pm Sat. **Admission** free; donations appreciated. *Tours* £3; free concessions. **Map** p399 M5.
Sir John Soane (1753-1837) was one of the leading architects and most obsessive collectors of his day. He acquired a huge raft of treasures during his lifetime, before turning his house into a museum so that 'amateurs and students' would be able to enjoy his collection. Much of the museum's appeal derives from its domestic atmosphere; it's the house of a rich art lover, where you're the lucky guest. Surfaces are covered with sculptures, paintings, furniture, architectural models, antiquities, jewellery and various odds and sods. Highlights include Hogarth's *Rake's Progress*, and the 3,300-year-old sarcophagus of an Egyptian pharaoh, but there's always some-thing around that will catch your eye: hundreds of plaster casts of Greek statues and many of Soane's architectural designs. For an atmospheric encounter, visit in the evening on the first Tuesday of the month, when the house is candlelit from the moment it gets dark. Tickets for Saturday tours go on sale at 2pm on a first-come, first-served basis. Generally, you may need to queue.

Clerkenwell & Farringdon

Map p402 N4-O5

Farringdon tube/rail.
Modern-day Clerkenwell epitomises the Cool Britannia of the 1990s. In the 1880s it was a slum; a century later it was full of abandoned factories and office space. Then artists began moving into empty warehouses and converting them into lofts. By the next decade, property developers had seen the area's potential, and nightclubs and restaurants followed. The neighbourhood's enduring destinations include the pioneering **St John** restaurant (*see p196*); gastropub the **Eagle** (159 Farringdon Road, 7837 1353); and nightclub **Fabric** (*see p318*). All are frequented by denizens of local photographic studios, advertising agencies and media companies (the *Guardian* newspaper is on Farringdon Road).

Clerkenwell has ancient roots. It was named after Clerk's Well: first mentioned in 1174 and rediscovered in 1924, this can be viewed through a window at 14-16 Farringdon Lane. The district grew up in the 12th century around the priory of St John of Jerusalem, of which all that remains is a gatehouse dating

Sightseeing

Walk this way Life's a stage

Performing London invites you to drown your sorrows on a pub crawl through the grim and grisly hinterland of the ancient city.

Start and finish: Farringdon Station
Length: Barely a mile
Time: Half an hour, plus libations

Projected to be the largest in the world, Farringdon Station was originally to be sited further south, stretching to the present Ludgate Circus and up to the Old Bailey. In the 1837 plan Farringdon was to incorporate all London's termini. More companies use this station than any other in Britain and soon it will serve Crossrail. From Farringdon, the first 'underground' in the world, 'the Drain', ran to King's Cross. Picture the celebrations to open the station in October 1863: an enormous banquet, held on the station platforms, for 700. Here's mud in your eye!

Turn right out of the station and cross over Farringdon Road. Trickle up **Greville Street**, formerly Pissing Alley, and drink in the **John Oldcastle** pub [map **1**], which honours the noble Lollard martyr. English Lollards began the Protestant revolution. Slightly further up on the right is a pub that appears in Dickens under a fictional name. Sup a pint o' porter in the One Tun pub [map **2**], then double-back and take the second right.

Walk on gilded splinters! **Saffron Hill** used to be the main north–south route before Farringdon Road was built in the 1830s. Tread softly past a building that is part of a very secret complex housing the Diamond Trading Company of Hatton Garden.

Precious gems are flown in from Amsterdam to the heliport on the roof, then re-buried deep beneath your feet. Diamonds on the soles of your shoes!

At the end of Saffron Hill, lurch up steps to **Charterhouse Street**. This is part of the orderly new road system that derived from Smithfield market, built in 1867. Above you a private footbridge of precious stones crosses the street. Diamonds in the sky! The Mohocks, a gang of noble hooligans, delighted in rolling old ladies down this hill. Bottoms up!

Drink in the memory of the tasty whiff of the **River Fleet**. Both its banks were the most notorious in London. Evil masterminds flourished locally: Fagin in fiction, Jonathan Wild in fact. To find out more you must come on the walk with us in real space and time.

Good health! Before the **Holborn Viaduct** was built, the route across the valley was laborious. Horses transporting freight frequently dropped dead from strain outside St Sepulchre's Church.

Swerve to your right before you reach the top. Pass a guarded entrance into the cul-de-sac of Ely Place. Here was the Bishop of Ely's palace, its garden laden with fruits, flowers and fountains. All that remains is the chapel, restored as a Catholic place of worship, containing strange figures of holy martyrs.

The end of Ely Place is sealed by a high wall, with a door through into **Bleeding Heart**

from 1504, now home to the **Museum & Library of the Order of St John** (*see p105*). The Carthusian monastery of Charterhouse, meanwhile, was founded in 1370. It became a private boys' school – since moved to Surrey – and is now a posh old people's home. The cloisters, the 14th-century chapel and the 17th-century library survive. The area's most fascinating religious institution is the enclave of **Ely Place**, once the site of the Bishop of Ely's impressive London palace. The gated road, lined by Georgian houses, leads up to **St Etheldreda** (*see p105*).

Over the centuries, a strong crafts tradition grew up in Clerkenwell, as French Huguenots and other immigrants chose to practise their

trades away from the City guilds. The area has not forgotten its roots: the Clerkenwell Green Association (www.cga.org.uk) still provides affordable studios for artists and craftspeople at **Pennybank Chambers** in St John's Square and **Cornwell House** on Clerkenwell Green.

In the early 19th century this area was favoured by Irish and Italian immigrants and radicals: Lenin edited his Bolshevik paper *Iskra* ('The Spark') from a back room, which has been preserved, in the **Marx Memorial Library** (37A Clerkenwell Green, 7251 6039). European Jews settled in **Hatton Garden**, transforming it into London's diamond district. For something a bit cheaper, **Leather Lane Market** west of here has clothes, food, electronics and caffs.

Yard, notorious thanks to Charles Dickens, who made it his symbol of London's lowest depths. The door is seldom open; you can get in via Greville Street, or view the scene with your imagination. Legend tells us how one night Lady Hatton was seen dancing here with a sinister figure. Dawn revealed her body, her heart ripped out and lying beside her – still beating. The devil likes to dance…

Retracing your footsteps slightly, duck down an alley now on your right, Ely Court, to find one of London's most charming secrets. Drink in the **Mitre** pub [map **3**], where a tree has grown through the lounge bar. Legend says Queen Elizabeth I danced here, which is conceivable since she wangled the property for her favourite, Sir Christopher Hatton. Duck out the other end of the alley, emerging in **Hatton Garden**, and turn left. Near this spot Mary Godwin had a coach waiting for her to elope with the poet Shelley.

Cross Holborn Circus to enter **Holborn Viaduct**. Pause on this Arch of Triumph and ponder its significance. On our walk you learn why it is the hub of all Victorian imperial dreams. Beware, this view is threatened by a new mega block.

At the far end, looking right, is the site of Newgate Prison, where the Old Bailey now stands. Get blazed in the **Viaduct Tavern** pub opposite [map **4**; *see p226* **Gin palaces**], a classic gin palace, which boasts it was the first in the City to be lit by electricity.

Your route back to Farringdon – up Giltspur Street and left into Grand Avenue, then Cowcross Street – takes you through **Smithfield** meat market, which has many of London's grisliest associations, animal and otherwise, and some of its oldest pubs. Down the hatch!

● **Performing London** (www.performing london.co.uk) provides a variety of guides and musicians to conduct curious and imaginative explorers through the dingy lanes and alleys of London, treating them to hymns, bawdy songs, lewd poems and holy rants en route.

Museum & Library of the Order of St John

St John's Gate, St John's Lane, EC1M 4DA (7324 4000/www.sja.org.uk/history). Farringdon tube/rail. **Open** 10am-5pm Mon-Fri; 10am-4pm Sat. *Tours* 11am, 2.30pm Tue, Fri, Sat. **Admission** free. *Tours* free. Suggested donations £5; £3.50 concessions. **Map** p402 O4.

Sick pilgrims arriving in Jerusalem in the 12th century were indebted to a group of monks from the local Benedictine Abbey for their care. These monks went on to form the Order of the Hospital of St John of Jerusalem and their story is told in this unspectacular museum. It has some exhibits on the order's history, both abroad and in London, and a multimedia feature about the work of the modern Ambulance Brigade, founded by the order.

St Etheldreda

14 Ely Place, EC1N 6RY (7405 1061). Chancery Lane tube or Farringdon tube/rail. **Open** 8.30am-7pm daily. **Admission** free; donations appreciated. **Map** p402 N5.

St Etheldreda is Britain's oldest Catholic church and London's only surviving example of 13th-century Gothic architecture. Only saved from the Great Fire of London by a change in the wind, this is the last remaining building of the Bishop of Ely's palace. The crypt still exists beneath the original chapel, which is a dark and atmospheric place, untouched by traffic noise. The church's 1960s stained-glass windows are gorgeous. The strawberries once grown in the gardens of Ely Place were said to be the finest in the city, even receiving plaudits in Shakespeare's *Richard III*.

Bloomsbury & Fitzrovia

Pretty squares, academic chairs and urban regeneration.

British Museum. *See p107*.

Bloomsbury

Map p399

Chancery Lane, Holborn or Tottenham Court Road tube.

The attraction of Bloomsbury cannot be pinned down to one thing alone, like the British Museum, say, or those elegant squares and Georgian terraces, so redolent of the area's literary past. Instead, its charm lies more in the sum of its parts, in an afternoon spent wandering through leafy, open spaces, peering into museum display cabinets and losing yourself in the throngs of a student café.

But for all its intellectual cachet, Bloomsbury hasn't always been a refuge for the high-minded (back in 1086, for instance, the neighbourhood was a breeding ground for pigs). What's more, its pretty floral name also has humdrum origins: it's taken from 'Blemondisberi', or 'the manor of William Blemond', who acquired the area in the early 13th century. It remained rural until the 1660s, when the fourth Earl of Southampton built Bloomsbury Square around his house, though none of the original architecture remains. The Southamptons intermarried with the Russells, the Dukes of

Bedford, and both families developed the area as one of London's first planned suburbs. During the next couple of centuries, they built a series of grand squares and streets, laid out in the classic Georgian grid style: check out Bedford Square (1775-80), London's only complete Georgian square, and huge Russell Square, now an attractive public park. Gower Street is also an uninterrupted stream of classic Georgian terraced houses.

Things are not so posh now (witness the aforementioned students), but the area's shabby grandeur is undeniably charming. And the streets are speckled with blue plaques, reading like a 'who's who' of English literature: William Butler Yeats once lived at 5 Upper Woburn Place; Edgar Allan Poe lived at 83 Southampton Row; Mary Wollstonecraft lived on Store Street, the birthplace of Anthony Trollope (he was born at No.6). Then there's Charles **Dickens' House**, at 48 Doughty Street, now a museum (*see p109*). As for the famous Bloomsbury Group, its headquarters was at 50 Gordon Square, where EM Forster, Lytton Strachey, John Maynard Keynes, Clive and Vanessa Bell and Duncan Grant would discuss literature, art and politics. Virginia and Leonard Woolf lived at 52 Tavistock Square. Gordon Square also holds an allure for orientalists – the erudite **Percival David Foundation of Chinese Art** is at No.53 (7387 3909) – but the real academia is clustered around Bloomsbury's western borders. Here, Malet Street, Gordon Street and Gower Street are dominated by the **University of London**. The most notable building is **University College**, on Gower Street, founded in 1826 and built in the Greek Revival style by William Wilkins, the architect responsible for the National Gallery. Inside lies one of the strangest exhibits in London: the preserved remains of philosopher Jeremy Bentham, who introduced the world to utilitarianism. The massive **Senate House**, on Malet Street, holds the university's biggest library. It was a particular favourite of Hitler's: had Germany won the war, he had planned to make his headquarters here. South of the university lies the fabled **British Museum** (*see right*), with its collection of the world's riches, not the least of which are the marble friezes from the Parthenon in Athens.

Such grand institutions may have put Bloomsbury on the map, but aficionados claim that the real delights lie in hidden pockets. **Sicilian Place**, a pedestrianised stretch of colonnaded shops that links Bloomsbury Way with Southampton Row, is one such. Note that **St George's Bloomsbury** (Bloomsbury Way, 7405 3044), a Hawksmoor church, is closed until late 2005 as it undergoes a £10 million restoration project. North-east of here is Lamb's Conduit Street, a convivial area with a good selection of old-fashioned pubs and stylish restaurants. At the top of this street lies wonderful **Coram's Fields** (*see p273*), a children's park (adults are only admitted if accompanied by a child) built on the former grounds of Thomas Coram's Foundling Hospital, which provided for abandoned children. The legacy of the great Coram family is now commemorated in the beautiful **Foundling Museum** (*see p270* **Suffer the children**). Tucked away behind the studentland is **Mecklenburgh Square**, and to the north-west lies budget hotel-land and **Cartwright Garden**. **Woburn Walk** is a pleasant stretch of shops and cafés.

It's not all Georgian grandeur. Take the **Brunswick Centre**, just opposite Russell Square tube station. When it was built in 1973, Patrick Hodgkinson's concrete jungle was hailed as the future for community living: a complex of shopping centre, flats, a cinema and an underground car park. Thirty years on, modernism's young dream is Bloomsbury's worst eyesore. Still, cartoon fans drop into the **Cartoon Art Trust** (*see right*), film buffs love

the **Renoir Cinema** (*see p283*), and fossicking readers frequent Skoob Russell Square (No.10, 7278 8760) for second-hand books. For new ones, there's the massive Waterstone's (*see p236*) on Gower Street; for alternative ones **Gay's the Word** (66 Marchmont Street, 7278 7654) and Bookmarks (1 Bloomsbury Street, 7637 1848) is all left-wing tomes.

British Museum

Great Russell Street, WC1B 3DG (7636 1555/ recorded information 7323 8783/www.thebritish museum.ac.uk). Russell Square or Tottenham Court Road tube. **Open** *Galleries* 10am-5.30pm Mon-Wed, Sat, Sun; 10am-8.30pm Thur, Fri. *Great Court* 9am-6pm Mon-Wed, Sun; 9am-11pm Thur-Sat. *Highlights tours (90mins)* 10.30am, 1pm, 3pm daily. **Admission** free; donations appreciated. *Temporary exhibitions* prices vary. *Highlights tours* £8; £5 concessions. **Credit** *Shop* AmEx, DC, MC, V. **Map** p399 K5.

Officially London's most popular tourist attraction, the museum is a neo-classical marvel built in 1847 by Robert Smirke, one of the pioneers of the Greek Revival style. Also impressive is Norman Foster's glass-roofed Great Court, the largest covered space in Europe, opened in 2000. This £100m landmark surrounds the domed Reading Room, where Marx, Lenin, Thackeray, Dickens, Hardy and Yeats once worked (now home to a modern information centre).

Star exhibits include Ancient Egyptian artefacts – the Rosetta Stone, statues of the pharaohs, mummies – and Greek antiquities, such as the marble friezes from the Parthenon. The Celts gallery has the Lindow Man, killed in 300 BC and preserved in peat. In 2003 the Wellcome Gallery of Ethnography opened, with an Easter Island statue and regalia from Captain Cook's travels.

The King's Library opened in 2004. The finest neo-classical space in London, it is home to a new permanent exhibition, 'Enlightenment: Discovering the World in the 18th Century', a 5,000-piece collection devoted to the formative period of the museum. Its remit covers physics, archaeology and the natural world, and it contains objects as diverse as 18th-century Indonesian puppets and a beautiful orrery.

You won't be able to see everything in one day, so buy a souvenir guide (£7) and pick out the showstoppers, or plan several visits. The 90-minute 'greatest hits' tour (£8, bookable at the information desk) and EyeOpener tours focus on specific aspects of the collection. Scheduled exhibitions for 2005 include 'Creating celebrity: Kabuki actors, artists and poets in 19th-century Osaka' (7 Apr-26 June 2005), 'Ancient Persia' (Sept 2005-Jan 2006) and 'Sasanian coins: religion and propaganda in Ancient Iran' (23 June 2005-Jan 2006).

Cartoon Art Trust

7 Brunswick Centre, Bernard Street, WC1N 1AF (7278 7172/www.cartoonarttrust.org.uk). Russell Square tube. **Open** 10am-5pm Tue-Sat. **Admission** free; donations appreciated. **Credit** *Shop* AmEx, MC, V. **Map** p399 L4.

Sightseeing

Cross purposes

Plans to regenerate raggedy old King's Cross and give it the full Eliza Doolittle makeover (with a view to attracting a better class of punter and, more specifically, tourist) have been discussed ad nauseam. But now, riding on the back of the Channel Tunnel Rail Link (CTRL), it seems that King's Cross is finally due to see some real changes. When the tunnel is finished in 2007, Eurostar trains will arrive at a new international terminal at St Pancras, with passengers disembarking beneath a glass extension designed by Sir Norman Foster. The CTRL is an incredible engineering undertaking: the average depth of the tunnel under London will be 24metres (79feet), with a maximum depth of 50metres (165feet). Working under the Euston Road, engineers are breaking through the oldest rail tunnels in the world – built in the mid 1800s, the brick tunnels are as strong today as when they were first constructed.

The new extension to St Pancras will double the length and number of platforms to receive the Eurostar trains and the old part of the station (built in 1865) will be cleaned and restored. Other networks that converge on St Pancras are also being overhauled including a refurbishment of King's Cross underground. The old train depot will be opened up to provide state-of-the-art concourses, waiting areas, shops and restaurants.

Long infamous for its prostitutes, drug dealers and tramps, and associated with some of the worst aspects of inner city decay, the surrounding area is undergoing a £37.5 million makeover, which is expected to create around 20,000 jobs and 1,800 new homes. This is largely being welcomed by local communities, where poverty and prosperity are mixed together and 60 per cent of residents are from ethnic minorities. But some residents are concerned that they haven't been consulted over the plans and fear that, as in many other parts of London, they will be pushed out by rising prices and gentrification. Developers say they are working with the community and council to ensure that many of the new homes will remain affordable for locals.

The regeneration work could also be a major draw for creative industries. 'The vision is very much of new streets and public spaces, a lot of very good, ordinary buildings with some very exciting buildings interspersed amongst them, real mixes of shops, restaurants, hotels, apartments, and other residential areas,' says Roger Madelin, chief executive of Argent St George, which is carrying out most of the work. If handled sensitively King's Cross could become a blueprint for future developments of this kind, where a mix of low cost homes and upmarket Manhattan-style lofts sit side by side in a thriving, creative neighbourhood. If not, the planned glittering plazas and gleaming offices will ring a hollow note of warning.

If you like your artwork caricatured and captioned, you're in for a real treat here. Exhibitions in this small, light space tend to last for a few months at a time and vary from the themed (such as the 'Grin and Blair it' collection of 100 drawings charting the trials and tribs of Tony's career) to the general. A small shop sells cards, books and other silliness.

Dickens' House

48 Doughty Street, WC1N 2LX (7405 2127/ www.dickensmuseum.com). Chancery Lane or Russell Square tube. **Open** 10am-5pm Mon-Sat; 11am-5pm Sun. *Tours* by arrangement. **Admission** £5; £4 concessions; £3 5-15s; £14 family. **Credit** *Shop* AmEx, DC, MC, V. **Map** p399 M4.

London is scattered with plaques marking the many addresses where the peripatetic Charles Dickens lived but never settled, including Devonshire Terrace near Paddington and Camden's Bayham Street, but this is the only one of the author's many London homes that is still standing. Dickens lived here for three years between 1837 and 1840 while he wrote *Nicholas Nickleby* and *Oliver Twist*. Restored to its former condition, the house is packed with Dickens ephemera. There are personal letters, all sorts of manuscripts and his writing desk.

Petrie Museum of Archaeology

University College London, Malet Place, WC1E 6BT (7679 2884/www.petrie.ucl.ac.uk). Euston Square, Goodge Street or Warren Street or tube. **Open** 1-5pm Tue-Fri; 10am-1pm Sat. **Admission** free; donations appreciated. **Map** p399 K4.

If you get lost while looking, don't give up, the Petrie *is* hard to find (the entrance is through the UCL Science Library), but it's worth it. The rather gloomy interior and 1950s wooden display cabinets give it all a kind of 'Indiana Jones on home leave' vibe, and some of the labelling is suitably professorial (read: dry). But there's fun to be had among the various girly bits: make-up pots, grooming accessories, jewellery, and a dress dating back to 2800 BC. Some things never change. Check out the coiffured head of a mummy with eyebrows and lashes intact.

St Pancras New Church

Euston Road (corner of Upper Woburn Place), NW1 2BA (7388 1461/www.stpancraschurch.org). Euston tube/rail. **Open** 12.45-2pm Wed; noon-2pm Thur; 9.15-11am, 3-5pm Sat; 7.45am-noon, 5.30-7.15pm Sun; occasional lunchtimes Tue, Fri. *Services* 8am, 10am, 6pm Sun; 1.15pm Wed. *Recital* 1.15pm Thur. **Admission** free. **Map** p399 K3.

Built in 1822, this church is a spectacular example of the Greek Revivalist style. At the time of its construction, it was, at £89,296 the most expensive church to be built in London apart from St Paul's. Inspired by the Erechtheion in Athens, its most notable feature is its Caryatid porches, entrances to the burial vaults. The interior is more restrained but has beautiful 19th-century stained-glass windows. Free lunchtime concerts (Thursdays, 1.15pm) soothe the jangled nerves of local workers with performances by violinists, pianists and sopranos.

Somers Town & King's Cross

Map p399

Euston or King's Cross tube/rail.

Now earmarked for extensive regeneration (*see p109* **Cross purposes**), Somers Town and King's Cross look set to see significant changes over the coming years. The former, situated on the north side of Euston Road between St Pancras and Euston stations, is where Dickens located his darker characters, and where locals lived in fear of the 'Somers Town mob'. Even today the area exudes a gritty realism (which basically means it's a dump). **Euston Station** is a bleak 1960s building that replaced Philip Hardwick's tragically beautiful Victorian structure. **St Pancras Station**, by contrast, has a gorgeous Victorian glass and iron train shed fronted by Sir George Gilbert Scott's Gothic hotel, the Midland Grand. This building is now **St Pancras Chambers** and, at press time, was still open to the public for tours (7304 3921), pending redevelopment work.

To the east lies **King's Cross**, which is the kind of place your mother warned you about. Immortalised in Neil Jordan's *Mona Lisa* and various TV dramas, the area is notoriously seedy, and a favourite of prostitutes and junkies. It only gets worse, as north of here is pure industrial wasteland. But that's cool: there are now a few hip clubs springing up in the area. And you can bet when the Eurostar terminal opens at St Pancras in 2007, grimy King's Cross will be gentrified beyond belief.

The British Library

96 Euston Road, NW1 2DB (7412 7332/www. bl.uk). Euston Square tube/Euston or King's Cross tube/rail. **Open** 9.30am-6pm Mon, Wed-Fri; 9.30am-8pm Tue; 9.30am-5pm Sat; 11am-5pm Sun. **Admission** free; donations appreciated. **Map** p399 K3.

The judgement 'one of the ugliest buildings in the world', famously passed by a Parliamentary committee, has been just one of the controversies that have dogged the new British Library since it opened in 1997. The project went overbudget by £350m, and took 20 years to complete (longer than St Paul's and 15 years behind schedule). When it finally opened, architecture critics ripped it to shreds.

But don't judge a book by its cover: the interior is spectacular, all white marble, glass and light. In the piazza sits Antony Gormley's sculpture *Planets*, a new addition in 2003. In the John Ritblat Gallery, the library's main treasures are displayed: the Magna Carta, the Lindisfarne Gospels and original manuscripts from Chaucer. There's fun stuff, too: Beatles lyric sheets, first editions of *The Jungle Books* and archive recordings of everyone from James Joyce to Bob Geldof. The library is also famous for its 80,000-strong stamp collection. The focal point of the building is the King's Library, a six-storey glass-walled tower that houses George III's collection.

This is one of the greatest libraries in the world, with 150 million items. Each year, it receives a copy of every publication produced in the UK and Ireland.

St Pancras Old Church & St Pancras Gardens

Pancras Road, NW1 1UL (7387 4193). Mornington Crescent tube/King's Cross tube/rail/46, 124 bus. **Open** *Gardens* 7am-dusk daily. *Services* 9am Mon-Fri; 9.30am Sun; 7pm Tue. **Admission** free. **Map** p399 K2.

The Old Church, whose site may date back to the fourth century, has been ruined and rebuilt many times. The current structure is handsome, but it's the churchyard that delights, recently restored after a long period of neglect. Among those buried here are writer William Godwin and his wife, Mary Wollstonecraft; over this grave, daughter Mary Godwin (author of *Frankenstein*) declared her love for poet Percy Bysshe Shelley. The grave of Sir John Soane is one of only two Grade I listed tombs (the other is Karl Marx's, in Highgate Cemetery, *see p155*); its dome influenced Sir Giles Gilbert Scott's design of the classic British phone box.

Fitzrovia

Map p399

Tottenham Court Road or Goodge Street tube.

Fitzrovia may not be as famous as Bloomsbury, but its history is just as rich. Squeezed in between Gower Street, Oxford Street, Great Portland Street and Euston Road, it only became known as Fitzrovia during the 20th century. The origins of its name are hazy: some believe it comes from Fitzroy Square, which was named after Henry Fitzroy, the son of Charles II. Others insist that the neighbourhood was named after the famous **Fitzroy Tavern** (7580 3714) at 16 Charlotte Street, London bohemia's ground zero for much of the 20th century. Once a favourite with radicals and artists, regulars included Dylan Thomas, George Orwell, Aleister Crowley and Quentin Crisp.

The neighbourhood's radical roots go deep. In 1792 Thomas Paine lived at 154 New Cavendish Street – the same year he published *The Rights of Man* and incurred governmental wrath. His friend Edmund Burke lived at 18 Charlotte Street. During the early 19th century the district became a hotbed of Chartist activity and working men's clubs. Later, Karl Marx attended Communist meetings in Tottenham Street, Charlotte Street and Rathbone Place. He was also a regular on the Tottenham Court Road pub scene: his favourites included the Rising Sun (No.46); the Court (No.108); the Mortimer Arms (No.174); and the Jack Horner (then known as the Italian, No.236).

A century later, Fitzrovia played pop. In the 1960s the Stones played gigs at the 100 Club (100 Oxford Street). A young Bob Dylan made his British debut singing at the King & Queen Pub (1 Foley Street) in 1962. Concert scenes for the Beatles' *A Hard Day's Night* were filmed at the Scala Theatre, then at 21-25 Tottenham Street. Pink Floyd and Jimi Hendrix were regulars at the Speakeasy at 50 Margaret Street. As flower power declined, punk took over. Regular performers at the 100 Club included the Sex Pistols, Siouxsie and the Banshees, the Damned and the Clash. At this time, Fitzrovia was descended upon by squatters. Boy George lived in squats on Great Titchfield Street, Warren Street and Carburton Street, while he wrote 'Do You Really Want to Hurt Me?'.

During the 1980s Fitzrovia's raffish image was transformed when the media moved in. ITN started broadcasting from 48 Wells Street, and Channel 4's first office was at 60 Charlotte Street in 1982. The BBC's simple, pared-down Broadcasting House had been on the western fringe of the area – 2-8 Portland Place – since 1922. But for a bit of the old bohemian scruff, head to seedy Hanway Street, a dark, urine-scented alley lined with late-night Spanish bars.

All Saints

7 Margaret Street, W1W 8JG (7636 1788/www. allsaintsmargaretstreet.org.uk). Oxford Circus tube. **Open** 7am-7pm daily. *Services* 7.30am-8am, 1.10pm, 6pm, 6.30pm Mon-Fri; 7.30am, 8am, 6pm, 6.30pm Sat; 8am, 10.20am, 11am, 5.15pm, 6pm Sun. **Admission** free. **Map** p398 J5.

This 1850s church was designed by William Butterfield, one of the great Gothic Revivalists. It is squeezed into a tiny site, but its soaring architecture and lofty spire – the second-highest in London – disguise this fact. Its lavish interior is one of the city's most striking, with rich marble, flamboyant tile work, and glittering stones built into its pillars.

Pollock's Toy Museum

1 Scala Street (entrance on Whitfield Street), W1T 2HL (7636 3452/www.pollocksmuseum.co.uk). Goodge Street tube. **Open** 10am-5pm Mon-Sat. **Admission** £3; £1.50 3-16s; free under-3s. **Credit** *Shop* MC, V. **Map** p398 J5.

A shrine to a pre-PlayStation era, and housed in a creaky Georgian townhouse, Pollock's is crammed with vintage toys to raise a nostalgic smile in adults and a resentful stare from the Ritalin generation. The museum is also famed for its toy theatres.

Dickens' House. *See p109.*

Marylebone

Stroll in the park, shop on the high street, slap J-Lo's waxwork arse.

Maps p395 & p398

*Baker Street, Bond Street, Edgware Road, Great
Portland Street, Marble Arch, Oxford Circus or
Regent's Park tube.*

Marylebone has been an affluent residential
neighbourhood since its development in the
18th and 19th centuries, but over the past
ten years it has become an increasingly
fashionable enclave. The curving high street
that once displayed a slightly fusty line-up
of shops is now the heart of what has been
rebranded 'Marylebone Village'. Its character
is still evolving, but the current mix of low-key
restaurants, lively bars, tasteful chain shops
and independents is luring visitors and
Londoners alike. While Marylebone is
bounded by heaving Oxford Street to the south
and Regent's Park to the north, thundering
Marylebone Road marks the end of the 'village'.

The area has not always been so genteel.
It was once made up of two ancient manors,
Lileston (Lisson) and Tyburn (named after a
stream that flowed into the Thames). In the
14th century they were violent places. Tyburn
was the site of a famous gallows until 1783, a
spot marked by a plaque on the traffic island
at **Marble Arch**.

The sumptuous
Wallace Collection.
See p113.

After the original parish church was
demolished in 1400, a new one was built near
the top of what is now **Marylebone High
Street**. It was called St Mary by the Bourne, a
name that came to cover the entire village. This
had been abbreviated to Marylebone by 1626.

Although nothing remains of the first two
parish churches, the foundations of the third –
damaged in the war, demolished in 1949 – were
preserved as the **Memorial Garden of Rest**.
Due to building works to the neighbouring
St Marylebone School, the garden is closed
until November 2006. The fourth church, on
Marylebone Road, was built to accommodate a
rapidly growing population in 1817. It was here
that Elizabeth Barrett of 50 Wimpole Street
secretly married fellow poet Robert Browning
in 1846. Dickens, who lived next door at 1
Devonshire Terrace (demolished in 1959),
had his son baptised in the church.

In the 16th century the northern half of
Marylebone – now **Regent's Park** – became
a royal hunting ground, while the southern
section was bought up by the Portman family.
Two centuries later, the Portmans developed
many of the elegant streets and squares that
lend the locale its dignified air. Some, such as
Bryanston Square and **Montagu Square**,
have survived well; others, such as **Cavendish
Square**, marred by an ugly brick wall and
underground car park, are less attractive. One
of the squares, laid out in 1761, still bears the
Portman name; another, 1776's **Manchester
Square**, is home to the **Wallace Collection**
(*see p113*). **Harley Street** and **Wimpole
Street** have been associated with highbrow
healthcare since the mid 19th century.

Running parallel to both, **Portland Place**
was the glory of 18th-century London. At its
other end, **Langham Place**, where it links
with John Nash's handsome **Regent Street**,
is the BBC's HQ, **Broadcasting House**,
currently undergoing major redevelopment.
Next door is Nash's only remaining church,
All Souls (1822-4), which daringly combines
a Gothic spire and classical rotunda. Over the
road is the Langham Hotel, which was the
first of London's grand hotels (1865); further
north is the **Royal Institute of British
Architects**, before the street forks into Park
Crescent, opposite Regent's Park. A few blocks
west by York Gate, the **Royal Academy of**

Music, another Nash design, founded in 1822, has a small museum (7873 7373; 12.30-6pm Mon-Fri; 2-5.30pm Sat, Sun).

Further west, opposite Marylebone railway station, is the **Landmark Hotel**. Originally the Great Central, it was the last significant Victorian hotel to be built in the golden age of steam (1899). It was closed in 1939, used as offices, then redeveloped as a hotel in 1986.

North of Marylebone Road, the landscape gives way to 1950s and '60s housing at Lisson Grove. It's worth taking a detour to Bell Street for the cutting-edge **Lisson Gallery** (*see p289*) as well as a couple of small second-hand bookshops. Church Street is a popular local food and general market that is rapidly gentrifying at its eastern end, thanks to **Alfie's Antiques Market** (*see p235*).

Around Marylebone High Street

It may be a clichéd moniker, but this picturesque shopping street does have a genuine 'village' feel, maintaining a delicate balance between independent shops and chains. On the whole, the more interesting shops are towards **Marylebone Road**, including beautiful Edwardian Daunt Books (Nos.83-4, 7224 2295) and eclectic clothes boutique Sixty 6 (No.66, 7224 6066). The area is becoming a magnet for foodies with a clutch of gourmet shops on **Moxon Street**, which leads to the site of the weekly farmers' market on Sundays (in the Cramer Street car park behind Waitrose, 10am-2pm). There are also some great restaurants.

To experience the neighbourhood's original character, duck into narrow **Marylebone Lane**. In tiny corner pub the Golden Eagle at No.59 (7935 3228) there are nostalgic singalongs around the piano, and 104-year-old lunchroom-deli Paul Rothe & Son (No.35, 7935 6783) is presided over by the original Rothe's white-coated grandson and great-grandson. Hemmed in between buildings behind Spanish Place, **St James's** (22 George Street) has a surprisingly soaring Gothic interior (1890). The church stands opposite the site of a Spanish chapel around the corner from the former embassy and contains objects from the older building, including Alfonso XIII's personal standard. Its Lady Chapel was designed by JF Bentley, architect of Westminster Cathedral. Vivien Leigh wed barrister Leigh Holman here in 1932. But a more interesting example of ecclesiastical architecture lies to the west on Crawford Street. **St Mary's, Wyndham Place**, which was designed by British Museum architect Sir Robert Smirke and completed in 1824, is a dramatic example of the Greek Revival style, set in a stone courtyard.

Wallace Collection

Hertford House, Manchester Square, W1U 3BN (7935 0687/www.wallacecollection.org). Bond Street tube. **Open** 10am-5pm Mon-Sat; noon-5pm Sun. **Admission** free. **Credit** *Shop* AmEx, MC, V. **Map** p398 G5.

Presiding over leafy Manchester Square, this handsomely restored late 18th-century house contains a collection of furniture, paintings, armour and objets d'art. It all belonged to Sir Richard Wallace, who, as the illegitimate offspring of the fourth Marquess of Hertford, inherited the treasures his father amassed in the last 30 years of his life. There's room after room of Louis XIV and XV furnishings and Sèvres porcelain, galleries of lush paintings by Titian, Velázquez, Boucher, Gainsborough and Reynolds – Franz Hals's *Laughing Cavalier* is one of the best-known masterpieces. The attractive Café Bagatelle, in the glass-roofed courtyard, ranks among the top London museum eateries.

Regent's Park

With its varied landscape, from formal flowerbeds to extensive, recently renovated playing fields, Regent's Park (open 5am-dusk daily) is one of London's most treasured green spaces. But it wasn't created for public pleasure; indeed, the masses weren't allowed in until 1845. Originally Henry VIII's 'chase', the park was designed in 1811 by John Nash, Crown Architect and friend of the Prince Regent, as a private residential estate to raise royal revenue. The Regency terraces of the **Outer Circle**, the road running around the park, are still Crown property, but of the 56 villas planned, only eight were built. Development of the Royal Park, with its botanic and zoological gardens, took almost two more decades, but rehabilitation after wartime damage and general neglect in the mid 20th century was not completed until the late 1970s. As well as the famous zoo (*see p114*), it has a boating lake (home to several unusual wildfowl species), tennis courts, several cafés offering really quite decent food and a lovely open-air theatre (*see p335*). To the west of the park is the London Central Mosque, built in 1978.

Just south of the park on Marylebone Road is tourist attraction *extraordinaire* **Madame Tussauds** (*see p114*). Nearby, **Baker Street**, which leads to Oxford Street, is forever associated with a certain fictional detective. The **Sherlock Holmes Museum** at No.221B (7935 8866, www.sherlock-holmes.co.uk) occupies the fictional detective's address and contains atmospheric room sets, but serious Sherlockians

Plastic fantastic: **Madame Tussauds**. *See p113.*

may want to check out the Sherlock Holmes Collection of books, journals, photos and film scripts around the corner at Marylebone Library (7641 1039, by appointment only).

London Zoo

Regent's Park, NW1 4RY (7722 3333/www.london zoo.co.uk). Baker Street or Camden Town tube, then 274, C2 bus. **Open** *End Oct-mid Mar 10am-4pm daily. Mid Mar-end Oct 10am-5.30pm daily.* **Admission** *£12.70; £10.20 concessions; £9 3-15s; free under-3s; £38 family.* **Credit** AmEx, MC, V. **Map** p398 G2.

Opened in 1828, this was the world's first scientific zoo, and today umbrella charity ZSL stresses its commitment to worldwide conservation. The zoo's habitats keep pace with the times – the elephants have been given room to roam at sister site Whipsnade Wild Animal Park in Bedfordshire, and the penguins have been moved from Lubetkin's famous modernist pool. This year (2005) sees a new walk-through squirrel monkey enclosure, and there are future plans for an African rainforest development. It's advisable to follow the recommended route to avoid missing anything in the 36-acre site; check the daily programme of events to get a good view at feeding times.

London Planetarium & Madame Tussauds

Marylebone Road, NW1 5LR (0870 400 3000/ www.madame-tussauds.com). Baker Street tube. **Open** *9.30am-6pm daily (last admission 5.30pm), times vary during holiday periods.* **Admission** *9.30am-3pm £19.99; £15.99 concessions; £14.99 5-15s; £72 family ticket (internet booking only). 3-5pm £15.99; £12.99 concessions; £11.99 5-15s, £62 family. 5-5.30pm £11, £9 concessions, £6 5-15s; £44 family.* **Credit** AmEx, MC, V. **Map** p398 G4.

As you enter the first room, 'Blush', you're dazzled by fake paparazzi flashbulbs, and starry-eyed kids can even take part in a 'Divas' routine with real dancers as well as immobile likenesses of Britney, Beyoncé and Kylie. A cunningly posed wax snapper provides a double-take moment. Surprisingly, visitors are encouraged to touch the figures; you can smack J-Lo's bottom or stroke Brad Pitt's soft face

– he's the first figure to be made of silicone. Other rooms contain public figures past and present, from Henry and six of his wives to a young-looking Blair and Bush, by way of the Fab Four circa 1964. Waxworks are constantly being added to keep up with new stars, movies and TV shows. Below stairs, the Chamber of Horrors surrounds you with hanging corpses and eviscerated victims of torture. For an extra £2 over-12s can be terrorised by serial killers in the Chamber Live. Children love the kitsch 'Spirit of London Ride' – you climb aboard a moving black taxi pod for a whirlwind trundle through 400 years of the city's history. Dazed, you're ushered into the Planetarium for a ten-minute digital show, before exiting through the huge gift shop.

South to Oxford Street

Heading south, Marylebone High Street turns into Thayer Street, then Mandeville Place. Across Wigmore Street, famous for the **Wigmore Hall** (*see p304*), narrow shop- and café-lined pedestrian alleyway St Christopher's Place widens to a fountain courtyard, which in summer is filled with tables from the surrounding cafés. Carrying on after it contracts – to even narrower alley Gees Court – will take you to pedestrian- and traffic-choked **Oxford Street**, packed with big chains department stores and tourist tat.

Marble Arch, another Nash creation, marks Oxford Street's western extent. This unremarkable monument was intended to be the entrance to Buckingham Palace but, discovered to be too puny, was moved to this site in 1851. Only members of the Royal Family and some military types are allowed by law to walk through the central portal.

A more modern landmark, the iconic **BT Tower** (60 Cleveland Street) was given Grade II listed status in 2003, and has now revamped the illuminations that crown its observation deck. The slick new design, courtesy of London-based creative agency Rufus Leonard, is intended to introduce BT's new global logo.

Mayfair & St James's

Snooty, royal and surprisingly quiet.

Mayfair

Map p400 H7

Bond Street or Green Park tube.

Not for nothing is this the most expensive property on a Monopoly board. It may sport one of the prettiest names in London (deriving from the fair that used to take place here each May), but Mayfair is austere, important and untouristy. Over the centuries, many of London's biggest wigs have chosen this as their neighbourhood, and it's not hard to see why.

It is generally agreed that Mayfair is the area between Oxford Street, Regent Street, Piccadilly and Park Lane. When it was all rolling green fields at the edge of London town, it belonged to the Grosvenor and Berkeley families, who bought the land in the mid 1600s. In the 1700s they developed the pastures into a posh new neighbourhood. In particular they built a series of squares surrounded by elegant houses – although the three biggest squares, Hanover, Berkeley and the immense Grosvenor, are ringed by offices and embassies these days. The most famous of these, Grosvenor (that's 'Grovener'), is where you'll find the drab US Embassy. Finished in 1960, it takes up one whole side of the square and its only decoration is a fierce-looking eagle, a lot of protective fencing and some heavily armed police. Out front, a big statue of President Eisenhower has pride of place, although there's also a grand statue of President Franklin D Roosevelt standing nobly in the square nearby. When in London, Eisenhower stayed at the painfully expensive hotel **Claridge's** (*see p53*), a block away on Brook Street.

The toffs are still in residence elsewhere in Mayfair, and the tone of the area remains sky-high. It has always been smart: the Duke of Wellington is its most distinguished former resident – he briefly lived at 4 Hamilton Place, before moving to **Apsley House** (*see p116*) – but he has stiff competition from Admiral Lord Nelson (147 New Bond Street), Benjamin Disraeli (29 Park Lane), Florence Nightingale (10 South Street) and Sir Robert Peel (16 Upper Grosvenor Street). Brook Street has its musicians: GF Handel lived at No.25 and Jimi Hendrix briefly next door at No.23. These adjacent buildings have been combined into a museum dedicated to Handel's memory (*see p116*).

Crowded, noisy Oxford Street to the north is least typical of Mayfair's consumer facilities. Other than a handful of good department stores it's a chain-store rat race. More representative are **New Bond Street**, the designer drag, and **Cork Street**, gallery row. The most famous Mayfair shopping street is **Savile Row** (*see p246*), the land of made-to-measure suits of the highest quality. At No.15 is the estimable Henry Poole & Co, which, over the years, has cut suits for clients including Napoleon Bonaparte, Charles Dickens, Winston Churchill and Charles de Gaulle. No.3 was the home of Apple Records, the Beatles' recording studio. The fabulous four famously played their last gig here in February 1969, up on the roof.

Savile Row leads on to the equally salubrious **Conduit Street**, from where you can follow St George Street into **Hanover Square**. Here you'll find **St George's Church**, built in the 1720s and once everybody's favourite place to get married. Among the luminaries who said their vows at the altar were George Eliot and Teddy Roosevelt. Handel, who married nobody, attended services here.

While all of this is so very chi-chi, the area around **Shepherd Market** (named after a food market set up here by architect Edward Shepherd in the early 18th century) is perhaps the true heart of the neighbourhood. From 1686 this was where the raucous May Fair was held, until it was shut down for good in the late 18th century after city leaders complained of 'drunkenness, fornication, gaming and lewdness'. Today, it seems a pleasant, upscale area with a couple of fine pubs (Ye Grapes at 16 Shepherd Market and the Shepherd's Tavern at 50 Hertford Street) and some of London's most agreeable pavement dining. But, in keeping with its background, you'll often also see prostitutes working from tatty apartment blocks whose accommodation probably bears little resemblance to the clutch of sophisticated hotels – the Hilton, the Dorchester, the Metropolitan and the Inter-Continental – moments away on Park Lane.

Faraday Museum

Royal Institution, 21 Albemarle Street, W1S 4BS (7409 2992/www.rigb.org). Green Park tube.
Open 10am-5pm Mon-Fri. *Tours* by arrangement.
Admission £1.50p concessions; children. *Tours* £5.
Credit MC, V. **Map** p400 J7.

This small museum in the building where Michael Faraday was professor has a re-creation of the lab where he discovered the laws of electromagnetics. It's probably of interest only to those of a scientific bent, but there is a variety of 19th-century scientific equipment to admire, including the electromagnetic induction ring with which Faraday, in 1831, created the first transformer.

Handel House Museum

25 Brook Street (entrance at rear in Lancashire Court), W1K 4HB (7495 1685/www.handelhouse. org). Bond Street tube. **Open** 10am-6pm Tue, Wed, Fri, Sat; 10am-8pm Thur; noon-6pm Sun. **Admission** £4.50; £3.50 concessions; £2 6-15s; free under-5s. **Credit** MC, V. **Map** p400 J7.
George Frideric Handel moved to Britain from his native Germany aged 25 and settled in this Mayfair house 12 years later, remaining here until his death in 1759. The house has been beautifully restored with original and recreated furnishings, paintings and a welter of the composer's scores. The programme of events here is surprisingly dynamic for a museum so small: there are activities tilted at kids every Saturday, recitals every Thursday and most days there's somebody playing in the Rehearsal Room. And we won't be forgetting the Beer & Baroque evening in a hurry.

Piccadilly & Green Park

Map p400 H8

Green Park or Hyde Park Corner tube.
Grandiose **Piccadilly** links the traffic-strewn bear-pit of **Hyde Park Corner** with the pickpocket heaven of **Piccadilly Circus** (*see below*). Its undeniably charming name comes from the fancy suit collars ('picadils') favoured by the posh gentlemen who once paraded down its length. It's not really very high class any more, but you can still see remnants of its glossy past in the Victorian shopping arcades, designed to protect shoppers from mud and horse manure and continuing to offer an exclusive service to toffs. One of the nicest is the **Burlington Arcade**. According to archaic laws still on the books, it is illegal to sing, whistle or hurry in the arcade, and there are top-hatted beadles on the job to catch anybody doing any of the above. Just next door to the Arcade, the **Royal Academy of Arts** (*see p117*) lures with innovative arts exhibitions. Across Piccadilly from the Academy, it's virtually impossible to pass the wonderfully overwrought, mint green veneer of the department store **Fortnum & Mason** (*see p236*) without stepping inside.

The simple-looking church at No.197 is **St James's** (*see p117*). This was the personal favourite of its architect Sir Christopher Wren, a fact that may come as a surprise to those who would expect him to have had a soft spot for glorious St Paul's. There's often a market out front, and a handy coffeeshop with outdoor seating is tucked into a corner behind it.

A few doors further down Piccadilly, the old-fashioned uniforms sported by the doormen and the excellent 1950s-style lighted sign leave no doubt that you've reached the **Ritz**, one of the city's best-known hotels and *the* place to go for afternoon tea. The simple green expanse just beyond the Ritz is the aptly named **Green Park**. Once a plague pit, where the city's many epidemic victims were buried, it may not be able to match the grandeur of Regent's Park or the sheer scale of Hyde Park, but it has its charms, most evident in the spring, when its gentle slopes are covered in bright daffodils (there are no planted flowerbeds here, hence the name). **Buckingham Palace** (*see p117*) and its extensive gardens lie at its southern tip. **St James's Park**, just across the Mall, with its lovely views and exotic birdlife, does rather overshadow Green Park's bland greensward. Originally a royal deer park for St James's Palace, its pastoral landscape owes its influence to John Nash, who redesigned it in the early 19th century under the orders of George IV. The view of Buckingham Palace from the bridge over the lake is wonderful, especially at night when the palace is floodlit. The lake is now a sanctuary for wildfowl, among them pelicans (fed at 3pm daily) and Australian black swans.

Continuing down Piccadilly, which gets noisy and hectic in short order, you work your way past the queues outside the Hard Rock Café (*see p203*) to the Duke of Wellington's old homestead, **Apsley House**, and on to **Wellington Arch** (*see p118*), both at Hyde Park Corner.

Apsley House: The Wellington Museum

149 Piccadilly, W1J 7NT (7499 5676/www.english-heritage.org.uk). Hyde Park Corner tube. **Open** 11am-5pm Tue-Sun. **Tours** by arrangement. **Admission** £4.50 (includes audio guide); £3 concessions; £2.30 under-18s; £15 family. **Tours** phone in advance. **Credit** MC, V. **Map** p400 G8.
Called No.1 London because it was the first London building one encountered on the road from the village of Kensington, Apsley House was built by Robert Adam in the 1770s. The Duke of Wellington had it as his London residence for 35 years. Though his descendants still live here, some rooms are open to the public and contain interesting trinkets: Goya's Wellington portrait shows the Iron Duke after he defeated the French in 1812. An X-ray of the painting in 1966 showed that Wellington's head had been brushed over that of Joseph Bonaparte, Napoleon's brother: Goya had been working on the portrait when he found out Wellington had been victorious, so he adjusted the painting accordingly.

Compact and bijou **Buckingham Palace**.

Buckingham Palace & Royal Mews

SW1A 1AA (7766 7300/Royal Mews 7766 7302/
www.royal.gov.uk). Green Park or St James's Park
tube/Victoria tube/rail. **Open** *State Rooms* early
Aug, Sept 9.30am-5pm daily. *Royal Mews* Oct-July
11am-4pm daily; Aug, Sept 10am-5pm daily. Last
admission 45mins before closing. **Admission** *Palace*
£12.95; £11 concessions; £6.50 5-16s; £32.50 family;
free under-5s. *Royal Mews* £5.50; £4.50 concessions;
£3 5-16s; free under-5s; £14 family. **Credit** AmEx,
MC, V. **Map** p400 H9.

The world's most famous palace, built in 1703, was
intended as a house for the Duke of Buckingham,
but George III liked it so much he bought it for his
young bride Charlotte. His son, George IV, hired
John Nash to convert it into a palace. Thus construction on the 600-room palace began, but the project was beset with disaster from the start. Nash was
fired after George IV's death – he was too flighty
apparently – and the reliable but unimaginative
Edward Blore was hired to finish the job. After critics saw the final result, they dubbed him 'Blore the
Bore'. What's more, Queen Victoria, who was the
first royal to live here, hated the place, calling it 'a
disgrace to the country'.

Judge for yourself. In August and September,
while the Windsors are off on their holidays, the
State Apartments – used for banquets and investi-
tures – are open to the public. After the initial thrill
of being inside Buckingham Palace, it's not all that
interesting, save for the Queen's Gallery, which contains highlights of Liz's art collection. An exhibition
of 17th-century works, 'Enchanting the Eye: Dutch
Paintings of the Golden Age', runs until 6 November.

Around the corner, on Buckingham Palace Road,
the Royal Mews holds those royal carriages that are
rolled out for the Royals to wag their hands from on
very important occasions. Best of Show award goes
to Her Majesty's State Coach, a breathtaking, double gilded affair built in 1761.

Royal Academy of Arts

Burlington House, Piccadilly, W1J 0BD (7300 8000/
www.royalacademy.org.uk). Green Park or Piccadilly
Circus tube. **Open** 10am-6pm Mon-Thur, Sat, Sun;
10am-10pm Fri. **Admission** varies. **Credit** AmEx,
DC, MC, V. **Map** p400 J7.

Britain's first art school was founded in 1768 and
moved to the extravagant Palladian Burlington
House a century later. It's best known these days for
its galleries, which stage a roster of populist temporary exhibitions (there is a small permanent collection on show; make an appointment with the
librarian to use the archives). Exhibitions scheduled
for 2005 include Turkic art until 12 April and
Matisse textiles from March till 30 May. The
Academy's biggest event is the Summer Exhibition,
which for 236 years has drawn from works entered
by the public. Some 12,000 pieces are submitted each
year, with ten per cent making it past the judges.

St James's Church Piccadilly

197 Piccadilly, W1J 9LL (7734 4511/www.st-james-
piccadilly.org). Piccadilly Circus tube. **Open** 8am-7pm
daily. Evening events times vary. **Admission** free.
Map p400 J7.

Consecrated in 1684, St James's is the only church
Sir Christopher Wren built on an entirely new site.
It's a calming building without architectural airs or
graces but not lacking in charm. It was bombed to
within an inch of its life in World War II, but was
painstakingly reconstructed. The lovely plasterwork around the sanctuary was reformed by using
the bits that remained of the original as a model. It
is still the building's only real frill. This is a busy
church, as along with its inclusive ministry, it runs
a counselling service, stages regular classical concerts, provides a home for the William Blake Society
(the poet was baptised here) and hosts markets in
its churchyard: antiques on Tuesday, arts and crafts
from Wednesday to Saturday.

Wellington Arch

Hyde Park Corner, W1J 7JZ (7930 2726/www. english-heritage.org.uk). Hyde Park Corner tube. **Open** *Apr-Sept* 10am-6pm Wed-Sun. *Oct* 10am-5pm Wed-Sun. *Nov-Mar* 10am-4pm Wed-Sun. **Admission** £3; £2.30 concessions; £1.50 5-16s; free under-5s. **Credit** MC, V. **Map** p400 G8.

Built in the 1820s to mark Britain's triumph over Napoleonic France, Decimus Burton's Wellington Arch was moved from its original Buckingham Palace location to Hyde Park Corner in 1882. It was initially topped by a statue of Wellington, but since 1912 Captain Adrian Jones's *Peace Descending on the Quadriga of War* has finished it with a flourish. It was restored and opened three years ago, and has three floors of displays about the history of the arch. From the balcony, you can see the Houses of Parliament and Buckingham Palace, though trees will probably obstruct your view in summer.

Piccadilly Circus & Regent Street

Maps p398 J6, p400 J7 & p401 K7
Oxford Circus or Piccadilly Circus tube.

Undeniable landmark though it is, the Piccadilly Circus of today is an uneasy mix of the tawdry and the grandiose, and would certainly not correspond to what its architect John Nash had planned for it. His original 1820s design for the intersection of two of the West End's most elegant streets was an elegant circle of curved frontages. But 60 years later, Shaftesbury Avenue muscled its way in, to create the present lopsided effect; in an attempt to compensate, a delicate statue in honour of child-labour abolitionist Earl Shaftesbury was

Fantastic voyagers

Friday 26 March 2004, number 98, Holborn (Red Lion Square) to Willesden. Friday 4 June 2004, number 8, Bow Church to Victoria. Black Friday, 3 September 2004: number 9, Aldwych to Hammersmith; number 390, Marble Arch to Archway; number 73, Victoria to Tottenham. The last journeys of London's iconic Routemaster buses. On each route, regulars took one last ritual ride and retired bus workers a last trip down memory lane. Journalists observed them. Conductors and passengers bantered; sweets were handed around. When the buses reached the depot for the last time, they were pensioned off, along with some of their conductors. The

scene will be played out on all remaining Routemaster routes until the last bus is withdrawn from service in late summer 2005.

Around the world, waves of incredulity. How could the authorities so readily scrap a vehicle that has become internationally symbolic of the capital? Not just any old red double-decker bus, but the open-backed, conductor-staffed bus that was purpose-built specifically for use in London 50 years ago and still seems ideally adapted to its role. Like any design classic, it not only does its job well, it is beautiful too. No icon will ever say 'London' so well or so democratically. It's a bit like Paris getting rid of the Eiffel Tower.

installed. Its subject was the Angel of Christian Charity, but it looks like Eros and so now is thus known. His unseeing eyes have gazed on further indignities: the arrival of the billboards in 1910, the junkie culture of the 1980s and the continual invasion of tourist tack: overpriced pizza and uninteresting arcades.

Connecting Piccadilly Circus to Oxford Circus to the north and Pall Mall to the south, Regent Street is a broad, curving boulevard designed by Nash in the early 1800s to separate the wealthy of Mayfair from the working classes of Soho. The grandeur of the sweeping road is impressive – although much of Nash's architecture was destroyed in the early 20th century, some does survive. It's an elegant shopping sweep now, home to famous children's emporium **Hamleys** (*see p258*)

and the landmark **Liberty** store (*see p237*), with far more class than Oxford Street despite the inevitable incursion of the chains.

St James's

Map p400 J7-J8

Green Park or Piccadilly Circus tube.
One of central London's quieter parts, St James's does not get many visitors – nor many Londoners, for that matter. Bordered by Piccadilly, Haymarket, the Mall and Green Park, it's even posher than Mayfair, its comrade-in-swank north of Piccadilly. This is a London that has remained unchanged for centuries: it's all very charming in its way, although it remains resolutely rich and gently conceited all the same.

Why? The answer, of course, is prosaic. Times have changed. Regulations (European), litigations (accidents are more frequent on Routemasters; there were three fatalities in 2003), and more egalitarian times. There's little room for pushchairs, and wheelchair users can forget it. As a spokesperson for Transport for London said: 'We're running a transport system, not a museum.'

It's an unarguable point, though it's hard to believe that there isn't some public service role that the Routemaster could usefully fill. And if there isn't, it makes it all the more disappointing that the Routemaster's 'bendy bus' replacement, a one-person operated

single decker comprising two articulated cars, is no design classic. It certainly has advantages – higher capacity (if you like standing), improved safety and accessibility – but it's far from being ideal when it comes to some of the narrow, winding roads it plies, nor much of a pleasure to ride. And it won't be gracing many postcards.

If you want to make the comparison yourself, look out for a Routemaster 'heritage route', which is planned (at press time in no detail) to keep the buses on the streets and in front of camera lenses after the main fleet is withdrawn. If you're visiting before then, catch one if you can.

Sightseeing

The material needs of the venerable gents of St James's are met by the anachronistic shops and restaurants of Jermyn Street and St James's Street, with the timewarp shopfronts, among them cigar retailer James J Fox (19 St James's Street, 7930 3787) and upmarket cobbler John Lobb (No.9, 7930 3665). To stroll around the alleys is to step back in time, and up in class.

Around the corner from St James's Street is the Queen Mother's old gaff, **Clarence House** (*see below*). Now the official London residence of Prince Charles and his sons Harry and William, it recently opened to the public. Very near to Clarence House, **St James's Palace** was originally built as a residence for Henry VIII in 1532. It has remained the official residence of the sovereign throughout the centuries, despite the fact that since 1837 the monarchs have all actually lived at nearby Buckingham Palace. It has great historic significance to the monarchy: Mary Tudor surrendered Calais here, Elizabeth I lived here during the campaign against the Spanish Armada, and Charles I was confined here before his execution in 1649.

Today St James's Palace is used by the Princess Royal and various minor royals, and it is, essentially, the address of the now largely defunct government of the monarch. Tradition still dictates that foreign ambassadors to the UK are officially known as 'Ambassadors to the Court of St James's'. Although the palace is closed to the public, you can attend Sunday services at the historic **Chapel Royal** (Oct-Good Friday; 8.30am, 11.15am).

Across Marlborough Road lies the **Queen's Chapel**, which was the first classical church to be built in England. Designed by the mighty and prolific Inigo Jones in the 1620s for Charles I's intended bride of the time, the Infanta of Castile, the chapel now stands in the grounds of **Marlborough House** and is only open to the public during Sunday services (Easter-July; 8.30am, 11.15am). The house itself was built by Sir Christopher Wren.

Two other notable St James's mansions stand nearby and overlook Green Park. The neo-classical **Lancaster House** was rebuilt in the 1820s by Benjamin Dean Wyatt for Frederick, Duke of York, and impressed Queen Victoria with its splendour. Closed to the public, it's now used mainly for government receptions and conferences. A little further north, on St James's Place, is the beautiful, 18th-century **Spencer House**, ancestral townhouse of the late Princess Diana's family and now infrequently open as a museum and art gallery.

Reached from the west via King Street or the Mall, **St James's Square** was the most fashionable address in London for the 50 years after it was laid out in the 1670s: some seven dukes and seven earls were residents by the 1720s. Alas, no private houses survive on the square today, though among the current occupants is the prestigious **London Library**. This private library was founded by Thomas Carlyle in 1841 in disgust at the inefficiency of the British Library.

Further east, overlooking the Mall, is **Carlton House Terrace**, which was built by Nash in 1827-32 on the site of Carlton House. When the Prince Regent came to the throne as George IV, he decided his home was not ostentatious enough for his elevated station and levelled what Horace Walpole had once described as 'the most perfect palace' in Europe. Nos.8 and 9 Carlton House Terrace, currently occupied by the Royal Society, were converted into a single building as the Germany Embassy during the Nazi era; their interiors renovated by Albert Speer, Hitler's architect.

Clarence House

SW1A 1AA (7766 7303/www.royal.gov.uk). Green Park tube. **Open** *Aug-mid Oct* 9.30am-6pm daily (last admission 5pm). **Admission** £5.50; £3 5-16s; free under-5s. **Tours** All tickets for the guided tours are timed and must be pre-booked. **Credit** AmEx, MC, V. **Map** p400 J8.

Standing austerely beside St James's Palace, Clarence House was built between 1825 and 1827, based on designs by John Nash. It was built for Prince William Henry, Duke of Clarence, who lived there as King William IV until 1837. During its history, the house has been much altered by its many royal inhabitants, the most recent of whom was the Queen Mother, who lived there until she died in 2002. Prince Charles and his two sons have since moved in, but parts of the house are open to the public in summer: five receiving rooms and the small but significant art collection, strong in 20th-century British art, accumulated by the Queen Mother. Among the art on display is a lovely 1945 portrait of her by Sir James Gunn. There's also a painting by Noël Coward and others by John Piper, WS Sickert and Augustus John. Tickets are hard to come by and tend to sell out by the end of August.

Spencer House

27 St James's Place, SW1A 1NR (7499 8620/ www.spencerhouse.co.uk). Green Park tube. **Open** *House* Feb-July, Sept-Dec 10.30am-5.45pm (last admission 4.45pm) Sun. *Restored gardens* spring, summer (phone to check). **Admission** Tour only £6; £5 concessions, 10-16s. No under-10s. **Map** p400 J8.

Designed by John Vardy and built for John Spencer, who became Earl Spencer the year before his house was completed, this 1766 construction is one of the capital's finest examples of a Palladian mansion. The eponymous Spencers moved out just over a century ago and the lavishly restored building is now used chiefly as offices and for corporate entertaining, hence the limited access.

Soho

Sleazy does it.

Old Compton Street. *See p122.*

Soho's present is also, to a large extent, its past. The area has had many different characters during its long and fruitful life, alternately wealthy and poor, cultured and seedy. Today the area, bounded by the four Circuses (Oxford, Piccadilly, Cambridge and St Giles) is not dominated by any single coterie. Businessmen, celebs, journalists, hookers, market traders, immigrants, tourists and queers all cosy up in what is still just about London's spiciest square mile, its skinny avenues and buzzing streetlife (at least in the east) defining the area more than any one community.

Documented Soho really begins in the Middle Ages, when the area was a rural idyll used as a hunting ground by London's aristocracy. It was after the Great Fire of 1666 that Soho became residential, when thousands were forced to relocate. Around this time, Soho also got its first wave of immigrants: Greek Christians (hence Greek Street) fleeing Ottoman persecution, and French Protestants (Huguenots) forced out of France by Louis XIV. Soon, the only trace of the neighbourhood's pastoral roots was its name: the huntsmen who once rode the verdant pastures here used to cry 'So-ho!' when they spotted their prey.

As the immigrants poured into Soho, wealthy residents moved out. The architect John Nash encouraged this social apartheid in 1813, when he designed Regent Street to provide what he called 'a complete separation between the Streets occupied by the Nobility and Gentry [Mayfair], and the narrower Streets and meaner houses occupied by mechanics and the trading part of the community'. With Nash's kind of thinking ruling the day, Soho became one of Britain's worst slums during the 19th century.

Change came again soon enough, however. The early years of the 20th century saw showgirls, prostitutes and artists (of a variety of stripes) define the area's character, with the 1950s prime time for the latter. Painter Francis Bacon and photographer John Deakin lunched and boozed their way around the area; Britain's earliest rock 'n' roll singers congregated at the long-since closed 2 i's Coffee Bar at 59 Old Compton Street. In 1962 Georgie Fame started his sweat-soaked residency at the Flamingo Club (33-37 Wardour Street); the nearby Marquee (then at 90 Wardour Street, now in Leicester Square; *see p309*) hosted early gigs by Jimi Hendrix and Pink Floyd.

The sex industry expanded to a phenomenal degree in the 1960s and '70s. At one point, there were well over 200 sex-related businesses here, many allowed to operate by a police force on the take from the owners. But soon after the corruption was uncovered, Westminster Council clamped down; in the mid 1980s the number of strip joints, porn cinemas and sex shops in the area fell by 80 per cent (although a hardy few continue to prosper). By and large, though, the gay community moved in to replace them: while pubs such as the **Golden Lion** on Dean Street had long been the haunt of gay servicemen (as well as writer Noël Coward), the '90s saw myriad gay bars, restaurants and shops set up on Old Compton Street and the nearby streets.

The future? As ever, it's impossible even to speculate what may become of this area. In many places, there are already the first telltale

Go-go gone

It looked like the end of an era. After 46 years as the doyen of Soho strip joints, Raymond Revuebar closed its doors to punters in 2004. The exotic dancers packed away their feather boas and peephole bras. The giant birthday cake that girls used to leap out of was quietly wheeled off stage.

Now, Soho's most famous strip club has been reinvented as a gay nightclub and cabaret. Too 2 Much is the brainchild of club impresario Paul Richardson, who honed his skills at the Sanctuary, Shadow Lounge and Heaven (for all, see pp294-300). The new club promises more of the same, with go-go boys decked out in neon pink hot-pants and a 'leave your inhibitions in the cloakroom' policy on the door.

But before you write off Raymond's as another vanished piece of seedy Soho, spare a moment to consider the history of Britain's first ever licensed strip club.

Before Raymond's came along, nude dancing in public was prohibited by order of the Lord Chamberlain. The most risqué show in town was Revuedeville at the Windmill Theatre off Piccadilly Circus, where topless models posed motionless in a series of static tableaux. (Punters would toss small change at them in the hope of provoking something approaching animation.)

The rules didn't, it turned out, apply to private members clubs. In 1958 a touring cabaret clairvoyant named Paul Raymond obtained the lease for a former restaurant on Brewer Street and staged Britain's first ever moving striptease show. It's safe to say that Soho has never looked back.

Dancing in the buff might seem pretty tame by modern standards, but in the 1950s the arrival of Raymond Revuebar was rather like a Chippendale walking into a nunnery. Everyone wanted a piece of it. The only prerequisite was money, which meant that businessmen, footballers, entertainers and gangsters all signed up to become members of the hottest new club in town and Paul Raymond became fabulously rich on the proceeds.

Raymond soon extended his sleaze empire to include West End stage shows and top-shelf magazines such as *Men Only* and *Club International*. By the 1960s the Revuebar was almost respectable. Olivia Newton-John appeared here with Pat Carroll, and the comedian Peter Richardson got his first big break at Raymond's before forming the hugely successful Comic Strip comedy troupe.

signs of homogenisation: an identikit bar here, a nationwide supermarket chain there. And with the sky-high rents showing no signs of dropping, it could very easily get worse. That said, though, it'd be a fool who'd bet on this most characterful and gutsy of neighbourhoods going the way of nearby Covent Garden. Soho has, and always has had, a resilient nature.

Old Compton Street & around

Map p399 K6

Leicester Square or Tottenham Court Road tube.
All human life hangs on **Old Compton Street**, Soho's Main Street. Either in the bars, shops, cafés (try the venerable **Patisserie Valerie**, No.44) and restaurants on the street, or just

When lap-dancing arrived in Britain in the 1990s, Raymond's went into steady decline. Although the legendary 'Festival of Erotica' show had everything from can-can girls to snake charmers, Raymond's upmarket striptease looked increasingly tepid compared to the full-frontal Goings On at American-style gentlemen's clubs in out-of-town locations with more liberal local bylaws. In 1997 Paul Raymond sold the bar to a rival club owner and vanished from the public eye.

The *coup de grâce* for Raymond's came in 2004 when the club's application for a table-dancing licence was rejected and the leaseholder simultaneously pushed up the rent. By an extraordinary coincidence, that leaseholder was none other than Soho Estates, a ruthlessly commercial property agency owned by... (guessed it yet?) a certain Paul Raymond.

Today Paul Raymond is Britain's 56th richest man, with a property portfolio valued at £590 million. Despite owning half of Soho, Raymond likes to keep a hand in the nudie business, with a porn website based on a virtual-reality Soho street.

As for the Revuebar, the bar-girls may have gone, but the spirit of Raymond's lives on at Too 2 Much. The new owners have retained the red velour wallpaper and Bohemian crystal chandeliers, and glamorous hosts still greet punters at the door.

Too 2 Much

11-12 Walker's Court, off Brewer Street, Soho, W1F 0ED (7437 4400/www.too2 much.com). Leicester Square or Piccadilly Circus tube. **Open** *5pm-4am Tue-Sat.* **Performances** *7pm.* **Admission** £10. **Credit** *AmEx, MC, V.*

passing through en route to somewhere else. On Fridays and Saturdays, gangs of tight-shirted, close-cropped straights rub shoulders with herds of tight-shirted, close-cropped gays. But while the uniforms are the same, the accessories are not: the straight guys are the ones carrying the half-drunk lager pints, the queens the ones with the gym-built bodies.

The place buzzes; if not quite 24/7, then certainly 17/ or 18/7. Also joining the fray are gaggles of girls out on the razzle, lairy stag parties down from the north, illegal minicab drivers touting for work (don't even think about it), elderly jazz buffs en route to the local jazz club, and confused tourists either heading to or leaving the immensely popular production of

Abba musical *Mamma Mia!* at the Prince of Wales Theatre (*see p337*). At dawn, club-goers wander distractedly along the traffic-free street, the homeless finally settle down to sleep in doorways and the street cleaners move in to begin mopping up in preparation for the locals to do it all over again tomorrow.

A couple of stone's throws north of Old Compton Street, **Soho Square** forms the neighbourhood's northern gateway. This tree-lined quadrangle was initially called King Square, and a weather-beaten statue of Charles II stands in the centre. It's held up pretty well: not as grand as it once was (traffic cruises around it all day and night, waiting for one of the area's few parking meters to become available), but popular with local workers, who pack the grass in summer. Jackie Leven and Kirsty MacColl wrote songs about the square; the latter, who died in 2000, has a bench dedicated to her on the south side. Two churches provide spiritual nourishment, but the area is dominated by the advertising and film industries: the British Board of Film Classification and 20th Century Fox both have their offices here.

The two streets that link Old Compton with Soho Square are rich with history. Casanova and Thomas de Quincey once lodged on **Greek Street**, though the street's now notable mainly for the gloriously old-fashioned **Gay Hussar** restaurant (No.2, 7437 0973). Neighbouring **Frith Street**, formerly home to Constable, Mozart and William Hazlitt, is livelier, thanks chiefly to the presence of legendary jazz club **Ronnie Scott's** (*see p314*) and similarly mythologised all-night café **Bar Italia** (*see p206*). The latter, above which John Logie Baird demonstrated his TV for the first time, feels like the centre of the world on busy nights, the whole of London and beyond revolving around its overworked espresso machine.

Dean Street, just west of Frith Street, has an equally colourful history, mostly composed of the bohemian characters who got drunk in its pubs. Dylan Thomas – surprise, surprise – held marathon drinking sessions at the York Minster (south of Old Compton Street at No.49), then nicknamed 'the French Pub' for its association with Charles de Gaulle and the Free French resistance movement. It's now called the **French House** (*see p223*), and still retains its louche charm. Also along here is the members-only **Groucho Club** (No.44), where members of London's media industry quench their thirsts and powder their noses, and the **Sunset Strip** (No.30), the sole remaining legitimate strip club in Soho (in contrast to the unlicensed places further west, the prices are reasonable and the girls actually take their clothes off). Hard to

believe that Karl Marx, who lived both at No.28 and No.44 for a time, would have approved of either. Further north is the **Soho Theatre** (*see p340*), which has fast cemented a reputation for its programme of new plays and comedy, and the **Crown & Two Chairmen** (No.31), arguably the best old-school pub in Soho.

Wardour Street, the next street along, is less interesting, its buildings predominantly providing homes to an assortment of film and TV production companies. On Wardour Street just to the south of Old Compton Street is the churchyard of **St Anne's**; bombed during the Blitz, only the 19th-century tower remains. Those with a keen eye and an expansive record collection will clock the next street along from the cover of the Oasis album (*What's the Story*) *Morning Glory?*, and **Berwick Street** (four streets west of Greek Street, for those not paying attention at the back) repays the favour. This road and those just off it are awash with independent record stores, selling everything from speciality dance 12-inches at premium prices to chart favourites at prices several pounds below those offered at the chain stores on Oxford Street.

The music retailers are joined on Berwick Street by two other cottage industries: the fruit and veg salesmen who make up the bulk of the street market (*see p256*; come late in the afternoon for the bargains), and the prostitutes who conduct their trade at the top of a number of scruffy stairwells; handwritten signs in doorways advertise the doubtless bargainous likes of 'Busty Model 1st Floor'. At the southern end of Berwick Street, what remains of the Soho sex industry is at its most visible. Tiny **Walkers Court** (linking Berwick and Brewer Streets) and even smaller **Tisbury Court** (joining Wardour and Rupert Streets) are lined with insalubrious strip joints that lure punters with the promise of untold bodily riches and then send them away again a half-hour later with a bar bill running to several hundred pounds and nary a tit in sight. Nearby **Rupert Street** is home to several other establishments that perform similar cash-guzzling services on the young, the dumb and the desperate.

Broadwick Street, just off Berwick Street, is famous for a couple of reasons: it was the birthplace of William Blake, and the epicentre of a severe cholera outbreak in 1854. Local doctor John Snow became convinced that the disease was transmitted by polluted water and had the street's water pump closed. Snow's hypothesis proved correct, leading to a breakthrough in epidemiology. The doctor is commemorated by a handle-less replica water pump and in the name of the street's pub (where very little water is drunk).

West Soho

Map p401 K7

Piccadilly Circus tube.

West of Berwick Street, Soho grows noticeably quieter; there are fewer bars and almost no restaurants around here, a minor miracle when you consider the none-more-central location. The roads that spout off Brewer Street don't offer a great deal of note, either, but **Great Windmill Street**, which runs south of Brewer Street, offers the perfect illustration of Soho's changing mores. In 1932 the **Windmill Theatre** embarked on its now-legendary 'revuedeville' shows with erotic 'tableaux', which were adapted to comply with a law that dictated that such shows, if they existed at all, could feature stationary naked girls. Some 70 years later, it's now a lap-dancing joint, the premises opposite and around it filled with unlicensed clip joints of the kind found in the vicinity of Walkers and Tisbury Courts.

North of Brewer Street, things grow calmer for a while, with **Golden Square** now home to some of the area's grandest residential buildings. Just north of here is **Carnaby Street**: four decades ago the epitome of swinging London and then a rather seamy commercial backwater, it's recently undergone a revival of sorts. On Carnaby Street and **Newburgh Street**, a mix of independent and familiar shops trade happily and, in some cases, lucratively off the area's history. The sole reason to visit **Argyll Street**, which runs north to Oxford Street, is the grand old **London Palladium** theatre.

Chinatown & Leicester Square

Map p401 K7

Leicester Square tube.

Shaftesbury Avenue, which wends its way down from New Oxford Street to Piccadilly Circus, is the heart of Theatreland (*see p333*). During the late Victorian period, seven grand theatres were built here; six of them still stand. Chinese shops and restaurants mark it as the northern edge of **Chinatown**, a district that extends to Leicester Square.

Soho has always attracted immigrants, but the Chinese were relative latecomers: most arrived in the 1950s from Hong Kong. Migrating west from their original location in Limehouse in the Docklands, and attracted by the cheap rents along Gerrard and Lisle Streets, thousands of Chinese moved in, and soon the neighbourhood developed its distinctive Chinese personality. The ersatz oriental gates,

Soho Square. *See p124.*

stone lions and pagoda-topped phone boxes suggest a Chinese theme park, but, in reality, this is a close-knit residential and working enclave. **Gerrard Street** is the glitziest spot, crammed with restaurants and twinkly lights.

Just south of here is **Leicester Square**, which, in the 17th and 18th centuries, used to be one of London's most exclusive addresses. By the 19th century, as Soho became a ghetto, the aristos moved out, and they've never really returned. These days, despite a recent-ish remodelling, it's still no fun: most Londoners avoid the cheap fast fooderies, expensive cinemas and deafness-inducing buskers, and so should you. However, it's not all bad news. The south side of the square is where you'll find the **tkts** booth (*see p333*), operated by the Society of London Theatres and retailer of cut-price tickets to that day's theatre shows. (The other ticket shops in or near the square are unofficial and often rather more expensive.) And north in Leicester Place is the **Prince Charles Cinema** (*see p285*), which screens an eclectic mix of recent movies (and the occasional cult classic) at knockdown prices, and the French Catholic church of **Notre Dame de France**, which contains murals by Jean Cocteau.

Covent Garden & St Giles's

From high opera to street theatre: London at play.

Secluded **Neal's Yard**. *See p129.*

Covent Garden

Maps p399 & p401 L6-L7

Covent Garden or Leicester Square tube.

Londoners of old were pretty straightforward when it came to christening a district. Thus Covent Garden belonged to the Convent of St Peter at Westminster and, extraordinarily, the Strand was just that – the strand line – of the Thames. The dissolution of the monasteries saw Covent Garden lose its ecclesiastical connection as the land was granted by the Crown to John Russell, first Earl of Bedford. It was the fourth earl, Francis Russell, who set the area on its way, building houses 'fitt for the habitacions of *Gentlemen* and men of ability' and earning a tidy profit in the process.

As architect, Russell hired Inigo Jones, a man whom talent alone had dragged from the dim prospects due to a clothworker's son to being the most fashionable builder in the land. Taking inspiration from the Palladian designs he had

studied in Italy, Jones built an open square, with St Paul's Church forming the western boundary and the remaining three sides consisting of tall terraced houses opening to a central courtyard. In 1639, as now, fashionable London flocked to the 'in' designer and tenants were soon paying £150 a year for the houses.

The square's status as a fashionable residence waned when in 1656 the fifth Earl of Bedford was granted a royal charter for a flowers, fruit, roots and herbs market in Covent Garden. The air grew thick with the smell of roasting java as coffee houses sprang up, catering for the literary and theatrical folk – Henry Fielding, James Boswell, Alexander Pope and David Garrick over the years – who patronised the area's theatres, gambling dens and brothels. A count in 1722 tallied 22 gambling houses, and the magistrate Sir John Fielding remarked that 'One would imagine that all the prostitutes in the kingdom had picked upon the rendezvous.' The market thrived for three centuries, gradually picking up business from its competitors until it became London's pre-eminent fruit and veg wholesaler, employing about 1,000 porters. It remained in the Bedfords' hands until 1918, having been upgraded with the addition of several new buildings and market halls.

In 1974, when the restored market was moved south to Vauxhall, property developers pegged the area for more unwanted office blocks, and it was only through mass squats and demonstrations that the area was saved. Today, though the piazza itself is eschewed by Londoners, the area as a whole, especially to the north, is an example of planning gone right. Not only is there a thriving residential community but there's also an interesting mix of shops and small businesses on generally quiet streets, along with a sprinkling of cultural venues carrying on the theatrical heritage. All in all, then, this makes it some of the most pleasant wandering territory.

Covent Garden Piazza

Little remains of Jones's original piazza, but it's nonetheless an attractive galleried square, with lots of outdoor restaurant seating in summer and no cars allowed. Tourists flock here for a combination of gentrified shopping and less predictable street performances. The majority of the latter take place under the portico of **St Paul's** (*see below*). Shoppers favour the old covered market (7836 9136, www.coventgarden market.co.uk), now a collection of small stores, many of them with a twee, touristy appeal. The **Apple Market**, in the North Hall, has arts and crafts stalls every Tuesday to Sunday, and antiques on Monday.

Across the road, the cheaper, tackier **Jubilee Market** (7836 2139) – once a flower market – deals mostly in novelty T-shirts and unofficial calendars, although it, too, is filled with antiques every Monday and crafts on a weekend.

London's Transport Museum

Covent Garden Piazza, WC2E 7BB (7379 6344/ www.ltmuseum.co.uk). Covent Garden tube. **Open** 10am-6pm Mon-Thur, Sat, Sun; 11am-6pm Fri. **Admission** £5.95; £4.50 concessions; free under-16s when accompanied by an adult. **Credit** MC, V. **Map** p401 L6.

You don't have to be a trainspotter to enjoy this well-managed museum, which charts the history of public transport in the city centre from 19th-century horse-drawn carts to the present day, with plenty of actors and interactive displays bringing the journey to life. Kids clamber on the electric trams and pretend to drive the bus; older enthusiasts marvel at the development of a genuine urban aesthetic. There's also an exhibition of promotional posters for mass transit systems, and a good gift shop.

Royal Opera House

Covent Garden, WC2E 9DD (7304 4000/www. royaloperahouse.org). Covent Garden tube. **Open** 10am-3.30pm Mon-Sat. **Admission** free. *Stage tours* £8; £7 concessions. **Credit** AmEx, DC, MC, V. **Map** p401 L7.

Are opera lovers firebugs? It seems unlikely, but how else to explain the Royal Opera's regular appointments with the loss adjusters? The current building is the third on the site, the second having been leased in 1855 to John Anderson who had already seen two theatres burnt down and promptly added a third. But that's the least of the dramas associated with this stage. Handel premièred *Samson*, *Judas Maccabaeus* and *Solomon* here among many other works. Frenzied opera lovers twice rioted against ticket price rises, for 61 nights in 1809, while the 1763 fracas came within an iron pillar of bringing down the galleries. When actors did manage to get in front of the lights, they then promptly collapsed, Peg Woffington and Edmund Keane doing so during *As You Like It* and *Othello* respectively. Productions for 2005 include *La Traviata*, *Turandot* and *Die Walküre*, and, from the Royal Ballet, *Swan Lake* and *Ondine*.

St Paul's Covent Garden

Bedford Street, WC2E 9ED (7836 5221/www. actorschurch.org). Covent Garden tube or Charing Cross tube/rail. **Open** 9am-4.30pm Mon-Fri; 9am-12.30pm Sun. *Services* 1.10pm Wed; 11am Sun. *Choral Evensong* 4pm 2nd Sun of mth. **Admission** free; donations appreciated. **Map** p401 L7.

Known as the Actors' Church for its association with Covent Garden's Theatreland, this plain Tuscan pastiche was designed by Inigo Jones in 1631. Actors commemorated on its walls range from those now lost beyond Lethe – AR Philpott, 'Pantopuck the Puppetman' – to those destined for ambrosian immortality – Vivian Leigh, 'Now boast thee, death, in thy possession lies a lass unparallel'd'. George Bernard Shaw set the first scene of *Pygmalion* under the church's portico, and the first known victim of the plague, Margaret Ponteous, is buried in the pleasant churchyard, a calm place to ease one's feet.

Theatre Museum

Tavistock Street (entrance Russell Street), WC2E 7PR (7943 4700/www.theatremuseum.org). Covent Garden tube. **Open** 10am-6pm Tue-Sun. Last entry 5.30pm. **Admission** free. **Credit** AmEx, MC, V. **Map** p401 L6.

The various colourful threads of Covent Garden's theatrical history are spun into a vivid tapestry in this little museum. The permanent galleries form an intriguing window into the heroes of a bygone age – David Garrick, Edmund Kean, Eliza Vestris – as well as the plays that cast them into the public eye. There are daily make-up classes and costume workshops, while larger exhibitions include an interactive biography of the Redgrave family and a potted history of *The Wind in the Willows*, and its journey from the paper to the stage.

Sightseeing

River Cruises

Discover The Heart of London

HOPPER PASS

UNLIMITED one-day travel between Embankment, Waterloo, Bankside, Tower of London and Greenwich.

CIRCULAR CRUISES

MULTI LINGUAL COMMENTARY

A premier 50-minute, non-stop, multi-lingual circular cruise from Embankment Pier, taking in all of the river's key attractions.

CATAMARAN CRUISERS

T: **020 7987 1185**   E: **info@bateauxlondon.com**
www.catamarancruisers.co.uk

Elsewhere in Covent Garden

The area is nothing if not a mixture: from opposite ends of **St Martin's Lane** – and the social spectrum – Stringfellows, once a dodgy nightclub, now an even dodgier lap-dancing establishment (7240 5534, www.stringfellows. co.uk) faces down the **Coliseum** (7836 0111, www.eno.org; *see p303* **London Coliseum**), newly restored home of the **English National Opera**. Meanwhile, neighbouring alleys in the shadow of the Wyndham and Albany theatres exude an overpowering old world charm; from the nook and cranny antiques stores of Cecil Court to the clockwork-operated gas lighting of **Goodwin's Court**, which nightly illuminates a row of bow-fronted 17th-century housing.

Further towards the piazza, most of the older, more unusual shops have been superseded by a homogenous mass of cafés and by the time you reach the far end of King Street, Covent Garden offers only token gestures towards its colourful history. High-profile fashion designers (and a few trendy up-and-comers supported by their celebrity parents) have all but domesticated **Floral Street**, **Long Acre** and, most noticeably, **Neal Street**, but more interesting shopping experiences await on **Monmouth Street** and **Earlham Street**. On the latter, a traditional butcher's and a family ironmonger's look on to cult clothing stores, specialist bookshops and a flower market.

At one end of Earlham Street is the **Seven Dials** roundabout, which was named after both the number of sundials incorporated into the central monument (the seventh being formed by the pillar itself) and streets branching off it. The original pillar, a notorious criminal rendezvous, was removed in 1773. A stone's throw from Seven Dials, **Neal's Yard** is known for its co-operative cafés mingling cheerfully with herbalists, head shops and wholefoods.

Towards Holborn, Covent Garden becomes less distinguished. **Endell Street** is perhaps most noticeable for the queues leading to the ace chippie Rock & Sole Plaice (No.47, 7836 3785). These days **Drury Lane** is largely ignored even by theatre-goers: the current Theatre Royal (the first was built there in 1663) opens on to Catherine Street, with its excess of restaurants vying for the attention of pre- and post-performance diners. Meanwhile, the historical depravity of the area is remembered at the **Bow Street Magistrates Court**, home to author and one-time magistrate Henry Fielding's Bow Street Runners (the original precursors to the Metropolitan Police), as well as the site of Oscar Wilde's notorious conviction, in 1895, for committing 'indecent acts'. Finally, the **Freemasons' Hall** – the impressive white building at the point where Long Acre becomes Great Queen Street (7831 9811) – is worth a peek, if only for its solemn, symbolic architecture.

That this is a residential neighbourood is evident in peaceful **Ching Court**, off Shelton Street, and the beautiful **Phoenix Garden** (21 Stacey Street, 7379 3187), *rus in urbs* writ large, where willow trees, fruit trees and honeysuckle attract many birds and lunchtime dreamers.

St Giles in the Fields. *See p130.*

Sightseeing

Don't go there

You can only take so much cute, and Covent Garden Piazza is one of those places that, unless they have a particular reason to visit, Londoners tend to leave to the tourists. If you want to follow local advice, you'll also take good care to avoid the following:

Chain steakhouses

Often prominently placed near theatres staging long-running shows, their salads wilting in the window, these are eschewed by locals who know from past experience and a history of health citations that the food here is neither nice, good for you nor necessarily free of staff saliva.

Buckingham Palace etc

Royal London soars over the heads of most locals, who view the Changing of the Guard as an irritating traffic obstacle. Few have, in fact, ever witnessed it, unless they've had family or map-flapping friends come to town.

Any cocktail bar with pink neon trim

Cocktails are cool again. But only when served in hotel or restaurant bars or places that look like aircraft hangars. Such places do *not* include those joints heralded by fizzing, spluttering neon. Also to be avoided: drinks whose names include a synonym for sex.

Oxford Street

A necessary evil on occasion, but, especially now that the traditional old hop-on hop-off Routemaster buses are being pensioned off, a blocked artery. Londoners follow the parallel side streets, which are not only quieter but vastly more interesting.

McDonald's & Burger King

Actually, we're lying: locals do come here, sometimes. But we're not on holiday and you are. London has thousands of brilliant restaurants that aren't replicated in cities across the world: you should be eating at those instead. *See pp192-219.*

Madame Tussaud's

We're not knocking it, though why largely static replicas should be interesting in this day and age we're not quite sure. We just don't go there. Probably this is because there's always such a queue. We're always so bleeding busy.

Leicester Square

What square? No gracious public space, this, but a holding tank for buskers and ticket queues. Dive in and out of the cinema and don't hang around, or we might trip over you, turned hostile by the urban angst caused by abominable city planning.

St Giles's

Map p399 L6
Tottenham Court Road tube.

The reality of St Giles's may never have lived up to the legend, but immortalised so unfavourably in Hogarth's *Gin Lane*, and described with such venom by neighbour Charles Dickens, this once-squalid area can nonetheless be considered to have improved significantly in recent years, despite being overshadowed by the much-reviled **Centrepoint** office tower. Indeed, the dozen or so acres of predominantly Irish slums, which struck such fear into the heart of central London, remained a threat until the Metropolitan Board of Works scattered their inhabitants to make way for New Oxford Street in 1847. After an alarmingly effective mopping-up operation, all that remains of those dangerous days is the original church of **St Giles in the Fields** just behind Centrepoint on the High Street, which, in its current form dates back to the early 1700s, although there's been a

house of prayer on this site for more than 900 years. Just along the road, a pub known to Elizabethans simply as the Bowl mercifully offered last pints to condemned men on their walk from Newgate to the gibbet at Tyburn. Don't be put off, however: the Angel (61 St Giles Street, 7240 2876), which now stands in its place, is a great little pub.

Beyond this, St Giles's is probably best known for the musical heritage of **Denmark Street**, affectionately known as Tin Pan Alley, and once home to Regents Sound Studios, where the Stones recorded 'Not Fade Away' and the Kinks cut their first demo. The Small Faces were signed at the Giaconda Café, where Bowie also met his first band, and the Sex Pistols wrote 'Anarchy in the UK' in what is now a guitar shop at No.6. These days, instrument sales and repairs are what Denmark Street does best (expect to be serenaded by an army of bedroom guitar soloists 'testing' the latest Fenders), although the **12 Bar Club** (*see p313*) remains the city's most intimate songwriters' venue.

Charing Cross Road is very big on books. Remaining our favourite is the still-traditional if now more efficient Foyles (*see p235*), its place ensured in our affections since the day we attempted to find the *Spiritual Exercises of St Ignatius Loyola* and were directed to the sports department. Still, the real gems are to be found in the smaller, specialised and second-hand stores including Henry Pordes Books (arts and humanties; No.58-60, 7836 9031) and Al Hoda (7240 8381), which is also an Islamic study centre. Cult crews can snap up comics and movie memorabilia at Comic Showcase (No.63, 7434 4349) or VinMagCo (No.55, 7494 4064).

The Strand & Embankment

Map p401 M7

Embankment tube/Charing Cross tube/rail.
In 1292 the body of Eleanor of Castile, consort to Edward I, completed its funerary procession from Lincoln to the Westminster end of the Strand, then marked by the last of 12 elaborate crosses, reconstructed in 1863 behind the railings of Charing Cross Station. Strange to think that back then this bustling street – which connects Westminster to the City in a narrow, unbroken thread, as its name suggests – once ran directly beside the Thames.

Like much of Covent Garden, the Strand has endured its fair share of slings and arrows throughout history. As far back as the 14th century, the street was lined with waterside homes and gardens for the well-educated and well-to-do, and was still a highly reputable part of London at the time when Inigo Jones was poring over plans for the main square. Just as his piazza proved too small for the swelling market, so the Strand proved too thin for the wave of licentiousness rushing to fill the void left by the fleeing upper classes. It was a notorious blackspot for poverty and prostitution until the second half of the 19th century, when Sir Christopher Wren suggested the creation of a reclaimed embankment to ease congestion and house the main sewer.

By the time George Newnes's *Strand* magazine was introducing its readership to Sherlock Holmes (1891), things were starting to look up. While never quite regaining the composure of more central parts of Covent Garden (there's little among its collection of overbearing office blocks and underwhelming restaurants to really fire the imagination today), Richard D'Oyly Carte's Savoy Theatre, created in the 1880s to host Gilbert and Sullivan operas and pre-dating the world-famous hotel by eight years, gives some indication of how its fortunes began to change once again after the reinforced concrete Embankment was completed.

The **Embankment** itself can be approached down **Villiers Street**. Cut down Embankment Place to **Craven Street**, where at No.36 the American writer, scientist, philosopher and statesman Benjamin Franklin lived for 16 years from 1762. The London-based Benjamin Franklin House Foundation is working to restore the crumbling building where Franklin conducted his experiments and entertained, and make it into a museum (see www.rsa.org.uk/franklin). A few steps down the road, at No.32, there's a plaque in honour of another famous past resident, the German poet Heinrich Heine.

Back to the Embankment, whence a number of boat tours with on-board entertainment, such as the Bateaux London restaurant (7839 3572) and the jolly Queen Mary floating nightclub (7240 9404), embark. On dry land stands **Cleopatra's Needle**, a stone obelisk first erected in Egypt under Pharaoh Tothmes III in 1500 BC, and which underwent truly epic adventures (not least of which was its being abandoned and then rescued after a storm in the Bay of Biscay in the 19th century) before being repositioned on the Thames in 1878. **Embankment Gardens**, on the opposite side of the road, is a tranquil park with an annual programme of free summer music played out on its small public stage.

Centrepoint. *See p130.*

Sightseeing

Westminster

The heavyweights of London's sightseeing world.

Here's the London that the folks back home need to know that you've been and seen: Trafalgar Square, Houses of Parliament, Westminster Abbey, Big Ben – wham, bam, you've done the classic sights of London (and you'll have to leave for other pleasures, thin on the ground in this monumental centre). Westminster has been at the heart of the Church and monarchy for almost 1,000 years, since Edward the Confessor built his 'West Minster' and palace on marshy Thorney Island in the 11th century. Politics came to the fore in the 14th century, when the first Parliament met in the abbey. Today the splendid Houses of Parliament provide an iconic backdrop for holiday photos: go on, put yourself in the picture beneath Big Ben. Everyone does.

Trafalgar Square

Map p401 K7

Leicester Square tube or Charing Cross tube/rail.
The centrepiece of London was conceived by the Prince Regent, later George IV, who was obsessed with building monuments to imperial Britain. He commissioned John Nash to create a grand square to pay homage to Britain's naval power and raise the tone of the area. It wasn't laid out until 1840, after the King's death, but Nash certainly did as he was told. The focal point is **Nelson's Column**, a tribute to the heroic Horatio, who died during the Battle of Trafalgar in 1805. This Corinthian column, designed by William Railton, is topped by a statue of Nelson by neo-classical architect Charles Barry. Hitler was so impressed by the monument that he ordered bombers not to touch it, hoping to erect it in Berlin once he had conquered Britain. The granite fountains were added in 1845 (then redesigned by Lutyens in 1939); and the bronze lions – the work of Edwin Landseer – in 1868. Statues of George IV and a couple of Victorian military heroes anchor three of the square's corners; modern sculpture takes up the fourth plinth, from spring 2005 the 15-foot (4.5-metre) *Alison Lapper Pregnant*, by Marc Quinn. Neo-classical buildings overlook the square: James Gibbs's **St Martin-in-the-Fields** (*see p133*), and one of the world's great art museums, the **National Gallery** (*see below*).

Trafalgar Square has always been one of the city's natural meeting points, even more

Big Ben clock tower. *See p136.*

so since it was semi-pedestrianised in 2003. Many protest marches finish here, and it's a boisterous spot on New Year's Eve. The Summer in the Square events (*see p266*) are further enlivening it. Technically, this is the geographical centre of London: on a traffic island on the south side (look for the statue of King Charles I on horseback) there's a plaque to prove it. This is the point from which all distances on signposts are measured and all street numbers ascend.

National Gallery

Trafalgar Square, WC2N 5DN (7747 2885/ www.nationalgallery.org.uk). Leicester Square tube/Charing Cross tube/rail. **Open** (incl Sainsbury

Wing) 10am-6pm Mon, Tue, Thur-Sun; 10am-9pm Wed. *Tours* 11.30am, 2.30pm daily; 6.30pm Wed. **Admission** free. *Special exhibitions* prices vary. **Credit** Shop MC, V. **Map** p401 K7.
Founded in 1824, this is a national treasure. From a mere 38 paintings at the start, the collection has grown into one of the greatest in the world, with more than 2,000 western European paintings. There are masterpieces from virtually every school of art, starting with 13th-century religious works and culminating in Van Gogh. You name it, they're here: da Vinci, Raphael, Rubens, Rembrandt, Van Dyck, Caravaggio, Turner, Constable, Gainsborough, Monet, Cézanne, Picasso... You can't see everything in one visit, but guided tours take in the major works and there are excellent free audio guides.

The Sainsbury Wing concentrates on the early Renaissance period, with an emphasis on Italian and Dutch painters. In the North Wing, look out for masterpieces by Rubens, Rembrandt and Vermeer. The East Wing has a strong collection of English paintings, include Constable's *The Hay Wain*, Turner's romantic watercolours and works by Gainsborough, Reynolds and Hogarth. The real big-ticket items, however, are the Impressionist paintings: Monet's *Water Lilies* series, Van Gogh's *Chair* and Seurat's *Bathers at Asnières* are the stars.

The gallery is midway through a £21m renovation. A new entrance from Trafalgar Square opened in September 2004, along with a splendidly refurbished Central Hall, used as a Renaissance gallery to showcase, currently, works by Titian, and a glass-roofed inner courtyard. Public facilities including information centres, cloakrooms and cafés are also being upgraded to a standard befitting a gallery of this status as works continue.

Major exhibitions in 2005 are 'Caravaggio: the Final Years' (23 Feb-22 May); 'Stubbs and the Horse' (29 June-25 Sept); and 'Rubens: from Italy to Antwerp' (26 Oct-15 Jan 2006). Smaller free shows focus on John Virtue's London paintings (9 Mar-5 June); still lifes in 'The Stuff of Life' (14 July-2 Oct); and Renaissance reconstruction photographer Tom Hunter (7 Dec-15 Mar 2006).

National Portrait Gallery
2 St Martin's Place, WC2H 0HE (7306 0055/www. npg.org.uk). Leicester Square tube/Charing Cross tube/rail. **Open** 10am-6pm Mon-Wed, Sat, Sun; 10am-9pm Thur, Fri. *Tours* throughout Aug, times vary. **Admission** free. *Special exhibitions* prices vary. **Credit** AmEx, MC, V. **Map** p401 K7.
Subjects of the portraits hanging here range from Tudor royalty to present-day celebrities, of interest for contributions not only to history but to culture, sport, science, business and government. Londoners drop in frequently, partly because it has a personal feel to it, a result of the subject matter, its manageable size and its attractive design, and partly because there's a lovely restaurant on the top floor.

The portraits are organised chronologically from top to bottom: start on the second floor and work your way down. One of the gallery's most prized

possessions is the only known portrait of William Shakespeare. It also forms a fascinating 'who's who' of medieval monarchy: there's a room devoted to pictures of Mary, Queen of Scots, and a portrait of Henry VIII by Holbein. Dickens, Darwin and Disraeli (the latter painted by Millais) are among those on the first floor. Recent historical figures include union leader Arthur Scargill and his nemesis Margaret Thatcher, photographed by Helmut Newton. She didn't have much time for him, and it shows. New to the collection are footballer David Beckham, architect John Pawson, novelist Margaret Drabble, broadcaster Sue MacGregor and a squadron of Athens 2004 successes, including boxer Amir Khan.

Exhibitions for 2005 include: portraits by photographer Lee Miller (3 Feb-30 May); 'Conquering England: Ireland in Victorian London' (9 Mar-19 June); in collaboration with the BBC, 'The World's Most Photographed' (6 July-30 Oct); and a major exhibition of 'Self-Portrait Painting 1500-2000' (20 Oct-29 Jan 2006).

St Martin-in-the-Fields
Trafalgar Square, WC2N 4JJ (7766 1100/Brass Rubbing Centre 7930 9306/box office evening concerts 7839 8362/www.stmartin-in-the-fields.org). Leicester Square tube/Charing Cross tube/rail. **Open** *Church* 8am-6.30pm daily. *Services* 8am, 5.30pm Mon-Fri; 1pm, 5pm, 6pm (not 5.30pm) Wed; 9am Sat; 8am, 10am, noon, 2.15pm, 5pm, 6.30pm Sun. *Brass Rubbing Centre* 10am-6pm Mon-Sat; noon-6pm Sun. *Evening concerts* Thur-Sat & alternate Tue 7.30pm. **Admission** free. *Brass rubbing* £2.90-£15. *Evening concerts* prices vary. **Credit** MC, V. **Map** p401 L7.
A church has stood on this site since the 13th century, 'in the fields' between Westminster and the City; this one was built in 1726 by James Gibbs, who designed it in a curious combination of neo-classical and baroque styles. This is the parish church for Buckingham Palace (note the royal box to the left of the gallery), but it is perhaps best known for its classical music concerts (*see p304*). It also has a good café, a small gallery and the London Brass Rubbing Centre. Its churchyard contains the graves of painters Reynolds and Hogarth. There are plans for a £34m refurbishment that would give it wheelchair-accessible toilets and a glazed pavilion entrance.

Around the Mall

Map p401 K7
Leicester Square tube or Charing Cross tube/rail.
From Trafalgar Square, the grand processional route of the Mall passes beneath Aston Webb's 1910 Admiralty Arch to the Victoria Memorial. The road was not designed as a triumphal approach to **Buckingham Palace** (*see p117*) at the other end, despite being tarmacked in pink to match the Queen's forecourt: Charles II had the street laid out before the palace was even a royal residence. He wanted a new place for 'pallemaille', a popular game that involved

hitting a ball through a hoop at the end of a long alley. Nearby Pall Mall, his favourite pitch, had become too crowded for the sport.

As you walk along the Mall, look out on the right for **Carlton House Terrace**, the last project completed by John Nash before his death. It was built on the site of Carlton House, which was George IV's home until he decided it wasn't fit for a king and built Buckingham Palace to replace it. Part of the terrace now houses the multidisciplinary **Institute of Contemporary Arts** (ICA; *see below*).

On the south side of St James's Park the Wellington Barracks, home of the Foot Guards, contains the **Guards' Museum** (*see below*). At the park's southern end is Birdcage Walk, named after the aviary that James I built there. Nearby are the Georgian terraces of Queen Anne's Gate and Old Queen Street.

Guards' Museum

Wellington Barracks, Birdcage Walk, SW1E 6HQ (7414 3428). St James's Park tube. **Open** 10am-4pm daily (last entry 3.30pm). **Admission** £2; £1 concessions; free under-16s. **Credit** *Shop* AmEx, MC, V. **Map** p400 J9.

The Changing of the Guard is one of London's great spectacles (*see p262* **Pomp & ceremony**). This small museum, founded in the 17th century under Charles II, records the history of the British Army's five Guards regiments. It contains mainly uniforms and paintings, set to martial music, plus some curios. A new exhibition honours the regiments' involvement in the Crimean War, complete with damaged cutlery and bullet-riddled uniforms. The shop has a good selection of toy soldiers.

ICA Gallery

The Mall, SW1Y 5AH (box office 7930 3647/ www.ica.org.uk). Piccadilly Circus tube/Charing Cross tube/rail. **Open** *Galleries* noon-7.30pm daily. **Membership** *Daily* £1.50, £1 concessions Mon-Fri; £2.50, £1.50 concessions Sat, Sun; free under-14s. *Annual* £30; £20 concessions. **Credit** AmEx, DC, MC, V. **Map** p401 K8.

Founded in 1948 by the anarchist Herbert Read, the ICA still revels in a remit that challenges traditional notions of art from its incongruously establishment-looking home. Scores of challengers have held their first exhibitions here: Henry Moore, Picasso, Max Ernst, Damien Hirst, Helen Chadwick and Gary Hume. Its cinema shows London's artiest films, its theatre stages performance art and quality gigs and its art exhibitions are always talking points. All this is achieved to the high presentation standards befitting a national institution. The annual Beck's Futures exhibition and art prize features the best of contemporary painting, sculpture, photography, installation and video (mid Mar-mid May).

Whitehall to Parliament Square

Map p401 L8-L9

Westminster tube or Charing Cross tube/rail.

You're in civil servant territory now. Lined with faux-imperial government buildings, the long, gentle curve of Whitehall is named after Henry VIII's magnificent palace, which burned to the ground in 1698. The street is still home to the Ministry of Defence, the Foreign Office and the Treasury among others. They're closed to the public, but pop into the **Whitehall Theatre** (No.14) for a peek at its gorgeous art nouveau interior. Halfway down the street, the **Horse Guards** building faces the **Banqueting House** (*see below*), London's first Italianate building.

Nearby is Edwin Lutyens's plain memorial to the dead of both world wars, the **Cenotaph**, and, on **Downing Street** (closed off by iron security gates), the equally plain homes of the prime minister and chancellor, at Nos.10 and 11. At the end of King Charles Street, home of the Foreign Office, sit the **Cabinet War Rooms** (*see p136*), the operations centre used by Churchill during World War II air raids, alongside which a new Churchill Museum opens in early 2005.

At the end of Whitehall, **Parliament Square** has architecture on an appropriately grand scale. Constructed in 1868, it features the fantastical, neo-Gothic **Middlesex Guildhall** (1906-13) on the west side. Just behind that is **Westminster Central Hall** with its great black dome, used for conferences (the first assembly of the United Nations was held here in 1946) and Methodist church services. The buildings overlook the shady square with its statues of British politicians, such as Disraeli and Churchill, and one outsider, Abraham Lincoln, who sits sombrely to one side. Protesters often encamp themselves here, to the increasing displeasure of the authorities – a worrying sign of the times.

Nearby, **Westminster Abbey** (*see p138*) is the most venerable ancient building in central London. Much smaller, **St Margaret's Church** (*see p138*) stands beside it: Pepys and Churchill were married here and it's still a popular choice for society weddings.

If it is true, as some say, that few buildings in London really dazzle, the extravagant **Houses of Parliament** (*see p136*) are an exception. Although formally still known as the Palace of Westminster, the only surviving part of the medieval royal palace is Westminster Hall (and the **Jewel Tower**, just south of Westminster Abbey, *see p138*). One note: the legendary **Big Ben** is actually the name of the bell, not the clock tower that houses it. In its shadow, at the end of Westminster Bridge, stands a statue of the warrier Boudicca and her daughters gesticulating toward Parliament.

Banqueting House

Whitehall, SW1A 2ER (7930 4179/www.hrp. org.uk). Westminster tube/Charing Cross tube/ rail. **Open** 10am-5pm Mon-Sat. **Admission** £4; £3 concessions; £2.60 5-15s; free under-5s. **Credit** MC, V. **Map** p401 L8.

Designed by the great neo-classicist Inigo Jones in 1622, this was one of the first Palladian buildings in London. It is also the only surviving part of Henry VIII's Whitehall Palace, which burned down in 1698. The cool simplicity of the exterior belies the sumptuous ceiling in the beautifully proportioned first-floor hall, painted by Rubens no less. Charles I commissioned the Flemish artist to glorify his father James I, 'the wisest fool in Christendom', and celebrate the divine right of the Stuart kings. A bust over the entrance commemorates the fact that Charles was beheaded here in 1649. The event is marked annually on 31 January with a small ceremony and service. Call to check the hall is open before you visit: the building sometimes closes for corporate and government functions. Lunchtime concerts are held here on the first Monday of every month except August.

Cabinet War Rooms & Churchill Museum

Clive Steps, King Charles Street, SW1A 2AQ (7930 6961/www.iwm.org.uk). St James's Park or Westminster tube. **Open** 9.30am-6pm daily. Last

Watermarks What lies beneath

'The St Lawrence is mere water. The Missouri muddy water. The Thames is liquid history.' So declared politician John Burns to an American visitor in 1929. This may sound like so much patriotic bombast (well, it probably was), but Burns had a point. The Thames is a remarkable repository of historical artefacts, thousands of which have been unearthed from its mud in recent centuries. Many fell in, some were deliberately placed. All tell something of London's past.

Pre-Roman communities put votive offerings in the water for ritual or religious reasons, and the city's museums bulge with Stone Age axe-heads, Bronze Age spears and Iron Age daggers. One of the most impressive pieces is the Iron Age Battersea Shield, a decorative beauty in bronze and red glass that was found in the water near Battersea Bridge and is now on display at the British Museum.

More recent items include the clamps that the Romans used to castrate priests of the goddess Cybele; the Seax of Beagnoth, a ninth- to tenth-century knife with the only complete inscription of the Anglo-Saxon runic alphabet in existence; toys dating back to the 13th century that changed academic ideas about medieval childhood; and the Great Seal (metal not mammal), netted by a fisherman in 1689, the year after James II had dropped it into the river as he fled London, hoping, fatuously, to sabotage William of Orange's attempts to gain the throne.

Historians studying the Victorian period have long owed a debt of gratitude to the early 19th-century sewers that spewed directly into the Thames carrying many household items with them. And we're talking full-blown furniture, as well as buttons and buckles. A journalist wrote in 1867 that when the River Fleet, a Thames tributary, flooded through the cellars of Clerkenwell, it caused an 'exciting spectacle of clamorous men and women in boats, surrounding the mouth of the great sewer, watching for the appearance of their goods'.

Archaeologists of the future will have their work cut out to analyse the detritus that modern London leaves behind: the Port of London Authority removes 3,000 tons of solid waste from the river each year. In years past, people could earn a living from the foreshore: from the coal that fell off the barges to the riverine bones that could be ground up and used as manure. Nowadays, these 'mudlarks' are amateurs, stepping cautiously over supermarket trolleys and mattresses, and usually reporting finds of interest to the Museum of London.

There is also, of course, a bodily element to the Thames's content. A horde of Bronze Age skulls belonging to Celtic men aged between 25 and 35 was found near Battersea in the 19th century and 48 skulls from the second century AD were found in the City; both sets were probably laid for votive reasons. Sadly, death caused by the river is not rare either. Bathers, Civil War soldiers, fishermen and walkers... all have been swept away. Even now, 80 to 100 people drown in the waters each year although 80 per cent of those are reckoned to be suicides.

entry 5pm. **Admission** £10; £8 concessions; £5 unemployed; £5/£4 disabled; £8/£7 group ticket per person; free under-15s. (All prices include audio guides.) **Credit** MC, V. **Map** p401 K9.

A serious and informative blast from the past, this small underground set of rooms was Churchill's war bunker. Almost nothing has been changed since it was closed on 16 August 1945: every book, chart and pin in the map room remains in place, as does the BBC microphone he used when making his famous addresses to the nation. Churchill's bedroom, the setting for his catnaps, displays a chamber pot and nightshirt; the Transatlantic Telephone Room had a hotline to the White House; and there's also a collection of Churchill's papers and speeches. The Churchill Suite comprises the PM's private rooms, including a kitchen and his wife's bedroom. The furnishings are spartan, vividly evoking the wartime atmosphere. The audio guide's sound effects – wailing sirens, Churchill's wartime speeches – add to the nostalgia. A new state-of-the-art Churchill Museum opens in February 2005, promising to take visitors entertainingly through the life of the leader many still consider Britain's finest.

Houses of Parliament

Parliament Square, SW1A 0AA (Commons information 7219 4272/Lords information 7219 3107/tours information 0870 906 3773/www. parliament.uk). Westminster tube. **Open** (when in session) *House of Commons Visitors' Gallery* 2.30-10.30pm Mon; 11.30am-7.30pm Tue, Wed; 11.30am-7.30pm Thur; 9.30am-3pm Fri. *House of Lords Visitors' Gallery* from 2.30pm Mon-Wed; from 11am Thur, occasional Fri. *Tours* summer recess only; phone for details. **Admission** Visitors' Gallery free. *Tours* £7; £5 concessions; free under-5s. **Credit** *Tours* MC, V. **Map** p401 L9.

This neo-Gothic extravaganza is so spectacular it's enough to make you want to go into politics. The ornate architecture is the ultimate expression of Victorian self-confidence, even if its style was a throwback to the Middle Ages. Completed in 1860, it was the creation of architect Charles Barry, who won the architectural competition to replace the original Houses of Parliament, which were destroyed by fire in 1834. Barry was assisted on the interiors by Augustus Pugin. The original palace was home to the young Henry VIII, until he upped sticks to Whitehall in 1532. Although the first Parliament was held here in 1275, Westminster did not become its permanent home until Henry moved out. Parliament was originally housed in the choir stalls of St Stephen's Chapel where members sat facing each other from opposite sides, and the tradition continues today. The only remaining parts of the original palace are the Jewel Tower and the almost mythically historic Westminster Hall, one of the finest medieval buildings in Europe.

In all, there are 1,000 rooms, 100 staircases, 11 courtyards, eight bars and six restaurants (plus a visitors' cafeteria). None of them is open to the public, but you can watch the Commons or Lords in

The **Cabinet War Rooms**, where Winston Churchill spent his finest hours.

session from the galleries. In truth, there's not much to see: most debates are sparsely attended and unenthusiastically conducted. Visitors queue at St Stephen's Entrance (it's well signposted) and, in high season, may wait a couple of hours. (Note that in 2004, following a couple of flour-bomb throwing security scares, there was talk of restricting public access.) The best spectacle is Prime Minister's Question Time at noon on Wednesday, but you need to book advance tickets through your MP or embassy, who can also arrange tours. Parliament goes into recess in summer, at which times tours of the main ceremonial rooms, including Westminster Hall and the two houses, are available to the general public.

Jewel Tower

Abingdon Street, SW1P 3JY (7222 2219/www. english-heritage.org.uk). Westminster tube. **Open** *Apr-Oct* 10am-5pm daily. *Nov-Mar* 10am-4pm daily. **Admission** (EH) £2.60; £2 concessions; £1.30 5-16s; free under-5s. **Credit** MC, V. **Map** p401 L9.

Emphatically not the home of the Crown Jewels, this old stone tower was built in 1365 to house Edward III's gold and silver plate. It's still worth a look, though, because, along with Westminster Hall, it is the only surviving part of the medieval Palace of Westminster. From 1621 to 1864 the place stored Parliamentary records, and it contains an exhibition on Parliaments past. On the ground floor, look out for the ninth-century Rhenish sword dug up in the gardens over the road in 1948.

St Margaret's Church

Parliament Square, SW1P 3PL (7654 4840 www.westminster-abbey.org). St James's Park or Westminster tube. **Open** 9.30am-3.45pm Mon-Fri; 9.30am-1.45pm Sat; 2-5pm Sun (times may change at short notice due to services). *Services* 11am Sun; phone to check for other days. **Admission** free. **Map** p401 K9.

Some of the most impressive pre-Reformation stained glass in London can be found here. The east window (1509) commemorates the marriage of Henry VIII and Catherine of Aragon. Later windows celebrate Britain's first printer, William Caxton, buried here in 1491, explorer Sir Walter Raleigh, executed in Old Palace Yard, and writer John Milton (1608-74), who married his second wife, Katherine Woodcock, here. Founded in the 12th century, this historic church was demolished in the reign of Edward III, but rebuilt from 1486 to 1523. Since then it has been restored many times. As the official church of the House of Commons since 1614, its bells are rung when a new Speaker is chosen. Above the doorway is a bust of Charles I, looking across the street at a statue of his old adversary, Cromwell.

Westminster Abbey

20 Dean's Yard, SW1P 3PA (7222 5152/tours 7654 4900/www.westminster-abbey.org). St James's Park or Westminster tube. **Open** *Chapter House, Nave & Royal Chapels* 9.30am-3.45pm Mon, Tue, Thur, Fri; 9.30am-7pm Wed; 9.30am-1.45pm Sat. *Abbey Museum* 10.30am-4pm Mon-Sat. *Cloisters* 8am-6pm Mon-Sat. *College Garden* Apr-Sept 10am-6pm Tue-Thur; Oct-Mar 10am-4pm Tue-Thur. Last entry 1hr before closing. *Services* 7.30am, 8am, 12.30pm, 5pm Mon-Fri; 8am, 9am, 3pm Sat; 8am, 10am, 11.15am, 3pm, 5.45pm, 6.30pm Sun. **Admission** £7.50; £5 concessions; free under-11s with paying adult; £15 family. **Credit** MC, V. **Map** p401 K9.

Westminster Abbey has been synonymous with British royalty since 1066, when Edward the Confessor built a church on the site just in time for his own funeral: it was consecrated eight days before he died. Since then, a 'who's who' of monarchy have been buried here, and, with two exceptions (Edwards V and VIII), every English monarch since William the Conqueror (1066) has been crowned in the abbey. In October 2005 the St Edward Millennium celebrates the 1,000th anniversary of the Confessor's birth with a variety of special events.

Of the original abbey, only the Pyx Chamber (the one-time royal treasury) and the Norman undercroft remain; the Gothic nave and choir were rebuilt in the 13th century; the Henry VII Chapel, with its spectacular fan vaulting, was added in 1503-12; and Nicholas Hawksmoor's west towers completed the building in 1745.

The interior is cluttered with monuments to statesmen, scientists, musicians and poets. Poets' Corner contains the graves of Dryden, Samuel Johnson, Browning and Tennyson – although it has plaques for many more, most are buried elsewhere. The centrepiece of the octagonal Chapter House is faded 13th-century tiled floor, while the Little Cloister with its pretty garden offers respite from the crowds, especially during free lunchtime concerts (call for details). Worth a look, too, are ten statues of 20th-century Christian martyrs in 15th-century niches over the west door. Come early, late, or on midweek afternoons to avoid the crowds.

Millbank

Map p401 L10-L1

Pimlico or Westminster tube.

Millbank runs along the river from Parliament to Vauxhall Bridge. Just off here is **Smith Square**, home to **St John's Smith Square**, an exuberant baroque fantasy built as a church in 1713-28, but now a venue for classical music (*see p302*) with a basement bar-restaurant. Nearby, on Lord North Street, is a clutch of fine Georgian houses – one of the most prestigious addresses in London. By the river, the Victoria Tower Gardens contain a statue of suffragette leader Emmeline Pankhurst, a cast of Rodin's glum-looking *Burghers of Calais* and the Buxton Drinking Fountain, which commemorates the emancipation of slaves.

Further along the river, just north of Vauxhall Bridge, stands the **Tate Britain** gallery (*see p139*). With its excellent collection of British art, it occupies the former site of the

Millbank Penitentiary, one of Britain's fouler Victorian prisons, which was demolished in 1890. Overshadowing the Tate is the 387-foot (240-metre) **Millbank Tower**, erstwhile home to the Labour Party. Across the river, the cream and green-glass block is the rather conspicuous HQ of the external security service, MI6.

Tate Britain

Millbank, SW1P 4RG (7887 8000/www.tate. org.uk). Pimlico tube/C10, 77A, 88 bus. **Open** 10am-5.50pm daily. *Tours* 11am, noon, 2pm, 3pm Mon-Fri; noon, 3pm Sat, Sun. **Admission** free. *Special exhibitions* prices vary. **Credit** *Shop* MC, V. **Map** p401 K11.

Tate Modern (*see p83*), its younger, sexier sibling, seems to get all the attention, but don't forget the Britain: it contains London's second great collection of art, after the National Gallery. With the opening of the Modern, oodles of space was freed up to accommodate the collection of British art from the 16th century to the present day.

The collection fills the 'something for everyone' remit that you'd hope from a gallery whose exhibits span five centuries. It takes in works by artists such as Hogarth, the Blakes (William and Peter), Gainsborough, Constable (who gets three rooms all to himself), Reynolds, Bacon and Moore. Turner is particularly well represented, even more so since 2003 when the gallery recovered two classics – *Shade and Darkness – The Evening of the Deluge* and *Light and Colour (Goethe's Theory)* – that were stolen in 1994. And Tate Modern doesn't have a monopoly on contemporary artists: there are works here by Howard Hodgkin, Lucian Freud and David Hockney. The shop is well stocked with posters and art books, and the restaurant highly regarded.

You can also have the best of both art worlds, thanks to the Tate-to-Tate boat service (*see p83*).

Exhibitions planned for 2005 include 'Turner Whistler Monet' (10 Feb-15 May); 'Joshua Reynolds – The Creation of Celebrity' (26 May-25 Sept); 'A Picture of Britain', celebrating British landscape painters (16 June-4 Sept); 'Degas, Sickert and Toulouse-Lautrec – Modern Life in Britain and France 1870-1910' (6 Oct-9 Jan 2006); and the annual Turner Prize (27 Oct-22 Jan 2006).

Victoria & Pimlico

Maps p400 J11

Pimlico tube or Victoria tube/rail.

Victoria Street, stretching from Parliament Square to Victoria Station, links political London with a rather more colourful and chaotic backpackers' London. Victoria Coach Station is a short distance away in Buckingham Palace Road; Belgrave Road provides an almost unbroken line of cheap and fairly grim hotels.

Not to be confused with the Abbey in Parliament Square, **Westminster Cathedral** (*see below*) is part-hidden by office blocks, and

comes as a pleasant surprise. The striking, red-brick Byzantine church was built between 1896 and 1903. Continuing along Victoria Street towards Parliament Square, you come to **Christchurch Gardens**, burial site of Thomas ('Colonel') Blood, the 17th-century rogue who nearly got away with stealing the Crown Jewels. A memorial is dedicated to the suffragettes, who held meetings at Caxton Hall, visible on the far side of the gardens. **New Scotland Yard**, with its famous revolving sign, is in Broadway, but there's nothing much else to see there. **Strutton Ground**, on the other side of Victoria Street, has a small market. Richard Rogers's **Channel Four Building** is on the corner of Chadwick and Horseferry Roads.

At the other end of Victoria Station from Victoria Street, smart **Pimlico** fills the triangle of land formed by Chelsea Bridge, Ebury Street, Vauxhall Bridge Road and the river. Thomas Cubitt built the elegant white stone streets and squares in the 1830s. The posh neighbourhood was immortalised in one of the great Ealing Comedies, *Passport to Pimlico*, in which the residents discover that their district is technically part of France. In general, though, Pimlico is residential and a bit dull for tourists, although many stay on the Belgrave Road.

Westminster Cathedral

Victoria Street, SW1P 1QW (7798 9055/www. westminstercathedral.org.uk). Victoria tube/ rail. **Open** 7am-7pm Mon-Fri, Sun; 8am-7pm Sat. *Services* 7am, 8am, 10.30am, 12.30pm, 1.05pm, 5.30pm Mon-Fri; 8am, 9am, 10.30am, 12.30pm, 6pm Sat; 8am, 9am, 10.30am, noon, 5.30pm, 7pm Sun. **Admission** free; donations appreciated. *Campanile* £3; £1.50 concessions. **No credit cards**. **Map** p400 J10.

Westminster Abbey might be more famous, but Westminster Cathedral is spectacular in its own bizarre way. Part wedding cake, part sweet stick, this neo-Byzantine confection is Britain's premier Catholic cathedral, built in 1895-1903 by John Francis Bentley, who was inspired by the Hagia Sophia in Istanbul. The land on which it is built had been a bull-baiting ring and a pleasure garden before being bought by the Catholic Church in 1884. With such a festive exterior, you'd expect an equally ornate interior. Not so: the inside has yet to be finished. Even so, you can get a taste of what the faithful will achieve from the magnificent columns and mosaics (made from more than 100 kinds of marble). Eric Gill's sculptures of the Stations of the Cross (1914-18) are world renowned. Simple and objective, they were controversial at time of installation, labelled Babylonian and crude. Westminster Cathedral's nave is the broadest in England, and dark wood floors and flickering candles add to the drama. The view from the 273ft (83m) bell tower is superb: best of all, it's got a lift.

South Kensington & Knightsbridge

Where to smarten up your mind and your wardrobe.

Science Museum. *See p141.*

South Kensington

Map p397 D9-D10

Gloucester Road or South Kensington tube.
Welcome to London's intellectual hub, an area where it's hard to walk 100 paces without chancing upon some august museum or lofty institute. This situation owes much to Queen Victoria's husband Prince Albert, who was one of the leading lights behind the establishment of a complex of cultural and academic institutions in South Kensington using the profits of 1851's landmark Great Exhibition. Consequently, the **Natural History Museum**, with its dinosaurs and volcanoes, sits cheek by jowl with the technology-stuffed **Science Museum** and the endlessly aesthetic **Victoria & Albert Museum** (for all three, *see p141*). Don't let

their proximity tempt you to 'do' all three in a day. Each contains an encyclopedia's worth of content: they are best inspected at a more leisurely pace, and reward multiple visits.

South Kensington's Victorian flowering was residential as well as cultural. This was a prime area for planned estate development (much of it on farmland), resulting in an unusual degree of uniformity. Elegant terraces of family houses sprang up, in retrospective Georgian style. Some of these are now occupied by numerous international institutes (French, German, Polish, Islamic); other cultural institutions also cluster here. On Prince Consort Road, the **Royal College of Music** (7589 3643) offers concerts and a museum containing 700 instruments dating from 1480, open from 2pm to 4.30pm on term-time Wednesdays. The **Royal**

Geographical Society (1 Kensington Gore, 7591 3000) has statues of Ernest Shackleton and David Livingstone on its frontage and runs a lively programme of events.

Natural History Museum
Cromwell Road, SW7 5BD (7942 5000/www. nhm.ac.uk). South Kensington tube. **Open** 10am-5.50pm Mon-Sat; 11am-5.50pm Sun. **Tours** every half-hour, 11am-4pm daily. **Admission** free. *Exhibitions* prices vary. **Credit** MC, V. **Map** p397 D10.
Built to hold the zoological specimens that were rapidly filling the British Museum, this stunning museum thrills from the moment of entry. The Diplodocus skeleton that excites all the children isn't even the biggest creature here: that honour belongs to the blue whale in the Mammals room. The museum splits into Life and Earth galleries, with the former including a dinosaur display with all the photos, models and paintings you could desire, and a Creepy Crawlies zone that comprehensively sorts your mites from your ants. The Earth Galleries are entered through a suspended globe: within minutes you can relive the Kobe earthquake in a supermarket simulator or drool over gemstones in Earth's Treasury. Alternatively, bring your rocks to the Earth Lab for a comparison with the museum's own. The recently opened Darwin Centre has an incredible 22 million exhibits in alcohol-filled jars. This is a full-on research centre, holding many of the original 'type' specimens from which species were first identified. There are daily opportunities to meet curators and researchers, and the tours (roughly six per day, every hour, booking essential) take you around the working sections, including the bizarre Tank Room, which contains specimens of the largest animals. The Wildlife Garden is open to the public between May and September.

Science Museum
Exhibition Road, SW7 2DD (7942 4454/www.science museum.org.uk). South Kensington tube. **Open** 10am-6pm daily. **Admission** free. *Exhibitions* prices vary. **Credit** AmEx, MC, V. **Map** p397 D9.
Ignore the unprepossessing entrance hall, because the fireworks begin just around the corner. This is a marvellous place with enough buttons, lights and interaction to delight children, and plenty of serious displays for the adults. The museum aims to make science interesting and accessible to an audience that might have thought of it as just another school subject. It demonstrates how science filters down through myriad elements of daily life, with displays on engines, cars, planes, ships, farming, medicine and computers. The new Energy exhibition uses a variety of interactive displays – dancefloor mats and electrocution among them – to show how energy powers every aspect of life, and there's more interactive fun in the hands-on Launch Pad gallery. There's a five-storey IMAX cinema, and the Dana Centre (open weekdays only), an informal venue with bar and restaurant for adults to voice their concerns, and raise questions, about contemporary science issues. Children aged eight to 11 can, with an accompanying adult, stay overnight on the regular Science Nights (eight in 2005; ring for details).

Victoria & Albert Museum
Cromwell Road, SW7 2RL (7942 2000/ www.vam.ac.uk). South Kensington tube. **Open** 10am-5.45pm Mon, Tue, Thur-Sun; 10am-10pm Wed, last Fri of mth. **Tours** daily; phone for details. **Admission** free. *Exhibitions* prices vary. **Credit** MC, V. **Map** p397 E10.
As spick 'n' span as any London attraction, the V&A is the peacock of the city's museum world. It parades a world-beating array of decorative arts, with around four million pieces of furniture, textiles, ceramics, sculpture, paintings, posters, jewellery and metalwork. It is sometimes hard to fathom exactly what the museum stands for (particularly since the name doesn't exactly help) but you should come and then make up your own mind. Items are grouped by theme, origin or age, and the map is not the most useful of navigational tools. Far better to wander idly and try to spot connections between, say, a cone-breasted Gaultier catsuit and Italian Renaissance sculpture. (The V&A's collection of the latter is the finest outside Italy.)

Less obviously child-oriented than its neighbouring museums, the V&A strikes a welcome note of calm. The world galleries on the ground floor have displays including beautiful Japanese swords and armour, while the highlights of the British galleries include Canova's *The Three Graces* and Henry VIII's writing desk. A new, permanent architecture gallery opened in November 2004, the first of its kind in the UK. Exhibitions for 2005 include 'Spectres, When Fashion Turns Back' (22 Feb-8 May), a look at how the past influences fashion, and 'International Arts and Crafts' (17 Mar-24 July), an exploration of the Arts and Crafts style. A display of Queen Maud of Norway's outfits will be displayed until early 2006.

Hyde Park & Kensington Gardens

Maps p394 & p395
Hyde Park Corner, Knightsbridge, Lancaster Gate or Queensway tube.
If the parks are the lungs of London, then this 1.5-mile-long space does most of the breathing. Residents and visitors in their thousands come here to walk, picnic, play sport, take a rowing boat out, listen to brass bands, admire art in the Serpentine Gallery (*see p114*), stroll around the points of interest, go horseriding (7723 2813) or just slump into a deckchair. It gets busy in summer, but there's always space for those seeking peace away from the footballers, rollerbladers and Frisbee throwers.

Snatched from the monks of Westminster Abbey by Henry VIII for hunting grounds, the parks were first opened to the public in the reign of James I in the early 17th century, although they were only frequented by the upper echelons of society. At the end of the 17th century, William III, suffering from asthma and averse to the dank air of Whitehall Palace, relocated to the village of Kensington and made his home in Kensington Palace. A corner of Hyde Park was sectioned off to make grounds for the palace, and although today the two merge, Kensington Gardens was closed to the public until King George II opened it on Sundays to those in formal dress only – soldiers, sailors and servants were not welcome.

These days, soldiers have an integral role in the park's life: at 10.30am each day (9.30am on Sundays), after a warm-up in the park, the Household Cavalry leaves its barracks near the Prince of Wales Gate and trots in full ceremonial dress to Whitehall for the Changing of the Guard. There are plenty of less formal attractions in Hyde Park, however, not least of which is the Serpentine Lake. Several sculptures of note include GF Watts's violently animated *Physical Energy*, a delightful bronze of Peter Pan and Jacob Epstein's depiction of *Rima, Spirit of Nature*, the unabashed nakedness of which inspired such anger upon its unveiling in 1925 that it was tarred and feathered twice for its sins. Hyde Park is also a focus for freedom of speech. It became a hotspot for mass demonstrations in the 19th century and remains so today – a march against war in Iraq in 2003 was the largest in its history. The legalisation of public assembly in the park led to the establishment of **Speakers' Corner** in 1872, where ranters both sane and bonkers have the floor. This isn't the place to come for balanced, political debate, but Marx, Engels, Lenin, Orwell and the Pankhursts all attended. Those with young children may feel more comfortable at the **Diana, Princess of Wales Memorial Playground** (*see p274*) or the memorial fountain (*see p143* **Water palaver**).

Kensington Palace

W8 4PX (7937 9561/www.hrp.org.uk). Bayswater, High Street Kensington or Queensway tube. **Open** *Mar-Oct* 10am-5pm daily; *Nov-Feb* 10am-4pm daily. **Admission** (LP) £10.80; £7.20 5-15s; £8.20 concessions; £32 family. **Credit** AmEx, MC, V. **Map** p394 B8.

Far more intimate than other, more regal palaces, Kensington exudes a warm, homely feel that visitors are quick to associate with its famous recent resident, Princess Diana, who had apartments here from 1981. A series of her dresses, including the blue silk number in which she danced with John Travolta at the White House, are permanently displayed alongside the Royal Ceremonial Dress Collection, an exhibition of royal and court dress dating from the 18th century. Until mid July 2005 there will also be an exhibition of 12 outfits from different stages of the Queen's life. Those preferring to avoid the entry fees to the State Apartments (the palace itself is closed to visitors) can still walk around the exquisite sunken gardens or take tea in the Orangery (dating from 1704) with its charming topiary gardens.

Don't judge the **Serpentine Gallery** by its staid exterior. *See p144.*

Water palaver

The grand opening on 6 July 2004 – and
ignominious closing a fortnight later – of the
Princess Diana Memorial Fountain in Hyde
Park unplugged a torrent of jocund tabloid
headlines like the above, for the silly season.
The fountain – more of a babbling moat,
actually – was conceived by US architect
Kathryn Gustafson. It's a circular granite
channel, with water pouring on to it and
flowing in two different directions, draped
'like a necklace' on a grassy slope near
the Serpentine bridge. The design is said
to reflect the personality of the princess,
which may be true – although the fountain's
cruellest critics likened it to a storm drain.
In any case, it's certainly caused enough
controversy, as did the late, lamented Diana.

There has been wrangling around the
fountain since 1999, when the project was
first dreamed up. A design competition was
launched in September 2001, narrowed down
to a shortlist of two in December of that year.
One, an avant-garde submission by Bombay-
born British artist Anish Kapoor, was
described as 'possibly shocking'. The other,
Gustafson's granite creation, was thought
more restrained and elegant. Many felt this
was more to Diana's taste, especially as the
idea behind the shallow, babbling stream on
a hillside was that children could gambol
happily in its sparkling waters. The princess,
once the world's most famous nursery school
teacher, liked to see children having fun.
Diana's mother's comments about a 'lack
of grandeur' were brushed aside, and
Gustafson it was who won the competition.

Work on the 700 tons of Cornish granite
chugged on for a year and the fountain
opened on schedule. The Queen, unveiling a
plaque and looking vaguely bemused as she
regarded the rushing water, referred to her
late daughter-in-law as a 'remarkable human
being'. Joining in the celebration, Diana's
brother, her two sons, and her ex-husband
all admired the watery tribute to an
'extraordinary' woman.

When the top brass had gone, however,
and ordinary folk, including hundreds of
Dianaphiles from all over the world,
converged on the fountain, the trouble began.
Not helped by unseasonally wet and stormy
weather, the grassy verges became mud
slicks under the onslaught of many paddling
feet. Wind-blown leaves clogged up the

system and caused an overflow. Worst of
all, the granite became slippery with algae,
causing several people to fall and hurt
themselves. At that point, the fountain was
closed and engineers brought in to roughen
the granite surface of the stone. The fountain
was reopened after health and safety checks.

These days visitors to the memorial
must approach the rushing water via a
roped-off walkway, stopping on the way to
be entertained by the fanatical poems and
tributes to the People's Princess pinned to
a tree by the entrance. Once they're in the
ring of bright water, however, restraint is
called for. A number of wardens (there were
seven in operation when we dropped by to
cool our heels) police the memorial, checking
there's no litter-dropping, dog-washing or
paddling. It's strictly toe-dangling only. It
doesn't seem the warm and inclusive
design that Kathryn Gustafson had planned.
Past articles celebrating this respected
architect's designs as 'acts of healing'
sound rather wistful in the aftermath of
the summer storms in Hyde Park.

Serpentine Gallery

*Kensington Gardens (nr Albert Memorial), W2 3XA
(7402 6075/www.serpentinegallery.org). Lancaster
Gate or South Kensington tube.* **Open** 10am-6pm
daily. *Tours* 3pm Sat. **Admission** free; donations
encouraged.

You tend to stumble across the Serpentine Gallery,
tucked away in the middle of the park, far from any
other building. The delicate 1930s tea pavilion belies
the vigour and variety of its contents, and the gallery
courts controversy with challenging exhibitions
by modern artists. 2005 sees work by Tomoko
Takahashi (Feb-June), who specialises in making art
from rubbish, followed by Argentina's Rirkrit
Tiravanija, gaining increasing renown for his interactive works. Each year, an architect who has not
previously completed a building in the UK designs
an outdoor pavilion, which plays host to the Park
Nights programme of open-air screenings, readings
and talks (May-Sept). The 2005 pavilion, which will
completely encompass the gallery, will be the work
of Dutch practice MVRDV with Arup.

Albert Memorial

*Kensington Gardens (opposite Royal Albert Hall),
SW7. South Kensington tube.*

'It would upset my equanimity to be permanently
ridiculed and laughed at in effigy,' suggested Prince
Albert in 1851. Well, the world should be glad that
his wishes were ignored because the Albert
Memorial is one of the great sculptural achievements
of the Victorian period. Created by Sir George
Gilbert Scott and unveiled in 1876 – 15 years after
Albert's death from typhoid – the Prince is surrounded on all sides by marble statues of famous
poets and painters, while pillars are crowned with
depictions of the sciences, and the arts are represented in a series of intricate mosaics. Overhead, the
dramatic 180ft (55m) spire is inlaid with many semi-
precious stones. The overall effect is perhaps best
appreciated from the Royal Albert Hall, opposite.

Knightsbridge

Maps p397 F9

Knightsbridge or South Kensington tube.

Knightsbridge may no longer be plagued by
highwaymen, but that doesn't mean people
aren't still leaving the area with their wallets
significantly the lighter. This is a modern-day
shopper's paradise. The vogueish **Harvey
Nichols** (*see p237*) still holds sway over the
top end of **Sloane Street**, where urban
princesses graze the shopping bags. Expensive
brands dominate on this otherwise
unremarkable road, which feels a bit like
Bond Street's staid sister, but Gucci, Chanel
and Christian Dior let you know you're in a
moneyed neighbourhood. More understated
is **Beauchamp Place**, a peaceful road with
plenty of good restaurants to break up the
haute, not to say haughty, couture.

That's all well and good, of course, but this
is Knightsbridge, and Knightsbridge means
one thing in the eyes of the wave of tourists
flooding Brompton Road each afternoon:
Harrods (*see p236*). From its tan bricks to
its olive green awning and green-coated
doormen, Harrods is an instantly recognisable
retailing legend. If you ever wondered if it's
only tourists who come here, take a look at the
line of chauffeured cars waiting round the back.
Originally a family grocer's, the world's most
famous department store now employs 5,000
people and takes over £1.5 million per day.
Under owner Mohammed Al Fayed it is ageing
gracefully, but Harrods wasn't without its
misspent youth: its first aeroplane was sold
in 1919, and in 1967 the Prince of Albania
purchased a baby elephant for Ronald Reagan.

Brompton and Belgravia serve primarily
as residential catchment areas for wealthy
families who imagine they couldn't survive
without Harrods' dog-grooming service on their
doorstep. It's perhaps not surprising to find a
pillar of penitence like the **Oratory Catholic
Church** (*see below*) amid the excess.

There's not much else in Brompton to fire
the imagination, however, bar Arne Jacobson's
Danish Embassy building (55 Sloane Street)
and the prospect of peering into other people's
living rooms. Belgravia is a little better, if still
lacking in atmosphere, but it does have a few
nice pubs tucked away behind its serious
marble parades: the Nag's Head (53 Kinnerton
Street, 7235 1135) and the Grenadier on Wilton
Row (No.18, 7235 3074) are worth seeking out.
St Paul's Knightsbridge, on Wilton Place, is
an appealing Victorian church with scenes from
the life of Jesus in ceramics tiling the nave, and
a wonderful wood-beamed ceiling. Otherwise,
the area is characterised by a cluster of foreign
embassies around Belgravia Square.

Oratory Catholic Church

*Thurloe Place, Brompton Road, SW7 2RP (7808
0900/www.bromptonoratory.com). South Kensington
tube.* **Open** 6.30am-8pm daily. *Services* 7am, 10am,
12.30am, 6pm daily; 7am, 8.30am, 10am, 11am,
12.30am, 4.30pm, 7pm Sun. **Admission** free;
donations appreciated. **Map** p397 E10.

The second-biggest Catholic church in the country,
after Westminster Cathedral, the Oratory was completed in 1884. It feels older, however, partly because
of its Baroque Italianate style but also because many
of its florid marbles, mosaics and statuary pre-date
the structure. Mazzuoli's late 17th-century apostle
statues, for example, once stood in Siena cathedral.
The combined effect of the treasures in shimmering
candlelight is awe inspiring. During the Cold War,
the church was used by the KGB as a dead letter box.
A stronghold of traditional Catholicism, the 11am
Sunday mass sung in Latin is particularly glorious.

Chelsea

Only Elvis Costello didn't want to go there.

Maps p396 & p397

Sloane Square tube.

Once famous for its painters, poets and air of design-led cool, today Chelsea is more about tanned bodies and bursting bank accounts. The heart of both 1960s swinging London and 1970s punk London, in the 21st century Chelsea epitomises the city's take on café society. The cost of living has seen off all but the most successful painters and punks, replacing them with financiers and footballers. There is still plenty to excite, but you need to get off the **King's Road** (the main thoroughfare) to unearth any historical treasures.

At the end of the King's Road closest to the tube station, **Sloane Square** gets its name from Sir Hans Sloane (1660-1753), a physician and canny entrepreneur who bought the Manor of Chelsea and saved the famously restorative **Chelsea Physic Garden** (*see p146*) from decline. His heirs are the Cadogans, who still own the large Chelsea Estate and a number of other properties. The **Royal Court** theatre (*see p335*), with its reputation for avant-garde performances, looks imperiously out over the square towards the King's Road, past Peter Jones, the polished department store beloved of lunching ladies from the Shires.

Overall, the King's Road is not what it once was, although it remains one of London's prime people-watching strips. Once the trendiest street in the city, it still has a few independent boutiques and antiques markets (including Antiquarius, *see p229*), but its glory days are largely over. Back in the swinging '60s, it became a focal point for designers such as Mary Quant (whose shop, Bazaar, stood at No.138) who dared the city to wear their creations. In the 1970s it became the bedrock for the punk movement, when Vivienne Westwood's shop, Sex, made headlines with its outlandish approach to style. It was there that Malcolm McLaren famously met John Lydon and Sid Vicious, and from that shop that the Sex Pistols reportedly got their names. Westwood still has a shop there (World's End, No.430) where the floor slopes drunkenly and the clock outside counts backwards, but the fashions within don't shock like they used to, which is somewhat symbolic of the King's Road itself, now much like a particularly posh high street, all Gaps and Starbucks. One of the bright spots is Bluebird,

(No.350, 020 7559 1000), in the 1923 garage of the record-breaking car, a Terence Conran restaurant. Gorgeous food, but it doesn't come cheap: it's easy to imagine what Sid Vicious would think of the street now.

Between the King's Road and Chelsea Embankment, the grounds of the **Royal Hospital** are best known these days as the site of the flashy, posh celebrity-magnet **Chelsea Flower Show** (*see p261*), but for 51 weeks of the year the area is quiet and peaceful, as befits a place of sanctuary for retired soldiers (*see p147* **Chelsea Pensioners**). The old Ranelagh Gardens, where the Flower Show was opened in 1742 and once had an ornamental lake, a Chinese Pavilion and large rococo rotunda encircled by stalls for tea and wine drinking. The surrounding shrubbery and wooded paths were meeting and posing places for nobility and society.

Riverside Chelsea

Continuing down Royal Hospital Road toward the **Chelsea Physic Garden** (*see p146*), and just past the **National Army Museum**, you pass **Tite Street**, where Whistler once had a studio, and where dramatist Oscar Wilde lived (at No.34) before his arrest for gross indecency at the Cadogan Hotel. Late Victorian Chelsea, when Whistler and Wilde socialised there, was self-consciously stylish.

The heart of the original Chelsea village is **Chelsea Old Church** (*see p146*), where the saint and statesman Thomas More once sang in the choir. More's river-facing home, Beaufort House, is long gone. You can still see parts of the original orchard wall bordering the gardens of the houses on the west side of Paulton's Square off Beaufort Street. More's country life ended in 1535 when he was thrown into the Tower of London by Henry VIII for refusing to swear to the Act of Succession and the Oath of Supremacy. L Cubitt Bevis's statue of the 'man for all seasons' stands outside the Old Church.

The artists and writers' community in Chelsea was centred at the western end of Chelsea Embankment, on **Cheyne Walk**, where the fashionable houses have changed little over the years. Blue plaques are thick on the walls: George Eliot at No.4; Pre-Raphaelite painter DG Rossetti at No.16; JM Whistler at

Chelsea Physic Garden.

No.96; JMW Turner at No.119. Thomas Carlyle lived on **Cheyne Row**, north of the Walk, and his house is open to view (*see below*).

Further west, **Lots Road Power Station**, once the power behind London Underground, became a target for property developers when the last generator was turned off in October 2002 but it remains resolutely unconverted. Upriver from there, the transformation of **Chelsea Harbour** from industrial wasteland into opulent offices, swish hotels, shops, restaurants and marina has made it a playground for the rich and famous.

Carlyle's House

24 Cheyne Row, SW3 5HL (7352 7087/www. nationaltrust.org.uk). Sloane Square tube/11, 19, 22, 39, 45, 49, 219 bus. **Open** *Apr-Oct* 2-5pm Wed-Fri; 11am-5pm Sat, Sun. **Admission** (NT) £4; £2 5-16s. **Map** p397 E12.

This house witnessed lively argument and tension when the prim scholar lived here from 1834 with his wife Jane, their days filled with visits from the Victorian glitterati, including Dickens, Tennyson, Darwin, Browning and Trollope. In the well preserved house visitors can see the original decor, furniture, books and pictures, and at the top is the 'sound-proofed' study where the writer insisted on complete quiet as he spent 13 years slaving at *The History of Frederick the Great*.

Chelsea Old Church

Cheyne Walk, Old Church Street, SW3 5DQ (7352 5627/www.chelseaoldchurch.org.uk). Sloane Square tube/11, 19, 22, 49, 319 bus. **Open** 2-4pm Tue, Thur; *Services* 8am, 10am, 11am; *Evensong* 6pm. **Admission** free; donations appreciated. **Map** p397 E12.

Most of the ancient church, which dates back to the 13th century, was destroyed by a bomb in 1941. The Thomas More Chapel remains on the south side, and legend has it that his headless body is buried somewhere under the walls, but his head, after being spiked on London Bridge (as was the custom in the brutal 16th century) was rescued and buried in a family vault in St Dunstan's Church, Canterbury.

Chelsea Physic Garden

66 Royal Hospital Road (entrance in Swan Walk), SW3 4HS (7352 5646/www.chelseaphysicgarden. co.uk). Sloane Square tube/11, 19, 239, bus. **Open** *Apr-late Oct* noon-5pm Wed; 2-6pm Sun. *Tours* times vary. **Admission** £5; £3 5-16s, concessions (not incl OAPs). *Tours* free. **Credit** *Shop only* AmEx, MC, V. **Map** p397 F12.

This therapeutic garden was founded in 1673 by the Worshipful Society of the Apothecaries of London, and remains a draw today. The garden's objective was to provide medical students with the means to study plants used in healing, and Sir Hans Sloane (for whom Sloane Square is named) helped to develop it in the early 18th century. The 3.8-acre (1.5-hectare) grounds are used today for research and education, with many of the beds tended by volunteers. The garden was opened to the public in 1983, but hours are limited. Free tours conducted by entertaining volunteers trace the history of the medicinal beds, where mandrake, yew, feverfew and other herbs are grown for their efficacy in treating illness.

National Army Museum

Royal Hospital Road, SW3 4HT (7730 0717/ www.national-army-museum.ac.uk). Sloane Square tube/11, 19, 239 bus. **Open** 10am-5.30pm daily. **Admission** free. **Map** p397 F12.

This disarmingly friendly museum can often seem rather emptier than it deserves to be. But it's enthusiastically run and boasts a full events calendar of interest to many. Families can come here for fun (and edifying) workshops in which historians dressed as soldiers explain life in the past; amateur historians can come for the lectures. The museum is on four floors, with an art gallery at the top alongside a display about the modern army and its developing roles. Other galleries include the 'Road to Waterloo', where visitors can see three short films over an enormous model of the battle employing 70,000 model soldiers, and a skeleton that's supposedly Napoleon's favourite horse, Marengo. There's also a fascinating trench mock-up in the recently enlarged 'World at War 1914-1946' exhibition and a Tudor cannon – the oldest object in the museum – in the section on the army's early years.

Chelsea Pensioners

The Royal Hospital in Chelsea is not your average old folks' home, but then the Chelsea Pensioners are not your average old folks. About 350 of them live here, all of them ex-soldiers. Their quarters, the Royal Hospital, was founded in 1682 by Charles II (the inspiration for the hospital came from Louis XIV's Hôtel des Invalides in Paris). The building was designed by Sir Christopher Wren and took a decade to complete, with later adjustments added by Robert Adam and Sir John Soane, who also designed the infirmary destroyed by bombing in 1941. A new infirmary opened 20 years later.

Retired soldiers are eligible to apply for a final posting here if they are over 65, in receipt of an Army or War Disability Pension for Army Service (this they hand over to pay for their keep) and free of obligation to support a wife and family. The in-pensioners are organised into companies, along military lines, with a governor and other officers, including medical officers, a quartermaster and a chaplain, but they are free these days to have leave of absence or holidays. In fact, life is much easier for them now than it was back in the 18th century, when they were obliged to stand guard shifts throughout the night, to protect the road from the Royal Hospital to St James's.

Today in-pensioners have their own club room, amenity centre, billiards room, library, bowling green and gardens. Some work in the museum, which tells you more about the life of a pensioner from the 17th century to the present day. Free to enter, the museum has a mock-up of an in-pensioner's room, designed by Wren, and there are paintings, ceremonial arms, medals bequeathed by former residents and uniforms on display.

The familiar scarlet coat and tricorn hat the old soldiers wear for ceremonial duties date back to the 18th century. They march to a military band, each wearing an oak leaf in their buttonhole, on Oak Apple Day. The leaves are laid at the statue of Charles II, to commemorate the day the King climbed into an oak tree to escape Cromwell's men. The red coats aren't in evidence when you visit the hospital on an ordinary day: dark trousers and pale blue shirts are the standard mufti for relaxing at home.

Royal Hospital Chelsea

Royal Hospital Road, SW3 4FR (7730 0161/www.chelsea-pensioners.co.uk). Sloane Square tube/11, 19, 22, 137, 211, 239 bus. **Open** 10am-noon, 2-4pm Mon-Sat *(May-Sept also 2-4pm Sun).* **Admission** free. **Map** p397 F12.

Sightseeing

North London

Where luvvies live and the famous lie at rest.

Camley Street Natural Park. *See p149.*

Camden

Camden Town or Chalk Farm tube.

Over the past few decades, this has become one of London's most fashionable addresses. But, like many newly desirable areas, Camden Town has had a long association with lowlife. Cheap lodging houses dominated the area around the time when the Regent's Canal was laid out in 1816, and it was rough in Victorian times, too, at least according to Charles Dickens, who grew up in Bayham Street. In later decades Irish and Greek immigrants laid down roots here, and by the 1960s this indisputably poor area had earned itself a raffish, bohemian character.

Around this time, arty types, among them writer Alan Bennett, saw the potential of the tall, spacious houses and elegant crescents, and moved into the area. White-collar professionals followed, and today Camden has a middle-class flavour: residents now shun the markets and buy their provisions from Nicholas Grimshaw's high tech Sainsbury's supermarket on Camden Road. Yet the area retains an edge: every night, Camden Town tube is garlanded with exotica, whether punks and goths in full regalia or the less photogenic (but basically harmless) junkies.

Teenagers and students love the area for **Camden Market** (*see p149*), but this once-alternative hangout has become one of London's big tourist attractions, which means crowds can be unpleasant and real bargains are few and far between. Within the market, the worthwhile stalls include collectibles in the Stables, and the crafts and unusual homewares in the main Market Hall, but to get to them you will have to persist through litter, grime and too many people trying too hard to have a good time. There is, of course, more to the neighbourhood than Camden High Street and the market, but you'd do best to explore it out of market hours to avoid the rabble.

The **Roundhouse** on Chalk Farm Road opened in 1846 as a steam-engine repair depot before becoming a music venue in the 1960s, hosting gigs by the likes of Pink Floyd, Jimi Hendrix and the Doors. Now it is being redeveloped as a performance space and young people's media centre (7424 9991). Work should be completed by autumn 2005. The lovely **Jewish Museum** (*see p149*), just off Parkway, is a gem, a reflection of the area's cultural diversity. But Camden is let down by its eating and drinking options; there are some grim bars and restaurants round here. In addition to the few suggestions in our Restaurants & Cafés chapter, try a cheap cake or seafood pasta dish from one of the Portuguese cafés on Plender Street or excellent pub food at the Engineer (65 Gloucester Avenue, 7722 0950), and then cool down with an ice-cream at Marine Ices (8 Haverstock Hill), a local institution.

Camden Market

Camden Market *Camden High Street, junction with Buck Street, NW1 (7278 4444).* **Open** 9.30am-5.30pm daily.
Camden Canal Market *off Chalk Farm Road, south of junction with Castlehaven Road, NW1 9XJ (7485 8355/www.camdenlock.net).* **Open** 9am-6.30pm Fri-Sun.
Camden Lock *Camden Lock Place, off Chalk Farm Road, NW1 8AF (7485 3459/www.camden lockmarket.com).* **Open** 10am-6pm daily.
Electric Ballroom *184 Camden High Street, NW1 8QP (7485 9006/www.electric-ballroom.co.uk).* **Open** 10am-6pm Sat, Sun; *record & film fairs occasional Sats throughout the year.*
Stables *off Chalk Farm Road, opposite junction with Hartland Road, NW1 8AH (7485 5511/ www.camdenlock.net).* **Open** 9.30am-5.30pm daily (reduced stalls Mon-Fri).
All *Camden Town tube.*

If you value elbow space, you won't like Camden Market. The place heaves with locust-plague numbers of people (mostly tourists), particularly at weekends when the greatest number of stalls are open. And as a market, it's far from inspiring. The section just next to the tube station continues to flog cheap sunglasses and cut-price interpretations of current fashions; the rest bears little resemblance to the cutting-edge place it was years ago. The Electric Ballroom sells second-hand clothes and young designers' wares, but it's neither cheap nor particularly exciting. Camden Lock Market, set around a courtyard next to Regent's Canal, is nicer: it has crafty shops and stalls selling funky lighting, contemporary fashion, ethnic homewares, arts, antiques and more. In the Stables Yard, what was once an open-air space selling combat gear and crochet jumpers is now full of permanent clothes and food huts, rather like an alternative shopping mall. In the railway arches, upmarket, permanent retro stalls and clubwear outlets have taken over, though some outlets selling antiques and 20th-century design furniture remain. In the area beside the canal is an avenue of yet more food stalls, from Indian to Mexican and from French to Lebanese. Here you'll also find interesting craft stalls selling bags and accessories.

Jewish Museum, Camden

Raymond Burton House, 129-131 Albert Street, NW1 7NB (7284 1997/www.jewishmuseum.org.uk). Camden Town tube. **Open** 10am-4pm Mon-Thur; 10am-5pm Sun. **Admission** £3.50; £2.50 OAPs; £1.50 5-16s; free under-5s. **Credit** MC, V.

One of a pair (its sister is in Finchley; *see p156*), Camden's Jewish Museum provides a fascinating insight into one of Britain's oldest immigrant communities. Different aspects of six centuries of Jewish life are illustrated through oil paintings, artefacts from a tailor's 'sweatshop', silver and chinaware, and photographs and passports. The museum also has one of the world's finest collections of Jewish ceremonial art, including a collection of silver Hanukkah candlesticks, spice boxes and an amazing 16th-century Italian synagogue ark, brought to Britain in the 19th century by an Englishman who had picked it up while doing his European Grand Tour. Audio-visual programmes provide information on Jewish festivals and Jewish life, while temporary exhibitions in 2005 include 'Passover: From Moses to Matzah' (until June).

Around Camden

Primrose Hill, to the north of Camden, with its gracious terraces, is as pretty as the actors, pop stars and writers who live there. The main shopping street, Regent's Park Road, is a pleasant mix of independent cafés, quality gastropubs and restaurants, and smart shops. Not so far away, **Kentish Town**, with its bargain stores, looks grubby by comparison.

South and east of Camden, bucolic **Camley Street Natural Park** (*see p272*) is the London Wildlife Trust's flagship reserve. The still-operative **Regent's Canal** (*see p152* **Watermarks**), which runs along one side of the park, opened in 1820 to provide a working waterway to link east and west London; the **London Canal Museum** (*see p150*) has all the history, along with a giant ice well.

Even the food's blinding at **Camden Market**.

London Canal Museum

12-13 New Wharf Road, King's Cross, N1 9RT (7713 0836/www.canalmuseum.org.uk). King's Cross tube/rail. **Open** 10am-4.30pm (last admission 3.45pm) Tue-Sun. **Admission** (LP) £3; £2 concessions; £1.50 8-16s; free under-8s. **Credit** MC, V. **Map** p399 L2.

The warehouse containing this small museum on the Regent's Canal's Battlebridge Basin was built in the 1850s by Carlo Gatti, an Italian immigrant who made a fortune importing ice from Norway's frozen lakes to the vast ice well that's open to view in the museum floor. Photos and videos tell the Gatti story, and further footage and exhibitions explore the hardships endured by those who made their living on the canals. There are intricate models of boats upstairs and a barge cabin in which visitors can sit. But the museum could do more to exploit a subject matter so pivotal to London's industrial history.

St John's Wood

St John's Wood or Swiss Cottage tube.

Rural calm prevailed in St John's Wood until well into the 19th century, when the only developments around the wooded hills and meadows were smart stucco villas. The pure air attracted artists, scientists and writers: Mary Anne Evans (aka George Eliot) often held receptions at her house. A blue plaque marks the house at 44 Grove End Road once owned by the artist Sir Lawrence Alma-Tadema, but, sadly, the interior is closed to the public.

In the 19th century the inexpensive but pretty houses suited rich men, who used them to house their mistresses. The building work carried out by the Great Central Railway in 1894 destroyed the rural calm, but sensitive redevelopment during the 1950s has left the area smart, desirable and fabulously expensive – just take a look at the chic boutiques of the exceedingly couth High Street. However, **Lord's**, the world's most famous cricket ground (*see below*), is the reason most people visit, but Beatles fans have their own motives. Grove End Road leads to **Abbey Road**, made famous by the Fab Four when its recording facility was still officially called EMI Studios (No.3). The crossing outside is always busy with tourists scrawling their names on the wall.

Up the Finchley Road from St John's Wood, you'll find that a **Swiss Cottage** actually exists, its black-and-white timbers smiling coyly at visitors. The structure is on the site of a Swiss-style tavern at the Junction Road Toll Gate. The excitement stops at the entrance but don't leave without sampling the cakes at **Louis Hungarian Pâtisserie** (12 Harben Parade, 7722 8100).

Lord's Tour & MCC Museum

Marylebone Cricket Club, Lord's, St John's Wood Road, NW8 8QN (7616 8595/www.lords.org). St John's Wood tube/13, 46, 82, 113, 139, 274 bus. **Open** *Oct-Mar* noon, 2pm daily. *Apr-Sept* 10am, noon, 2pm daily. **Admission** £7; £5.50 concessions; £4.50 5-15s; free under-5s; £20 family. **Credit** MC, V.

Despite a reputation as die-hard stick-in-the-muds, the wearers of the famous egg-and-bacon striped tie have nonetheless come to love the NatWest Media Centre, the stunning raised pod that dominates the self-proclaimed home of cricket. The Centre joins the portrait-bedecked Long Room on the guided tour (you'll need to book), along with the expected collection of battered bats, photos and blazers. There's plenty of WG Grace ephemera, a stuffed sparrow felled by a ball in 1936 and, of course, the Ashes. No matter how often the Aussies win 'em (though we've got our fingers crossed for 2005's contest), you can rest assured that cricket's holy grail – the story of whose creation is related with appealing dryness – will remain here.

'A gentleman's private park': **Kenwood House**. *See p154.*

Hampstead

Golders Green or Hampstead tube/Hampstead Heath rail.

Like many rural villages on the fringes of the city, Hampstead was a popular retreat in times of plague. Its undulating thoroughfares and protected heath ensured that urbanisation never happened and the village remains exclusive to this day. For centuries, it has been the favoured roosting place for literary and artistic bigwigs; Keats and Constable called it home in the 19th century, while modernist and surrealist artists such as Barbara Hepworth and Henry Moore lived the village London idyll here in the 1930s.

Hampstead tube station stands at the top of the steep High Street. The twin lines of higgledy-piggledy terraces that make up Church Row, one of Hampstead's most beautiful streets, lead down to **St John at Hampstead** (7794 5808), a less ostentatious cemetery than its near-neighbour Highgate, but just as restful and bucolic. Among those of note buried here are Constable and, in an unmarked plot, the comedian Peter Cook, who lived nearby.

Close too, on Holly Hill, is Hampstead's antique Holly Bush pub (*see p227*), which was painter George Romney's stable block until he moved to rustic Hampstead to get over his obsession with Nelson's paramour, Lady Hamilton. Another minute's climb will bring you to **Fenton House** (*see p152*), while the celestially inclined should potter round the corner to **Hampstead Scientific Society Observatory** (Lower Terrace, 8346 1056).

East of Heath Street, a maze of attractive streets shelters **Burgh House** on New End Square, a Queen Anne house that now contains a small museum, and **2 Willow Road** (*see p154*), the residence that émigré Hungarian architect Ernö Goldfinger built in the 1930s. Nearby, off Keats Grove, is **Keats House** (*see p154*), where the poet did most of his best work. The bullet-marked Magdala pub on South Hill Park (No.2A, 7435 2503) is where Ruth Ellis shot her former boyfriend in 1955 and became the last woman to be hanged in Britain.

Hampstead Heath, the inspiration for CS Lewis's Narnia, is the city's countryside. Its charming contours and woodlands conspire to make it feel far larger and more rural than it is (something over a mile in each direction): you can quite easily get lost here, especially if you're looking for a particular group of picnickers, as most people are on summer weekends. The views of London from the top of **Parliament Hill** are stunning; on hot days, the murky bathing ponds (men's, women's and mixed, open daily all year) are a godsend. There's also a great lido at Gospel Oak (7485 3873). Pick up a map from one of the information points on the heath, which can also advise you of concerts held on summer Sundays. At the north end of the park is **Kenwood House** (*see p154*).

Camden Arts Centre

Arkwright Road, corner of Finchley Road, NW3 6DG (7472 5500/www.camdenartscentre.org). Finchley Road tube/Finchley Road & Frognal rail. **Open** 10am-6pm Tue, Thur-Sun; 10am-9pm Wed. **Admission** free. **Credit** *Shop only* MC, V.

Following a lengthy £4m refurbishment, this innovative centre dedicated to contemporary visual art reopened in 2004. The money has been spent on new galleries and studios, a café and landscaped gardens. Among 2005's shows will be 'An Aside', an exhibition running from February to May involving film and video, curated by Tacita Dean, and an exhibition of African artists' work (including an African artist-in-residence) in July and August as part of the Londonwide Africa 2005 project.

Fenton House

*3 Hampstead Grove, NW3 6RT (7435 3471/
information 01494 755563/www.nationaltrust.
org.uk). Hampstead tube.* **Open** *Mar* 2-5pm Sat,
Sun. *Apr-Oct* 2-5pm Wed-Fri; 11am-5pm Sat, Sun.
Tours phone for details. **Admission** (NT) £4.80;
£2.40 5-15s; free under-5s. *Joint ticket with 2 Willow
Road* £6.40. **No credit cards**.

Devotees of early music will be impressed by the
collection of harpsichords, clavichords, virginals
and spinets housed at this William and Mary
house. The bequest was made on condition that
qualified musicians be allowed to play them, so
you might be lucky enough to hear them in action
(otherwise, phone for details of the fortnightly
summer concerts held here). The porcelain collection won't appeal to everyone – the 'curious
grotesque teapot' certainly lives up to its billing –
but for fans, there's work by Meissen and
Rockingham. The gardens are a delight (£1 unless
you're visiting the house), with the small orchard
coming into its own for October's Apple Day
celebration. Out of season, enjoy the exterior: join
the walking tours that begin in the 1930s at

Watermarks Regent's Canal

It's a pleasurable irony that a relic of the
Industrial Revolution should provide one of
London's most gorgeous getaways. No, it's
not exactly the Venice of the north. But the
Regent's Canal is one of the city's most
cherishable anachronisms all the same:
an eight-and-a-half-mile stretch of waterway
offers a parallel reality to the hustle-heavy
city that overlooks it. Where once cargo
was pulled by horses on the towpath, now
this route has become a scenic path from
Docklands up to Islington and Camden Town
and then, through the top of Regent's Park,
to Little Venice and Paddington.

Like many grand designs, it was a financial
farrago. It was first mooted in 1810, to join
the Grand Union Canal (which reaches up to

Manchester) to the Thames at Limehouse.
Over the course of the next decade it received
some severe setbacks: the canal's promoter,
Thomas Homer, ran off with a large sum of
cash in 1815. A nifty new hydro-pneumatic
lock design by William Congreve, famous for
his invention of the rocket, was discarded
for something more conventional in 1819.

John Nash, the architect who designed
Regent's Park, was the director of the
project. His relationship with the Prince
Regent enabled him to get the future George
IV to lend his name to it. They even got some
Government financial assistance as part of
a plan to tackle unemployment after the
Napoleonic Wars ended in 1815. Slowly,
painfully, it all got done.

2 Willow Road (*see p154*) and take you back in time through Georgian and Edwardian Hampstead to end up here (£6; 01494 755572).

Freud Museum

20 Maresfield Gardens, NW3 5SX (7435 2002/ www.freud.org.uk). Finchley Road tube. **Open** noon-5pm Wed-Sun. **Admission** £5; £2 concessions; free under-12s. **Credit** MC, V.

After Anna Freud's death in 1982, the house she and her father Sigmund shared for the last year of his life became a museum. The analyst's couch sits in

the study, round glasses and unsmoked cigars setting the scene, and the copious library is impressive, but more intellectual or biographical context would be appreciated by the uninitiated. Extracts from Freud's writings require a good deal of concentration to piece together. Upstairs is Anna's room (with another couch and handloom) and a gallery. This is one of the few buildings in London to have two blue plaques: commemorating both father and daughter (she was a pioneer in child psychiatry), they were unveiled by comedian John Cleese in 2002.

Finally, the canal opened on 1 August 1820. It cost £772,000, well over twice the original estimate. And although trade flourished – with its first year's 120,000-ton cargo load increasing to the million-ton mark through the century – it was always in the shadow of the even-more-flourishing railway network. Various attempts were made to convert the canal route itself to a railway.

Commercial canal usage steadily declined during the 20th century, except during World War II when the canals offered an important alternative to the overworked railways. But the last horse-drawn barges didn't disappear until 1956; commercial traffic had pretty much puttered away by 1968, when the towpaths were first opened to the public.

Any stretch of the canal is worth a stroll, but the most popular patches are those between the Canal Museum at King's Cross (*see p110*) and Camden Town, and particularly from Camden Town to Little Venice. The museum itself (*see p150*) could do with an update, though its location in an old ice warehouse – used for storing imported Norwegian ice – in Battlebridge Basin is emblematic of the way the canal's industrial trappings have been transformed over the past few decades. The rest of the basin used to include engineering works, a marmalade factory and a Guinness bottling plant – now it's surrounded by offices, and is home to residential narrowboats (which are also clustered behind King's Cross Station and towards Little Venice).

The towpath runs on the north side of the canal, taking you under the fast-redeveloping King's Cross, with one gasholder left of the seven that were there until the building of the Channel Tunnel Rail Link. Further up, on the opposite side, is the Camley Street Natural Park (*see p272*), a small nature reserve created from derelict land in 1985. The

canal's diverse wildlife includes crayfish, coots, moorhens, grey herons, cormorants and the ubiquitous mallard ducks. Not to mention a seal, known as Simone, who occasionally surfaces at the docklands end. And the thousands of terrapins descended from the unwanted pets decanted into the canal at the end of the Teenage Mutant Ninja Turtles craze.

A few hundred yards along, before the Camden Road bridge, there are some enviable canalside houses that look more Cornwall than Camden. Then, by perfect contrast, you get to see the futuristic silver housing that architect Nicholas Grimshaw built with his iconic, postmodern Sainsbury's in 1988, before heading into – well, actually, under – the tourist scrum of Camden Market. Here, you have the option of hopping on one of the riverboat cruises that run in summer and on winter weekends between Camden and Little Venice (London Waterbus Company, 7482 2660; Jenny Wren 7485 4433; Jason's Canal Boat Trip 7286 3428).

Whether travelling by boat or by foot, the section west of Camden offers some of the lushest foliage as you head into Regent's Park and, indeed, right through the zoo. There's a specially created wildflower embankment just past the zoo that makes this section a popular haunt for butterflies. Once you're past the park, a slightly less luscious inner-city area precedes the posh-again Little Venice.

Every city needs its escape hatches. And whenever you make use of the Regent's Canal, even if only as a shortcut, it feels like a true escape from the noise of the big city above. Fusing industrial history with a fish-eye view of the parts of town you can't otherwise see, it's an important reminder that sometimes the backwaters are just as important as the main stream.

Keats House

Keats Grove, NW3 2RR (7435 2062/www.
keatshouse.org.uk). Hampstead Heath rail/
Hampstead tube/24, 46, 168 bus. **Open** *Apr-Oct*
noon-5pm Tue-Sun. *Nov-Mar* 10am-4pm Tue-Sun.
Tours 3pm Sat, Sun. **Admission** £3; £1.50
concessions; free under-16s. **Credit** MC, V.

The Romantic poet made his home here from 1818
to 1820, when he left for Rome (where he died of
tuberculosis the following year, aged 25). Today it
attracts obscene numbers of visitors every year. As
well as mooching through the rooms, you can attend
events and talks in the poetry reading room and see
a display on Keats's sweetheart, Fanny Brawne,
who lived next door. The garden in which he wrote
'Ode to a Nightingale' is a pleasant place to wander
in romantic reverie.

Kenwood House/Iveagh Bequest

Hampstead Lane, NW3 7JR (8348 1286/www.
english-heritage.org). Hampstead tube/Golders Green
tube, then 210 bus. **Open** *Apr-Sept* 10am-5.30pm
Mon, Tue, Thur, Sat, Sun; 10.30am-5.30pm Wed, Fri.
Oct closes at 5pm. *Nov-Mar* closes at 4pm. *Tours* by
appointment only. **Admission** free; donations
appreciated. *Tours* £3.50; £2.50 concessions; £1.50
under-16s. **Credit** AmEx, MC, V.

Built in 1616 as a manor house, Kenwood House was
remodelled for the first Earl of Mansfield by Robert
Adam in 1760, whose decision as Chief Justice in a
test case in 1772 made it illegal to own slaves in
England. The house stayed in the Mansfield family
until 1924, when brewing magnate Edward Guinness
bought it, filling it with his art collection. Now English
Heritage is in charge of the perfect interiors, endors-
ing his wish 'that the atmosphere of a gentleman's
private park should be preserved'. Art includes
Vermeer's *The Guitar Player*, Rembrandt's self-portrait, works by Hals and Van Dyck and French rococo scenes by Boucher and Pater. In the green-grey
music room, Gainsborough's *Countess Howe* presides
over a harem of society beauties. Outside, Humphrey
Repton's landscape remains mostly unchanged from
its creation in 1793. Repton meant it to be walked, and
the ivy arch leading from the flower garden to a raised
terrace with lovely views over the lakes is one of his
famous 'surprises'. Part of Kenwood's grounds is now
listed as a Site of Special Scientific Interest, for its four
species of bat and nine Nationally Scarce inverte-
brates. The old brewhouse is now the Brew House
Restaurant, and does a terrific breakfast. In July and
August there are concerts by the lake.

2 Willow Road

2 Willow Road, NW3 1TH (7435 6166/www.
nationaltrust.org.uk). Hampstead tube/Hampstead
Heath rail. **Open** *Mar, Nov* noon-5pm Sat. *Apr-Oct*
noon-5pm Thur-Sat (last entry 4.30pm). *Tours* noon,
1pm, 2pm. **Admission** £4.60; £2.30 5-15s; free
under-5s. *Joint ticket with Fenton House* £6.30.
No credit cards.

This strange and atmospheric building is the
National Trust's only example of international

modernism. James Bond author Ian Fleming was so
annoyed by its architect, Ernö Goldfinger – also
resonsible for some bleak blocks of flats – that he
named one of his villains after him. The light pouring through the windows is a feature in itself, and
the perfect functionalism of original fixtures and fittings is a revelation. Designed and built by the
Austro-Hungarian Goldfinger in 1939 as a terrace of
three houses (the two others are still occupied), it also
contains works by Max Ernst and Henry Moore.

Highgate

Archway or Highgate tube.

Highgate's name comes from a tollgate that
once stood on the site of the Gate House pub on
the High Street. Dinky shops now predominate
there, but a villagey vibe still remains.

Legend has it that Dick Whittington, as
he walked away from the city at the foot of
Highgate Hill, heard the Bow bells peal out
'Turn again Whittington, thrice Mayor of
London'. The event is commemorated on the
Whittington Stone, near the hospital of the
same name. Yet the area is today best known
for the twin burial grounds of **Highgate
Cemetery** (*see p155*), the newer of which is
the last resting place of Karl Marx. Adjoining
it is beautiful **Waterlow Park** (7272 2825),
donated to Londoners by low-cost housing
pioneer Sir Sydney Waterlow in 1889. This
underappreciated hillside area has ponds, a
mini aviary, tennis courts and, in 16th-century
Lauderdale House, a garden café.

Further down Swains Lane, peep through
the Gothic entrance to **Holly Village**, a private
village built in 1865. Hornsey Lane, on the other
side of Highgate Hill, leads you to **Archway**,
a Victorian viaduct offering vertiginous views
of the City and the East End. The famous
Archway Bridge has long been popularly
known as Suicide Bridge – the first recorded
jumper took the leap in 1908. The recent
addition of fencing has made this vast cast-
iron Victorian arch rather harder to use as a
launching pad into the afterlife.

If this depresses you, hurry away east
down Hornsey Lane to comfortable, middle-
class **Crouch End**. Here, the 1895 clock
tower and the **Hornsey Town Hall** preside
over a pleasant community. The High Street
is an eclectic mix of boutiques and decent
restaurants: try the Turkish Mazgal (19
Topsfield Parade, 8340 3194).

North of Highgate tube, shady **Highgate
Woods** were mentioned (under another name)
in the Domesday Book. Nowadays, this is a
conservation area with a nature trail, a
children's playground and plenty of space for
picnics and ball games.

Sightseeing

Highgate Cemetery

Swains Lane, N6 6PJ (8340 1834/www.highgate-cemetery.org). Archway tube/143, 210, 271 bus.
Open East Cemetery *Apr-Oct* 10am-5pm Mon-Fri;
11am-5pm Sat, Sun. Last entry 4.30pm. *Nov-Mar*
10am-4pm Mon-Fri; 11am-4pm Sat, Sun. Last entry
3.30pm. West Cemetery *tours Apr-Oct* 2pm Mon-Fri;
hourly 11am-4pm Sat, Sun. *Nov-Mar* hourly 11am-
3pm Sat, Sun. **Admission** *East Cemetery* £2. *West
Cemetery tours* £3; £1 1st child 8-16 (others pay full
price); prior booking advisable. *Camera permit* £1.
No video cameras. No under-8s. **No credit cards.**
Highgate Cemetery is London's most famous graveyard, marked by its dramatic tombs of towering
angels and curling roses. Celebrity spotters will be
delighted with the Karl Marx and George Eliot
memorials in the East Cemetery, but the West
Cemetery (accessible only on guided tours) is the real
highlight. It is a breathtaking place: long pathways
wind through tall tombs, gloomy catacombs and
remarkably elaborate funerary architecture (plus the
bones of poet Christina Rossetti and chemist Michael
Faraday). The cemetery closes during burials.

Islington

Map p402

Angel tube/Highbury & Islington tube/rail.
Henry VIII owned houses for hunting in this
once-idyllic village, but by the 19th century
it was already known for its shops, theatres
and music halls. From 1820, the arrival of the
Regent's Canal brought industrial slums,
and Islington declined into one of the poorest
boroughs in London. However, like so much
of the city, its Georgian squares and Victorian
terraces have been gentrified in the past 30
years. These days, despite stubborn pockets of
poverty, this is a wealthy middle-class area, as
is clear when you emerge from Angel tube and
walk along Upper Street, past the glass façade
of the Business Design Centre (and, opposite,
hoary old Camden Passage antiques market,
see p235), along the side of the triangular Green
and up towards **Highbury**. En route, you'll
take in countless boutiques, the Screen on the
Green cinema, the Almeida Theatre (*see p339*)
and the Union Chapel (*see p310*).

Taking this route you'll graze the south
entrance of the new N1 Centre shopping mall,
near the Angel; among its largely mainstream
tenants are a Gap, a music venue (the Carling
Islington Academy), a big and loud Vue
cineplex and lots of mainstream chain stores.
This behemoth is but a symptom of the influx
of high-street names into the area over the past
decade, turning a unique locale into something
more standard-issue.

You might spy some cabbies nearby: Penton
Street, at the end of Chapel Market, is where all
cab drivers once chewed down a pencil trying to

pass 'the Knowledge', a detailed exam based on
London streets and buildings that all London's
cabbies must pass.

On the way along Upper Street, take a detour
to **Canonbury Square**, a Regency square
once home to George Orwell (No.27) and Evelyn
Waugh (No.17A). Worth a look is the **Estorick
Collection of Modern Italian Art** (*see
p156*), while to the east is the tranquil New
River, beside the less than tranquil Marquess
Estate. It turns out that New River is neither
new nor a river, but a 17th-century commercial
water conduit that is now a park.

Just beyond the end of Upper Street is
Highbury Fields, where 200,000 Londoners
fled to escape the Great Fire of 1666. Smart
Highbury is best known as home to author Nick
Hornby's beloved Arsenal football club, who
play at the small but perfectly formed art deco
Highbury Stadium. There's a museum
(Avenell Road, 7704 4000) and occasional
guided tours. A new ground with a capacity
more befitting Arsenal's status is being built
down the road in time for the 2006/7 season.

Estorick Collection. *See p156.*

Sightseeing

Estorick Collection of Modern Italian Art

39A Canonbury Square, N1 2AN (7704 9522/ www.estorickcollection.com). Highbury & Islington tube/rail/271 bus. **Open** 11am-6pm Wed-Sat; noon-5pm Sun. **Admission** £3.50; £2.50 concessions; free under-16s, students. **Credit** MC, V.

Eric Estorick was a US political scientist, writer and art collector whose interest in the Futurists began in the 1950s. The collection he amassed includes work by some fine Italian Futurists, such as Balla's *Hand of the Violinist* and Boccioni's *Modern Idol*, as well as pieces by Carra, Marinetti, Russolo and Severini. The museum has a library with over 2,000 books on modern Italian art, a shop and a café. Temporary exhibitions in 2005 include 'Futurist Skies: Italian Aeropainting' (to March) and 'Power and Persuasion: Avant-garde Graphic Design and Photomontages in Europe, 1916-36' (23 Mar-5 June).

Dalston & Stoke Newington

Dalston: Dalston Kingsland rail/30, 38, 56, 67, 149, 242, 243, 277 bus. Stoke Newington: Stoke Newington rail/73 bus.

Bishopsgate starts in the City, passes Shoreditch, becomes Kingsland Road and runs north to Dalston and Stoke Newington, past the Hassidic enclave of Stamford Hill, and out of London.

Though scruffy and, at times, intimidating, **Dalston** is a vibrant place, with shops, market stalls, cafés and all-night restaurants and clubs catering to the area's immigrant communities (chiefly Afro-Caribbean and Turkish).

Stoke Newington has been labelled, not inaccurately, as the place people move to when they can't afford Islington. Stoke Newington Church Street has a number of good restaurants: Rasa (No.55, 7249 1340) is famed for its meat-free Indian cooking. For shoppers, there are gifts and second-hand book and clothes stores and the fascinating Cookson's Junk Yard (121 Marton Road, 7254 9941). **Clissold Park** (7923 3660) is a lovely green space with a small zoo, tennis courts, a lake and a tearoom; rather more other-worldly is the wildlife-filled **Abney Park Cemetery** (7275 7557), a rambling old boneyard that's also a nature reserve. Among the notables buried within are Salvation Army founder William Booth and painter Edward Calvert. Rare butterflies, woodpeckers and bats are the live attractions for nature lovers.

Further north

The tidy suburban streets at north London's perimeter are enlivened by the immigrant communities that have made them their home. Golders Green, Hendon and **Finchley** have large Jewish communities, the last of these

home to north London's second **Jewish Museum** (80 East End Road, 8349 1143, *see also p149*), where the focus is on Jewish social history and there's an exhibition tracing the life of Leon Greenman, a British Jew who survived Auschwitz. He's in his 90s now but still comes in on Sundays to speak about his experiences.

Golders Green is the focus of a growing population of both Chinese and Japanese City workers, with the Oriental City shopping mall (399 Edgware Road, 8200 0009) supplying their shopping needs. There's been a Jewish cemetery on Hoop Lane since 1895; cellist Jacqueline du Pré is buried here. Meanwhile, TS Eliot, Marc Bolan and Anna Pavlova ended up at **Golders Green Crematorium** (8455 2374).

The neighbourhoods of **Tottenham** and **Haringey** have sizeable Greek Cypriot, Turkish Cypriot and Kurdish communities; aside from occasional clashes, the groups live side by side in **Green Lanes**, where food-related business success is evident in the thriving kebab shops, bakeries and supermarkets. Finally, **Alexandra Palace** is as good a reason as any to visit Muswell Hill.

Alexandra Park & Palace

Alexandra Palace Way, N22 7AY (park 8444 7696/ information 8365 2121/boating 8889 9089/www. alexandrapalace.com). Wood Green tube/Alexandra Palace rail/W3, W7, 84A, 144, 144A bus. **Open** *Park* 24hrs daily. *Palace* times vary.

'The People's Palace', when it opened in 1873, was supposed to provide affordable entertainment for all. It burned to the ground just 16 days later. Rebuilt, it became the site of the first TV broadcasts by the BBC in 1936, but in 1980 was destroyed by fire once more. The born-yet-again palace has remained upright for the past 24 years and yields panoramic views of London. Its grounds provide a multitude of attractions – ice skating, boating, pitch-and-putt – while its entertainment and exhibition centre hosts fairs and events. Indoors, experimental theatre titans Complicité plan to revive the atmospheric music hall to stage Dickens's *Our Mutual Friend* in 2005.

Royal Air Force Museum Hendon

Grahame Park Way, NW9 5LL (8205 2266/www.raf museum.org). Colindale tube/Mill Hill Broadway rail/ 32, 226, 292, 303 bus. **Open** 10am-6pm daily. *Tours* times vary; *specialised tours* advance booking. **Admission** free; *specialised tours* £20 for 12 people. **Credit** AmEx, MC, V.

Claiming to be the birthplace of aviation in Britain, Hendon Aerodrome currently houses more than 70 aircraft, among them WWI Fokkers, WWII Spitfires and Cold War-era Valiants, together with all manner of aviation memorabilia. Following redevelopment work at the museum, a new exhibition traces the history of aviation. There's an interactive show about the Battle of Britain and a Red Arrows flight simulator and a 'touch and try' Jet Provost cockpit.

East London

Terrorised by Jack the Ripper and bombed in the Blitz, the old East End is the focal point of a new, multicultural London.

Whitechapel & Spitalfields

Maps p403 & p405

Aldgate, Aldgate East, Shoreditch or Whitechapel tube.
Whitechapel and Spitalfields form the beating heart of the East End, but don't expect cockney patois and pearly kings and queens. Centuries of immigration have made this one of the most multicultural parts of London. First to arrive were French Huguenots (Protestant refugees)

in the 18th century, followed by Irish and Germans in the early 19th century and Jewish refugees from Eastern Europe at the start of the 20th. As the Jews prospered and headed to north London, Bangladeshis and Indians moved in. Now, inevitably, City Man is making his mark. The area is going rapidly upmarket, and houses that were built for refugees are now changing hands for half a million pounds. Bars, pavement cafés and trendy shops are springing up on every corner, particularly around Brick

19 Princelet Street. *See p159.*

Lane and **Spitalfields Market** (*see p256*).
But the past isn't so easily supressed, nor the
area so easily gentrified. Original London
Walks' (www.walks.com) Jack the Ripper
option remains popular, and there is plenty of
raw material for the irreverent Back Passages
of Spitalfields (www.backpassageswalks.co.uk).

Whitechapel

Named for a vanished chapel on Whitechapel
Road, this area of wholesale clothing shops and
curry houses is the surprising location for the
art nouveau **Whitechapel Art Gallery** (*see
below*), next to Aldgate East station. While art
buffs browse the modern art inside, bargain-
hunters trawl the nearby street markets on
Wentworth Street and Whitechapel Road for
cheap clothes and imported 'fancy goods'. On
Sundays, **Petticoat Lane Market** (*see p255*)
takes up most of the streets behind Aldgate East.

For a taste of the old East End, pick up a
tub of cockles from Tubby Isaac's seafood
stall on the corner of Whitechapel High Street
and Goulston Street, and stroll east along
Whitechapel Road to the **Whitechapel Bell
Foundry** (No.80-82, 7247 2599). This piece of
living history has been churning out bells since
1570, including Big Ben and the Liberty Bell.
You can tour by arrangement, or visit the free
museum from 9am to 4pm Monday to Friday.
Just down the road, the **Bombay Saree
House** is where Joseph Merrick – the Elephant
Man – was exhibited as a sideshow freak,
before being rescued by surgeon Sir Frederick
Treves, as explained in the fascinating **Royal
London Hospital Archives & Museum**
(St Philip's Church, Newark Street, 7377 7608,
open 10am-4.30pm Mon-Fri).

Victorian Whitechapel was battered in
the Blitz, but a few relics survive. The derelict
Tower House, tucked away behind the East
London Mosque on Fieldgate Street, is where
Jack London went undercover to experience
life as an East London pauper; Joseph Stalin
also rented a room here before embarking on
his rampage through Russia. A few doors down,
New Tayyab's excellent Pakistani cooking (83-
99 Fieldgate Street, 7247 6200) is a fine contrast
to the generic curry houses on Brick Lane.

While Jack the Ripper terrorised Whitechapel
in the 1880s, this honour passed to the Kray
twins in the 1960s. Ronnie Kray was finally
arrested after shooting George Cornell dead at
the Blind Beggar pub (337 Whitechapel Road)
in March 1966. Plenty of revolutionaries have
been drawn to Whitechapel over the centuries;
as well as Stalin, Vladimir Lenin and George
Bernard Shaw both put in an appearance and
a gang of Russian anarchists barricaded
themselves into a house on Sidney Street in
1911 and took pot-shots at police and soldiers
led by Winston Churchill. Closer to the City,
the **Women's Library** (7320 2222/www.the
womenslibrary.ac.uk) on Old Castle Street
offers challenging exhibitions devoted to
women's history and suffrage.

Whitechapel Art Gallery

*80-2 Whitechapel High Street, E1 7QX (7522
7888/www.whitechapel.org). Aldgate East tube/15,
25, 205, 253 bus.* **Open** 11am-6pm Tue, Wed, Fri-
Sun; 11am-9pm Thur. *Tours* 2.30pm occasional Sun.
Admission free; 1 paying exhibition a yr, phone for
details. **Map** p405 S6.

An unexpected cultural treat in this bustling commercial area, Whitechapel Art Gallery has been
exposing East Enders to contemporary art for more
than a century. The line up for 2005 includes ama-

teur films by Polish factory workers, photographs by Richard Prince and a 'story of modern art' show with work by Manet, Bacon, Warhol and Cindy Sherman. The gallery café was designed by Turner Prize nominee Liam Gillick and there's a regular programme of live music, poetry and film on Thursday nights, plus free guided tours on Sunday.

Spitalfields

It used to be possible to pick up houses in Spitalfields for a song, but that was before this became east London's most desirable address. Today, this up-and-coming district is populated by a mixture of artists, office workers, East End cockneys and Bangladeshi immigrants. Whether things stay this way remains to be seen; the City is encroaching ever deeper into Spitalfields and Norman Foster's shimmering Gherkin (Swiss Re Building) looms over he area like a harbinger of things to come.

The centre point of Spitalfields is the (deliberately) domineering **Christ Church Spitalfields** (Commercial Street, 7247 7202). A long restoration completed in 2004 has better revealed architect Nicholas Hawksmoor's intent, and confirmed its status as one of London's finest churches, to rival Wren's. It's flanked by tall, shuttered Huguenot houses, particularly along **Fournier Street** and **Wilkes Street**. Around the corner at **19 Princelet Street** (7247 5352, www.19princelet street.org.uk), you can tour the unrestored house of an 18th-century silk merchant, which doubled as a synagogue for Spitalfield's Jewish community. Currently, it's only open a handful of Sundays each year (see the website for details) but there are plans to turn it into a permanent museum of immigration. On the far side of Commercial Street, the wonderful **Dennis Severs' House** (see below) keeps more regular hours.

Facing Christ Church Spitalfields on Commercial Street is covered Spitalfields Market (see *p256*), which offers organic foodstuffs, retro fashions and an impressive collection of ethnic food stalls every Sunday. The market is under continuing threat from developers; check www.smut.org.uk for news of its survival. Across the road, the Ten Bells pub (84 Commercial Street, 7366 1721) is where prostitutes who evaded Jack the Ripper got ripped on cheap gin.

Dennis Severs' House

18 Folgate Street, E1 6BX (7247 4013/www.dennis severshouse.co.uk). Liverpool Street tube/rail. **Open** 2-5pm 1st & 3rd Sun of mth; noon-2pm Mon following 1st & 3rd Sun of mth; Mon eves (times vary). **Admission** £8 Sun; £5 noon-2pm Mon; £12 Mon eves. **No credit cards. Map** p403 R5.

One block north of Spitalfields Market, this splendid Huguenot home contains one of the East End's more unusual attractions. This curious 'still-life drama' was the brainchild of eccentric American artist Dennis Severs, and each room in the house is set up to recreate the sights, sounds and smells of a different period. Severs used to evict guests who failed to appreciate his vision and visitors are still asked to maintain a reverential silence.

Brick Lane

Long an emblem of London's multicultural harmony, Brick Lane's reputation took a few knocks when Asian youths firebombed the Pride of Spitalfields pub on **Heneage Street** in 2003. Things have settled down since then and the area has regained its mysterious and unjustified reputation as *the* place in London to do curry. It has a busy evening scene as restaurant touts compete to lure parties off the streets. If you do want to eat here, credible curry houses that won't try and drag you through the door include sleek Café Naz (Nos.46-48, 7247 0234) and down-home Sweet & Spicy (No.40, 7247 1081). Every Sunday, Brick Lane hosts a sprawling old-fashioned street market (see *p255*).

Brick Lane changes character as you head north from the historic **Jamme Masjid** mosque, a 1740s Huguenot chapel that functioned as a synagogue until 1976. Nearby, the old Truman Brewery has been redeveloped as a hangout for self-conscious arts and media types. A dusting of interesting fashion, crafts, vintage and antiques shops is scattered among the leather-shop lock-ups of Brick Lane and thriving cross street Cheshire Street.

A reminder of Brick Lane's Jewish heritage can be seen at the 24-hour Brick Lane Beigel Bake at No.159, where the food is good, fast, cheap and flung at you unceremoniously.

Shoreditch & Hoxton

Map p403

Old Street tube/rail.

Although it stands within spitting distance of the Square Mile, **Shoreditch** is a much more chaotic affair. Ravaged by bombing raids in World War II, the area lost half of its population and continued in a state of quiet decay until the mid 1990s, when Young British Artists like Tracey Emin (see *p96* **My kind of town**) and Damien Hirst chose to make the area their own. The scene caught fire, and **Hoxton** (technically north of Old Street but used as the modern, happening name for the whole Shoreditch area) became the centre of a modern bohemian scene, with upmarket art galleries (particularly White Cube, the commercial hub of Young British Artists' work; *see p292*) and DJ bars (*see pp321-324*) of variable quality but measurable attitude. At weekends, the revelry is centred on **Hoxton Square** (formerly Hoxton Fields), where the playwright Ben Jonson killed actor Gabriel Spencer in a duel in 1598.

In fact, there are links to the stage all over Shoreditch. James Burbage founded London's first theatre on the corner of Great Eastern Street and New Inn Yard in 1576, before Shakespeare and some disgruntled Burbage employees seized the timbers in lieu of rent and used them to build the Globe (*see p83*). In Victorian times, Shoreditch gained a mixed reputation for its boisterous music halls; the Queen of the Halls herself, Marie Lloyd, was born in Hoxton in 1870.

As with Spitalfields, the City is encroaching deeper and deeper into Shoreditch. As rents have gone skywards, many artists have headed north or east, where the cost of living is more within the realms of reason, though the stalwart Vietnamese community at the southern end of Kingsland Road is still hanging on, with the estimable Sông Quê (*see p216*) one of several Vietnamese canteens catering to visitors to the nearby **Geffrye Museum** (*see below*).

Geffrye Museum

Kingsland Road, E2 8EA (7739 9893/ recorded information 7739 8543/www.geffrye-museum.org.uk). Liverpool Street tube/rail then 149, 242 bus/Old Street tube/rail then 243 bus. **Open** 10am-5pm Tue-Sat; noon-5pm Sun. *Almshouse tours* 11am, noon, 2pm, 3pm, 4pm of 1st Sat of mth. **Admission** *Museum* free; donations appreciated. *Almshouse tours* £2; free under-16s. **Credit** *Shop* MC, V. **Map** p403 R3.

Housed in a close of Georgian almshouses, the Geffrye Museum is a wonderfully serene place to wander for a couple of hours. The houses were converted into a museum of interior design in 1914, offering a chronological sequence of room interiors from the 1600s to the present day. Fans of retro furniture will love the chintzy 1930s and 1960s living rooms. There's an exhibition space with shows by local designers, an airy restaurant and a herb garden that offers a delightfully fragrant stroll on summer afternoons.

Bethnal Green & Hackney

The terraced streets of Bethnal Green were used as a location for the movie *The Krays* but the terrible twins were actually born just down the road in Hoxton's Stean Street. This used to be one of the poorest areas in London, but most of the slums were torn down in the 1960s and replaced with public housing. The new 'streets in the sky' failed to greatly improve life for local residents, whereas the remaining Victorian terraces, on the other hand, have now become highly desirable residences because of their proximity to the City.

Although impoverished, Bethnal has a handful of saving graces. The **Bethnal Green Museum of Childhood** (*see below*) contains a fascinating collection of toys and games for kids. A short walk away is **Columbia Road**, which erupts into a riot of colour every Sunday for the weekly flower market and snoozes prettily the rest of the week.

North of Bethnal Green, the London borough of **Hackney** is known for its incompetent town council and the gloriously restored **Hackney Empire** (*see p162* **Age of Empire**), rescued from ignominy as a bingo hall by a troupe of alternative comedians. Central Hackney is undergoing something of a renaissance; the art deco town hall on **Mare Street** is now flanked by the revamped Empire, the thoroughly modern Technology Learning Centre and Hackney Museum and music venue Ocean (*see p310*). South across London Fields, **Broadway Market** has changed almost overnight from a neglected market street that you had to be very careful about visiting at night to a vital artery mixing old London pie and mash with New London moules-frites and cappuccino, with a lovely Saturday market.

During the 19th century, Hackney was the testing ground for a number of Victorian social experiments, including the benevolent-sounding Children's Friend Society, which put waifs and strays to work as farm labourers before shipping them off to Canada, Australia and Rhodesia (Zimbabwe). Looking around today, it's hard to believe that most of this area was farmland as recently as the 1850s. A short walk from Mare Street, **Sutton House** (*see p161*), is the oldest house in the East End.

Bethnal Green Museum of Childhood

Cambridge Heath Road, E2 9PA (8983 5200/ recorded information 8980 2415/www.museumof childhood.org.uk). Bethnal Green/Cambridge Heath tube/rail. **Open** 10am-5.50pm Mon-Thur, Sat, Sun. **Admission** free; donations appreciated. **Credit** MC, V.

This quirky museum has been collecting children's toys since 1872, so you're almost guaranteed to find some lost plaything from your past. Predictably, there are plenty of hands-on activities for kids, including dressing-up boxes, giant draughts, a working zoetrope and free art and craft workshops in the summer holidays. Adults will enjoy the old board games and quirky toys such as the special Hong Kong reunification issue Barbie doll. Upstairs, there's an astounding collection of doll's houses, dating from 1673 all the way up to 2001.

Sutton House

2 & 4 Homerton High Street, E9 6JQ (8986 2264/ www.nationaltrust.org.uk). Bethnal Green tube then 253, 106, D6 bus/Hackney Central rail. **Open** *Historic rooms* 1-5pm Fri, Sat; 11.30am-5pm Sun. *Café, gallery, shop* 11.30am-5pm Wed-Sun. *Tours* 1.30pm, 3.30pm 1st Sun of mth. **Admission** £2.50; 50p 5-16s; free under-5s; £5.50 family. *Tours* free on admission. **Credit** MC, V.

That Sutton House escaped the bulldozers is a minor miracle as the house was occupied by squatters as recently as 1985. Now beautifully restored, this red-brick Tudor mansion offers a stately home experience in the heart of the East End. Built in 1535 for Henry VIII's first secretary of state, Sir Ralph Sadleir, this is east London's oldest home. You may get lucky and catch a glimpse of the Blue Lady, one of several resident ghosts. There are plenty of special events and activities, including Saturday talks by local historians (call for details).

Mile End & Bow

Bow Church, Bow Road or Mile End tube.

Like Hackney, **Mile End** consisted mostly of common land until the 1800s, when the fields and marshes vanished under row after row of terraced houses. Devastating bombing in World War II was followed by the construction of vast tracts of community housing, but some impressive green areas remain, including **Mile End Park**, which was remodelled in 2003 at a cost of £25 million. A year on, the park is a little overgrown, but there are some fantastic features, including a grass-covered 'living bridge', wetland nature areas and a tiny art gallery (7364 3106). At the southern end, Copperfield Road is home to the interesting **Ragged School Museum** (*see p162*).

Modern Mile End has a strongly South Asian vibe, but this was a Jewish area right up until World War II. The first Jewish cemetery in London was established here in 1657. The area also has some unlikely nautical links: the **Trinity Almshouses** near the junction of Mile End Road and Cambridge Heath Road were built for '28 decayed masters and commanders' in 1695. Just down the road is a rather beleaguered statue of William Booth, who founded the Salvation Army here in 1865.

North of Mile End, at the confluence of the Grand Union and Hertford Union canals, stand the manicured lawns and rose gardens of **Victoria Park**. Protected from development by poor transport links, the surrounding streets are lined with smart Georgian houses. There's a bijou cluster of curiosity shops, gastropubs and cafés at the junction of Victoria Park Road and Grove Road.

Broadway Market. *See p160.*

Sightseeing

Age of Empire

It isn't often that the little man defeats the big developers, but that was what happened with the Hackney Empire. Built in 1901 by celebrated architect Frank Matcham (who also created the Coliseum off Trafalgar Square), the Empire was one of London's most famous variety venues, hosting everyone from Charlie Chaplin to music hall queen Marie Lloyd.

Yet Hackney Council was planning to turn this wonderful Edwardian extravagance into a multi-storey carpark as recently as 1986. Mercifully, the theatre was rescued by an independent theatre group, who have just completed a £16 million facelift, restoring the Empire to its original 1900s splendour.

The decline of the Empire was a sorry tale. With audiences deserting in droves for cinema and television, the variety theatre closed its doors in February 1956; the final performance was a somewhat dubious 'black impersonation' act by vaudeville star GH Elliott. It was briefly used as a studio for the TV talent show *Oh Boy* – launching the career of Sir Cliff Richard – before it was converted into a Mecca bingo hall. The opulent interior was painted over and the façade was stripped of its distinctive terracotta towers and statue of Euterpe, the Muse of Music. The bingo hall never

did very well and in 1986, Hackney Council announced plans to tear it down and build a carpark in its place.

Salvation came in the form of Roland Muldoon, leader of the touring comic theatre group CAST. Muldoon had been commissioned by the Greater London Council (GLC) to create new venues for variety and stand-up comedy and after remortgaging his house to raise money, he reopened the Empire as a venue in 1986. Considering the satirical nature of CAST performances, this could easily have been a subversive plot by the left-wing GLC to stir up opposition to the Conservative government of Margaret Thatcher. Outspoken celebrities to be launched from the springboard of the reinvented Empire included Harry Enfield, Paul Merton, Julian Clary, and French and Saunders.

In 2001, Muldoon and team embarked on a massive renovation scheme with funding from the Arts Council, the Heritage Lottery and Hackney Council. Predictably, the pot of government money was woefully inadequate, so celebrities from the world of comedy were drafted in to help fundraise, including restoration-obsessed comic Griff Rhys Jones. There were a few minor hiccups. The fundraising was so successful that the Heritage Lottery withdrew £200,000 of its contribution. Then the construction firm

---

Bow, to the east, has long been a gateway between London and the east of England. Legend has it that the bow-shaped bridge that gave the area its name was constructed on the orders of Queen Matilda, wife of Henry I, after she got soaked while fording the River Lea. The area later became a major centre for milling grain and gunpowder, particularly around **Three Mills Island** (*see below*). On the next island east, Joseph Bazalgette's Gothic **Abbey Mill** was built in 1868 to disguise a Victorian sewage pumping station.

Ragged School Museum

46-50 Copperfield Road, E3 4RR (8980 6405/www.raggedschoolmuseum.org.uk). Mile End tube. **Open** 10am-5pm Wed, Thur; 2-5pm 1st Sun of mth. *Tours* by arrangement; phone for details. **Admission** free; donations appreciated.

Ragged schools were an early experiment in public education and thousands of East End urchins were schooled here by the famous Dr Barnardo in the 19th century. This surprisingly good museum gives a history of each of the Tower Hamlets, touching on education, poverty, industry, wartime devastation and

immigration. There's a recreation of a typical ragged classroom where historical re-enactments are staged for visiting school children.

Three Mills Island

Three Mill Lane, E3 3DU (8980 4626/www.house mill.com). Bromley-by-Bow tube. **Open** 11am-4pm 1st Sun of mth. *Tours* *June-Sept* 2-4pm Sat. *May-Oct* 2-4pm Sun. **Admission** £3; £1.50 concessions; free under-16s. **No credit cards**.

This large island in the River Lea takes its name from the three mills that used to grind flour and gunpowder here until the 18th century. The House Mill, built in 1776, is the oldest and largest tidal mill in Britain and it now houses a museum of early industrial history. The island offers pleasant walks on warm days and there's a small café and a crafts market on the first Sunday of the month.

Walthamstow

Walthamstow tube/rail.

As well as being the stomping ground of now departed boy band East 17, Walthamstow won Time Out's search for London's best village in

---

employed for the renovation went bankrupt with 90 per cent of the work completed, leading to a desperate last-minute push to scare up an extra £1 million to finally get the job done.

But it was worth it in the end. The restorers have revived most of the original details, including acres of lush velvet upholstery and gilded scrollwork, and the terracotta domes and statue on the façade. Blending the old with the new, the façade also features the words 'Hackney Empire' spelled out in giant terracotta letters.

Future projects range from theatre and music shows designed to highlight local talent to stand-up comedy, body-building competitions and opera. There are even two new theatrical spaces: the 100-seat Acorn Theatre and 250-seat Bullion Room. All in, the Empire looks well set to achieve its prime objective – which is, according to Muldoon, to provide 'everything for everybody'. Old-fashioned, po-faced theatre is dead; long live variety!

Hackney Empire

291 Mare Street, E8 1EJ (8985 2424/www.hackneyempire.co.uk). Bethnal Green tube then 106, 254, D6 bus/bus 38, 55, 48.

2003, so it must be doing something right. Traditionally working class, the area is now attracting waves of middle-class homebuyers who have been priced out of the housing market any closer to the centre.

The area around Walthamstow Central station is fairly pedestrian, but the streets to the east are full of historical treasures. Just off Hoe Street, **St Mary's Walthamstow** is plain on the outside, but parts of the interior date back to the 16th century. The surrounding cemetery doubles as a nature reserve. The cottage-like **Vestry House Museum** (8509 1917, open 10am-1pm, 2-5.30pm Mon-Fri, 10am-1pm, 2-5pm Sat), full of interesting local memorabilia is a short walk along Vestry Road. Back in the centre, **Walthamstow Market** is Europe's longest street market.

Walthamstow's other attractions are further north on Forest Road. West of the junction with Hoe Street is the art deco **Walthamstow Town Hall**; head east and you'll find peaceful **Lloyd Park**, with duck ponds, an aviary and a scented garden. The grand Georgian house at the entrance contains the **William Morris Gallery** (*see p164*). To the north, over the A406, lies **Walthamstow Stadium** (*see p327*), London's best-known greyhound track.

From Walthamstow Central station, it's three stops by train (about every 15 minutes) to Chingford, the gateway to spectacular **Epping Forest**. We have the Victorians to thank for saving this splendid green lung: in 1878, Parliament granted the City of London the power to buy land within 25 miles (40 kilometres) of the city centre to be used for the recreation of city dwellers.

The huge park is two thirds primeval forest; Henry VIII used to come here to hunt for deer and poachers. (The punishment for successful poachers was death; unsuccessful poachers only lost their hands.) Queen Elizabeth I maintained a hunting lodge in Epping Forest that has now been converted into a free museum (8529 6681, open 1pm-4pm Wed-Sun). The forest is a wonderful space for walking, jogging, cycling, riding and picnicking; stop in at the visitors' centre (8508 0028) for information and maps.

William Morris Gallery

Lloyd Park, Forest Road, E17 4PP (8527 3782/ www.lbwf.gov.uk/wmg). Walthamstow Central tube/rail/34, 97 bus. **Open** 10am-1pm, 2-5pm Tue-Sat, 1st Sun of mth. *Tours* phone for details. **Admission** free; donations appreciated. **Credit** *Shop* MC, V.

Artist, socialist and wallpaper mogul, William Morris lived in this house until 1856, so it's appropriate that it was chosen to house the only gallery in London highlighting his work. You don't have to be an Arts and Crafts buff to appreciate the wonderful wallpaper, fabric, stained glass and ceramics produced by Morris and his colleagues.

Leyton

South of Walthamstow, suburban **Leyton** sits at the bottom of the green Lea Valley. Some haphazard redevelopment after World War II means it falls short of the standard set by its northern neighbour, but the **Lee Valley Park** is good for walking and there's an ice rink, nature reserve and riding stable on Lea Bridge Road (www.leevalleypark.org.uk).

German bombers were drawn to Leyton by its gas and waterworks, some of which were redeveloped as the **WaterWorks Nature Reserve** (Lea Bridge Road; 8988 7566). The water-filter beds here were built to fight a cholera epidemic in 1849 but now provide a home for 322 species of plant, 25 species of breeding birds and scores of pitch and putt golfers, open 8am to dusk daily.

Docklands

Shadwell or Wapping tube/Various stops on the Docklands Light Railway (DLR).

For many, Docklands is a living memorial to the values of Thatcher's Britain. In the 1980s and '90s, working-class neighbourhoods along the river were bulldozed without planning constraint to make way for high-rise office buildings, marinas and loft developments. Modern Docklands is London's answer to Manhattan, a towering cityscape of skyscrapers, plazas and coffee franchises.

That Docklands exists at all is testament to the resilience of the financial sector. Developers faced protests from local residents from day one and numerous construction projects had to be rescued from bankruptcy, including Canary Wharf itself. The whole project almost went belly up after the IRA blew up a car bomb near Canary Wharf in 1996. Fortunately, Docklands was bailed out by HSBC and Citigroup, who built their own soaring skyscrapers in the shadow of Canary Wharf.

Although the redevelopment destroyed a way of life, it was largely inevitable. Labour unrest, the collapse of the Empire and the development

of deep-draught container ships all contributed to the closure of the docks during the 1960s. Today, some 55,000 people commute daily to work at Canary Wharf.

Thames Clippers (7977 6892, www.thames clippers.com) provides daily ferry connections between various jetties in Docklands and central London. The Thames Path (www. nationaltrails.gov.uk) provides excellent insights into riverside development.

St Katharine's & Wapping

Just east of Tower Bridge, **St Katharine's** has been putty in the hands of developers since 1828, when 1,250 cottages, a brewery and the 12th-century church of St Katharine demolished to make way for a grandiose development known as St Katharine's Dock. In the 1960s, the development was reinvented as St Katharine's Haven, and became the first of the Docklands redevelopments. Now a yacht marina, it houses century-old barges, plush modern motor launches, as well as a fleet of upmarket pubs and restaurants catering to wealthy condo owners.

East of St Katharine's, **Wapping** was the setting for one of London's biggest industrial disputes in 1986, when 6,000 print workers from Rupert Murdoch's newspaper company, News International went on strike. Murdoch sacked the strikers and hired blackleg electricians to run the printing presses, triggering violent demonstrations.

In 1598 historian John Stowe described **Wapping High Street** as a 'filthy strait passage, with alleys of small tenements or cottages… built and inhabited by sailors' victuallers'. A surprising number of these historic pubs survive today, including the 1545 **Town of Ramsgate** (No.62), where 'hanging judge' George Jeffreys was captured in 1688 while trying to escape to Europe disguised as a woman. Other notable patrons include Captain Bligh and Fletcher Christian of HMS *Bounty* fame, and 'Colonel' Blood, who attempted to steal the Crown Jewels in 1671.

Down the road at No.108, the Captain Kidd pub commemorates the execution of privateer William Kidd at **Execution Dock** in 1701. Right up until the 19th century, convicted pirates were dragged to this gruesome spot near Wapping New Stairs and publicly hanged at low tide. Further east, ever-busy boozer the Prospect of Whitby (*see p228*) dates from 1520 and once counted Pepys, Dickens and Turner among its regulars. Opposite, the red-brick London Hydraulic Power Company building (1890) is now the **Wapping Project** (*see p292*), an impressive restaurant and art space.

Inland, a large mural at St George's Town Hall on Cable Street commemorates the day in October 1936 when working-class locals rose up in support of their Jewish neighbours and blocked a march by fascist Blackshirts led by Sir Oswald Mosley. On Cannon Street Road, St George-in-the-East is yet another brooding Hawksmoor structure.

Limehouse

Sandwiched between Wapping and the Isle of Dogs, **Limehouse** is named after medieval lime kilns, but this was historically a seafaring neighbourhood. A 1610 census revealed that half of its working population were mariners. There are handsome Victorian wharfs along **Narrow Street**, and Charles Dickens used the tiny, dark and still superb Grapes (*see p228*) as the model for the Six Jolly Fellowship Porters Tavern in *Our Mutual Friend*.

Inland on Limehouse Road, St Anne's Limehouse is another imposing Hawksmoor structure, with the second highest spire in Britain after Big Ben tower. Opposite is the art-deco pile of the **Sailor's Society Mission**. Britain's first wave of Chinese immigrants,

mainly seafarers, settled here in the 19th century, giving the area a reputation for gambling and opium dens: Oscar Wilde's Dorian Gray came here to buy opium and Limehouse was the hideout for Sax Rohmer's outrageously stereotyped villain, Fu Manchu.

Isle of Dogs

The Isle of Dogs is not an island but the land contained in the prominent loop in the east river. But for centuries it had an island culture and a fierce sense of community. It was the area hardest hit by the collapse of the Port of London docks and most damaged by the 1980s redevelopments, which planted their triumphal totem, Canary Wharf Tower, bang in its heart.

Many of the docks here played a pivotal role in the development of the British Empire, most notably the **East** and **West India Docks**, which unloaded spices, sugar, tea, rum, coconut fibre and timber from India and the Caribbean well into the 20th century. The area took an incredible pounding during World War II; at the height of the Blitz, the docks were hit by German bombing raids on 57 consecutive nights. The story is powerfully told at the

Sightseeing

Rich Mix

'The attraction of Rich Mix is that it is a mirror of the East End. And when you walk around Shoreditch, people are very separate in their communities – the fashion crowd don't mix with the architecture crowd, let alone different races mixing. One thing we want to do is bring these people together.' So says Keith Kahn, chief executive of Rich Mix, an enormous £16 million performance venue at the top of Brick Lane that's due to open in autumn 2005.

The centre, formerly an old garment warehouse, is being converted by the cutting-edge Penoyre & Prasad Architects. Once open, it will feature a multiscreen cinema (showing everything from the latest Hollywood blockbusters to Asian art house), gallery spaces, recording studios, an IT suite, a digital cultural archive, a café and bar, and affordable workspace for creative and cultural business enterprises. It will also house two of the UK's leading music training agencies, CM (Community Music) and Asian Dub Foundation Education, an offshoot of the pop group Asian Dub Foundation, which has been involved in supporting Rich Mix from the outset. The centre will also be one of the bases for Guildhall University.

'In Tower Hamlets we have one of the biggest groups of refugees in Britain. Many immigrant groups are still at a stage where they don't have funding for social activities or to develop networks. This is where Rich Mix can come in,' says musician John Pandit from Asian Dub Foundation. 'Recently, a Somali woman from an outreach project I'm involved in said to me, "You know. I've always wanted to get into music." Soon I'll be able to say to her, "Well come here, learn the basics – you can even do a degree-type course."'

But Rich Mix is a million miles away from the old-style community arts projects – as well as impacting on the lives of local communities, its state-of-the-art performance, art and film facilities are intended to draw tourists from across the globe. 'We represent the new culture of London: the younger, different and digital culture, both global and local. The ideal visitor here is someone from New York rubbing shoulders with a local lad,' says Kahn.

Rich Mix

39-47 Bethnal Green Road, E1 6HZ (www.richmix.org.uk). Liverpool Street tube/rail. **Map** *p403 R4.*

Museum in Docklands.

Museum in Docklands (*see below*) on West India Quay. Despite the intensity of the bombing, it was the development of modern container ships that ultimately spelled doom for the Port of London. Dock operations shifted to Tilbury, where the Thames was deeper, and the Isle of Dogs went into rapid decline. By the 1980s the area was so run-down that Stanley Kubrick chose it as a stand-in for war-torn Vietnam in his 1987 movie *Full Metal Jacket*.

After two decades of development, the area has been reinvented as a futuristic metropolis, with Japanese-style gardens, perky apartment complexes, subterranean shopping malls and the elevated Docklands Light Railway (DLR) snaking through the skyscrapers. The grandest structure here is still Cesar Pelli's rocket-shaped **Canary Wharf Tower**, more properly known as One Canada Square. With 50 occupied floors, it's been the tallest building in the UK since 1991. A shopping centre occupies its lower floors. Canary Wharf was joined in 2002 by the **Citigroup Centre** and **HSBC Tower**, Britain's second- and third-tallest buildings.

Clones of these giant towers are proliferating across the island, where concrete architecture and new ecological projects mix with the scant remnants of the original local housing, wharves and street layout, with gap-toothed vistas to water wherever you look. One remnant of traditional East End culture is **Billingsgate Fish Market** (open 5-8.30am Tue-Sat) just across the footbridge from Canary Wharf.

Heading south, **Island Gardens** offers a gorgeous view across the Thames towards Greenwich, said to be Wren's favourite vista during his construction of the Old Royal Naval College. Nearby, you'll find one end of the Victorian foot tunnel (lift service 7am-7pm Mon-Sat, 10am-5.30pm Sun) that surfaces beside the *Cutty Sark* on the south bank.

As for the name 'Isle of Dogs', the popular theory is that Henry VII kept his hunting dogs here. However, it's also propounded that Canary Wharf used to receive goods from the Canary Islands, corrupted from the Latin *Canariae Insulae* – literally, 'Isles of Dogs'.

Museum in Docklands

No.1 Warehouse, West India Quay, Hertsmere Road, E14 4AL (recorded information 0870 444 3856/box office 0870 444 3855/www.museumindocklands. org.uk). West India Quay DLR or Canary Wharf tube. **Open** 10am-6pm Mon, Tue, Thur-Sun; 10am-8pm Wed. **Admission** (unlimited entrance for 1 year) £5, £3 concessions, free under-16s. **Credit** MC, V. This huge and interesting museum sprawls over several floors of a tastefully restored Georgian warehouse. It doesn't shirk from covering the controversies surrounding the redevelopment of Docklands, and the contemporary galleries are every bit as interesting as those covering ancient maritime history. Many displays are narrated by people who were involved and the section on the Docklands at War is both harrowing and moving. The ticket is valid for up to a year; useful, as there's a lot to see here.

Further east

East of the Isle of Dogs, the Beckton DLR stop offers good views across the river to the Millennium Dome. Alight at Royal Victoria or Custom House and you can stroll around vast Royal Victoria Dock to peaceful **Thames Barrier Park** (7511 4111/www.thames barrierpark.org.uk) on North Woolwich Road. Opened in 2001, this was London's first entirely new park in half a century, and the lush sunken garden offers grand views over the futuristic **Thames Barrier** (*see p171*). Further east, near City Airport, is the jolly little **North Woolwich Old Station Museum** (Pier Road, 7474 7244, open 1-5pm Sat, Sun, closed Dec).

South-east London

Thames-side, then south to countryside.

Rotherhithe

Rotherhithe tube.
Redriffe, as **Rotherhithe** used to be known,
was a shipbuilding village with the beloved
mariners' church of **St Mary** at its heart
(open only for services). The Pilgrim ship, the
Mayflower, sailed from here in 1620; its master,
Christopher Jones, was buried in St Mary's
churchyard in 1622. Today the cobbly streets
are all part of a conservation area; Rotherhithe's
warehouses and docks are the focus of
aspirational riverside living, and rickety old
riverside pubs, such as the Mayflower (117
Rotherhithe Street, 7237 4088), attract tourists
and post-office suits rather than rum-soaked
smugglers. The Thames Path offers views of
yet more stylish pads, north and south, but an
atmospheric slice of old Rotherhithe awaits at
the **Brunel Engine House & Tunnel
Exhibition** (*see right*).

Out of the conservation area, the **Norwegian
Church & Seamen's Mission** lies at the
mouth of another tunnel, the stinky Rotherhithe
car one. There are several Scandinavian
churches around here, a relic of Rotherhithe's
historical links with Nordic sailors, which date
right back to the Vikings. Across Jamaica Road,
the beautifully restored **Southwark Park** is
London's oldest municipal park and has a
community art gallery (open Wed-Sun) with a
café, a lovely old bandstand, landscaped lake
and refurbished playgrounds.

Brunel Engine House & Tunnel Exhibition

*Brunel Engine House, Railway Avenue, SE16 4LF
(7231 3840/www.brunelenginehouse.org.uk).
Rotherhithe tube.* **Open** 1-5pm Sat, Sun. *Tours* by
appointment only. **Admission** £2; £1 concessions;
free under-5s; £5 family (2+2). **No credit cards**.
The story of the Eighth Wonder of the World, which
is what the Victorians called the first underwater
tunnel, is told in this museum, housed in the original engine house. The Thames Tunnel was designed
by Marc Isambard Brunel with the help of his more
famous son, Isambard Kingdom Brunel – the only
time they worked together. The main thrust of the
exhibition is the construction of the tunnel, finished
in 1843, and now used for the East London tube line.

Deptford & Greenwich

*Cutty Sark DLR for Maritime Greenwich or Deptford
Bridge DLR/Greenwich DLR/rail/Deptford or Maze
Hill rail.*
River views being at a premium, apartment
blocks continue to stack up along the banks
of the Thames at Deptford. Follow the
muddy creeks inland, however, and you find
a traditional working-class neighbourhood.
Deptford High Street has a rowdy market and
a couple of historic pie and mash shops. The
ridiculously handsome **St Paul's Church**
(Mary Ann Gardens, 8692 0989), built in Roman
baroque style by Thomas Archer around 1712-
30, dominates the area. It was rededicated in
September 2004 after refurbishment.

Dulwich Picture Gallery.
See p173.

Sailors in the 17th century worshipped at **St Nicholas's Church**, on Deptford Green (8692 8848). The crumbly skull-and-crossbone carvings on its gate piers lend it a forbidding air. Christopher Marlowe is rumoured to be buried here following a fatal brawl in Deptford tavern; there is certainly a plaque recording his death. The church is usually unlocked in the morning, but ring before you visit.

With its handsome Georgian and Regency architecture and air of a decadent seaside resort, **Greenwich** earned its reputation when it was a playground for Tudor royalty. Henry VIII and his daughters Mary I and Elizabeth I were all born here – Greenwich Palace was Henry's favourite residence. The palace fell into disrepair under Cromwell, and during the reign of William and Mary, who preferred Hampton Court and Kensington, it was designated as the Royal Naval Hospital. The hospital is now the **Old Royal Naval College** (*see p170*).

If you take a riverboat to Greenwich Pier you disembark in the shadow of the slowly disintegrating **Cutty Sark** (*see p169*). The entrance to the Greenwich Foot Tunnel, which takes you under the Thames to Island Gardens and Docklands, is also here. **Greenwich Tourist Information Centre** (0870 608 2000) is based in the Royal Naval College and is a useful first point of call.

Walk past the Old Royal Naval College with the river on your left, and you'll reach the

Trafalgar Tavern, a favourite haunt of Thackeray, Dickens and Wilkie Collins. Tiny Crane Street, on the far side of the pub, leads to Trinity Hospital, which in 1617 provided a home to '21 retired gentlemen of Greenwich'. The path continues as far as the attractive Cutty Sark Tavern, dating from 1695.

Back in town, busy **Greenwich Market** (*see p255*) pulls in the tourists at weekends, but the area's loveliest bits are away from the centre, either along the riverside walk or around the prettiest of the Royal Parks, **Greenwich Park**, with the Wren-designed **Royal Observatory** (*see p170*) at the top of the hill (a shuttle bus – Apr-Sept, £1.50, 8859 1096 – can take you up there from Cutty Sark Gardens) and the **National Maritime Museum** (*see p169*) and **Queen's House** (*see p170*) at the bottom. In between there are beautiful formal gardens, deer enclosures and avenues of historic trees. In 1616 James I commissioned Inigo Jones to rebuild the Tudor Greenwich Palace within Greenwich's historic park. The palace became **Queen's House**, England's first Palladian villa. The parkland was later redesigned by André Le Nôtre, who landscaped Versailles for Louis XIV. At the southern end of the park is the **Ranger's House** (*see p170*).

Two different worlds lie at opposite compass points from Greenwich. North, on Greenwich Peninsula, sits the empty **Millennium Dome**, destined to become a sport and leisure complex

My kind of town 'Mad' Frankie Fraser

During the 1960s just the name Frankie Fraser would have hardened criminals sprinting for the door. Frank Fraser – 'Mad' Frankie to anyone who rubbed him up the wrong way – was a henchman for the Richardson brothers, who ran a rival gangland empire to the Kray twins on the south side of the river. Like the Krays, Frankie loved his mum and wouldn't hear a bad word said about another gangster. He was also tougher than the school hamster at Borstal. During his criminal career, Frankie was involved in more notorious gangland capers than most people have had hot dinners. Today he plays a more sedate role, running guided tours of gangland sites in the capital (7708 5682, www.madfrankiefraser.co.uk).
Where would you take visitors to London?
I'd take them to old London. Manze's pie and mash shop in Tower Bridge Road (No.87, 7407 2985), then the Blind Beggar pub in Whitechapel (337 Whitechapel Road, 7247

at the heart of a new town made up of acres of much-needed cheap housing. To the south, **Maze Hill** runs from Trafalgar Road, forming the eastern boundary of Greenwich Park. The castle-like house on the hilltop was built by architect and playwright John Vanbrugh, who lived here from 1719 to 1726.

Maze Hill leads to **Blackheath**'s grassy expanses – hemmed by incessant traffic and surrounded by smart Georgian homes. Some of Britain's earliest sports clubs started here: the Royal Blackheath Golf Club (1745), the Blackheath Hockey Club (1861) and the Blackheath Football Club (which actually plays rugby; 1862).

Cutty Sark

King William Walk, SE10 9HT (8858 3445/ www.cuttysark.org.uk). Cutty Sark DLR/Greenwich DLR/rail. **Open** 10am-5pm daily (last entry 4.30pm). **Admission** £4.25; £3.25 concessions; £10.50 family; group rates available. **Credit** MC, V.

The world's only Grade I listed ship and last surviving tea clipper, built by Hercules Linton in 1869, has been in dry dock for 50 years. The *Cutty Sark* is in a parlous state after doing sterling service as a tourist attraction, and it's calculated that it will cost about £25m to keep her open beyond 2007. Whether the Heritage Lottery Fund will be able to help is a moot point (an application for a grant of £11.75m was under consideration as we went to press). The lower decks house an extensive exhibition on the clipper's history, plus paintings, models and the world's largest collection of carved and painted figureheads.

Fan Museum

12 Crooms Hill, SE10 8ER (8305 1441/www.fan-museum.org). Cutty Sark DLR/Greenwich DLR/rail. **Open** 11am-5pm Tue-Sat; noon-5pm Sun. **Admission** £3.50; £2.50 concessions; free under-7s; free OAPs, disabled 2-5pm Tues. **Credit** MC, V.

A pair of smartly restored Georgian townhouses is home to more than 3,000 hand-held folding fans, although they're not all exhibited at the same time – antique fans need to be rested. The Orangery is a beautiful room, all hand-painted murals and exquisite furnishing: take tea there with your little finger cocked on Tuesdays and Sunday afternoons.

National Maritime Museum

Park Row, SE10 9NF (8858 4422/information 8312 6565/www.nmm.ac.uk). Greenwich DLR/rail/Maze Hill rail. **Open** *July, Aug* 10am-6pm daily. *Sept-June* 10am-5pm daily. **Admission** free. **Credit** MC, V.

This most elegant museum charts the nation's seafaring history. There is a lot to get around, even if you eschew the special exhibitions (which usually charge admission). Of the permanent galleries, 'Explorers' is devoted to naval pioneers, 'Passengers' is a paean to glamorous old ocean liners, and 'Maritime London' tells the capital's nautical history through old prints and model ships. Upstairs, 'Seapower' covers naval battles from Gallipoli to the Falklands and the 'Art of the Sea' is the world's largest maritime art collection. On level 3, the 'All Hands' gallery has children learning Morse code, navigating Viking longboats or steering a modern passenger ferry. 'Nelson and Napoleon' is the big

Sightseeing

6195). Next, that beautiful, old Italian church in Clerkenwell, St Peter's, and the Old Bailey, where my life hung in the balance when I was nicked for murder. And lastly, New Scotland Yard, where it's alleged I slung the ashes of my victims...

Where do you like to go for peace and quiet?

I'd go to Soho Square. When you're in the square, it's unbelievable. All around you, there's all these streets, all this hustle and bustle, but sitting in the square itself, it's lovely.

What place for you is quintessentially London?

East Lane Market in Peckham. It's packed to capacity. It's where Charlie Chaplin was born. It's got old London pubs. There's been murders committed down there. It's got everything.

Where would you go to feel a sense of history?

That would be Soho again. There's something about it. It's all still the same, though, of course, these days when I go to Soho for a drink, there's people coming up for my autograph and everything.

What is your favourite building or landmark in London?

That would be Tower Bridge. It's the history. The first man to be beheaded in the Tower was a Scottish rebel called Fraser, so I feel right at home there.

What is your favourite quirky feature of London?

Everybody loves London. You can't help it. It's extremely tolerant. We take in everyone from all round the world and that's wonderful.

Where would you go for an ideal London night out?

I'd go to the Savoy. It's a beautiful building and I can see right across to where I was born. It's lovely to think that when I was a kid, I used to do penny for the guy right outside.

exhibition of 2005 (7 July-13 Nov), marking the 200th anniversary of the Battle of Trafalgar. Summer also sees the opening of a new permanent gallery entitled 'Your Ocean', showing how life depends on the sea.

Old Royal Naval College

King William Walk, SE10 9LW (8269 4747/www.
greenwichfoundation.org.uk). Cutty Sark DLR/
Greenwich DLR/rail. **Open** 10am-5pm daily.
Admission free. **Credit** MC, V.

Built by Sir Christopher Wren in 1696, these buildings were originally a hospital and are now part of the University of Greenwich. The public are allowed into the rococo chapel and Painted Hall; the amazing painted tribute to William and Mary took artist Sir James Thornhill 19 years to complete. For his efforts, he was paid £6,685 2s 4d – just £3 per square yard. In 1806 the body of Lord Nelson was laid in state here. In the chapel there are free organ recitals on the first Sunday of each month.

The Greenwich Gateway Visitor Centre, in the Pepys Building, has an exhibition on 2,000 years of Greenwich history as well as visitor information.

Queen's House

Park Row, SE10 9NF (8312 6565/www.nmm.ac.uk).
Greenwich DLR/rail/Maze Hill rail. **Open** 10am-5pm daily. **Admission** free. **Credit** MC, V.

Designed by Inigo Jones in 1616 for James I's wife, Anne of Denmark, the Queen's House was his first attempt at Palladian architecture. The interior contains the National Maritime Museum's art collection, with works by Hogarth and Gainsborough. A magnificent colonnade connects the building to the National Maritime Museum (*see p169*). An exhibition of maritime photography mounted by the National Trust and Magnum (working title: 'The Coast Exposed') runs from 23 March 2005.

Ranger's House

Chesterfield Walk, SE10 8QX (8853 0035/
www.english-heritage.org.uk). Cutty Sark DLR/
Greenwich DLR/rail/Blackheath rail. **Open** Apr-Sept 10am-5pm Wed-Sun. **Admission** (EH) £5; £3.80 concessions; £2.50 5-15yrs. **Credit** MC, V.

Once a 'grace and favour' home to the Greenwich park ranger, this pretty 18th-century villa had been converted into council-owned changing rooms by 1902. English Heritage eventually refurbished the place, which now houses the treasure amassed by millionaire diamond magnate Julius Wernher, who died in 1912. His collection of 19th-century art, including jewellery (he had the biggest collection of Renaissance jewellery in the world), bronzes, tapestries, furniture, porcelain and paintings is most unusual – enamelled skulls, jewel-encrusted reptiles and miniature coffins are among the more bizarre exhibits. Phone to confirm opening hours.

Royal Observatory & Planetarium

Greenwich Park, SE10 9NL (8312 6565/www.rog.
nmm.ac.uk). Greenwich DLR/rail/Maze Hill rail.
Open 10am-5pm daily. **Admission** free.
Credit MC, V.

Built for Charles II by Wren in 1675, this observatory now examines the life of John Flamsteed, the Royal Astronomer assigned the task of mapping the heavens. A series of set-piece rooms evokes the Flamsteed household. Elsewhere, there are cases of clocks and watches, from hourglasses to an astonishingly accurate atomic clock. The dome houses the largest refracting telescope in the country. In the courtyard is the Prime Meridian Line – star of a billion snaps of tourists with a foot in each hemisphere. Up the hill from the Observatory, the Planetarium offers a range of guided tours to the stars; these take place at 2.30pm and 3.30pm daily (£4; £2 children).

There are changes afoot round here. The 'Time and Space' project, partly financed by the Heritage Lottery Fund, will by 2007 open up one-third of the site previously closed to visitors. The site remains open while work is in progress.

Charlton & Woolwich

Charlton, Woolwich Arsenal or Woolwich Dockyard rail.

A pleasant cycle path takes the intrepid from Blackheath to the once well-to-do area of **Charlton**, which still retains villagey charm. Until 1872 the area was the focus of the rowdy Charlton Horn Fair (recompense from King John for seducing a local miller's wife). Today **Charlton House** is the main attraction. Its once-grand terrace looks out over Charlton Park. More parkland – Maryon Wilson Park – takes you north to Woolwich Church Street and the river, spanned by London's lifeline, the **Thames Barrier** (*see p171*).

Woolwich has an intriguing naval and military history. The Woolwich Arsenal was established in Tudor times as the country's main source of munitions and, by World War I, stretched 32 miles along the river. The arsenal was closed in 1967, but some beautiful buildings have been preserved. The chief visitor attraction is **Firepower** (*see p171*); south of here, the **Royal Artillery Barracks** has the longest Georgian façade in the country.

The **Woolwich Ferry** crosses to **North Woolwich** every 15 minutes or so. It's a free service, and has been since 1889, when today's diesel-driven chuggers replaced the paddle steamers that had been in use since the 14th century. The ferry will carry you to the **North Woolwich Old Station Museum** (*see p166*) on the other side of the Thames.

Charlton House

Charlton Road, SE7 8RE (8856 3951/
www.greenwich.gov.uk). Charlton rail/53, 54, 380,
422 bus. **Open** by appointment 9am-10.30pm Mon-Fri; 10am-4pm Sat. **Admission** free.

Sublime and ridiculous collide in delightful old Charlton House. One of the finest examples of Jacobean architecture in the country, built between

1607 and 1612, the place has been adapted for use by the community as a library and meeting rooms for local groups. The Mulberry tearoom, where pensioners sit and read their library books, has a huge ornate fireplace. Outside, the brickwork is crumbly and subject to graffiti; lager cans lie under benches in the Jacobean herb garden and the views over scruffy Charlton Park are less than inspiring. Beside the car park, a spreading mulberry tree that dates from 1608 still bears fruit in season.

Firepower

Royal Arsenal, Woolwich, SE18 6ST (8855 7755/ www.firepower.org.uk). Woolwich Arsenal rail. **Open** *Nov-Mar* 11am-5pm Fri-Sun (last entry 4pm); *Apr-Oct* 10.30am-5pm Wed-Sun (last entry 4pm). **Admission** £5; £4.50 concessions; £2.50 5-16s; free under-5s; £12 family. **Credit** MC, V.
Since the completion of Phase Two of the development, the Royal Artillery Museum has become a must-see for devotees of military hardware. Exhibits trace the evolution of artillery from primitive catapults to nuclear warheads. There's an affecting introductory film in the Breech cinema, then visitors are bombarded from all sides by a multimedia presentation called 'Fields of Fire', which covers various 20th-century wars. Other galleries in this building include the Gunnery Hall (full of howitzers and tanks), the Real Weapon gallery (which shows you how guns work) and the medal gallery. Phase Two, opened by Dame Vera Lynn on 31 March 2004, includes a collection of trophy guns and the Cold War gallery, which focuses on the 'monster bits' (ginormous tanks and guns). The first-floor Command Post is child-friendly, with a paintball range and a walk-in Anderson shelter.

Thames Barrier Visitors' Centre

1 Unity Way, SE18 5NJ (8305 4188/www. environment-agency.gov.uk). North Greenwich tube/Charlton rail/161,177, 180, 472 bus. **Open** *Apr-Sept* 10.30am-4.30pm daily. *Oct-Mar* 11am-3.30pm daily. **Admission** (LP) £1; 75p concessions; 50p 5-16s; free under-5s. **Credit** MC, V.
The world's largest adjustable dam was completed in 1982 at a cost of £535m. The nine shiny metal piers anchor massive steel gates that can be raised from the riverbed to protect London from surge tides: the barrier has saved the city 67 times. The visitors' centre on the south bank shows how the barrier was built, how it works and those bits of London that would be submerged if it didn't. Check the website for dates of monthly partial test-closures. In 2005 a full-scale test takes place on 8 May, part of the barrier's 21st birthday celebrations.

at the **Brit Oval** (*see p325*) to watch county and international cricket matches. Off Kennington Lane are elegant streets: Cardigan Street, Courtenay Street and Courtenay Square all have neat neo-Georgian terraced houses.
A short walk north takes you to the **Imperial War Museum** (*see below*), beyond which lies London's roundabout of shame, the **Elephant & Castle**, the centre of an area historically called Newington. Currently comprising a stained red 1960s shopping mall containing low-grade chains, all marooned in a whirl of traffic, this horror's days are numbered. The Elephant & Castle Regeneration scheme (www.elehantandcastle.org.uk) and the London Development Agency plan to rework the entire area by 2012. Hurrah.

Imperial War Museum

Lambeth Road, SE1 6HZ (7416 5000/www.iwm. org.uk). Lambeth North tube/Elephant & Castle tube/rail. **Open** 10am-6pm daily. **Admission** free. **Credit** AmEx, MC, V. **Map** p404 N10.
The lump of Berlin Wall outside this heavyweight museum bears the legend in graffiti 'Change your Life'. The relic faces a pair of colossal warship artillery pieces, setting the scene for an impressive display of military might inside – tanks, planes, submarines and jeeps all salvaged from past world wars. Beyond the hardware, the life-changing awfulness of war is exposed. On the lower ground floor, you're plunged into Word War I with its smelly Trench Experience peopled by bloodied, waxen cannon fodder, or you can take a right into World War II and the teeth-chattering Blitz Experience. In between there's a countdown clock face, whose minute hand ticks off the number of people killed in war. When we visited it stood at 103,807,575. And counting. The Holocaust Exhibition on the third floor traces the history of anti-Semitism and the rise of Hitler. Shocking images of brutality and suffering make it unsuitable for children under 14, but it's the vast collection of salvaged shoes, clothes, spectacles and other mementos, as well as testimonials from survivors, that break the heart. On the fourth floor, 'Crimes Against Humanity', covering genocide and ethnic violence in our time, leaves you in no doubt about the cost of war (over-16s only). Exhibitions for 2005 include, until 31 July, 'Great Escapes' – some of the audacious escape attempts made by Allied POWs in World War II. Spring 2005 launches 'The Children's War', looking at the conflict of 1939-45 through the eyes of British children. 'Lawrence of Arabia' (autumn 2005) marks the 70th anniversary of the death of TE Lawrence.

Kennington & the Elephant

Kennington tube/Elephant & Castle tube/rail.
Kennington Park is the remains of a common where, during the 18th and 19th centuries, John Wesley and other preachers addressed large audiences. Nowadays the Surrey faithful gather

Camberwell & Peckham

Denmark Hill or Peckham Rye rail.
Trafficky Camberwell Green is a frantic crossroads from which, travelling west, you reach Kennington and the Oval (*see p325*). Choose east and you pass **St Giles Church**,

an imposing early Victorian structure by Sir George Gilbert Scott of St Pancras fame. Further down towards Peckham lies Camberwell College of Arts on Peckham Road and the **South London Gallery** (*see below*), two reasons why estate agents compare arty Camberwell with trendy Hoxton.

Linking Camberwell to Peckham, **Burgess Park** was created by filling in the Grand Surrey Canal and razing rows of houses. Walking through it to Peckham takes you to a canal path cycleway that runs past the peculiar-looking **Peckham Library**, for which architect Will Alsop won awards. **Peckham Rye Common**, once grazing land, is an airy stretch with ornamental gardens. At the top, Honor Oak and Forest Hill look down over suburban south-east London and Kent. The **Horniman Museum** (*see below*) is the best reason for taking to these hills.

Horniman Museum

100 London Road, SE23 3PQ (8699 1872/ www.horniman.ac.uk). Forest Hill rail/363, 122, 176, 185, 312, 356, P4, P13 bus. **Open** 10.30am-5.30pm daily. **Admission** free; donations appreciated. **Credit** AmEx, MC, V.

Travelling tea trader Frederick J Horniman assembled a great number of curiosities, first in his home at Forest Hill and later, in 1901, in this jolly art nou-veau museum. In the recently smartened natural history gallery, skeletons, pickled fauna and stuffed birds in old-fashioned glass cases are presided over by a large walrus. The African Worlds gallery has Egyptian mummies, ceremonial masks and a huge Ijele masquerade costume. In the Music Room, the walls are hung with hundreds of instruments of every type, with touch-screens on tables for you to hear their sound and a 'Hands On' room for visitors to bash away. There's also an aquarium, cases of exotic reptiles and an observation beehive in the Environment Room. The gardens, with their animal enclosure and elegant conservatory, are lovely, and the spacious café a welcome pit stop.

To coincide with the Africa 2005 festivities taking place across the country, the Horniman is mounting 'A Celebration of African Culture', with a display of textiles and related material from the museum's extensive collection (Apr-Jan 2006). 'Amazon to Caribbean' (opening Oct 2005) highlights the cultural links of these areas.

South London Gallery

65 Peckham Road, SE5 8UH (7703 6120/www.south londongallery.org). 12, 36, 171 bus. **Open** noon-6pm Tue, Wed, Fri-Sun; noon 8.30pm Thur. **Admission** free. Founded in 1868, this forward-thinking gallery's original principal was biologist TH Huxley, grandfather of novelist Aldous. Saskia Olde-Wolbers, Beck's Futures award-winner, presents a new collection at the South London from 11 May 2005.

Dulwich & Crystal Palace

Crystal Palace, East Dulwich, Herne Hill, North Dulwich or West Dulwich rail.

Comfortable Dulwich Village is home to a boys' public school and the **Dulwich Picture Gallery** (*see below*). West of it, Herne Hill is like a halfway point between posh, white Dulwich and multicultural Brixton (*see p175*).

Car drivers pay a toll to pass through College Road from Dulwich to reach **Crystal Palace Park**. The Crystal Palace, built by Joseph Paxton for the Great Exhibition of 1851, was moved here and made Sydenham a tourist attraction, until the glittering structure burned down in 1936. Steps, balustrades and headless statues mark where the great palace once commanded views over parkland and the south-eastern suburbs. Now you look down on to Crystal Palace Sports Centre, which is going to need much work if it is to handle Olympic duties in 2012. In fact, the whole park is due to get some much-needed attention. Meanwhile, the 'monsters' (the remains of a Victorian prehistoric theme park created by Benjamin Waterhouse-Hawkins), restored in 2003, sit menacingly around the tidal lake. The **Crystal Palace Park Museum** (Anerley Hill, 8676 0700, open 11am-5pm Sun & bank holidays), is housed in the former engineering school where John Logie Baird invented TV.

Dulwich Picture Gallery

Gallery Road, SE21 7AD (8693 5254/www.dulwich picturegallery.org.uk). North Dulwich or West Dulwich rail. **Open** 10am-5pm Tue-Fri; 11am-5pm Sat, Sun. **Admission** £4; £3 concessions; free under-16s, students, unemployed, disabled. **Credit** MC, V.

Sir John Soane's neo-classical building, which inspired the National Gallery's Sainsbury Wing and the Getty Museum in Los Angeles, was the first public art gallery. Inside is a roll-call of greats: Rubens, Van Dyck, Cuyp, Poussin, Raphael and Reynolds. Exhibitions for 2005 incude works by Antony Gormley (2 May-30 July); an exhibition of the early work of Graham Sutherland (15 June-25 Sept) and a Beatrix Potter retrospective (12 Oct-22 Jan 2006).

Further south-east

Pilgrims, as caricatured by Geoffrey Chaucer, followed Watling Street, the old Roman road, out of London, passing through what were once Kentish villages on their way to Canterbury. Watling Street is now the A207 and the villages are London suburbs, such as **Bexleyheath**. This was where the founder of the Arts and Crafts Movement, William Morris, chose to settle in the **Red House** (*see right*), designed for him by Philip Webb. Today Bexleyheath's triumvirate of stately buildings is well worth

the pilgrimage by train from London Bridge. Near the Red House, in Danson Park, lies **Danson Mansion**, an 18th-century Palladian villa, restored by the Bexley Heritage Trust (01322 526574) and open to visitors from Easter 2005. More award-winning gardens, this time containing a Tudor mansion, are at **Hall Place** (Bourne Road, Bexley, Kent DA5 1PQ, 01322 526574/www.hallplaceandgardens.com).

South of the pilgrims' way, **Eltham** was well known to Londoners, and particularly to Chaucer, who served as the clerk of works during improvements to **Eltham Palace** in the reign of Richard II. In fact, the unfortunate clerk was mugged on his way to work there.

Eltham Palace

Court Yard, off Court Road, SE9 5QE (8294 2548/ www.english-heritage.org.uk). Eltham rail. **Open** *Feb, Mar 2005* 10am-4pm Wed-Fri, Sun. *Apr-Oct 2005* 10am-5pm Mon-Wed, Sun. *Nov-Mar 2006* 10am-4pm Mon-Wed, Sun. **Admission** (EH) *House & grounds (incl audio tour)* £7; £5.30 concessions; £3.50 5-16s; free under-5s; £19.50 family (2+2). *Grounds only* £4.50; £3.40 concessions; £2.30 5-16s; free under-5s. **Credit** MC, V.

A royal residence from the 13th century through to Henry VIII's heyday, Eltham Palace fell out of favour in the latter part of Henry's reign. It was not until 1931 that it came back under public gaze, thanks to the vision of Stephen Courtauld and his wife Virginia. The Courtaulds commissioned a luxorious art deco house to stand among the relics of the old palace. The Great Hall with its stained glass and intricate hammer-beam roof – pressed into service for parties, concerts and banquets – plus a 15th-century stone bridge over the moat and various medieval ruins, are all that's left of the original. The interior is all polished veneer and chunky marble, with mod cons such as concealed lighting, underfloor heating and room-to-room vacuuming system. Even the Courtaulds' ring-tailed lemur, Mah Jongg, lived the life of Riley in specially designed quarters.

Red House

13 Red House Lane, Bexleyheath, Kent DA6 8JF (01494 755588/www.nationaltrust.org.uk). Bexleyheath rail, then 10min walk or taxi from station. **Open** (pre-booked guided tour only) *Oct-Feb* 11am-3.30pm Wed-Sun. *Mar-Sept* 11am-4.15pm Wed-Sun. **Admission** (NT) £5; £2.50 children; £12.50 family. **No credit cards.**

William Morris's Society for the Protection of Ancient Buildings was part of the movement that gave rise to the National Trust and in 2003 the Trust bought his old home. Morris lived here for just five years, but it embodies his philosophy. Beautifully detailed stained glass, tiling, paintings and items of furniture remain in the house, but there is plenty still to uncover. Fundraising is an ongoing concern if it is to be restored to its original splendour – 'the beautifullest place on earth' as Burne-Jones put it. There's a tearoom in the grounds. Pre-booked guided tours only.

Sightseeing

South-west London

From Brixton's urban hymns to Richmond's park life.

Vauxhall, Stockwell & Brixton

Vauxhall tube/rail, Stockwell tube, Brixton tube/rail.
Vauxhall has a hedonistic history. Already back in the 18th century the **Vauxhall Pleasure Gardens** were London's number one playground. With its Chinese pavilion, orchestras, fountains and lamp-lit 'lovers' walks', it attracted pleasure-seekers from all walks of life. Samuel Pepys described its amusements as 'mighty divertising'; William Thackeray said it attracted 'loose characters'; while John Keats wrote a 'Sonnet to a Lady Seen for a Few Moments in Vauxhall'.

Alas, the gardens were closed in 1859, but Vauxhall's hedonistic origins live on: in recent years, it has become the capital's gay village, teeming with late-night clubs. The grande dame of the scene is the crumbling **Royal Vauxhall Tavern** (*see p296* for Duckie club), behind which lie the remains of the Pleasure Gardens – a drab park called Spring Garden. The park gained notoriety in 1996 when the Real IRA

used it to launch a mortar bomb at the **MI6 Building**. Some critics were disappointed the bomb didn't destroy it: the flamboyant cream and emerald structure divides opinion. So does the adjacent St George's Wharf, a glitzy, ziggurat-style apartment complex nicknamed the 'five ugly sisters' for its green glass towers. For a glimpse of old Vauxhall, visit lovely, leafy **Bonnington Square**, a bohemian enclave with a chilled café and lavender-filled garden.

With the arrival of the railway in the 1840s, the sleepy village of **Stockwell** became prime commuter territory. Nowadays, its main drag is an unappealing stretch of housing estates and heavy traffic. By contrast, the backstreets are packed with Victorian gems: notably, Albert Square, Durand Gardens and Stockwell Park Crescent. A blue plaque at 87 Hackford Road tells us it was Vincent van Gogh's home from 1873 to 1874. Stockwell's biggest claim to fame, however, is **Little Portugal**, a characterful string of Portuguese cafés, shops and tapas bars along South Lambeth Road. The most famous is Bar Estrela (115 South Lambeth Road, SW8, 7793 1051).

An unlikely haven for hedonists: the **Royal Vauxhall Tavern**.

It's hard to believe, but edgy **Brixton** once consisted of farmers' fields. But when Vauxhall Bridge opened in 1816, city slickers slowly trickled in. Brixton Prison, off Jebb Avenue, opened in 1820 and gained a reputation as one of the harshest in London (this still holds true). The first treadmill, invented by Sir William Cubitt, was used there to grind corn until 1921.

In the 1860s the railways and trams reached Brixton. City merchants built large houses and before long Brixton was a thriving commuter town. In 1880 Electric Avenue, later to be immortalised in Eddy Grant's song, became one of the first shopping streets lit by electricity. Between the wars, wealthy residents moved out and the mansions were turned into cheap boarding houses. The working classes, particularly theatre folk, flocked to the area: former prime minister John Major was raised here by his circus-performer father.

Brixton's personality changed dramatically during the 1950s and '60s with the arrival of immigrants from the West Indies. A generation later, tensions between black residents and police reached boiling point. The infamous riots of 1981, 1985 and 1995 erupted around Railton Road and **Coldharbour Lane**. Problems remain, particularly drug-related crime, but the mood is upbeat. Gentrification – see Trinity Gardens or Josephine Avenue for a glimpse at genteel Brixton – hasn't pushed out the anarchists and artists. And the sizeable black population, almost a third of local residents, lives alongside a growing gay community.

During the day, the Brixton buzz is best experienced by strolling chaotic **Brixton Market** (*see p254*). On your wanderings, visit the Black Cultural Archives (378 Coldharbour Lane, 7738 4591), the Brixton Art Gallery (35 Brixton Station Road, 7733 6957) or the Juice Bar (407 Coldharbour Lane, 7738 4141). The Brixton Academy (*see p309*) is one of London's premier rock venues. For old-school Brixton, check out the deliciously bohemian Effra pub (38A Kellet Road, SW2, 7274 4180) and the splendid 1911 Ritzy Cinema (*see p284*).

Battersea

Clapham Junction rail.
Battersea is one of south London's yuppiest neighbourhoods. Its origins were more humble: 1,000 years ago it was a small Saxon farming settlement ('Batrices Ege', or Badric's Island), and, until the 19th century, its chief occupation was market gardening. But the coming of the railways changed that: **Clapham Junction** became the city's bustling transport hub (it's Europe's busiest railway junction). It wasn't long before the fields became factories.

The most distinctive piece of industrial architecture is **Battersea Power Station**, Sir Giles Gilbert Scott's 1933 structure (just east of Chelsea Bridge). Closed in 1983, the building is slated to be restored as a business and entertainment complex. But the area is best known for the **Battersea Dogs' Home**.

Battersea Park, just west of the dogs' home, was once a rough old place, popular with duellers, drunkards and criminals. But it was relandscaped in the mid 19th century, and in 1951 became the site of the Pleasure Gardens for the Festival of Britain. Today the riverside promenades, Peace Pagoda (built by Japanese monks and nuns in 1985 to commemorate Hiroshima Day), boating lake and fountains all look lovely. There's a children's zoo (closed winter, 7924 5826) and a small art gallery (the Pumphouse, 7350 0523).

West of the park, past Albert Bridge, is Battersea Bridge, rebuilt in 1886-90 to Joseph Bazalgette's designs. Further along the river is the wedge-shaped glass tower **Montevetro**. Designed by Richard Rogers, these high-tech luxury flats have been dubbed 'Monster Vetro' by some locals. By contrast, the adjacent **St Mary's Battersea** oozes historical grace: William Blake was married here, American traitor Benedict Arnold was buried here, and JMW Turner came here to paint the river.

Clapham & Wandsworth

Clapham Common tube/Wandsworth Common or Wandsworth Town rail.
During the 17th century Londoners fled the city in droves, chased by plague and fire. Many sought the clean air of Clapham. Among the early residents were Captain Cook and Samuel Pepys. In the 19th century the area became synonymous with the Clapham Sect, a group of wealthy Anglicans known for their 'muscular Christianity', that worshipped at **Holy Trinity Church** (on the edge of the common). By the 20th century Clapham was in decline, but gentrification during the '90s has turned it into one of south London's most desirable addresses.

The heart of the neighbourhood lies around the gorgeous **Clapham Common**. Abbeville village, south-east of the tube station, is brimming with smart shops and cafés; **Clapham Old Town**, north-east of the common along the Pavement, is another upscale area, featuring traditional pubs and shops. Across the road lies the common: by day it's popular with joggers and footballers; by night, gay cruisers let off steam in the woods.

To the west lies 'Nappy Valley', so called because of the many young middle-class families who reside there (it falls between

Sightseeing

Clapham Common and Wandsworth Common). They're are out in force on Saturdays, pushing their prams along Northcote Road, lined with smart shops, bars and restaurants; carnivores must try the superb Gourmet Burger Kitchen (No.44, 7228 3309). Nearby **Wandsworth Common** is even prettier than Clapham: the north-west side is dominated by a big old Victorian heap, the Gothic Royal Victoria Patriotic Building. The building was originally an asylum for orphans of the Crimean War; during World War II, it became a POW camp.

Putney, Barnes & Kew

Putney Bridge tube, Barnes rail, Kew Gardens tube/rail, Kew Bridge rail.

Peaceful, riverside **Putney** was once a humdrum fishing and farming community. Then it became popular with Tudor celebrity commuters such as Thomas Cromwell. These days it's familiar to millions as the starting point of the annual Varsity Boat Race (*see p261*). The river takes on a semi-rural aspect at Putney Bridge; looking back down the Thames,

Watermark Wandling free

THE WANDLE TRAIL

Tony Trude
Moored his houseboat
'Land of Cockaign'
And watched river life
The boat sunk
In 2001

The recent history of the River Wandle is typical of the slow recovery of London's waterways from a series of open sewers to the kind of sparkling streams that you might even be able to picnic beside without grimacing every time the wind changes.

The nine-mile stretch from Croydon down to the Thames at Wandsworth has always been too fast-flowing for boating, but for the emerging fabrics industry in the 19th century there was no better place to site mills and water wheels, and textile magnates William Morris and Arthur Liberty dominated the riverbanks during this era. However, along with the production of printed oriental silks came chemicals and effluent, and by around 1950 virtually all life had been extinguished from the river itself, with riverbank habitats

suffering almost as much. The balance swung back in nature's favour after the winding-down of the manufacturing industry in the 1970s and the eventual closure of the mills, which finally gave the Wandle the chance to regenerate. Teams of local people worked tirelessly at weekends to haul rusting kitchen appliances out of the river and into skips, kicking off a monumental clean-up effort. This coincided with a helpful revamp of the area's sewerage network and some invaluable assistance from the Environment Agency in repopulating the river with fish.

Today the river, which flows out of ponds at Carshalton and Beddington, provides a contrast of the picturesque and the still rather grim. At the southern end of the Northern Line, Morden Hall Park demonstrates that you can catch glimpses of London's skyline, but upstream, it's all trees.

The **WWT Wetland Centre** (*see below*) lies on the other side of **Barnes Common**. The main road across the expanse, Queen's Ride, humpbacks over the railway line below. It was here, on 16 September 1977, that singer Gloria Jones drove her Mini off the road, killing her passenger, T-Rex singer Marc Bolan. The slim trunk of the sycamore tree hit by the car is now covered with notes, poems and declarations of love. Steps lead to a bronze bust of the star.

there's more to Morden than a post-pubbing, temple-throbbing, eye-rubbing 1am surprise as the last tube reaches its terminus. 125 acres (51 hectares) of meadow and woodland are bisected neatly by the river, with handy signposts to guide you through the marshes and the buzzing of passing trams on the recently opened Croydon Tramlink. Nearby, the redeveloped Merton Abbey Mills – once the site owned by Liberty's – is now the home of a small theatre and a thriving market selling organic produce, books and pottery, with a functioning waterwheel as a reminder of its industrial past.

Further north the river snakes through industrial estates and derelict land, with the Wandle Trail footpath, which runs the river's length, presenting us with the best (kingfishers, grey herons) and also the worst (abandoned shopping trolleys, unimaginative graffiti). Behind the Wimbledon Greyhound Stadium and the clutch of DIY and carpet superstores is an open space that was once Wandle Valley Sewage Works. Thanks to a regeneration programme, this has undergone an unlikely transformation into the Wandle Meadow Nature Park, having seen off a bid to site Wimbledon's football stadium here. A trail of buzzing electric pylons provides an unlikely canopy for a nature trail but the local wildlife seems unperturbed.

If you continue along to the basin where the Wandle finally flows into the Thames you'll find Young's brewery, where beer has been produced since 1581. Traditional methods are still used to produce a range of ales and to spread that distinctive, but fairly unpleasant, smell of hops throughout the Wandsworth one-way system. Cheers.

Further west, **Kew** is famed for its gardens (properly known as the **Royal Botanic Gardens**; *see below*) and its royal, bucolic air.

Royal Botanic Gardens

Kew, Richmond, Surrey TW9 3AB (8332 5655/ information 8940 1171/www.kew.org). Kew Gardens tube/rail/Kew Bridge rail/riverboat to Kew Pier. **Open** *Late Mar-Aug* 9.30am-6.30pm Mon-Fri; 9.30am-7.30pm Sat, Sun, bank holidays. *Sept, Oct* 9.30am-6pm daily. *Late Oct-early Feb* 9.30am-4.15pm daily. *Early Feb-late Mar* 9.30am-5.30pm daily. **Admission** (LP) £8.50; £6 concessions; free under-16s. **Credit** AmEx, MC, V.

Kew Gardens has several claims to fame: it's got the world's biggest plant collection, oldest palm tree and largest collection of orchids. Designed in the 1770s by Lancelot 'Capability' Brown, its lush, landscaped beauty represents the pinnacle of English gardening. Not just a pretty face, Kew is a major centre for horticultural research. After all, it boasts plants, trees and shrubs from all over the globe; some of these date back hundreds of years.

For the most flamboyant floral displays, come in the spring: in April/May, look out for blossoming lilacs, cherries, crab apples and magnolias or the carpets of bluebells by Queen Charlotte's cottage; in May/June, the rhododendrons and azaleas are at their peak. But there's plenty of action in the winter, too: snowdrops, heather and hellebores bloom in January; look out for crocuses, daffodils and forsythia from mid February to March.

The gardens are spread out over 300 gorgeous acres so there's a lot of ground to cover. The Kew Explorer train from Victoria Gate offers a 35-minute overview (£3; £1.50 concessions). The Woodland Garden is the stuff of fairy tales; the Redwood Grove has a treetop walkway at 33ft (10m); and the romantic lake is prime marriage-proposal territory. All the walking will make you hungry: luckily, there are tearooms scattered throughout, including the impressive Orangery restaurant.

The sultry Palm House hosts a greatest hits medley of the tropics: palms, bamboo, tamarind, mango and fig trees, not to mention fragrant hibiscus and frangipani. The Temperate House, meanwhile, features the *pendiculata sanderina*, the Holy Grail for orchid hunters, whose petals grow to 3ft (0.9m) long.

Highlights for 2005 include 'Gardens of Glass', a major exhibition of glass sculptures by American artist Dale Chihuly (27 May-8 Jan 06).

WWT Wetland Centre

Queen Elizabeth's Walk, SW13 9WT (8409 4400/ www.wwt.org.uk). Hammersmith tube, then 283 bus/Barnes rail/33, 72 bus. **Open** *Mar-Oct* 9.30am-6pm daily (last entry 5pm). *Nov-Feb* 9.30am-5pm daily (last entry 4pm). **Admission** £6.75; £5.50 concessions; £4 4-16s; free under-4s; £17.50 family. **Credit** MC, V.

A mere 4 miles (6.5km) from central London, the WWT Wetland Centre feels worlds away. The setting is straight out of the Norfolk Broads: ponds,

Sightseeing

rushes, rustling reeds and wildflower gardens. The teeming bird life – 150 species at last count – sends twitchers into fits of ecstasy. Botanists ponder its 27,000 trees and 300,000 aquatic plants; naturalists swoon at the 300 varieties of butterfly, 20 types of dragonfly, four species of bat and water vole.

It wasn't always this pretty. Until 1989 the site consisted of four huge concrete reservoirs owned by Thames Water. But when the reservoirs were made redundant, naturalist Sir Peter Scott transformed the 105 acres (42ha) into this wonderful wetland habitat. Soon the marshy oasis became the equivalent of avian five-star hotel – the kind of place where grown men squeal in delight when they spot a mealy redpoll, chiff-chaff or white-spotted bluethroat.

The visitors' centre features a 'who's who' of bird life and a decent café with an outdoor terrace.

Wimbledon

Wimbledon tube/rail.

Once the tennis tournament (*see p328*) is finished, wealthy Wimbledon reverts to leafy, sleepy type. Wimbledon's **Centre Court** shopping centre holds many high-street chains; the handsome, Edwardian **Wimbledon Theatre** is big on Christmas pantomime (seasonal plays for children) and touring musicals. Wimbledon High Street is a picturesque, villagey stretch dotted with smart shops, bars and restaurants.

But the neighbourhood's biggest draw is **Wimbledon Common**, a huge, wild and partly wooded expanse crossed by paths, horse tracks, a golf course and, of course, Wombles, although we can't guarantee sightings of Uncle Bulgaria. The common also has a windmill with a volunteer-run tearoom (Windmill Museum, Windmill Road, 8947 2825), where Robert Baden-Powell wrote *Scouting for Boys* in 1908. For something stronger, a couple of pubs provide refreshment: the Fox & Grapes (Camp Road, 8946 5599) and Hand in Hand (7 Crooked Billet, 8946 5720). East of the common is **Wimbledon Park**, with its large boating lake, and the **All England Lawn Tennis Club**.

Tooting, an up-and-coming area east of Wimbledon, has been optimistically billed as 'the New Clapham' by inflationary estate agents. But it's certainly true that **Tooting Common**, with its gorgeously retro Lido, rivals its more famous northern neighbour. And though the area has a long way to go in terms of trendy bars and eateries, it is renowned for its Indian restaurants. Three of the best include Radha Krishna Bhavan (86 Tooting High Street, 8767 3462), Kastoori (188 Upper Tooting Road, 8767 7027) and Vijaya Krishna (114 Mitcham Road, 8767 7688).

Design historians should make a pilgrimage to **Colliers Wood**: bizarrely, this bland suburb was once the Arts and Crafts capital of the world. In 1881 William Morris opened his textiles workshops here, taking advantage of the rushing River Wandle for power. When Morris died, another textiles legend moved in: Arthur Liberty (of Regent Street fame). To see his old workshops, follow the river path down to **Merton Abbey Mills**, a quaint enclave famous for its weekend market. The William Morris pub (8540 0216) sits prettily on the river by the waterwheel.

Wimbledon Lawn Tennis Museum

Centre Court, All England Lawn Tennis Club, Church Road, SW19 5AE (8946 6131/www. wimbledon.org/museum). Southfields tube/39, 93, 200, 493 bus. **Open** 10.30am-5pm daily; ticket holders only during championships. **Admission** (LP) £6; £5 concessions; £3.75 5-16s; free under-5s. **Credit** AmEx, MC, V.

From the starchy, serious-looking Victorian players to the foul-mouthed celebrities of today, this popular museum traces the history of tennis. Items on show include dresses worn by the Williams sisters and Boris Becker's shoes. A theatre replays classic matches and a gallery showcases tennis-related art from across the generations. Guided tours culminate in a visit to the hallowed Centre Court.

Richmond

Richmond tube/rail.

Despite the constant roar of planes overhead, Richmond retains much of its villagey charm. Parts of it are so bucolic, you wonder if the District line hasn't dropped you in Cambridge by mistake. Originally known as Shene, the area has been linked with royalty for centuries: Edward III had a riverside palace here in the mid 1300s; Henry VII loved it so much he built a palace here in 1501 – and renamed it Richmond after his favourite earldom in Yorkshire.

These days, all that's left of the palace where Elizabeth I spent her last few summers (she died here in 1603) is the gateway on **Richmond Green**. This picturesque spot was once the site of royal jousting tournaments; now locals sun themselves here or play cricket. The green is surrounded by antiquated alleyways (Brewer's Lane), old cloistered pubs and the elegant **Richmond Theatre**. Also of interest is the **Church of St Mary Magdalene**, on Paradise Road, which blends a myriad of architectural styles ranging from 1507 to 1904.

The riverside promenade is very strollable. It's dotted with pubs, ranging from chains to more atmospheric spots, such as the White Cross (8940 6844): with its 'entrance at high tide' (the river floods regularly), the pub has watched the waters run by since 1835. **Richmond Bridge**, built in 1774 and the oldest surviving crossing

Sightseeing

on the Thames, has cafés tucked beneath it and magnificent, sweeping views up top.

But Richmond's pièce de résistance is the ruggedly beautiful **Richmond Park**. The largest park in London, it's one of the last vestiges of the magnificent oak woodland that once encircled the city. Wonderfully uncultivated, it's suited to riding, rambling and off-road cycling. The park also forms a natural habitat for wildlife, such as free-roaming red and fallow deer. Buildings include **Pembroke Lodge**, the childhood home of philosopher Bertrand Russell (now a café), and the Palladian splendour of **White Lodge**; Isabella Plantation offers a winding walk through landscaped gardens with streams and ponds.

Museum of Richmond

Old Town Hall, Whittaker Avenue, Richmond, Surrey TW9 1TP (8332 1141/www.museumof richmond.com). Richmond tube/rail. **Open** *May-Sept* 11am-5pm Tue-Sat; 1-4pm Sun. *Oct-Apr* 11am-5pm Tue-Sat. **Admission** free. **No credit cards**.
Housed in Richmond's old town hall, a lovely Victorian building near the river, this small museum charts the town's development as a royal resort and fashionable haven for high society.

Further south-west

If the water table allows, follow the river from Richmond on a pastoral walk to Petersham and Ham, or take in one of a handful of country villas in the area, among them **Ham House** (*see below*) and **Marble Hill House** (*see right*). Further along, the river meanders around Twickenham to **Strawberry Hill** (8240 4224), home of Horace Walpole, author of *The Castle of Otranto*, and the first significant building of the Gothic Revival, and, after a leisurely trip through suburban Kingston, arrives at **Hampton Court Palace** (*see right*).

Ham House

Ham, Richmond, Surrey TW10 7RS (8940 1950/ www.nationaltrust.org.uk/hamhouse). Richmond tube/rail, then 371 bus. **Open** *Gardens* 11am-6pm or dusk if earlier Mon-Wed, Sat, Sun. *House* 1-5pm Mon-Wed, Sat, Sun. **Admission** £7.50; £3.75 5-15s; £18.75 family (2+2). *Garden only* £3.50; £1.75 5-15s; free under-5s; £8.75 family (2+2). **Credit** MC, V.
Built in 1610 for one of James I's courtiers, this lavish red-brick mansion is one of the most outstanding Stuart properties in the country. The grand interior is filled with period furnishings: rococo mirrors, ornate tapestries and a table in the dairy supported on sculptures of cows' legs. The formal grounds attract the most attention: there's a trellised Cherry Garden dominated by a statue of Bacchus. The tearoom in the old orangery turns out historic dishes (lavender syllabub, anyone?) using ingredients from the restored Kitchen Gardens.

Hampton Court Palace

East Molesey, Surrey KT8 9AU (0870 751 5175/ 24hr information 0870 752 7777/advance tickets 0870 753 7777/www.hrp.org.uk). Hampton Court rail/riverboat from Westminster or Richmond to Hampton Court Pier (Apr-Oct). **Open** *Palace* Apr-Oct 10.15am-6pm Mon, 9.30am-6pm Tue-Sun; Nov-Mar 10.15am-4.30pm Mon, 9.30am-4.30pm Tue-Sun (last entry 1-hr before closing). *Park* dawn-dusk daily. **Admission** (LP) *Palace, courtyard, cloister & maze* £11; £8.70 concessions; £7.70 5-15s; free under-5s; £35 family (max 5 people). *Maze only* £3.50; £2.50 5-15s. *Formal Gardens only* £4; £3 concessions; £2 5-15s. **Credit** AmEx, MC, V.
Remembered for chopping off Anne Boleyn's head, having six wives and bringing about the English Reformation, Henry VIII is one of history's most unforgettable monarchs. And this Tudor palace – nicknamed 'Magnificence-upon-Thames' – is a suitably spectacular monument to the King. It was built in 1514 by Cardinal Wolsey, Henry's high-flying Lord Chancellor. But Henry liked it so much, he seized it for himself in 1528. For the next 200 years it was a focal point in English history: Elizabeth I was imprisoned in a tower by her jealous and cautious elder sister Mary I; Shakespeare performed here in 1604; and after the Civil War, Oliver Cromwell was so besotted by the building that he ditched his puritanical principles and moved in.

Centuries later, the palace still dazzles. But its vast size can be daunting, so take advantage of the costumed guided tours. If you go it alone, start with King Henry VIII's State Apartments, which include the Great Hall, noted for its splendid hammerbeam roof, stained-glass windows and elaborate religious tapestries; in the Haunted Gallery, the ghost of Catherine Howard – Henry's fifth wife, executed for adultery in 1542 – can reputedly be heard shrieking.

The King's Apartments, added in 1689 by Sir Christopher Wren, are notable for a splendid mural of Alexander the Great, painted by Antonio Verrio. The Queen's Apartments and Georgian Rooms feature similarly elaborate paintings, chandeliers and tapestries. The Tudor Kitchens are great fun, with their giant cauldrons, fake pies and blood-spattered walls (no vegetarians in those days). But the palace's most spectacular sights are outside: the exquisitely landscaped gardens include the world's oldest vine, the famous maze and tranquil Thames views. Just outside its borders, visitors can hire a horse and carriage for a ride through Hampton Court Park.

The major exhibition for 2005 is 'Suffragettes, Soldiers & Servants: Behind the Scenes of Hampton Court Palace 1750-1950'.

Marble Hill House

Richmond Road, Twickenham, Middx TW1 2NL (8892 5115/www.english-heritage.org.uk). Richmond tube/rail/St Margaret's rail/33, 90, 490, H22, R70 bus. **Open** *Apr-Sept* 10am-6pm Mon-Fri; 10am-2pm Sat; 10am-5pm Sun. *Oct* 10am-4pm daily. **Admission** £4; £2.80 concessions; £1.90 5-15s; free under-5s. **Credit** MC, V.

Marble Hill House. *See p180.*

Ah, royal love. Sometimes dangerous – think of Henry VIII – but seldom unprofitable. Thus King George II spared no expense to please his mistress. Not only did he build this perfect Palladian house (1724) for his lover Henrietta Howard, he almost dragged Britain into a war while doing so: by using Honduran mahogany to build the grand staircase, he sparked a diplomatic row with Spain. But it was worth it. Over the centuries, this stately mansion has welcomed the great and the good alike: luminaries such as Alexander Pope, Jonathan Swift and Horace Walpole were all entertained in the opulent Great Room. And the grounds are home to England's oldest black walnut tree (which would, in itself, make a formidable staircase). Picnic parties are welcome; so are athletes (there are tennis, putting and cricket facilities). Ferries regularly cross the river to neighbouring Ham House (*see p180*). A programme of concerts and events runs in summer.

Orleans House Gallery

Riverside, Twickenham, Middx TW1 3DJ (8831 6000/www.richmond.gov.uk/orleanshouse). Richmond tube, then 33, 490, H22, R68, R70 bus/St Margaret's/ Twickenham rail. **Open** *Apr-Sept* 1-5.30pm Tue-Sat; 2-5.30pm Sun. *Oct-Mar* 1-4.30pm Tue-Sat; 2-4.30pm Sun. **Admission** free. **Credit** MC, V.

Secluded in 6 acres (6.4ha) of gardens, this lovely Grade I listed riverside house was constructed in 1710. It was built for someone called James Johnson, the then-secretary of state for Scotland. But it wasn't named after him. That honour went to the Duke of Orleans, Louis-Philippe, who lived here between 1800 and 1817 in exile from Napoleonic France (he later returned and claimed the throne). Although it was partially demolished in 1926, the building retains James Gibbs's neo-classical Octagon Room, housing the impressive Richmond-upon-Thames art collection, a soothing pictorial record of the surrounding countryside from the early 1700s to the present. Temporary exhibitions include plenty of modern and contemporary work.

Rugby Museum/ Twickenham Stadium

Twickenham Rugby Stadium, Rugby Road, Twickenham, Middx TW1 1DZ (8892 8877/ www.rfu.com). Hounslow East tube, then 281 bus/ Twickenham rail. **Open** *Museum* 10am-5pm Tue-Sat; 11am-5pm Sun (last entry 4.30pm). *Tours* 10.30am, noon, 1.30pm, 3pm Tue-Sat; 1pm, 3pm Sun. **Admission** £9; £6 concessions; £30 family. **Credit** AmEx, MC, V.

The impressive Twickenham Stadium is the home of English rugby union. Tickets for international matches are extremely hard to come by, but this little museum offers some compensation. Tours take in the England dressing room ('sights, sounds and smells') – a great place to indulge your Lawrence Dallaglio fantasies. Visitors can experience the rush of adrenaline standing in the players' tunnel, or drop in on the Members Lounge, the Presidents Suite and the Royal Box. A permanent collection of memorabilia charts the game's development from the late 19th century. Highlights include the oldest jersey in existence (1871), the Calcutta Cup contested by England and Scotland, and, until November 2005, the Rugby World Cup (thanks to England's 2003 victory). Video snippets recall classic matches; a simulated scrum machine tests your strength. Temporary exhibitions change about every six months.

West London

Go west, my son, from the glamour of Notting Hill to Chiswick's riverside calm.

The North–South (of the river) divide is London's most touted pycho-geographical distinction, but East–West is a more telling one. London's west is perceived as less 'real', less 'happening' and less storied than the east: more metropolitan but less urban; fashionable rather than cool (though that particular barometer is wavering at the moment). West London is full of rich artists' and architects' children; east London is where they now come to slum it with the real people (where they once would have gone to Notting Hill for the same reason).

It's true that outside the central areas, the urban edge can be deeply buried among rows of suburban housing and busy roads, but there is plenty to admire, starting with the expansive architecture of Notting Hill, the riverside appeal of Chiswick and some very fine historic houses.

Paddington & Bayswater

Maps p394 & p395

Bayswater, Lancaster Gate or Queensway tube/ Paddington tube/rail.

Named after Padda, an ancient Anglo-Saxon chieftain who settled here, Paddington was for centuries just a rural backwater, isolated from the rest of London. For part of the 18th century, it served as a stomping ground for French Huguenots, but its role changed with the building of Paddington Station in 1838. The original station was built of wood, but was replaced in 1854 by the magnificent structure designed by Isambard Kingdom Brunel.

The area soon descended into seediness, plagued by overcrowding and poverty in Victorian times. The grim situation prevailed throughout the 20th century, but today those behind the massive Paddington Waterside project, one of the most high-profile urban regeneration projects in Europe, are giving the area a major facelift. The areas around West End Quay, the Point and Paddington Central and Basin are already gleaming; by 2006 a new urban quarter will feature restaurants, offices and other businesses.

To the south and west of Paddington, the area known as **Bayswater** started life as a grand estate for the Bishop of London's trustees. However, the original crescent was abandoned, and its smart houses built into pretty squares that became fashionable during

Victorian times. Alas, the huge houses became too dear to maintain and many were sold off or demolished; these days the area is a mishmash of grubby-fronted hotels, expensive apartments and touristy shops and restaurants. At the southern edge runs Bayswater Road, a straight, tree-lined thoroughfare facing **Hyde Park**. A blue plaque to Sir James Barrie, of *Peter Pan* fame, adorns No.100.

A left turn at the northern end of busy **Queensway** leads into trendy **Westbourne Grove**. The eastern limits host a number of top-notch restaurants, including excellent Middle Eastern options, and interesting shops. But the Grove's western end, towards Notting Hill, is distinctly posher, with organic haven Fresh & Wild, antiques shops and, particularly on Ledbury Road, chic clothes boutiques.

Alexander Fleming Laboratory Museum

St Mary's Hospital, Praed Street, W2 1NY (7886 6528/www.sg.nhs.uk/about/fleming_museum). *Paddington tube/rail.* **Open** 10am-1pm Mon-Thur. By appointment 2-5pm Mon-Thur; 10am-5pm Fri. **Admission** £2; £1 concessions, 5-16s; free under-5s. **No credit cards. Map** p395 D5.

Explore the room in which Alexander Fleming discovered penicillin in 1928 and then watch a ten-minute video detailing his pioneering work. Among the artefacts preserved from Fleming's day is the fungus-infested Petri dish in which he first saw his miraculous 'mould juice' in action.

Maida Vale & Kilburn

Kilburn, Kilburn Park, Maida Vale or Warwick Avenue tube.

Extending from Marble Arch up past Paddington, **Edgware Road** is long, straight and jammed with traffic. Its southernmost end – Marble Arch to Praed Street – is interesting for its colourful collection of Middle Eastern businesses, including many of the best kebab shops in London. North of St John's Wood Road, Edgware Road turns into **Maida Vale**, the road – and the neighbourhood it splits – named after the British victory over the French at the Battle of Maida in southern Italy in 1806.

It's affluent round here, and prettified immensely by the canal-fronted area known as **Little Venice**. From here, you can walk or take a waterbus down Regent's Canal to

London Zoo (*see p152* **Watermarks**). Aside from the waterway, the area's main point of interest is a large pub called Crocker's Folly (24 Aberdeen Place, 7286 6608). It was built as a hotel in 1898 by entrepreneur Frank Crocker, who'd received a tip-off that a new rail terminus was to be built opposite. When a Marylebone area half a mile away was instead chosen for the station site, a distraught Crocker hurled himself off the roof.

Dashing through the green **Paddington Recreation Ground**, where Roger Bannister pounded the track practising for the world's first under-four-minute mile run, you'll reach **Kilburn**, whose **High Road** is well known for its pubs crammed with Irish expats. This is the best bet in town for a proper St Patrick's Day celebration. However, its finest feature is undoubtedly the excellent **Tricycle** (*see p340*), a theatre, gallery and cinema.

A load of hot (dry) air

Porchester Spa is one of the few surviving examples of the Victorian Turkish baths that proliferated in Britain after being introduced in 1856 by eccentric diplomat David Urquhart and Irish physician Richard Barter. Today we think of Turkish baths in terms of leisure and pleasure, but they were originally introduced for hygienic and medical reasons.

Thousands died of cholera in the early 1800s, when most people had no easily accessible running water. Baths and Washhouses Acts passed in the 1840s allowed local authorities to build baths and laundries at public expense. Urquhart argued that Turkish baths got you cleaner, and were cheaper to provide than hot water baths. Most of the earliest Turkish baths were opened by working-class proprietors.

Medicine in the latter part of the 19th century was still very hit and miss. Not only were there no cures for complaints such as rheumatism and gout, but there were no safe ways to ease the pain. Patent medicines and quack cures were rife. The wealthy tried the spartan cold water cure available at hydros. But Dr Barter found, at his hydro in Blarney, Ireland, that the often-curative fever produced by wrapping patients in cold, water-soaked sheets was more easily, and pleasantly, produced by sweating in a Turkish bath.

During a stint as First Secretary at the British Embassy in Constantinople in the 1830s, Urquhart frequented humid hot air baths, or hammams. Bathers spent time in a series of rooms, each hotter than the last, making them sweat profusely. After a scrub and massage – together called shampooing – they relaxed with a Turkish coffee in the cooling room.

Urquhart and Barter knew that to be most effective in cleansing the body and easing its aches and pains, their baths had to be hotter than hammams, whose maximum temperature was limited by the humidity that

came from having washbasins in the hot rooms. To create dry heat, they based their baths on the ancient Roman baths, or *thermae*, where washing facilities were separated from hot rooms, and invigorating cold plunge pools were added. If, as in hammams, there were also steam rooms, they were located apart from the dry areas.

Bathers using Turkish baths to cleanse themselves or ease their aches and pains soon found that the bath was also enjoyable and relaxing, leading to its growing popularity. Over 600 British establishments are so far known, but there were probably many more.

Yet the unlucky Victorians of Westminster never got their affordable Turkish baths. There was a proposal to build them in 1874, but the local authority couldn't agree where to put them. Not until 1929 was Porchester Hall opened. Even then the Turkish and Russian vapour baths, with their Axminster carpets and kidney-shaped icy plunge pool, were an afterthought – substituted at the last moment for two shops.

Today the baths are still very much in use, and a pleasure to experience, with their vast tiled spaces, original art deco fittings and slightly institutional tone. This must be one of the only spas in town where bacon sandwiches are still on the menu.
Malcolm Shifrin.
● For more information, see Malcolm Shifrin's Victorian Turkish Baths at www.victorianturkishbath.org

Porchester Spa

The Porchester Centre, Queensway, W2 5HS (7792 3980). Bayswater tube. **Open** *Women only* 10am-10pm Tue, Thur, Fri; 10am-4pm Sun. *Men only* 10am-10pm Mon, Wed, Sat. *Mixed couples* 4-10pm Sun. Last admissions 2hrs before closing. **Admission** £18.95; £26.75 couples. **Credit** MC, V. **Map** p394 C5.

Notting Hill

Map p394 A7

Notting Hill Gate or Westbourne Park tube.
Initially farmland, old *Knottynghull* has gone
from gracious (18th century) via poor, white
working class (1950s) and bohemian (1960s to
1980s), to astronomically expensive (no thanks
to the blockbuster film *Notting Hill*). **Notting
Hill Gate**, into which you'll emerge from the
tube station, will disappoint those expecting the
vibrant streets of the Hugh Grant film. But do
not despair: the Notting Hill you seek is just
around the corner.

From Notting Hill Gate, follow Pembridge
Road to **Portobello Road**, a narrow winding
street that's home to a number of cafés,
bars, restaurants, delis and shops, the newly
refurbished **Electric** cinema (*see p284*) and,
towards the northern end on Fridays and
Saturdays, a flea market with hip vintage
clothes, shoes and accessories (*see p255*).
Some of the area's best shops are actually
just off Portobello Road. At its northern end,
for instance, **Golborne Road** has excellent
antiques shops and Portuguese pâtisseries such
as the Lisboa (No.57, 8968 5242). The street
also has the **Trellick Tower**; built in 1973
by architect Ernö Goldfinger and considered
by some to be a hideous eyesore and by others
a significant piece of modern architecture. You
might wonder about the concordance of Ernö's
name with a James Bond villain? That's the
penalty for irritating Ian Fleming.

Besides the film, Notting Hill is most
famous for the annual **Notting Hill Carnival**
(*see p264*). The event was introduced in 1959
as a celebration of the West Indian immigrants
who first moved to the area in the 1950s.
The carnival continues, though most of the
immigrant families who first created the event
have long since been priced out of the area.

East of Portobello Road, the **Westbourne
Park** area is scruffy but hip, particularly
around All Saints Road, which has been
colonised by quirky little boutiques. At the
top of Ladbroke Grove, meanwhile, is one
of London's famously spooky boneyards,
Kensal Green Cemetery.

Kensal Green Cemetery

*Harrow Road, Kensal Green, W10 4RA (8969
0152/www.kensalgreen.co.uk). Kensal Green tube.*
Open *Apr-Sept* 9am-6pm Mon-Sat; 10am-6pm Sun.
Oct-Mar 9am-5pm Mon-Sat; 10am-5pm Sun. *Tours*
2pm Sun; *tours incl catacombs* 2pm 1st & 3rd Sun of
mth (bring a torch). **Admission** free. *Tours* £5
donation; £4 concessions. **No credit cards.**
The Duke of Sussex, sixth son of King George III,
made it clear his remains should not be buried in the
usual place (Windsor). Instead, he chose Kensal

Green Cemetery for his resting place, his patronage
making it a socially acceptable venue for the lofty
dead. The scale of the monuments shows that the
wealthy were happy to invest in stonemasonry.
William Makepeace Thackeray, Isambard Kingdom
Brunel and Anthony Trollope lie here, but many of
the most eye-catching graves are of less famous folk.

Kensington & Holland Park

Maps p394-p397

High Street Kensington or Holland Park tube.
From rich farmland (*Chenesit*) listed in the
Domesday Book of 1086 to a prosperous
rural parish prized in the 17th century for
its proximity to London, **Kensington** has
attracted the affluent for years. The district
first developed around Holland House (1606)
and Campden House (1612), and the area was
described by one historian in 1705 as a place
'inhabited by gentry and persons of note'.
It's as smart today as it's always been.

Kensington High Street offers a mix of
shops stretching along the busy main road,
while the surrounding streets and squares
are lined by imposing townhouses. The
most famous square is just behind the art deco
splendour of Barker's department store (No.63;
built 1905-13). **Kensington Square** still looks
noble and sports a generous display of plaques
for its residents of distinction, such as
Thackeray (No.16) and John Stuart Mill (No.18).

At the foot of Kensington Church Street is
the church of **St Mary Abbots**, a superb
example of Victorian Gothic style designed by
Sir George Gilbert Scott and built in 1872. It has
the tallest spire in London (250 feet/85 metres),
as well as fine stained-glass windows that
include the famous 'Healing' window funded
by the Royal College of Surgeons.

Further west is the wonderfully
romantic **Holland Park**, whose Japanese-style
1991 Kyoto Garden commemorates the long-
lasting friendship between Britain and Japan.
Beautiful woods and formal gardens surround
the reconstructed Jacobean **Holland House**,
named after an early owner, Sir Henry, Earl
of Holland. The house suffered serious bomb
damage during World War II and only the
ground floor and arcades survived. The
restored east wing contains the most
dramatically sited youth hostel in town
(*see p70*), and the summer ballroom has
been converted into a contemporary restaurant.
Open-air operas are staged in the park under
a canopy during the summer, and there's an
adventure playground with tree-walks and
rope swings. Among the historic houses
worth a visit are **Leighton House** and **Linley
Sambourne House** (for both, *see p186*).

Giving the Goldfinger. **Trellick Tower**.

Now that's a headdress. **Notting Hill Carnival**. *See p184*.

Leighton House

12 Holland Park Road, W14 8LZ (7602 3316/ www.rbkc.gov.uk/leightonhousemuseum). High Street Kensington tube. **Open** 11am-5.30pm Mon, Wed-Sun. *Tours* 2.30pm Wed, Thur; by appointment other times (min group of 12). **Admission** £3; £1 concessions, children (children at school in borough free). **Credit** MC, V. **Map** p396 A9.

This gorgeous Victorian house was the residence and studio of Victorian artist Frederic, Lord Leighton (1830-96). Its highly decorative rooms and halls are adorned with his paintings and drawings, including *The Death of Brunelleschi*. Other works of art are by contemporaries such as John Everett Millais and Edward Burne-Jones. The house was designed in 1864 by Leighton in collaboration with architect George Aitchison. In addition to temporary exhibitions, there are regular talks, tours and recitals.

Linley Sambourne House, about ten minutes' walk away (18 Stafford Terrace), was the home of cartoonist Edward Linley Sambourne. Classical Italianate in style, the house was built in the 1870s and Sambourne and his wife furnished it in the fashionable style of the period. Scheduled guided tours by costumed actors take place on the weekends; otherwise, plain-clothed weekday tours can be booked through the Leighton House switchboard.

Earl's Court & Fulham

Maps p396 & p397

Earl's Court, Fulham Broadway or West Brompton tube.

This district originally housed the courthouse of the earls of Warwick and Holland, who owned the area. The two earls are immortalised in the naming of **Warwick Road** and **Holland Park** in neighbouring Kensington.

Grand landowners notwithstanding, the area was a mere hamlet until the 1860s, when the Metropolitan Railway purchased farmland nearby to build Earl's Court station. A fairground was built on some neglected land near the tracks in 1887, where its founder JR Whitley erected the country's first – also, at that time, the world's largest – Ferris wheel in the mid 1890s. Today the site hosts the gigantic Earl's Court Exhibition Centre, built in 1937 and which now accommodates a full calendar of trade shows, pop concerts and large-scale events such as the Ideal Home Show.

During the early 1900s many of Earl's Court's residential properties were turned into flats, drawing a large immigrant population to the area. The biggest was the Australian influx of the 1950s, '60s and '70s, which earned Earl's Court the nickname 'Kangaroo Court'. A clutch of budget hotels, hostels and pubs continue to fly the flag. In the 1970s the area glammed up a bit and became a popular gay haunt for a while; Queen's Freddie Mercury lived in Logan Place before moving to Stafford Terrace in the 1980s.

Just south-east of Earl's Court station, connecting Old Brompton Road and Fulham Road, is **Brompton Cemetery**. This huge Victorian burial ground, consecrated in 1840, has elaborate stonemasonry and grand funereal architecture, and is the final resting place of suffragette Emmeline Pankhurst. The grounds are a lovely spot in which to wander. This is a popular pick-up spot among gay men, so ignore any rustlings in the undergrowth.

Nearby neighbourhoods **Parson's Green** and **Fulham** are both affluent. The former is centred around a small green that once supported, well, a parsonage, the existence of which was first recorded in 1391. This was considered the aristocratic part of Fulham in the 1700s, housing the great and good of both court and commerce. Nearby, and best accessed from Barons Court tube station, is the Queen's Club, where the pre-Wimbledon Stella Artois tennis tournament is held. Also in the area is **Fulham Palace** (*see below*), which is inside pretty **Bishop's Park**, along the Thames Path.

Fulham Palace

Bishop's Avenue, off Fulham Palace Road, SW6 6EA (7736 3233). Putney Bridge tube/14, 74, 220, 414, 430 bus. **Open** *Mar-Oct* 2-5pm Wed-Sun. *Nov-Feb* 1-4pm Thur-Sun. *Tours* 2pm 2nd & 4th Sun of mth. **Admission** free; under-16s must be accompanied by adult. *Tours* £3; free under-16s. **No credit cards.**
The foundations of Fulham Palace can be traced back to 704, when the property was granted to Bishop Wealdheri. Tours of the palace as it stands now – a hotchpotch of architectural styles, having been the home of successive Bishops of London for around 700 years – are only available on certain Wednesdays and Sundays. For the rest of the time, a small museum housing a number of artefacts goes a little way towards satiating curiosity.

Shepherd's Bush & Hammersmith

Goldhawk Road, Hammersmith or Shepherd's Bush tube.
Shepherd's Bush is loosely organised around its triangular, eight-acre (3.2 hectare) patch of grass generally known as Shepherd's Bush Green. In truth, this is only the name of the road that bounds it on two sides, the grassy area itself being officially called Shepherd's Bush Common. Either way, there's not a whole lot to see; it's merely a glorified traffic island that separates Uxbridge Road and Goldhawk Road.

Shepherd's Bush first gained recognition in the late 1700s, after the highwayman Sixteen-String Jack was captured here. Nowadays the area's main draws are the **Bush Theatre**, a highly regarded centre for new writing (*see p339*), the **Shepherd's Bush Empire**, one of London's leading music venues (*see p310*), and **Shepherd's Bush Market** (just east of the railway viaduct off Goldhawk Road), which features stalls selling African and Caribbean food and clothing every day except Sunday.

Thanks to a huge chunk of council and EU funding, this neighbourhood – known for its tatty shops, ankle-deep litter and obvious social problems – is undergoing major redevelopment. The W12 shopping centre has been made over, and a number of restaurants and a 12-screen cinema have opened. More interesting is the proposed West London Tram Project. If approved, it will link Shepherd's Bush with nearby western neighbourhoods by 2009.

To the north of Shepherd's Bush is White City, home of the massive **BBC Television Centre** (*see below*). Across the road, developers are building what is likely to be one of Europe's biggest retail parks: 1.4 million square feet (427,000 square metres) in size, it's due to open in 2007. Further north of White City, **Wormwood Scrubs** is infamously home to an imposing Victorian jail. To lighten the mood, a section of parkland outside the prison walls has been designated a nature reserve.

South of Shepherd's Bush is the busier **Hammersmith** area, whose giant roundabout and flyover can't help but dominate, though it also offers riverside strolls. It's a centre for entertainment, including the **Carling Apollo Hammersmith**, which hosts live music events; some alternative theatrical work comes courtesy of the **Lyric Hammersmith** (*see p340*), whose main auditorium has a gloriously old-fashioned interior and a grand proscenium arch; while the **Riverside Studios** (*see p335*) is home to three theatre stages, a gallery and a rep cinema. But the area's main attraction is the beautiful, over-the-top **Hammersmith Bridge**, the city's oldest suspension bridge.

BBC Television Centre Tours

Wood Lane, W12 7RJ (0870 603 0304/www.bbc.co.uk/tours). White City tube. **Tours** by appointment only Mon-Sat. **Admission** £7.95; £6.95 concessions; £5.95 10-16s, students; £21.95 family. No under-9s. **Credit** MC, V.
Tours of the BBC include visits to the news desk, the TV studios and the Weather Centre, though you must book ahead to secure a place. To be part of a TV audience log on to www.bbc.co.uk/whatson/tickets, where you can apply for free tickets.

Chiswick

Turnham Green tube/Chiswick rail.
Leaving behind the tarmacked swoops of
Hammersmith and walking west alongside
the river from Hammersmith Bridge, you'll
eventually reach the elegantly aloof **Chiswick
Mall**, a mile-long riverside stretch of grand
17th- to 19th-century townhouses, the colourful
flowers and wrought-iron verandas heralding
your arrival in the wealthy suburb of Chiswick.
The nearby **Fuller's Griffin Brewery**, just
off Chiswick Mall on Chiswick Lane South, has
stood on the same site since the 17th century.
Nearby, Chiswick Mall ends at **St Nicholas
Church**. Only the ragstone tower of the 15th-
century building remains, the rest of the church
being 19th century. Gravestones commemorate
local painters Hogarth and Whistler, but they're
actually buried elsewhere.

Other Chiswick attractions include the
Palladian **Chiswick House** and **Hogarth's
House**; further west is the **Kew Bridge
Steam Museum** (for all, *see below*). The
much-loved **Musical Museum** is currently
undergoing a move from an old, damp church
building into new, custom-built premises,
slated for a 2005 opening; for full details,
see www.musicalmuseum.co.uk.

South of here, overlooking Kew Gardens
from the opposite side of the river, is Tudor
Syon House (*see right*). A pretty, riverside
promenade, just east of Kew Bridge on the north
side of the river, runs by the mini village of
Strand-on-the-Green, which offers two splendid
pubs, the Bell & Crown and the City Barge.

Chiswick House

*Burlington Lane, W4 2RP (8995 0508/www.english-
heritage.org.uk). Turnham Green tube, then E3 bus
to Edensor Road/Hammersmith tube/rail, then 190
bus/Chiswick rail.* **Open** *Apr-Oct* 10am-5pm Wed-Fri,
Sun; 10am-2pm Sat. Closed Nov-Mar. **Admission**
(EH) £3.70; £2.80 concessions; £1.70 5-16s; free
under-5s. **Credit** MC, V.
Richard Boyle, third Earl of Burlington, designed
this lovely Palladian villa in 1725. As a leading
patron of the arts, he sought to create a temple of
culture in which he could entertain the cream of society and support writers like Pope, Swift, Gay and
Thomson, the composer Handel and artists Kent,
Leoni and Rysbrack. Sculptures by Rysbrack of
Burlington's heroes, Inigo Jones and Palladio, stand
in front of the house. William Kent was responsible
for much of the interior. The gorgeous reception
rooms interconnect with a magnificent central
saloon. The grounds, designed by Lord Burlington
with Kent and Charles Bridgeman, are a triumph of
early 18th-century garden design. There's plenty to
admire, including a gateway originally designed by
Inigo Jones in 1621 and erected at Chiswick in 1738.

Hogarth's House

*Hogarth Lane, Great West Road, W4 2QN
(8994 6757). Turnham Green tube/Chiswick
rail.* **Open** *Apr-Oct* 1-5pm Tue-Fri; 1-6pm Sat,
Sun. *Nov, Dec, Feb, Mar* 1-4pm Tue-Fri; 1-5pm
Sat, Sun. **Admission** free; donations appreciated.
No credit cards.
This early 18th-century house was the country
retreat of painter, engraver and social commentator
William Hogarth. Fully restored in 1997 for the
300th anniversary of Hogarth's birth, it now functions as a gallery displaying most of his celebrated
engravings, including *Gin Lane*, *Marriage à la Mode*
and a copy of *Rake's Progress*.

Kew Bridge Steam Museum

*Green Dragon Lane, Brentford, Middx TW8 0EN
(8568 4757/www.kbsm.org). Gunnersbury tube/Kew
Bridge rail/65, 237, 267, 391 bus.* **Open** 11am-5pm
daily. **Admission** *Mon-Fri* £4; £3 concessions;
£2 5-15s; free under-5s; £10 family. *Sat, Sun* £5.20;
£4.20 concessions; £3 5-15s; free under-5s; £15.95
family. **Credit** MC, V.
Housed in a Victorian riverside pumping station,
this museum explores the city's use and abuse of
water. For some, the highlight is a walk through a
section of the London ring main waterpipe. On weekends (11am-5pm) the engines are in steam; one of the
biggest working examples in the world, a Cornish
beam engine built in 1845 for use in the tin mines,
stirs into motion at 3pm.

Syon House

*Syon Park, Brentford, Middx TW8 8JF (8560 0883/
www.syonpark.co.uk). Gunnersbury tube/rail, then
237, 267 bus.* **Open** *House* (24 Mar-31 Oct only)
11am-5pm Wed, Thur, Sun. *Gardens (year-round)*
10.30am-dusk daily. *Tours* by arrangement.
Admission *House & gardens* £7.25; £5.95
concessions; £16 family. *Gardens only* £3.75; £2.50
concessions; £9 family. *Tours* free. **Credit** MC, V.
The land around this turreted Tudor mansion,
embellished by successive tenants during the 16th
century, belonged to the Syon Monastery. It was
dedicated to the Bridgettine order in 1415 until the
dissolution of the monasteries by Henry VIII. It was
here that Catherine Howard, Henry's fifth wife, spent
a miserable Christmas before her execution in 1542.

The building was converted into a house in 1547
for the Duke of Northumberland, who still uses it as
his London home. The neo-classical interior was created by Robert Adam in 1761. Paintings by Van
Dyck, Gainsborough and Reynolds hang inside. The
duke's most valuable painting, *The Madonna of the
Pinks* by Raphael, was loaned to the National
Gallery (*see p132*) from 1992, but he determined to
sell it to raise funds to maintain Syon and Alnwick
(his place in Northumberland). After a struggle, the
gallery raised the necessary £22m to purchase the
work, with the help of the Heritage Lottery Fund.

A collection of 1960s buildings includes the
London Butterfly House, where more than 1,000
specimens flutter and settle, at least, until it closes

Literature with attitude

There's a strong tradition for exploring the extraordinary in the literary magazine – freedom in the bright idea, experimentation over mainstream – which makes it a happy home for writers both established and new. This is due in part to the fact that there is so little money in the medium and so, to most involved, it is a labour of love driven far more by personal creative interests than the fickle tastes of an audience.

But what happens when you have a young, talented literary editor with ample financial backing, and enough contacts to make a magazine as commercially viable as *Vogue*? Well, then you have *Zembla*.

Westbourne Grove's *Zembla* is an 'International Literary Magazine' produced on glossy paper, with ad spreads for Dior, Marc Jacobs and the VW Phaeton V10 before you even get to the contents page, and a strong visual image courtesy of Frost Design. All this may have purists dismissing it as style over substance, but on closer look this is a magazine about words – and some very fine words at that. First, take the title, with its wink at Vladimir Nabokov (Zembla is a fictional 'distant northern land' and homeland to the narrator of *Pale Fire*), and then look at the word itself, which is not only visually striking, but also starts with the letter Z and ends with an A, and sings of the magazine's primary

aim to have 'fun with words'. 'I consider *Zembla* to be part of a developing literary world,' says editor Dan Crowe, who founded the magazine in autumn 2003. The world of *Zembla* is more celebratory than critical, involving quirky ideas like interviews with the dead, such as Henry James, and getting novelists to review their own books. It also packs in the talent. 'The birth of the magazine coincided with the birth of a number of very talented writers,' says Crowe, 'a number of whom are writing for us, which makes me very proud. For instance, we've had Robert MacFarlane from the start and he's won a number of awards and is on the Booker Prize jury this year.' Other writers include Mark Leyner, James Flint and Hari Kunzru, as well as previously unpublished authors.

But *Zembla* is also cannily marketed: the 'international' stamp gets it distributed all over the world and it enjoys a place on British Airways' first-class flights, as well as being a hit with the fashion world. 'The magazine is a bit like a club,' says Crowe. 'And the fashion world is keen to buy membership because there aren't that many smart, attractive magazines around.' Lily Dunn.
● For more details, see www.zembla magazine.com. Lily Dunn is editor of literary magazine *Matter*.

in September 2005. There's also a walk-in aviary of tropical birds, and the Aquatic Experience (8847 4730), which counts crocodiles and piranhas among its largely piscatorial residents. Plans are under way for a large hotel to be built in the park in the next few years. The house and park's glittering film career includes a scene stealing performance in Robert Altman's *Gosford Park*.

Further west

The birthplace of Britain's film industry and the country's first purpose-built film studios, **Ealing Studios** put the westerly suburb of Ealing on the map. A team of filmmakers and developers owns the old site, where classic comedies like *Kind Hearts and Coronets, The*

Kyoto Garden, Holland Park. *See p184.*

Ladykillers and *Passport to Pimlico* were produced, and has converted the historic buildings into offices and production units. Movies aside, Ealing offers handy shopping (at the Broadway Centre), eating and drinking, which makes such gems as **Walpole Park**, home to **Pitzhanger Manor (PM) Gallery & House**, worth the long tube ride out west. Further west still, in the middle of Osterley Park, is **Osterley House** (for both, *see below*), another Robert Adam undertaking.

Just north of here, **Southall** has been revitalised by Indian immigrants, their presence bringing authentic cuisine to countless restaurants lining the Broadway. The golden dome of the **Gurdwara Sri Guru Singh Sabha Southall** can be seen from all over the area; don a headscarf – provided if you don't have one to hand – and remove your shoes to enter what is, with capacity for 3,000 people, the largest Sikh place of worship outside India. Free vegetarian food is available to all visitors in the langar, the communal kitchen.

To the north, **Wembley** is best known as the home of the famous stadium, which closed in 2000. Construction of the new 90,000-seater **Wembley National Stadium** has been dogged by controversy and financial problems, but is due to be completed in 2006; already completed and visible from as far as Canary Wharf, the supporting arch is tall enough for the London Eye to be rolled underneath. For details, check www.wembleystadium.com.

Nearby **Neasden** is famous for the multi-billion-rupee **Shri Swaminarayan Mandir** temple, built here by a Hindu sect in 1995. It required 5,000 tons of marble and limestone and the work of around 1,500 sculptors for an enterprise unprecedented in this country since

cathedral-building in the Middle Ages. As well as a large prayer hall, the complex contains a conference hall, a marriage suite, sports facilities, a library and a health clinic. Modest attire is strongly advised. For details, check www.mandir.org.

Osterley House

Osterley Park, off Jersey Road, Isleworth, Hounslow, Middx TW7 4RB (8232 5050/recorded information 01494 755566/www.nationaltrust.org.uk/osterley). Osterley tube. **Open** *Park* 9am-7.30pm (dusk if earlier) daily, year-round. *House* Mar 1-4.30pm Sat, Sun; Apr-Oct 1-4.30pm Wed-Sun. **Admission** (NT) *House* £4.90; £2.40 5-15s; £12.20 family. *Park* free. In 1761 Scottish architect Robert Adam was commissioned to transform Osterley from a crumbling Tudor mansion into a swish neo-classical villa. He did so in spectacular style, creating friezes, pilasters and ornate ceilings over the course of 19 years. The National Trust oversees a number of events throughout the year, from ghost walks to conservation mornings; ring or check the website for details. From March to October, the Jersey Galleries stage contemporary art exhibitions.

PM Gallery & House

Walpole Park, Mattock Lane, Ealing, W5 5EQ (8567 1227/www.ealing.gov.uk/pmgallery&house). Ealing Broadway tube/rail. **Open** *May-Sept* 1-5pm Tue-Fri, Sun; 11am-5pm Sat. *Oct-Apr* 1-5pm Tue-Fri; 11am-5pm Sat. *Tours* by arrangement. **Admission** free. Aside from one early wing (the west one) designed by George Dance, Pitzhanger House is the work of Sir John Soane, who bought the house as his weekend retreat in 1800 and then rebuilt it. After Soane sold it in 1810, the house was owned by several notables, among them Spencer Perceval, the only British prime minister to have been assassinated. To celebrate the 250th anniversary of Soane's birth in 2003, the property honoured him with a special exhibition, and the house and gallery were given a new title.

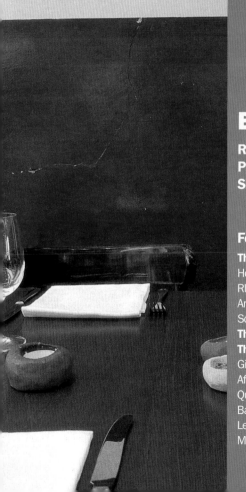

Eat, Drink, Shop

Restaurants & Cafés	**192**
Pubs & Bars	**220**
Shops & Services	**233**

Features

The best Restaurants	193
Hot plates?	200
RIP, classic caffs	204
And the winner is…	207
School of toque	213
The best Drinking holes	220
The best Hip to sip	223
Gin palaces	226
After hours	230
Quality street	240
Bargain abasement	244
Let us eat cake!	248
Mushroom for manoeuvre	253

Restaurants & Cafés

Put your money where your mouth is.

Medcalf.
See p196.

Alongside New York, London ranks as the world's most dynamic and varied culinary destination. Every year, millions of pounds are spent in every corner of the city, in its cafés and bargain eateries, its pizza joints and local bistros through to its international temples of fine dining, where a bottle of wine can cost more than most people would spend on a car. You'll find food from every corner of the globe, from Armenia to Vietnam, with some of the more prevalent ethnic cuisines reaching unprecedented heights: **Hakkasan** (*see p201*) was the UK's first Chinese to be awarded a Michelin star, **Nahm** (*see p211*) the first Thai.

The best is not always the most famous, of course. Sometimes fame is a product solely of itself – celebrity for celebrity's sake. Thus, we have Jordan and places like the **Ivy** (*see p210*), with paparazzi out front and homely British comfort food inside.

On the other hand, some restaurants deserve their headlines. You'll have nearly as much trouble getting a reservation at **Gordon Ramsay**, whether in Claridge's hotel (*see p205*) or in Chelsea (*see p213*), as you will at the Ivy,

but the food makes it worth the time spent on hold. And the same can be said of chef Jamie Oliver's venture, **Fifteen** (*see p216*) – the subject of a television documentary in both the US and Britain before it opened, it's booked up months in advance, but not only is the food stellar, it's all for a very good cause.

DOS AND DON'TS

Not all London restaurants insist on reservations. We've indicated those places where booking is essential, but it's always best to reserve in advance where possible.

Some London places are entirely non-smoking and others allow smoking anywhere; some set aside sections for smokers. If you're passionate either way, it's best to call ahead.

Tipping is standard practice; ten to 15 per cent is usual. Some restaurants add service to the bill, so double-check or you may tip twice.

We've listed a range of meal prices for each place. However, restaurants often change their menus, so these prices are only guidelines.

For the best places to eat with kids, *see p271*; for more on eating out in London, buy the annual

Time Out Eating & Drinking Guide (£10.99) and, for a remarkable range of budget dinners, *Time Out Cheap Eats in London* (£6.99).

The South Bank & Bankside

Cafés & brasseries

Konditor & Cook
10 Stoney Street, SE1 9AD (7407 5100). London Bridge tube/rail. **Open** 7.30am-6pm Mon-Fri; 8.30am-4pm Sat. **Main courses** £2.10-£4.75. **Credit** AmEx, MC, V. **Map** p404 P8.
This is one of our favourite mini chains. Here, the interior is minimalist, staff are professional rather than chatty, and sandwiches are varied and great value at around £2.75. The cakes, tarts and biscuits are deservedly legendary.
Other locations: throughout the city.

Tate Modern Café: Level 2
2nd Floor, Tate Modern, Sumner Street, SE1 9TG (7401 5014/www.tate.org.uk). Southwark tube/London Bridge tube/rail. **Open** 10-11.30am, 11.30am-3pm daily; 3-5.30pm Mon-Thur, Sun; 3-6pm, 6-9.30pm Fri, Sat. **Main courses** (lunch) £7.95-£11. **Credit** AmEx, DC, MC, V. **Map** p404 O/P8.
Hungry Tate Modernists can find sustenance in this spacious café-restaurant, and take a break from staring at art by staring at the riverbank through the floor-to-ceiling windows. Three menus (breakfast, lunch and afternoon) are offered during the day, plus tapas on late-opening nights.

Fish

Livebait
41-45 The Cut, SE1 8LF (7928 7211/www.santeonline.co.uk/livebait). Southwark tube/Waterloo tube/rail. **Open** noon-11pm Mon-Sat; 12.30-9pm Sun. **Main courses** £9.75-£29. **Credit** AmEx, DC, MC, V. **Map** p404 N8.
Livebait is always great for a pre- or post-event meal, particularly this branch, which is close to the Old and New Vics and to the South Bank. You can expect a clean, functional interior and superior seafood, deftly served.
Other locations: throughout the city.

Gastropubs

Anchor & Hope
36 The Cut, SE1 8LP (7928 9898). Southwark tube or Waterloo tube/rail. **Open** 5-11pm Mon; 11am-11pm Tue-Sat. **Main courses** £10.80-£14. **Credit** MC, V. **Map** p401 M8.
A low-key yet deliriously popular combination of relaxed bar area and slightly more formal dining room, A&H has an imaginative menu and some great, affordable wines and sherries. Food ranges to such unusual combinations as snail, preserved rabbit and watercress salad (delicious, by the way).

Global

Baltic
74 Blackfriars Road, SE1 8HA (7928 1111/www.balticrestaurant.co.uk). Southwark tube. **Open** noon-3pm, 6-11.15pm Mon-Sat; noon-10.30pm Sun. **Main courses** £9.50-£14. **Credit** AmEx, MC, V. **Map** p404 N8.
Baltic's spacious interior, complete with its 'wall of amber' bar and amber sculptures, makes a terrific setting for the modern, varied menu and beautiful, efficient waiting staff. The food manages what is a rare combination for an eastern European restaurant: it's both adventurous *and* authentic.

Tas
72 Borough High Street, SE1 1XF (7403 7200/www.tasrestaurant.com). London Bridge tube/rail. **Open** noon-11.30pm Mon-Sat; noon-10.30pm Sun. **Main courses** £4.95-£14.45. **Credit** AmEx, MC, V. **Map** p404 P9.
Modern and rather chic, with designer chairs, wooden floors and polished fittings, this branch of the Tas mini chain manages to pack in plenty of

The best Restaurants

For Atkins dieters
Gaucho Grill (*see p199*); **St John** (*see p196*); **Smiths of Smithfield** (*see p199*).

For grazers
Cígala (*see p199*); **Club Gascon** (*see p196*); **Drunken Monkey** (*see p195*); **Flâneur Food Hall** (*see p196*); **Yokoso Sushi** (*see p196*).

For green cuisine
The Gate (*see p219*); **Heartstone** (*see p215*); **Manna** (*see p215*); **Morgan M** (*see p214*); **The Place Below** (*see p196*).

For guzzlers
Arkansas Café (*see p215*); **Bamboula** (*see p217*); **Christopher's** (*see p210*); **Harlem** (*see p218*); **Rodizio Rico** (*see p219*).

For silencing the kids
Eagle Bar Diner (*see p199*); **Gourmet Burger Kitchen** (*see p217*); **Hard Rock Café** (*see p203*); **Lucky 7** (*see p218*); **Maison Bertaux** (*see p206*); **Ramen Seto** (*see p209*); **Rock & Sole Plaice** (*see p210*); **Wagamama** (*see p214*).

For snacking before a show
Anchor & Hope (*see left*); **Belgo Centraal** (*see p209*); **Christopher's** (*see p210*); **Konditor & Cook** (*see left*); **Livebait** (*see left*).

Eat, Drink, Shop

LUNCH & DINNER
CRUISES

Relax for lunch or indulge in a luxurious dinner cruise aboard Bateaux London's elegant restaurant vessel whilst you cruise past London's breathtaking landmarks along the Thames.

BATEAUX
LONDON

TEL: 020 7925 2215
EMAIL: info@bateauxlondon.com
www.bateauxlondon.com

London   *   New York   *   Paris

people without ever seeming overcrowded. Excellent Turkish cuisine comes as standard.
Other locations: throughout the city.

Modern European

Oxo Tower Restaurant, Bar & Brasserie

8th Floor, Oxo Tower Wharf, Barge House Street, SE1 9PH (7803 3888/www.harveynichols.com). Blackfriars or Waterloo tube/rail. **Open** noon-2.30pm, 6-11pm Mon-Sat; noon-3pm, 6.30-10pm Sun. **Main courses** £17.50-£26. **Credit** AmEx, DC, MC, V. **Map** p404 N7.

There's something of the production line about the Brasserie at Oxo Tower: diners are processed through their allotted time slot in a rather soulless fashion, with industrial noise levels a further incentive to eat up and go. The view is impressive; the food mostly delivers; and the place is certainly lively – but if you require a little peace and quiet, look elsewhere.

The City

Cafés & brasseries

De Gustibus

53-55 Carter Lane, EC4V 5AE (7236 0056/www. degustibus.co.uk). St Paul's tube/Blackfriars tube/rail. **Open** 7am-5pm Mon-Fri. **Main courses** £4.95-£7.25. **Credit** MC, V. **Map** p404 O6.

One of the UK's leading bakers, De Gustibus makes artisan breads for restaurants and luxury loaf lovers, but also runs cafés. This branch looks a bit dated, but sells great sandwiches and some tasty sweet treats.
Other locations: 53 Blandford Street, Marylebone, W1U 7HL (7486 6608); 4 Southwark Street, Borough, SE1 1TQ (7407 3625).

Chinese

Drunken Monkey

222 Shoreditch High Street, E1 6PJ (7392 9606/ www.thedrunkenmonkey.info). Liverpool Street tube/rail/35, 47, 242, 344 bus. **Open** noon-11.30pm Mon-Fri; 6pm-midnight Sat; noon-11.30pm Sun. **Main courses** £4.50-£6.50. **Credit** AmEx, MC, V. **Map** p403 R4.

If you want Chinese food in the pub, you'll be delighted by Drunken Monkey. The owners serve dim sum, but have ditched the daytime-only serving and the traditional tea. Instead, dumplings and simple meals come with cocktails, wines and beers.

Fish

Sweetings

39 Queen Victoria Street, EC4N 4SA (7248 3062). Cannon Street tube/rail/Bank tube/DLR. **Open** 11.30am-3pm Mon-Fri. **Main courses** £10.50-£24.50. **Credit** AmEx, MC, V. **Map** p404 O7.

Drunken Monkey. *See p196.*

Everything about this City haunt is old school, from the mahogany-topped counters and efficient staff to the suited gents eating unfussy fare accompanied by buttered sliced bread and silver tankards of ale.

French

1 Lombard Street

1 Lombard Street, EC3V 9AA (7929 6611/www. 1lombardstreet.com). Bank tube/DLR. **Open** noon-3pm, 6-10pm Mon-Fri. **Main courses** £27.50-£29.50. **Credit** AmEx, DC, MC, V. **Map** p405 Q6/7.

This domed and whitewashed brasserie (a Grade II listed former banking hall) is filled with a cacophony of bankers and lawyers taking advantage of the relative bargain offered by the set lunch menu. A splendid location at the heart of the Square Mile, but the food's a mixed bag and prices undeniably steep.

Japanese

City Miyama

17 Godliman Street, EC4V 5BD (7489 1937). St Paul's tube/Blackfriars tube/rail. **Open** noon-2pm, 6-9.30pm Mon-Fri; 6-9.30pm Sat. **Main courses** £9-£25. **Credit** AmEx, DC, MC, V. **Map** p404 O6.

For a relatively formal City joint, Miyama puts on a surprisingly warm welcome, with a jolly greeter who leads customers (brokers, Japanese workers) down from the ground-floor sushi and teppan areas to the basement dining room. It's a small, old-fashioned and overstaffed space, but the food is good.

Yokoso Sushi

40 Whitefriars Street, EC4Y 8BH (7583 9656).
Blackfriars tube/rail. **Open** 11am-10pm Mon-Fri.
Set meals £7.50-£11.50 incl miso soup. **Credit**
AmEx, MC, V. **Map** p404 N6.
Tricky to find (there's just a sign and a doorway
at street level), this butterscotch-walled basement
kaiten diner is usually packed nonetheless. Expect
to find tasty, affordable snacks on the belt.

Mediterranean

Eyre Brothers

70 Leonard Street, EC2A 4QX (7613 5346/
www.eyrebrothers.co.uk). Old Street tube/rail.
Open noon-3pm, 6.30-11pm Mon-Fri; 6.30-11pm
Sat. **Main courses** £13-£25. **Service** 12.5%.
Credit AmEx, DC, MC, V. **Map** p403 Q4.
A winning combination of Shoreditch stylishness
(inventive lighting, long banquettes), a friendly atmosphere and enjoyable Portuguese-based food makes
this the benchmark for newer London restaurants.

Modern European

Bonds

Threadneedles, 5 Threadneedle Street, EC2R 8BD
(7657 8088/www.theetongroup.com). Bank tube/
DLR. **Open** noon-2.30pm, 6-10pm Mon-Fri. **Main**
courses £17.50-£25. **Credit** AmEx, DC, MC, V.
Map p405 Q6.
Due to its location in the City, Bonds is far livelier
during the day than of an evening, once the stock-
brokers and *FT* readers have gone home. Dishes are
peppered with goodies such as pigs' cheeks, smoked
eel, bone marrow and frogs' legs aïoli.

Vegetarian & organic

The Place Below

St Mary-le-Bow, Cheapside, EC2V 6AU (7329 0789/
www.theplacebelow.co.uk). St Paul's tube/Bank tube/
DLR. **Open** 7.30-11am, 11.30am-2.30pm, 2.30-3.30pm
Mon-Fri. **Main courses** £5.50-£7.50. **Credit** MC, V.
Map p404 P6.
An oasis of calm in the City, this is an ideal spot
for breakfast before facing the office. Browse the
morning papers with fortifying toasted oat porridge
with maple syrup and cream, fruit salads or muesli.
Good, strong Illy coffee is a bargain 80p. Soups with
own-made bread reward lunchtime visitors.

Holborn & Clerkenwell

British

Medcalf

40 Exmouth Market, EC1R 4QE (7833 3533). Angel
tube/Farringdon tube/rail/38 bus. **Open** 10am-11pm
Mon-Fri; 7-11pm Sat; noon-10.30pm Sun. **Main**
courses £8.50-£12. **Credit** MC, V. **Map** p402 N4.

This former butcher's shop pitches itself perfectly
for the locale: by day it's a diner, offering breakfast
and lunch to local workers; from mid-afternoon to
mid-evening there's an inventive bar menu; by night
it's a drinking den, with DJs playing on Friday and
Saturday nights.

St John

26 St John Street, EC1M 4AY (7251 0848/4998/
www.stjohnrestaurant.com). Farringdon tube/rail.
Open noon-3pm, 6-11pm Mon-Fri; 6-11pm Sat.
Main courses £13-£19. **Credit** AmEx, DC,
MC, V. **Map** p402 O3.
Its whitewashed walls, steel kitchen counters and
telltale signs of a previous incarnation as a smoke
house have won St John favour with carnivores in
City suits. The menu is renowned for its flashes of
gore (offal, pigs' tails, brains), but many trad British
dishes are also regulars, with an emphasis on sea-
sonal produce guaranteeing bright, fresh flavours.
Other locations: St John Bread & Wine, 94-96
Commercial Street, Spitalfields, E1 6LZ (7247 8724).

Cafés & brasseries

Flâneur Food Hall

41 Farringdon Road, EC1M 3JB (7404 4422).
Farringdon tube/rail. **Open** noon-3pm, 6-10pm
Mon-Fri; 6-10pm Sat. Brunch served 9am-4pm Sat,
Sun. **Main courses** £8.50-£15.50. **Credit** AmEx,
DC, MC, V. **Map** p402 N4/5.
This food hall restaurant charms immediately with
its Wonderland atmosphere and enthusiastic staff.
It's a handsomely converted warehouse with an ele-
ment of whimsy in the improbably tall shelves and
shapely wooden tables. Food is impeccably fresh,
making picnic-style dishes such as a charcuterie or
cheese plate (with great bread) a default order.

French

Club Gascon

57 West Smithfield, EC1A 9DS (7796 0600).
Barbican tube/Farringdon tube/rail. **Open** noon-
2pm, 7-10pm Mon-Thur; noon-2pm, 7-10.30pm Fri;
7-10.30pm Sat. **Main courses** £5.30-£29. **Tapas**
£6-£16.50. **Credit** AmEx, MC, V. **Map** p402 O5.
Renowned as a foie gras specialist, Club Gascon
is, as you might assume, a plush, pricey venue, but
it is no bastion of conservatism. From conception to
presentation, the food is witty, challenging and
imaginative. So is the environment, with lots of
incongruous shapes and materials assembled into
clubby, natural warmth.

Gastropubs

Coach & Horses

26-28 Ray Street, EC1R 3DJ (7278 8990/www.the
coachandhorses.com). Farringdon tube/rail. **Open**
11am-11pm Mon-Fri; 6-11pm Sat; noon-3pm Sun. **Main**
courses £9.95-£13.95. **Credit** MC, V. **Map** p402 N4.

Dry your eyes, Cinders: you've reached the **Coach & Horses**.

Like the pumpkin and mice depicted in its logo, the Coach & Horses has been the object of an impressive feat of conjuring: where once a traditional boozer stood, there is now a stylish, sophisticated gastropub. The decor is discreet, the menu is full of tempting, unfussy dishes, and the wine list is usefully annotated. The few outside tables are perfect for languid summer afternoons.

Perseverance

63 Lamb's Conduit Street, WC1N 3NB (7405 8278). Holborn or Russell Square tube. **Open** 12.30-11pm Mon-Sat; 12.30-10.30pm Sun. **Main courses** £8-£14. **Credit** AmEx, DC, MC, V. **Map** p399 M4/5.

Dramatically different from the boisterous and be-flocked pub below, the discreet first-floor restaurant is an intimate little space. The menu is a short and none-too-ambitious roster of European standards, but what it does, it does well.

Global

Gaucho Grill

125-126 Chancery Lane, WC2A 1PU (7242 7727/ www.thegauchogrill.co.uk). Chancery Lane tube. **Open** noon-11pm Mon-Fri. **Main courses** £9-£20. **Credit** AmEx, DC, MC, V. **Map** p399 M5, p404 N6.

Cowhide stools and racks of Mendozan plonk may allude to the Argentine countryside, but this Gaucho Grill is a refined steakhouse for City slickers. There are usually more people sipping cocktails on the ground floor than dining upstairs.

Other locations: throughout the city.

Modern European

Bank Aldwych

1 Kingsway, WC2B 6XF (7379 9797/www. bankrestaurants.com). Holborn or Temple tube. **Open** 7.30-10.30am, noon-3pm, 5.30-11pm Mon-Fri; 11.30am-3pm, 5.30-11pm Sat; 11.30am-3pm, 5.30-9.30pm Sun. **Main courses** £10.80-£21. **Credit** AmEx, DC, MC, V. **Map** p399 M6.

This place is as impressive as it was when it opened in 1996, from the vast chandelier, the huge bar area where cocktails are supped, the mirrored walls along the chef's station to the slick dining area beyond. Nor has the kitchen lost its edge: first-class food is served by efficient staff.

Smiths of Smithfield

67-77 Charterhouse Street, EC1M 6HJ (7251 7950/ www.smithsofsmithfield.co.uk). Farringdon tube/rail. **Open** noon-3pm, 6-11pm Mon-Fri; 6-10.45pm Sat. **Main courses** £9.50-£11.50. **Credit** AmEx, DC, MC, V. **Map** p402 O5.

Staying true to its roots as a former market store, Smiths retains an industrial, New York warehouse feel. Of the four storeys, the ground floor serves breakfast, brunch and other casual fare; the next level up is a cocktail and champagne bar; the second floor is a lively brasserie; the third a fine-dining restaurant. A one-stop-shop by any other name.

Spanish

Cigala

54 Lamb's Conduit Street, WC1N 3LW (7405 1717/ www.cigala.co.uk). Holborn or Russell Square tube. **Open** noon-10.45pm Mon-Fri; 12.30-10.45pm Sat. **Main courses** £10-£17. **Tapas** £2-£8. **Credit** AmEx, DC, MC, V. **Map** p400 H7/J6.

One of a cluster of restaurants on Lamb's Conduit Street, Cigala is a slick, modern operation with crisp white and pine decor. Despite the trendy aesthetics, the menu remains traditional and unshowy. If you're after tapas, head down to the basement bar or nab one of the pavement tables.

Moro

34-36 Exmouth Market, EC1R 4QE (7833 8336/ www.moro.co.uk). Farringdon tube/rail/19, 38 bus. **Open** 12.30-2.30pm, 7-10.30pm Mon-Fri; 7-10.30pm Sat. **Main courses** £13.50-£17.50. **Credit** AmEx, DC, MC, V. **Map** p402 N4.

With praise from all sides, a top-selling cookbook and near-permanently busy tables, Moro has set the style for restaurants offering an imaginative English take on Mediterranean food traditions – in this case, from Spain and North Africa.

Fitzrovia

American

Eagle Bar Diner

3-5 Rathbone Place, W1T 1HJ (7637 1418/www. eaglebardiner.com). Tottenham Court Road tube. **Open** noon-11pm Mon-Wed; noon-11.30pm Thur, Fri; 11am-midnight Sat; 11am-6pm Sun. **Main courses** £4-£8.75. **Credit** MC, V. **Map** p399 K5.

This trendy, cool, reliably good restaurant is an oasis off the hellish hustle of Oxford Street. The look is posh diner – leather banquettes at arty angles, high-backed green booths and a slick bar at the front – and the menu is much the same. The superb, juicy hamburgers are a must.

Indian

Rasa Samudra

5 Charlotte Street, W1T 1RE (7637 0222/ www.rasarestaurants.com). Goodge Street tube. **Open** noon-3pm, 6-10.45pm Mon-Sat; 6-10.45pm Sun. **Main courses** £6.25-£12.95. **Credit** AmEx, MC, V. **Map** p398 J5.

That Rasa Samudra – the seafood specialist of the small chain of Keralite restaurants that began many years ago in lowly Stoke Newington – is among the best venues for Indian food in London is beyond doubt. Yet what you won't get are the modern Indian flourishes. Here, tradition triumphs over fusion; presentation owes nothing to nouvelle cuisine; and design statements are largely confined to the vivid pink frontage. Recommended.

Other locations: throughout the city.

Italian

Carluccio's Caffè
8 Market Place, W1W 8AG (7636 2228/
www.carluccios.com). Oxford Circus tube. **Open**
7.30am-11pm Mon-Fri; 10am-11pm Sat; 10am-10pm
Sun. **Main courses** £4.85-£10.95. **Credit** AmEx,
MC, V. **Map** p398 J6.
Although deservedly popular, this cleverly conceived luncheonette – the original West End branch
of what has become a widespread chain – has perhaps become a little dishevelled. But when food is
so reasonably priced and delicious, such faults are
easy to forgive. **Other locations:** throughout the city.

Sardo
45 Grafton Way, W1T 5DQ (7387 2521/www.sardo-
restaurant.com). Warren Street tube. **Open** noon-
3pm, 6-11pm Mon-Fri; 6-11pm Sat. **Main courses**
£8.90-£18. **Credit** AmEx, DC, MC, V. **Map** p398 J4.
This Sardinian tratt has acquired a reputation as the
place restaurant reviewers go when they're spending their own money. It's easy to see why: the many
well-executed dishes on the menu are, like the decor
and service, unpretentious and of a high standard.

Modern European

Pied à Terre
34 Charlotte Street, W1T 2NH (7636 1178/www.
pied.a.terre.co.uk). Goodge Street or Tottenham
Court Road tube. **Open** 6.15-11pm Mon; 12.15-
2.30pm, 6.15-11pm Tue-Fri. **Main courses** £27.
Credit AmEx, MC, V. **Map** p398 J5.
Pied à Terre goes out of its way to provide a
realistically priced and completely relaxing gourmet
experience, so if fine dining is an arena into which
you've never ventured, then this intimate, softly lit
restaurant is an edifying place to start.

Oriental

Busaba Eathai
22 Store Street, WC1E 7DS (7299 7900). Goodge
Street or Tottenham Court Road tube. **Open** noon-
11pm Mon-Thur; noon-11.30pm Fri, Sat; noon-10pm
Sun. **Main courses** £5.10-£9.80. **Credit** AmEx, MC,
V. **Map** p399 K5.
This is a shared-table, bench-seating, no-smoking,
no-booking restaurant. Sound familiar? This nifty
Thai concept joint was created by Alan Yau, who

Hot plates?

Chefs working at the top of their profession
the world over are renowned for their magpie-
like habit of stealing ideas from each others'
menus and depositing them among their own
plats du jour without so much as a nod or
a thank you. While this may be accepted
protocol among the top toques, it can
produce a kind of dizzying effect on the
punters, who find themselves falling prey to
serious bouts of *déjà mangé* as they discover
the same fashionable dish bobbing up on a
dozen different menus. So, in the interests
of safeguarding the dining public's sanity,
we have decided to name and shame some
of the current worst offenders.

Let's start with the starters, and the
ubiquitous carpaccio. These slivers of cured
raw beef used only to be found among the
antipasti of certain Italian restaurants, yet
now they have swaggered (with their favourite
sidekicks, Parmesan Shavings and Pile Of
Rocket) on to every even vaguely international
or modern European menu in town. Just as
common, although less traditional in its
origins, is the pairing of cooked oysters or
scallops with some kind of spicy sausage,
almost always that trusty 21st-century
standby, chorizo. Then there are the savoury
panna cottas: don't get us started on those...

Pork also features prominently among
the main-course contenders, although, to
be absolutely precise, we should say that
the belly does. A swine's stomach, it would
seem, is never safe, judging by the frequency
with which they appear on menus having been
subjected to the trials of slow-roasting,
braising and other time-consuming, flavour-
infusing treatments. Speaking of treatments,
many of London's main courses have been
finished with one of the following fashionable
techniques: the drizzling of oils; the frothing
of soups and sauces into a 'cappuccino';
the flaking of dried products (padron peppers
being a particular fave). And one final word
on main-course homogeny: it would seem
that practically every second dish has the
provenance of its ingredients meticulously
listed. Crab is from Cornwall, beef is from
the black-foot, white-eared, long-horn stock
of Western Skye, every scallop has been
gathered painstakingly by hand, each and
every bream ensnared on a line. Enough,
we say, is enough.

Lastly, a quick word about dessert. Where
carpaccio has come to represent the clichéd
beginning of the menu, chocolate fondant has
become this year's sticky end.

But, hey, there are worse ways to go.

also conceived Wagamama and runs top Chinese restaurants Hakkasan (*see below*) and Yauatcha (*see p207*). Its green curry is still the best in town. **Other locations**: 106-110 Wardour Street, Soho, W1F OTR (7255 8686).

Hakkasan
8 Hanway Place, W1T 1HD (7907 1888).
Tottenham Court Road tube. **Open** noon-3.15pm, 6-11.30pm Mon-Wed; noon-3.15pm, 6pm-12.30am Thur, Fri; noon-4.30pm, 6pm-12.30am Sat; noon-4.30pm Sun. **Main courses** £11.50-£40. **Dim sum** £3.50-£16. **Credit** AmEx, MC, V. **Map** p399 K5.
Few London restaurants beat the thrill of descending the green slate staircase here. Incense smoke and outlandish flowers greet you as you enter a subtly lit space of dark latticed screens. Hakkasan breaks the Chinatown mould by offering fine, pricey Chinese food in a venue that satisfies both western and oriental tastes. The lunchtime dim sum is unrivalled in London, but you may have to ask for the menu.

Han Kang
16 Hanway Street, W1T 1UE (7637 1985).
Tottenham Court Road tube. **Open** noon-3pm, 6-11pm Mon-Sat. **Main courses** £6.50-£28. **Credit** AmEx, MC, V. **Map** p399 K5.
If you're after a calm, smoke-free oasis, look elsewhere. It seems that a large segment of London's Korean student population comes here for a quick bite (one-dish set menus with rice and soup range from £5 to £6.50) and a pack or two of fags at lunchtime. In the evening, the atmosphere is less frenetic. Table-top barbecues are a forte.

Marylebone

Fish & chips

Golden Hind
73 Marylebone Lane, W1U 2PN (7486 3644).
Bond Street tube. **Open** noon-3pm, 6-10pm Mon-Fri; 6-10pm Sat. **Main courses** £5-£10.70. **Credit** AmEx, MC, V. **Map** p398 G5.
Great chips, lovely fresh fish and a few unusual dishes to tempt adventurous palates (deep-fried mussels being a case in point). The gleaming stainless steel and Bakelite fish fryer typifies the beautifully preserved art deco interior.

Global

Original Tagines
7A Dorset Street, W1H 3SE (7935 1545/ www.originaltagines.com). Baker Street tube.
Open noon-3pm, 6-11pm daily. **Main courses** £9.50-£11.95. **Credit** MC, V. **Map** p398 G5.
One of London's very best Moroccan restaurants, Original Tagines eschews the gimmicky kasbah decoration so popular elsewhere and instead concentrates on what goes on in the kitchen. The menu is firmly traditional (couscous and tagines), but the cooking and presentation are very contemporary.

Inn the Park. *See p203.*

Providores & Tapa Room
109 Marylebone High Street, W1U 4RX (7935 6175/www.theprovidores.co.uk). Baker Street or Bond Street tube. **Open** noon-2.45pm, 6-10.45pm Mon-Sat; noon-2.45pm, 6-10pm Sun. **Main courses** £15-£22. **Tapas** £1.50-£9. **Credit** AmEx, MC, V. **Map** p398 G4/5.
Welcome to the refined upper reaches of fusion food. The ground-floor Tapa Room is the more casual space; it is open for posh breakfast fry-ups, brunchy snacks and global tapas. Upstairs, the Providores is a serene, clean-lined white room. Here, you can expect globe-trotting influences and ingredients from Asia to the Middle East.

Six-13
19 Wigmore Street, W1U 1PH (7629 6133/www.six13.com). Bond Street or Oxford Circus tube. **Open** noon-3pm, 5.30-10.30pm Mon-Thur. **Main courses** £17-£24. **Credit** AmEx, MC, V. **Map** p398 G6.
This smart, modern restaurant has a minimalist turquoise interior and well-crafted kosher cuisine.

Italian

Locanda Locatelli
8 Seymour Street, W1H 7JZ (7935 9088/www.locandalocatelli.com). Marble Arch tube. **Open** noon-3pm, 7-11pm Mon-Thur; noon-3pm, 7-11.30pm Fri, Sat. **Main courses** £16-£30. **Credit** AmEx, MC, V. **Map** p395 F6.

A highly enjoyable restaurant from the UK's foremost Italian chef, Locanda Locatelli specialises in high-end cuisine. And while recent reports of the cooking may have been disappointing, the pedigree of the kitchen is beyond doubt.

Middle Eastern

Levant

Jason Court, 76 Wigmore Street, W1U 2SJ (7224 1111/www.levantrestaurant.co.uk). Bond Street tube. **Open** noon-11.30pm Mon-Fri; 5.30-11.30pm Sat, Sun. **Main courses** £11.25-£25. **Credit** AmEx, DC, MC, V. **Map** p398 G6.
Levant aims at oriental fantasy – rose petals, carved screens, the occasional bellydancer – with loud music and a partyish atmosphere to egg diners on. And the food? Moroccan-style tagines to European-influenced dishes with a Lebanese slant.

Maroush

21 Edgware Road, W2 2JE (7723 0773/www.maroush.com). Marble Arch tube. **Open** noon-midnight daily. **Main courses** £12-£22. **Credit** AmEx, DC, MC, V. **Map** p395 F6.
There really is nowhere quite like Maroush. This branch of the successful London chain is housed in a handsome and spacious dark red basement (there's a café area upstairs) just made for after-dark. Meze are always super-fresh and beautifully presented. **Other locations**: Maroush Gardens, 1-3 Connaught Street, W2 2DH (7262 0222).

Modern European

Orrery

55 Marylebone High Street, W1M 3AE (7616 8000/www.orrery.co.uk). Baker Street or Regent's Park tube. **Open** noon-3pm, 7-11pm Mon-Sat; noon-3pm, 7-10.30pm Sun. **Main courses** £16.50-£30. **Credit** AmEx, DC, MC, V. **Map** p398 G4/5.
This top-of-the-line Conran outlet sets out to offer luxury: from the smiling greeters to the cigar list and giant digestifs trolley. The long space is white, airy and (of course) sleek. The haute cuisine cooking is refined, expensive and extremely delicate.

Oriental

Royal China

24-26 Baker Street, W1U 7AB (7487 4688/www.royalchinagroup.co.uk). Baker Street tube. **Open** noon-11pm Mon-Thur; noon-11.30pm Fri, Sat; 11am-10pm Sun. **Main courses** £7-£30. **Credit** AmEx, MC, V. **Map** p398 G4/5.
It pains us to write anything negative about the much-loved Royal China chain, which has been serving some of the best dim sum in London for years, but this branch looks in need of a revamp and a management shake-up. Happily, though, the kitchen remains on good form. **Other locations**: throughout the city.

Mayfair & St James's

The Americas

Hard Rock Café

150 Old Park Lane, W1K 1QZ (7629 0382/www.hardrock.com). Hyde Park Corner tube. **Open** 11.30am-midnight Mon-Thur, Sun; 11.30am-1am Fri, Sat. **Main courses** £7.25-£13.95. **Credit** AmEx, MC, V. **Map** p400 G8.
We've never understood why so many people visit all those Hard Rock Cafés dotted around the world. Could it be for the burgers, nachos and other generic hard-rocker fodder? Who knows? Or, indeed, cares? Not us. Not now, when it's been outpaced. For Rock spotters, though, this was the first one.

British

Dorchester Grill Room

The Dorchester, 53 Park Lane, W1A 2HJ (7317 6336/www.dorchesterhotel.com). Hyde Park Corner tube. **Open** 7-11am, 12.30-2.30pm, 6-11pm Mon-Sat; 7.30-11am, 12.30-2.30pm, 7-10.30pm Sun. **Main courses** £21-£30. **Credit** AmEx, DC, MC, V. **Map** p400 G8.
Resolutely old school and meticulously grand, the Grill Room, with its splendid tapestries and ornate banquettes, makes a fabulous setting for what is invariably a fine feed. Shamelessly, wonderfully, admirably, roast beef remains a speciality.

Inn the Park

St James's Park, SW1A 2BJ (7451 9999/www.innthepark.co.uk). Green Park or Piccadilly Circus tube. **Open** 8am-11am, noon-3pm, 6-10.30pm Mon-Fri; 9-11am, noon-4pm, 6-10.30pm Sat, Sun. **Main courses** £8.50-£17.50. **Credit** AmEx, MC, V. **Map** p401 K8.
This striking new venture in St James's Park has brought together a true roll-call of British talent. Food comes courtesy of restaurateur Oliver Peyton; the striking wooden building, partly covered by a turf roof, with a sweeping glass front and veranda, is by architect Michael Hopkins; while the chic, if sauna-like interior is by Tom Dixon (of Habitat fame). The park itself provides a bevy of ducks to potter past as you sip and scoff.

Cafés & brasseries

Victory Café

Basement, Gray's Antiques Market, South Molton Lane, W1K 5AB (7499 6801). Bond Street tube. **Open** 10am-6pm Mon-Fri. **Main courses** £2.75-£4.95. **No credit cards**. **Map** p398 H6.
Hidden in the basement of Gray's Antiques Market, the Victory Café is a quirky gem. The vibe is deliciously retro; the decor is a pastiche of post-war Britain; the menu is decidedly of the if-it-ain't-broke school of catering. Try the all-day English breakfast, an organic belt-buster.

RIP, classic caffs

Bob Stanley of St Etienne laments the loss of London's greasy spoons.

The queue for the last ever specials at the Copper Grill stretched halfway down Eldon Street by one o'clock. All bade farewell to one of London's finest caffs. The wooden banquettes, copper piping, city murals and fabulous '50s counter will all have been skipped by the time you read this. Ditto the Piccolo bar two doors down (it had the best Formica in town) and the Euro on Swallow Street.

The Italians are renowned conspiracy theorists. What would they make of the rapid disappearance of the café, their great contribution to London culture? My obsession with them began aged four, with a BBC kids' programme called *Joe* set in a transport caff (lorries! A jukebox!), and blossomed when I moved to London in the mid '80s, fuelled by Dexy's Midnight Runners' 'The Teams That Meet in Caffs', and the photo on the back of Madness's 'The Sun and the Rain'. The green-and-white luncheon voucher called to me. Thinking I was a kind of beatnik, I planned to while away my days over frothy coffee, reading Waterhouse, Mackay and Brautigan, and with like-minded souls, plot to bring down the government. My hangouts were the Regent Milk Bar on Edgware Road, Gattopardo at King's Cross, and the Oval Platter on Charing Cross Road.

Cafés were a haven – while everything else in the city seems to accelerate, the pace of life in a London caff is resolutely mid 20th century. The history appealed, too – Soho caffs like the New Piccadilly were just about the only remnants of the area's bohemian golden age when Francis Bacon, Colin Wilson and Adam Faith could all be at adjacent tables. The classic café sees no boundary between boho, biker and office boy. It's truly cosmopolitan.

Adrian Maddox, in his essential book *Classic Cafés*, considers the quality of the food to be less significant than the curve of a coffee-cup handle or the number of chrome pipes on an espresso machine. Perhaps this explains their demise: tea and toast costs a pound, liver and bacon three quid. Anyone can afford it, which is why the customers are such a cross-section of London life. To cover the current steep rent rises, a cup of tea should cost something like two pounds. This ain't going to happen. The result is that these independent traders are being squeezed out, replaced by identikit shops from Anywhere, UK. Many café owners are now close to retirement age and if the kids don't want to take over the business, it folds.

Happily there are exceptions: **Andrews** on Gray's Inn Road (No.160, 7837 1630) and **Pellicci's** on Bethnal Green Road (No.332, 7739 4873) have been handed down, hopefully secure for another generation. But the recently vacated Tea Rooms on Museum Street or Rendezvous on Maddox Street will be hard to replace in a brave new world of fast food and binge drinking.

● Saint Etienne's compilation *Songs for Mario's Café* (Discotheque Records) is out now.

French

Embassy
29 Old Burlington Street, W1S 3AN (7851 0956/ www.embassylondon.com). Green Park or Piccadilly Circus tube. **Open** noon-3pm, 6-11.30pm Tue-Fri; 6-11.30pm Sat. **Main courses** £14.50-£25. **Credit** AmEx, MC, V. **Map** p400 J7.

Gary Hollihead produces exquisite dishes in jewelled colours, with flavours perfectly balanced and ingredients just so. The only disappointment comes in the tacky corporate surroundings.

Indian

Tamarind
20 Queen Street, W1J 5PR (7629 3561/www. tamarindrestaurant.com). Green Park tube. **Open** noon-3pm, 6-11.30pm Mon-Fri; 6-11.30pm Sat; noon-2.30pm, 6-10.30pm Sun. **Main courses** £14.50-£22. **Credit** AmEx, DC, MC, V. **Map** p400 H7.

Dignified and luxurious, this elegant basement restaurant is synonymous with quality cooking, superlative service and a choice selection of wines. It's also a popular stomping ground for wealthy tourists and business folk on expense accounts.

Italian

Cecconi's
5A Burlington Gardens, W1S 3EW (7434 1500). Green Park tube. **Open** 8-11am, noon-3pm, 6.30-11.30pm Mon-Fri; 10am-4pm, 6.30-11.30pm Sat; 10am-4pm, 6.30-10.30pm Sun. **Main courses** £10-£27.50. **Credit** AmEx, DC, MC, V. **Map** p400 J7.

Sinking into the leather booths at this sexy and sophisticated restaurant gives a sense of excited anticipation. When on form, this is one of London's best Italian restaurants.

Middle Eastern

Al Sultan
51-52 Hertford Street, W1J 7ST (7408 1155/1166). Green Park or Hyde Park Corner tube. **Open** noon-midnight daily. **Main courses** £10-£12. **Credit** AmEx, DC, MC, V. **Map** p400 H8.

Very much a classic Mayfair Lebanese, Al Sultan comes complete with a prim interior, hypnotic Lebanese piped music, and a team of professional, uniformed waiting staff. Standards in the kitchen are suitably high.

Modern European

Le Caprice
Arlington House, Arlington Street, SW1A 1RT (7629 2239/www.caprice-holdings.co.uk). Green Park tube. **Open** noon-3pm, 5.30pm-midnight Mon-Sat; noon-4pm, 6pm-midnight Sun. **Main courses** £12.50-£25. **Credit** AmEx, DC, MC, V. **Map** p400 J8.

This long-time haunt of the old-school fashionable shows no sign of falling from its des-res(ervation) perch. Expensive without being exorbitant, the modern brasserie food that's on offer continues to please Le Caprice's glam clientele.

Gordon Ramsay at Claridge's
Claridge's Hotel, 55 Brook Street, W1A 2JQ (7499 0099/www.gordonramsay.com). Bond Street tube. **Open** noon-2.45pm, 5.45-11pm Mon-Fri; noon-3pm, 5.45-11pm Sat; noon-3pm, 6-11pm Sun. **Set lunch** £30 3 courses. **Set dinner** £55 3 courses, £65 6 courses. **Credit** AmEx, MC, V. **Map** p398 H6.

Perhaps you've heard of this guy? There are so many things we'd like to add about his beautiful hotel restaurant but, sadly, space doesn't permit it. Suffice to say, the quality of the cooking is peerless, the subtlety of the service beyond question and the sophistication of the surroundings a credit to both of the above. Some of the best food in the capital, served in the most glamorous yet relaxed atmosphere: an unmissable culinary experience.

The Ritz
150 Piccadilly, W1J 9BR (7493 8181/www.the ritzhotel.co.uk). Green Park tube. **Open** 7-10.30am, 12.30-2.30pm, 6-10.30pm Mon-Sat; 8-10.30am, 12.30-2.30pm Sun. **Main courses** £25-£56. **Credit** AmEx, MC, V. **Map** p400 J8.

It takes a brave team to renovate a hotel as revered as the Ritz, but the dining room is looking good. So, too, is the menu. The archaic old list has gone; in its stead, there's an equally grand, more modern and lighter incarnation that will knock your socks off.

The Wolseley
160 Piccadilly, W1J 9EB (7499 6996/www.the wolseley.com). Green Park tube. **Open** 7-11.30am, noon-2.30pm, 5.30pm-midnight Mon-Fri; 9-11.30am, noon-3pm, 5.30pm-midnight Sat; noon-3pm, 3.30-6pm Sun. **Main courses** £8.75-£26. **Credit** AmEx, DC, MC, V. **Map** p400 J7.

The handsome new venture from the team behind the Ivy (*see p210*) is a surprisingly egalitarian affair. The long opening hours mean that everyone can get in at short notice, even if just for breakfast, tea or a cocktail accompanied by superior bar snacks. And the sizeable, brasserie-style menu is surely a crowd-pleaser. A wonderful addition to London dining.

North African

Momo
25 Heddon Street, W1B 4BH (7434 4040/www. momoresto.com). Piccadilly Circus tube. **Open** noon-2.30pm, 7-11pm Mon-Sat; 7-10.30pm Sun. **Main courses** £14.50-£19.50. **Credit** AmEx, DC, MC, V. **Map** p400 J7.

Simply gorgeous, Momo is decked out like Rick's Café Américain (of *Casablanca* fame), staff are kitted out in custom-designed kasbah pop art T-shirts, and the menu supplements the standard tagines and couscous of Morocco with dishes such as baked cod, duck breast and sea bass. Maroc 'n' roll.

Oriental

Kaya

42 Albemarle Street, W1X 3FE (7499 0622/0633).
Green Park tube. **Open** noon-3pm, 6-11pm Mon-Sat;
6-11pm Sun. **Main courses** £7.50-£17. **Credit** MC,
V. **Map** p400 J7.

Korean restaurants don't very often do 'smart', but
you can count Kaya the honourable exception to that
rule. The restaurant creates a pervasive sense of
calm and order, and in surroundings that are very
easy on the eye. Aficionados will appreciate the
'chef's specials' section of the menu.

Kiku

17 Half Moon Street, W1J 7BE (7499 4208/
www.kikurestaurant.co.uk). Green Park tube.
Open noon-2.30pm; 6-10.15pm Mon-Sat; 5.30-
9.45pm Sun. **Main courses** £10-£28. **Credit**
AmEx, MC, V. **Map** p400 H8.

A stone's throw from Nobu (*see below*), Kiku is a
little less exciting and not very much cheaper than
its glamorous neighbour. If you've seen *Lost in
Translation*, the decor might strike you as having a
certain salaryman chic. The Japanese food, however,
is of undeniably high quality.

Nobu

*Metropolitan Hotel, 19 Old Park Lane, W1K 1LB
(7447 4747/www.noburestaurants.com). Hyde
Park Corner tube.* **Open** noon-2.15pm, 6-10.15pm
Mon-Thur; noon-2.15pm, 6-11pm Fri; 12.30-3pm,
6-11pm Sat; 12.30-3pm, 6-9.30pm Sun. **Main
courses** £5-£27.50 incl miso soup, rice & pickles.
Credit AmEx, DC, MC, V. **Map** p400 G8.

Nobu's tables are small and packed, and the low
ratio of customers to square feet is emphasised by
bright lighting and canteen noise levels. But the
cooking more than makes up for any such caveats:
the fusion of Japanese and Peruvian traditions
served here is no longer novel, but can still inspire
surprise and delight.

Other locations: Ubon, 34 Westferry Circus,
Docklands, E14 8RR (7719 7800).

Soho & Chinatown

British

Lindsay House

*21 Romilly Street, W1V 5AF (7439 0450/
www.lindsayhouse.co.uk). Leicester Square tube.*
Open noon-2.30pm, 6-11pm Mon-Fri; 6-11pm
Sat. **Main courses** (lunch) £18-£22. **Credit**
AmEx, DC, MC, V. **Map** p398 J6.

To be buzzed into this elegant restaurant (and there
is a buzzer; it deters the riff-raff, don't you know) is
to be given a passport to a world where cured foie
gras is rolled in spiced gingerbread, where butter-
poached haddock comes with parsnip cream, and
where ordinary cheeses are usurped by the likes of
stinking bishop with brioche. Wonderful.

Cafés & brasseries

Bar Italia

*22 Frith Street, W1V 5PS (7437 4520/www.bar
italiasoho.co.uk). Leicester Square, Piccadilly Circus
or Tottenham Court Road tube.* **Open** 24hrs Mon-
Sat; 7am-4am Sun. **Main courses** £3.20-£8. **Credit**
(noon-3am only) AmEx, DC, MC, V. **Map** p399 K6.

Still going strong after 55 years, Bar Italia is part of
the Soho furniture. All walks of life come here to
chat, sip coffee and people-watch. It's open round the
clock most days (and gets very busy from midnight
onwards). Excellent panini.

Maison Bertaux

*28 Greek Street, W1V 5LL (7437 6007). Leicester
Square, Piccadilly Circus or Tottenham Court Road
tube.* **Open** 8.30am-8pm daily. **Main courses** £1.30-
£2.90. **No credit cards.** **Map** p399 K6.

Furnished with wonky tables and chairs that
have seen better days, this Soho institution has no
written menus – what you see is what you get. It's
quite a sight, though: French pâtisserie, freshly
baked breads and flavoursome savouries.

Pâtisserie Valerie

*44 Old Compton Street, W1D 4TY (7437 3466/
www.patisserie-valerie.co.uk). Leicester Square,
Piccadilly Circus or Tottenham Court Road tube.*
Open 7.30am-8.30pm Mon, Tue; 7.30am-9pm
Wed-Fri; 8.30am-9pm Sat; 9.30am-7pm Sun. **Main
courses** £3.75-£7.95. **Credit** (over £5) AmEx, DC,
MC, V. **Map** p399 K6.

Indulgent cakes, marzipans and typically French
breads provide a feast for the senses at this landmark Old Compton Street pastry shop and café. The
upstairs is often less busy than the rather gloomy
ground floor, but it's markedly less atmospheric.
Other locations: throughout the city.

Chinese

Imperial China

*White Bear Yard, 25A Lisle Street, WC2H 7BA
(7734 3388/www.imperial-china.co.uk). Leicester
Square or Piccadilly Circus tube.* **Open** noon-11.30pm
Mon-Sat; 11.30am-10.30pm Sun. **Main courses**
£6-£24. **Credit** AmEx, MC, V. **Map** p401 K7.

A year on, the revamped ex-China City is still
elegant. The dim sum list has some of the tastiest
delicacies to be had in London. Pride of place goes
to the ethereal fried taro paste croquettes (yu kok).

ECapital

*8 Gerrard Street, W1D 5PJ (7434 3838). Leicester
Square or Piccadilly Circus tube.* **Open** noon-11.30pm
Mon-Thur; noon-midnight Fri, Sat; noon-10.30pm
Sun. **Main courses** £8.50-£22. **Credit** AmEx, DC,
MC, V. **Map** p401 K6/7.

ECapital is the only place in London to specialise
in the food of Shanghai and eastern China. The best
Chinese food in London it ain't but we recommend
it for a taste of the East.

Fook Sing

25-26 Newport Court, WC2H 7JS (7287 0188).
Leicester Square or Piccadilly Circus tube. Open
11am-10.30pm daily. **Main courses** £3.90-£4.30.
No credit cards. Map p401 K7.
The newest wave of Chinese cooking to reach
London comes from the coastal province of Fujian,
across the strait from Taiwan, to which a large
section of this tiny café's menu is devoted. Very good.

Mr Kong

21 Lisle Street, WC2H 7BA (7437 7341/9679).
Leicester Square or Piccadilly Circus tube. Open noon-
2.45am Mon-Sat; noon-1.45am Sun. **Main courses**
£5.90-£26. **Credit** AmEx, DC, MC, V. **Map** p401 K7.
There's a raft of enticing dishes to be savoured here:
proper Chinese food, intricately prepared. Yet there
are drawbacks, chief among them the cramped
ground-floor and stuffy basement dining areas.

New World

1 Gerrard Place, W1D 5PA (7734 0396).
Leicester Square or Piccadilly Circus tube. Open
11am-11.45pm Mon-Sat. **Main**
courses £4.90-£10.50. **Credit** AmEx, DC, MC, V.
Map p401 K7.
You'll be asked to wait in line if you visit three-
storey New World after noon on Sunday. Despite its
vast size, the restaurant's elaborately decorated
dining rooms will be packed full of mostly Chinese
diners enthusiastically picking dim sum from heated
trolleys. Stick out the queue and you'll see why.

Yauatcha

15 Broadwick Street, W1F 0DE (7494 8888).
Oxford Circus tube. Open noon-11pm Mon-Sat;
noon-10pm Sun. **Main courses** £3.50-£12.
Credit AmEx, MC, V. **Map** p398 J6.

Costing £4.2 million, deeply chic Yauatcha is the
latest venture from restaurateur Alan Yau. Taking
up residence in the basement of Richard Rogers' new
Ingeni building, it serves food that is, as you might
expect, quite exquisite. Oh, and there's a kick-ass
tearoom on the ground floor.

Yming

35-36 Greek Street, W1D 5DL (7734 2721/www.
yming.com). Leicester Square, Piccadilly Circus or
Tottenham Court Road tube. Open noon-11.45pm
Mon-Sat. **Main courses** £5-£10. **Credit** AmEx,
DC, MC, V. **Map** p399 K6.
Avoiding the usual run of Cantonese dishes, Yming
likes to be different. Its adventurous spirit doesn't
always pay off, but the corner site with wrap-around
windows makes for bright and comfortable lunches.

French

L'Escargot Marco Pierre White

48 Greek Street, W1D 4EF (7437 2679). Leicester
Square or Tottenham Court Road tube. Open noon-
2.15pm, 6-11.30pm Mon-Fri; 5.30-11.30pm Sat. **Main**
courses £12.95-£14.95. **Credit** AmEx, DC, MC, V.
Map p399 K6.
Pristine-suited maîtres d', swarms of classically
garbed waiters, a clientele that's largely suits and
the elderly: it's formal and expensive, but the first-
class food is worth very nearly every penny.

La Trouvaille

12A Newburgh Street, W1F 7RR (7287 8488/
www.latrouvaille.co.uk). Oxford Circus tube. Open
noon-3pm, 6-11pm Mon-Sat; noon-3.30pm Sun.
Set lunch £16.95 2 courses; £19.75 3 courses.
Set dinner £24.50 2 courses; £29.50 3 courses.
Credit AmEx, DC, MC, V. **Map** p398 J6.

And the winner is...

Every year, *Time Out* recognises the best of
London's eating and drinking establishments
with a series of awards. The combination
of our experience – we anonymously review
2,000 of the capital's restaurants each year –
and the votes of *Time Out* readers results in
a unique list that rewards the excellent but
unfeted alongside the celebrated and well-
known. Below we have listed the winners
in each category of the 2004 awards.

Best bar
Milk & Honey. *See p224.*

Best pub
The Sultan. *See p232.*

Best local restaurant
Medcalf. *See p196.*

Best gastropub
Coach & Horses. *See p196.*

Best family restaurant
Frizzante at City Farm. *See p271.*

Best Chinese restaurant
Hakkasan. *See p201.*

Best cheap eat
The Vincent Rooms. *See p211.*

Best vegetarian meal
Manna. *See p215.*

Best design
Loungelover. *See p228.*

Best new restaurant
The Wolseley. *See p205.*

Eat, Drink, Shop

If you're after a quirkily romantic dinner, La Trouvaille will do the trick. Its setting on one of Soho's more characterful backstreets is appealing, as is its decor, and its fanciful French cuisine wins points for inventiveness and flair. A find indeed.

Indian

Masala Zone
9 Marshall Street, W1F 7ER (7287 9966/www.real indianfood.com). Oxford Circus tube. **Open** noon-3pm, 5.30-11pm Mon-Fri; 12.30-11pm Sat; 12.30-3.30pm, 6-10.30pm Sun. **Main courses** £5.50-£11. **Credit** MC, V. **Map** p398 J6.
Deserving its popularity, Masala Zone has Wagamama-fied Indian dining. And the canteen vibe, the fast throughput and (at peak times) the queues aren't at the expense of authenticity. For dinner, the combination thali is a good idea. **Other locations:** 80 Upper Street, Islington, N1 0NP (7359 3399).

Red Fort
77 Dean Street, W1D 3SH (7437 2115/www.redfort. co.uk). Leicester Square or Tottenham Court Road tube. **Open** noon-2.15pm, 5.45-11pm Mon-Fri; 5.45-11pm Sat. **Main courses** £12.50-£20. **Credit** AmEx, MC, V. **Map** p399 K6.
The elegant Red Fort continues to attract a big-walleted clientele. Cooking remains inspired by the regal traditions of Lucknow, and is characterised by myriad, complex-tasting spice mixes. The service is impeccable, enhanced by the calm modernity of the decor (ancient urns, a sleek water feature).

Italian

Quo Vadis
26-29 Dean Street, W1T 6LL (7437 9585/www. whitestarline.org.uk). Leicester Square or Piccadilly Circus tube. **Open** noon-2.30pm, 5.30-11pm Mon-Fri; 5.30-11pm Sat. **Main courses** £10.50-£19. **Credit** AmEx, DC, MC, V. **Map** p399 K6.
Irreverent decor that combines Hirst-esque art (skeleton and butterfly collections), stained glass and clubby seating makes Quo Vadis an amusing and comfortable restaurant in which to while away the evening. The menu blends classic and innovative Italian, with the dishes superbly presented.

Modern European

Alastair Little
49 Frith Street, W1D 4SG (7734 5183). Leicester Square or Tottenham Court Road tube. **Lunch served** noon-3pm, 6-11.30pm Mon-Fri; 6-11.30pm Sat. **Main courses** £16.50-£21.50. **Credit** AmEx, MC, V. **Map** p399 K6.
The man himself is no longer wielding the pans, but Little's guiding principles of simplicity and quality remain paramount at this iconic Soho culinary beacon (which celebrates its 20th birthday in 2005). The ever-evolving menu is always finely tuned to the season, and gently inventive.

Andrew Edmunds
46 Lexington Street, W1F 0LW (7437 5708). Oxford Circus or Piccadilly Circus tube. **Lunch served** 12.30-3pm, 6-10.45pm Mon-Fri; 1-3pm,

Columbus would have loved **1492**.
See p218.

6-10.45pm Sat; 1-3pm, 6-10.30pm Sun. **Main
courses** £7.95-£13. **Credit** MC, V. **Map** p398 J6.
This gloriously unselfconscious sliver of a restaurant has long thumbed its nose at decorative and culinary fashion. The interior suggests passé wine bar meets gentleman's club; the food is superior peasant fare: simple, hearty and fairly priced, yet perfectly pitched and cooked with aplomb.

Gay Hussar
*2 Greek Street, W1D 4NB (7437 0973). Tottenham
Court Road tube.* **Open** 12.15-2.30pm, 5.30-10.45pm
Mon-Sat. **Main courses** £9.50-£16.50. **Credit**
AmEx, DC, MC, V. **Map** p399 K6.
This place easily lives up to its legendary political reputation. Stuffed full of Westminster caricatures and guffawing diners, the Gay Hussar is worth visiting for the atmosphere alone. The menu is also deservedly famous.

Oriental

Kulu Kulu
*76 Brewer Street, W1F 9TX (7734 7316). Oxford
Circus, Piccadilly Circus or Tottenham Court Road
tube.* **Open** noon-2.30pm, 5-10pm Mon-Fri; noon-3.45pm, 5-10pm Sat. **Main courses** £1.20-£3.60.
Credit MC, V. **Map** p397 E10.
You're allocated just 45 minutes to grab what you want and eat it at this frills-free, wallet-friendly exponent of conveyor-belted meal delivery. Japanese efficiency is required.
Other locations: 39 Thurlow Place, South Kensington, SW7 (7589 2225).

Ramen Seto
*19 Kingly Street, W1B 5PY (7434 0309). Oxford
Circus or Piccadilly Circus tube.* **Open** noon-10pm
Mon-Sat. **Main courses** £5-£8.50. **Credit** MC, V.
Map p398 J6.
A fresh lick of paint, wood panelling and a change of furniture spruced up Ramen Seto in spring 2004. It's not a place for fine dining, but it can hit the spot if you're ravenous and don't want to spend more than a tenner per head.

Vegetarian & organic

Mildred's
*45 Lexington Street, W1F 9AN (7494 1634). Oxford
Circus or Piccadilly Circus tube.* **Open** noon-11pm
Mon-Sat. **Main courses** £6.25-£7.95. **No credit
cards. Map** p399 K6.
A winning combination of tasty food (and big portions), good service and a relaxed and unpretentious atmosphere in the heart of Soho, Mildred's will deliver nothing to your plate that has endured any greater suffering than the odd spot of peeling or a bit of harmless julienning.

Covent Garden & St Giles's

Belgian

Belgo Centraal
*50 Earlham Street, WC2H 9LJ (7813 2233/
www.belgo-restaurants.com). Covent Garden or
Leicester Square tube.* **Open** noon-11pm Mon-Thur;

noon-11.30pm Fri, Sat; noon-10.30pm Sun. **Main courses** £8.75-£17.95. **Credit** AmEx, DC, MC, V. **Map** p399 L6.

This cavernous warehouse-deluxe basement built its rep on high-quality moules frites, great beers, fun service and an energetic atmosphere. But recent reports indicate a decline in standards; hopefully, though, this is just a temporary glitch.

Other locations: 72 Chalk Farm Road, Camden, NW1 8AN (7267 0718).

British

The Savoy Grill

The Savoy, Strand, WC2R 0EU (7420 2065/ www.gordonramsay.com). Covent Garden or Embankment tube/Charing Cross tube/rail. **Open** noon-2.45pm, 5.45-11pm Mon-Fri; noon-3pm, 5.45-11pm Sat; noon-3pm, 6-10.30pm Sun. **Set menu** (lunch, 5.45-6.45pm Mon-Sat) £30 3 courses. **Credit** AmEx, MC, V. **Map** p399 L6.

Here you'll find the work of Savile Row tailors amply displayed, and you'll be able to watch the futures of Harley Street cardiologists steadily secured: the Savoy Grill has lost none of its aristo cachet. What's more, Marcus Wareing's rejuvenation of its menu goes beyond superb.

Simpson's-in-the-Strand

100 Strand, WC2R 0EW (7836 9112/www. simpsons-in-the-strand.com). Embankment tube/Charing Cross tube/rail. **Open** 7.15-10.30am, 12.15-2.30pm, 5.30-10.45pm Mon-Fri; 12.15-2.30pm, 5.30-10.45pm Sat; noon-3pm Sun. **Main courses** £19.50-£23.50. **Credit** AmEx, DC, MC, V. **Map** p400 L7.

Popular with wealthy tourists, and a haunt of wine-swilling expense-accounters, Simpson's has panache even if the cooking does occasionally dip to boarding school standards. Endearingly nostalgic, then, but a long way from the cutting edge.

Cafés & brasseries

Zoomslide Café

The Photographers' Gallery, 5 Great Newport Street, WC2H 7HY (7831 1772). Leicester Square tube. **Open** 11am-5.30pm Mon-Wed, Fri, Sat; 11am-7.30pm Thur; noon-5.30pm Sun. **Main courses** £1.65-£4.25. **No credit cards. Map** p401 K6.

Tucked away in one of the two Photographers' Gallery buildings on Great Newport Street, Zoomslide doubles as an exhibition space. Food runs to a few sarnies and a handful of good, fresh salads.

Fish

J Sheekey

28-32 St Martin's Court, WC2N 4AL (7240 2565/ www.caprice-holdings.co.uk). Leicester Square tube. **Open** noon-3pm, 5.30pm-midnight Mon-Sat; noon-3.30pm, 6pm-midnight Sun. **Main courses** £10.75-£29.75. **Credit** AmEx, DC, MC, V. **Map** p399 K6.

Elegant and discreet, with simple but sublime food, plus a more upmarket class of celebrity, J Sheekey shares many wonderful things with its sister restaurant, the Ivy (*see below*). Sadly, though, it also shares the same booking nightmare, viz that you'll never get a table unless you book months in advance.

Fish & chips

Rock & Sole Plaice

47 Endell Street, WC2H 9AJ (7836 3785). Covent Garden tube. **Open** 11.30am-11pm Mon-Sat; noon-10pm Sun. **Main courses** £8-£14. **Credit** MC, V. **Map** p399 L6.

There has been a chippy on this site since 1871 and, while taramasalata, Efes beer and pitta point to the current owners' Turkish roots, the name of the game is still good old-fashioned British fish and chips.

French

The Admiralty

Somerset House, Strand, WC2R 1LA (7845 4646/ www.somerset-house.org.uk). Temple tube. **Open** noon-2.30pm, 6-10.30pm Mon-Sat; noon-2.30pm Sun. **Main courses** £16.50-£22.50. **Credit** AmEx, DC, MC, V. **Map** p401 L7.

Hidden within the old Navy Office in the wing of Somerset House overlooking the Thames, the Admiralty has an admirable setting. Also, it maintains a strong reputation for quality cuisine. So why, then, are its gracious high-ceilinged dining rooms often so sparsely populated? Beats us.

Modern American/European

Christopher's

18 Wellington Street, WC2E 7DD (7240 4222/www. christophersgrill.com). Covent Garden tube. **Open** noon-3pm, 5-11pm Mon-Fri; 11.30am-3pm, 5-11pm Sat; 11.30am-3pm Sun. **Main courses** £12-£28. **Credit** AmEx, DC, MC, V. **Map** p401 L6/7.

Christopher's remains one of London's best restaurants for modern American cuisine. The decor of the first-floor restaurant is cool and contemporary, with cream and chocolate tones, and the ground-floor bar is excellent for cocktails.

The Ivy

1 West Street, WC2H 9NQ (7836 4751/www. caprice-holdings.co.uk). Leicester Square tube. **Open** noon-3pm, 5.30pm-midnight Mon-Sat; noon-3.30pm, 5.30pm-midnight Sun. **Main courses** £9.25-£35. **Credit** AmEx, DC, MC, V. **Map** p399 K6.

Among the world's most famous restaurants – and notorious for its ages-in-advance booking policy – the Ivy continues to fill its celeb quota, much to the delight of the paparazzi who haunt the place. And the quality of the trademark comfort cuisine is as high as ever. Our only complaint: the service on our last visit was not as good as it could have been.

Vegetarian & organic

Food for Thought
31 Neal Street, WC2H 9PR (7836 9072).
Covent Garden tube. **Open** 9.30-11.30am, noon-5pm,
5-8.30pm Mon-Sat; noon-5pm Sun. **Main courses**
£3-£6.50. **No credit cards. Map** p399 L6.
The antithesis of the ultra-trendy, wallet-bashing
boutiques and shoe shops of Neal Street, FfT is
unpretentious, reliable and great value. Diners share
tables in the small narrow basement to enjoy a daily
changing, globally inspired menu.

World Food Café
1st Floor, 14 Neal's Yard, WC2H 9DP (7379 0298).
Covent Garden tube. **Open** 11.30am-4.30pm Mon-Fri;
11.30am-5pm Sat. **Main courses** £4.85-£7.95.
Credit MC, V. **Map** p399 L6.
The clue is in the name: from the colourful framed
prints on whitewashed walls and the world music
soundtrack to the menu, global influences abound
at this cheery café.

Westminster

Cafés & brasseries

Café in the Crypt
Crypt of St Martin-in-the-Fields, Duncannon Street,
WC2N 4JJ (7839 4342/www.stmartin-in-the-fields.
org). Embankment tube/Charing Cross tube/rail.
Open 11.30am-3pm, 5-7.30pm Mon-Wed; 11.30am-
3pm, 5-10.15pm Thur-Sat; noon-3pm, 5-7.30pm Sun.
Main courses £5.95-£7.50. **No credit cards.**
Map p401 L7.
This cavernous self-service café is hidden in the
centuries-old crypt below St Martin-in-the-Fields
church, minutes from the National Gallery, the Mall
and other key sights. A daily rotating menu offers
large salad platters (probably best to avoid the over-
dry veggie tartlet) plus more substantial options.

The Vincent Rooms
Westminster Kingsway College, Vincent Square,
SW1P 2PD (7802 8391/www.westking.ac.uk). St
James's Park tube/Victoria tube/rail. **Open** noon-
1.15pm Mon-Fri. **Main courses** £6.50-£8.50.
Credit MC, V. **Map** p401 K10.
Celebrated chefs (Jamie Oliver included) have
trained at Westminster Kingsway College, and the
Vincent Rooms is where the mettle of current
students is tested. They produce a daily brasserie
menu of affordable yet delicious modern European
cuisine. Expect to dine alongside staff, pupils and a
few clued-up Londoners.

Indian

Cinnamon Club
The Old Westminster Library, Great Smith Street,
SW1P 3BU (7222 2555/www.cinnamonclub.com).
St James's Park or Westminster tube. **Open**
7.30-9.30am, noon-2.30pm, 6-10.45pm Mon-Fri; 6-
10.45pm Sat. **Main courses** £11-£26. **Credit**
AmEx, DC, MC, V. **Map** p401 K9.
Chef Vivek Singh has put the Cinnamon Club at the
forefront of Indian food in Britain. Classic dishes are
cooked with due diligence, plus the odd unexpected
twist. The setting is a conversion of a grand 19th-
century library, with cinnamon-hued banquettes
and crisp tablecloths.

Quilon
41 Buckingham Gate, SW1E 6AF (7821 1899/
www.thequilonrestaurant.com). St James's Park tube.
Open noon-2.30pm, 6-11pm Mon-Fri; 6-11pm Sat.
Main courses £8-£23. **Credit** AmEx, DC, MC, V.
Map p400 H9/J9.
Named after a town in Kerala, Quilon's large dining
room is decorated with a strange mishmash of
colonial-style wicker chairs and pretty mosaics; it
also has a smart bar. But while Quilon is charming
(and popular with tourists), it's expensive. You can
eat South Indian food that's just as good, if not
better, elsewhere for less. At Rasa Samudra, for
example (*see p199*).

Oriental

Nahm
The Halkin, Halkin Street, SW1X 7DJ (7333 1234/
www.halkin.como.bz). Hyde Park Corner tube. **Open**
noon-2.30pm, 7-11pm Mon-Fri; 7-11pm Sat; 7-10pm
Sun. **Main courses** £19.50-£21.50. **Credit** AmEx,
DC, MC, V. **Map** p400 G9.
The old cliché 'never judge a book by its cover' is
nowhere more appropriate than at this gem of a
restaurant, located within the Halkin hotel. For
despite a dull, slightly odd interior that features
muted gold surfaces and net curtains, David
Thompson's award-spangled interpretation of the
'Royal Thai' cuisine of ancient Bangkok is among the
best in the UK. The £47 set dinner is an extraordinarily generous banquet.

Knightsbridge & South Kensington

Global

Jakob's
20 Gloucester Road, SW7 4RB (7581 9292).
Gloucester Road tube. **Meals served** 8am-10pm
Mon-Sat; 8am-5pm Sun. **Main courses** £6.50-£11.
Credit AmEx, MC, V. **Map** p396 C9.
Jakob's looks like a friendly, local Italian deli. It is
actually a friendly, local Armenian deli with a vast
choice of unexpectedly good and authentic dishes.
To be unfair to Armenian food, which warrants far
a more extravagant description, it is something of
a mix between Italian, Greek, Turkish and Iranian
cuisines. Vegetarian lasagne and spinach filo pie are
both recommended.

French

Racine

239 Brompton Road, SW3 2EP (7584 4477).
Knightsbridge or South Kensington tube/14, 74
bus. **Open** noon-3pm, 6-10.30pm Mon-Fri; noon-
3.30pm, 6-10.30pm Sat; noon-3.30pm, 6-10pm Sun.
Main courses £9.50-£18.75. **Credit** AmEx, MC, V.
Map p397 E10.

Very chic, very Knightsbridge and a little bit hard-
edged, Racine is the essence of a Parisian brasserie
transported to London. Draw aside the theatrical
drape that shields the door and you'll step into a
room lined with mirrors and deep-green banquettes,
filled with enthusiastic diners. The source of their
enthusiasm? Chef Henry Harris's gorgeous French
bourgeois food.

Japanese

Zuma

5 Raphael Street, SW7 1DL (7584 1010/www.
zumarestaurant.com). Knightsbridge tube.
Open noon-2pm, 6-11pm Mon-Sat; noon-2.30pm Sun.
Main courses £3.50-£28.50. **Credit** AmEx, DC,
MC, V. **Map** p397 F9.

Has Zuma taken over from Nobu as the capital's
most glamorous dining spot? Possibly, if the wait
(several weeks) for a reservation is anything to go
by. Not to mention the strict two-hour sittings. Still,
the food remains compellingly good, helped by
service that is well informed and friendly (up until
the two-hour deadline). The biggest problem
remains what to choose from the extensive menu.

Modern European

Boxwood Café

The Berkeley Hotel, Wilton Place, SW1X 7RL (7235
1010/www.gordonramsay.com). Hyde Park Corner
or Knightsbridge tube. **Open** noon-3pm, 6-11pm
Mon-Fri; noon-4pm, 6-11pm Sat, Sun. **Main courses**
£13.50-£25. **Service** 12.5%. **Credit** AmEx, MC, V.
Map p400 G9.

Is it a café, or is it a fine-dining restaurant? The informal name and mouth-watering menu suggest the
former, but the starched linen, silver leaf walls and
dark lacquered furniture suggest the latter. We
suggest you go and see for yourself, since Gordon
Ramsay has again produced a fantastic place in
which to eat and be pampered, only this time with
considerably less stress on your wallet.

Spanish

Cambio de Tercio

163 Old Brompton Road, SW5 0LJ (7244 8970/
www.cambiodetercio.com). Gloucester Road or South
Kensington tube. **Open** 12.30-2.30pm, 7-11.30pm Mon-
Sat; 12.30-2.30pm, 7-11pm Sun. **Main courses** £13.50-
£15.50. **Credit** AmEx, DC, MC, V. **Map** p396 C11.

It's a mystery to us. Occasionally someone reports
having had a bad experience at Cambio de Tercio.
In the interests of science, we've really tried to have
one too, but every meal we've had here has been
great, sometimes wonderful and, most recently,
reaching new heights. Simply put, this place serves
some of the most sophisticated modern Spanish
cooking in London.

Chelsea

Gastropubs

Lots Road Pub & Dining Room

114 Lots Road, SW10 0RJ (7352 6645). Fulham
Broadway tube, then 11 bus/Sloane Square tube,
then 11, 19, 22 bus. **Open** noon-10pm Mon-Thur,
Sun; noon-10.30pm Fri, Sat. **Main courses** £8-£13.
Credit MC, V. **Map** p397 D13.

If all gastropubs were like Lots Road, the world
would be a happier place. A sunny chrome-fitted
bar, beautifully finished oak floors, colourful
abstract paintings and good quality food, provided
at reasonable prices, add up to a chic and cheerful
atmosphere. Well-kept ales and a fine wine list, with
a commendable range available by the glass, mean
our happiness is complete.

Indian

Chutney Mary

535 King's Road, SW10 0SZ (7351 3113/www.real
indianfood.com). Fulham Broadway tube/11, 22 bus.
Open 6.30-11pm Mon-Fri; 12.30-2.30pm, 6.30-11pm
Sat; 12.30-3pm, 6.30-10.30pm Sun. **Main courses**
£12.50-£24. **Credit** AmEx, DC, MC, V. **Map** p397 C13.
Service can be overbearing at this renowned establishment. Chutney Mary has two contrasting dining
spaces: a bright, verdant conservatory out back, and
a dark cavern of an interior with vibrant artwork,
entirely lit by flickering candles. The food is sometimes a little too flamboyant, but the desserts will
leave your stomach singing the place's praises.

Modern European

Bibendum

Michelin House, 81 Fulham Road, SW3 6RD (7581
5817/www.bibendum.co.uk). South Kensington tube.
Open noon-2.30pm, 7-11.30pm Mon-Fri; 12.30-3pm,
7-11.30pm Sat; 12.30-3pm, 7-10.30pm Sun. **Main
courses** £19-£42. **Credit** AmEx, DC, MC, V.
Map p397 E10.

The figurehead of the good ship Conran remains an
attractive venue. The spectacular dining room, on
the first floor of the Michelin building – above the
Bibendum Oyster Bar – has a real sense of occasion,
dominated by the original 1930s rich blue Michelin
Man stained-glass windows. Nor does the food shy
away from the rich and robust: come expecting luxury on a plate, with prices to match.

Gordon Ramsay

68-69 Royal Hospital Road, SW3 4HP (7352 4441/ 3334/www.gordonramsay.com). Sloane Square tube. **Open** noon-2pm, 6.30-11pm Mon-Fri. **Set meal** £65 3 courses, £80 7 courses. **Credit** AmEx, DC, MC, V. **Map** p397 F12.

Those less passionate about fish than Mr Ramsay may be stuck for choice at his flagship enterprise: six of the eight starters contain fish, as do half the mains. But that's our sole criticism. Waiting staff really know what they're doing, and the cooking, as you'd expect, is unimpeachable. If you haven't been here, start saving. Book at least a month in advance.

Oriental

Hunan

51 Pimlico Road, SW1W 8NE (7730 5712). Sloane Square tube. **Open** 12.30-2.30pm, 6-11pm Mon-Sat. **Set meal** £31-£150 per person (minimum 2). **Credit** AmEx, DC, MC, V. **Map** p400 G11.

As the name makes clear, this is Hunan cuisine. That means many dishes will be hottish, although none should be fiercely so. Clear soup with minced pork and ginger, served in a bamboo tube, is an example of the excellent grub on offer. A meal here isn't cheap, but it is worth it.

School of toque

Ever felt inspired to bump your culinary skills up a notch but never found the time to sign up for a course? Well, why not make some room in your plans to drop into one of the venues below and spend a few hours learning how to make that roux sauce or blanch your veggies? All offer short courses that give visiting foodies a hands-on taste of London's culinary expertise.

A good first port of call is the Notting Hill bookshop **Books for Cooks** (4 Blenheim Crescent, W11 1NN, 7221 19992), where an upstairs kitchen is the venue for three-hour (£25) classes on themes as diverse as Asian street food and Italian Easter treats. In Marylebone, kitchenware mecca **Divertimenti** (33-34 Marylebone High Street, W1U 4PT, 7935 0689) offers lunchtime demos and

short classes (from £20) on essential techniques and contemporary culinary preoccupations: everything from knife skills to sushi making.

Also in Marylebone is **Caldesi** (15-17 Marylebone Lane, W1U 2NB, 7935 1144), a Tuscan restaurant that offers Sunday lunch cookery sessions, in which students learn how to cook a three-course meal before sitting down to a good feed and some fine wine themselves (£100 incl food and wine).

If cooking leaves you cold, tap into another skillset by taking cocktail classes from barmeister Tino Bezzillo at **Zeta** restaurant's rated bar (35 Hertford Street, Mayfair, W1J 7SD; *pictured*). They cost £30 (samples included) and usually run early on Saturday and Tuesday evenings. Book in advance.

French

Morgan M

489 Liverpool Road, Islington, N7 8NS (7609 3560). Highbury & Islington tube/rail. **Open** 7-10.30pm Tue; noon-2.30pm, 7-10.30pm Wed-Fri; 7-10.30pm Sat; noon-2.30pm Sun. **Set lunch** £19.50 2 courses, £23.50 3 courses. **Set dinner** £30 3 courses. **Credit** DC, MC, V.

Chef-patron Morgan Meunier, who was previously at the Admiralty (*see p210*), opened Morgan M in late summer 2003. His cooking style has remained much the same, so, as before, there's a 'garden' menu as well as the à la carte. Almost unheard of in a French restaurant, that consists of six courses (plus cheese) that will delight any vegetarian. Neither the staff nor the venue are stuffy, even though the latter lacks a bit of buzz.

Gastropubs

Wells

30 Well Walk, Hampstead, NW3 1BX (7794 3785/ www.thewellshampstead.co.uk). Hampstead tube. **Open** noon-3pm, 7-10pm Mon-Thur; noon-3pm, 7-10.30pm Fri, Sat; noon-3pm, 7-9.30pm Sun. **Set lunch** (Mon-Fri) £14.50 2 courses, £19.50 3 courses (Sat, Sun) £20 2 courses, £25 3 courses. **Set dinner** £24.50 2 courses, £29.50 3 courses. **Credit** AmEx, DC, MC, V.

This leafy Hampstead backwater must be one of London's prettiest quarters, and the Wells is no disgrace to its surroundings. The ground-floor bar is where the cheaper menu operates, while upstairs a more formal space has some beautiful Georgian windows and a pricier modern British menu.

Global

Afghan Kitchen

35 Islington Green, Islington, N1 8DU (7359 8019). Angel tube. **Open** noon-3.30pm, 5.30-11pm Tue-Sat. **Main courses** £4.50-£6. **No credit cards**. **Map** p402 O2.

A recent redecoration has given the tiny Afghan Kitchen a slightly trendier edge, but it remains essentially the same. The dining areas (one upstairs, one down) are tiny, so guests crowd around communal tables. Sensibly, the menu is kept short; food is prepared in advance and reheated to order.

Mango Room

10 Kentish Town Road, Camden, NW1 8NH (7482 5065/www.mangoroom.co.uk). Camden Town tube. **Open** 6pm-midnight Mon; noon-3pm, 6pm-midnight Tue-Sat; noon-11pm Sun. **Main courses** £9.50-£12.50. **Credit** MC, V.

Split into two rooms with raw brickwork, comfortably worn wooden floors, and large, abstract Keith Haringesque pictures, Mango Room subtly fuses the Caribbean with international influences. Dishes such as ackee and avocado or curried goat sit nicely with lamb steak or mussels in coconut sauce.

Mediterranean

Café Corfu

7 Pratt Street, Camden, NW1 0AE (7267 8088/ www.cafecorfu.com). Camden Town or Mornington Crescent tube. **Open** noon-10.30pm Tue-Thur, Sun; noon-11.30pm Fri; 5-11.30pm Sat. **Main courses** £7.95-£12.95. **Credit** MC, V.

With its attractive bar and cavernous back room often full to capacity, Café Corfu may be enjoying the benefits of a comfortable middle age but its cooking still wipes the floor with most Greek eateries. The Greek wine list is also among the best in town.

Sariyer Balik

56 Green Lanes, Stoke Newington, N16 9NH (7275 7681). Bus 141, 341. **Open** 5pm-1am daily. **Main courses** £6.50-£10. **No credit cards**.

This outstanding Turkish fish restaurant is a little off the beaten track, but it's worth the effort. The interior is tiny (though there's more seating in the basement) and painted black; fishing nets are suspended from the ceiling. The pan-fried anchovies are a succulent revelation.

Oriental

Wagamama

11 Jamestown Road, Camden, NW1 7BW (7428 0800/www.wagamama.com). Camden Town tube. **Open** noon-11pm Mon-Sat; noon-10pm Sun. **Main courses** £5.50-£9.25. **Credit** AmEx, MC, V.

Everyone's a bit blasé about noodle bars – a high-street staple nowadays – but it pays to remember that Wagamama is one of the originals, and one of the best. Its gleaming, smoke-free environment, perky staff and a wholesome menu are appealing – especially for families – though not everyone likes the communal tables and resultant noise. **Other locations**: throughout the city.

Turkish

19 Numara Bos Cirrik

34 Stoke Newington Road, N16 7XJ (7249 0400). Dalston Kingsland rail/76, 149, 243 bus. **Meals served** noon-midnight daily. **Main courses** £5-£8. **Credit** MC, V.

This strip of Stoke Newington Road is unequalled in London for great Turkish cafés; Mangal 2 (No.4), Somine (131 Stoke Newington High Street) and Mangal Ocakbasi (10 Arcola Street) are other favourites in the vicinity. But here, the secret is simple: enormous portions of perfect grills. Eschew starters: once a grill is ordered, a large salad and cold starters will be brought – usually onion in chilli, and onion in pomegranate and turnip sauce – plus warm bread. Cheap, simple and friendly.

Vegetarian & organic

Heartstone

106 Parkway, Camden, NW1 7AN (7485 7744).
Camden Town tube. **Open** 8.30am-9pm Tue;
8.30am Wed-Fri; 8.30am-9pm Sat; 10am-4pm Sun.
Main courses £9.50-£15. **Credit** MC, V.
There's no avoiding the word: this is a very mellow
spot – bright, calm and decorated in white and mauve.
Organic food is presented with a clever, modern sense
of style. The menu is mainly veggie, but there are non-
veg options such as great house burgers.

Manna

4 Erskine Road, NW3 3AJ, Chalk Farm (7722
8023). Chalk Farm tube. **Open** 6.30-11pm daily.
Brunch served 12.30-3pm Sun. **Main courses**
£8.95-£12.75. **Credit** MC, V.
Tucked around the corner of Primrose Hill's main
drag, Manna is an unpretentious mix of the veggie
world's old and new. Decorated simply with lots of
wood and candles, it may seem trad, but the elegant,
thoughtful and modern food will remind you that
this is one of the brightest stars of green cuisine.

East London

For family-friendly café **Frizzante@City**
Farm, *see p271.*

Cafés & brasseries

Brick Lane Beigel Bake

159 Brick Lane, Spitalfields, E1 6SB (7729 0616).
Liverpool Street tube/rail/8 bus. **Open** 24hrs daily.
No credit cards. Map p403 S4.
Once part of a vibrant Jewish community, the Brick
Lane bakery now serves local Bangladeshi residents
and assorted night-time revellers. But the style hasn't
changed. Bagels are boiled, then baked, and day and
night the smell of rye bread and challah wafts down
the street. The staff are famously brisk; don't dither.

Jones Dairy Café

23 Ezra Street, Bethnal Green, E2 7RH (7739
5372). Bethnal Green tube/26, 48, 55, 149, 243
bus. **Open** 9am-3pm Fri, Sat; 8am-3pm Sun. **Main**
courses £2-£5. **No credit cards. Map** p403 S3.
On Sunday mornings, when the Columbia Road
Flower Market is in full bloom, this adorable little
operation gets overrun by green-fingered locals well
aware that it has the best bread in the area and the
finest bagels this side of Brick Lane.

Global

Arkansas Café

Unit 12, Old Spitalfields Market, Spitalfields, E1 6AA
(7377 6999). Liverpool Street tube/rail. **Open** noon-
2.30pm Mon-Fri; noon-4pm Sun. Dinner served by
arrangement. **Main courses** £5-£14.50. **Credit** MC,
V. **Map** p403 R5.

Morgan M. *See p214.*

This wonderfully eccentric restaurant hovering on
the edge of Spitalfields Market is justifiably popular. Its Arkansan owner, Bubba, presides over the
barbecue pit, greeting customers with a wave of his
spatula while he cooks huge piles of tender beef
brisket, pork ribs, perfect duck and juicy chicken.

Armadillo

41 Broadway Market, Bethnal Green, E8 4PH (7249
3633/www.armadillorestaurant.co.uk). Bethnal Green
tube, then 106, 253 bus/26, 48, 55 bus. **Open** 6.30-
10.30pm daily. **Main courses** £9.50-£16.50. **Credit**
AmEx, DC, MC, V.
São Paulo-born chef Rogerio David puts together an
eclectic and changing menu at this stylish, laid-back
neighbourhood restaurant, plundering dishes and
ingredients from right across Latin America.

The Real Greek

15 Hoxton Market, Hoxton, N1 6HG (7739 8212/
www.therealgreek.co.uk). Old Street tube/rail/26,
48, 55, 149, 243 bus. **Open** noon-3pm, 5.30-10.30pm
Mon-Sat. **Main courses** £12.90-£15.90. **Credit** MC,
V. **Map** p403 R3.
The Real Greek, a lodestar for the chattering classes
of Shoreditch (and much further afield), offers classy
mainland cooking, the like of which you won't find
elsewhere in London. It shares singular premises
(a former Victorian mission hall) with Mezedopolio,
a less formal, baby version of the restaurant proper.
The moussaka is to die for.

Home cooking, **Harlem** style. *See p218.*

Indian

Café Spice Namaste

16 Prescot Street, Whitechapel, E1 8AZ (7488 9242/ www.cafespice.co.uk). Aldgate or Tower Hill tube/ Tower Gateway DLR. **Open** noon-3pm Mon-Fri, 6.15-10.30pm Mon-Fri; 6.30-10.30pm Sat. **Main courses** £9.95-£15.95. **Credit** AmEx, DC, MC, V. **Map** p405 S7.

Bombay-born Parsi chef-owner Cyrus Todiwala is famous for taking the best from the gamut of Indian cuisines and adding exciting twists. Expect the likes of venison and duck tikka, Goan wild boar sausages in a rich vindaloo sauce, seafood samosas and king scallops with ginger and chilli.

Italian

Fifteen

15 Westland Place, Hoxton, N1 7LP (0871 330 1515/ www.fifteenrestaurant.com). Old Street tube/rail. **Open** noon-2.30pm, 6.30-9.30pm Mon-Sat. **Main courses** £25-£29. **Credit** AmEx, MC, V. **Map** p403 Q3.

Jamie Oliver's Fifteen was a hit the day it opened in November 2002; even now, getting a table in the restaurant requires much phone work (with recorded prompts from Jamie himself). It's expensive – a recent headline-courting starter of (albeit fancy) beans on toast weighed in at £7. But the profits *do* go to a good cause, and the food is generally pukka, larverly etc.

Middle Eastern

Hookah Lounge

133 Brick Lane, Shoreditch, E1 6SB (7033 9072). Shoreditch tube/8 bus. **Open** 11am-10.30pm Mon-Thur, Sun; 11.30am-midnight Fri, Sat. **Credit** (over £10) AmEx, MC, V. **Map** p403 S4.

Part vintage emporium, part den of eastern exotica (low seating, cushions, arabesque accoutrements), everything in Hookah Lounge looks as if it came out of an attic. The menu lists soft drinks with an eastern touch and a big selection of coffees, cocktails and whatnot. You can smoke a hookah too, if you like.

Vietnamese

Sông Quê

134 Kingsland Road, Hackney, E2 8DY (7613 3222). Old Street tube/rail/26, 48, 55, 67, 149, 242, 243 bus. **Open** noon-3pm, 5.30-11pm Mon-Sat; noon-11pm Sun. **Main courses** £4.40-£5.60. **Credit** AmEx, MC, V. **Map** p403 R3.

Despite all the plaudits heaped upon it, Sông Quê has resisted the temptation to ratchet up the prices. And while its functional decor is not much to write home about, fabulous cooking continues to secure its status as a must-visit Vietnamese in an increasingly crowded market. More than 20 types of pho are on offer, including some terrific rarities.

South-east London

Fish & chips

Sea Cow
37 Lordship Lane, East Dulwich, SE22 8EW (8693 3111). East Dulwich rail/176, 196 bus. **Open** noon-11pm Tue-Sat. **Main courses** £7-£10. **Credit** MC, V.
Sea Cow adopts a refreshingly simple approach to the business of eating fish. At the front is the wet fish counter with its gleaming mounds of ice; next to that the fryer, where you can order takeaway portions; and beyond that some hefty wooden tables and bench seating if you want to eat in. The fish and chips are arguably the best in London.

Modern European

Inside
19 Greenwich South Street, Greenwich, SE10 8NW (8265 5060/www.insiderestaurant.co.uk). Greenwich rail/DLR. **Open** 6.30-11pm Tue; noon-2.30pm, 6.30-11pm Wed-Fri; 11am-2.30pm, 6.30-11pm Sat; noon-3pm Sun. **Main courses** £10.95-£16. **Credit** MC, V.
Inside resembles a less expensive version of the bar-restaurant you'd find in a boutique hotel. The menu is one of those where you want to try everything. In short, this is a top neighbourhood restaurant.

South-west London

Cafés & brasseries

The Lavender
171 Lavender Hill, Battersea, SW11 5TE (7978 5242). Clapham Junction rail. **Open** noon-3pm, 7-11pm Mon-Fri; noon-4pm, 7-11pm Sat; noon-4pm, 7-10.30pm Sun. **Main courses** £7.50-£12.80. **Credit** AmEx, MC, V.
This cosy, lavender-fronted brasserie, with endearingly mismatched tables and chairs, emits a welcoming hum. The menu chalked up on the blackboard is inviting and varied in style, featuring European fare with occasional Asian flourishes. **Other locations**: 112 Vauxhall Walk, Vauxhall, SE11 5ER (7735 4440); 24 Clapham Road, Clapham, SW9 0JG (7793 0770).

French

Chez Bruce
2 Bellevue Road, Wandsworth, SW17 7EG (8672 0114/www.chezbruce.co.uk). Wandsworth Common rail. **Open** noon-2pm, 6.30-10.30pm Mon-Fri; 12.30-2.30pm, 6.30-10.30pm Sat; noon-3pm, 7-10pm Sun. **Set lunch** £23.50 3 courses (Mon-Fri), £25 3 courses (Sat), £29.50 3 courses (Sun). **Set dinner** £32.50 3 courses. **Credit** AmEx, DC, MC, V.
Bruce Poole's scintillating restaurant is approaching its tenth year, but remains Wandsworth's top venue. It's not stuffy, partly because diners give the impression they've just dropped into their local caff – and yet are excited to be here – and although the space is compact, ample bow windows make the most of the common. Dishes are robust with strong French or Mediterranean influences.

Global

Bamboula
12 Acre Lane, Brixton, SW2 5SG (7737 6633). Brixton tube/rail. **Open** 11am-11pm Mon-Fri; noon-11pm Sat; 3-11pm Sun. **Main courses** £6.90-£8.50. **Credit** MC, V.
Though the celebrated Sunday buffet is no more, Bamboula still does a brisk trade. Sunshine-yellow walls, rampant greenery, wicker chairs and a bamboo bar recreate a beach hut atmosphere. The menu features standard Caribbean favourites served in generous portions, with the ackee and saltfish among the best we've ever had.

Canyon
The Towpath, Richmond Riverside, Richmond, Surrey TW10 6UJ (8948 2944). Richmond tube/rail. **Open** 11am-3.30pm, 6-10.30pm Mon-Fri; 11am-3.30pm, 6-10.30pm Sat, Sun. **Main courses** £11-£19. **Credit** AmEx, MC, V.
An evening at this breezy riverside restaurant is always a pleasure. With striking views of the Thames and an extensive outdoor terrace, Canyon is the perfect location for dramatic summer sunsets. On the downside, the Southwestern-influenced menu is short and perhaps due for a change of direction. Still, the service is great and the puddings are delicious.

Gourmet Burger Kitchen
44 Northcote Road, Battersea, SW11 1NZ (7228 3309/www.gbkinfo.co.uk). Clapham Junction rail/49, 77, 219, 345 bus. **Open** noon-11pm Mon-Fri; 11am-11pm Sat; 11am-10pm Sun. **Main courses** £4.95-£7.25. **Credit** MC, V.
Standing proud at more than half a foot high, Gourmet Burger Kitchen's burgers are 100% Aberdeen Angus Scotch beef, shaped into thick patties and cooked to your liking (medium-rare to well done), served in a sourdough roll topped with sesame. You'll need two hands to eat them.

Italian

Enoteca Turi
28 Putney High Street, Putney, SW15 1SQ (8785 4449). East Putney tube/Putney Bridge rail/14, 74, 270 bus. **Open** noon-2.30pm, 6.30-11pm Mon-Thur; noon-2.30pm, 6.30-11.30pm Fri, Sat. **Main courses** £14-£17. **Credit** AmEx, DC, MC, V.
A polished outfit offering Prada style at Putney prices, Enoteca Turi is decorated in mottled tones of rich terracotta and shantung gold. Saying the wine list is comprehensive does not begin to do it justice, and each dish on the main menu features a symbol indicating the best wine to accompany it. Staff are pleasant, capable and discreet.

Modern European

The Glasshouse
14 Station Parade, Kew, Surrey TW9 3PZ (8940 6777). Kew Gardens tube/rail. **Open** noon-2.30pm, 7-10.30pm Mon-Thur; noon-2.30pm, 6.30-10.30pm Fri, Sat; 12.30-2.45pm, 7.30-10pm Sun. **Set lunch** £17.50 3 courses; (Sun) £25 3 courses. **Set dinner** £32.50 3 courses; (tasting menu) £45. **Credit** AmEx, MC, V.
Two sides of this wedge-shaped dining room are glass. On warm days, the windows are thrown open and the flood of light makes everyone look ten years younger. On the whole, the diners are old enough to appreciate this benefit almost as much as they do the warm atmosphere and great food.

Oriental

Tsunami
5-7 Voltaire Road, Clapham, SW4 6DQ (7978 1610). Clapham North tube. **Open** 6-11pm Mon-Thur; 6-11.30pm Fri; noon-11.30pm Sat. **Main courses** £6.95-£16.50. **Credit** AmEx, MC, V.
Daylight pours into Tsunami from a large skylight and even larger windows across dark-wood tables, white walls and tropical flowers. The kitchen's performance wavers between distinguished and quite ordinary, but on a good day you'll be washed away.

West London

American

1492
404 North End Road, Fulham, SW6 1LU (7381 3810/www.1492restaurant.com). Fulham Broadway tube. **Open** 12.30-3pm, 6pm-midnight Mon-Fri; 11am-3pm, 6pm-midnight Sat, Sun. **Main courses** £8.50-£17. **Credit** AmEx, MC, V. **Map** p396 A12.
1492 specialises in pan-Latin American food, offering dishes that hail from Mexico to the Caribbean – and no tacky Tex-Mex or ponchos. Burnt sienna paintwork, exposed brickwork, dark wood and colourful paintings provide a casual setting.

Harlem
78 Westbourne Grove, Notting Hill, W2 5RT (7985 0900/www.harlemsoulfood.com). Bayswater or Notting Hill Gate tube. **Open** 10.30am-midnight daily. **Service** 12.5%. **Credit** AmEx, DC, MC, V. **Map** p394 B6.
This trendy new wood-panelled restaurant-bar serves excellent soul food, described as Southern-style 'home cooking'. Portions are vast; service, from hip young things, is cool but friendly enough.

Lucky 7
127 Westbourne Park Road, Westbourne Park, W2 5QL (7727 6771). Royal Oak or Westbourne Park tube. **Open** 7am-11pm Mon-Sat; 9am-10.30pm Sun. **Main courses** £4.25-£7.95. **No credit cards.** **Map** p394 A5.

The worst thing about this Tom Conran stylised take on the US diner is its size: it's tiny, just a handful of big booths that you will likely be called on to share with strangers. The best thing about Lucky 7 is the food. The menu is short and sweet, consisting of a few hamburgers (many of them fish or vegetarian), sides, salads and ice-cream.

Cafés & brasseries

Lisboa Patisserie
57 Golborne Road, Ladbroke Grove, W10 5NR (8968 5242). Ladbroke Grove or Westbourne Park tube/23, 52 bus. **Open** 8am-8pm Mon-Sat; 8am-7pm Sun. **Credit** MC, V.
If London isn't overcome with one giant urge for *pasteis de nata* – those delectable Portuguese egg custard tarts – you can't blame Lisboa. With three other deli/pâtisseries throughout London, the firm is doing its best to spread the word. This, the original branch, contains the bakery.

Fish

Fish Hoek
8 Elliott Road, Chiswick, W4 1PE (8742 0766). Turnham Green tube. **Open** 6-10.30pm Mon; noon-2.30pm, 6-10.30pm Tue-Sun. **Main courses** £9.75-£30. **Credit** MC, V.
This lovely restaurant specialises in South African fish dishes. It's a small, bright space decorated with sepia-tinged fishing photos that can get uncomfortably crammed, especially on weekends, but such considerations soon fade thanks to a buoyant atmosphere, knowledgeable service from South African staff, and great cooking.

French

La Trompette
5-7 Devonshire Road, Chiswick, W4 2EU (8747 1836). Turnham Green tube. **Open** noon-2.30pm, 6.30-10.45pm Mon-Sat; 12.30-3pm, 7-10.30pm Sun. **Set lunch** £21.50 3 courses; (Sun) £25 3 courses. **Set dinner** £32.50 3 courses, £42.50 4 courses. **Credit** AmEx, MC, V.
This vibrant space – tan leather ceiling, mushroom-coloured, bamboo-textured walls – is usually filled with a wide range of enthusiastic diners, from first dates to old friends to families with young children. Quite an achievement for a local, although the crew behind this establishment has something of a pedigree. Great cooking comes as standard.

Gastropubs

Cow Dining Room
89 Westbourne Park Road, Westbourne Park, W2 5QH (7221 0021). Royal Oak or Westbourne Park tube. **Open** 7-11pm Mon-Fri; noon-2.30pm, 7-11pm Sat; 12.30-3.30pm, 7-10.30pm Sun. **Main courses** £13-£18. **Credit** MC, V. **Map** p394 A5.

The clocks seem to have been set back to the 1950s at this airy, lace-curtained upstairs room, which offers classy reinventions of old-fashioned British standards. Similar dishes feature on the fishy menu served in the pub downstairs.

Global

Mandalay

444 Edgware Road, Paddington, W2 1EG (7258 3696). Edgware Road tube. **Open** noon-2.30pm, 6-10.30pm Mon-Sat. **Main courses** £3.90-£6.90. **Credit** AmEx, DC, MC, V. **Map** p395 E4.
Mandalay has been a *Time Out* favourite for years. Who couldn't love the place? OK, so the Edgware Road location isn't salubrious, and the decor does little to evoke 'the mysterious East', but the food is a revelation: Burmese cooking combines elements of Thai, Indian and southern Chinese. Book.

Rodizio Rico

111 Westbourne Grove, Bayswater, W2 4UW (7792 4035). Bayswater tube. **Open** 6-11.30pm Mon-Fri; noon-4.30pm, 6-11.30pm Sat; 12.30-10.30pm Sun. **Set buffet** £11.90 vegetarian, £18 barbecue. **Credit** MC, V. **Map** p394 B6.
Modelled on the urban churrascarias (busy, ranch-like steakhouses) found throughout Brazil, Rodizio Rico is centred on the meat that is served up on a sword and taken from table to table. There's a smallish self-service salad selection, but the main reason for paying the all-you-can-eat rate is the meat.

Indian

Zaika

1 Kensington High Street, Kensington, W8 5NP (7795 6533/www.zaika-restaurant.co.uk). High Street Kensington tube. **Open** noon-2.45pm, 6.30-10.45pm Mon-Fri; 6.30-10.45pm Sat; noon-2.45pm, 6.30-9.45pm Sun. **Main courses** £12.50-£19.50. **Credit** AmEx, DC, MC, V. **Map** p394 C8.
Zaika's beautiful split-level dining room is tastefully done up in shades of terracotta, charcoal and plum, and decorated with carved antiques and discreetly placed screens. The cooking is inventive, modern and plate-lickingly delicious.

Italian

Assaggi

1st Floor, 39 Chepstow Place, Notting Hill, W2 4TS (7792 5501). Bayswater, Queensway or Notting Hill Gate tube. **Open** 12.30-2.30pm, 7.30-11pm Mon-Fri; 1-2.30pm, 7.30-11pm Sat. **Main courses** £16.95-£19.95. **Credit** DC, MC, V. **Map** p394 B6.
Although above a pub, this simply designed small room is a pleasure to dine in, with enchanting flower arrangements, well-kept window boxes and vibrant walls and artwork. The modern take on Italian cooking is generally superb, and the service hits the pitch-perfect note of being attentive yet unhurried.

Rosmarino

1 Blenheim Terrace, St John's Wood, NW8 0EH (7328 5014). St John's Wood tube. **Lunch served** noon-2.30pm, 7-10.30pm Mon-Fri; noon-3pm, 7-10.30pm Sat; noon-3pm, 7-10pm Sun. **Set lunch** (Mon-Thur) £14.50 2 courses, £19.50 3 courses. **Set meal** (lunch Fri-Sun; dinner daily) £22.50 2 courses, £27.50 3 courses, £32.50 4 courses. **Credit** AmEx, DC, MC, V.
The charming terrace at the front of this property has been enclosed with glass, making 18 more seats available for use all year round. And that's a good thing too: a menu of classic dishes and innovative flavour combinations keeps supplying Rosmarino's many regulars with reasons to come back.

Oriental

E&O

14 Blenheim Crescent, Ladbroke Grove, W11 1NN (7229 5454/www.eando.nu). Ladbroke Grove or Notting Hill Gate tube. **Open** noon-3pm, 6-10.30pm Mon-Sat; 1-3pm, 6-10pm Sun. **Main courses** £6-£21.50. **Credit** AmEx, DC, MC, V.
This is one hip and stylish restaurant. Cream walls, huge circular lampshades and dark-wood slatted walls create a simple, oriental feel that is reflected in the interesting pan-Asian menu. The small bar (with its range of spirits on ceiling-suspended glass shelves) is always packed.

Mandarin Kitchen

14-16 Queensway, Bayswater, W2 3RX (7727 9012). Bayswater or Queensway tube. **Open** noon-11.30pm daily. **Main courses** £5.90-£25. **Credit** AmEx, DC, MC, V.
The Mandarin is a reliable bet for spankingly fresh seafood, and a magnet for discerning east Asians. Don't expect to be thrilled by the decor, though, which is steadfastly 1970s with its undulating, textured ceiling and smoked-glass mirrors; the street frontage is so nondescript you'd walk straight past if you didn't know better.

Vegetarian & organic

The Gate

51 Queen Caroline Street, Hammersmith, W6 9QL (8748 6932/www.gateveg.co.uk). Hammersmith tube. **Open** noon-2.45pm, 6-10.45pm Mon-Fri; 6-10.45pm Sat. **Main courses** £7.95-£13. **Credit** AmEx, MC, V.
The Gate's younger sibling closed in 2004, but this trendsetting restaurant still has much to shout about. Diners flock here in their droves, and chef-proprietors Adrian and Michael Daniel continue to demonstrate a profound grasp of Middle Eastern, Mediterranean and Asian ingredients and cooking techniques. The surroundings help: the bright, sunny interior comes alive with flickering candle-light in the evenings. In a city that is short of truly world-class vegetarian restaurants, the Gate isn't just a beacon of hope – it's the future.

Eat, Drink, Shop

Pubs & Bars

Raise a glass to the best of London's boozers.

London's drinking scene has been experiencing something of a purple patch in the last few years. And still there's a constant array of new venues opening, not to mention old venues being revamped or relaunched and publicised as the next best thing since wheat and hops were first fermented. But guff and gush aside, more and more venues are, if not quite living up to the hype, at least turning out to be very good. There's no doubt that overall standards are consistently rising – quite possibly because the public is becoming ever more demanding.

The ongoing gastropub phenomenon is a reflection of the 1990s surge of interest in what goes on in the kitchen; now, any pub or bar worth its salt and pepper has a daily changing blackboard menu. Drinks are catching up too. Heavily advertised lagers still dominate bar counters, but there's evidence that we no longer swallow the ad men's pitches: independent and specialist beers are a big growth area. It's also easier to get properly made, innovative cocktails.

But the best advice we can give is to start the night with a tube ticket: the days of the West End being home to the best bars are over. Try Hoxton and Shoreditch in the east, Notting Hill and Ladbroke Grove in the west and Brixton in the south and you'll not only find some excellent bars, but you'll also see London at its most cosmopolitan.

Should you find your drinking rudely interrupted by a ringing bell and the cry 'Time Please!' we apologise. There's not an adult in London who has not been frustrated by the arcane law that means, without a special licence, pubs may only be open between the hours of 11am and 11pm (noon to 10.30pm on Sunday). But, thankfully, this is set to change: pubs and bars will be able to apply for a licence that enables them to open 24 hours daily by, if all goes to plan, November 2005. Further changes are also on the cards in the form of a much-debated ban on smoking in public places (*see p29* **No butts?**).

The best Drinking holes

For shaking the silver
Sosho (*see p228*); **Townhouse** (*see p225*).

For resistance to change
Coach & Horses (*see p223*).

For oriental-style opulence
Hakkasan (*see p223*).

For Londoners at play
Embassy Bar (*see p227*); **Mother Bar** (*see p228*); **Tongue & Groove** (*see p220*).

For obsessive spirit stockpiling
Baltic (*see p226*); **Boisdale** (*see p224*); **Salt Whisky Bar** (*see p224*).

For going to market
Market Porter (*see p221*); **Smiths of Smithfield** (*see p222*).

For gastropub gorging
Anchor & Hope (*see p193*); **Coach & Horses** (*see p196*); **Lots Road Pub & Dining Room** (*see p212*); **Seven Stars** (*see p222*); **White Horse** (*see p232*).

For old fashions and good beers
Royal Oak (*see p221*); **Star Tavern** (*see p225*); **Wenlock Arms** (*see p228*).

For new fashions and speciality beers
Jerusalem Tavern (*see p222*); **Lowlander** (*see p224*).

For the view
Vertigo 42/Twentyfour (*see p221*).

For the river
City Barge (*see p232*); **White Swan** (*see p232*).

For the history
French House (*see p223*); **Ye Olde Cheshire Cheese** (*see p221*).

For fine wines
Bleeding Heart Tavern (*see p221*); **Cork & Bottle** (*see p223*).

For a guest appearance
Blue Bar (*see p227*).

For a full survey of London drinking options we suggest you pick up a copy of the annual *Time Out Pubs & Bars Guide* (£8.99).

Central London

The South Bank & Bankside

Archduke
Concert Hall Approach, South Bank, SE1 8XU (7928 9370). Waterloo tube/rail. **Open** 8.30am-11pm Mon-Fri; 11am-11pm Sat. **Credit** AmEx, DC, MC, V. **Map** p401 M8.
This meeting place for arts lovers has a touch of class. Contemporary food (think marinated vegetable and goat's cheese focacia), hanging plants and glass walls are accompanied by decent wine-quaffing; most bottles cost between £15 and £20.

Market Porter
9 Stoney Street, Borough, SE1 9AA (7407 2495). London Bridge tube/rail. **Open** 6am-8.30am, 11am-11pm Mon-Fri; noon-11pm Sat; noon-10.30pm Sun. **Credit** AmEx, MC, V. **Map** p404 P8.
Open from 6am for the benefit of Borough Market traders, the Porter is always busy. With eight real ales, it deserves to be. Cosmetic tweaks have slightly spoilt the ancient fittings, but this is still a fine place, at all hours.

Royal Oak
44 Tabard Street, Borough, SE1 4JU (7357 7173). Borough tube/London Bridge tube/rail. **Open** 11.30am-11pm Mon-Fri. **Credit** MC, V. **Map** p404 P9.
The handsome, wonderfully maintained Royal Oak is the only pub in the capital tied to excellent Lewes ale-brewer Harvey's. Undemonstrative, welcoming – one of London's finest.

The City

Black Friar
174 Queen Victoria Street, EC4V 4EG (7236 5474). Blackfriars tube/rail. **Open** 11.30am-11pm Mon-Sat; noon-9.30pm Sun. **Credit** AmEx, MC, V. **Map** p404 O6.
An extraordinary wedge-shaped pub with an art nouveau façade and an interior of Edwardian marble, mosaics and pillared fireplaces. Expect a fairly decent range of real ales, bland corporate pub food and a smoky atmosphere.

Jamaica Wine House
St Michael's Alley, EC3V 9DS (7929 6972/www. massivepub.com). Monument tube/Bank tube/DLR. **Open** 11am-11pm Mon-Fri. **Credit** AmEx, MC, V. **Map** p405 Q6.
Said to be the site of the first London coffee house and a haunt of Jamaican plantation owners, this place was rebuilt after the Great Fire and converted into a pub at the end of the 19th century. Recent modern additions were slightly misjudged, but the mahogany interior continues to age nicely.

Seven Stars for excellence. *See p222.*

Vertigo 42
Tower 42, 25 Old Broad Street, EC2N 1HQ (7877 7842/www.vertigo42.co.uk). Bank tube/DLR/ Liverpool Street tube/rail. **Open** noon-3pm, 5-11pm Mon-Fri (reservation essential). **Credit** AmEx, DC, MC, V. **Map** p402 N5.
Smartly dressed City types are prepared to queue for the 600ft (185m) drinking experience at the top of this office block. There are two swanky bars: Twentyfour (on the 24th floor), with views of St Paul's and Tower Bridge; 18 floors nearer God is Vertigo 42, with spectacular views of London and three counties beyond. Booking is essential.

Ye Olde Cheshire Cheese
145 Fleet Street, EC4A 2BU (7353 6170/www. yeoldecheshirecheese.com). Blackfriars tube/rail. **Open** 11am-11pm Mon-Sat; noon-2.30pm Sun. **Credit** AmEx, DC, MC, V. **Map** p404 N6.
The Cheese might look closed, but it probably isn't: its anonymous dark frontage conceals a dingy alley entrance. Built over medieval cellars, it's a warren of wooden settles, boards and sawdust, once familiar to Dickens, Conan Doyle and Dr Johnson.

Holborn & Clerkenwell

Bleeding Heart Tavern
Bleeding Heart Yard, 19 Greville Street, Farringdon, EC1N 8SQ (7242 2056/www.bleedingheart.co.uk). Farringdon tube/rail. **Open** 11am-11pm Mon-Fri. **Credit** AmEx, DC, MC, V. **Map** p402 N5.

This wooden-floored pub oozes a rich history of bloody murders and royal weddings. The superb wine list runs to 450 varieties; the food is modern, French and tasty.

Café Kick

43 Exmouth Market, Clerkenwell, EC1R 4QL (7837 8077/www.cafekick.co.uk). Farringdon tube/rail. **Open** noon-11pm Mon-Sat. *Spring/summer* also 1-10.30pm Sun. **Credit** MC, V. **Map** p402 N4.

The sweetest of venues, Café Kick is a multi-hued shack dotted with football memorabilia. The scout hut aesthetics are the setting for competitive hi-jinks, courtesy of three René Pierre babyfoot tables. Euro beers and tapas food accompany the action. **Other locations**: Bar Kick, 127 Shoreditch High Street, Shoreditch, E1 6JE (7739 8700).

Jerusalem Tavern

55 Britton Street, Farringdon, EC1M 5NA (7490 4281). Farringdon tube/rail. **Open** 11am-11pm Mon-Fri. **Credit** AmEx, MC, V. **Map** p402 O5.

A marvellously mad little pub, the Jerusalem is all niches, nooks and crannies. It is the sole London outpost of St Peter's Brewery in Suffolk, which specialises in ales flavoured with fruits and spices.

Match EC1

45-47 Clerkenwell Road, Clerkenwell, EC1M 5RS (7250 4002/www.matchbar.com). Farringdon tube/rail. **Open** 11am-midnight Mon-Fri; 5pm-midnight Sat. **Credit** AmEx, DC, MC, V. **Map** p402 N4/O4.

There is no great mystery to Match's success: the cocktail list is put together by 'king of cocktails' Dale DeGroff and the bartenders are equally inspirational. Their love of Brambles, Dark & Stormys and, above all, the Martini, knows no bounds. Match's sibling bars are in the West End (37-38 Margaret Street, 7499 3443) and Shoreditch (*see p228*).

Seven Stars

53-54 Carey Street, Holborn, WC2A 2JB (7242 8521). Chancery Lane, Holborn or Temple tube. **Open** 11am-11pm Mon-Fri; noon-11pm Sat. **Credit** AmEx, MC, V. **Map** p399 M6.

An outstanding little place, built in 1602 and still intact. Lawyers from the Royal Courts opposite love its excellent beers and superior lunches, its low-beamed ceilings, narrow settles and rough plaster.

Smiths of Smithfield

67-77 Charterhouse Street, Farringdon, EC1M 6HJ (7251 7950/www.smithsofsmithfield.co.uk). Farringdon tube/rail. **Open** 7am-11pm Mon-Thur; 7am-midnight Fri; 10.30am-midnight Sat; 9.30am-10.30pm Sun. **Credit** AmEx, DC, MC, V. **Map** p402 O5.

Bang opposite Smithfield Market, this all-in-one cocktail bar, brasserie and restaurant is spread over four floors of an impressive listed building. The serious drinking part of the operation is a vast warehouse room with bare concrete, steel columns and industrial light fittings. The space is abuzz all day long, serving a café menu and breakfast until 5pm. Post-work it gets very boozy indeed. *See also p199.*

You can do minimalist when you get home: **Loungelover**. *See p228.*

Bloomsbury & Fitzrovia

Bradley's Spanish Bar
42-44 Hanway Street, Fitzrovia, W1T 9DE (7636 0359). Tottenham Court Road tube. **Open** noon-11pm Mon-Sat; 3am-10.30pm Sun. **Credit** MC, V. **Map** p399 K6.
Ever-popular, poky and tacky, this little bar tucked among the vinyl junkie-yards lures young(ish) drinkers. The draught beer is good, if pricey; the jukebox sounds aren't as kitsch as they used to be.

Eagle Bar Diner
3-5 Rathbone Place, Fitzrovia, W1T 1HJ (7637 1418/www.eaglebardiner.com). Tottenham Court Road tube. **Open** noon-11pm Mon-Wed; noon-midnight Thur-Fri; 10am-midnight Sat; 11am-6pm Sun. **Credit** MC, V. **Map** p399 K5.
This postmodern diner is a prime dine-and-drink spot on the busy Soho/Noho border. High-backed green snugs with sofas in front face a long zinc bar. Staff are cocktail savvy and DJs man the decks from Thursday to Saturday. *See also p199.*

Hakkasan
8 Hanway Place, W1T 1QL, Fitzrovia (7907 1888). Tottenham Court Road tube. **Open** noon-2.45pm, 6-11.30pm Mon-Wed; noon-2.45pm, 6pm-12.30am Thur, Fri; noon-4.30pm, 6pm-12.30am Sat; noon-4.30pm, 6-11.30pm Sun. **Credit** AmEx, MC, V. **Map** p399 K5.
A blossom-scented staircase leads to an impossibly polite reception, where you're gestured past a sumptuous Chinese restaurant (*see p201*) to the cocktail counter. Kumquat, ginger, lemongrass, Nashi pears and rose-petal syrup fuse sublimely with Ketels, Matusalems, rice wines and ginseng spirits. Brilliant.

Lamb
94 Lamb's Conduit Street, Bloomsbury, WC1N 3LZ (7405 0713). Holborn or Russell Square tube. **Open** 11am-11pm Mon-Sat; noon-4pm, 7-10.30pm Sun. **Credit** AmEx, MC, V. **Map** p399 M4.
This Grade II listed structure boasts a gorgeous Victorian interior: mahogany island bar and etched glass snob screens. Plus superb Young's bitters.

Nordic
25 Newman Street, Fitzrovia, W1T 1PN (7631 3174/www.nordicbar.com). Tottenham Court Road tube. **Open** noon-11pm Mon-Fri; 6-11pm Sat. **Credit** AmEx, MC, V. **Map** p398 J5.
A stylish Scandinavian bar with an excellent range of vodkas and beers, plus fun shooters and cocktails (Lapp Dancer, Dyslexic Tobogganist). The authentic smörgåsbord is reasonably priced (£1.50-£3.50). Skol!

Soho & Leicester Square

Ain't Nothin' But? The Blues Bar
20 Kingly Street, W1B 5PZ (7287 0514). Oxford Circus or Piccadilly Circus tube. **Open** 6pm-1am Mon-Wed; 6pm-2am Thur; noon-3am Fri, Sat; 7.30pm-midnight Sun. **Credit** MC, V. **Map** p398 J6.

For down 'n' dirty blues and a late drink you can't do much better than this compact bar. The hand-painted signs and tiny balcony-style stage give it the feel of a Louisiana blues club; bands play each night.

Coach & Horses
29 Greek Street, W1V 5DH (7437 5920). Leicester Square or Piccadilly Circus tube. **Open** 11am-11pm Mon-Sat; noon-10.30pm Sun. **Credit** MC, V. **Map** p399 K6.
Despite the famously ill-tempered behaviour of landlord Norman Balon ('the West End's rudest landlord', proclaims the pub sign), the Coach stands fast as the welcome refuge for a motley crew of (ir)regulars. Sandwiches are still only £1.

Cork & Bottle
44-46 Cranbourn Street, WC2H 7AN (7734 7807). Leicester Square tube. **Open** 11am-11.30pm Mon-Sat; noon-10.30pm Sun. **Credit** AmEx, DC, MC, V. **Map** p401 K7.
One of those eccentric little places that make London special, the Cork is an underground world of wine, squeezed between purveyors of sex and kebabs. The wine list and food choices are excellent and the atmosphere is intimate (cosy alcoves a speciality).

French House
49 Dean Street, W1D 5BG (7437 2799). Leicester Square or Piccadilly Circus tube. **Open** noon-11pm Mon-Sat; noon-10.30pm Sun. **Credit** AmEx, DC, MC, V. **Map** p399 K6.

Eat, Drink, Shop

Push the door marked 'Poussez' beneath flapping tricolours, and enter history. The French House was a London base for De Gaulle and his Resistance cohorts, and a drinking den for Brendan Behan and Dylan Thomas. A similar arty, cliquey and defiant mood has lingered on. In Gallic style, they don't serve in pints – Breton cider is popular, but not as apt as a pastis and a raise of the glass.

Milk & Honey
61 Poland Street, W1F 7NU (7292 9949/0700 655469/www.mlkhny.com). Oxford Circus tube. **Open** 6-11pm Mon-Fri; 7-11pm Sat (reservation only). **Credit** AmEx, DC, MC, V. **Map** p398 J6.
Billed as London's most secret bar, Milk & Honey has the unmarked door and ring-for-entry arrangement of a Prohibition speakeasy. Add the dimly lit booths, highly professional staff and sublime cocktails and it's obvious why it won best bar in the *Time Out* Eating and Drinking Awards, 2004. Anyone can visit. Just phone in advance and make a reservation.

Player
8 Broadwick Street, W1F 8HN (7494 9125/www. thplyr.com). Tottenham Court Road tube. **Open** 5.30pm-midnight Mon-Wed; 5.30pm-1am Thur, Fri; 7pm-1am Sat. **Credit** AmEx, DC, JCB, MC, V. **Map** p398 J6.
Dimly lit, thoroughly seductive and potently alcoholic, this could be Soho's classiest basement boozing joint. Drinks can be mixed economy (£6.50), business (£8) or first (£10) – and the higher the price, the better the quality of the spirit. A discreet, little known place.

Marylebone

Dusk
79 Marylebone High Street, W1U 5JZ (7486 5746). Baker Street tube. **Open** 10am-11pm Mon-Sat; 10am-10.30pm Sun. **Credit** MC, V. **Map** p398 G4.
Gastropub food and a long wine list make Dusk a fine spot for lunch or an afternoon swifty, but in the evenings it's a different story. Marylebone's smartly clad office workers pile in and the music is turned up; conversation grows intense and flirtatious.

Salt Whisky Bar
82 Seymour Street, W2 2JB (7402 1155). Marble Arch tube. **Open** noon-1am Mon-Sat; noon-midnight Sun. **Credit** AmEx, MC, V. **Map** p395 F6.
Fashionably dark – it's barely illuminated by pretty tea-lights and an underlit perspex bar counter – Salt is a fabulous whisky bar, attached to a more ordinary restaurant. Islay malts, American rye and even Japanese whiskies are just the tip of phenol heaven.

Mayfair & St James's

Guinea
30 Bruton Place, W1J 6NL (7499 1210/www. theguinea.co.uk). Bond Street or Green Park tube. **Open** 11am-11pm Mon-Fri; 6.30-11pm Sat. **Credit** AmEx, DC, MC, V. **Map** p400 H7.

Tucked away in a quiet mews off Berkeley Square, the Guinea is the province of expensively suited gentlemen who drop in for dark-wooded ambience, Young's beers and award-winning pies.

Red Lion
1 Waverton Street, W1J 5QN (7499 1307). Green Park tube. **Open** 11.30am-11pm Mon-Fri; 6-11pm Sat; noon-3pm, 6-10.30pm Sun. **Credit** AmEx, MC, V. **Map** p400 H7.
Never less than crowded, despite its obscure location, the Red Lion is a wonderful, old-fashioned pub with dark wood, discreet lighting and fires. There's a generous selection of draught beers to drink; for eats, try the Cumberland sausage and mash, which is something of a local institution.

Covent Garden & St Giles's

Gordon's
47 Villiers Street, WC2N 6NE (7930 1408/ www.gordonswinebar.com). Embankment tube/ Charing Cross tube/rail. **Open** 11am-11pm Mon-Sat; noon-10pm Sun. **Credit** AmEx, DC, MC, V. **Map** p401 L7.
This atmospheric, subterranean wine bar has enough squalor-chic to pass for a set from a lavish production of *Les Misérables*. In summer, tables in the alley alongside are highly coveted.

Lamb & Flag
33 Rose Street, WC2E 9EB (7497 9504). Covent Garden tube. **Open** 11am-11pm Mon-Thur; 11am-10.45pm Fri, Sat; noon-10.30pm Sun. **Credit** MC, V. **Map** p401 L7.
Among the few surviving wooden-framed buildings in London, the Lamb & Flag (once known as the Bucket of Blood) is also one of the very few bearable boozers in Covent Garden. It's invariably thronging with drinkers – especially on summer nights.

Lowlander
36 Drury Lane, WC2B 5RR (7379 7446/www. lowlander.com). Covent Garden or Holborn tube. **Open** noon-11pm daily. **Credit** AmEx, MC, V. **Map** p399 L6.
A high-ceilinged barn of a place, Lowlander offers a complete Dutch and Belgian face-filling experience. Beer options include Trappist, fruit and wheat varieties. Tables fill up quickly, so it pays to come early.

Westminster

Boisdale
13 Eccleston Street, SW1W 9LX (7730 6922/ www.boisdale.co.uk). Victoria tube/rail. **Open** 1am Mon-Fri; 7pm-1am Sat. **Admission** £10 after 10pm Mon-Sat; £3.95 if already on premises. **Credit** AmEx, DC, MC, V. **Map** p400 H10.
The Boisdale is a veritable tartan industry spanning high-class cuisine, fine wines, grandes marques of champagne, 150 malt whiskies and – improbably – vintage cigars. Jazz bands play regularly.

Still the **Pride of Spitalfields**. *See p228.*

Red Lion

48 Parliament Street, SW1A 2NH (7930 5826/ www.thespiritgroup.com). Westminster tube. **Open** 11am-11pm Mon-Fri; 11am-9pm Sat; noon-8pm Sun. **Credit** MC, V. **Map** p401 L9.

There's been a tavern here since 1434, but this particular incarnation has existed since 1900, hence the mahogany and etched-glass fittings. The silent TV screens are perpetually tuned in to the BBC Parliamentary Channel, which should give you a good idea of who the regulars are.

Knightsbridge & South Kensington

Nag's Head

53 Kinnerton Street, SW1X 8ED (7235 1135). Hyde Park Corner or Knightsbridge tube. **Open** 11am-11pm Mon-Sat; noon-10.30pm Sun. **No credit cards. Map** p400 G9.

From its country-store frontage on a cobbled mews through to the stone-flagged bar, this is a boozer's dream pub, with more quirks than Quentin Crisp's wardrobe. Add a no-mobiles policy and draught Adnams and you have a ridiculously perfect pub.

Star Tavern

6 Belgrave Mews West, SW1X 8HT (7235 3019/www. fullers.co.uk). Hyde Park Corner or Knightsbridge tube. **Open** 11am-11pm Mon-Sat; noon-10.30pm Sun. **Credit** AmEx, MC, V. **Map** p400 G9.

A stately home among London pubs, the Star boasts a large sitting room warmed by real fires. It has the history to match the looks, with several decades of roguish colour involving East End crims and West End celebs. The ales are kept in beautiful condition.

Townhouse

31 Beauchamp Place, SW3 1NU (7589 5080/ www.lab-townhouse.com). Knightsbridge tube. **Open** 4-11.30pm Mon-Fri, Sun; noon-midnight Sat. **Credit** AmEx, MC, V. **Map** p397 F10.

Gin palaces

'All is light and brilliancy.' So said Charles Dickens of the gin palace in *Sketches by Boz* (1836). These 'splendid mansions', he went on, were filled with 'stone balustrades, rosewood fittings, immense lamps, and illuminated clocks.' But he wasn't a fan. Gin palaces, or 'gin shops', attracted the poor, for all the wrong reasons. '[The] gin-palaces of Drury Lane... are lighthouses which guide the thirsty "sweater" on the road to ruin' said Max Schlesinger in *Saunterings in and about London* (1853). The greed of the pub companies – not just a 21st-century sin, by any means – was largely to blame. Spirit retailers devised the gin palace as a means to compete with the 'beer shops', which enjoyed more lenient licensing laws: gin had caused havoc and riots; beer was seen as harmless (witness Hogarth's *Gin Lane* and *Beer Street*). With their lights and finery, gin palaces were designed to be desirable refuges from slum life. It worked. First appearing around 1830, they numbered around 5,000 in the capital by the 1850s.

Only a handful still exist, and many examples have had their glory diminished by brash modern fittings. Take the **Paxton's Head** (153 Knightsbridge, Knightsbridge, SW1X 7PA, 7589 6627): gorgeous dark wood, snob screens (wood-and-etched-glass panels dividing seats to create greater privacy) and marble-topped tables – shame about the games machines. Others have been thoughtfully kept, and make a great escape from the chain gang. (But forget the gin: a pint and a pack of crisps is the norm.)

Starting centrally, the **Princess Louise** (208-209 High Holborn, Holborn, WC1V 7EP, 7405 8816; *pictured*), built in 1872, is

missing only its original partitions (gin palaces were split into bar, saloon and numerous other drinking areas). What remains is a magnificent horseshoe wooden bar, complete with clock; a moulded ceiling and intricately carved woodwork; all reflected in tall engraved mirrors. The patrons are slightly crusty, but the interior is like a pub

With its discreet front, you'd hardly notice Townhouse was there. But this is an establishment well worth getting to know – the Collins and Martini cocktails are superb, and the variety of spirits is dizzying. A tad pretentious, but staff are pleasant.

Chelsea

Apartment 195

195 King's Road, SW3 5ED (7351 5195/ www.apartment195.co.uk). Sloane Square tube/11, 22 bus. **Open** 4-11pm Mon-Sat. **Winter** 4-10.30pm Sun. **Credit** AmEx, MC, V. **Map** p397 F11.
It's been some time since there was anything on the King's Road to get the blood racing, but this place

does it. Quality booze is served by a good-looking bartending crew, and the dimly lit room with leather seating and open fires has pulling power too.

Waterloo

Baltic

74 Blackfriars Road, SE1 8HA (7928 1111/www. balticrestaurant.co.uk). Southwark tube. **Open** noon-11pm daily. **Credit** AmEx, DC, MC, V. **Map** p404 N8.
Baltic is a jewel. The design – a long, thin bar area of alcoves, banquettes and button stools – is breathtaking. Then there's the drinks menu, featuring almost every vodka known to Poles, and some known to Siberians. The food is superb too.

cathedral. In Soho, the 1866 **Argyll Arms** (18 Argyll Street, Soho, W1F 7TP, 7734 6117) is where many tourists and shoppers admit defeat over half-pints and pub pies. The real reason to come here is for the rich endowment of Victorian etched mirrors, snob screens and mahogany; the original layout is intact, too – a corridor leads to the large back saloon past three small snug bars. For knockout Victoriana near Victoria Station, the **Albert** (52 Victoria Street, Pimlico, SW1H 0NP, 7222 5577) is a fabulous confection of hand-cut glass, carved dark wood and old gas light fittings, built in the 1860s to honour the Empress's departed prince. Ignore the tourist-baiting T-shirts relating to the MPs who have drunk here, and enjoy the ornate cocoon.

In the City, where many of the old-timers of the London pub world are still standing, is the 1869 **Viaduct Tavern** (126 Newgate Street, The City, EC1 7AA, 7600 1863), slap bang across the road from the Old Bailey court. The lawyers, clients and relatives who traditionally drink here after long trials may be too tired or distraught to notice the carved mahogany bar, the giant gilt and silver mirrors and the restored original tiling. Take in the busts of 16 Victorian hanging judges and vow to keep your nose clean. Up in north London is the **Island Queen** (87 Noel Road, Islington, N1 8HD, 7704 7631). Swathed in wood and etched glass, it celebrates nautical glory with a wave-damaged wooden figurehead, palm leaves and prints of ships; a vast island bar presides over the middle of the lofty single room.

Belgravia

Blue Bar

The Berkeley, Wilton Place, SW1X 7RL (7235 6000/www.savoygroup.com). Hyde Park Corner tube. **Open** 4pm-1am Mon-Sat. **Credit** AmEx, DC, MC, V. **Map** p400 G9.
Stepping from the lobby of host hotel the Berkeley into the Blue Bar can feel like gatecrashing the fashion shoot for Italian *Vogue*'s Brit-set special. And it is the perfect setting for such assembled gorgeousness: a cocktail bar in the classic mould, but stylish and hip with it. Classic cocktails go for around £10 a time; there are seriously premium spirts and the vintagest of champagnes, too.

Clifton

96 Clifton Hill, St John's Wood, NW8 0JT (7372 3427). Maida Vale or St John's Wood tube. **Open** noon-11pm Mon-Sat; noon-10.30pm Sun. **Credit** AmEx, MC, V.
The Clifton's discreet location and calming pinewood interiors have preserved an ambience fit for a king. The clientele are well catered for with summer barbecues and hot toddies during colder months. High-brow board games keep the intelligentsia amused.

Embassy Bar

119 Essex Road, Islington, N1 2SN (7226 7901/ www.embassybar.com). Angel tube/38, 56, 73 bus. **Open** 4.30pm-midnight Sun-Thur; 4.30pm-2am Fri, Sat. **Admission** £3 after 9pm Fri; £4 after 9pm Sat. **Credit** MC, V. **Map** p402 O1.
A golden leaf pattern on the walls and a stylish wood-panelled ceiling give the Embassy the feel of a gentleman's playground. Downstairs a DJ spins for a tightly packed but ample dancefloor. Expect very little elbow room at weekends.

Hill

94 Haverstock Hill, Belsize Park, NW3 2BD (7267 0033/www.geronimo-inns.co.uk). Belsize Park or Chalk Farm tube. **Open** 4pm-midnight Mon-Thur; noon-midnight Fri, Sat; noon-10.30pm Sun. **Credit** MC, V.
The Hill is a design dream, combining stylish Victorian dandyism with playful '70s chic. Although the crowd mainly consists of rich north London trendies, the atmosphere is surprisingly relaxed.

Holly Bush

22 Holly Mount, Hampstead, NW3 6SG (7435 2892/ www.hollybush-hotel.co.uk). Hampstead tube. **Open** noon-11pm Mon-Sat; noon-10.30pm Sun. **Credit** MC, V.
One of the oldest and most picturesque drinking haunts in Hampstead, the Holly Bush is well hidden up a tiny backstreet. It has four bars, low ceilings, wood and plaster walls, and a real coal fire great for toe-warming after winter walks on the heath.

Keston Lodge

131 Upper Street, Islington, N1 1QP (7354 9535/ www.kestonlodge.com). Angel tube. **Open** noon-11.30pm Mon-Thur, Sun; noon-2am Fri, Sat. **Credit** MC, V. **Map** p402 N2.
A cut above most of the drinking gambits on Upper Street, Keston Lodge is a Hoxton-esque, warehouse-chic type of place, with the added luxuries of table service, half-decent cocktails and good music.

Lock Tavern

35 Chalk Farm Road, Camden, NW1 8AJ (7482 7163/www.locktavern.co.uk). Camden Town tube. **Open** noon-11pm Mon-Sat; noon-10.30pm Sun. **Credit** MC, V.
With dark wood and leather sofas, this place has a gentleman's club-meets-old man's-pub vibe. There's also a roof terrace overlooking Camden Lock, and a ramshackle beer garden perfect for summer pints.

Monkey Chews

2 Queen's Crescent, Chalk Farm, NW5 4EP (7267 6406/www.monkeychews.com). Chalk Farm tube. **Open** 5-11pm Mon-Thur; 5pm-midnight Fri; noon-midnight Sat; noon-10.30pm Sun. **Credit** MC, V.

A safe distance from the main Camden scrum, Monkey Chews is black on the outside and low-lit and low-slung on the inside. The bohemian air brings in a young crowd, who chill out during the week and let off steam to DJs at the weekends.

Shakespeare

57 Allen Road, Stoke Newington, N16 8RY (7254 4190). Stoke Newington rail/bus 73, 476. **Open** 5-11pm Mon-Thur; noon-midnight Fri, Sat; noon-10.30pm Sun. **Credit** MC, V.

The decor is fag-stained and the draught beer (Litovel) rather poor, but the Shakey is still very much its own pub, drawing a faithful clientele of arty, hard-drinking locals. The impeccable jukebox runs a nightly service from jazz to punk.

Wenlock Arms

26 Wenlock Road, N1 7TA (7608 3406/www. wenlock-arms.co.uk). Old Street tube/rail/55, 205, 214, 394 bus. **Open** noon-midnight Mon-Sat; noon-10.30pm Sun. **No credit cards. Map** p402 P3.

A real rough diamond of a boozer, and runner-up for best pub in *Time Out*'s Eating and Drinking Awards, 2004. The Wenlock boasts an excellent beer selection, and simple, traditional no-fuss decor.

East London

Florist

255 Globe Road, Bethnal Green, E2 0JD (8981 1100). Bethnal Green tube/rail/8 bus. **Open** 3-11pm Mon, Tue; noon-11pm Wed-Sat; noon-10.30pm Sun. **Credit** MC, V.

This East End corner pub was transformed a year ago from a grungy old boozer into a warm assembly of burgundy walls and battered leather sofas. The cognoscenti go for the cocktails – they're the business, and an incredible £5.

Grapes

76 Narrow Street, Limehouse, E14 8BP (7987 4396). Westferry DLR. **Open** noon-3pm, 5.30-11pm Mon-Fri; noon-11pm Sat; noon-10.30pm Sun. **Credit** AmEx, DC, MC, V.

This superb little pub is steeped in Dickensian charm, and is a real treat in summer if you can find space on the small riverside deck. Best of all, there's no music to disturb the convivial hubbub.

Home

100-106 Leonard Street, Shoreditch, EC2A 4RH (7684 8618/www.homebar.co.uk). Old Street or Liverpool Street tube/rail. **Open** 5.30pm-midnight Mon-Sat. **No credit cards. Map** p403 Q4.

There certainly is no place like Home, one of the true Hoxton originals. The beers (Asahi, Budvar and Staropramen) could be improved, as could the music on occasion, but overall, this is still a pack leader.

Loungelover

1 Whitby Street, Shoreditch, E1 6JU (7012 1234/ www.loungelover.co.uk). Liverpool Street tube/rail. **Open** 6pm-midnight Mon-Thur; 6pm-1am Fri; 7pm-1am Sat. **Credit** AmEx, MC, V. **Map** p403 S4.

This place is a paragon of high camp, stuffed with gaily coloured anatomical models, painted fairground gallopers and myriad light fittings. In such surrounds it has to be cocktails, ordered off a list that runs to around 16 pages.

Mother Bar

333 Old Street, Hoxton, EC1V 9LE (7739 5949/ www.333mother.com). Old Street tube/rail/55 bus. **Open** 8pm-3am Mon-Wed; 8pm-4am Thur-Sun. **Credit** MC, V. **Map** p403 R3.

The kind of thing that London does so well: subversive, tacky and bolshy. On busy nights you may have to queue, but once in you get a large dollop of decent music and discoball dancing to go with your Red Stripe, Guinness or Boddington's.

Pride of Spitalfields

3 Heneage Street, Spitalfields, E1 5LJ (7247 8933). Aldgate East or Whitechapel tube. **Open** 11am-11pm Mon-Sat; noon-10.30pm Sun. **No credit cards. Map** p403 S5.

That Brick Lane still has this decent pub on its doorstep is fortuitous: a recent firebomb attack could have ruined it. But following a refurb, it's now comfier than ever: the red carpet is lusher and the wood panelling smarter. The open fire is very welcome too.

Prospect of Whitby

57 Wapping Wall, Shadwell, E1W 3SH (7481 1095). Wapping tube. **Open** 11.30am-11pm Mon-Sat; noon-10.30pm Sun. **Credit** AmEx, DC, MC, V.

Built in 1520 and last remodelled in 1777, this historic pub has aged gracefully. The pewter-topped counter, stone-flagged floors, giant timbers and pebbled windows have all been preserved. Enjoy the river views but beware the coach parties.

Smersh

5 Ravey Street, Shoreditch, EC2A 4QW (7739 0092). Liverpool Street or Old Street tube/rail. **Open** 5pm-midnight Mon-Fri; 7pm-midnight Sat. **Credit** (over £10) AmEx, MC, V.

This idiosyncratic DJ bar is as unpretentious as it gets in Hoxton waters. 'Smersh' originally meant 'Death To Spies', so the walls are papered with Soviet propaganda. Music could be country and western one night, northern soul another; the Polish vodkas and Euro beers are top-notch.

Sosho

2 Tabernacle Street, Shoreditch, EC2A 4LU (7920 0701/www.sosho3am.com). Moorgate or Old Street tube/rail. **Open** noon-10pm Mon; noon-midnight Tue; noon-1am Wed; noon-2am Thur; noon-3am Fri; 7pm-3am Sat. **Admission** £3-£5 after 9pm Thur-Sat. **Credit** AmEx, DC, MC, V. **Map** p403 Q4.

An award-winning member of the Match family (*see also p222*), Sosho is a classy purveyor of stirred and shaken delights. Try cocktail impresario Dale DeGroff's Perfect Agave with Cuervo Tradicional, lychee, strawberries and home-made ginger beer. DJs play on weekends.

South-east London

Ashburnham Arms

25 Ashburnham Grove, Greenwich, SE10 8UH (8692 2007). Greenwich rail/DLR. **Open** noon-11pm Mon-Sat; noon-10.30pm Sun. **Credit** MC, V.

The exemplary Ashburnham has beer for the cognoscenti, food for the choosy and a back garden for the kids. The intimate front bar is embellished by a roaring fire in winter, pub cricket XI gatherings in summer and bar billiards all year round.

North Pole

131 Greenwich High Road, Greenwich, SE10 8JA (8853 3020/www.northpolegreenwich.com). Greenwich rail/DLR. **Open** noon-11pm Mon-Sat; noon-10.30pm Sun. **Credit** AmEx, MC, V.

The zebra stripes have faded on the bar stools, but this place is still a success with the area's young drinkers. Set on a rather dismal stretch of road, it has a buzzy walk-in lounge bar, underground dance club and a classy upstairs restaurant.

Trafalgar Tavern

Park Row, Greenwich, SE10 9NW (8858 2909/ www.trafalgartavern.co.uk). Cutty Sark Gardens DLR/Maze Hill rail. **Open** 11.30am-11pm Mon-Sat; noon-10.30pm Sun. **Credit** MC, V.

The future-focused **Lonsdale**. *See p232.*

This historic pub was founded on the site of the Old George Inn in 1837, as a tribute to naval hero Horatio Nelson. After the ignominy of serving as hostel for destitute seamen, it was painstakingly restored in the late '60s, which means there's all the mahogany panelling and stone fireplaces you'd expect, complementing a fine riverside terrace.

South-west London

Bread & Roses

68 Clapham Manor Street, Clapham, SW4 6DZ (7498 1779/www.breadandrosespub.com). Clapham Common or Clapham North tube. **Open** noon-11pm Mon-Sat; noon-10.30pm Sun. **Credit** MC, V.
A spacious hostelry with a minimalist interior and a traditional pub atmosphere. There's good beer, music, Sunday lunches and comedy nights. Children are allowed in until 9pm.

Dogstar

389 Coldharbour Lane, Brixton, SW9 8LQ (7733 7515/www.thedogstar.com). Brixton tube/rail. **Open** noon-2am Mon-Thur, Sun; noon-4am Fri, Sat. **Admission** £3 10-11pm, £5 after 11pm Fri, Sat. **Credit** AmEx, MC, V.
Over the years nothing much has changed here, but there's life in the old dog yet. In fact, this Brixton pioneer is still a hotspot, pulling a friendly throng of punters with retro pop, hip hop and drum 'n' bass.

Drawing Room & Sofa Bar

103 Lavender Hill, Battersea, SW11 5QL (7350 2564/www.galleryrestaurant.co.uk). Clapham Junction rail/77, 77A, 345 bus. **Open** noon-11pm Mon-Sat; noon-10.30pm Sun. **Credit** MC, V.
This quirky bar (think Mad Hatter meets Louis XIV) has a relaxed atmosphere and a great selection of aperitifs, enjoyed by a young boho crowd.

After hours

Most boozers still chuck you out at 11pm. They have to, according to the still sadly unchanged (as we go to press) licensing laws. But while late licences are in too short supply in order to meet the demand, they are still held by around 350 London venues.

The bad news? You often have to pay for the privilege, particularly on the weekend, when a few quid invariably buys you access to rowdy drunken scenes in a nondescript and often over-crowded room. Many hotel bars, such as the **American Bar** (*pictured*), **Blue Bar** and **Long Bar** (for all, *see below*), also keep long hours, but don't rock up expecting to start a party – unless, of course, you really are an international plaything.

The late-night spots (open until at least midnight) listed below are among the capital's best bets. Some charge admission – indicated in the listings. If you're looking for clubs and DJ bars, *see pp315-324*.

Central

Ain't Nothin' But? The Blues Bar (Soho, *see p223*); **Blue Bar** (Belgravia, *see p223*). **Boisdale** (Westminster, *see p224*); **Eagle Bar Diner** (Fitzrovia, *see p223*); **Hakkasan** (Fitzrovia, *see p223*); **Match EC1** (Clerkenwell, *see p222*); **Player** (Soho, *see p224*); **Salt Whisky Bar** (Marylebone, *see p224*); **Smiths of Smithfield** (The City, *see p222*); **Townhouse** (Knightsbridge, *see p225*).

North London

Embassy Bar (*see p227*); **Hill** (*see p227*); **Monkey Chews** (*see p228*).

East London

Home (*see p228*); **Loungelover** (*see p228*); **Mother Bar** (*see p228*); **Smersh** (*see p228*); **Sosho** (*see p228*).

South-west London

Dogstar (*see p230*); **Sand** (*see p231*); **South London Pacific** (*see p232*); **Tongue & Groove** (*see p232*).

West London

Lonsdale (*see p232*); **Tom & Dick's** (*see p232*).

Other good bets

Beating the curfew is particularly tricky in central London, so below we've gathered together a list of bars where you can get a drink past the witching hour – without having to pay up at the door.
Akbar *77 Dean Street, Soho, W1D 3SH (7437 2525/www.redfort.co.uk). Leicester Square or Piccadilly Circus tube.* **Open** until 1am Mon-Sat. **Map** p399 K6.
Exotic looker – with the cocktails to match.
American Bar *Savoy Hotel, Strand, Covent Garden, WC2R 0EU (7836 4343/www.the-savoy.com). Charing Cross tube/rail.* **Open** until 1am Mon-Sat. **Map** p401 L7/M6.
Superlative use of the silver shaker – as you'd expect at the Savoy. Dust off your glad rags.
Cafe Bohème *13 Old Compton Street, Soho, W1D 5JQ (7734 0623/www.cafe boheme.co.uk). Leicester Square tube.* **Open** until 3am Mon-Sat. **Map** p399 K6.
Pavement tables and Belgian beer.

Duke's Head

8 Lower Richmond Road, Putney, SW15 1JN (8788 2552). Putney Bridge tube/265 bus. **Open** 11am-11pm Mon-Sat; noon-10.30pm Sun. **Credit** AmEx, DC, MC, V.

This grand old Victorian pub is the perfect spot for watching the annual battle of the blues in the Oxford and Cambridge boat race. The handful of picnic tables offer ringside seats if the weather holds.

Fire Stables

27-29 Church Road, Wimbledon, SW19 5DQ (8946 3197). Wimbledon tube/rail, then 93, 200, 493 bus. **Open** 11am-11pm Mon-Sat; 11.30am-10.30pm Sun. **Credit** MC, V.

The Fire Stables is the very successful result of a gastropub overhaul comprising scuffed leather sofas, an open kitchen and international wines and beers. Sink into a comfy seat and prepare to linger.

Sand

156 Clapham Park Road, Clapham, SW4 7DE (7622 3022/www.sandbarrestaurant.co.uk). Clapham Common tube/35, 37 bus. **Open** 6pm-2am Sun. **Admission** £5 after 9.30pm Fri, Sat; £8 after 11pm Sat. **Credit** MC, V.

The vibe is seductive and accessible, the desert theme is understated (not a stuffed camel to be seen) and the music is funky. A fine establishment.

Ship

41 Jew's Row, Wandsworth, SW18 1TB (8870 9667/www.theship.co.uk). Wandsworth Town rail. **Open** 11am-11pm Mon-Sat; noon-10.30pm Sun. **Credit** AmEx, DC, MC, V.

Nestled in between rusting skips just shy of the Thames, the Ship has a great riverside beer garden – the scene of some serious barbecues in summer. There's an excellent wine list, decently priced.

International *116 St Martin's Lane, Covent Garden, WC2N 4BF (7655 9810). Leicester Square tube/Charing Cross tube/rail.* **Open** until 2am Mon-Sat. **Map** p401 L7.
Cosmopolitan destination for the well-heeled.

Lab *12 Old Compton Street, Soho, W1D (7437 7820). Leicester Square tube.* **Open** until midnight Mon-Sat. **Map** p399 K6.
Pioneer of the quality cocktail craze, still maintains its popularity.

Langley *5 Langley Street, Covent Garden, WC2H 9JA (7836 5005/www.thelangley. co.uk). Covent Garden tube.* **Open** until 1am Mon-Sat. **Map** p399 L6.
Thumping music, loud conversation and booze.

Long Bar *Sanderson Hotel, 50 Berners Street, Fitzrovia, W1T (7300 1400). Tottenham Court Road tube.* **Open** until 12.30am Mon-Sat. **Map** p398 J5/6.
Starck-inspired hotel bar, pricey and posey.

Point 101 *101 New Oxford Street, St Giles's, WC1A (7379 3112). Tottenham Court Road.* **Open** until 2am Mon-Thur; 2.30am Fri, Sat; midnight Sun. **Map** p399 K6/L5.
Drinks and DJs set in Centre Point concrete.

Crobar *17 Manette Street, Soho, W1D (7439 0831). Tottenham Court Road tube.* **Open** until 3am Mon-Sat. **Map** p399 K6.
A loveable shack, providing a home for the heavy metal fraternity.

Jerusalem *33-34 Rathbone Place, Fitzrovia, W1T 1GN (7255 1120). Tottenham Court Road tube.* **Open** until midnight Tue, Wed; 1am Thur-Sat. **Map** p399 K5.
Popular basement bar-restaurant.

Ruby Lounge *33 Caledonian Road, King's Cross, N1 9BU (7837 9558). King's Cross tube/rail.* **Map** p399 L2/M2. **Open** until 1am Thur; 2am Fri, Sat.
Inexpensive cocktails, DJs and young fun.

Thirst *53 Greek Street, Soho, W1D 3DR (7437 1977/www.thirstbar.com). Tottenham Court Road tube.* **Open** until 3am Mon-Sat. **Map** p399 K6.
Funky-by-rote, but popular with sassy Sohoites.

Eat, Drink, Shop

South London Pacific

340 Kennington Road, Kennington, SE11 4LD
(7820 9189/www.southlondonpacific.com).
Kennington or Oval tube. **Open** 6pm-1am Thur;
6pm-2am Fri, Sat. Occasionally 6pm-1am Wed, Sun.
Admission £3 before 10pm, £5 after 10pm Fri, Sat.
Credit MC, V.
This lounge bar-nightclub has a tacky South Seas
theme that admirably refuses to take itself too seriously: Easter Island totems, Hawaiian table football
and retro pinball. Innovative venture, iffy location.

Sultan

78 Norman Road, Wimbledon, SW19 1BT (8542
4532). Colliers Wood/South Wimbledon tube. **Open**
noon-11pm Mon-Sat; noon-10.30pm Sun. **Credit** MC, V.
Winner of the 2004 *Time Out* Eating and Drinking
Awards for best pub, this friendly family-run estab-
lishment is a must for the beer enthusiast as the sole
London outpost of Salisbury's Hop Black brewery.
Decor is in the no-nonsense school of local pubbery.

Tongue & Groove

50 Atlantic Road, Brixton, SW9 8JN (7274 8600).
Brixton tube/rail. **Open** 9pm-2am Wed; 9pm-3am
Thur-Sat; 9pm-2am Sun. **Admission** £3 after 11pm
Fri, Sat. **Credit** AmEx, DC, MC, V.
Lustrous decor and a cool-list clientele give this bar
its slick, classy aura. Arrive early for cocktails and
the easy lounge vibe (which gathers tempo as the
night goes on), or brace yourself for a queue.

West London

City Barge

27 Strand-on-the-Green, Chiswick, W4 3PH (8994
2148). Gunnersbury tube/rail/Kew Bridge rail.
Open 11am-11pm Mon-Sat; noon-10.30pm Sun.
Credit AmEx, DC, MC, V.
Situated amid the finery of Kew's riverside
mansions, this boozer bedecked in boating para-
phernalia is a classic. Have a wander down from the
bridge on a summer's evening – a better place to stop
off for a pint is hard to imagine.

Dove

19 Upper Mall, Hammersmith, W6 9TA (8748
5405). Hammersmith or Ravenscourt Park tube.
Open 11am-11pm Mon-Sat; noon-10.30pm Sun.
Credit AmEx, MC, V.
On a turn of the Thames made famous by the
Oxbridge Boat Race, the Dove is a 17th-century ode
to the great English boozer. Although occasionally
rowdy, the fantastically low-beamed ceiling and fine
summer terrace make it difficult to flaw.

Elgin

96 Ladbroke Grove, W11 1PY (7229 5663).
Ladbroke Grove tube. **Open** 11am-11pm Mon-Sat;
noon-10.30pm Sun. Meals served noon-10pm daily.
Credit AmEx, MC, V.
This listed boozer bristles with urban chic. Most of
today's punters take the elaborate stained glass,
carved mahogany, etched mirrors and decorative

tiles for granted. Take a look: you'll not find better
this side of the 1890s.

Grand Union

45 Woodfield Road, Westbourne Park, W9 2BA
(7286 1886). Westbourne Park tube. **Open** noon-
11pm Mon-Sat; noon-10.30pm Sun. **Credit** MC, V.
A fashionable crowd frequents this much-loved,
reassuringly scruffy local. There's good gastropub
food and beer, plus alfresco boozing on the patio.

Lonsdale

44-48 Lonsdale Road, Notting Hill, W11 2DE
(7228 1517/www.thelonsdale.co.uk). Notting Hill
Gate/Ladbroke Grove tube. **Open** 6pm-midnight
Mon-Sat; 6pm-11.30pm Sun. **Credit** AmEx, MC, V.
Map p394 A6.
This exclusive joint feels like the relaxation deck of a
futuristic spacecraft – so gorgeous that you'll double
your style quotient just by sitting in it. Luckily, the
mood is a bit more relaxed than the decor.

Trailer Happiness

177 Portobello Road, Ladbroke Grove, W11 2DY
(7727 2700/www.trailerhappiness.com). Ladbroke
Grove/Notting Hill Gate tube. **Open** 5pm-midnight
Tue-Fri; 6pm-midnight Sat. **Credit** AmEx, MC, V.
Map p394 A6.
The decor at this Portobello newcomer is fairly neg-
ligible 1970s Woolworths kitsch, but the attention
is on the spotlit bar and the preparation of some
absolutely killer cocktails – very good value at £6.

Tom & Dick's

30 Alexander Street, Bayswater, W2 5NU (7229
7711/www.tomanddicks.com). Royal Oak tube. **Open**
6.30pm-midnight Mon-Sat; noon-10.30pm
Sun. **Credit** AmEx, MC, V. **Map** p394 B5.
A luscious yet homely little drinking haunt that's
two parts camp to one splash of calculated cool. A
fruity cocktail menu and excellent spicy Indian
snacks add to the mix.

White Horse

1-3 Parsons Green, SW6 4UL (7736 2115/
www.whitehorsesw6.com). Parsons Green tube.
Open 11am-11pm Mon-Sat; 11am-10.30pm Sun.
Credit AmEx, MC, V.
The boozer of choice for posh locals has earned the
nickname Sloaney Pony. Don't be put off – the menu
is exemplary and the beers are a joy. The front
terrace provides a grand view of the green.

White Swan

Riverside, Twickenham, Middx, TW1 3DN
(8892 2166/www.massivepub.com). Twickenham/
St Margaret's rail. **Open** *Winter* 11am-3pm, 5.30-
11pm Mon-Thur; 11am-11pm Fri, Sat; noon-10.30pm
Sun. *Summer* 11am-11pm Mon-Sat; noon-10.30pm
Sun. **Credit** MC, V.
With its magnificent riverside view and rickety
charm, the White Swan is something of a classic. On
match days at Twickenham, the place gets overrun
with rugby fans; at most other times it's all about
having a beer and relaxing.

Eat, Drink, Shop

Shops & Services

This is shoppers' paradise. Bag it.

In shopping terms, London is the centre of the universe. Well, OK, New York may have the edge, but London is giving it a run for its money.

Everyone knows that **Oxford Street** is the place to find most chain stores and department stores, but it can be a teeming, noisy, even unpleasant experience. It's also increasingly full of tat, especially at the northern end. Head to the quirkier parts of London – there are plenty of interesting boutiques selling designer 'street' fashion around **Hoxton** and **Spitalfields** to the east and **Westbourne Park** in the west.

Marylebone High Street has a good mix of homewares, independent food shops and salons.

Head for **Covent Garden** or **Knightsbridge** for expensive designer fashion, **Soho** for music and funkier clothes, **Charing Cross Road** for bookstores (new and antiquarian) and the **King's Road** for (expensive) homewares and kids' stuff. Your adolescent children may want to skulk around **Camden**, but most adult Londoners avoid this tourist attraction.

THE BASICS

Central London shops are open late one night a week, usually till 7pm or 8pm. Those in the West End (Oxford Street to Covent Garden) are open until late on Thursdays, while Wednesday is late opening in Chelsea and Knightsbridge.

Sweet **Liberty**.
See p237.

For more listings and reviews, buy the extensive *Time Out Shopping Guide* (£9.99).

Antiques

Islington, Kensington and Chelsea are the three antiques centres in London. *Antiques Trade Gazette* (www.antiquestradegazette.com), the *Collector* (www.artefact.co.uk) and *Antique Collecting* (www.antique-acc.com) have listings on dealers, plus details of auctions. **Greenwich Market** has a sizeable antiques section, as does **Portobello Road** (for both, *see p255*).

Alfie's Antique Market

13-25 Church Street, Marylebone, NW8 8DT (7723 6066/www.alfiesantiques.com). Edgware Road tube/Marylebone tube/rail. **Open** 10am-6pm Tue-Sat. **Credit** varies. **Map** p395 E4.
The bigger spaces at Alfie's tend to belong to 20th-century decorative arts, antiques and vintage clothing. Vincenzo Caffarella has some stunning pieces, particularly lighting; Ian Broughton has '30s to '50s kitsch. You can also find advertising posters, telephones, china and jewellery. The top floor is the best.

Antiquarius

131-141 King's Road, Chelsea, SW3 5EB (7351 5353/ www.antiquarius.co.uk). Sloane Square tube, then 11, 19, 22 bus. **Open** 10am-6pm Mon-Sat. **Credit** varies. **Map** p397 E12.
With its well-kept shops, this is a more pleasant venue than the often shabby arcades. It's a good source of Arts and Crafts and Aesthetic Movement objects, stunning antique Baccarat glass, jewellery, clocks and watches. The French-owned Art Deco Pavilion has stylish furniture, lamps, photo frames and cigarette accessories. Everything is negotiable.

Camden Passage

Camden Passage, off Upper Street, Islington, N1 5ED (7359 0190/www.antiquesnews.co.uk/ camdenpassage). Angel tube. **Open** *General market* 7am-4pm Wed; 7am-5pm Sat. *Book market* 8.30am-6pm Thur. **Credit** varies. **Map** p402 O2.
The market held in this pedestrianised backstreet near Angel majors in costume jewellery, silver plate and downright junk – but that doesn't mean you can't find rare items at good prices. More interesting are the dealers in the surrounding arcades, who open to coincide with the market.

Grays Antique Market & Grays in the Mews

58 Davies Street, W1K 5LP, & 1-7 Davies Mews, Mayfair, W1K 5AB (7629 7034/www.graysantiques. com). Bond Street tube. **Open** 10am-6pm Mon-Fri. **Credit** varies. **Map** p398 H6.
A liveried doorman greets you as enter Grays from South Molton Street: here small shops sell jewellery; further back, there are silver, glass and other antiques. The more varied dealers in the Mews building makes hunting for affordable presents more rewarding there.

Books

General

Blackwell's

100 Charing Cross Road, St Giles's, WC2H 0JG (7292 5100/www.blackwell.co.uk). Tottenham Court Road tube. **Open** 9.30am-8pm Mon-Sat; noon-6pm Sun. **Credit** AmEx, MC, V. **Map** p399 K5.
One of the capital's pre-eminent academic booksellers, Blackwell's offers a very broad selection of titles covering the whole spectrum of academic disciplines. The perfect place to pick up that *Foucault for Beginners*. **Other locations**: throughout the city.

Books etc

421 Oxford Street, W1C 2PQ (7495 5850/www. booksetc.co.uk). Bond Street tube. **Open** 9.30am-8pm Mon-Wed, Sat; 9.30am-8.30pm Thur, Fri; 11.30am-6pm Sun. **Credit** AmEx, DC, MC, V. **Map** p399 J6.
Run by the US Borders Group, Inc – which also owns the UK based Borders Superstores – Books etc is a pared-down version of its larger sibling. Stores carry a healthy selection of general interest material and run offers on the current mainstream bestsellers. **Other locations**: throughout the city.

Borders Books & Music

203 Oxford Street, Oxford Circus, W1D 2LE (7292 1600/www.borders.co.uk). Oxford Circus tube. **Open** 8am-11pm Mon-Sat; noon-6pm Sun. **Credit** AmEx, MC, V. **Map** p398 J6.
Offering an extensive selection of general interest and specialist titles spread over five floors, plus a decent CD/video/DVD section and a commendable stationery and magazine area (lots of US imports) at ground level. A smattering of comfortable chairs are provided as well as a coffee shop. **Other locations**: throughout the city.

Foyles

113-119 Charing Cross Road, Soho, WC2H 0EB (7437 5660/www.foyles.co.uk). Tottenham Court Road tube. **Open** 9.30am-8pm Mon-Sat; noon-6pm Sun. **Credit** AmEx, DC, MC, V. **Map** p399 K6.
The transformation is complete. This cherished independent, once renowned for its haphazard and unruly appearance, now has clarity and purpose. About the only feature that remains is the incredible array of titles over its five floors. Punters can now spend the time they would have lost rummaging through its vast collection enjoying a drink in the coffee shop or connecting to the web via Wi-Fi.

London Review of Books

14 Bury Place, Bloomsbury, WC1A 2JL (7269 9030). Tottenham Court Road tube. **Open** 10am-6.30pm Mon-Sat; noon-6pm Sun. **Credit** AmEx, MC, V. **Map** p399 L5.
Half-owned by the eponymous literary-political journal, this fresh, well-laid-out shop is all polished wood, quiet conversation, passionate staff and a seriously informed selection of books. Frequent readings and talks are held here.

Eat, Drink, Shop

Waterstone's

82 Gower Street, Bloomsbury, WC1E 6EQ (7636 1577/www.waterstones.co.uk). Goodge Street or Warren Street tube. **Open** 9.30am-8pm Mon, Wed-Fri; 10am-8pm Tue; 9.30am-7pm Sat; noon-6pm Sun. **Credit** AmEx, DC, MC, V. **Map** p399 K4.

This bookseller houses second-hand and remainders plus an impressive collection of academic (and other) books at excellent prices. There's an outstanding selection of new books covering all topics, over four floors. Additional highlights include book-search facilities and frequent three-for-two deals.
Other locations: throughout the city.

Used & antiquarian

The weekly **Riverside Walk Market** (10am-5pm Sat, Sun and irregular weekdays) on the South Bank under Waterloo Bridge, sells plenty of cheap paperbacks.

Any Amount of Books

56 Charing Cross Road, Leicester Square, WC2H 0QA (7836 3697/www.anyamountofbooks.com). Leicester Square tube. **Open** 10.30am-9.30pm Mon-Sat; 11.30am-7.30pm Sun. **Credit** AmEx, MC, V. **Map** p401 K6.

Probably the most approachable of the booksellers on this stretch, Any Amount of Books is a literary treasure trove. All subjects are covered here, with large sections on literary criticism, biography, art, architecture, gender, history, medicine, and religion. There's also a small number of first-editions, plus trolleys of books outside at dirt-cheap prices.

Ulysses

40 Museum Street, Bloomsbury, WC1A 1LU (7831 1600). Holborn tube. **Open** 11am-6pm Mon-Sat. **Credit** AmEx, MC, V. **Map** p399 L5.

One of the premier bookshops for affordable modern first editions. The space has a smart, homely feel with plenty of scope for browsing. Prices tend to be between £35 and £100 (books for under £35 are housed in the basement).

Department stores

Fortnum & Mason

181 Piccadilly, St James's, W1A 1ER (7734 8040/ www.fortnumandmason.co.uk). Green Park or Piccadilly Circus tube. **Open** 10am-6.30pm Mon-Sat; (restaurant & food hall only) noon-6pm Sun. **Credit** AmEx, MC, V. **Map** p400 J7.

The ground-floor food hall is wonderfully over-the-top, with marbled pillars, chandeliers and long rows of tea, coffee and chocolates. The elegant, blissfully quiet upper levels feature women's fashion and accessories. There's also an excellent perfumery, home to the Clive Christian range (exclusive in London). Formal lunch or afternoon tea at the St James's Restaurant, and light meals and teas at the Fountain and Patio restaurants don't come cheap, but they're a real slice of London.

Harrods

87-135 Brompton Road, Knightsbridge, SW1X 7XL (7730 1234/www.harrods.com). Knightsbridge tube. **Open** 10am-7pm Mon-Sat. **Credit** AmEx, DC, MC, V. **Map** p397 F9.

Star department store **Harrods** deserves its name in lights.

Harrods is the mother of all upscale department stores, with floor after floor of expensive designer clothing overseen by surprisingly friendly staff who know you can't afford to buy but don't seem to mind you looking. And looking is fab – it costs nothing to soak up the ambience in the ground-floor Room of Luxury with accessories by the likes of Celine, Gucci, Dior and Hermès; or to linger amid the designs by MaxMara, Joseph, Armani, Dolce & Gabbana and Moschino. It's also fun to giggle at the over-the-top glitz that helped make the Harrods name. But for us it's the legendary food halls that are the biggest draw.

Harvey Nichols
109-125 Knightsbridge, Knightsbridge, SW1X 7RJ (7235 5000/www.harveynichols.com). Knightsbridge tube. **Open** *Store* 10am-8pm Mon-Fri; 10am-7pm Sat; noon-6pm Sun. *Café* 10am-10pm Mon-Sat; 10am-6pm Sun. *Restaurant* 10am-11pm Mon-Sat; 10am-6pm Sun. **Credit** AmEx, DC, MC, V. **Map** p397 F9.
Harvey Nicks is an elegant and urban one-stop shop for front-line fashion. The ground floor is a cosmetics junkie's paradise. The bag department has a well-chosen selection, showcasing Donna Karan and Stella McCartney's forays into armwear, and shoes are divine. For refreshment there's the light-suffused fifth-floor café, bar and restaurant.

John Lewis
278-306 Oxford Street, Oxford Circus, W1A 1EX (7629 7711/www.johnlewis.co.uk). Bond Street or Oxford Circus tube. **Open** 9.30am-7pm Mon-Wed, Fri, Sat; 9.30am-8pm Thur. **Credit** MC, V. **Map** p398 H6.
Knocking on for some 150 years of trade, John Lewis represents the best of British middle-class consumer values with its 'never knowingly undersold' prices. Nothing's super-stylish, but it's no longer embarrassingly outdated either, and the staff know what they're talking about. Recommended for buying, not browsing. All departments – and there are plenty of them – are well stocked; haberdashery and kitchenware are positively legendary.

Liberty
210-220 Regent Street, Oxford Circus, W1B 5AH (7734 1234/www.liberty.co.uk). Oxford Circus tube. **Open** 10am-7pm Mon-Wed; 10am-8pm Thur; 10am-7pm Fri, Sat; noon-6pm Sun. **Credit** AmEx, DC, MC, V. **Map** p398 J6
Its famous prints are coveted the world over, but tourists may not be aware of the rest of the riches behind Liberty's façade. Made up of two interlinked buildings, the store can be tricky to navigate. Menswear, women's shoes and lingerie are in the refurbished Regent House on Regent Street, as is the cosmetics department, which exudes sophistication. But for body and bath products, you need to hop over to the original Tudor House on Great Marlborough Street. This lovely 1920s building also houses the celebrated scarf hall and a new childrenswear section. The British Arts and Crafts movement lives on in the basement home collections and among the sumptuous oriental rugs on the third floor.

Marks & Spencer
458 Oxford Street, Oxford Circus, W1C 1AP (7935 7954/www.marksandspencer.co.uk). Marble Arch tube. **Open** 9am-9pm Mon-Fri; 9am-8pm Sat; noon-6pm Sun. **Credit** AmEx, DC, MC, V. **Map** p398 G6.
The basics for which M&S is famous are still present and reliable – cotton tees, everyday undies – but get much further into the store and you're met by a mind-blowing wall of subsections. M&S's homewares features lots of gilt and richly coloured curtains, plus furniture that sits somewhere between minimalist and cosy. This branch also has a third-floor café, a bureau de change and instant cash VAT refunds for those eligible, not to mention food and beauty halls. **Other locations**: throughout the city.

Selfridges
400 Oxford Street, Oxford Circus, W1A 1AB (0870 837 7377/www.selfridges.com). Bond Street or Marble Arch tube. **Open** 10am-8pm Mon-Fri; 9.30am-8pm Sat; noon-6pm Sun. **Credit** AmEx, DC, MC, V. **Map** p398 G6.
The ground floor is a heaving cosmetics and fragrance marketplace where you can't swing a Fendi bag without bumping into a display for Stila, MAC, Bobbi Brown, Nars or Benefit. If you enter via the luxury fashion accessories department you'll spot more names: Miu Miu, Celine, Fendi, Prada, Burberry… the layout doesn't always seem logical, but it's all here. The Superbrands section is dedicated to eight well-known designers (including Balenciaga). On the third floor, you can lose yourself in the excellent lingerie department.

Electronics
Tottenham Court Road has the city's main concentration of electronics and computer shops, but for good prices, expert advice and good guarantees on a limited range of the best products, go to **John Lewis** (*see above*).

Computers

Computer Exchange
32 Rathbone Place, Fitzrovia, W1T 1JJ (7636 2666/www.cex.co.uk). Tottenham Court Road tube. **Open** 10am-7pm Mon-Wed, Sat; 10am-8pm Thur, Fri; 11am-6pm Sun. **Credit** MC, V. **Map** p399 K5.
A budget-conscious and retro-gamers' paradise, CEX is the second-hand emporium par excellence, where you can pick up classic Intellivision and Atari consoles for £30-£40, plus Space Invaders, Pac-Man or Donkey Kong for around a tenner. Up-to-date titles (new and second-hand) are sold on the main floor, including Japanese and American imports.

Gultronics
264-7 Tottenham Court Road, Fitzrovia, W1T 7RH (7436 4120/www.gultronics.co.uk). Goodge Street or Tottenham Court Road tube. **Open** 10am-7pm Mon-Sat; 11am-5pm Sun. **Credit** AmEx, MC, V. **Map** p399 K5.

Eat, Drink, Shop

love arts & crafts
love fashion
love home
love food & drink
love health & beauty
love property
love market shopping

...you will love Old Spitalfields Market

"a vibrant mix of contemporary style and history"

"at the heart of the City's creative, fashionable East End, just a stone's-throw from Liverpool Street"

"over 300 shops, stalls and restaurants, plus special events, in and around the covered market"

"fun for all the family; buggy and wheelchair friendly"

HOW TO GET THERE
Brushfield Street, London E1
Rail / Underground: Liverpool St or Aldgate East
Local buses: 8, 242, 149 and 67

SOMETHING SPECIAL EVERY DAY
Open all year round
Shops, market stalls, restaurants

visit
spitalfields
.com

For further information, you'll love our website www.visitspitalfields.com

They sell most categories of consumer electronics, but it's the range of Toshiba and Sony laptops that makes Gultronics worth a visit. Prices are competitive and the shop stocks a good range of accessories.

Micro Anvika

245 Tottenham Court Road, Fitzrovia, W1T 7QT (7467 6000/www.microanvika.co.uk). Goodge Street or Tottenham Court Road tube. **Open** 9.30am-6pm Mon-Wed, Fri, Sat; 9.30am-6.30pm Thur; 11am-5pm Sun. **Credit** AmEx, MC, V. **Map** p399 K5.

Micro Anvika has good selection of Sony, Toshiba, IBM and other laptops supplemented by accessories galore and a nice line in gadgets and software. There's also an outlet in Selfridges.

General & audio-visual

Ask Electronics

248 Tottenham Court Road, Fitzrovia, W1T 7QZ (7637 0353/www.askdirect.co.uk). Tottenham Court Road tube. **Open** 9am-6pm Mon-Wed, Fri, Sat; 10am-8pm Thur; noon-6pm Sun. **Credit** AmEx, DC, MC, V. **Map** p399 K5.

Boasting 'more than 10,000 product lines from over 400 suppliers', Ask offers an excellent range of quality computers, cameras, hi-fis, gadgets and accessories from leading brands such as Sony, Panasonic and Pioneer. The store has a modern, stylish feel with well-displayed merchandise, prices are competitive and the staff knowledgeable.

Photography

Chains all around town can do one-hour delivery; our favourite is **Snappy Snaps**. **Boots** (*see p252*) has a reliable service at most branches, including digital services.

Jacobs Photo, Video & Digital

74 New Oxford Street, St Giles's, WC1A 1EU (7436 5544/www.jacobs-photo.co.uk). Tottenham Court Road tube. **Open** 9am-6pm Mon-Wed, Fri, Sat; 9am-8pm Thur. **Credit** AmEx, MC, V. **Map** p399 L5.

Though part of a nationwide chain, Jacobs feels friendly and the staff are well informed. It has an excellent range of compact, digital and SLR cameras and accessories, and one of the best tripod selections in town. Prices are competitive, with frequent special deals to be had. The second-hand department is also worth checking out. Next-day colour film processing is £4.99, while the one-hour service is £7.49.

Fashion

Boutiques

Austique

330 King's Road, Chelsea, SW3 5UR (7376 3663/ www.austique.co.uk). Bus 11, 19, 49. **Open** 10.30am-6.30pm Mon-Sat; noon-5pm Sun. **Credit** AmEx, MC, V. **Map** p397 D12.

Glamour kittens are scampering to this eclectic white-painted boudoir filled with iridescence and clothes by exclusive designers from Australia, Spain and Los Angeles, and Love Kylie and Elegantly Scant lingerie. They also stock Oliver Twist, voted denim label of the year by US Vogue.

Browns

23-27 South Molton Street, Mayfair, W1K 5RD (7514 0000/www.brownsfashion.com). Bond Street tube. **Open** 10am-6.30pm Mon-Wed, Fri, Sat; 10am-7pm Thur. **Credit** AmEx, DC, MC, V. **Map** p398 H6.

Joan Burstein's venerable shop has reigned supreme over London's boutiques for 30 years, and abdication seems a long way off. Among over 80 designers vying for favour are Diane von Furstenberg, Marc Jacobs, Chloé, Bottega Veneta, Sophia Kokosalaki, Goat and Etro. Labels exclusive to Browns include Zoran, Lainey Keogh and Worth. Those *sans* sugar daddy can peruse the almost-affordable diffusion and emergent-designer ranges, which are on offer at the adjacent Browns Focus. At No.50 there's a sale shop called Browns Labels for Less.

Other locations: 6C Sloane Street, Knightsbridge, SW1X 9LE (7514 0000).

The Cross

141 Portland Road, Holland Park, W11 4LR (7727 6760). Holland Park tube. **Open** 11am-5.30pm Mon-Sat. **Credit** AmEx, MC, V.

One of London's most successful boutiques. The rich mix of designers includes Megan Park, Betty Jackson, Mulberry and Clements Ribeiro. Rising stars include NY designer Jane Mayle and Andrew Roberts' exquisitely tailored suits for women. The biggest treat is the shop's own range of beautiful cashmere knitwear.

Koh Samui

65-67 Monmouth Street, Covent Garden, WC2H 9DG (7240 4280/www.kohsamui.co.uk). Covent Garden tube. **Open** 10am-6.30pm Mon, Sat; 10.30am-6.30pm Tue, Wed, Fri; 10.30am-7pm Thur; 11.30am-6pm Sun. **Credit** AmEx, DC, MC, V. **Map** p399 L6.

One of the capital's premier cutting-edge clothes emporiums. The collection is as strong as ever with old favourites Chloé, Marc by Marc Jacobs, Dries van Noten, Balenciaga and Missoni much in evidence plus a smattering of rising stars like Victim Grain.

Labour of Love

193 Upper Street, Islington, N1 1RQ (7354 9333). Highbury & Islington tube/rail. **Open** 10.30am-6.30pm Mon-Wed, Fri, Sat; 10.30am-7pm Thur; 12.30-5.30pm Sun. **Credit** MC, V. **Map** p402 O1.

This stylishly quirky boutique sells the wares of small, independent designers who are passionate about their craft. Recommended.

Miss Lala's Boudoir

144 Gloucester Avenue, Primrose Hill, NW1 8JA (7483 1888). Chalk Farm tube. **Open** 10.30am-6.30pm Mon-Wed, Fri, Sat; 10.30am-7pm Thur. **Credit** DC, MC, V.

Fine Rees' shop is a pretty, tongue-in-cheek take on a burlesque-queen emporium, billing itself a 'dressing-up shop for grown-up girls'. As you might expect from the name, cheeky lingerie labels are the stock in trade here, but it's not all sexy nothings – Miss Lala T-shirts embellished with sequins, crystals and glitter, Holly Golightly's cashmere cardies with faux-fur collars and cuffs, and the shop's signature tutu skirts (from £190) are typical beyond-the-bedroom alternative buys.

Budget/mid range chains

Other brands that are worth checking out include **Miss Selfridge** (36-38 Great Castle Street, entrance on Oxford Street, W1W 8LG, 7927 0214, www.miss-selfridge.net), which has tapped into the recent retro obsession via its Miss Vintage line, and **Dorothy Perkins** (189 Oxford Street, W1D 2JY, 7494 3769, www.dorothyperkins.co.uk), a more conservative bet for well-detailed wardrobe staples.

French Connection

396 Oxford Street, Oxford Circus, W1C 7JX (7629 7766/www.frenchconnection.com). Bond Street tube. **Open** 10am-8pm Mon-Wed, Fri; 10am-9pm Thur; 10am-7pm Sat; noon-6pm Sun. **Credit** AmEx, MC, V. **Map** p398 J6.
FCUK for England. Cool as FCUK. FCUK it… just some of the slogans recently emblazoned on French Connection's T-shirts. Though the risqué name suggests a streetwise image, the clothes are mostly on the comfortable side of cutting-edge, but high quality and with a modern, body-conscious fit. Menswear, accessories, a home range and beauty products mean you can FCUK up your whole life. Nothing is dirt cheap.

Karen Millen

262-264 Regent Street, Oxford Circus, W1R 5AD (7287 6158/www.karenmillen.com). Oxford Circus tube. **Open** 10am-7.30pm Mon-Wed, Fri, Sat; 10am-8pm Thur; noon-6pm Sun. **Credit** AmEx, DC, MC, V. **Map** p398 J6.
Sharp, sexy suits – the kind that demand to be worn with high heels – are the British designer's trademark,

Eat, Drink, Shop

Quality street

You don't need your finger on the fashion pulse to know that London is the place to buy quirky, cool lines in clothing, but catwalk chic at a snippet of the price? Londoners have long been watching the results of unions between top designers and stores like Topshop, Debenhams and New Look (as you'll witness by the stylish customers tussling over the latest Eley Kishimoto or Tatty Devine), but low-brow staples like Etam and Allders? One thing's for sure: the high street is going high fashion. What these stores are doing is collaborating with big-name designers, such as Duffer, Tracey Boyd and Clements Ribeiro who are doing high-street versions of their catwalk designs, sold at high-street prices; and the results are certainly worth pushing through the crowds for.

From the retailers' side, it's about turning a coin. Consider that Debenhams, which has been working with fashion names for the past ten years, recently shifted 10,000 John Rocha coats and you can see the attraction. Duffer's designer Joseph Pollard, who oversaw Saint George by Duffer for Debenhams (one of its most recent acquisitions), says: 'It's not in either of our interests if there isn't money to be made from this. Our range allows Debenhams to access a cooler area of the market and will generate a lot of money.' But money isn't everyone's motive. 'We don't look at it as a mass market

commercial opportunity at all,' says Jane Shepherdson, brand director at Topshop, which has been working with designers (starting with Hussein Chalayan) for six years, and sponsors the new Generation Award at London Fashion Week. 'We do it because we are seriously interested in design and keen to keep in touch with what's happening.'
So what's the difference between the high-street range and the real thing? Tracey Boyd says: 'My Boyd customer won't get the same thing by walking into Etam and buying from the "Love from Tracey Boyd" range, although the essence of Boyd is still there, with special things like embroidery, prints and sequins.' Which seems to be the winning formula: high-street collections, simplified and with less workmanship than catwalk pieces, still bear the designer label's signature aesthetic.

With competition so strong, the undoubted winner is the consumer, who can cherry-pick the best products. Provided prices are enticing. 'You can either go expensive real designer, or it's high street,' says Sarah Walter, New Look's fashion consultant – who brought the company Luella Bartley, Eley Kishimoto, Tatty Devine, Karen Walker and, more recently, tailoring whiz Pamela Blundell. 'Our prices are in line with the rest of the products.' As are Topshop's, where a Jonathan Saunders dress will be about £60; a fraction of his catwalk price tags.

but every sartorial need of the confident girl about town is catered for. Tailoring is reasonable but some separates are less good value.

Kookaï

257-259 Oxford Street, Oxford Circus, W1R 2DD (7408 2391/www.kookai.co.uk). Oxford Circus tube. **Open** 10am-7pm Mon-Wed, Sat; 10am-8pm Thur, Fri; noon-6pm Sun. **Credit** AmEx, DC, MC, V. **Map** p398 J6.

Oh là là! The shapes and detailing may change with the catwalk trends, but Kookaï's slinky, strappy tops, figure-skimming dresses and derrière-hugging trousers always exude Parisian sex appeal. And you don't have to be as petite as a young Bardot to wear them, as the clothes go up to size 16. Quality is good condsidering the prices – around £20 for a top and from £60 for a dress.

Monsoon

5-6 James Street, Covent Garden, WC2E 8BH (7379 3623/www.monsoon.co.uk). Covent Garden tube. **Open** 10am-8pm Mon-Sat; 11am-6pm Sun. **Credit** AmEx, DC, MC, V. **Map** p401 L6.

An eclectic collection with broad appeal, mixing boho looks and current trends. Prices won't break the bank (from £40 for a skirt or sweater, from £60 for a tailored jacket). Good for interesting eveningwear.

Oasis

12-14 Argyll Street, Oxford Circus, W1F 7NT (7434 1799/www.oasis-stores.com). Oxford Circus tube. **Open** 10am-7pm Mon-Wed, Fri, Sat; 10am-8pm Thur; noon-6pm Sun. **Credit** AmEx, MC, V. **Map** p398 J6.

This one has really come into its own, boasting high-profile celeb customers such as Sophie Ellis Bextor and Charlotte Church. Cuts are elegant with a demure retro feel echoed in the fabrics, and quality has improved dramatically. Several interesting sub-ranges have recently been introduced: New Vintage, based on thrift-shop finds and pretty Odile lingerie.

Topshop

36-38 Great Castle Street, Oxford Circus, W1W 8LG (7636 7700/www.topshop.co.uk). Oxford Circus tube. **Open** 9am-8pm Mon-Wed,

New Look.

Which means the only hardship left for shoppers is onerous task of deciding which range they should plump for.
Allders *499-517 Oxford Street, Mayfair, WC1 2BB (7855 4300/www.allders.com).*
Etam *508 Oxford Street, Marylebone, W1C 1NX (7629 1430/www.etam.com).*
Debenhams *334-348 Oxford Street, Marylebone, W1C 1JG (7580 3000/ www.debenhams.com).*
New Look *500-502 Oxford Street, Marylebone, W1C 7LH (7290 7860/www.newlook.co.uk).*
Topshop *36-38 Great Castle Street, Fitzrovia, W1W 8LG (7636 7700/www.topshop.co.uk).*

Fri, Sat; 9am-9pm Thur; noon-6pm Sun. **Credit** AmEx, DC, MC, V. **Map** p398 J6.

Topshop has worked hard to build up its now undisputed fashion cachet and widen its customer base. Recent innovations include free personal style advisers and a trendy maternity range. Topshop is known for nurturing young talent, and the Boutique on level -1 features designs by recent graduates alongside specially commissioned ranges by well-known avant garde designers. Descend even further into the bowels of 'the world's largest fashion store' to level -2 for the vintage department stuffed with gems such as 1970s Adidas tops and glitzy '80s frocks.

Zara

118 Regent Street, Oxford Circus, W1B 5SE (7534 9500/www.zara.com). Piccadilly Circus tube. **Open** 10am-7pm Mon-Wed, Fri, Sat; 10am-8pm Thur; noon-6pm Sun. **Credit** AmEx, DC, MC, V. **Map** p398 J6.

Spanish supremo Zara seems set for global domination with over 650 stores worldwide. The womenswear looks better than ever – these aren't mere catwalk knockoffs, but good-quality clothes in their own right. The Basic range is great for wardrobe staples at ridiculous prices. The Knightsbridge branch (79-81 Brompton Road, SW3 1DB, 7590 6990) also sells menswear, kids' clothes and Zara Home.

Miss Lala's Boudoir. Whatever would Tinky Winky think? *See p239*.

Children

Caramel

291 Brompton Road, South Kensington, SW3 2DY (7589 7001). South Kensington tube. **Open** 10am-6.30pm Mon-Sat; noon-5pm Sun. **Credit** AmEx, MC, V. **Map** p397 E9.

Ring the bell to enter this chicer-than-chic designer shop. The deliciously cuddly, cashmere pullover for six-month-olds (from £65) and teeny Prada trainers (£90) are for seriously label-led yummy mummies. There are rompers, skirts and trousers for children up to ten, plus accessories and the odd toy.

Children's Book Centre

237 Kensington High Street, Kensington, W8 6SA (7937 7497/www.childrensbookcentre.co.uk). High Street Kensington tube. **Open** 9.30am-6.30pm Mon, Wed, Fri, Sat; 9.30am-7pm Thur; noon-6pm Sun. **Credit** AmEx, MC, V. **Map** p396 A9.

A visit to this two-storey treasure trove yields far more than books. The ground level has a small selection of clothes, including the trendy Punky Fish label, plus accessories, stationery, posters and toys. Kids can try out computer games on the PC at the back.

Daisy & Tom

181-183 King's Road, Chelsea, SW3 5EB (7352 5000/www.daisyandtom.com). Sloane Square tube, then 11, 319, 22 bus. **Open** 9.30am-6pm Mon-Wed, Fri; 10am-7pm Thur, Sat; 11am-5pm Sun. **Credit** AmEx, MC, V. **Map** p397 E12.

A fun-packed emporium of quality kids' clothes, nursery equipment and toys, with lots of play opportunities and demos. Junior shoppers are entertained by the in-house puppet shows (every 25 minutes) and the traditional ground-floor carousel.

Primark

King's Mall, King Street, Hammersmith, W6 0PZ (8748 7119/www.primark.co.uk). Hammersmith tube. **Open** 9am-6pm Mon-Sat; 11am-5pm Sun. **Credit** MC, V.

Why so snobbish? This Irish bargain store has plenty of uses. Perfect for quick, cheap holiday extras. **Other locations**: throughout the city.

Sasti

8 Portobello Green Arcade, Ladbroke Grove, 281 Portobello Road, W10 5TZ (8960 1125/ www.sasti.co.uk). Ladbroke Grove tube. **Open** 10am-6pm Mon-Sat. **Credit** AmEx, MC, V.

Children with flamboyant tastes like it here. Little prima donnas love body warmers in pink fake fur or leopard-skin print and fluffy red coats with pink hearts. Boys like the POW! and ZAP! T-shirts. Look out for cowboy-style fringed denims and cute knickers with three layers of frilly netting.

Street

Bread & Honey

205 Whitecross Street, The City, EC1Y 8QP (7253 4455/www.breadnhoney.com). Barbican tube or Old Street tube/rail. **Open** 10am-6pm Mon-Thur; 10am-7pm Fri; 11am-5pm Sat. **Credit** AmEx, MC, V. **Map** p402 P4.

An eclectic collection of funky, upscale streetwear mixing familiar labels like Stüssy with young newcomers (Peruvian brand Misericordia) and hip brands like Treatyaself, Urino and Militia. As well as clothes, the store stocks accessories like Sweetfoot foam clogs and Reino jewellery, toys, books and magazines. There's even an on-site barber.

Concrete
35A Marshall Street, Soho, W1F 7EX (7434 4546/ www.concretelondon.com). Oxford Circus tube. **Open** 10.30am-6.30pm Mon-Fri; 11am-6.30pm Sat. **Credit** AmEx, MC, V. **Map** p398 J6.
Concrete is all about taking a chance on the new and the thought-provoking, with labels such as Asish, Maria Marta Fachinelli, Mansharey, Dubuc and Camilla Staerk making Concrete more than just a place to name-drop (though Kate Moss does shop here, among many other hip names). Designed like a rather decadent living room, it also has a section devoted to homeware and accessories.

Maharishi
19A Floral Street, Covent Garden, WC2E 9HL (7836 3860/www.emaharishi.com). Covent Garden tube. **Open** 10am-7pm Mon-Sat; noon-5pm Sun. **Credit** AmEx, MC, V. **Map** p399 L6.
Hemp clothing based on simple military shapes, with subtly tweaked camouflage patterns and embroidery. Eastern mysticism is key to what Maharishi is all about, so care labels on the garments contain positive messages dedicated to the wearer rather than to the clothes.

Microzine
66-67 Colebrooke Row, Islington, N1 8AB (7704 6667/www.microzine.co.uk). Angel tube. **Open** 11am-6pm Mon-Fri; 10am-7pm Sat; noon-6pm Sun. **Credit** MC, V, AmEx. **Map** p402 O2.
Microzine brings in fresh stock every month, all of it aimed straight at the kind of guy who reads *Arena*. Designed in the style of a disturbingly trendy bachelor pad, it provides all the blokeish ephemera you could ever wish for.

Urban Outfitters
36-38 Kensington High Street, Kensington, W8 4PF (7761 1001/www.urbanoutfitters.com). High Street Kensington tube. **Open** 10am-7pm Mon-Wed, Fri, Sat; 10am-8pm Thur; noon-6pm Sun. **Credit** AmEx, MC, V. **Map** p394 B8.
Much more than hip streetwear. At this aptly named American emporium, you can kit out your wardrobe and flat, and then even add to your record collection. Men's clothing comes courtesy of Surface to Air, John Smedley, Emperor's New Clothing and G Star, to name but a few. For women there's a similarly wide selection of brands. The staggering array of accessories includes bags and jewellery, plus funky underwear and an 'Urban Renewal' range of vintage clothing that gives old garments a new lease of life. **Other locations**: 42-56 Earlham Street, WC2H 9LA (7759 6390); 200-201 Oxford Street, W1D 1NU (7907 0800).

Weardowney Get-Up Boutique
9 Ashbridge Street, Marylebone, NW8 8DH (7258 3087/www.weardowney.com). Marylebone

tube/rail. **Open** 10am-4pm Mon-Sat. **Credit** AmEx, MC, V. **Map** p395 E4.
The Get-Up Boutique's exuberant knitwear features vintage-inspired wrap dresses and shrugs, frilly knickers and, for men, oversized stripy wool boxers. While many people live above their shop, Gail Downey and Amy Wear live inside theirs, complete with kids and a dog.

Underwear

Agent Provocateur
6 Broadwick Street, Soho, W1V 1FH (7439 0229/ www.agentprovocateur.com). Oxford Circus tube. **Open** 11am-7pm Mon-Sat. **Credit** AmEx, MC, V. **Map** p397 F10.
Agent Provocateur is the brainchild of Vivienne Westwood's son Joseph Corre and his partner Serena Rees. It serves up decadent sauciness but without descending into sleaze. Celebs and city boys alike flock here to be served by nubile staff wearing undersized pink nurses' unforms and killer heels. Prices can be high, but so is the quality, and there are some beautiful fabrics and details.
Other locations: 16 Pont Street, Knightsbridge, SW1X 9EN (7235 0229); Royal Exchange, Threadneedle Street, The City, EC3V 3LL (7623 0229); 18 Mansfield Street, Marylebone (7927 6999); 305 Westbourne Grove, W11 2QA (7243 1292).

Aware
25 Old Compton Street, Soho, W1D 5JN (7287 3789/www.awareunderwear.co.uk). Leicester Square tube. **Open** 11am-8pm Mon-Sat; noon-7pm Sun. **Credit** AmEx, MC, V. **Map** p399 K6.
This diminutive shop sells a comprehensive collection of men's designer labels. Expect to find boxers and briefs by Diesel, Puma, Dolce & Gabbana, Energie, Hom and Armani. Swimwear, close-fitting T-shirts and beachwear are also available.

Rigby & Peller
22A Conduit Street, Mayfair, W1S 2XT (7491 2200/www.rigbyandpeller.com). Oxford Circus tube. **Open** 9.30am-6pm Mon-Wed, Fri, Sat; 9.30am-7pm Thur. **Credit** AmEx, MC, V. **Map** p397 F9.
Her Majesty's corsetière has been measuring busts since 1939. The company prides itself on its free expert fitting service – highly trained staff can often accurately guess your size by sight. They offer bras ready made and made to measure. Styles tend to be ultra-feminine, and prices match the quality. Bespoke bras start at £250.
Other locations: 2 Hans Road, Knightsbridge, SW3 1RX (7589 9293).

Vintage

Bertie Wooster
284 Fulham Road, Fulham, SW10 9DW (7352 5662/ www.bertie-wooster.co.uk). Earl's Court or Fulham Broadway tube. **Open** 10am-6pm Mon-Wed, Fri; 10am-7pm Thur; 10am-4.30pm Sat. **Credit** MC, V.

Bargain abasement

London's obsession with the January sales.

Of course the term January sales is something of a misnomer. Wait till January? You must be joking! Most sales actually start on December 27 or even Boxing Day.

With sales, shopping becomes less of a leisure activity, more of a mission. No one knows this better than Londoners. We're used to queuing for buses, art exhibitions and lattes, so queues per se aren't the problem. Neither are the crowds. No, the trouble is the total lack of any form of shopping etiquette after everyone has rushed in. It's the free-for-all frenzy with every man, woman and child out for themselves.

If you think it's bad for the customer, spare a thought for those working on the shop floor. It can't be fun refereeing this scrum. Gather a bunch of assistants in the staff room of any of the capital's big department stores during sales time, and you'll hear tales of desperate shoppers making offers for empty shelves (yes, really), hiding items at the back of the rails (in the wrong department) while they go away and 'think about it'. Then there's the perennial problem faced by anyone working in footwear. One source at **Selfridges** (see p237), who wishes to remain anonymous, tells us that every year, at the end of a busy sales day, there is guaranteed to be at least one pair of old shoes left behind as someone sneaks out with a brand new pair on their feet.

Harrods (see p236), the world's most famous sale, is one of the few that is true to its January name, starting on the first Monday and ending on the last Saturday of the month. It also attracts the capital's most crazed shoppers – up to 30,000 on the first day (when takings have exceeded £14million). Its perfect moment of sales madness occurred when a dazed woman, laden with bags, stumbled into the gents,

and glared at the security guard before barking: 'Well, is this lift going up or down?'

But be prepared to queue: in 2003 a 17-year-old student made a record-breaking dash (12 seconds) for a Plasma screen TV reduced from £3,999 to £100, after waiting in a queue alongside more than 200 people, one of whom had been there for three and a half days.

Harvey Nichols (see p237), on the other hand, prides itself on being a little more sedate. The shoppers it attracts are more sophisticated, believes Heather Short, sales manager for first-floor fashions: 'Our customers walk quickly, but don't run.'

Sounds civilised. So what other tips does Short have for the urbane shopper? 'Do your homework and be destination specific,' she advises. 'Look at the stock before the sales start, try on possible purchases and befriend an assistant.' Tricky, no? 'It's easier than you imagine,' she says. 'It's essential to have someone on the shop floor who will recognise you. The layout is always different during sales, so you'll need help.'

Other ways to disassociate yourself from the bridge-and-tunnel brigade include leaving your heels at home, so you won't spend the day moaning about aching feet, and remembering to eat and drink (to restrict any dehydrated moment of madness). And 'Don't carry too much; in other words, leave both hands free,' says Harrods' Michael Mann.

Short recommends starting your sales shopping before Christmas at those stores that open. 'Our savviest customers know that the most reduced stock, which is at least one season old, is previewed on Christmas Eve,' she says. In other stores, the best bargains can always be found on the first and last days of the sales. The final day can especially be fruitful when prices are reduced even further.

If you're a man who likes to look sharp but can't afford Savile Row prices, this shop is the next best thing, selling top-quality, second-hand tailored suits, jackets, formal hats and handmade leather shoes. Pick up an immaculate suit for £110, a tweed jacket for £95 and pair of John Lobb shoes for around £25.

Butler & Wilson

189 Fulham Road, Chelsea, SW3 6JN (7352 8255/ www.butlerandwilson.co.uk). South Kensington tube. **Open** 10am-6pm Mon, Tue, Thur-Sat; 10am-7pm Wed; noon-6pm Sun. **Credit** AmEx, MC, V. **Map** p397 E11.

Better known for its range of bold and brash costume jewellery, Butler & Wilson will also show you a fantastic selection of vintage drama-queen clothes if you ask them nicely. There's a good choice of shawls, beaded 1920s dresses, sinuous bias-cut 1930s numbers and a fine collection of exotically oriental dresses and shawls. The shop stocks vintage Liberty and Dior, as well as dresses made from old Chanel and Hermès scarves. Prices are above average – a 1950s skirt will set you back £300 and over, dresses can go for up to £1,000.

The Girl Can't Help It/ Cad Van Swankster

G100, Alfie's Antique Market, 13-25 Church Street, Marylebone, NW8 8DT (7724 8984/www. sparklemoore.com). Edgware Road tube/Marylebone tube/rail. **Open** 10am-6pm Tue-Sat. **Credit** AmEx, MC, V. **Map** p395 E4.

Wonderfully chi-chi owner Sparkle Moore goes to New York regularly to stock up on fantastical American vintage lingerie. The adjoining stall is owned by Cad Van Swankster, who has lots of bar-themed wear for guys, from hand-painted 1940s ties to Hawaiian shirts and kitsch cufflinks.

Fashion accessories & services

General

Accessorize

22 The Market, Covent Garden, WC2 8HB (7240 2107/www.accessorize.co.uk). Covent Garden tube. **Open** 9am-8pm Mon-Fri; 10am-8pm Sat; 11am-7pm Sun. **Credit** AmEx, DC, MC, V. **Map** p401 L6.

This high-street staple keeps quality high and prices low. Accessories are regularly updated: woolly hats, striped scarves, bags and jewellery crop up each winter; flip flops and beach hats join the bags and jewellery for summer.

Other locations: throughout the city.

Doors by Jas MB

8 Ganton Street, Soho, W1F 7PQ (7494 2288). Oxford Circus tube. **Open** 10am-6pm Mon-Sat. **Credit** MC, V. **Map** p400 J7.

Jas Sehmbi's career has seen him go from designing record bags in Soho to creating one-offs for the Louis Vuitton store in Japan. Opened in May 2004, Doors is his latest project and fills a gap in the market, providing streetwise accessories for fashionable chaps.

Dry cleaning & laundry

Blossom & Browne's Sycamore

73A Clarendon Road, Notting Hill, W11 4JF (7727 2635/www.blossomandbrowne.co.uk). Holland Park tube. **Open** 8.30am-5.30pm Mon-Wed, Fri; 8.30am-4.30pm Thur; 8.30am-3pm Sat. **Credit** MC, V.

This venerable launderer and dry-cleaner caters to Her Maj. A two-piece suit costs from £10, an evening dress from £40. The 'jet-set' service for travellers cleans and repacks the contents of a suitcase. Alterations and repairs are undertaken, and delivery is free.

Danish Express

16 Hinde Street, Marylebone, W1M 5AR (7935 6306). Bond Street tube. **Open** 8.30am-5.30pm Mon-Fri; 9.30am-1.30pm Sat. **Credit** AmEx, MC, V. **Map** p398 G5.

Everything from sheets to shirts (£2.15). There's a 'bag wash' service, costing around £6.50 per six kilos.

Jewellery

Asprey

167 New Bond Street, Mayfair, W1S 4AR (7493 6767/www.asprey.com). Bond Street or Green Park tube. **Open** 10am-6pm Mon- Sat. **Credit** AmEx, DC, MC, V. **Map** p398 H6.

This imposingly grand flagship has recently undergone a major facelift; Keira Knightley was signed up as the label's 'face' to emphasise that there's a fresh aspect to this sophisticated, traditional jewellery. Which there isn't, really, despite updates to the classic Daisy range.

Angela Hale

5 Royal Arcade, 28 Old Bond Street, Mayfair, W1S 4SE (7495 1920). Green Park tube. **Open** 10am-6pm Mon-Sat. **Credit** AmEx, MC, V. **Map** p400 J7.

The romantic, whimsical aesthetics of Angela Hale's designs will make any girl swoon. This little boutique is awash with costume jewellery in any colour you care to name and set with Swarovski crystals.

Aurum

8 Avery Row, Mayfair, W1K 4AL (7499 9222/www. aurumgallery.com). Bond Street tube. **Open** 11am-6.30pm Mon-Wed, Fri; 11am-7pm Thur; 11am-5pm Sat. **Credit** AmEx, MC, V. **Map** p400 6H.

Aurum has just opened a branch in swish Mayfair, which showcases designs by some brilliant new talents of the jewellery world, including Scott Wilson, Tina Engell and Shaun Leane. Leane was crowned British Jewellery Designer of the Year in 2004, and celeb fans include David Bowie and Liv Tyler.

Other locations: 12 England's Lane, Hampstead, NW3 4TG (7586 8656).

Garrard

24 Albemarle Street, Mayfair, W1Y 4HT (7758 8520/www.garrard.com). Bond Street or Green Park tube. **Open** 10am-6pm Mon-Fri; 10am-5pm Sat. **Credit** AmEx, DC, MC, V. **Map** p400 J7.

The crown jewellers' flirtation with cool flourishes, thanks to Jade Jagger. Her input as creative director modernised Garrard's designs to such an extent that Missy Elliott has been sparkling in its bling-tastic creations. But those with traditional tastes still pay stratospheric prices for classic diamond jewellery.

Lesley Craze Gallery

33-35A Clerkenwell Green, Clerkenwell, EC1R 0DU (7608 0393/www.lesleycrazegallery.co.uk). Farringdon tube/rail. **Open** 10am-5.30pm Tue-Sat. **Credit** AmEx, DC, MC, V. **Map** p402 N4.

Diamonds aren't the focus here, but the jewellery is certainly cutting-edge. Over 100 designers are showcased, from as far afield as Australia, Japan and the Netherlands, working with precious metals and imaginative mixed media. From affordable to unthinkable.

Tiffany & Co

25 Old Bond Street, Mayfair, W1S 4QB (7409 2790/ www.tiffany.com/uk). Green Park tube. **Open** 10am-6pm Mon-Fri; 10am-5.30pm Sat. **Credit** AmEx, MC, V. **Map** p400 J7.

Eat, Drink, Shop

You might only be able to afford a £50 silver key-ring, but some of that Audrey Hepburn glamour will still rub off at the legendary Tiffany's. The range of diamond engagement rings (£800-£965,000) is to sigh for. Though famous for its diamonds, the company also has other ranges.
Other locations: Royal Exchange, Threadneedle Street, The City, EC3V 3LQ (7495 3511).

Shoes

Aldo
3-7 Neal Street, Covent Garden, WC2H 9PU (7836 7692/www.aldoshoes.com). Covent Garden, Holborn or Leicester Square tube. **Open** 10am-8pm Mon-Sat; noon-7pm Sun. **Credit** AmEx, MC, V. **Map** p399 L6.
For sheer choice at surprisingly cheap prices, it's hard to beat this vast Canadian shoe emporium, which is stocked with a dizzying array of styles for men and women. Top marks for interpreting catwalk styles at lower prices.
Other locations: 309 Oxford Street, W1C 2HW (7499 4348); 146-148 Oxford Street, W1D 1NB (7436 4940); 141 Kensington High Street, W8 6SU (7937 7996).

Audley
72 Duke of York Square, King's Road, Chelsea, SW3 4LY (7730 2902/www.audley.com). Sloane Square tube. **Open** 10am-6pm Mon, Tue, Thur-Sat; 10am-7pm Wed; noon-5pm Sun. **Credit** AmEx, MC, V. **Map** p397 F11.
Audley started life as a bespoke shoemaker, and it shows in the artful lines and fine details of these well-made shoes. Prices are in line with upper-end high-street chains (around £100 for shoes; £200 for boots). For an extra £75, you can have a pair made up in a different colour to match an outfit. A handmade-to-order service is planned for 2005.

Birkenstock
70 Neal Street, Covent Garden, WC2H 9PR (7240 2783/www.birkenstock.co.uk). Covent Garden or Leicester Square tube. **Open** 10.30am-7pm Mon-Wed, Fri, Sat; 10.30am-8pm Thur; noon-6pm Sun. **Credit** AmEx, MC, V. **Map** p399 L6.
Although it's moved to more spacious premises down the road, the only stand-alone Birkenstock store in the UK still has a queue outside most days, especially in the heat of summer. It offers the ultimate selection of the famous ergonomic sandals, clogs and shoes – including a groovy range styled by supermodel Heidi Klum.

Jimmy Choo
169 Draycott Avenue, Chelsea, SW3 3AJ (7584 6111/www.jimmychoo.com). South Kensington tube. **Open** 10am-6pm Mon, Tue, Thur-Sat; 10am-7pm Wed; 1-6pm Sun. **Credit** AmEx, MC, V. **Map** p397 E10.
It seems everywhere you go there's a Jimmy Choo outlet – Selfridges, Harvey Nicks, Bond Street, South Ken... Yet there seems to be no danger of Choo fatigue: eager buyers at all of the above splash out hundreds on each exquisitely made pair, and on the

equally popular matching bags. Shapes are sleek, ladylike and impeccably crafted, for day or night.

Kurt Geiger
65 South Molton Street, Mayfair, W1K 5SU (7758 8020/www.kurtgeiger.com). Bond Street tube. **Open** 10am-7pm Mon-Wed, Fri, Sat; 10am-8pm Thur; noon-6pm Sun. **Credit** AmEx, DC, MC, V. **Map** p398 H6.
The ubiquitous department-store label has shaken off the last vestiges of its staid image with designs that look like they stepped right off the catwalk at surprisingly affordable prices. There are lots of exciting shapes, colours and materials in both the main line and the younger, edgier kg label (from £29). In the slick flagship store, a selection of designer shoes is also on display.

Manolo Blahnik
49-51 Old Church Street, Chelsea, SW3 5BS (7352 3863). Sloane Square tube, then 11, 19, 22 bus. **Open** 10am-5.30pm Mon-Fri; 10.30am-5pm Sat. **Credit** AmEx, MC, V. **Map** p397 D11.
This small salon is remarkably low-key for such a globally celebrated designer. For more than 30 years a fiercely loyal clientele, including numerous (undisclosed) celebs, has sought out flattering, feminine heels with lots of striking details. The bad news? £300 upwards.

Tailors

Since the middle of the 19th century, **Savile Row**, Mayfair, W1, has been the traditional home of men's tailoring.

Consummate tailoring at **Ozwald Boateng**. *See p247.*

Ozwald Boateng

9 Vigo Street, Mayfair, W1X 1AL (7437 0620/
www.ozwaldboateng.com). Green Park tube. **Open**
10am-6pm Mon-Wed; 10am-7pm Thur-Sat. **Credit**
AmEx, MC, V. **Map** p400 J7.

One of the breed of cool tailors who colonised Savile
Row about a decade ago, Ozwald Boateng has a
fashion designer's flair – indeed, he's now creative
director for Givenchy menswear. In addition to the
bespoke service (from £3,000 for a suit), Boateng sells
made-to-measure (from £1,400) and ready-to-wear
(from £795). A cheaper diffusion line is sold at House
of Fraser, Oxford Street, and branches of Cecil Gee.

H Huntsman & Sons

11 Savile Row, Mayfair, W1S 3PF (7734 7441/
www.h-huntsman.com). Piccadilly Circus tube.
Open 9am-5.30pm Mon-Fri. **Credit** AmEx, DC,
MC, V. **Map** p400 J7.

This level of quality comes at a price – expect to shell
out over £3,000 for a suit handmade on the premises,
although ready-to-wear versions are available from
£1,000. Huntsman's also produces its own fabrics,
introducing new tweeds each year and resurrecting
designs from the archives.

Food & drink

Many department stores (*see p236*) have
fabulous food halls. For food markets, *see p256*.

Bakeries & pâtisseries

Along with those listed here, there are others in
the **Restaurants & Cafés** chapter (*see pp192-
219*). There are plenty of pâtisseries in Soho,
including on Old Compton Street, **Amato
Caffe/Pasticceria** (No.14, 7734 5733) and
Pâtisserie Valerie (No.44, 7437 3466).

& Clarke's

*122 Kensington Church Street, Kensington, W8
4BU (7229 2190/www.sallyclarke.com). Notting
Hill Gate tube.* **Open** 8am-8pm Mon-Fri; 8am-4pm
Sat. **Credit** AmEx, MC, V. **Map** p394 B8.

It's impossible to enter this shop and leave without a
purchase. Fresh bakes of impeccable quality include
oatmeal honeypot and rosemary, raisin and rock salt
loaves; you'll be tearing pieces off the fragrant fig
and fennel stick (£1.60) before you're out the door.
Breakfast croissants and brioche are also sold.
Sublime bitter chocolate truffles, sweet and savoury
biscuits, Italian olive oils, and seasonal own-label
chutneys and jams round off the range.

Jones Dairy

23 Ezra Street, Bethnal Green, E2 7RH (7739 5372/
www.jonesdairy.co.uk). Bus 26, 48, 55. **Open** *Shop*
8am-1pm Fri, Sat; 9am-2pm Sun. *Café* 9am-3pm Fri,
Sat; 8am-2pm Sun. **No credit cards. Map** p403 S3.

A visit to Jones is like stepping back in time. The
big marble counter, laden with free-range eggs, jams
and chutneys, is surrounded by baskets of seasonal

fruit and vegetables. Farm cheeses include beauties
like Montgomery's cheddars, Colston Bassett stiltons
and Appleby cheshires. Breads are sourced from
artisan bakers, and there are also bagels, croissants
(plain and almond) and pains au chocolat. The
attached café does a roaring trade on Sundays when
the Columbia Road flower market is in full swing.

Confectioners

L'Artisan du Chocolat

*89 Lower Sloane Street, Chelsea, SW1W 8DA
(7824 8365/www.artisanduchocolat.com). Sloane
Square tube.* **Open** 10am-7pm Mon-Sat. **Credit**
MC, V. **Map** p400 G11.

Combining both artistry and craftsmanship, Gerald
Coleman creates some of London's most innovative
chocolates. Unusual flavour combinations and top-
notch ingredients have won him high renown –
Heston Blumenthal is a long-standing fan of the
tobacco variety. House classics include delectable sea-
salted caramels and intense pavé truffles (£5/100g);
but there are also quirkier varieties such as ganaches
of green cardamom or Lapsang Souchong. There's a
stall at Borough Market on most Saturdays.

The Chocolate Society

*36 Elizabeth Street, Belgravia, SW1W 9NZ (7259
9222/www.chocolate.co.uk). Sloane Square tube.*
Open 9.30am-5.30pm Mon-Fri; 9.30am-4pm Sat.
Credit MC, V. **Map** p400 G10.

This society is dedicated to elevating chocolate
to its rightful status as one of life's gourmet delights.
The own-brand and Valrhona ranges are prime
examples of subtlety, aroma and flavour. During
the summer, a small café area offers divine hot
chocolate, brownies and ice-cream.

Pierre Marcolini

6 Lancer Square, Kensington, W8 4EH (7795 6611/
*www.pierremarcolini.co.uk). High Street Kensington
tube.* **Open** 10am-7pm Mon-Sat. **Credit** AmEx, MC,
V. **Map** p394 B8.

The god of Belgian chocolate has finally come to
London. This award-winning company is one of the
few to develop its chocolate all the way from the
selection of the bean to the final product, pralines
being the pièce de résistance. The shop showcases
over 100 different chocs, at £35 for a selection, treats
to savour, not scoff.

Delicatessens

The Delicatessen Shop

*23 South End Road, Hampstead, NW3 2PT
(7435 7315). Hampstead tube/Hampstead Heath
rail/24 bus.* **Open** 9.30am-7pm Mon-Fri; 9am-6pm
Sat. **Credit** MC, V.

The own-made pesto at this 40-year-old deli opposite
Hampstead Heath is such a vivid, summery green
that it looks as though it's been freshly pounded
with just-snipped basil. Other pasta sauces and

Let us eat cake!

After years of being obsessed with the French tart, Londoners are getting back to their roots with a revival of traditional cakes like your mum used to make. Get your teeth stuck into the following, and be proud of getting vanilla icing on your nose.

Hummingbird Bakery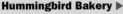

From the chocolate and vanilla cupcakes (topped with those all-important sprinkles) to lemon meringue pie, owner Tarek Malouf offers that deep southern comfort only given by true excess. Even the roll call of names is enough to add inches to your waistline: red velvet cake, chocolate chess pie, Brooklyn blackout cake and crumb-topped chocolate sponge. Get stuck in. *133 Portobello Road, Ladbroke Grove, W11 2DY (7229 6446). Ladbroke Grove or Notting Hill Gate tube.* **Open** 10am-6pm Tue-Thur; 10am-7pm Fri; 10am-6pm Sat; 10am-5pm Sun.

Sweet

After four years as one of the busiest stalls in Borough Market, Sweet recently opened its first shop in Exmouth Market. Unusual items include canneles de Bordeaux (small chewy cakes baked in copper cannele moulds) and Lamingtons (Australian sponge cakes, pictured; £1.50). Jammy. *64 Exmouth Market, Clerkenwell, EC1R 4QP (7713 6777). Farringdon tube/rail.* **Open** 7am-6pm Mon-Fri; 8am-4pm Sat. **Map** p402 4N.
◄

Baker & Spice

This top-end bakery, pâtisserie and traiteur chain sells tempting meringues, fruit tarts and fabulous breads. The cake are eminently wonderful, such as the orange and almond teacakes pictured here – gluten-free, they cost £2.25 each.
54-56 Elizabeth Street, Belgravia, SW1W 9PB (7730 3033). Victoria tube/rail. **Open** *8am-7pm Mon-Sat.* **Map** *p400 G10.* ▶

Treacle

'This is a tea shop, please do not use the C word,' is written on the blackboard of this quintessentially British and charming little shop. Pop in for a mug of builders' tea (£1 per cup), an adorable selection of mini and large cupcakes (with all types of sprinkles from silver balls to pink elephants, from 60p each; £5 per box), Victoria sponges (the likes of Jammy Dodger, £22) and post-war and contemporary ceramics.
160 Columbia Road, Bethnal Green, E2 7RG (7729 5657/www.treacleworld.com). Liverpool Street tube/rail, then 20min walk/bus 26, 48, ▼ *55.* **Open** *9.30am-3.30pm Sun.* **Map** *p403 S3.*

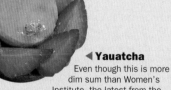

◀ **Yauatcha**

Even though this is more dim sum than Women's Institute, the latest from the man behind Wagamama, Busaba Eathai and Hakkasan has a tea parlour with cakes so beautiful you might find them very hard to eat. Take them away and use them as decoration, or enjoy them in-house with one of the 50 varieties of tea.
15 Broadwick Street, Soho, W1F 0DE (7494 8888). Oxford Circus tube. **Open** *TeaHouse noon-11pm daily.* **Map** *p398 J6.*

own-made fresh pasta are also notable; as are salamis, pepperoni, cheeses such as Ribblesdale (Yorkshire), fresh-roasted coffee and a luscious Tunisian almond and orange bread.

Flâneur Food Hall

41 Farringdon Road, Farringdon, EC1M 3JB (7404 4422). Farringdon tube/rail. **Open** 9am-10pm Mon-Sat; 9am-6pm Sun. **Credit** AmEx, DC, MC, V. **Map** p402 N4/5.

A huge, wood-panelled deli, with a large central service area, and a restaurant at the back. On display is a mind-boggling variety of pickles, preserves, sauces and honeys, plus an unusual variety of oils. Cheeses are attractively displayed on straw, many from Neal's Yard. Also on sale are wines, beers, breads and fresh fruit and veg. Own-made tarts, and cakes are also available. *See also p196.*

The Grocer on Elgin

6 Elgin Crescent, Notting Hill, W11 2HX (7221 3844/www.thegroceron.com). Ladbroke Grove or Notting Hill Gate tube. **Open** 9am-8pm Mon-Fri; 9am-7pm Sat; 10am-6pm Sun. **Credit** MC, V. **Map** p399 K6.

Nominated for this year's *Time Out Shopping Guide* awards, this cool, minimalist deli specialises in attractively packaged, preservative-free, ready-cooked meals from artisanal producers. Other goodies include wild boar and venison salami; stracchino yoghurt cheese; 'mother-in-law's tongue' bread; the Sugar Club range of spices and seasonings; and retro-packaged Starbrook Airlines chocolates.

Other locations: The Grocer on Warwick, 21 Warwick Street, Soho, W1R 5RB.

Megan's Delicatessen

571 King's Road, Chelsea, SW6 2EB (7371 7837/ www.megansdeli.com). Parsons Green or Fulham Broadway tube, then 11, 14, 22 bus. **Open** 8am-6pm Mon-Fri; 9am-6pm Sat. **Credit** AmEx, DC, MC, V. **Map** p396 C13.

Oils, vinegars, pickles, preserves and breads are displayed imaginatively in this stunningly laid-out deli. Don't miss homemade jams and bottles of rose petal, silver birch and rhubarb wines from Lurgashall Winery. A daily-changing menu of salads, hot dishes, soups and cakes is served in a pretty walled garden at the back. From September 2004 it plans to extend its opening hours, invite guest chefs, and offer buffet lunches.

Wines & spirits

Booze store **Oddbins** (www.oddbins.com for locations around London) is also hard to beat.

The Beer Shop

14 Pitfield Street, Hoxton, N1 6EY (7739 3701/ www.pitfieldbeershop.co.uk). Old Street tube/rail. **Open** 11am-7pm Tue-Fri; 10am-4pm Sat. **Credit** MC, V. **Map** p403 Q4.

A beer lover's mecca, packed with a constantly changing range of around 600 unusual bottled beers (and a few cans) from around the globe, with

Belgium and Britain making a sizeable contribution. Seven excellent beers are also brewed at Pitfield's organic brewery next door and for sale here.

Berry Bros & Rudd

3 St James's Street, Mayfair, SW1A 1EG (7396 9600/www.bbr.com). Green Park tube. **Open** 10am-6pm Mon-Fri; 10am-4pm Sat. **Credit** AmEx, DC, MC, V. **Map** p399 K6.

One of the more traditional London wine merchants (operating in St James's since the mid 17th century), but its shop demonstrates a modern take on the wine world. The 'Wines with Personality' list highlights the world's quirkier wine regions. Berry's wines are genuinely good, with a full range of classics and a characterful selection from the New World too. The average bottle price is still around £8 or £9, with frequent special offers and tastings.

Milroy's of Soho

3 Greek Street, Soho, W1V 6NX (7437 9311/www. milroys.co.uk). Tottenham Court Road tube. **Open** 10am-8pm Mon-Sat. **Credit** AmEx, MC, V. **Map** p399 K6.

London's most famous whisky specialist has been around for almost 40 years and stocks one of the biggest ranges in the city, with around 650 different types on offer. Recent expansion has enabled the team to bring in a full range of wines too.

Gifts & stationery

Some museum and gallery shops are also great for gifts. Try **Tate Modern** (*see p83*) for stylish gifts; the **British Museum** (*see p107*) for souvenirs and reproductions and the **Science Museum** (*see p141*) for toys.

Paperchase

213-215 Tottenham Court Road, Bloomsbury, W1T 9PS (7467 6200/www.paperchase.co.uk). Goodge Street tube. **Open** 9.30am-7pm Mon, Wed, Fri, Sat; 10am-7pm Tue; 9.30am-8pm Thur; noon-6pm Sun. **Credit** AmEx, MC, V. **Map** p399 K5.

Paperchase's flagship is a three-storey stationery superstore. The ground floor has calendars, cards, gift wrap and desk storage units, all lovely stuff. Kitsch bits and bobs, fridge poetry, pencils, pens, invitations and coloured notepaper are at the back. The first floor has a more upmarket range, from Lexon accessories, posh pens and clocks to picture frames. Artists' materials fill the second floor.

Other locations: throughout the city.

Smythson

40 New Bond Street, Mayfair, W1S 2DE (7629 8558/www.smythson.com). Bond Street tube. **Open** 9.30am-6pm Mon-Wed, Fri; 10am-6pm Thur, Sat. **Credit** AmEx, DC, MC, V. **Map** p399 H6.

An elegant selection of fine stationery and gifts for those who see the luxuries of creamy paper, bespoke gold stamping and hand-engraving as *de rigueur*. Other classy (and pricey) items include diaries, photo albums, manicure sets and wallets.

The Beer Shop: it does what it says on the can. *See p250.*

Beauty services

Several hotels also have excellent spa facilities open to the public, including the **Sanderson** (*see p49*) and the **Dorchester** (*p55*).

Calmia

52-54 Marylebone High Street, Marylebone, W1U 5HR (7224 3585/www.calmia.com). Baker Street tube. **Open** *Spa* 9am-9pm Mon-Sat; 10am-7pm Sun. *Store* 10am-7pm Mon-Sat; 10am-6pm Sun. **Credit** AmEx, MC, V. **Map** p398 G5.

Upstairs, a shop sells everything from herbal remedies to scented candles, designer clothes and yoga gear. Beauty brands stocked include Dermalogica, Dr Hauschka, Red Flower and Naturopathica. Downstairs in the spa, enjoy treatments such as Calmia Essential Harmony (£70), 60 minutes of manipulation and eventual meltdown. We rate this place highly.

The Refinery

60 Brook Street, Mayfair, W1K 5DU (7409 2001/ www.the-refinery.com). Bond Street tube. **Open** 10am-7pm Mon, Tue; 10am-9pm Wed-Fri; 9am-6pm Sat; 11am-5pm Sun. **Credit** MC, V. **Map** p398 H6.

This spa within an impressive Mayfair townhouse is designed entirely for men. The Refinery aims for a 'clubby' feel, and the expert staff cater for the likes of Pierce Brosnan. Treatments range from quick massages and facials (£20) to LaStone therapy (£100 for 90mins) and therapeutic massage.

This Works

18 Cale Street, Chelsea, SW3 3QU (7584 1887/ www.thisworks.com). Sloane Square tube. **Open** 10am-6pm Mon-Sat. **Credit** MC, V. **Map** p397 E11.

Set up by ex-*Vogue* health and beauty director Kathy Phillips, This Works sells aromatherapy products based on high-quality natural plant oils: shower oils, shower gels, hot stone burner and essences, body lotion. The must-have is the Orla Kiely-designed travel pouch, containing mini versions of the products. The adjacent treatment rooms offer massages using products from the range.

Urban Retreat

5th Floor, Harrods, Knightsbridge, 87-135 Brompton Road, SW1X 7XL (7893 8333/ www.harrods.com). Knightsbridge tube. **Open** 10am-7pm Mon-Sat. **Credit** AmEx, DC, MC, V. **Map** p397 F9.

This once-tired old salon has recently been transformed into a shrine to beauty. Still, the biggest news is the advent of the world's first Crème de la Mer facials (from £95 for an hour). Treatments use products such as Guinot, Thalgo and La Prairie. Specialist massages include the Hydrotherm Massage (£80 for an hour), during which warm water bags support you, so you don't turn over.

Cosmetics, skincare & perfume

Department stores (*see p236*) are the places to go for most upmarket make-up brands.

Aveda Lifestyle Institute

174 High Holborn, St Giles's, WC1V 7AA (7759 7355/www.aveda.com). Holborn tube. **Open** 9.30am-7pm Mon-Fri; 9am-6.30pm Sat. **Credit** AmEx, MC, V. **Map** p399 L6.

Since 1978 Aveda has flown the flag for environmentally sound beauty products and it's a boon that most of its goods – haircare, bodycare, make-up, teas, vitamins and more – are a pleasure to use. Look out for new hair products such as Control Granules, the extended Caribbean Therapy range. Plus point: a great travel range. Minus point: just that tad more expensive than feels justified.

Other locations: 28-29 Marylebone High Street, Marylebone, W1U 4PL (7224 3157).

Boots

75 Queensway, Bayswater, W2 4QH (7229 9266/www.boots.com). Bayswater tube. **Open** 9am-10pm Mon-Sat; noon-10pm Sun. **Credit** MC, V. **Map** p394 C6.

Beloved Boots is the king of all chemists, with an exhaustive product list and regular twofer offers. Not only does it stock all the basics, plus food and perfume, but, depending on the size of the store, also stretches to electrical goods, photo processing, sunglasses and upper-crust skincare brands. It continues to innovate, bringing free cholesterol testing, plus digital fertility monitors and even 'date rape' drug testing kits to the high street.
Other locations: throughout the city.

Kiehl's

29 Monmouth Street, Covent Garden, WC2H 9DD (7240 2411/www.kiehls.com). Covent Garden or Leicester Square tube. **Open** 10.30am-7pm Mon-Sat; noon-5pm Sun. **Credit** AmEx, MC, V. **Map** p399 L6.

Kiehl's was founded in New York more than 150 years ago, but it was only in 2002 that it set up its first UK store. Lots of natural ingredients, including deep-sea products in the new anti-ageing Abyssine face and eye cream.

MAC Cosmetics

109 King's Road, Chelsea, SW3 4PA (7349 0022/ www.maccosmetics.com). Sloane Square tube. **Open** 10am-6.30pm Mon-Sat; noon-5.30pm Sun. **Credit** AmEx, MC, V. **Map** p397 F11.

MAC is the first port of call for anyone who's serious about looking good. As well as perennially popular items such as Strobe Cream (great for giving the face a healthy sheen) and firmly established basics such as Shadesticks and Lipglasses, there are fantastic limited editions that always hit the mark.
Other locations: 28 Foubert's Place, Soho, W1F 7PR (7534 9222); 38 Neal Street, Covent Garden, WC2H 9PS (7379 6820).

Origins

51 King's Road, Chelsea, SW3 4ND (7823 6715/ www.origins.com). Sloane Square tube. **Open** 10am-6.30pm Mon, Tue, Thur, Fri; 10am-7pm Wed, Sat; noon-6pm Sun. **Credit** AmEx, MC, V. **Map** p397 F11.

Every once in a while Origins launches a product that takes the beauty world by storm. Take the White Tea Skin Guardian, for instance, which really does leave skin silky, or the Peace of Mind on-the-spot relief gel – scientifically proven to reduce tension, fatigue and even sadness (!). On the make-up front, there's a lovely new range of lipglosses and finishing powders.

Hairdressers

Diverse Hair

280 Upper Street, Islington, N1 2TZ (7704 6842). Angel tube/Highbury & Islington tube/rail. **Open** 11am-6pm Mon-Fri; 10am-5pm Sat. **Credit** AmEx, MC, V.

Michaeljohn cuts it.

A very friendly unisex salon, where all-comers are made welcome. Gently groovy music plays (which comes in very handy when you don't feel like chatting) and there's a laid-back atmosphere. Basic cuts cost £35.

Geo F Trumper

9 Curzon Street, Mayfair, W1J 5HQ (7499 1850/ www.trumpers.com). Green Park tube. **Open** 9am-5.30pm Mon-Fri; 9am-1pm Sat. **Credit** AmEx, DC, MC, V. **Map** p400 H7.

Old-style gentility is reflected in the curtained barbering booths, dark wood panelling, green leather chairs and red velvet curtains. Striving to remain unchanged since it was founded in 1875, Trumper's has earned the loyalty of its male clients. Haircuts and wet shaves both cost from £26.50, facials are £25 and £45, and shaving lessons from £45.

Mr Topper's

13A Great Russell Street, Bloomsbury, WC1B 3NH (7631 3233). Tottenham Court Road tube. **Open** 9am-6.30pm Mon-Sat; 11am-5.30pm Sun. **No credit cards**. **Map** p399 K5.

The large sign advertising cuts draws in a steady stream of traffic. Customers are waved towards a chair, the clippers come out, and the whole process is over in less than ten minutes. In terms of speed and humourlessness it's slightly reminiscent of a sheep-shearing station, but the cuts are good enough, and the place is constantly busy. Women have to pay a whole extra pound.
Other locations: throughout the city.

Michaeljohn

25 Albemarle Street, Mayfair, W1S 4HU (7629 6969/www.michaeljohn.co.uk). Green Park tube. **Open** 8am-6.30pm Mon, Sat; 8am-8pm Tue-Fri. **Credit** MC, V. **Map** p400 H7.

Michaeljohn is one of our favourites. In spite of its swanky Mayfair location, MJ continues to be a friendly but always consummately professional salon where you can get a great cut, colour and even manicure while your colour is doing its work. The client list is full to the brim with stars, politicians and people who want reliably good results. Cuts range from £60 to £150.

Sejour

3-5 Bray Place, Chelsea, SW3 (020 7589 1100) Sloane Square tube. **Open** Mon-Sat 8.30am-8pm. **Credit** MC, V. **Map** p397 F11.

Two stylists from the Nicky Clarke stable have created a salon that masquerades as an elegant and opulent boudoir. The mellow music is DJ-provided, the drinks are homemade smoothies, and the chairs have a control pad to determine what sort of back massage you'd like. You'll get a stunning kimono in rich red and gold to wear and the hair-dressing skills on offer are fantastic.

Opticians

David Clulow

185 King's Road, Chelsea, SW3 5EB (7376 5733/www.davidclulow.com). Sloane Square tube. **Open** 9.30am-6pm Mon, Tue, Thur-Sat; 9.30am-7pm Wed; noon-6pm Sun. **Credit** AmEx, DC, MC, V. **Map** p397 E12.

This smart and award-winning optician's is big on lenses, with the varieties on offer running to coloured and hand-painted made-to-order styles. In terms of frames, it stocks the usual suspects – Chanel, Gucci, Bulgari, Dolce & Gabbana, Oliver Peoples and Starck, as well as some lesser-known brands. Sunglasses start at £90.

Other locations: throughout the city.

Kirk Originals

29 Floral Street, Covent Garden, WC2E 9DP (7240 5055/www.kirkoriginals.com). Covent Garden tube. **Open** 11am-7pm Mon-Sat; 1-5pm Sun. **Credit** MC, V.

This shop is a byword for cool, with colourful, chunky retro-inspired frames. The new Wild collection (£199) features contrasting fluorescent colours. There are also original vintage sunglasses from the 1950s, '60s and '70s (£150). In true Covent Garden style, Kirk's often hosts in-store art exhibitions.

Homewares

Aria

295-296 Upper Street, Islington, N1 2TU (7704 1999/www.aria-shop.co.uk). Angel tube. **Open** 10am-7pm Mon-Fri; 10am-6.30pm Sat; noon-5pm Sun. **Credit** AmEx, MC, V.

This supremely trendy store stocks household items for the style-conscious, with items designed by big names like Alessi, Zack, Ella Doran and Philippe Starck. Classic items include Bialetti espresso makers; a range of retro-style Dualit toasters (£109-£195) and Marina Abramovic designed Illy cups (six for £69.95). A good bet for original gifts.

Conran Shop

Michelin House, 81 Fulham Road, Fulham, SW3 6RD (7589 7401/www.conran.com). South Kensington tube. **Open** 10am-6pm Mon, Tue, Fri; 10am-7pm Wed, Thur; 10am-6.30pm Sat; noon-6pm Sun. **Credit** AmEx, MC, V. **Map** p397 E10.

The Conran Shop was one of the very first retailers to embody the term 'lifestyle' by introducing a set

Mushroom for manoeuvre

Magic mushrooms have been hard to avoid in recent years. If you did Glastonbury, read the music press or have been to Camden, you can't move for joints making the most of the legal loophole. No surprise, then, that the **Camden Mushroom Company** has set up a branch in trendy Covent Garden. Its fungi are even pricier than the organic ones in Carluccio's, but, then, they do have an added hallucinogenic kick. 'A good degree of our customers are professionals whom one might not expect to find at a mushroom store,' says Lucy May, business manager. The company has doubled in size over the past three months, and, with prices ranging from £10 per 10g, business is set to keep booming – as long as the Home Office stays groovy.

The Camden Mushroom Company
Outside 40 Neal Street, W1 (no phone/www. camdenmushroomcompany.com). Covent Garden tube. **Open** 10.30am-6pm daily.

of cosmopolitan shoppers to the notion of buying everything for their home from a single place. Because of the product variation, there is something for everyone's budget, be it a ceramic vase for £20, a Norm 69 pendant light for £75 or an fabulous Aspen sofa for £1,595.

Other locations: throughout the city.

eatmyhandbagbitch

37 Drury Lane, Covent Garden, WC2B 5RR (7836 0830/www.eatmyhandbagbitch.co.uk). Covent Garden or Holborn tube. **Open** 10am-6pm Mon-Sat. **Credit** AmEx, MC, V. **Map** p399 L6.

Despite their shop's odd name, eatmyhandbagbitch's owners take a serious approach to 20th-century design. A new line in custom-made leather goods can create anything from a set of six coasters (£75) to that absolute must-have accessory, a travelling bar (£13,000). Although prices go into the thousands, repro versions of Baron Albrizzi's acrylic 1968 designs are priced from £75.

Design Museum Shop

28 Shad Thames, Bermondsey, SE1 2YD (7940 8753/www.designmuseum.org). Tower Hill tube/ London Bridge tube/rail. **Open** 10am-5.45pm daily. **Credit** AmEx, MC, V. **Map** p405 S9.

This is the place to visit for the latest gadgets and accessories from some of the hottest designers including Stefan Lindfors, Otto Rittweger and Marc Newson. Recent highlights included George Nelson's Ball and Spoke clock and Jacob Jensen telephones. More playful items stocked include the collection of Ugly dolls by Kim and Hovarth (£24.99).

Maisonette

79 Chamberlayne Road, Kensal Rise, NW10 3ND (8964 8444/www.maisonette.uk.com). Queen's Park tube/rail/Kensal Rise rail. **Open** 11am-6.30pm Tue-Sat. **Credit** AmEx, MC, V.

Amanda Sellers and Martin Barrells' sumptuous collection features glamorous ceramics, glassware and jewellery and some fabulous shaggy merino sheepskin rugs, set among some very cool vintage furniture like a great '60s Dutch sideboard (£550). Their bold and beautiful vintage scarf cushions are one of the store's biggest sellers, as are their ingenious line of paint-it-yourself kits containing canvases, paints and instructions.

SCP

135-139 Curtain Road, Shoreditch, EC2A 3BX (7739 1869/www.scp.co.uk). Old Street tube/rail. **Open** 9.30am-6pm Mon-Sat; 11am-5pm Sun. **Credit** MC, V. **Map** p402 R4.

In addition to a superb collection of well-executed, well-chosen contemporary furniture, SCP stocks an expansive range of up-to-date accessories, great lighting and some excellent design books. The shop features a clutch of respected designers, with Michael Sodeau among them. New designs that are worth a special mention include Matthew Hilton's Baude armchair and the solid wood Extending Table by the same designer.

Markets

The markets listed below are the most famous in the capital, and not too far away from the centre, or the tourist areas. There are some fantastic markets in more far-flung places. Down south in Battersea, **Northcote Road Market** (9am-5pm Thur-Sat) has lovely food stalls; in Hackney, **Ridley Road Market** (open 7am-5pm Mon-Sat) is fine for African specialities. Also notable for Afro/Caribbean goodies is Shepherd's Bush Market (*see p167*). To the amazement of Londoners **Camden Market** (Camden High Street, junction with Buck Street, NW1, 7278 4444) continues to draw the hordes (usually tourists) who come looking for cheap designer clothes and crafty things. If you're after a scrum you'll find it open daily (9.30am-5.30pm); head for **Stables Market** (off Chalk Farm Road, opposite junction with Hartland Road, NW1, 7485 5511) where the stalls and shops sell crafts, vintage clothing, antiques and food. **Petticoat Lane Market** (Middlesex Street, Goulston Street, New Goulston Street, Toynbee Street, Wentworth Street, Bell Lane, Cobb Street, Leyden Street, Strype Street, Old Castle Street, Cutler Street, E1, open 10am-2pm Mon-Fri, 9am-2pm Sun) sells mainly cheap clothes, toys and electronic goods, as well as beauty, jewellery and kitchen equipment, to a ramshackle crowd of locals.

General

Brick Lane Market

Brick Lane – north of railway bridge, Cygnet Street, Sclater Street, E1; Bacon Street, Cheshire Street, Chilton Street, E2. Spitalfields. Aldgate East or Shoreditch tube/Liverpool Street tube/rail. **Open** daybreak-2pm Sun. **Map** p403 S5.

This positively folkloric East End institution has stalls selling cheap soaps and razors, magazines, towels, bric-a-brac, second-hand clothes and old furniture, along with bagel shops, back-of-a-lorry hustlers and East End seafood stalls. The market spreads out along a number of narrow streets that are now lined with trendy clothes shops and expensive home accessories stores alongside Bangladeshi and Pakistani restaurants and sweetshops. The most browsable is Cheshire Street.

Brixton Market

Electric Avenue, Pope's Road, Brixton Station Road, Atlantic Road, Brixton, SW9 8JX. Brixton tube/rail. **Open** 8am-6pm Mon, Tue, Thur-Sat; 8am-3pm Wed (varies according to the weather).

Visiting Brixton's thronging market is like being plunged into another country. Electric Avenue is packed with stalls piled high with exotic fruit and veg – yams, plantains, mangoes, papaya and more – as well as fresh tomatoes, courgettes, carrots and other staples. Opposite the stalls are stores crammed with halal meats and an incredible variety of fish. Around Atlantic Road it's more clothes, towels and cheap wallets. 'Brixton Village' (previously Granville Arcade) houses African and Caribbean food stores, household goods, books, crafts and specialist hair and wig shops.

Greenwich Market

(General enquiries 8293 3110/www.greenwich market.net). Greenwich rail/DLR/Cutty Sark DLR/Maze Hill rail. **Open** *Antiques & Collectibles Market 7.30am-5.30pm Thur-Fri. Village Market Stockwell Street, 8am-5pm Sat, Sun. Arts & Crafts Market 9.30am-5.30pm Thur-Sun. Food Court 9.30am-5.30pm Sat, Sun.*

Greenwich has not one, but three markets. Heading into the town centre from the station you come first to the antiques market, a collection of bric-a-brac and junk that varies from tat to treasures. Next along is the Village Market, where a second-hand clothes flea market mingles with Chinese silk dresses, cheap trendy clothes, ethnic ornaments, CDs and more. Passing the food court – noodles, curries, Thai, etc – you come to the covered Crafts Market which is bristling with young designer-makers and ideal for gift-hunting. The central hub of stalls sells a delicious selection of olives, breads, jam doughnuts and chocolate brownies.

Portobello Road Market

Portobello Road, W10, W11; Golborne Road, W10. Ladbroke Grove, Notting Hill Gate or Westbourne Park tube. **Open** *General 8am-6.30pm Mon-Wed, Fri, Sat; 8am-1pm Thur. Antiques 5.30am-4.30pm Sat.* **Map** *p394 A6.*

Portobello Road is several markets rolled into one. Starting at the Notting Hill end are mainly antiques stalls selling toy soldiers, vases, bric-a-brac and general Victoriana. Further up you come to the food stalls, ranging from traditional fruit and veg to tasty cheeses, stuffed olives, organic biscuits and crackers, bratwurst and crêpes. Next up come clothes and jewellery, ranging from cheap trendy club-and casualwear to delightful craft bracelets and earrings. The cafés under the Westway are a good place to rest before plunging into the next section – new designers' clothes and vintage wear along the walkway to Ladbroke Grove, while on the right-hand side are random selections of bric-a-brac.

Spitalfields Market

Commercial Street, between Lamb Street & Brushfield Street, E1 (7247 8556). Liverpool Street tube/rail. **Open** *General market 10am-5pm Mon-Fri, Sun. Organic food market 10am-4pm Wed, Sun. Antiques market 9am-4pm Thur. Fashion & art markets 10am-4pm Fri. Records & books market 10am-4pm 1st and 3rd Wed.* **Map** *p403 R5.*

Historic Spitalfields Market and its gorgeous vaulted roof have already been the victim of City expansion; protesters are trying to keep the remaining square untouched. Surrounded by cool shops selling movie posters, second-hand books and modish vintage furniture, the stalls offer everything from handmade cards, dyed sheepskin rugs and craft jewellery to aromatherapy products, CDs and quirky fashions. There are cake and bread stalls and a mini food court selling grub from all over the world at bargain prices. A visit to Spitalfields is easily combined with a quick poke around Brick Lane (*see p254*).

Spitalfields Market.

Flowers

Columbia Road Flower Market

*Columbia Road, between Gosset Street
& the Royal Oak pub, Bethnal Green, E2
(www.columbia-flower-market.freewebspace.
com). Bus 26, 48, 55.* **Open** 8am-1pm Sun.
No credit cards. Map p403 S3.
You know you are nearing this popular street market when you see masses of greenery bobbing down
the surrounding streets, held aloft by happy gardeners. Alongside the masses of plant stalls selling
a diverse range of plants, there are great cafés and
an eclectic range of shops, selling everything from
ceramics to hats. Only open on Sundays, the market
is immensely popular so it's worth making the effort
to get there before 9am to avoid the crush or, alternatively, drop in just before closing time at 2pm for
bargains sold off costermonger style.

Food

Farmers' Markets are the way forward for
city folk who want to buy food that has been
grown, reared and prepared by the stallholder,
and produced reasonably locally. The most
central ones are in **Marylebone** (Cramer
Street car park, 7704 9659, open 10am-2pm
Sun), **Notting Hill** (car park behind
Waterstones, access via Kensington Place,
corner of Kensington Church Street, W8 7PR,
7704 9659, open 9am-1pm Sat) and **Pimlico**
(Orange Square, corner of Pimlico Road and
Ebury Street, 7704 9659, open 9am-1pm Sat).
For further information contact the **National
Association of Farmers' Markets** (0845
230 2150, www.farmers markets.net).

Berwick Street Market

*Berwick Street, Rupert Street, Soho, W1. Piccadilly
Circus or Tottenham Court Road tube.* **Open** 9am-
6pm Mon-Sat. **Map** p398 J6.

A traditional fruit and veg market in the seedy heart
of Soho, Berwick Street also has stalls selling flowers,
nuts, CDs, electric toothbrushes, sweets, knickers and
socks. The fresh produce is delicious, ranging from
vine tomatoes, new potatoes and strawberries to
mangoes, passion fruit, avocados and watermelons.
South beyond the Raymond Revue Bar are a few stalls
offering trendy jackets, combat gear and accessories.
Don't bother rising with the lark to catch the best
Saturday bargains – like the rest of Soho, Berwick
Street Market doesn't get going until a bit later.

Borough Market

*8 Southwark Street, SE1 1TL (7407 1002/www.
boroughmarket.org.uk). London Bridge tube/rail.*
Open noon-6pm Fri; 9am-4pm Sat. **Map** p405 P8.
Endorsed by many a celebrity chef, Borough Market
offers an exciting mix of food from all over the
world. Meat encompasses everything from chicken
to venison – and on Saturday lunchtime lengthy
queues wait patiently for a chorizo sandwich from
the stall selling Spanish goods from Brindisa (which
also has its own shop in Exmouth Market, EC1).
Add to this fresh fruit and veg of all varieties, organic goods (cakes, breads), exotic teas, flowers, olive
oils, dairy (cheeses, yoghurts), fish, beers and wines
and you've got the makings of a feast. Quality is
high and prices match that.

Music

Megastores

HMV

*150 Oxford Street, Oxford Circus, W1D 1DJ (7631
3423/www.hmv.co.uk). Oxford Circus tube.* **Open**
9am-8pm Mon, Wed, Fri, Sat; 9.30am-8pm Tue; 9am-
9pm Thur; 11.45am-6pm Sun. **Credit** AmEx, DC,
MC, V. **Map** p398 J6.
A huge store with the latest chart albums on prominent display. Each of the sections, from world to
country, folk, jazz, and so on, could be a shop in

Fopp.
See p257.

itself. Amazing deals are to be had on value box sets (from £10.99). Dance vinyl is well represented, with expert staff recruited to handwrite reviews on the latest house, nu-jazz and hip hop 12-inches. The highlight, a classical department with knowledgeable staff, is in the basement.
Other locations: throughout the city.

Virgin Megastore

14-16 Oxford Street, Fitzrovia, W1N 9FL (7631 1234/www.virgin.com). Tottenham Court Road tube. **Open** 10am-8.30pm Mon-Wed, Fri, Sat; 10am-9pm Thur; noon-6pm Sun. **Credit** AmEx, MC, V. **Map** p399 K6.

Virgin plays host to regular chart signings, and the entrance seems permanently blocked by young Busted fans. The store satisfies an Oxford Street crowd with a vast range of chart, rock and pop, although the vinyl selection is limited; the world, jazz, classical and folk sections are comprehensive. The basement has a coffee shop with listening posts, and sells guitars, keyboards and the like.
Other locations: throughout the city.

Specialist music shops

Soho's Berwick Street is a CD and LP mecca – **Selectadisc** (No.34) and **Sister Ray** (No.94) are strong on indie and mainstream, while **Reckless** (No.30) is good for mainstream; there are cut-price CDs at **Mr CD** (No.80).

Fopp

1 Earlham Street, St Giles's, WC2H 9LL (7379 0883/www.fopp.co.uk). Covent Garden or Tottenham Court Road tube. **Open** 10am-10pm Mon-Sat; 11am-6pm Sun. **Credit** AmEx, MC, V. **Map** p399 M6.

The Fopp motto, plastered over the shelves, is 'suck it and see'. This means you'll find all genres represented and juxtaposed, with prices low enough to let you try something new without fear. In the basement is a good sweep of vinyl, on the ground floor are new releases, and upstairs is a low-priced (from £5) mixture of everything from jazz and rock to world music. It's unpretentious and well thought out.

Harold Moores Records

2 Great Marlborough Street, Soho, W1F 7HQ (7437 1576/www.hmrecords.co.uk). Oxford Circus tube. **Open** 10am-6.30pm Mon-Sat; noon-6pm Sun. **Credit** AmEx, MC, V. **Map** p398 J6.

Harold Moores is famous for a few things: a marvellous used LP section in the basement, second-hand and deleted CDs, obscure and hard-to-get recordings and a range of historic performances by instrumentalists and singers. There's also a large contemporary and avant-garde section, and staff are rightly proud of their knowledge and expertise.

Honest Jon's

278 Portobello Road, Ladbroke Grove, W10 5TE (8969 9822/www.honestjons.com). Ladbroke Grove tube. **Open** 10am-6pm Mon-Sat; 11am-5pm Sun. **Credit** AmEx, DC, MC, V. **Map** p394 A6.

You won't find any of those new-fangled private listening posts at Honest Jon's: here the staff play whatever you choose to the rest of the customers over the house stereo system. Fortunately you can't go wrong with the own-label compilations of soul, ska, hip hop and funk, nor with any of the other vinyl on offer: it all sounds so amazingly good you'll look like a connoisseur. There's an excellent jazz section in the basement.

Rough Trade

130 Talbot Road, Ladbroke Grove, W11 1JA (7229 8541/www.roughtrade.com). Ladbroke Grove tube. **Open** 10am-6.30pm Mon-Sat; 1-5pm Sun. **Credit** AmEx, MC, V. **Map** p394 A5.

These days Rough Trade is almost too aware of its place in the history of underground music, with staff who seem to think they're Che Guevara for managing to stock the latest indie releases on CD and vinyl. Nevertheless, the shop continues to satisfy the many hunters after obscurities with whatever is six months ahead of the mainstream, from hip hop and house to guitar-based stuff. There's a good selection of world music too.
Other locations: 16 Neal's Yard, Covent Garden, WC2H 9DP (7240 0105).

Pharmacies

High-street chemists **Boots** (*see p252*) also runs pharmacies in many of its central locations, some of which stay open late.

Bliss Chemist

5-6 Marble Arch, Marylebone, W1H 7EL (7723 6116). Marble Arch tube. **Open** 9am-midnight daily. **Credit** AmEx, MC, V. **Map** p395 F6.

This store has a handy late-night pharmacy.

Sport & adventure

Ellis Brigham

Tower House, 3-11 Southampton Street, Covent Garden, WC2E 7HA (7395 1010/www.ellis-brigham.com). Covent Garden tube/Charing Cross tube/rail. **Open** 10am-7pm Mon-Wed, Fri; 10am-7.30pm Thur; 9.30am-6.30pm Sat; 11.30am-5.30pm Sun. **Credit** AmEx, MC, V. **Map** p401 L7.

This well-established mountain sports company has increased its coverage of camping, trekking and climbing. The ski selection is extensive during the season, and prices are generally lower than those of competitors. There are great bargains during the sales too. The big news, however, is the two-storey ice wall (*see p329* **The icing on the wall**).
Other locations: 178 Kensington High Street, Kensington, W8 7RG (7937 6889).

Farlows

9 Pall Mall, St James's, SW1Y 5LX (7484 1000/www.farlows.co.uk). Piccadilly Circus tube. **Open** 9am-6pm Mon-Wed, Fri; 9am-8pm Thur; 10am-6pm Sat. **Credit** AmEx, DC, MC, V. **Map** p400 J8.

Eat, Drink, Shop

All the world's a stage at **Benjamin Pollock's Toy Shop**.

Established back in 1840, London's destination for clothing and equipment for traditional British country pursuits has had an incredible £1.5 million refit. A magnificent rod room displays 320 fully assembled fishing rods. As well as heritage brands such as Hardy's and Barbour, the store stocks more modern gear including Simms jackets and Patagonia clothes, bags and accessories.

Lillywhites

24-36 Lower Regent Street, St James's, SW1Y 4QF (0870 333 9600/www.sports-soccer.co.uk). Piccadilly Circus tube. **Open** 10am-9pm Mon-Sat; noon-6pm Sun. **Credit** AmEx, DC, MC, V. **Map** p401 K7.

Since being bought by the kSports Soccer group, Britain's most famous sports store now caters to fewer activities (lacrosse, equestrian, diving and the like have gone). On the plus side, the emphasis is now on value for money, so you can pick up all the gear you need for cricket, golf, football, and racket sports at very competitive prices.

Toys & games

In addition to the shops listed here, also check out the toy and game sections at the department stores (*see p236*) and some of the children's shops (*p242*). For computer games, try the music megastores (*see p256*).

Benjamin Pollock's Toyshop

44 The Market, Covent Garden Piazza, WC2E 8RF (7379 7866/www.pollocks-coventgarden.co.uk). Covent Garden tube. **Open** 10.30am-6pm Mon-Sat; 11am-4pm Sun. **Credit** AmEx, MC, V.

Best known for its toy theatres, Pollock's is an educational wonderland. The most popular self-assembly paper theatre is Jackson's (£5.95), with its set and characters for the ballet *Cinderella*. Other items on sale include marionettes, glove and finger puppets and French musical boxes (£37.50). Collectors pop in for antiques and handmade bears (from £82), but there are quirky pocket-money toys too.

Cheeky Monkeys

202 Kensington Park Road, Ladbroke Grove, W11 1NR (7792 9022/www.cheekymonkeys.com). Ladbroke Grove tube. **Open** 9.30am-5.30pm Mon-Fri; 10am-5.30pm Sat. **Credit** MC, V.

These lovely modern toy shops are strong on presentation and good at stocking unusual, attractive and fun products. Monkeys have some of London's best fancy dress (from smart soldiers to tigers and frogs, alongside Angelina Ballerina tutus). Then there's Playstack, a brilliant vertical puzzle system that comes with a book telling the story of, say, *Jack and the Beanstalk*. Pocket money toys and gifts (for around £1.99) tend to be offbeat.

Other locations: throughout the city.

Hamleys

188-196 Regent Street, Soho, W1B 5BT (0870 333 2455/www.hamleys.com). Oxford Circus tube. **Open** 10am-8pm Mon-Sat; noon-6pm Sun. **Credit** AmEx, MC, V. **Map** p400 J7.

The largest toy shop in the world (allegedly) is a loud, frenetic, exciting experience. The ground floor is where the latest fun toys are demonstrated; it also accommodates a mountain of soft toys. The basement is the Cyberzone, full of games consoles and high-tech gadgets. The first floor has items of a scientific bent, and bear depot. On second is everything for pre-schoolers. Third is girlie heaven with departments for dressing up, make-up and so on. Fourth has remote-controlled vehicles, plus die-cast models. Fifth is Lego World, with its own café.

Mystical Fairies

12 Flask Walk, Hampstead, NW3 1HE (7431 1888/www.mysticalfairies.co.uk). Hampstead tube. **Open** 10am-6pm Mon-Sat; 11am-6pm Sun. **Credit** MC, V.

Fairy creatures hang from the ceiling on beaded swings and lend their wings to little girls' rucksacks. Is there anything in this shop that doesn't sparkle in a magical and mystical way? Fairy costumes and balletwear are available in great profusion and the basement doubles up as twinkly party venue.

Arts & Entertainment

Festivals & Events	**260**
Children	**268**
Comedy	**275**
Dance	**278**
Film	**281**
Galleries	**287**
Gay & Lesbian	**294**
Music	**301**
Nightlife	**315**
Sport & Fitness	**325**
Theatre	**332**

Features

Pomp and ceremony	262
Taking the air	266
Suffer the little children	270
Gongs show	276
Super troupers	279
Brother, can you spare 15 quid?	286
Space invaders	291
The best Gay venues	295
Walk this way Famous footsteps	296
London Coliseum	303
Asian explosion	307
Grime time	308
Jock in a box	319
Day is the new night	323
The rise of the Roman empire	326
The icing on the wall	329
A pint and a play	336

Map

Theatreland	333

Festivals & Events

So much to do, so little time.

London Marathon. *See p261.*

If there's one thing that Londoners do well, it's throw a party. The city's full programme of festivals and events reflects, and benefits from, the many varied interests and cultures of its visitors and residents; from bhangra to beluga, every walk of life gets to strut its stuff. Recent years have also seen some imaginative sponsored seasons and one-off events, such as 2004's Art Car Boot Fair in Vauxhall, when contemporary artists of some renown sold rather sweet budget works out of car boots. Such events are seldom confirmed very far in advance, so check the listings in *Time Out* magazine to be sure you don't miss out.

January-March 2005

London International Boat Show

ExCeL, 1 Western Gateway, Royal Victoria Dock, Docklands, E16 1XL (0870 060 0246/www. schroderslondonboatshow.com). Custom House DLR. **Date** 6-16 Jan.

For 50 years this maritime convention has been showing off leisure boats to keen crowds. This year will be the second time the show will be in the spacious Docklands venue and will feature historic boats and an indoor watersports arena, as well as showcasing new vessels.

London International Mime Festival

Various venues across London (7637 5661/ www.mimefest.co.uk). **Date** 15-30 Jan.

Surely the quietest festival the city has to offer, LIMF will invite 20 companies from the UK and abroad to perform a variety of shows for all ages. This year's highlight is Barcelona-based El Tricicle, who will perform a slapstick show at the South Bank's Queen Elizabeth Hall chronicling, of all things, the history of the chair. Free brochures available via phone or website.

Chinese New Year Festival

Around Gerrard Street, Chinatown, W1, Leicester Square, WC2 & Trafalgar Square, WC2 (7851 6686/www.chinatownchinese.com). Leicester Square or Piccadilly Circus tube. **Date** 13 Feb. **Map** p401 K7.

Traditional event to welcome in the new year, which in 2005 will be the Year of the Rooster. Celebrations begin at 11am with a children's parade from Leicester Square gardens to Trafalgar Square, where the lion and dragon dance teams perform traditional dances. And there are, of course, firework displays (at lunchtime and at 5pm).

London Art Fair

Business Design Centre, 52 Upper Street, Islington,
N1 0QH (7359 3535/www.londonartfair.co.uk).
Angel tube. **Date** 19-23 Jan. **Map** p402 N2.
More than 100 galleries get involved in this contemporary art fair. Millions of pounds will change hands during the five-day event.

Great Spitalfields Pancake Day Race

Spitalfields Market (entrance on Commercial
Street or Brushfield Street), Spitalfields, E1 6AA
(7375 0441). Liverpool Street tube/rail. **Date** 8 Feb.
Map p403 R5.
This traditional tomfoolery starts at 12.30pm, with teams of four tossing pancakes as they run, all for a good cause, of course. Call in advance if you want to take part, or just show up if all you're after is seeing any number of pancakes hit the pavement.

International Tourist Guide Day

Various venues across London (7403 1115/
www.blue-badge.org.uk). **Date** 21 Feb.
Members of the public are invited to sample, free of charge, a range of walks and tours given by qualified Tourist Board registered guides.

St Patrick's Day Parade & Festival

Various venues across London (7983 4100/
www.london.gov.uk). **Date** 13 Mar.
This year the capital's celebrations for the Irish community promise to build on the success of last year's party. Supported by the Mayor, a thousands-strong parade through central London will be followed by a free party. Expect plenty of Irish music and dancing, arts and crafts and activities for all ages.

Oxford & Cambridge Boat Race

Thames, from Putney to Mortlake (01225 383483/
www.theboatrace.org). Putney Bridge tube/Putney
rail. **Date** 27 Mar.
The 151st race will take place during the afternoon, probably at 4pm. Huge crowds line the Thames from Putney to Mortlake for this annual elitist grudge match, with the riverside pubs in Mortlake and Hammersmith the most popular (read: obscenely crowded and packed with toffs) vantage points. For those who care: Oxford is in the dark blue, Cambridge is in the light blue.

April-June 2005

Mosaïques Festival

Institut Français, 17 Queensberry Place, South
Kensington, SW7 2DT, & Ritzy Cinema, Brixton,
SW2 1JG (7073 1350/www.institut-
francais.org.uk/mosaiques). South Kensington tube &
Brixton tube/rail. **Date** Call or check the website.
During its week-long celebration of world culture, the Mosaïques Festival offers a diverse programme of films, talks, musical performances, evening events and discussions on related topics.

London Marathon

Greenwich Park to the Mall via the Isle of Dogs,
Victoria Embankment & St James's Park (7902
0200/www.london-marathon.co.uk). Maze Hill rail &
Charing Cross tube/rail. **Date** 17 Apr.
As one of the world's biggest metropolitan marathons, this event attracts 35,000 starters, including a few in outrageous costumes. Would-be runners must apply by the previous October to be entered in the ballot. Spectators are advised to arrive early; the front runners reach the 13 mile mark near the Tower of London at around 10am.

London Harness Horse Parade

Battersea Park, Albert Bridge Road, Battersea,
SW11 (01737 646132). Battersea Park or
Queenstown Road rail/97, 137 bus. **Date** 28 Mar.
Map p397 F13.
An Easter Monday parade of more than 300 working horses, donkeys and mules with their various commercial and private carriages. The horses assemble from 9am; main parade noon-1pm.

National Science Week

Various venues (www.the-ba.net). **Date** 11-20 Mar.
Annual festival encompassing a wide variety of events from hands-on shows for youngsters to discussions for adults to celebrate all aspects of science and technology.

May Fayre & Puppet Festival

St Paul's Church Garden, Bedford Street, Covent
Garden, WC2E 9ED (7375 0441/www.alternative
arts.co.uk). Covent Garden tube. **Date** 8 May.
Map p401 L7.
Celebrating the first recorded sighting of Mr Punch in England (by Pepys, in 1662), this free event offers puppetry galore from 10.30am to 5.30pm.

Chelsea Flower Show

Grounds of Royal Hospital, Royal Hospital Road,
Chelsea, SW3 4SR (7649 1885/www.rhs.org.uk).
Sloane Square tube. **Date** 24-28 May. **Map** p397 F12.
The hysteria that builds up around this annual flower show has to be seen to be believed. Fight your way past the rich old ladies to see perfect roses bred by experts, or to get ideas for your own humble plot. But not on the first two days, as those are open only to Royal Horticultural Society members; the show closes at 5.30pm on the final day, with display plants sold off from 4.30pm.

Spitalfields Festival Fringe

Various venues (7375 0441/www.alternative
arts.co.uk). Liverpool Street tube/rail. **Date** 1-30 June.
A month-long programme of events, the Spitalfields Festival Fringe encompasses theatre, comedy and visual arts in and around Spitalfields.

▶ Specialist festivals are listed in our Arts & Entertainment chapters. For dates of public holidays in the UK, *see p377.*

Playtex Moonwalk

Start & finish at Hyde Park, W1 (01483 741 430/
www.walkthewalk.org). **Date** 18 June. **Map** p395 F7.
Charity night walk to raise money for breast cancer
research. The 15,000-odd – men included – wear specially decorated bras to walk the 26.2 mile route.

Coin Street Festival

Bernie Spain Gardens (next to Oxo Tower Wharf),
SE1 9PH (7401 3610/www.coinstreet.org).
Southwark tube/Waterloo tube/rail. **Date** June-Aug.
Map p404 N7.
Not one but a series of eight or so culturally themed
weekday and weekend events celebrating different
communities in the capital. Events take place on the
South Bank and include music, dance and performance events for all ages with craft and refreshment
stalls at each one. Celebrating Sanctuary is held during Refugee Week in June and Capital Age (call for
details) is for the older community.

Kew Summer Festival

Royal Botanic Gardens, Kew, Richmond, Surrey
TW9 3AB (8332 5655/www.kew.org). Kew Gardens
tube/rail/Kew Bridge rail. **Date** May-Sept.
Each season at the botanical gardens has its own
programme of events, with the summer one lasting
the longest. The festival theme changes each year
and there are special activities on bank holidays,
such as bluebell walks in May.

Pomp and ceremony

Ceremony of the Keys

Tower of London, Tower Hill, The
City, EC3N 4AB (08707 515177/
www.hrp.org.uk). Tower Hill tube/
Tower Gateway DLR. **Date** daily.
Maximum *Apr-Oct* party of 7, *Nov-*
Mar party of 15. **Map** p405 R7.
Dating back 700 years, this is the
ceremony in which the Yeoman
Warders lock the entrances to
the Tower of London at 9.53pm
every evening. The ticketed public
assembles at the West Gate at
9pm, and it's all over by 10pm,
when the last post sounds. See
the website for details concerning
ticket application.

Changing of the Guard

Buckingham Palace, St James's,
SW1A 1AA (7321 2233/
www.royal.gov.uk). Green Park
or St James's Park tube/Victoria
tube/rail. **Ceremonies** *Apr-Aug* 11.30am
daily. *Sept-Mar* alternate days (may be
cancelled in wet weather). **Map** p400 H9.
Horse Guards & St James's Palace,
SW1A 1BQ. **Ceremonies** 11am Mon-Sat;
10am Sun. **Map** p401 K8.
One of the regiments of Foot Guards, in their
scarlet coats and bearskin hats, lines up in
the forecourt of Wellington Barracks from
10.45am; at 11.27am the soldiers march,
accompanied by their regimental band, to
Buckingham Palace for the changing of the
sentries in the palace forecourt. At Horse
Guards in Whitehall, the Household Cavalry
mount the guard (10am-4pm daily); they then
ride to Whitehall via the Mall from Hyde Park
for the daily changeover (pictured).

Gun Salutes

Green Park, Mayfair & St James's, W1, &
Tower of London, The City, EC3. **Dates** 6 Feb
(Accession Day); 21 Apr (Queen's birthday);
2 June (Coronation Day); 10 June (Duke of
Edinburgh's birthday); 11 June (Trooping
the Colour); State Opening of Parliament
(*see p267*); 13 Nov (Remembrance Sunday);
and state visits. **Map** p400 H8.
The King's Troop of the Royal Horse Artillery
makes a mounted charge through Hyde Park,
sets up the guns and fires a 41-gun salute
(at noon, except on the occasion of the
State Opening of Parliament) opposite the
Dorchester Hotel. Not to be outdone, the
Honourable Artillery Company fires a 62-gun
salute at the Tower of London at 1pm.

Arts & Entertainment

Architecture Week

Various venues (www.architectureweek.co.uk).
Date 17-26 June.
Celebrates contemporary architecture with a programme of events, exhibitions, talks and tours plus an open practice initiative that allows the public into selected architecture practices.

Jazz Plus

Victoria Embankment Gardens, Villiers Street, Westminster, WC2R 2PY (7375 0441/ www.alternative arts.co.uk). Embankment tube. **Date** 7 June-26 July. **Map** p399 L7.
Free lunchtime concerts are performed by a variety of contemporary jazz musicians.

Royal National Theatre Summer Festival

South Bank, SE1 9PX (7452 3400/www.national theatre.org.uk). Waterloo tube/rail. **Date** June-Aug. **Map** p401 M7.
This lively ten-week free festival of music, street theatre and films is held outside the National Theatre on the South Bank.

Derby Day

Epsom Downs Racecourse, Epsom Downs, Surrey KT18 5LQ (01372 470047/www.epsomderby.co.uk). Epsom rail, then shuttle bus. **Date** 4 June.
The most important flat race of the season has a carnival mood, but if you want comfort or a good view, be prepared to pay for it.

London Garden Squares Weekend

Various venues across London (http:myweb. tiscali.co.uk/london.gardens/home.htm).
Date 11-12 June.
All those enchanting little private parks around the wealthy parts of town that tempt you but then lock you out are opened up for this event only. Maps are available to guide you to the green oases all over London (gardens vary from Japanese-style retreats to secret 'children-only' play areas).

Meltdown

South Bank Centre, Belvedere Road, South Bank, SE1 8XX (08703 800400/www.rfh.org.uk). Embankment tube/Waterloo tube/rail. **Date** Last 2 wks in June. **Map** p401 M8.
This enormously successful festival of contemporary culture at the South Bank Centre invites a guest curator each year. A varied selection of bosses in recent years have included Nick Cave, David Bowie and Morrissey. It's perhaps unsurprising, then, that the gigs and special events tend towards the unpredictable (and are occasionally brilliant).

Trooping the Colour

Horse Guards Parade, Whitehall, Westminster, SW1A 2AX (7414 2479). Westminster tube/Charing Cross tube/rail. **Date** 11 June. **Map** p401 K8.
Though the Queen was born on 21 April, this is her official birthday celebration. At 10.45am she makes the 15-minute journey from Buckingham Palace to Horse Guards Parade, then scurries back home to watch a midday Royal Air Force flypast and receive a formal gun salute from Green Park.

Beating Retreat

Horse Guards Parade, Whitehall, Westminster, SW1A 2AX (booking 7414 2271). Westminster tube/Charing Cross tube/rail. **Date** 1-2 June. **Map** p401 K8.
This ineffably patriotic ceremony begins at 7pm, with the 'Retreat' beaten on drums by the Mounted Bands of the Household Cavalry and the Massed Bands of the Guards Division.

Wimbledon Lawn Tennis Championships

PO Box 98, Church Road, Wimbledon, SW19 5AE (8944 1066/recorded information 8946 2244/www.wimbledon.org). Southfields tube/ Wimbledon tube/rail. **Date** 20 June-3 July.
The world's most prestigious tennis tournament and, when it's not raining, the best. Actually, even when it *is* raining. *See also p328.*

Summer in the Square

Trafalgar Square, Westminster, WC2 (7983 4100/ www.london.gov.uk). Embankment tube/Charing Cross tube/rail. **Date** July-Aug.
An annual programme of free (and usually fun) live cultural performances for all ages, Summer in the Square is keenly supported by the Mayor of London.

City of London Festival

Venues across the City, EC2-EC4 (7377 0540/ www.colf.org). Bank, Barbican, Moorgate & St Paul's tube/Blackfriars, Cannon Street & Farringdon tube/rail. **Date** 27 June-13 July.
Now in its 43rd year, the City of London Festival takes place in some of the finest buildings in the Square Mile including livery halls and churches. The programme is traditional classical music, such as concerts from the London Symphony Orchestra, as well as more unusual offerings from the worlds of jazz, dance, visual art, literature and theatre.

Henley Royal Regatta

Henley Reach, Henley-on-Thames, Oxon RG9 2LY (01491 572153/www.hrr.co.uk). Henley-on-Thames rail. **Date** 29 June-3 July.
First held in 1839, Henley is now a five-day affair, and about as posh as it gets. Boat races range from open events for men and women through club and student crews to junior boys.

July-September 2005

Pride London

Parade from Hyde Park, W1, to Trafalgar Square, WC2 (7494 2225/www.pridelondon.org). Hyde Park Corner tube/Charing Cross tube/rail. **Date** Festival Fortnight from 18 June; parade & rally 2 July.
London's proud-to-be-gays and lesbians throw their annual, good-natured (and free) bash that begins with a colourful and festive march from Hyde Park

Arts & Entertainment

to Trafalgar Square via Park Lane, Piccadilly, Whitehall and Victoria Embankment. This year's parade, which leaves Hyde Park at 1pm, ends with a rally in Trafalgar Square in the evening. It promises to be bigger than ever this year in anticipation of Europride 2006. Festival Fortnight is a mix of cultural performances in various venues.

Rhythm Sticks

South Bank Centre, Belvedere Road, South Bank, SE1 8XX (08703 800400/www.rfh.org.uk). Embankment tube/Waterloo tube/rail. **Date** July. **Map** p401 M8.

Each year, Rhythm Sticks takes a week to celebrate everything that bangs, crashes and, indeed, pings. Performers come from all corners of the world and play in the widest possible range of styles.

Tango Al Fresco

Regent's Park, NW1 (07970 599445). Regent's Park tube. **Date** July-Aug. **Map** p398 G3.

Annual outdoor social dance event held on three Sundays. Put on your dancing shoes and tango to your heart's delight from 2pm to 6pm. Tango novices can join a lesson at 1pm. Money raised from the small charge is donated to tree planting in the park.

Greenwich & Docklands International Festival

Various venues in Greenwich & Docklands (8305 1818/www.festival.org). **Date** July.

An array of free theatrical, musical and site specific events are held across east London and in the vicinity of Canary Wharf combining community arts with grander projects.

Soho Festival

St Anne's Gardens & St Anne's Community Centre, Soho, W1D 6AE (7439 4303/ www.thesohosociety.org.uk). Tottenham Court Road tube. **Date** 10 July. **Map** p401 K7.

Stalls, music, displays by local artists and an alpine horn-blowing contest bring locals and guests together in aid of the Soho Society.

Sprite Urban Games

Clapham Common, SW4 (0870 902 0444/ www.spriteurbangames.com). **Date** 22-24 July.

Three days of skateboarding, BMXing and skating, plus trade stands and gaming tents, accompanied by a soundtrack of hip hop, punk and rock from live bands and DJs.

BBC Sir Henry Wood Promenade Concerts

Royal Albert Hall, Kensington Gore, South Kensington, SW7 2AP (box office 7589 8212/ www.bbc.co.uk/proms). Knightsbridge or South Kensington tube/9, 10, 52 bus. **Date** 15 July-10 Sept. **Map** p397 D9.

This annual event brings together an eclectic range of mostly classical concerts over the course of two months. Most are televised, but there's nothing like seeing them in person. *See also p306.*

Respect Week & Festival

Venue tbc (7983 4100/www.london.gov.uk). **Date** July (call for details).

This huge, free anti-racist music and entertainment festival is supported by the Mayor of London.

Fruitstock

Regent's Park, NW1 (8600 3939/www.fruit stock.com). Regent's Park tube. **Date** Aug.

Although seemingly unlikely organisers, the Innocent fruit smoothies drink company's free summer bash has proved extremely popular in past years. This year, the third, will be pretty much the same: plenty of live music, a dance tent, posh food stalls, a farmers' market, activities for children and the chance to laze in the park on a rug with your pals.

Great British Beer Festival

Olympia, Hammersmith Road, Kensington, W14 8UX (01727 867201/www.camra.org.uk). Kensington (Olympia) tube/rail. **Date** 2-6 Aug.

Oh, yes. If ever there was a city that could host a beer fest, it's this one. Tens of thousands of visitors are expected to sample over 500 real ales plus 200 foreign beers and lager, cider and perry at this boozetastic event. Hiccups and belches are guaranteed. As are hangovers.

Notting Hill Carnival

Notting Hill, W10, W11 (www.lnhc.org.uk). Ladbroke Grove, Notting Hill Gate & Westbourne Park tube. **Date** 28-29 Aug.

It calls itself Europe's biggest street party, and that may be true, as thousands of revellers show up each year to drink warm beer and wander about in posh Notting Hill. There is occasional live music and relentless and unavoidable sound systems (loaded on to trucks, followed by unglamorous dancers in T-shirts). There's a costume parade, but all too often you miss it because of the crowds (and probably a surfeit of warm beer).

Trafalgar Great River Race

Thames, from Ham House, Richmond, Surrey, to Island Gardens, Greenwich, E14 (8398 9057/www.greatriverrace.co.uk). **Date** 17 Sept.

More than 260 'traditional' boats, from Chinese dragon boats to Viking longboats, vie in the UK traditional boat championship over a 22-mile (35km) course. This year's race commemorates Nelson's victory in the Battle of Trafalgar in 1805. The race begins at 2.30pm with the winners reaching the finish from around 5.30pm. Best viewing point is Richmond Bridge on the riverside and along the South Bank, Millennium Bridge and Hungerford Bridge.

Brick Lane Festival

Brick Lane & Allen Gardens, E1 (7655 0906/ www.visitbricklane.com). Aldgate East tube/ Liverpool Street tube/rail. **Date** Sept (tbc). **Map** p404 S5/6.

This colourful annual celebration of Spitalfields' multicultural communities past and present is everything the Notting Hill Carnival (*see above*) isn't.

Pride London.
See p263.

It is a festive, enjoyable event of food, music, dance and performance, rickshaw rides, stilt-walkers, clowns and jugglers. The main stage showcases world music acts, while the children's area has fun-fair rides, inflatables and workshops.

Regent Street Festival

Regent Street, W1 (7152 5853/www.regent-street. co.uk). Oxford Circus or Piccadilly Circus tube. **Date** 4 Sept. **Map** p399 J6.

Celebrate central London with fairground attractions, theatre, street entertainers and storytelling, as well as a variety of live music.

City of London Flower Show

Guildhall, Gresham Street, The City, EC2 2EJ (8472 3584/www.cityoflondon.gov.uk). Bank or Mansion House tube/Moorgate or Liverpool Street tube/rail. **Date** 5-6 Sept.

Annual event encompassing floral displays, crafts, stalls and more taking place in one of the City's most historic buildings.

Mayor's Thames Festival

Between Westminster & Blackfriars Bridges (7928 8998/www.thamesfestival.org). Blackfriars or Waterloo tube/rail. **Date** 17-18 Sept.

Always fun and occasionally spectacular, this waterfest runs from noon to 10pm all weekend and is highlighted by a lantern procession and firework finale on Sunday evening. But before the pyrotechnics kick off, there are food and crafts stalls in a riverside market, environmental activities and creative workshops, and a lively assortment of dance and music performances.

Open House London

Various venues (09001 600 061/ www.openhouselondon.org). **Date** 17-18 Sept.

An annual event that allows architecture lovers free access to more than 500 fascinating buildings all over the capital, from palaces to private homes to the latest and greatest office spaces. Apply for a buildings guide from the end of August and plan your route, remembering that you'll need to book ahead to gain access to certain buildings.

October-December 2005

Punch & Judy Festival

Covent Garden Piazza, Covent Garden, WC2 (7836 9136/www.coventgardenmarket.co.uk). Covent Garden tube. **Map** p401 L7. **Date** 3 Oct.

More funny-voiced domestic incidents involving the crocodile, a policeman and Mr Punch giving Judy a few slaps (and, vice versa). This special puppet fest celebrates the shows so beloved of Samuel Pepys.

Pearly Kings & Queens Harvest Festival

St Martin-in-the-Fields, Trafalgar Square, Westminster, WC2N 4JJ (7766 1100/www.pearly society.co.uk). Embankment tube/Charing Cross tube/rail. **Map** p401 L7. **Date** 2 Oct.

Pearly kings and queens – so-called because of the shiny white buttons sewn in elaborate designs on their dark suits – have their origins in the 'aristocracy' of London's early Victorian costermongers, who elected their own royalty to safeguard their interests. Now charity representatives, today's pearly monarchy gathers for this 3pm thanksgiving service in their traditional 'flash boy' outfits.

Trafalgar Day Parade

Trafalgar Square, Westminster, WC2 (7928 8978/www.sea-cadets.org/www.trafalgar200.org). Charing Cross tube/rail. **Date** 23 Oct. **Map** p401 K7.

Taking the air

Brits are renowned for their climactic fortitude, but in recent years a combination of warm summers, patio heaters and new venues has conspired to lure this hardy breed outdoors in their masses. Suddenly, it seems London's gone all Mediterranean.

New developments are taking this to heart. The Tower Environs scheme at the Tower of London has successfully created a modern, spacious area on Tower Hill where free events are staged, while in central London, completion of work on the north side of Trafalgar Square in summer 2003 created a pleasant piazza. This year will be the fifth 'Summer in the Square' (7983 4100, www.london.gov.uk), a free programme of cultural events in the square such as live dance and street theatre which last year attracted some 250,000 people.

The Serpentine's Summer Pavilion summer events programme is also in its fifth year and although plans for this year's structure are still awaiting approval at the time of going to press it promises to be spectacular: a giant, grassy 'mountain' will cover the building housing the Serpentine Gallery (see p144).

The South Bank's Royal National Theatre (see p335) has created a space especially for outdoor events: from June through August Theatre Square hosts all manner of unstuffy entertainments, from guerilla theatre to outdoor film screenings.

Another summer highlight is Somerset House (see p102), where a welcome oasis of calm can be found in the large fountained courtyard – except during July the weeks when it hosts its annual series of concerts. In previous years the likes of Lemon Jelly, Goldfrapp and Bebel Gilberto have played well against the background of classical.

Come winter, there's been an explosion in outdoor ice rinks. The old favourite, occupying Liverpool Street Station's back parlour, is Broadgate Circle (7505 4068, www.broadgate ice.co.uk), which has the longest period of operation (from late October to early April). It's now been joined by Somerset House (late Nov-late Jan), Hampton Court (Dec-mid Jan; see p180), Duke of York Square, King's Road, SW3 (early Dec-early Jan; 7730 7978) and Kew Gardens (Dec-early Jan; www.kew gardensicerink.com; see p177).

This year's commemoration of Nelson's victory at the Battle of Trafalgar (21 Oct 1805) will include a special service at St Paul's Cathedral in addition to the usual event in which more than 500 sea cadets parade with marching bands and musical performances culminating in the laying of a wreath at the foot of Nelson's Column.

London Film Festival

National Film Theatre, South Bank, SE1 8XT (7928 3535/www.lff.org.uk). Embankment tube/Waterloo tube/rail. **Date** Oct-Nov. **Map** p401 M8.

Attracting big-name actors and directors and offering the public the chance to see around 150 new British and international features, the LFF centres on the NFT (*see p285*) and the Odeon West End (*see p283*). For other London film festivals, *see p286*.

Diwali

Trafalgar Square, Westminster, WC2 (7983 4100/ www.london.gov.uk). Charing Cross tube/rail. **Date** Nov (call for details).

This annual Festival of Light is celebrated by the capital's Asian community.

State Opening of Parliament

House of Lords, Palace of Westminster, Westminster, SW1A 0PW (7219 4272/ www.parliament.uk). Westminster tube. **Date** Mid-late Nov (call for details). **Map** p401 L9.

In a ceremony that has changed little since the 16th century, the Queen officially reopens Parliament after its summer recess. You can only see what goes on inside on telly, but if you join the throngs on the streets, you can watch Her Maj arrive and depart in her Irish or Australian State Coach, attended by the Household Cavalry.

London to Brighton Veteran Car Run

From Serpentine Road, Hyde Park, W1 (01280 841062/www.lbvcr.com). Hyde Park Corner tube. **Date** 6 Nov. **Map** p395 E8.

Get up at the crack of dawn to catch this parade of around 500 vintage motors, none of which exceeds 20mph on the way to Brighton, setting off from Hyde Park between 7.30am and 9am, aiming to reach Brighton before 4pm. Otherwise, join the crowds lining the rest of the route, which wends down via Westminster Bridge.

Bonfire Night

Date 5 Nov.

This annual pyrotechnic frenzy sees Brits across the country gather – usually in inclement weather – to burn a 'guy' (an effigy of Guy Fawkes, who notoriously failed to blow up James I and his Parliament in the Gunpowder Plot of 1605) on a giant bonfire, and set off loads of fireworks. Most public displays are held on the weekend nearest 5 November; among the best in London are those at Battersea Park, Alexandra Palace and Crystal Palace. Alternatively, try to book a late ride on the relevant nights on the British Airways London Eye (*see p77*).

Lord Mayor's Show

Various streets in the City (7332 3456/ www.lord mayorsshow.org). **Date** 12 Nov.

Today's the day when, under the conditions of the Magna Carta, the newly elected Lord Mayor of London is presented to the monarch or to their justices for approval. Amid a procession of about 140 floats and more than 6,000 people, the Lord Mayor leaves Mansion House at 11am and travels through the City to the Royal Courts of Justice on the Strand, where he makes some vows before returning to Mansion House by 2.30pm. The procession will take around an hour and a quarter to pass you, wherever you stand. The event is rounded off by a firework display from a barge moored on the Thames between Waterloo and Blackfriars Bridges.

Remembrance Sunday Ceremony

Cenotaph, Whitehall, Westminster, SW1. Charing Cross tube/rail. **Date** 13 Nov. **Map** p401 L8.

In honour of those who lost their lives in World Wars I and II, the Queen, the Prime Minister and other dignitaries lay wreaths at the Cenotaph, Britain's memorial to 'the Glorious Dead'. After a minute's silence at 11am, the Bishop of London leads a service of remembrance.

Christmas Lights & Tree

Covent Garden (7836 9136/www.covent gardenmarket.co.uk); Oxford Street (7976 1123/www.oxfordstreet.co.uk); Regent Street (7152 5853/www.regent-street.co.uk); Bond Street (www.bondstreetassociation.com); Trafalgar Square (7983 4234/www.london.gov.uk). **Date** Nov-Dec.

Though the Christmas lights on London's main shopping streets are an increasingly commercialised proposition), much of the childhood wonder still remains in the glittering lights on St Christopher's Place, Marylebone High Street, Bond Street and Kensington High Street. The giant fir tree in Trafalgar Square each year is a gift from the Norwegian people, in gratitude for Britain's role in liberating their country from the Nazis.

The London International Horse Show

Olympia, Hammersmith Road, Kensington, W14 8UX (0870 733 0733/www.olympiahorseshow.com). Kensington (Olympia) tube/rail. **Date** 13-19 Dec.

This annual extravaganza for equestrian enthusiasts has dressage, showjumping, and much more.

New Year's Eve Celebrations

Date 31 Dec.

Celebratory events in London tend to be local in nature, though Trafalgar Square has traditionally been an unofficial gathering point. Otherwise, many of the city's nightclubs hold ludicrously expensive New Year parties. If you're feeling up to it the next morning, the extremely raucous New Year's Day Parade starts at Parliament Square at noon, and finishes at Berkeley Square, taking in Whitehall, Trafalgar Square and Piccadilly.

Arts & Entertainment

Children

The kids'll be all right in this city.

London Zoo. *See p273.*

For weekly listings consult *Time Out*'s Children pages. Better still, buy *Time Out London for Children* (£9.99), which details the provision for children in London's museums, galleries, leisure centres and parks. Note that a family Travelcard is excellent value, especially at weekends, when two adults and up to four children can all travel Zones 1 and 2 for £2.80.

Area guide

In the localities we list below, the attractions are all within convenient walking distance of one another, there are green spaces for picnicking on and playing in and, crucially, you can get away from the endless traffic.

The South Bank to Bankside p75

Children love the **British Airways London Eye** (*see p77*), the nearby **London Aquarium** (*p77*) and the **BFI London IMAX Cinema** (*p285*). Summertime in this area is lively, thanks to adventures laid on by the free **Coin Street Festival** (*see p262*) and at the **National**

Theatre's alfresco events centre Theatre Square. Walking east takes you to Clink Street and its museum, and on to the **Golden Hinde** (*see p81*), famed for its party and sleepover programme. Further on, Tooley Street gives (accompanied over-tens) a thrill courtesy of the **London Dungeon** (*see p86*). **HMS Belfast** (*see p83*) is the ultimate war-game location.

The City p88

The **Tower of London** (*see p99*) can keep kids busy all day, as can the **Museum of London** (*see p100*). From here, you can head west along the London Wall and descend the steps by the old Roman fort to the Barber Surgeons' garden, thence to the **Barbican** (*see p333*) with its children's library, Saturday films and occasional free foyer events.

Covent Garden p126

Children are most diverted by the performances on the piazza, but best of all is the excellent **Theatre Museum** (the thespian arm of the

Arts & Entertainment

V&A), where school holidays see free events and workshops for children. **London's Transport Museum** (*see p127*) is a hit with under-tens, who love the activity trails, climb-on buses and the tube simulator.

Trafalgar Square p132

The remodelling of Trafalgar Square means that pram pushers no longer have to brave an unceasing flow of traffic to get from the fountains and Nelson's Column to the **National Gallery** (*see p132*). Apart from its vast art collection, this extraordinary institution has paintings trails to follow, and weekend activities for children on the second Saturday and Sunday of each month. The **National Portrait Gallery** (*see p133*) has an interactive IT gallery and frequent school holiday events. Nearby, **St Martin-in-the-Fields** (*see p133*) has a Brass Rubbing Centre.

South Kensington p140

Often the first choice for a family museum visit, the **Natural History Museum** (*see p141*) has the Dinosaurs Gallery, the Creepy Crawlies gallery and an earthquake mock-up in the Earth Galleries. The **Science Museum** (*see p141*) has hands-on activities, Science Nights and sleepovers for eight- to 11-year-olds. In the **V&A Museum** (*see p141*), there are children's workshops and activities at weekends.

Greenwich p167

The best way to reach Henry VIII's favourite place is by boat. From **Greenwich Pier**, it's a short walk to the **National Maritime Museum**, with its interactive galleries and frequent workshops and storytelling sessions. The **Cutty Sark** (*see p169*) needs all the visitors it can get. In **Royal Greenwich Park** free events take place during the summer.

Childcare & advice

Parentline Plus (0808 800 2222, www.parent lineplus.org.uk) gives confidential advice on being a parent; **4Children** (7512 2112/info line 7512 2100/www.4children.org.uk) is about after-school clubs and family services. **Simply Childcare** (7701 6111, www.simply childcare.com) offers childcare listings.

Childminders

6 Nottingham Street, Marylebone, W1U 5EJ (7935 3000/2049/www.childminders.co.uk). **Open** 8.45am-5.30pm Mon-Thur; 8.45am-5pm Fri; 9am-4.30pm Sat. **Rates** £5.20-£6.90/hr. **Credit** AmEx, MC, V. **Map** p398 G5.

A large agency with more than 1,500 babysitters, mainly nurses, nannies and infant teachers (all with references), who live in London or the suburbs.

Pippa Pop-ins

430 Fulham Road, Chelsea, SW6 4SN (7731 1445/ www.pippapopins.com). **Open** 8.15am-6pm Mon-Fri. **Rates** Sessions £40-£80. **Credit** MC, V. **Map** p398 G5.

A nursery school and kindergarten whose staff host parties, holiday activities and a crèche. **Other locations**: 165 New King's Road, Chelsea, SW6 1DU (7731 1445).

Universal Aunts

PO Box 304, SW4 0NN (daytime childminding 7738 8937/evenings 7386 5900/www.universalaunts.co.uk). **Open** 9.30am-5pm Mon-Thur; 9.30am-4pm Fri. **Rates** Agency fee from £15. Childminding from £8.50/hr. Babysitting from £5/hr. **No credit cards**.

This London agency, founded in 1921, provides reliable people to babysit, to meet children from trains, planes or boats, or to take them sightseeing.

City farms

Contact the **British Federation of City Farms** (0117 923 1800, www.farmgarden.org. uk) for a complete list.

Freightliners City Farm

Paradise Park, Sheringham Road, off Liverpool Road, Islington, N7 8PF (7609 0467/www.freight linersfarm.org.uk). Caledonian Road or Holloway Road tube/Highbury & Islington tube/rail. **Open** Summer 10am-4.45pm Tue-Sun. Winter 10am-4pm Tue-Sun. **Admission** free; donations appreciated.

Many of the cows, goats, pigs and poultry are rare breeds. Giant Flemish rabbits are the biggest you will see anywhere; guinea fowl run amok in other animals' pens; exotic cockerels with feathered feet squawk alarmingly; bees fly around their hives.

Mudchute City Farm

Pier Street, Isle of Dogs, E14 3HP (7515 5901/ www.mudchute.org). Crossharbour or Island Gardens DLR. **Open** 9am-4pm daily. **Admission** free; donations appreciated.

Ducks, chickens, goats, pigs, llamas, sheep and some cattle all live here. There's a small aviary and petting corner for bunny-hugging. Depending on the time of year, children can help the farmers bottle-feed lambs, shear sheep, milk goats or collect eggs.

Vauxhall City Farm

24 St Oswald's Place, Tyers Street, Vauxhall, SE11 5JE (7582 4204). Vauxhall tube/rail/2, 36, 44, 77, 360 bus. **Open** 10.30am-4pm Wed-Sun. **Admission** free; donations appreciated.

This farm project was created from a couple of acres of derelict land back in 1977. The farmyard inhabitants include pigs, donkeys, goats, chickens, rabbits and guinea pigs, all thriving under the adoring gaze of visiting children. Vauxhall City Farm runs workshops and special needs riding sessions.

Arts & Entertainment

Suffer the little children

Hogarth decreed that the place should also be the first public art gallery. Many artists, including Gainsborough, Reynolds and Wilson, donated their work, while Handel gave performances of his *Messiah* at the hospital chapel, and left a fair copy of the score to the hospital in his will.

The museum recounts this period, using pictures, manuscripts and objects, timelines and interactive exhibits including a lottery machine that describes the lucky-dip selection procedure that once determined which, out of the hundreds of abandoned babies presented, could stay. Even more tragic is the case full of mementos left by mothers for their babies.

British society's sentimental attitude toward its pampered young is not just a 21st-century phenomenon. The idealisation of innocent babes was all the rage in fashionable Georgian society, where a 'bleeding heart' provided evidence of a lady's refinement. Children born in poverty around that time were duly grateful, however, because it was only when royalty espoused the child welfare cause in 1739 that plans for Thomas Coram's Foundling Hospital came to fruition.

The **Foundling Museum**, which opened in June 2004, recalls the social history of the Foundling Hospital with exhibitions on the original buildings, the lives of the children who grew up in them and the work of compassionate shipwright and sailor Captain Thomas Coram and other benefactors.

When Coram returned to England from America in 1720, he was appalled by the numbers of abandoned children he saw on the streets. He resolved to build a 'Hospital for the Maintenance and Education of Exposed and Deserted Young Children' and petitioned royalty – George I – for patronage, at first without much luck. The second George, or rather his wife Caroline, who took a sentimental interest, proved more amenable. A charter for the hospital was signed in 1739. Royal favour paved the way for other benefactors, notably the artist William Hogarth and the composer George Frideric Handel, who both became governors.

Also displayed are artworks donated to the hospital, including the Hogarth series featuring *Gin Lane*, depicting the levels of drunken despair among the poor. On the top floor, the Gerald Coke collection consists of cases of Handeliana – scores and busts, the composer's will and a quartet of 'musical chairs', from whose ear-level speakers sitters can select extracts from his greatest works.

Young visitors to the museum are made much of. They're given well-equipped activity packs to help them explore the collections. Depending on their age, they can study the art and create pictures of their own, or play with puzzles and toys. No one need feel left out; this is, in every sense of the word, a child-friendly place.

The Foundling Museum

40 Brunswick Square, Bloomsbury, WC1N 1AZ (7841 3600/www.foundlingmuseum. org.uk). Russell Square tube. **Open** 10am-6pm Tue-Sat; noon-6pm Sun. **Admission** £5; £3 concessions; free under-16s. **Credit** MC, V. **Map** p399 L4.

Eating & drinking

See also chapter **Restaurants & Cafés** *p192*
for **Smiths of Smithfield**, **Wagamama** and
Carluccio's Caffè, all loved by kids.

Blue Kangaroo

555 King's Road, Fulham, SW6 2EB (7371 7622/
www.thebluekangaroo.co.uk). Fulham Broadway tube,
then 11, 19, 22 bus. **Meals served** 9.30am-7pm
Mon-Fri; 9.30am-8.30pm Sat, Sun. **Main courses**
£8-£16. **Credit** AmEx, MC, V. **Map** p396 C13.
The bouncy Blue Kangaroo sits on a frenetic indoor
playground, but the food and service appease the
adults. The children's menu (£4.95 with a drink) lists
own-made all-breast chicken nuggets, chunky real
burgers and crud-free organic sausages; a mixed-
leaf salad can replace chips, if required.

Boiled Egg & Soldiers

63 Northcote Road, Battersea, SW11 1NP (7223
4894). Clapham Junction rail, then 319 bus. **Open**
9am-6pm Mon-Sat; 9am-4pm Sun. **Main courses**
£3.95-£4.95. **No credit cards**.
On weekdays, after nursery, or Saturday afternoons,
after the park, the café is packed with families.
Breakfasts are lovely, from fry-ups to humble five-
minute eggs, with toastie soldiers. Afternoon teas,
with cucumber sandwiches, own-made cakes and
cookies are another big attraction.

Bush Garden Café

59 Goldhawk Road, Shepherd's Bush, W12 8EG
(8743 6372). Goldhawk Road tube. **Open** 8am-5pm
Mon-Sat. **Main courses** £3.90-£4.60. **Credit**
(min £10) AmEx, MC, V.
This wholesome café and quality grocery shop has
a back garden with a playhouse. The fare is all
health-giving produce: fruit juice, pressed to order
(£2.20); salads and quiches; veg hot-pots, soups and
bean salads. For children, there's Marmite on toast,
beans on toast and boiled eggs, all priced at £1.50.

Dexter's Grill

20 Bellevue Road, Wandsworth, SW17 7EB (8767
1858). Wandsworth Common rail. **Meals served**
noon-11pm Mon-Fri; 10am-11pm Sat, Sun. **Main**
courses £6.50-£14. **Credit** AmEx, MC, V.
The good quality nursery food available for young
children (shepherd's pie, cheesy broccoli pasta and
bangers and mash, made with some organic ingredients) is a big draw for Dexter's. Kids with more
fast-food inclinations can have small-sized burgers,
baby back ribs, hot dogs, fish and chips or all-day
breakfasts. Puddings include a sundae with loads of
extra toppings served separately.

Frizzante@City Farm

1A Goldsmith's Row, Hackney, E2 8QA (7739
2266/www.frizzanteltd.co.uk). Bus 26, 48, 55.
Meals served 10am-4.30pm Tue-Sun. **Main**
courses £4.50-£6.50. **No credit cards**.
Winner of the *Time Out* Best Family Restaurant
gong, this Italian café is down on the farm. Food

ordered from the kitchen hatch includes steak sandwiches, vegetarian or meaty pies and quiches, big
salads, and a children's menu of either pasta or ultra-
thin, delicious pizzas (£2.50). Failing that you can
choose from the lovely hot daily specials.

Giraffe

46 Rosslyn Hill, Hampstead, NW3 1NH (7435 0343/
www.giraffe.net). Hampstead tube. **Brunch served**
8am-4pm Mon-Fri; 9am-5pm Sat, Sun. **Lunch**
served noon-4pm Mon-Fri; noon-5pm Sat, Sun.
Dinner served 5-11pm Mon-Fri; 6-11pm Sat, Sun.
Credit AmEx, MC, V.
Each branch of Giraffe has a great family location:
check the website for the other six. Giraffe's flexi-
bility is the key to its success: you can pop in for
breakfast, brunch, lunch, dinner or just a quick
snack from the globally eclectic menu. The children's menu has both meat-based and veggie
options. Kids also love the huge shakes and juices
with the giraffe-shaped straws.

Rainforest Café

20 Shaftesbury Avenue, Soho, W1D 7EU (7434
3111/www.therainforestcafe.co.uk). Piccadilly Circus
tube. **Meals served** noon-9pm Mon-Thur; noon-
8pm Fri; 11.30am-8pm Sat; 11.30am-10pm Sun.
Main courses £9.95-£15.95. **Credit** AmEx, DC,
MC, V. **Map** p401 K7.
A steamy rainforest mockup, and the city's largest
no-smoking restaurant, whose menu for children
includes interestingly named thematic burgers, ribs,
pizza, chicken and pasta.

Smollensky's on the Strand

105 Strand, Covent Garden, WC2R 0AA (7497
2101/www.smollenskys.co.uk). Embankment tube/
Charing Cross tube/rail. **Meals served** noon-
midnight Mon-Wed; noon-12.30am Thur-Sat; noon-
5.30pm, 6.30-10.30pm Sun. **Main courses** £8.85-
£19.95. **Set meal** (noon-7pm, after 10pm Mon-Fri)
£10 2 courses, £12 3 courses. **Credit** AmEx, DC,
MC, V. **Map** p401 L7.
Saturdays and Sundays are (smoke-free) family
affairs at Smollensky's, when the flustered staff grin
winningly at the children underfoot. Entertainers –
balloon-modelling clowns, jolly jesters and face-
painters – are wheeled in to do their stuff. Children
choose between hot dogs, fish, chicken or burgers
with curly fries, or go for pasta or pizza. For adults
there are steaks, seafood and veggie choices.

TGI Friday's

6 Bedford Street, Covent Garden, WC2E 9HZ (7379
0585/www.tgifridays.co.uk). Covent Garden or
Embankment tube/Charing Cross tube/rail. **Meals**
served noon-11.30pm Mon-Sat; noon-11pm Sun.
Main courses £7.15-£16.35. **Credit** AmEx, MC, V.
Map p401 L7.
Children at TGI are plied with balloons, activity
sheets and crayons and there are occasional entertainers (ring for details). The whole experience is a
delight for small people, a tad headachey for parents. Food is classic American restaurant fare.

Arts & Entertainment

Entertainment

Cinema

These cinemas have screenings for children at weekends. For full listings, *see p281* **Film**. **Clapham Picture House**, **Electric Cinema**, **Everyman**, **NFT**, **Rio**, **Ritzy**.

Puppets

Little Angel Theatre

14 Dagmar Passage, off Cross Street, Islington, N1 2DN (7226 1787/www.littleangeltheatre.com). Angel tube/Highbury & Islington tube/rail, then 4, 19, 30, 43 bus. **Open** *Box office* 10am-6pm Mon-Fri; 9.30am-4.30pm Sat, Sun. **Tickets** £7.50; £5 children. **Credit** MC, V.

London's only permanent puppet theatre. Shows cover a huge range of styles and the calendar is peppered with shows by touring companies from across the country eager to work with the theatre's rare proscenium arch. Most productions are aimed at audiences aged five and over. A Saturday Puppet Club runs alongside most major productions.

Puppet Theatre Barge

Opposite 35 Blomfield Road, Little Venice, W9 2PF (7249 6876/www.puppetbarge.com). Warwick Avenue tube. **Box office** 10am-8pm daily. **Children's shows** *Term-time* Sat, Sun. *School holidays* daily. **Tickets** £7.50; £7 under-16s, concessions. **Credit** MC, V.

The barge's combination of high-quality puppet shows – courtesy of Movingstage Productions – and the loveliness of the location remains unique. Small and cosy (there are just 60 seats), the barge is moored on the towpath in Little Venice between November and June. Between July and October, the barge embarks on a summer tour of the Thames.

Theatre

Half Moon Young People's Theatre

43 White Horse Road, Stepney, E1 0ND (7709 8900/ www.halfmoon.org.uk). Limehouse DLR/rail. **Open** *Box office* 10am-6pm Mon-Fri; 10am-4pm Sat. **Tickets** £5; £3.50 under-18s, concessions. **Credit** MC, V.

The Half Moon is a pillar of creativity, uniting young people regardless of race, gender or financial situation. Its fully accessible theatre is home to two studios, between them offering an annual calendar of performances for kids from six months old.

Polka Theatre

240 The Broadway, Wimbledon, SW19 1SB (8543 4888/www.polkatheatre.com). South Wimbledon tube/Wimbledon tube/rail, then 57, 93, 219, 493 bus. **Open** *Phone bookings* 9.30am-4.30pm Mon; 9am-6pm Tue-Fri; 10am-5pm Sat. *Personal callers* 9.30am-4.30pm Tue-Fri; 10am-5pm Sat. **Tickets** £5-£14. **Credit** AmEx, MC, V.

A dedicated young people's theatre with a highly praised programme of events. Daily shows are staged by touring companies in the main auditorium (10.30am, 2pm), with weekly performances – rarely featuring more than two actors, and often puppet-based – taking place in the Adventure Theatre for those younger than four.

Unicorn Theatre for Children

Tooley Street, SE1 (7700 0702/www.unicorn theatre.com).

The Unicorn's brand new purpose-built theatre in Southwark is scheduled to open at the end of 2004. This renowned company continues to tour an exciting programme of theatre for children.

Science & nature

Camley Street Natural Park

12 Camley Street, King's Cross, NW1 0PW (7833 2311/www.wildlondon.org.uk). King's Cross tube/rail. **Open** *May-Sept* 9am-5pm Mon-Thur; 11am-5pm Sat, Sun. *Oct-Apr* 9am-dusk Mon-Thur; 10am-4pm Sat, Sun. Closed 20 Dec-1 Jan. **Admission** free. **Map** p399 L2.

The London Wildlife Trust's flagship reserve is in an unpromising part of town, but has a pond for dipping in, meadow and woodland for minibeast hunting and staff committed to spreading the environmental message. The visitors' centre is a rustic cabin stuffed with bird, bat and spider studies and information on urban flora and fauna. Check the LWT website for bookable kids' events here.

London Wildlife Trust Centre for Wildlife Gardening

28 Marsden Road, East Dulwich, SE15 4EE (7252 9186/www.wildlondon.org.uk). East Dulwich or Peckham Rye rail. **Open** 10.30am-4.30pm Tue-Thur, Sun. **Admission** free.

This nature reserve was created on a disused bus depot. Children can wander through a range of natural habitats, from wilderness to cultivated, including woodland, marshland and kitchen garden. There's a froggy pond area, a plant nursery, a play area and sandpit. The visitors' centre – used by school parties – has tanks of fish and stick insects.

Museums & galleries

All London's top museums have a children's programme of some sort. Some of the best include workshops, storytelling sessions and trails that take place at weekends and during school hols at **Tate Modern** (*see p83*) and **Tate Britain** (*see p139*). Children join the Young Friends of the **British Museum** (*see p107*) for a chance to stay the night. The **National Army Museum** (*see p146*), often forgotten in the stampede to neighbouring South Kensington's Albertopolis, presents army life entertainingly, as does the family-friendly **Imperial War Museum** (*see p171*).

The **Museum of Childhood at Bethnal Green** (*see p160*) has art and craft workshops and soft-play sessions at weekends. The **Ragged School Museum** (*see p162*), a Victorian classroom preserved from 1908, will learn 'em. The **Horniman Museum** (*see p172*) and the **Livesey Museum for Children** (682 Old Kent Road, SE15 1JF, 7639 5604/www. liveseymuseum.org.uk, open 10am-4.30pm Tue-Sat) justify the tube-free pilgrimage into south-east London. Both are free; the Livesey is designed for under-12s, with themed interactive displays (check the website for upcoming exhibitions) and the Horniman has a music room, gardens, animals and shows for children during summer. The **Wimbledon Lawn Tennis Museum** (*see p179*) offers an inspired range of activities. The **Royal Air Force Museum Hendon** (*see p156*) has an imaginative programme for young visitors.

Spaces to play

Regent's Park (*see p113*) has two boating lakes (one for children), four playgrounds, loads of sporting facilities and an open-air theatre, as well as the fabulous **London Zoo** (*see p114*). **Kensington Gardens** (*see p141*) has the Diana, Princess of Wales playground (*see p143* **Water palaver**). The grounds of **Syon House** (*see p188*) include indoor and outdoor play areas. **Hampstead Heath** (*p151*) and Parliament Hill are great for views and kite-

flying. **Highbury Fields** (*see p155*) has an unusually varied playground. **Battersea Park** (*see p175*) has a decent adventure playground and a small children's zoo. **Crystal Palace Park** (*see p173*) has huge model dinosaurs and a maze as well as the usual play equipment. **Dulwich Park** has recumbent bikes and trikes for hire and a busy but well-maintained playground. The longest walks can be had at **Richmond Park** (*see p180*), where kids can cycle (bike hire available), spot herds of red and fallow deer and visit the Isabella Plantation. In east London, elegant **Victoria Park** (*see p161*) has a central playground, tennis courts, a bowling green, fallow deer, ducks and geese. Scruffy **Mile End Park** has go-karts, a children's playground and eco-themed holiday activities. **West Ham Park** has the edge for children's sporting events and free summer activities for little ones.

To find out about safe, supervised play areas, get in touch with **Kids** (7520 0405, www.kids-online.org.uk), which has six playgrounds across London where disabled and able-bodied children aged five to 15 can play safely.

Coram's Fields

93 Guilford Street, Bloomsbury, WC1N 1DN (7837 6138/info@coramsfields.org.uk). Russell Square tube. **Open** *Apr-Sept* 9am-7pm daily. *Oct-Mar* 9am-6pm daily. **Admission** free (adults only admitted if accompanied by child under 16). **Map** p399 L4/M4. This bit of Captain Coram's land was given to London's children in 1936. There are lawns, sand-

Crystal Palace Park.

pits, a football pitch, a basketball court and play areas with climbing towers, a helterskelter chute, swings and an assault-course pulley. There's also a café, animal enclosures (sheep, goats, ducks, rabbits and an aviary) and for the under-threes a drop-in playgroup and occasional clowns' visits in summer.

Diana, Princess of Wales Memorial Playground

Nr Black Lion Gate, Broad Walk, Kensington Gardens, W8 2UH (7298 2117/recorded information 7298 2141/www.royalparks.gov.uk). Bayswater or Queensway tube/12, 94, 148 bus. **Open** *Summer* 10am-7.30pm. *Winter* 10am-4pm (unaccompanied adults may enter between 9.30am-10am) daily. **Admission** free, all adults must be accompanied by a child. **Map** p394 C7.

The focal point is a pirate ship in a sea of fine white sand. Children enjoy scaling the rigging, the ship's wheel, cabins, pulleys and ropes. Beyond these lies the teepee camp: a trio of wigwams. The treehouse encampment has walkways, ladders, slides and 'tree phones'. The playground's attractions appeal to the senses: scented shrubs, willows and bamboo, footfall chimes and touchy-feely sculpture engage young visitors. Much of the equipment has been designed for use by children with special needs.

Discover

1 Bridge Terrace, Stratford, E15 4BG (8536 5555/ www.discover.org.uk). Stratford tube/rail/DLR. **Open** *Term-time* 10am-5pm Tue-Thur, Sat, Sun. *School holidays* 10am-5pm daily. **Admission** *Garden* free. *Story Trail* £3; £2 concessions. **No credit cards**.

This interactive play centre for children aged two to seven is all about making stories. There's plenty to do, both indoors and out. The garden has a space rocket to climb in, slides and chunky wooden climbing frames, living willow tunnels for hide and seek, a wet-play area and picnic benches. It's a beautiful resource for local children in a bleak area. Inside the centre, Story Builders help children play their imaginary games as they wander through a whole series of settings. Regular weekend and holiday activities.

Indoor playgrounds

Bramley's Big Adventure

136 Bramley Road, North Kensington, W10 6TJ (8960 1515/www.bramleysbig.co.uk). Latimer Road tube/295 bus. **Open** 10am-6pm Mon-Fri; 10am-6.30pm Sat, Sun. **Admission** *School days* £4.40 5-adult; £3.90 under-5s; £2.50 under-2s. *Weekends & school holidays* £4.80 5-adult; £4.40 under-5s; £3 under-2s. **Credit** AmEx, MC, V.

Bramley's indoor adventure playground (slides, ball ponds, monkey swings) rings to the shrieks of feral children. Parties are a popular option.

Tiger's Eye

42 Station Road, Merton, SW19 2LP (8543 1655/ www.tigerseye.co.uk). South Wimbledon tube . **Open** 10am-6pm Tue-Sun. **Admission** £4.50 2-10s; £2.25 under-2s. **Credit** MC, V.

The barn-like Tiger's Eye is an indoor play centre for kids up to the age of ten. The soft-play equipment has a height restriction of 4ft 9in (1.44m).

Theme parks

Call to check parks are open before you set out.

Chessington World of Adventures

Leatherhead Road, Chessington, Surrey KT9 2NE (0870 444 7777/www.chessington.com). **Getting there** *By train* Chessington South rail, then 71 bus. *By car* J9/10 off M25/M26. **Open** *Apr-Nov* 10am-5pm or 6pm daily. *Late July-early Sept* 10am-7pm daily; times may vary according to special events. Height restrictions vary on rides. **Admission** £28 (accompanying child free); £18 additional under-12s; £18 concessions. Check website for advance bookings for fast-track entry. **Credit** MC, V.

Chessington is now happy to leave most of the white-knuckle stuff to its sister park, Thorpe (*see below*). It has reinvented itself as a family-friendly theme park, and to that end 90% of the rides and attractions are suitable for the under-12s.

Legoland

Winkfield Road, Windsor, Berks SL4 4AY (0870 504 0404/www.legoland.co.uk). **Getting there** *By train* Windsor & Eton Riverside or Windsor Central rail. *By car* J3 off M3 or J6 off M4. **Open** *Mid Mar-early Nov* 10am-5pm or 6pm (during summer holidays) or 7pm (Aug) daily. **Admission** *Peak (school holidays)* £23; £20 3-15s, concessions. *Off-peak* £21; £19 3-15s, concessions. **Credit** MC, V.

Brilliant, but a pricey option for a family, Legoland is full of fun. Miniland contains the greatest concentration of Lego bricks in the park. Some 35 million have been used to create scenes from Europe, including memorable London landmarks, such as the London Eye and the Tower of London. Then there's the Driving School, which gives its successful participants a Legoland driver's licence, the Lego Safari and two mildly thrilling rides. Toddlers love Duplo Land and the shows in the four theatre venues around the complex. Expect queues.

Thorpe Park

Staines Road, Chertsey, Surrey KT16 8PN (0870 444 4466/www.thorpepark.com). **Getting there** *By train* Staines rail, then 950 bus. *By car* J11/13 off M25.* **Open** *Apr-late July, early Sept-early Nov* 9.30am-5pm weekdays; 9.30am-6pm weekends. *Late July-early Sept* 9.30am-7pm daily. Height restrictions vary, depending on rides. **Admission** £28; £21 children, concessions; £78 family (2+2, 1+3); free under-4s. Check website or phone for advance bookings; allow 24hrs to process advance ticket purchases. **Credit** AmEx, MC, V.

Thorpe markets itself as white-knuckle central; its rides have macho names – like Nemesis Inferno, a legs-dangling swoop through 2,460ft (750m) of suspended track, turning through 360° loops. Colossus is the world's first ten-looping coaster. Tidal Wave is one of the highest water-drop rides in Europe.

Comedy

Heard the one about the great stand-up scene?

When jobbing comedians from overseas decide to make their name, they usually come here. Why? Well, though there's no major festival to speak of – nothing on the scale of Edinburgh, or Brighton, at any rate – there is a sophisticated, bustling scene that populates atmospheric pub basements and fine purpose-built venues with top-notch names, character comedy, ventriloquists, impressionists, improv artists, satirists, double acts and folk you've seen off the telly who started their names on the circuit and feel like going back to their roots.

A word of warning for summer visitors: you'll find that most smaller clubs close during August when all and sundry head up north for the Edinburgh Festival, whose successes rejuvenate the autumn circuit. Lastly, it's good to see legendary promoter Malcolm Hardee back in action again at Up the River in Rotherhithe, bringing the best names on the circuit to the dark dank alliterative depths of Surrey Quays.

Major venues

Amused Moose Soho

Moonlighting, 17 Greek Street, Soho, W1D 4DR (8341 1341/www.amusedmoose.co.uk). Leicester Square or Tottenham Court Road tube. **Shows** 7.45pm Thur, Fri; 7.30pm Sat. **Admission** £5-£12. **No credit cards. Map** p399 K6.
This well-established Soho club now has a welcome addition on the road leading up to the heights of Hampstead, and continues apace with its quality bills of stand-up and character comedy and courses for performers and writers. In recent years, *Time Out* Live Award-winners Eddie Izzard, Adam Bloom and Noel Fielding have appeared.
Other locations: The Enterprise, Haverstock Hill, NW3 (8341 1341).

Banana Cabaret

The Bedford, 77 Bedford Hill, Balham, SW12 9HD (8673 8904/www.bananacabaret.co.uk). Balham tube/ rail. **Shows** 9pm Fri, Sat. **Admission** £10 Fri, £7 concessions; £14 Sat, £10 concessions. **No credit cards.**
The well-known venue with the drum-shaped stage is where Mark Thomas used to warm up for his politically charged TV shows. Skilful and experienced comics take up most nights, with around four or five solo stand-ups on the bill. At the same venue, but not part of the Banana Cabaret, is the New Act Night at the Bedford (Tue).

Bearcat Club

Turk's Head, 28 Winchester Road, Twickenham, Middx TW1 1LF (8891 1852/www.bearcat comedy.co.uk). St Margaret's rail. **Shows** 8.45pm Sat. **Admission** £10 non-members; £9 members. **No credit cards.**
October 2004 marked the 20th anniversary of the loveable Bearcat, which has made its name churning out strong bills of stand-up to the well-to-do denizens of Twickenham.

Bound & Gagged

The Fox, 413 Green Lanes, Palmers Green, N13 4JD (8450 4100/www.boundandgaggedcomedy.com). Palmers Green rail/329, W2, W6 bus. **Shows** 8.15pm doors, 9.15pm show Fri. **Admission** £8; £5 concessions. **No credit cards.**
The scruffy Tufnell Park outpost may have closed, but this plush Palmers Green venue is still going strong. Its huge management roster includes the likes of Phill Jupitus, Gina Yashere and Omid Djalili – a good sampling of the type of acts you might see.

Canal Café Theatre

Bridge House, Delamere Terrace, Little Venice, W2 6ND (7289 6054). Warwick Avenue tube. **Shows** Newsrevue 9.30pm Thur-Sat; 9pm Sun. Ring box office for details of other shows. **Admission** £5-£10; £4-£8 concessions. **No credit cards. Map** p294 C4.
The Canal Café's most famous resident is the political satire Newsrevue, a topical mix of sketches and songs updated every week. Past alumni include Rory Bremner and Josie Lawrence.

Chuckle Club

Three Tuns Bar, London School of Economics, Houghton Street, Holborn, WC2A 2AL (7476 1672/ www.chuckleclub.com). Holborn tube. **Shows** 7.45pm Sat. **Admission** £10; £8 concessions. **No credit cards. Map** p399 M6.
Eugene Cheese (real name: Paul) has been compering this fun night for as long as we can remember. His trademark warm-up – the 'Chuckle Club Song' – is worth the admission fee alone. As for the bills: they're consistently high quality, and go down a treat with the cheap beer (at LSE union prices).

Comedy Café

66-68 Rivington Street, Shoreditch, EC2A 3AY (7739 5706/www.comedycafe.co.uk). Liverpool Street or Old Street tube/rail. **Shows** 8.30pm Wed-Sat. **Admission** £14 Sat; £10 Fri; £5 Thur; free Wed. **Credit** MC, V. **Map** p403 R4.
A purpose-built venue in Shoreditch is bound to host some fun, and the Comedy Café doesn't disappoint. You won't necessarily find the biggest names on the

circuit, but you'll get a fine calibre of comedic talent, usually in the form of four stand-ups a night and open spots on Wednesdays.

Comedy Store
1A Oxendon Street, St James's, SW1Y 4EE (Ticketmaster 08700 602 340/www.thecomedy store.co.uk). Leicester Square or Piccadilly Circus tube. **Shows** 8pm Tue-Thur, Sun; 8pm, midnight Fri, Sat. Occasional Mon shows. **Admission** £13-£15; £8 concessions. **Credit** MC, V. **Map** p401 K7.
If any comedy club is the stuff of legend, it's this one. After an inauspicious start above a Soho strip club in the 1970s, the Store established itself as the spiritual home of alternative comedy; today the club still hosts some of the best names on the circuit. On Wednesdays and Sundays there is improv from the Comedy Store Players; Tuesdays offer the topical and innovative Cutting Edge show. Stand-up bills usually dominate the rest of the week.

Gongs show

Some are judged by industry executives, others are judged by those who really know the business. Whatever your feelings on awards ceremonies, they provide a useful starting point on the new faces to watch in the capital. This was the 2004 honours list.

Love them or loathe them, the most high-profile of the bunch are the Perrier Awards. An unexciting nominee list yielded a surprise winner in solo actor-turned-comic Will Adamsdale, whose show was a spoof centred around a motivational guru. Best Newcomer was another send-up character comic – punk parody Will Hodgson. Egyptian American Ahmed-Ahmed created a buzz as the winner of the first Richard Pryor Award for Ethnic Comedy while stand-up Andrew 'Poor Little Ginger Boy' Lawrence won the Amused Moose Star Search. The long-running So You Think You're Funny Award produced a winner from the other side of the world – Aussie new-boy Nick Sun.

Every January the Hackney Empire announces the winner of its regular New Act Night competition – comedian Peter Aterman won in 2004 with his amusing comic-theatrical set pieces. And just before it all gets too worthy, you can be sure of some more loony offerings, too: one comedy club in Edinburgh launched the Ginger Award for — you guessed it – 'the best red, auburn or ginger-haired comic at the 2004 festival'.

Downstairs at the King's Head
2 Crouch End Hill, Crouch End, N8 8AA (pub 8340 1028/office 01920 823265/www.downstairsatthe kingshead.com). Finsbury Park tube/rail, then W7 bus. **Shows** 8.30pm Thur, Sat, Sun. **Admission** £4 Thur; £8 Sat; £7 Sun. **No credit cards**.
Comedian Sean Lock says this is the best club in London; most punters won't deny that it's one of the friendliest. On Wednesdays, the Sketch Club is a showcase for sketch and character comedy. Thursdays see the Try Out Nights, where 15 newish comics take to the stage. Don't worry, they're not all newbies: there are also established comics who use the occasion to try out new material.

Ha Bloody Ha
Ealing Studios, Ealing Green, St Mary's Road, Ealing, W5 5EP (8566 4067/www.headlinerscomedy. biz). Ealing Broadway tube/rail. **Shows** 8.45pm Fri, Sat. **Admission** £8. **No credit cards**.
This comedy club, a west London institution, takes place at the legendary Ealing Studios. Bills here – largely stand-up oriented – are strong ones. The club is also the main thrust behind July's annual Ealing Comedy Festival, which traditionally takes place at Walpole Park on Mattock Lane.

Hampstead Clinic
Downstairs at the White Horse, 154 Fleet Road, Hampstead, NW3 2QX (7485 2112). Belsize Park tube/Hampstead Heath rail. **Shows** 8.30pm Sat. **Admission** £7; £5 concessions. **Credit** MC, V.
This small cellar scores points for being one of the most atmospheric and intimate venues in town. Stand-up bills stick to the tried and tested.

Headliners
The George IV, 185 Chiswick High Road, Chiswick, W4 2DR (8566 4067/www.headlinerscomedy.biz). Turnham Green tube. **Shows** 9pm Fri; 8.30pm Sat. **Admission** £10. **Credit** MC, V.
West London's first purpose-built comedy club, now over two years old, has gone down a treat with the locals thanks to its smart but unfussy surroundings. Expect lively audiences and strong stand-up bills.

Jongleurs Comedy Club
Battersea *Bar Risa, 49 Lavender Gardens, SW11 1DJ. Clapham Junction rail.* **Shows** 8.30pm Fri, Sat. **Admission** £16.
Bow *221 Grove Road, E3 1AA. Mile End tube.* **Shows** 8.30pm Fri, Sat. **Admission** £14-£15.
Camden *Dingwalls, Camden Lock, Chalk Farm Road, NW1 8AB. Chalk Farm tube.* **Shows** 8.30pm Fri, Sat. **Admission** £16-£17.
All information 0870 787 0707/box office 7564 2500/www.jongleurs.com. **Credit** AmEx, MC, V.
The first Jongleurs venue opened in 1983. Since then, the chain has grown so fast, you could call it the Starbucks of comedy (hell, there's even a branch in Magaluf). That said, the line ups here include some of the biggest names in the business. Love it or loathe it, the format is the same at each venue: quality bills, plus a restaurant, a bar and a disco afterwards.

Comedy Café. *See p275.*

Lee Hurst's Backyard Comedy Club

231 Cambridge Heath Road, Bethnal Green, E2 0EL (77393122/www.leehurst.com). Bethnal Green tube/rail. **Shows** 8pm Thur; 8.30pm Fri, Sat. **Admission** £5 Thur; £10-£12 Fri; £11-£13 Sat. **Credit** AmEx, MC, V.

Comedian Lee Hurst made his name on the popular TV game show *They Think It's All Over*. Hurst's goggle box enhanced clout has helped to ensure the 400-capacity east London venue can attract top names – usually three a night, plus a compere (Hurst is there most nights). There's a restaurant upstairs.

Red Rose Comedy Club

129 Seven Sisters Road, Finsbury Park, N7 7QG (7281 3051/www.redrosecomedy.co.uk). Finsbury Park tube/rail. **Shows** 9pm Sat. **Admission** £8; £6 concessions. **No credit cards**.

Established in 1987 and situated at the back of a Labour club, this comedy institution was originally set up by Ivor Dembina. Expect a bill of top names and quality up-and-comers, plus a late bar until 1am.

Up the Creek

302 Creek Road, Greenwich, SE10 9SW (8858 4581/www.up-the-creek.com). Greenwich DLR/rail. **Shows** 9pm Fri; 8.30pm Sat. **Admission** £10 Fri, £6 concessions; £14 Sat, £10 concessions. **Credit** AmEx, DC, V.

Some say audiences here are the most discerning on the circuit; others argue that they're just the rowdiest. Whatever they are, Up the Creek regulars come in droves for the strong bills (mostly stand-up sets).

Up the River

4 Odessa Street, Rotherhithe, SE16 7LU (7231 7134). Surrey Quays tube. **Shows** telephone for details. **Admission** £10; £6 concessions. **No credit cards**.

London's newest club, situated in a former nightclub

('it's a bit 1970s,' reckons founder Malcolm Hardee), is located in the depths of Rotherhithe, and holds 350 punters. Those who venture out will be justly rewarded with some terrific names – Jo Brand, Jenny Eclair and Jerry Sadowitz among them. Catering comes courtesy of chef French Fred.

Other venues

Brixton Comedy Club *The Hobgoblin, 95 Effra Road, Brixton, SW2 1DF (7633 9539/www.brixton comedy.co.uk). Brixton tube/rail.* **Shows** 8.30pm Sun.

Comedy Brewhouse *Camden Head, 2 Camden Walk, Camden Passage, Islington, N1 8DY (7359 0851). Angel tube.* **Shows** 9pm Fri, Sat.

Covent Garden Comedy Club *20 Upper St Martin's Lane, Covent Garden, WC2 (07960 071340). Leicester Square tube.* **Shows** 8.30pm Fri, Sat.

Hampstead Comedy Club *The Washington, 50 England's Lane, Hampstead, NW3 4UE (7928 1035/www.hampsteadcomedy.co.uk). Belsize Park or Chalk Farm tube.* **Shows** 9pm Sat.

Hen & Chickens Theatre *109 St Paul's Road, Highbury Corner, Islington, N1 2NA (7704 2001/ www.henandchickens.com). Highbury & Islington tube/rail.* **Shows** 8pm Mon, Sun.

Laughing Horse Soho *Coach & Horses, 1 Great Marlborough Street, Soho, W1F 7HG (bookings 07796 171190/www.laughinghorse.co.uk). Oxford Circus tube.* **Shows** 8.30pm Tue, Sat. Also at Camden, Richmond and Wimbledon.

Mirth Control *Lower Ground Bar, 269 West End Lane, NW6 1QS (7431 2211/www.mirthcontrol.org. uk). West Hampstead tube/rail.* **Shows** 7.45pm Wed.

Oxford Street Comedy Club *The Wheatsheaf, 25 Rathbone Place, Fitzrovia, W1T 1JB (7580 1585). Tottenham Court Road tube.* **Shows** 9pm Sat.

Pear-Shaped in Fitzrovia *Fitzroy Tavern, 16 Charlotte Street, Fitzrovia, W1T 2LY (7580 3714). Goodge Street tube.* **Shows** 8pm Wed.

Arts & Entertainment

Dance

It's moving stuff.

The unpronounceable, inimitable **Cholmondeleys** and **Featherstonehaughs**. *See p279.*

London arguably has one of the most varied and sophisticated dance scenes in the world, and savvy programming by major venues, supplemented by activities in a plethora of smaller spaces, ensures that the art form thrives year-round. What's more the city is bursting with classes for dance lovers, in genres from flamenco, Egyptian, African, street and swing to all varieties of Latin dance.

Check the Dance listings in the weekly *Time Out* magazine for the most comprehensive, up-to-date information on what to see and where to go, or try the website www.londondance.com. For information on specific companies, *see p279* **Super troupers**, and for more on the popular annual **Dance Umbrella** festival, contact the Place (*see below*).

Major venues

Barbican Centre

Silk Street, The City, EC2Y 8DS (0845 120 7553/ www.barbican.org.uk). Barbican tube/Farringdon or Moorgate tube/rail. **Box office** *In person*

10am-8pm Mon-Sat; noon-8pm Sun daily. *Phone bookings* 9am-8pm daily. **Tickets** £5-£40. **Credit** AmEx, MC, V. **Map** p402 P5.

The year-round Barbican International Theatre Event (BITE) programme, now in its eighth year, has gradually turned this arts centre into a major player on London's dance scene. Dance is just one component of BITE (for theatrical productions, *see p333*), but a very vital one. The Barbican frequently co-commissions works in collaboration with both continental and American theatres.

The Place

17 Duke's Road, Bloomsbury, WC1H 9PY (7387 0031/www.theplace.org.uk). Euston tube/rail. **Box office** 10.30am-6pm Mon-Fri; noon-6pm Sat; 8pm on performance evenings. **Tickets** £5-£15. **Credit** MC, V. **Map** p399 K3.

This internationally recognised dance venue provides top-notch professional training as well as classes in all genres for all levels. The 300-seat theatre presents innovative contemporary dance from around the globe. The 2005 season opens in January with *Resolution!*, an annual platform for young artists who can boast a different triple-bill nightly. In autumn the venue is used by Dance Umbrella, the UK's top dance festival. The Place is home base for the Richard Alston Dance Company and also offers extended residencies to a variety of young creative talents.

Royal Opera House
Bow Street, Covent Garden, WC2E 9DD (box office 7304 4000/www.royal operahouse.org.uk). Covent Garden tube. **Box office** 10am-8pm Mon-Sat. **Tickets** £3-£175. **Credit** AmEx, DC, MC, V. **Map** p401 L7.

This magnificent theatre's main stage is home to the Royal Ballet, where you can see stars of the calibre of Carlos Acosta, Darcey Bussell, Alina Cojocaru and Sylvie Guillem. For 2005, company director Monica Mason has programmed an exceptional season celebrating the centenary of Frederick Ashton, the company's founding choreographer.

Ticket prices start cheap (excellently located standing-room places and more dicey restricted views on the far edges of the auditorium) and end high. The ROH complex has a pair of more affordable spaces: the Linbury Studio Theatre, a 420-capacity theatre, with a good reputation for mid-scale West End music and dance productions, and the Clore Studio Upstairs, used for rehearsals, workshops and experimental performances. Programming responsibility for both spaces, linked together under the name of ROH2, lies with ex-Royal dancer Deborah Bull.

The ROH's main lobby, the Vilar Floral Hall, is one of the most handsome public spaces anywhere in London. It also serves as the venue for afternoon tea dances, usually twice a month. A 90-minute backstage tour is available most days of the week.

Sadler's Wells Theatre
Rosebery Avenue, Finsbury, EC1R 4TN (box office 0870 737 7737/www.sadlerswells.com). Angel tube. **Box office** *In person* 10am-8.30pm daily. *Phone bookings* 9am-8.30pm daily. **Tickets** £10-£40. **Credit** AmEx, MC, V. **Map** p402 N3.

One of the premier dance venues in the world, with the most exciting performance line-up in town. Top international companies from Pina Bausch and William Forsythe to major British troupes such as Rambert Dance Company and Birmingham Royal Ballet are showcased throughout the year. The 1,500-seat theatre is augmented by the small Lilian Baylis Theatre where more experimental works can be seen. Several Dance Umbrella performances are seen here each year, including the innovative 'Stand Up for Dance' series, which gives punters a chance to see top dance groups for just £5.

South Bank Centre
Belvedere Road, South Bank, SE1 8XX (box office 0870 380 0400/recorded information 7921 0973/www.rfh.org.uk). Waterloo tube/rail. **Box office** 11am-8pm daily; 11am-9pm on performance evenings. *Phone bookings* 9am-8pm daily. **Tickets** £5-£75. **Credit** AmEx, MC, V. **Map** p401 M8.

This multi-building complex regularly presents British and international dance companies in three theatres: the huge Royal Festival Hall, the medium-sized Queen Elizabeth Hall and the pocket-sized Purcell Room. Extensive ongoing renovations will be continuing throughout 2005, necessitating the closure of the RFH for 18 months from July. The inconvenience is balanced by the promise of big improvements of both the stages and public spaces.

Other venues

Chisenhale Dance Space
64-84 Chisenhale Road, Bow, E3 5QZ (8981 6617/www.chisenhaledancespace.co.uk). Bethnal Green/Mile End tube. **Open** *Enquiries* 10am-6pm Mon-Sat. **Tickets** free-£10. **Credit** MC, V.

Super troupers

If you want to make doubly sure you're not missing out on an amazing performance that you just didn't hear about in time, try having a quick trawl of the websites of some prominent London-based dance companies. Among these are the cutting-edge team of the all-female **Cholmondeleys** (pronounced Chumlees) and male **Featherstonehaughs** (Fanshaws), the brainchild of Lea Anderson, an inventive and irreverent iconoclast. For both, see www.thecholmondeleys.org. **DV8 Physical Theatre** (www.dv8.co.uk) is another highly acclaimed, innovative company, while the excellent **Candoco** (www.candoco.co.uk) integrates the work of disabled and non-disabled dancers in often-stunning performances. **Rambert Dance Company** (www.rambert.org.uk), the oldest and largest of the country's contemporary operations, prides itself on its accessible but thoughtful productions, such as the recent *Five Brahms Waltzes in the Manner of Isadora Duncan*. Also with a good reputation for challenging and varied contemporary dance is the **Henri Oguike** company (www.henrioguikedance.co.uk).

On a grander scale, the **English National Ballet** needs no introduction, but for information on the season's projects and performances (such as flawless renditions of classics like *Romeo & Juliet* and *The Nutcracker*), check www.ballet.org.uk. For information on the prestigious **Royal Ballet**, contact the Royal Opera House (*see left*). Lastly, the current productions of Matthew Bourne's highly respected company **New Adventures** can be found at www.new-adventures.net.

This seminal research centre for contemporary dance and movement-based disciplines runs various workshops and community projects, as well as a summer school. Celebrating its 21st anniversary in 2004/5, this season's schedule promises to be especially rich in experimentation.

The Circus Space

Coronet Street, Hoxton, N1 6HD (7613 4141 ext 226/www.thecircusspace.co.uk). Old Street tube/rail. **Open** 9am-10pm Mon-Fri; 10.30am-6pm Sat, Sun. **Classes** phone for details. **Membership** free. **Credit** MC, V. **Map** p403 R3.

Courses and workshops in all types of circus arts are run at this superb venue, from casual juggling to red-nose training for staff development, take place in this Hoxton venue. It also presents physical, choreographed performances in its impressive space (a former turbine hall). Aerial dance is one of the trends of the moment, with mainstream modernist choreographers such as Fin Walker experimenting with off-the-ground dancing.

Greenwich Dance Agency

Borough Hall, Royal Hill, Greenwich, SE10 8RE (8293 9741/www.greenwichdance.org.uk). Greenwich DLR/rail. **Box office** 9.30am-5.30pm Mon-Fri. **Classes** £3.75-£5. **Tickets** £7-£12. **Credit** MC, V.

Several of the country's best young companies and dance artists reside in this handsome old venue, where a variety of classes and workshops are complemented by an inventive programme of shows.

ICA

The Mall, Westminster, SW1Y 5AH (box office 7930 3647/www.ica.org.uk). Piccadilly Circus tube/Charing Cross tube/rail. **Box office** noon-9.30pm daily. **Tickets** £5-£20. **Membership** *Daily* £1.50, £1 concessions. *Weekend* £2.50; £1.50 concessions. Free under-14s. **Credit** AmEx, DC, MC, V. **Map** p401 K8.

This trendsetting arts centre sometimes hosts movement-based theatre and performance with an avant-garde or technological bent.

Jacksons Lane

269A Archway Road, Highgate, N6 5AA (8341 4421/www.jacksonslane.org.uk). Highgate tube. **Open** 10am-11pm daily. *Phone bookings* 10am-7pm daily. **Tickets** £4.50-£10. **Credit** MC, V.

This community centre puts on many performances and activities, including contemporary dance – Zone 3 in autumn 2004, for instance, commissioned work from some of the UK's brightest emerging choreographers. Classes range from ballet to breakdance.

Laban Centre

Creekside, Lewisham, SE8 3TZ (information 8691 8600/tickets, from Greenwich Theatre 8858 7755/www.laban.org). Deptford DLR/ Greenwich DLR/rail. **Open** 10am-6pm Mon-Sat; or until start of performance on performance evenings. **Tickets** £1-£15. **Credit** MC, V.

This independent conservatoire for contemporary dance training and research runs undergraduate and postgrad courses. Its stunning, award-winning

£22m premises include an intimate auditorium for shows by Laban's resident company Transitions and dance performances from visiting companies, as well as frequent student showcases.

Riverside Studios

Crisp Road, Hammersmith, W6 9RL (8237 1000/box office 8237 1111/www.river sidestudios.co.uk). Hammersmith tube. **Box office** noon-9pm daily. **Tickets** £4.50-£25. **Credit** MC, V.

This arts and media centre occasionally presents British and international contemporary dance and physical theatre in three auditoria.

Dance classes

As well as all-rounders like the Greenwich Dance Agency and Danceworks, London has a number of educational specialists. Cecil Sharp House offers fun classes in a variety of folk dance styles from around the world, while the London School of Capoeira teaches that uniquely pretty Brazilian fusion of dance, gymnastics and martial arts.

Cecil Sharp House English Folk Dance & Song Society

2 Regent's Park Road, Camden, NW1 7AY (7485 2206/www.efdss.org). Camden Town tube. **Enquiries** 9.30am-5.30pm Mon-Fri. **Classes** £5-£8.50. **Credit** AmEx, MC, V.

Dance Attic

368 North End Road, Fulham, SW6 1LY (7610 2055/www.danceattic.com). Fulham Broadway tube. **Open** 9am-10pm Mon-Fri; 10am-5pm Sat, Sun. **Classes** £4-£6. **Membership** £2/day; £40/6mths; £70/yr. **Credit** MC, V. **Map** p396 A12.

Danceworks

16 Balderton Street, Mayfair, W1K 6TN (7629 6183/www.danceworks.net). Bond Street tube. **Open** 9am-10pm Mon-Fri; 9.30am-6pm Sat, Sun. **Classes** £4-£10. **Membership** £2-£4/day; £40/mth; £60-£120/yr. **Credit** AmEx, MC, V. **Map** p398 G6.

Drill Hall

16 Chenies Street, Fitzrovia, WC1E 7EX (7307 5060/www.drillhall.co.uk). Goodge Street tube. **Open** 10am-9.30pm daily. **Classes** £5-£25. **Courses** £30-£100. **Credit** AmEx, MC, V. **Map** p399 K5.

London School of Capoeira

Units 1 & 2, Leeds Place, Tollington Park, Finsbury Park, N4 3RQ (7281 2020/www.londonschool ofcapoeira.co.uk). Finsbury Park tube/rail. **Classes** phone for details. **No credit cards. Map** p399 K3.

Pineapple Dance Studio

7 Langley Street, Covent Garden, WC2H 9JA (7836 4004/www.pineapple.uk.com). Covent Garden tube. **Open** 9am-9.30pm Mon-Fri; 9am-6pm Sat; 10am-6pm Sun. **Classes** £5-£8. **Membership** £2/day; £4/evening; £25/mth; £65/quarter; £140/yr. **Credit** AmEx, MC, V. **Map** p399 L6.

Film

London's interesting and independent screens refuse to be multiplexed away.

On location: *28 Days Later.*

London loves film, and its Cinemascope-wide spectrum of picture houses is a testament to this wide and varied appetite for all things celluloid. From the pile 'em high multiplexes screening blockbusters, prequels and sequels via loved locals and respected rep houses to exclusive members-only bars/cinemas, the film scene is pretty varied. This is not the case outside the city centre, though. Some London boroughs have fewer cinemas than the national average – poor old Lewisham in south London hasn't a single one. Only if you're a Bollywood fan is it worth travelling much out of the centre. The racy potboilers and all-singing, all-dancing romances unfold mostly in the suburbs, and places like the Grade II listed **Himalaya Palace** (*see p285*) justify a long journey in search of the exotic.

In the city centre, though, there are a number of first-run cinemas whose varied programmes stand out from the crowd. The **Curzon Soho** (*see p283*) and **Ritzy** (*p284*) lead the pack of new-look arthouse 'miniplexes' offering a mix of new independent releases, classic matinées and

special seasons and events, along with bars and cafés where you can linger afterwards and discuss auteurs and actors with fellow cineastes. The **ICA** (*see p283*) and the **Other Cinema** (*p283*) can be relied upon to provide arty, edgy, political and rare fare. The **Riverside** (*see p285*) maintains a steady programme of thoughtful repertory double-bills, but the **National Film Theatre** (*p285*) is London's best-appointed showcase for the cinematic treasures of the past. The **Prince Charles** (*see p285*) screens recent releases on rotation, offering the chance to see things you missed when all the other cinemas were showing them, for the cheapest prices in town.

For cinema news see *Time Out* magazine each week. *Time Out* also publishes a fat and fantastic *Film Guide* (£19.99).

Films released in the UK are classified under the following categories: **U** – suitable for all ages; **PG** – open to all, parental guidance is advised; **12A** – under-12s only admitted with an over-18; **15** – no one under 15 is admitted; **18** – no one under 18 is admitted.

First-run cinemas

The closer to Leicester Square, the more you pay. Many cinemas charge less on Mondays or before 5pm from Tuesday to Friday; call them for details. Book ahead if you're planning to see a blockbuster on the weekend of its release: new films emerge in the UK on Fridays.

Central London

Apollo West End
19 Lower Regent Street, Mayfair, W1Y 4LR (0871 223 3444/www.apollocinemas.co.uk). Piccadilly Circus tube. **Screens** 5. **Tickets** £12.50; £8.50 before 5pm. **Credit** MC, V. **Map** p400 J7.

Barbican
Silk Street, The City, EC2Y 8DS (information 7382 7000/bookings 7638 8891/www.barbican.org.uk). Barbican tube/Moorgate tube/rail. **Screens** 3. **Tickets** £7; £5.50 concessions; £4.50 Mon. **Credit** AmEx, MC, V. **Map** p402 P5.

Chelsea Cinema
206 King's Road, Chelsea, SW3 5XP (7351 3742). Sloane Square tube. **Screens** 1. **Tickets** £7.50-£8.50. Early shows £5.50; £3.50 concessions. **Credit** AmEx, MC, V. **Map** p397 E12.

Curzon
Mayfair *38 Curzon Street, Mayfair, W1J 7TY (7495 0500/www.curzoncinemas.com). Green Park or Hyde Park Corner tube.* **Screens** 2. **Tickets** £8.50; £5.50 concessions (selected times). Early shows £5.50. **Credit** AmEx, MC, V. **Map** p400 H8.
Soho *99 Shaftesbury Avenue, Soho, W1D 5DY (information 7292 1686/bookings 7734 2255/www.curzoncinemas.com). Leicester Square or Piccadilly Circus tube.* **Screens** 3. **Tickets** £8.50; £5.50 concessions (selected times). Early shows £5.50. **Credit** AmEx, MC, V. **Map** p401 K6.

Empire
4-6 Leicester Square, Soho, WC2H 7NA (0870 010 2030/www.uci.co.uk). Leicester Square or Piccadilly Circus tube. **Screens** 3. **Tickets** £8-£10; £5-£5.50 concessions (selected times). Early shows £5.50-£6.50. **Credit** AmEx, MC, V. **Map** p401 K7.

ICA Cinema
Nash House, The Mall, St James's, SW1Y 5AH (information 7930 6393/bookings 7930 3647/www.ica.org.uk). Piccadilly Circus tube/Charing Cross tube/rail. **Screens** 2. **Tickets** £6.50; £5.50 concessions. Early shows £4.50. Membership £20-£30/yr. **Credit** AmEx, DC, MC, V. **Map** p401 K8.

Odeon
Covent Garden *135 Shaftesbury Avenue, Covent Garden, WC2H 8AH (0871 224 4007/www.odeon.co.uk). Leicester Square or Tottenham Court Road tube.* **Screens** 4. **Tickets** £9; £6 concessions (select times). 2-5pm £5; before 2pm (Mon-Fri only) £4. **Credit** AmEx, MC, V. **Map** p399 K6.

Leicester Square *Leicester Square, Soho, WC2H 7LP (0871 224 4007/www.odeon.co.uk). Leicester Square tube.* **Screens** 1. **Tickets** £11.50-£13. Early shows £7-£8. **Credit** AmEx, MC, V. **Map** p401 K7.
Mezzanine *next to Odeon Leicester Square, Soho, WC2H 7LP (0871 224 4007/www.odeon.co.uk). Leicester Square tube.* **Screens** 5. **Tickets** £8.50. Early shows £5. **Credit** AmEx, MC, V. **Map** p401 K7.
Marble Arch *10 Edgware Road, Marylebone, W2 2EN (0871 224 4007/www.odeon.co.uk). Marble Arch tube.* **Screens** 5. **Tickets** £9; £6 concessions (select times). Early shows £6. **Credit** AmEx, MC, V. **Map** p395 F6.
Panton Street *11-18 Panton Street, Soho, SW1Y 4DP (0871 224 4007/www.odeon.co.uk). Piccadilly Circus tube.* **Screens** 4. **Tickets** £8.50; £5.50. Early shows £4. **Credit** AmEx, MC, V. **Map** p401 K7.
Tottenham Court Road *30 Tottenham Court Road, Fitzrovia, W1T 1BX (0871 224 4007/www.odeon.co.uk). Tottenham Court Road tube.* **Screens** 3. **Tickets** £8.50; £5.80 concessions. Early shows £5.80. **Credit** AmEx, MC, V. **Map** p399 K5.
Wardour Street *10 Wardour Street, Soho, W1D 6QF (0871 224 4007/www.odeon.co.uk). Leicester Square or Piccadilly Circus tube.* **Screens** 4. **Tickets** £5. **Credit** AmEx, MC, V. **Map** p401 K7.
West End *40 Leicester Square, Soho, WC2H 7LP (0871 224 4007/www.odeon.co.uk). Leicester Square tube.* **Screens** 2. **Tickets** £11.50; £7 concessions (select times). Early shows £7. **Credit** AmEx, MC, V. **Map** p401 K7.

The Other Cinema
11 Rupert Street, Soho, W1D 7PR (information 7437 0757/bookings 7734 1506/www.picturehouses.co.uk). Leicester Square or Piccadilly Circus tube. **Screens** 2. **Tickets** £8; £4.50 concessions (selected times). Early shows & Mon £4.50. No concessions available Fri-Sun. **Membership** £25 single; £43 joint; £15 students; £6 mailing list. **Credit** MC, V. **Map** p401 K7.

Renoir
Brunswick Square, Bloomsbury, WC1N 1AW (7837 8402/www.artificial-eye.com). Russell Square tube. **Screens** 2. **Tickets** £7.50. Early shows £5; £3.50 concessions. **Credit** MC, V. **Map** p399 L4.

Screen on Baker Street
96-98 Baker Street, Marylebone, W1U 6TJ (box office 7935 2772/7486 0036/www.screencinemas.co.uk). Baker Street tube. **Screens** 2. **Tickets** £7. Early shows £5. **Credit** MC, V. **Map** p398 G5.

UGC
Haymarket *63-65 Haymarket, Chinatown, SW1Y 4RQ (box office 0871 200 2000/0870 777 2775/www.ugccinemas.co.uk). Piccadilly Circus tube.* **Screens** 3. **Tickets** £8.50; £5.50 concessions (selected times). Early shows £4 before noon. **Credit** AmEx, MC, V. **Map** p401 K7.
Chelsea *279 King's Road, Chelsea, SW3 5EW (box office 0871 200 2000/7376 4744/www.ugccinemas.co.uk). Sloane Square tube, then 11, 19, 22, 319 bus.* **Screens** 4. **Tickets** £8.30; £4.90 concessions. Early shows £4.50. **Credit** AmEx, MC, V. **Map** p397 E12.

Arts & Entertainment

Shaftesbury Avenue *30 Coventry Street, Soho,*
W1D 7AQ (box office 0871 200 2000/7434 0032/
www.ugccinemas.co.uk). Piccadilly Circus tube.
Screens 7. **Tickets** £8.50; £5.50 concessions
(selected times). Early shows £5.50. **Credit** AmEx,
MC, V. **Map** p401 K7.

Vue West End
Leicester Square, Soho, WC2H 7AL (0871 224
0240/www.myvue.com). Leicester Square tube.
Screens 9. **Tickets** £10-£11; £8 concessions.
Early shows £8.50. **Credit** MC, V. **Map** p401 K7.

Outer London

Clapham Picture House
76 Venn Street, Clapham, SW4 0AT (information
7498 2242/bookings 7498 3323/www.picturehouses.
co.uk). Clapham Common tube. **Screens** 4. **Tickets**
£7.50; £4.50 concessions; no concessions Fri-Sun;
£5.50 for all before 6pm. **Credit** MC, V.

Electric Cinema
191 Portobello Road, Notting Hill, W11 2ED (7908
9696/www.the-electric.co.uk). Ladbroke Grove or
Notting Hill Gate tube. **Screens** 1. **Tickets** £10-
£12.50; £5-£7.50 Mon. **Credit** AmEx, MC, V.

Everyman Cinema Club
5 Hollybush Vale, Hampstead, NW3 6TX (08700
664777/www.everymancinema.com). Hampstead
tube. **Screens** 2. **Tickets** £9 (gallery £15); £7.50
concessions (select times). **Credit** MC, V.

Gate Cinema
87 Notting Hill Gate, Notting Hill, W11 3JZ (7727
4043/www.gatecinema.co.uk). Notting Hill Gate tube.
Screens 1. **Tickets** £9; £4.50 concessions (select
times). Early shows £7. **Credit** MC, V.
Map p394 A7.

Notting Hill Coronet
103 Notting Hill Gate, W11 3LB (7727 6705/www.
coronet.org). Notting Hill Gate tube. **Screens** 2.
Tickets £7; £4.50 concessions (select times). Early
shows £4.50; all tickets Tue £3.50 . **Credit** MC, V.
Map p394 A7.

Odeon
Camden Town *14 Parkway, Camden, NW1 7AA*
(0871 224 4007/www.odeon.co.uk). Camden Town
tube. **Screens** 5. **Tickets** £8; £6 concessions; £5.50
seniors/children (selected times). **Credit** AmEx,
MC, V.

Kensington *263 Kensington High Street,*
Kensington, W8 6NA (0871 224 4007/www.odeon.
co.uk). Earl's Court/High Street Kensington tube.
Screens 6. **Tickets** £9.10; £6 concessions (select
times). Early shows £6. **Credit** AmEx, MC, V.
Map p396 A9.

Swiss Cottage *96 Finchley Road, Swiss Cottage,*
NW3 5EL (0871 224 4007/www.odeon.co.uk). Swiss
Cottage tube. **Screens** 6. **Tickets** £8.20; £5.50-
£5.80 concessions (select times). Early shows £5.80.
Credit AmEx, MC, V.

Phoenix
52 High Road, Finchley, N2 9PJ (box office 8444
6789/8883 2233/www.phoenix cinema.co.uk). East
Finchley tube. **Screens** 1. **Tickets** £4-£7; £4-£5.50
concessions (selected times). Early shows *Mon-Fri*
£4.25-£4.75; *Sat, Sun* £4.50-£5.50. **Credit** MC, V.

Rio Cinema
107 Kingsland High Street, Dalston, E8 2PB (7254
6677/www.riocinema.org.uk). Dalston Kingsland
rail/30, 38, 56, 76, 149, 236, 242, 243, 277 bus.
Screens 1. **Tickets** £7; £5.50 concessions. Early
shows, all shows Mon £5/£4. Late shows £6.
Credit AmEx, MC, V.

Ritzy
Brixton Oval, Coldharbour Lane, Brixton, SW2 1JG
(bookings 7733 2229/www.picturehouses.co.uk).
Brixton tube/rail. **Screens** 5. **Tickets** £7; £5
concessions; £4.50 Mon. Early shows £2.50.
Credit MC, V.

Screen on the Green
83 Upper Street, Islington, N1 0NP (7226 3520/
www.screencinemas.co.uk). Angel tube. **Screens** 1.
Tickets £7. Early shows, all shows Mon £4.80.
Credit MC, V. **Map** p402 O2.

Screen on the Hill
203 Haverstock Hill, Belsize Park, NW3 4QG (7435
3366/www.screencinemas.co.uk). Belsize Park tube.
Screens 1. **Tickets** £8; £5 concessions (selected
times). Early shows, all shows Mon £5.50. **Credit**
MC, V.

Tricycle Cinema
269 Kilburn High Road, Kilburn, NW6 7JR
(information 7328 1900/bookings 7328 1000/
www.tricycle.co.uk). Kilburn tube. **Screens** 1.
Tickets £7; £6 concessions (selected times);
£4.50 Mon. **Credit** MC, V.

UCI
Whiteleys *2nd Floor, Whiteleys Shopping Centre,*
Queensway, Bayswater, W2 4YL (0870 010 2030/
www.uci-cinemas.co.uk). Bayswater or Queensway
tube. **Screens** 8. **Tickets** £8; £4/£5 concessions
(selected times). Early shows £5.75. **Credit** AmEx,
MC, V. **Map** p394 C6.

UGC
Fulham Road *142 Fulham Road, Chelsea, SW10*
9QR (0871 200 2000/www.ugccinemas.co.uk). South
Kensington tube. **Screens** 6. **Tickets** £8.30;
£5.50 concessions (select times). Early shows
£4.50. **Credit** AmEx, MC, V. **Map** p397 D11.

Vue
Finchley Road *255 Finchley Road, Swiss Cottage,*
NW3 6LU (0871 224 0240/www.myvue.com).
Finchley Road tube. **Screens** 8. **Tickets** £8.30;
£5.70 concessions. Early shows £5-£6. **Credit** MC, V.

Islington *Parkfield Street, Islington, N1 0PS (0871*
224 0240/www.myvue.com). Angel tube. **Screens** 9.
Tickets £8.30; £5.70 concessions. Early shows
£5-£6. **Credit** MC, V.

Curzon Soho. *See p283.*

Shepherd's Bush *West 12 Centre, Shepherd's Bush Green, Shepherd's Bush, W12 8PP (0871 224 0240/www.myvue.com). Shepherd's Bush tube.* **Screens** 12. **Tickets** £6.90; £5 concessions. Early shows £5. **Credit** MC, V.

Repertory cinemas

Several first-run cinemas also offer a more limited selection of rep-style fare. These include the **Barbican**, **Clapham Picture House**, **Curzons Mayfair** and **Soho**, **Electric**, **Everyman**, **ICA**, **Phoenix**, **Rio**, **Ritzy** and **Tricycle**.

Ciné Lumière
Institut Français, 17 Queensberry Place, South Kensington, SW7 2DT (7073 1350/www.institut. ambafrance.org.uk). South Kensington tube. **Screens** 1. **Tickets** £7; £5 concessions; £5 members. **Credit** MC, V. **Map** p397 D10.

National Film Theatre (NFT)
South Bank, SE1 8XT (information 7633 0274/ bookings 7928 3232/www.bfi.org.uk/nft). Embankment tube/Waterloo tube/rail. **Screens** 3. **Tickets** £7.90; £6 concessions. **Credit** AmEx, MC, V. **Map** p401 M7.

Prince Charles
7 Leicester Place, Leicester Square, WC2H 7BY (bookings 7494 3654/www.princecharlescinema.com). Leicester Square tube. **Screens** 1. **Tickets** £3-£4 non-members; £1.50-£3 members. **Credit** MC, V. **Map** p401 K7.

Riverside Studios
Crisp Road, Hammersmith, W6 9RL (8237 1111/ www.riversidestudios.co.uk). Hammersmith tube. **Screens** 1. **Tickets** £5.50; £4.50 concessions. **Credit** MC, V.

Watermans Arts Centre
40 High Street, Brentford, Middx TW8 0DS (8232 1010/www.watermans.org.uk). Brentford or Kew Bridge rail. **Screens** 1. **Tickets** £6.50 non-members; £5.85 members; £4.50 concessions. **Credit** MC, V.

Bollywood cinemas

Belle-Vue Cinema, Willesden
95 High Road, Willesden Green Library, NW10 (8830 0823). Willesden Green tube. **Screens** 1. **Tickets** *Bollywood* £6; £4 all day Wed. *Hollywood* £5; £4 all day Tue. *All films* £4 Mon-Fri before 5pm.

Boleyn Cinema
7-11 Barking Road, Newham, E6 1PW (8471 4884/ www.boleyncinema.co.uk). Upton Park rail. **Screens** 3. **Tickets** £5; £3.50 Tue. Early shows £3.50. **No credit cards.**

Himalaya Palace
14 South Road, Southall, Middx UB1 3AD (8813 8844/ www.himalayapalace.co.uk). Southall rail. **Tickets** £4.95-£5.95. *Early shows* £3.95. **Credit** MC, V.

Safari Cinema, Harrow
Station Road, Harrow, Middx HA1 2TY (8426 0303/www.safaricinema.com). Harrow & Wealdstone tube/rail. **Tickets** £6; £4 concessions. Early shows £4. **Credit** AmEx, MC, V.

Uxbridge Odeon
The Chimes Shopping Centre, Uxbridge, Middx UB8 1GD (0871 224 4007/www.odeon.co.uk). **Screens** 9. **Tickets** £6.80; £4.70-£5 concessions. Early shows £5.80. **Credit** AmEx, MC, V.

IMAX

BFI London IMAX Cinema
1 Charlie Chaplin Walk, South Bank, SE1 8XR (0870 787 2525/www.bfi.org.uk/imax).Waterloo tube/rail. **Screens** 1. **Tickets** £7.90; £4.95 children; £6.50 concessions; free under-3s. **Credit** AmEx, MC, V. **Map** p401 M8.
The biggest screen in the country for 3-D delight.

Science Museum IMAX Theatre
Exhibition Road, South Kensington, SW7 2DD (0870 870 4868/www.sciencemuseum.org.uk). South Kensington tube. **Screens** 1. **Tickets** £7.50; £6 concessions. **Credit** AmEx, MC, V. **Map** p397 D9.
A big noise in a big museum. *See also p141.*

Arts & Entertainment

Halloween Short Film Festival

ICA (7766 1407/www.shortfilms.org.uk). **Dates** 13-16 Jan 2006 (phone to check).

A shorts showcase with a punk/DIY bent.

Human Rights Watch International Film Festival

7733 2229/www.hrw.org/iff. **Dates** 17-24 Mar 2005.

Screens fiction, documentary and animated films.

London Lesbian & Gay Film Festival

National Film Theatre, South Bank, SE1 8XT (7928 3232/www.llgff.org.uk). Embankment tube/Waterloo tube/rail. **Dates** Spring 2005. **Map** p401 M7.

186 new and restored films from around the world.

onedotzero

ICA (7766 1407/box office 7930 3647/ www.onedotzero.com). **Dates** May 2005.

Showcase of moving-image innovation.

Rushes Soho Shorts Festival

www.sohoshorts.com. **Dates** July 2005.

Around 60 short films and music videos by new directors are screened for free at venues across Soho.

Portobello Film Festival

Westbourne Studios & other venues (8960 0996/ www.portobellofilmfestival.com). **Dates** 5-21 Aug 2005.

'London's biggest filmic free-for-all': an open-access neighbourhood film and video jamboree.

BFM International Film Festival

ICA, Prince Charles & Rio (7766 1407/8531 9199/ www.bfmmedia.com). **Dates** Sept 2005.

This *Black Filmmaker*-programmed festival shows works from inside and outside the mainstream.

Resfest

NFT (7928 3232/www.resfest.com). Embankment/ Waterloo tube. **Dates** Sept-Oct 2005.

International travelling festival of new wave digitally inflected shorts and more, akin to onedotzero.

Raindance

Shaftesbury Avenue cinemas (7287 3833/www.rain dance.co.uk). Leicester Square tube. **Dates** Oct 2005.

Britain's largest indie film festival.

London Film Festival

Venues around London (7928 3232/www.lff.org.uk). **Dates** Oct/Nov 2005.

The biggest film festival in the UK, now in its 48th year, is a broad church; for further details, *see p267.*

Brother, can you spare 15 quid?

The movies have traditionally prided themselves on being a democratic art form – a modern mass medium that makes everyone equal in the dark. In the niche-friendly noughties, though, the trend is for the luxury ambience of exclusive movie dens, free from the popcorn-munching waft of the hoi polloi. Of course, the arts crowd has always been able to huddle at firmly alternative cinemas such as the Renoir (pictured), ICA and the Other Cinema, but for those willing to pay a premium for the elite experience, London now hosts a handful of defiantly first-class picture palaces.

In particular, the well-to-do of Hampstead and Notting Hill have seen their long-standing independent locals re-emerge as top-whack, top-drawer plush pads: at the Everyman Cinema Club (*see p284*), or Portobello's Electric Cinema (*see p284*), refashioned by the owners of Soho House, you can pay up to £15 per person for a leather armchair or a two-seat sofa, with a wine bar at the back of the auditorium. And if even a public cinema sounds like too much exposure, try Soho's private-members' Rex Cinema and Bar (21 Rupert Street, W1, 020 7287 0102), the Everyman's Private Screening Lounge, or the weekend dinner and film screenings at the Covent Garden Hotel (*see p57*), Charlotte Street Hotel (*p49*) and One Aldwych (*p59*).

Galleries

Invest some time, and maybe a little cash, in the stars of tomorrow.

The right **Approach**. *See p290.*

Two highly succesful art fairs held concurrently in Regent's Park Zoo during the autumn of 2004 once again put London in the international spotlight. The largest of these, the **Frieze Art Fair** (www.friezeartfair.com), attracted 150 important contemporary galleries from Europe and America to the capital, while the more modest **Zoo Art Fair** (www.artprojx.com) allowed some of London's smaller commercial spaces to muscle in on the action. And in many ways, these two projects encapsulate London's art scene, with Frieze on the one hand an indicator of the city's status on the international stage, and Zoo, organised by young gallerist David Risley and curator Soraya Rodriguez, a typically vibrant platform for fresh talent, showcasing as it did 26 new galleries and artist-run spaces.

But despite the efforts of 2004 to bring the focus to the fringe – notably with the relaunch of **Whitechapel Art Gallery**'s (*see p158*) East End Academy, an open-submission competition for emerging artists based in east London – the year has been dominated by high-profile developments in the museums and major spaces. Much of the activity has remained in central London, with several West End spaces,

such as **Gagosian** and **Haunch of Venison** (for both, *see p289*), showcasing their second sites. Elsewhere, refurbishment has been the order of the day with **Camden Arts Centre** (*see p151*) and the **South London Gallery** (*see p293*) reopening after extensive facelifts. But in general times remain pretty tough for London's alternative non-profit-making and artist-run spaces.

Some galleries close in August, and many also have little to see between shows, so if in doubt phone ahead or consult *Time Out* magazine. A free brochure, *New Exhibitions of Contemporary Art*, is available at galleries or at www.newexhibitions.com.

Central

Anthony Reynolds Gallery
60 Great Marlborough Street, Soho, W1F 7BG (7439 2201/www.anthonyreynolds.com). Oxford Circus tube. **Open** 10am-6pm Tue-Sat. **No credit cards. Map** p398 J6.

▶ For details of public galleries and exhibition spaces, *see* **Sightseeing**.

Richard Billingham and Mark Wallinger are two high-profile artists represented by Anthony Reynolds. In 2002 the gallery moved to this beautifully converted building.

Gagosian

8 Heddon Street, Mayfair, W1B 4BU (7292 8222/www.gagosian.com). Oxford Circus or Piccadilly Circus tube. **Open** 10am-6pm Tue-Sat; by appointment Mon. **No credit cards**. **Map** p400 J7.

US super-dealer Larry Gagosian ('Go-Go' to his friends) opened this London branch in 2000, and has since brought over a wealth of big names – not least Andy Warhol and Jasper Johns – as well as lesser-known US and European artists. In May 2004 Cy Twombly was the first artist to be shown at Gagosian's second site near King's Cross (6-24 Britannia Street, WC1X 9JD, 7841 9960), converted from a former garage by architects Caruso St John.

Haunch of Venison

6 Haunch of Venison Yard, Mayfair, W1K 5ES (7495 5050/www.haunchofvenison.com). Bond Street tube. **Open** 10am-6pm Mon-Wed, Fri; 10am-7pm Thur; 10am-5pm Sat. **Credit** AmEx, MC, V. **Map** p398 H6.

Previously leased as a project space by Anthony d'Offay (who retired in 2001), Haunch is now run by Harry Blain, a founder of Blains Fine Art (www.blains.co.uk), and Graham Southern, ex-director of the Anthony d'Offay Gallery. During 2004 the gallery focused on developing a more emerging programme for its second space (23 Bruton Street, W1J 6QH, 7495 5050), which opened with Berlin-based photographer Yannick Demmerle in July. Highlights of 2005 include Keith Tyson and Ian Munroe.

Hauser & Wirth

196A Piccadilly, Mayfair, W1J 9DY (7287 2300/www.hauserwirth.com). Piccadilly Circus tube. **Open** 10am-6pm Tue-Sat. **No credit cards**. **Map** p400 J7.

Founded in 1992 in Zurich, this Swiss-owned gallery opened a London branch in 2003 in an historic former bank designed by Sir Edwin Luytens. With a truly international group of artists, Hauser & Wirth represents big names such as Louise Bourgeois and Dan Graham, as well as home-grown talents Pipilotti Rist and painter Maria Lassnig.

Jerwood Space

171 Union Street, Bankside, SE1 0LN (7654 0171/www.jerwoodspace.co.uk). Borough or Southwark tube. **Open** 10am-6pm daily (during exhibitions; phone to check). **No credit cards**. **Map** p404 O8.

Just when we'd given up hope of ever again seeing cutting-edge contemporary art at the Jerwood Space, a new initiative was announced: a platform for young artists based on nominations by critics and curators, which so far has included Elizabeth Price and Tina O'Connell. The gallery also hosts the annual Jerwood Painting Prize, which with a first prize of £30,000 is the most valuable award for painting in the UK.

Lisson

29 & 52-54 Bell Street, Marylebone, NW1 5DA (7724 2739/www.lisson.co.uk). Edgware Road tube. **Open** 10am-6pm Mon-Fri; 11am-5pm Sat. **Credit** MC, V. **Map** p395 E5.

Tony Fretton's 1991 building is one of London's most beautiful spaces, making a superb platform for artists including Douglas Gordon, Dan Graham and the 'Lisson Sculptors': Anish Kapoor, Tony Cragg, Richard Wentworth and Richard Deacon. In 2002 a second space opened, which is also in Marylebone (52-54 Bell Street, NW1 5DA, 7724 2739). Expect Tatsuo Miyajima, Robert Mangold and Tony Cragg in 2005.

Sadie Coles HQ

35 Heddon Street, Mayfair, W1B 4BP (7434 2227/www.sadiecoles.com). Oxford Circus or Piccadilly Circus tube. **Open** 10am-6pm Tue-Sat. **No credit cards**. **Map** p400 J7.

Sarah Lucas, Elizabeth Peyton, John Currin… Sadie Coles represents some of the hippest artists from both sides of the Atlantic and continues to scour the globe for new talent. The upshot? This space, down a quiet Mayfair cul-de-sac, gets to show some of the hottest names in the business. In 2003 the gallery was extended to make room for an upstairs space, which allowed for a larger main gallery and an additional viewing area.

Sprüth Magers Lee

12 Berkeley Street, Mayfair, W1J 8DT (7491 0100/www.spruethmagerslee.com). Green Park tube. **Open** 10am-6pm Mon-Fri; 11am-4pm Sat. **No credit cards**. **Map** p400 H7.

Monika Sprüth and Philomene Magers oversee galleries in Cologne and Munich, where they represent major names such as Vito Acconci, Nan Goldin and John Baldessari. They opened their London branch in 2002 with business partner Simon Lee. Look out for Rosemary Trockel, Christopher Wool and Jenny Holzer in 2005.

Stephen Friedman

25-28 Old Burlington Street, Mayfair, W1S 3AN (7494 1434/www.stephenfriedman.com). Green Park or Piccadilly Circus tube. **Open** 10am-6pm Tue-Fri; 11am-5pm Sat. **No credit cards**. **Map** p400 J7.

Stephen Friedman is a shop-fronted space that shows international artists including Thomas Hirschorn, Yinka Shonibare and Yoshimoto Nara. In 2005 the gallery programme will feature Mamma Andersson and Mark Grotjahn.

Timothy Taylor Gallery

24 Dering Street, Mayfair, W1S 1TT (7409 3344/www.timothytaylorgallery.com). Bond Street tube. **Open** 10am-6pm Mon-Fri; 11am-5pm Sat. **No credit cards**. **Map** p398 H6.

Since opening in 2003, Timothy Taylor has gone some way to filling the gap left by the closure of the Anthony d'Offay Gallery in 2001. Shows by James Riley, Craigie Aitchison and Susan Hiller will ensure the trend continues in 2005.

Arts & Entertainment

Waddington Galleries

11 Cork Street, Mayfair, W1S 3LT (7437 8611/
www.waddington-galleries.com). Green Park or
Piccadilly Circus tube. **Open** 10am-6pm Mon-Fri;
10am-3pm Sat. **No credit cards. Map** p400 J7.
If it's a selection of blue-chip stock you're after, head
to Waddington Galleries. You're likely to find a
smörgåsbord of British and American modernism
in the gallery's changing displays, as well as solo
shows by UK and US big guns.

East

Since we have only been able to include a
limited selection of east London's myriad
galleries, you may want to do some exploring
of your own. In this case, we recommend a
visit to the gallery-packed corner of Hackney
where Cambridge Heath Road meets Mare
Street. Tudor Road, Broadway Market,
Wadeson and Vyner Streets are of
particular interest.

The Approach

Approach Tavern, 1st Floor, 47 Approach Road,
Bethnal Green, E2 9LY (8983 3878/www.theapproach
gallery.co.uk). Bethnal Green tube. **Open** noon-6pm
Wed-Sun; also by appointment. **No credit cards.**
By referring to the Approach as 'a great pub with a
gallery attached', most commentators get the measure
of this place entirely wrong. Certainly, the Approach
Tavern is a fine East End boozer but the gallery that
is located on the first floor is the real draw. Here
Jake Miller continues to show a fantastic range of
emerging artists, while maintaining a viable platform
for more established names such as Emma Kay and
Michael Raedecker.

Bloomberg Space

50 Finsbury Square, The City, EC2A 1HD (7330
7959). Moorgate tube/rail. **Open** 11am-6pm Tue-Sat.
No credit cards. Map p403 Q5.
In 2002 the eponymous financial company opened
this gallery, which is dedicated to commissioning
and exhibiting contemporary art. The curatorial
team of art-world figures Sacha Craddock, Graham
Gussin, Stephen Hepworth and David Risley has
ensured a diverse programme, including 'Art School'
in 2004 (a six-week programme of art tuition, production and discussion).

Chisenhale Gallery

64 Chisenhale Road, Bow, E3 5QZ (8981 4518/
www.chisenhale.org.uk). Bethnal Green or Mile
End tube/D6, 8, 277 bus. **Open** 1-6pm Wed-Sun.
No credit cards.
This former factory contains a dance space, artists'
studios and a large gallery. One of the few truly
independent spaces in the East End and a vital
part of the scene, Chisenhale has a built up a good
reputation for spotting the stars of tomorrow and
continues to commission fine work by young and
lesser-known artists.

Counter Gallery

44A Charlotte Road, Shoreditch, EC2A 3PD
(7684 8888/www.countergallery.com). Old Street
tube/rail. **Open** noon-6pm Thur-Sat. **Credit** MC, V.
Map p403 R4.
Responsible for such seminal shows as 'Modern
Medicine' in 1990, Carl Freedman is an old hand at
promoting young British art and, from this smart
Shoreditch gallery, continues to focus his attention
on new and emerging artists. Along with the
gallery, Freedman co-ordinates Counter Editions,
which produces prints and editions by such YBAs
as Mat Collishaw and Gary Hume.

Flowers East

82 Kingsland Road, Hoxton, E2 8DP (7920 7777/
www.flowerseast.com). Old Street tube/rail. **Open**
10am-6pm Tue-Sat; 11am-5pm Sun. **Credit** AmEx,
MC, V. **Map** p403 R3.
British painting is the dominant theme at Flowers
East and its three other spaces: Mayfair's Flowers
Central (21 Cork Street, W1S 3LZ, 7439 7766) and,
in the United States, Flowers Madison Avenue and
Flowers West (in New York City and Santa Monica,
respectively). This Kingsland Road branch also
contains Flowers Graphics.

Hales Gallery

Tea Building, 7 Bethnal Green Road, Shoreditch,
E1 6LA (7033 1938/www.halesgallery.com).
Liverpool Street or Old Street tube/rail. **Open**
11am-6pm Wed-Sat. **Credit** AmEx, DC, MC, V.
Map p403 S4.
Having helped put Deptford on the art map, last year
Hales moved east into the Tea Building, on the
corner of Shoreditch High Street and Bethnal Green
Road, opening with a group show of up-and-coming
artists featuring German muralist Lothar Götz and
Brit painter Danny Rolph.

Interim Art

21 Herald Street, Bethnal Green, E2 6JT (7729
4112). Bethnal Green tube. **Open** 11am-6pm
Wed-Sun; also by appointment. **No credit**
cards. Map p403 R3.
Maureen Paley's Interim Art has been here since
1999. The gallery represents Paul Noble (best known
for drawings of the fictitious town, Nobson), Turner
Prize-winners Wolfgang Tillmans and Gillian
Wearing, along with Becks Futures 2004 winner
Saskia Olde Wolbers.

Matt's Gallery

42-44 Copperfield Road, Mile End, E3 4RR
(8983 1771/www.mattsgallery.org). Mile End tube.
Open noon-6pm Wed-Sun; also by appointment.
No credit cards.
There are few galleries in town as well respected as
Matt's. Over two decades, it has commissioned
installations as memorable as *20:50*, Richard
Wilson's expanse of sump oil (now in the Saatchi
Gallery) and Mike Nelson's *Coral Reef*. Installation
continues to be the gallery's forte, with work by
Richard Grayson in 2005.

Modern Art

*10 Vyner Street, Hackney, E2 9DG (8980 7742/
www.modernartinc.com). Bethnal Green tube.*
Open 11am-6pm Thur-Sun; also by appointment.
No credit cards.
Modern Art is certainly one of the more elite spaces
in the East End. Opened by Stuart Shave and
Detmar Blow in 1998, the space boasts a diverse
international stable of artists such as German photographer Juergen Teller and Brit duo Tim Noble
and Sue Webster. A highlight of 2004 was a revival
of Kenneth Anger's seminal 1963 film *Invocation of
My Demon Brother*.

The Showroom

*44 Bonner Road, Bethnal Green, E2 9JS (8983
4115/www.theshowroom.org). Bethnal Green tube.*
Open 1-6pm Wed-Sun. **No credit cards**.

The Showroom has gained a reputation over the
years for its commitment to young artists. And, in
fact, it often commissions large-scale works at early
stages in artists' careers. The triangular space here
isn't easy to fill successfully, but it occasionally
works perfectly. For 2005 the typically diverse
programme includes graphic painter Diann Bauer
and a performance by Aaron Williamson.

Victoria Miro

*16 Wharf Road, Islington, N1 7RW (7336 8109/
www.victoria-miro.com). Angel tube or Old Street
tube/rail.* **Open** 10am-6pm Tue-Sat. **Credit**
MC, V. **Map** p402 P2.

One of the most fabulous art spaces anywhere, this
huge converted Victorian factory is always worth
a visit. Painting was the order of the day in 2004
with 'Extended Painting' featuring Anne Chu and

Space invaders

London artists, frustrated
by the lack of affordable
studio space and difficulty
getting their work shown,
have found a radical
solution: squatting.
'Art-squatters' are
increasingly taking
over disused buildings to
convert into work spaces
and stage exhibitions.
  Random Artists
(www.randomartists.org)
squat buildings for three
days at a time and put
on cultural events that
include live performance
as well as and
sculpture. They are also
planning tours to take
their next show to long-
term squats in Amsterdam
and Berlin. Check their
website for details on
how to submit your work.

  Found in Space (45 Tudor Road, E9 7SN,
www.foundinspace.co.uk) is a collective of
artists and musicians squatting a disused
factory in Haggerston. The group has taken
advantage of the landlord's prolonged
wrangles with the local council planning
department to set up a series of art studios.
Every six months FIS curates an exhibition,
while filmmakers can show their shorts in
the makeshift cinema (a projector and a
small row of comfy old sofas).

  At **491 Gallery** in Leytonstone (491 Grove
Green Road, E11 4AA, www.491gallery.com;
pictured), the resident squatters have an
unusually amicable agreement with the
landlord, which spares them the imminent
threat of eviction. The squat houses a core of
about 20 residents with many others involved
part-time. They hold some interesting events
– life drawing to a DJ set, anyone? There is
also a cinema, and their monthly parties
with live bands are a big draw.

Arts & Entertainment

Sprüth Magers Lee. *See p289.*

Grayson Perry, and 'Painting 2004' showcasing younger international talent. In 2005 expect shows from German artist Thomas Demand and New York painter Inka Essenhigh.

Vilma Gold
25B Vyner Street, Hackney, E1 9DG (8981 3344/ www.vilmagold.com). Bethnal Green tube. **Open** noon-6pm Thur-Sun. **Credit** MC, V. **Map** p403 R4.
Rachel Williams and Steven Pippet have a magic touch. The cognoscenti flock here for such fashionable fare as the neo-neo-expressionist paintings of Sophie von Hellermann and Markus Vater, or Andrew Mania's conglomerations of drawings, paintings, sculpture and found photographs.

Wapping Project
Wapping Hydraulic Power Station, Wapping Wall, Wapping, E1W 3ST (7680 2080/www.thewapping project.com). Wapping tube. **Open** noon-11pm Mon-Sat; noon-6pm Sun. **Credit** AmEx, DC, MC, V.
This magnificent converted hydraulic power station was originally intended to attract those working with film, video and the digital arts, but has hosted a wider range of genres, including modern dance. Elina Brotherus's videos of naked Finnish bathers sparked controversy in the local community in 2004. The space also houses a good restaurant.

White Cube
48 Hoxton Square, Hoxton, N1 6PB (7930 5373/ www.whitecube.com). Old Street tube/rail. **Open** 10am-6pm Tue-Sat. **Credit** AmEx, MC, V. **Map** p402 P4.
A rooftop extension has made room for a project space – 'Inside the White Cube' – with its own curator to be changed annually. Downstairs, the gallery hosted, in 2004, new sculptural installations by Antony Gormley and Polish artist Miroslaw Balka. The commercial hub of YBA art, White Cube's plans to open a further space in a former London Electricity substation in Mason's Yard, Piccadilly, have yet to be confirmed.

Wilkinson Gallery
242 Cambridge Heath Road, Bethnal Green, E2 9DA (8980 2662/www.wilkinsongallery.com). Bethnal Green tube. **Open** 11am-6pm Thur-Sat; noon-6pm Sun; also by appointment. **No credit cards.**
A series of smallish rooms over three floors, this excellent gallery, run by Anthony Wilkinson, represents mainly British and European artists, including Bob & Roberta Smith (aka Patrick Brill) whose knockabout text pieces and sculptures poke gentle fun at the art world, and artist/writer/curator Matthew Higgs. The 2005 programme is a painting-heavy line-up that includes solo shows for Brits Paul Housley and George Shaw.

South-east

Corvi-Mora
1A Kempsford Road, Kennington, SE11 4NU (7840 9111/www.corvi-mora.com). Kennington tube. **Open** 11am-6pm Tue-Sat. **No credit cards.**

Italian gallerist Tommasso Corvi-Mora brings a wealth of international art to this small space, which has become known for its multinational offerings. The flavour continues in 2005 with painter Jim Isermann and printmaker Dorota Jurczak.

Gasworks

155 Vauxhall Street, Oval, SE11 5RH (7582 6848/ www.gasworks.org.uk). Oval tube. **Open** noon-6pm Wed-Sun. **No credit cards.**
Part of the Triangle Arts Trust, this space comprises both a gallery and a collective of artists' studios, three of which are reserved for artists taking part in an ambitious international residency programme. The gallery provides a platform for artists who have had limited exposure in London. Following refurbishment, Gasworks reopened in 2004 with a new performance by Lali Chetwynd.

South London Gallery

65 Peckham Road, Peckham, SE5 8UH (7703 9799/ www.southlondongallery.org). Oval tube, then 436 bus/Elephant & Castle tube/rail, then 12, 171 bus. **Open** noon-6pm Tue, Wed, Fri-Sun; noon-8.30pm Thur. **No credit cards.**
Built in 1891 as a philanthropic venture, this is a cathedral-like space that has become one of the capital's foremost venues for contemporary art, and host to a remarkably varied programme. The gallery reopened after an extensive facelift in June 2004, and now has disabled access and improved facilities. The debut exhibition was an ambitious show by American sculptor Tom Friedman.

Other spaces

A number of museums are also listed in sightseeing chapters. These include the **Design Museum** (*see p88*), the **Geffrye Museum** (*see p160*) and the **V&A** (*see p141*).

Architectural Association

36 Bedford Square, Fitzrovia, WC1B 3ES (7887 4000/www.aaschool.ac.uk). Tottenham Court Road tube. **Open** 10am-7pm Mon-Fri; 10am-3pm Sat. **Credit** MC, V. **Map** 399 K5.
Talks, events, discussions and exhibitions: four good reasons for visiting these elegant premises. During the summer, the gallery shows work by graduating students of the AA School.

Crafts Council

44A Pentonville Road, Islington, N1 9BY (7278 7700/www.craftscouncil.org.uk). Angel tube. **Open** 11am-6pm Tue-Sat; 2-6pm Sun. **No credit cards.** **Map** p402 N2.
The Council showcases the nation's craft output and has recently begun to stage exhibitions that examine the crossovers between art and design. The finalists of the Jerwood Applied Art Prize are usually shown in autumn. Following the successful launch of 'Collect' in 2004, at the Victoria & Albert Museum (*see p141*), the art fair will run for a second year in January 2005.

Royal Institute of British Architects

66 Portland Place, Marylebone, W1B 1AD (7580 5533/www.architecture.com). Great Portland Street or Regent's Park tube. **Open** 10am-6pm Mon-Fri; 10am-5pm Sat. **Credit** MC, V. **Map** p398 H5.
Based in a monumental edifice built by Grey Wornham in 1934, the Royal Institute of British Architects (aka RIBA) has a gallery that celebrates the profession's great and good and showcases emerging architecture from around the world.

Photography

Michael Hoppen Contemporary

3 Jubilee Place, Chelsea, SW3 3TD (7352 4499/ www.michaelhoppengallery.com). Sloane Square tube. **Open** noon-6pm Tue-Sat; or by appointment. **Credit** AmEx, MC, V. **Map** p397 E11.
Shine Gallery was relaunched in the summer of 2004 as a new three-floor space under the new name of Michael Hoppen Gallery. Michael Hoppen continues to show a mixture of vintage and contemporary works. Look out for Chinese photographer Dodo Jinming and Ken Griffiths' images of the 'Three Ganges' irrigation project in 2005.

Photofusion

17A Electric Lane, Brixton, SW9 8LA (7738 5774/ www.photofusion.org). Brixton tube/rail. **Open** 10am-6pm Tue, Thur, Fri; 10am-8pm Wed; 11am-6pm Sat. **Credit** MC, V.
This place is the largest independent photography resource centre in town. Among 2004's impressive exhibitions were 'Physical Sites', in which Nigel Green and Naglaa Walker explored scientific environments. More of the same is expected in 2005.

Photographers' Gallery

5 & 8 Great Newport Street, Covent Garden, WC2H 7HY (7831 1772/www.photonet.org.uk). Leicester Square tube. **Open** 11am-6pm Mon-Sat; noon-6pm Sun. **Membership** £30/yr; £20/yr concessions. **Credit** AmEx, DC, MC, V. **Map** p401 K6.
A giant among photography galleries, this space hosts a huge range of diverse shows each year, while promoting photography around the country. In 2005 it will once more host the annual Deutsche Börse Photography Prize, which is the largest prize for photography in the UK.

Zelda Cheatle Gallery

99 Mount Street, Mayfair, W1K 2TQ (7408 4448/ www.zcgall.demon.co.uk). Bond Street or Green Park tube. **Open** 10am-6pm Tue-Fri; 11am-5pm Sat. **Credit** AmEx, MC, V. **Map** p400 G7.
Javier Silva Meinel's show of Peruvian portraits in 2004 was typical of the high standards set and met by this specialist in the exhibition and sale of vintage and contemporary photography. Exhibitions for 2005 include Abbas Kiarostami, who will be the first artist to show in the new premises, details of which were yet to be announced as we went to press.

Arts & Entertainment

Gay & Lesbian

Where the out go out.

Balans. *See p295.*

The pink pound, like it or loathe it, has done wonders for London's gay scene. Back in the 1970s, the gay village consisted of a few grotty pubs around Earl's Court tube and hordes of moustached men: a true clone zone. More recently, London's queer club scene became dominated by Muscle Marys, poppers and samey house music.

Not any more. Bar and club entrepreneurs have started to realise that variety is the spice of gay life. True, the Muscle Mary scene continues to grow as rapidly as those men's steroid-induced physiques (the proliferation of club nights in Vauxhall is astonishing). But times have changed: now other gay men, not to mention lesbians, have plenty of swell places for painting the town *rouge*. For a start, the indie love affair that began at **Popstarz** (*see p297*) a decade ago has produced children of its own, including mixed clubs such as **Duckie** (*see p296*), **Shinky Shonky** (*see p298*) and the **Ghetto** (*see p297*). Glamorous queeny gays have made a comeback, too: cocktail culture is taking over Soho, in venues such as the **Shadow Lounge, Sanctuary Soho, Shaun & Joe** and **Too 2 Much** (for all four, *see p300*), while lesbians have discovered their

inner supermodel in sexy women-only venues such as **Candy Bar** (*see p299*). Suburban gays have also come out of the closet, at various far-flung venues such as the **Two Brewers** (*see p300*), the **Black Cap** and **BJ's White Swan** (for both, *see p298*).

If you want to cut out the middleman – that is, the gay clubs – and get straight down to business, London is one enormous cruising ground. By night, **Hampstead Heath** is a veritable outdoor orgy (behind Jack Straw's Castle). **Clapham Common** is also crawling with lustful men (particularly in the southern portion of woodland) but is considered more dangerous than Hampstead Heath. Online cruising grounds include the popular **www.gaydar.co.uk**, **www.m4m4sex.com** and **www.outintheuk.com**. For lesbians the best site is **www.gingerbeer.co.uk**.

Also, gay film buffs have the huge annual **London Lesbian & Gay Film Festival** (*see p286*), and you can often see good gay indies at the **Other Cinema** (*see p283*) and plays at the **Soho Theatre** (*see p340*).

The **Pride Festival** (*see p263*) always seems to be on its last legs but in 2005 organisers will attempt to reverse this trend with a fortnight of cultural events, starting mid June and culminating on Pride Day on 2 July. For details go to www.PrideLondon.org or www.biggayout.co.uk.

The most celebrated gay shops are the excellent **Gay's the Word** bookshop (*see p107*), and 'shopping and fucking' emporiums **Clone Zone** (64 Old Compton Street, Soho, 7287 3530) and **Prowler** (3-7 Brewer Street, Soho, 7734 4031).

For a fuller take on gay London, pick up Time Out's *Gay & Lesbian London* guidebook (£9.99), and for weekly listings of clubs, meetings and groups, check the Gay & Lesbian section of *Time Out* magazine or free sheets *Boyz* and *QX*. On shop shelves, gay lifestyle is covered by *Gay Times, Attitude* and dyke bible *Diva*.

Cafés & restaurants

Balans
60 Old Compton Street, Soho, W1D 4UG (7439 2183/www.balans.co.uk). Leicester Square or Piccadilly Circus tube. **Open** 8am-5am Mon-Thur; 8am-6am Fri, Sat; 8am-2am Sun. **Admission** *After midnight* £5 Mon-Thur; £7 Fri, Sat. **Credit** AmEx, MC, V. **Map** p399 6K.
This buzzing brasserie is gay central. Stop in for a steak, omelette or salad – or just eye up the beefcake over a cheesecake. The nearby Balans Café, at No.34, serves up a shorter version of the menu. Both are open almost all night: good for a post-clubbing feast. **Other locations**: 249 Old Brompton Road, Earl's Court, SW5 9HP (7244 8838); 187 Kensington High Street, Kensington, W8 6SH (7376 0115).

First Out
52 St Giles High Street, St Giles's, WC2H 8LH (7240 8042/www.firstoutcafebar.com). Tottenham Court Road tube. **Open** 9am-11pm Mon-Sat; 11am-10.30pm Sun. **Credit** MC, V. **Map** p399 K6.
Opened in 1986, First Out was indeed London's first lesbian and gay café, with an emphasis on the lesbian. It's a right-on place, with a healthy veggie menu; if real men don't eat quiche, lesbians sure do. Decent prices, friendly vibe and a good basement bar, too.

Clubs

This town moves fast. This is especially true of Vauxhall, where clubs open and close more frequently than the closet door, though surely only an earthquake could stop scene stalwarts **G.A.Y.** or **Heaven**. Check listings in *Time Out* and scene mag *Boyz* for the latest.

Action
The Renaissance Rooms, off Miles Street, Vauxhall, SW8 1SD (07973 233377/www.action club.net). Oval tube/Vauxhall tube/rail. **Open** 11pm-6am 1st & 3rd Sat of mth. **Admission** £16; £11 members; £13 before midnight with flyer. **No credit cards**.

A hugely popular dance party for the muscle boy brigade, Action has a massive dance arena, heated outside terrace, plus cruise and chill-out rooms.

Club Kali
The Dome, 1 Dartmouth Park Hill, Dartmouth Park, N19 5QQ (7272 8153). Tufnell Park tube. **Open** 10pm-3am 1st & 3rd Fri of mth. **Admission** £7; £5 concessions. **No credit cards**.
The world's largest Asian music lesbian and gay club, Kali's big, barn-like venue echoes to the sounds of bhangra, Bollywood and plain old house music.

Club Motherfucker
Upstairs at the Garage, 20-22 Highbury Corner, Highbury, N5 1RD (7607 1818/www.mean fiddler.com). Highbury & Islington tube/rail. **Open** 9pm-3am last Fri of mth; 9pm-3am 2nd Sat of mth. **Admission** £5; £4 concessions. **No credit cards**.
CM's polysexual party features DJs Daughters of Kaos, Vic Voltaire and Miss Alabama Cherry. DJs play dirty punk and 'bad-taste' rock. Live bands, too.

Crash
Arch 66, Goding Street, Vauxhall, SE11 5AW (7793 9262). Vauxhall tube/rail. **Open** *Club* 10.30pm-6am 2nd & 4th Sat of mth. **Admission** £15; £12 with flyer or members. **Credit** DC, MC, V.
Crash headlines all-star DJs Steve Pitron, Severino, Paul Heron et al. Under the arches are four bars, two dancefloors, chill-out areas… and lots of muscles.

The best Gay venues

For bad boys
The Hoist. *See p299.*

For club freaks
Nag Nag Nag at Ghetto. *See p297.*

For cocktail queens
The Shadow Lounge. *See p300.*

For gay punks
Duckie. *See p296.*

For glamorous lesbians
Candy Bar. *See p299.*

For Kylie fans
Camp Attack at G.A.Y. *See p296.*

For muscle Marys
Action. *See left.*

For showtunes around the piano
Sanctuary Soho. *See p300.*

For silly boys and girls
Shinky Shonky. *See p298.*

Discotec

The End, 18 West Central Street, St Giles's, WC1A 1JJ (7419 9199/www.discotec-club.com). Holborn or Tottenham Court Road tube. **Open** 10pm-4am Thur. **Admission** £8; £6 before midnight. **Credit** *Bar* MC, V. **Map** p399 L6.

Fancy a 'midweekend' party spread over two dance-floors? Equipped with air-conditioning and great sounds, this is one of London's classiest venues, and it attracts a dressy crowd.

DTPM

Fabric, 77A Charterhouse Street, Clerkenwell, EC1M 6HJ (7749 1199). Barbican tube/Farringdon tube/rail. **Open** 10pm-late Sun. **Admission** £15; £11 members, concessions; £9 before 11pm with flyer. **Credit** *Bar* MC, V. **Map** p402 O5.

A busy polysexual club night with three dance-floors, DTPM plays house, R&B, hip hop and disco.

Duckie

Royal Vauxhall Tavern, 372 Kennington Lane, Vauxhall, SE11 5HY (7737 4043/www.duckie.co.uk). Vauxhall tube/rail. **Open** 9pm-2am Sat. **Admission** £5. **No credit cards**.

Expect 'post-gay vaudeville and post-punk pogo-ing' at this legendary dive. DJs the London Readers Wifes (*sic*) play the best retro set in town; Amy Lamé hosts bizarre cabaret.

Exilio Latino

The Phoenix, 37 Cavendish Square, Marylebone, W1G 0PP (07956 983230/www.exilio.co.uk). Oxford Circus tube. **Open** *Club* 10pm-3am Sat. **Admission** £6 before 11pm; £10 after 11pm. **No credit cards**. **Map** p399 M6.

In newly improved and even more comfortable sur-roundings, this popular lesbian and gay Latin music club is still going strong.

Fiction

The Cross, King's Cross Goods Yard, off York Way, King's Cross, N1 0BB (7749 1199/www.club-fiction.net). King's Cross tube/rail. **Open** 11pm-5am Fri. **Admission** £15; £11 concessions; £9 before 11.30pm; £11 before midnight with flyer. **Credit** *Bar* MC, V. **Map** p399 L2.

This polysexual club may be looking a bit straight these days but it's still a great night out. Three dancefloors, five bars and two outside terraces make it a great summer venue. DJs, including Fat Tony, play house grooves.

G.A.Y.

Astoria, 157-165 Charing Cross Road, Soho, WC2H 0EN (7434 9592/www.g-a-y.co.uk). Tottenham Court Road tube. **Open** 10.30pm-4am Mon, Thur; 11pm-4.30am Fri, Sat. **Admission** £3-£10; reductions with flyer. **No credit cards**. **Map** p399 K6.

Walk this way Famous footsteps

Following a prolonged period of escorting innumerable groups of US service personnel around Whitechapel on the 'Jack the Ripper' tour, and dodging rats and buckets of urine from the upper windows of pissed-off locals, Blue Badge guide Simon Rodway needed a change. So he devised two new walks aimed at a more sensitive crowd: one based on the suffragette movement and the other on Oscar Wilde. Neither is a million miles away from the well-trodden tourist trails, but they allow walkers to look at the city from a different perspective. As Simon says: 'There's much more to walking in London than Jack the Ripper. People like Christabel Pankhurst and Oscar Wilde played the cards fate dealt them as well as they could on the great stage of the West End. Although both were born outsiders, theirs are London stories.' Both walks focus on engrossing personal stories, which are gradually revealed en route.

The 'Women Behaving Badly' walk starts at Temple and follows the historic trail of charismatic Christabel Pankhurst and the suffragettes as they rampaged across the West End in their brave and brilliant campaign to win votes for women. It visits their HQ, the

court that sent many of them to prison, the scene of the celebratory 'Liberty Breakfasts' when hunger strikers were released, and the National Gallery, where Simon points out the scars that are still visible on Velazquez's *The Rokeby Venus*, left when Mary Richardson attacked it in 1914.

'Walk on the Wilde Side' starts at Villiers Street and follows Oscar through his West End playground during the fateful spring of 1895, when he started the disastrous proceedings for libel against his lover's father, the Marquis of Queensbury. Highlights include the Café Royal, where Wilde frequently held court, the Theatre Royal Haymarket, where his great social comedies were premiered, and the Savoy, where Oscar, Bosey and 'the love that dare not speak its name' checked in for three weeks, running up the modern equivalent of a £7,000 bar bill and unwittingly providing plenty of meaty evidence for Queensbury's accusation of 'posing as a sodomite'.

● 'Women Behaving Badly' and 'Walk on the Wilde Side' are two of the diverse London walking tours led by Simon Rodway (www.silvercanetours.com, 07720 715295).

The Shadow Lounge. *See p300.*

London's largest gay venue is something of a dump these days, but that doesn't bother the hordes of disco-bunnies who congregate to dance to poppy tunes and sing to Saturday PAs. Friday's Camp Attack is a must for Kylie fans.

Ghetto

5-6 Falconberg Court (behind the Astoria), Soho, W1D 3AB (7287 3726/www.ghetto-london.co.uk). Tottenham Court Road tube. **Open** 10.30pm-3am Mon-Thur; 10.30pm-4am Fri; 10.30pm-5am Sat; 10am-3pm Sun. **Admission** £2-£7 (free Mon). **No credit cards. Map** p399 K6.

Heading the backlash against London's snootier venues, this gritty indie club offers Nag Nag Nag for electro fans on Wednesday and Mis-Shapes for cool lesbians on Thursdays, while the Cock puts the spunk back into Soho on Fridays. Saturdays is long-running trash night Wig Out; Detox is on Sunday.

Heaven

The Arches, Villiers Street, Covent Garden, WC2N 6NG (7930 2020/www.heaven-london.com). Embankment tube/Charing Cross tube/rail. **Open** 10.30pm-3am Mon, Wed; 10.30pm-6am Fri; 10pm-5am Sat. **Admission** £1-£12. **Credit** *Bar* AmEx, DC, MC, V. **Map** p401 L7.

London's most famous gay club recently turned 25. The best nights are Popcorn (Mondays) and Fruit Machine (Wednesdays) – both upbeat early-week fun – but Heaven really comes alive on Saturdays, when gay revellers dance to commercial house.

Horse Meat Disco

South Central (formerly Duke's), 349 Kennington Lane, Vauxhall, SE11 5QY (7793 0903/www.horse meatdisco.co.uk). Vauxhall tube/rail. **Open** 1pm-1am 1st & 3rd Sun of mth. **Admission** £3 before 5pm, then £5. **Credit** *Bar* MC, V.

Bears and fashionistas come together at this hip but unpretentious club night held in a traditional gay boozer. Excellent DJs spin an eclectic mix, from dance, disco and soul to new wave and punk.

Orange

Fire, 39-41 Parry Street, Vauxhall, SW8 1RT (07905 035682/www.allthingsorange.com). Vauxhall tube/rail. **Open** 3am-noon Mon. **Admission** £12; £10 with flyer. **No credit cards.**

House music, bare torsos and the whiff of poppers are what to expect at this quintessential Vauxhall Sunday night/Monday morning dance club. Don't these guys have jobs?

Popstarz

Scala, 275 Pentonville Road, King's Cross, N1 9NL (7833 2022/www.popstarz.org). King's Cross tube/rail. **Open** 10pm-5am Fri. **Admission** £8; £5 members, students. **Credit** *Bar* MC, V. **Map** p399 L3.

The original indie gay party, Popstarz is a club of three parts. The Love Lounge plays disco and R&B, the Common Room plays indie and dance, and the Trash Room plays Kylie and kitsch. Expect a mixed, predominantly studenty crowd.

Arts & Entertainment

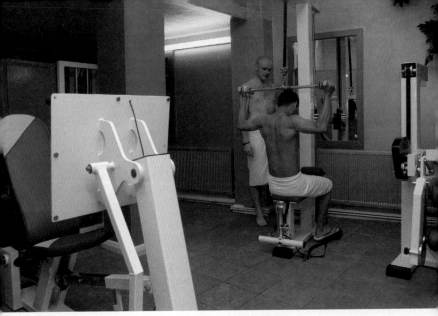

Shinky Shonky

Polar Bear, 30 Lisle Street, Soho, WC2H 7BA (7479 7981). Leicester Square tube. **Open** 10pm-3am Sat. **Admission** £6; £5 with flyer. **Credit** AmEx, MC, V. **Map** p401 K7.

Boogaloo Stu and the gang host a camp party where it's cool to act the fool. DJs spin pop, rock and disco. Plus, obnoxious live entertainment from the likes of Miss High Leg Kick and the Incredible Tall Lady.

Substation South

9 Brighton Terrace, Brixton, SW9 8DJ (7737 2095). Brixton tube/rail/N2, N3, N37, N109 bus. **Open** 10.30pm-2.30am Mon, Thur; 10.30pm-5am Fri; 10.30pm-6am Sat; 10pm-late Sun. **Admission** £4-£8. **No credit cards**.

This dark, edgy club is a south London fixture. Monday is underwear-only night with Y-Front; Wednesday is fetish night Boot Camp; Friday is funky house night Dirty Dishes. On Saturday there's Queer Nation, a house and garage night, followed by alternative shindig Marvellous on Sunday.

Pubs & bars

All of the venues listed below are open to both gays and lesbians, unless otherwise indicated.

Admiral Duncan

54 Old Compton Street, Soho, W1U 5UD (7437 5300). Leicester Square tube. **Open** noon-11pm Mon-Sat; noon-10.30pm Sun. **Credit** MC, V. **Map** p399 K6.

This traditional gay bar in the heart of Soho attracts a slightly older, down-to-earth crowd in a darkened setting. Bombed in a homophobic attack in 1999, this doughty old survivor is still going strong.

Barcode

3-4 Archer Street, Soho, W1D 7AP (7734 3342/ www.bar-code.co.uk). Leicester Square or Piccadilly Circus tube. **Open** 2.30pm-1am Mon-Sat; 2.30-10.30pm Sun. **Admission** £3 after 11pm Fri, Sat. **Credit** MC, V. **Map** p401 K7.

Just the ticket for those in search of a busy men's cruise bar on two levels, Barcode also has a dance-floor downstairs and a late licence.

BJ's White Swan

556 Commercial Road, The City, E14 7JD (7780 9870/www.bjswhiteswan.com). Aldgate East tube. **Open** 9pm-1am Mon; 9pm-2am Tue-Thur; 9pm-3am Fri, Sat; 5.30pm-midnight Sun. **Admission** £4 after 10pm Fri, Sat. **Credit** MC, V. **Map** p405 S6.

This large local attracts a loyal following, who come to savour the amateur male strip and drag shows, and to dance to commercial house music.

Black Cap

171 Camden High Street, Camden, NW1 7JY (7428 2721/www.theblackcap.com). Camden Town tube. **Open** noon-2am Mon-Thur; noon-3am Fri, Sat; noon-1am Sun. **Credit** MC, V.

Recently refurbished, this famous north London pub/club is renowned for its drag shows, and was once a second home to television's own Lily Savage.

The Box

Seven Dials, 32-34 Monmouth Street, Covent Garden, WC2H 9HA (7240 5828/www.boxbar.com). Leicester Square tube. **Open** 11am-11pm Mon-Sat; noon-10.30pm Sun. **Credit** MC, V. **Map** p399 L6.

By day, a popular café-bar for a mixed crowd, the Box transforms itself into a cruisey Muscle Mary hangout come nightfall.

Arts & Entertainment

Steamy **Chariots**. See p300.

Bromptons

*294 Old Brompton Road, Earl's Court, SW5 9JF
(7370 1344/www.bromptons.info). Earl's Court tube.*
Open 5pm-2am Mon-Sat; 5pm-midnight Sun.
Admission £1 10-11pm, £3 thereafter Mon-Thur;
£1 10-11pm, £5 thereafter Fri, Sat; £1 after 10pm, £3
thereafter Sun. **Credit** MC, V. **Map** p396 B11.
This busy men's pub-club with cabaret and strip-
pers lures a slightly older crowd with its unpretentious atmosphere.

Candy Bar

*4 Carlisle Street, Soho, W1D 3BJ (7494 4041/
www.candybar.easynet.co.uk). Tottenham Court Road
tube.* **Open** 5-11pm Mon-Sat; noon-
5-10.30pm Sun. **Admission** £5 after 9pm Fri, Sat; £3
after 10pm Thur. **Credit** *Bar* MC, V. **Map** p399 K6.
London's best-known lesbian bar attracts a mixed
clientele, from students to lipstick lesbians. Drinks
are pricey but there's a late licence at weekends.

Compton's of Soho

*51-53 Old Compton Street, Soho, W1V 5PN (7479
7961/www.comptons-of-soho.co.uk). Tottenham
Court Road tube.* **Open** noon-11pm Mon-Sat; noon-
10.30pm Sun. **Credit** AmEx, MC, V. **Map** p399 K6.
Popular with blokey gay men in bomber jackets,
Compton's cruisey atmosphere extends to both floors.

The Edge

*11 Soho Square, Soho, W1D 3QE (7439 1313/
www.edge.uk.com). Tottenham Court Road tube.*
Open noon-1am Mon-Sat; noon-10.30pm Sun.
Credit MC, V. **Map** p399 K6.
DJs play most nights at this busy polysexual bar set
out over several floors (including one with a piano
bar). It's also great for summer drinking, given the
proximity of Soho Square.

Escape Bar

*10A Brewer Street, Soho, W1F 0SU (7734 2626/
www.kudosgroup.com). Leicester Square tube.* **Open**
5pm-3am Mon-Sat. **Admission** £2 after 11pm Tue-
Thur; £3 after 10.30pm Fri, Sat. **Credit** AmEx, MC,
V. **Map** p401 K7.
This intimate gay dance bar has a large video screen
playing music videos to a mixed crowd.

G.A.Y. Bar

*30 Old Compton Street, Soho, W1D 4UR (7494
2756/www.g-a-y.co.uk). Leicester Square tube.* **Open**
noon-midnight daily. **Credit** MC, V. **Map** p399 K6.
If you like the Astoria's ever-popular G.A.Y. club
(*see p296*), and you probably do, then you'll love this
cheesy bar. Girls Go Down is the new women's bar
in the basement.

Glass Bar

*West Lodge, Euston Square Gardens, 190 Euston
Road, Bloomsbury, NW1 2EF (7387 6184/www.
glass-bar.co.uk). Euston tube/rail.* **Open** 5pm-late
Mon-Fri; 6pm-3am Sat. **Admission** £1-£2 Mon-Fri;
£5 after 10pm Sat. **No credit cards**. **Map** p398 J4.
This shabby-chic bar is hidden away in the west
stone lodge at the entrance to Euston Station. Knock
three times on the door, give the password 'Martina',
and pay your cover. Strictly women-only.

The Hoist

*Railway Arch, 47B&C South Lambeth Road,
Vauxhall Cross, Vauxhall, SW8 1RH (7735 9972/
www.thehoist.co.uk). Vauxhall tube/rail.* **Open**
8.30pm-midnight 3rd Thur of mth; 10pm-3am Fri;
10pm-4am Sat; 10pm-2am Sun. **Admission** £4 Thur;
£5 Fri, Sun; £10 Sat. **No credit cards**.
A popular men's fetish bar in an industrial setting,
the Hoist's dress code – leather, rubber and the like
– is taken seriously.

King William IV

*77 Hampstead High Street, Hampstead, NW3
1RE (7435 5747/www.kw4.co.uk). Hampstead tube/
Hampstead Heath rail.* **Open** 11am-11pm Mon-Sat;
noon-10pm Sun. **Credit** MC, V.
Attracting a vaguely affluent crowd, this old-fashioned gay local in swanky Hampstead is notable in
the summer months for its busy beer garden.

Kudos

*10 Adelaide Street, Covent Garden, WC2 4HZ (7379
4573/www.kudosgroup.com). Charing Cross tube/rail.*
Open noon-11pm Mon-Sat; noon-10.30pm Sun.
Credit AmEx, MC, V. **Map** p401 L7.
Right next to the Oscar Wilde memorial statue and
close to Charing Cross Station, this busy men's café-
bar attracts a mixture of scene queens, tourists and
men waiting for the next train back to suburbia.

Oak Bar

*79 Green Lanes, Newington Green, N16 9BU
(7354 2791). Manor House tube.* **Open** 5pm-
midnight Mon-Wed; 5pm-1am Thur; 5pm-3am
Fri, Sat; 1pm-midnight Sun. **Admission** free-£5.
Credit AmEx, MC, V.

Recent refurbs have given this lesbian mecca a funky new look, but its unpretentious attitude survives. It remains a mixed gay local by day and a lesbian stronghold by night.

Retro Bar
2 George Court, off Strand, Covent Garden, WC2N 6HH (7321 2811). Charing Cross tube/rail. **Open** noon-11pm Mon-Fri; 5-11pm Sat; 5-10.30pm Sun. **Credit** AmEx, MC, V. **Map** p401 L7.
True to its name, this mixed gay indie/retro bar plays '70s, '80s, goth and alternative sounds. Friendly atmosphere.

Rupert Street
50 Rupert Street, Soho, W1V 6DR (7292 7141). Leicester Square or Piccadilly Circus tube. **Open** noon-11pm Mon-Sat; noon-10.30pm Sun. **Credit** AmEx, MC, V. **Map** p401 K7.
This busy Soho bar has a distinctly '90s feel and attracts a slightly smarter, after-work crowd.

Sanctuary Soho
4-5 Greek Street, Soho, W1D 4DD (7434 3323). Tottenham Court Road tube. **Open** 5pm-2am Mon-Sat; 5pm-12.30am Sun. **Admission** £5 after 11pm Fri, Sat. **Credit** AmEx, MC, V. **Map** p399 K6.
Upstairs it feels like a private members' club at this upmarket venue for the gay cocktail crowd. On Fridays and Saturdays there's a lively piano bar singalong. Downstairs has a bar and dance area.

The Shadow Lounge
5 Brewer Street, Soho, W1F 0RF (7287 7988/ www.theshadowlounge.co.uk). Piccadilly Circus tube. **Open** 10pm-3am Mon-Wed; 9pm-3am Thur-Sat. **Admission** £3 after 11pm Mon-Wed; £5 after 10pm Thur; £5 before 10.30pm, £10 thereafter Fri, Sat. **Credit** AmEx, MC, V. **Map** p401 K7.
The original lounge bar and gay members' club, the Shadow Lounge is still popular with celebrities and gay wannabes alike. Funky decor, professional cocktail waiters and air-conditioning come as standard.

Shaun & Joe
5 Goslett Yard, Soho, WC2H 0EA (7734 9858/www.shaunandjoe.com). Tottenham Court Road tube. **Open** 6pm-4am daily. **Admission** £10 non-members after 10pm Fri, Sat (membership by invitation only). **Credit** MC, V. **Map** p399 K6.
A new members' bar and club from the team behind the Shadow Lounge (*see above*), S & J has fabulous decor, delicious cocktails and superb food.

Too 2 Much
11-12 Walker's Court, off Brewer Street, Soho, W1F 0ED (7437 4400/www.too2much.com). Leicester Square or Piccadilly Circus tube. **Open** 5pm-4am Tue-Sat. **Performances** 7pm. **Admission** £10. **Credit** AmEx, MC, V.
Remember the old Raymond's Revue Bar? Well, that's now died a death, and this glitzy new gay venue has risen from its ashes. Sleaze has been replaced by glamour: the bar has a smart lounge area and snazzy club space.

Two Brewers
114 Clapham High Street, Clapham, SW4 7UJ (7498 4971/www.the2brewers.com). Clapham Common tube. **Open** 5pm-2am Mon-Thur; 5pm-3am Fri, Sat; 4pm-12.30am Sun. **Admission** £1.50-£4. **Credit** AmEx, MC, V.
Recently refurbished, this Clapham gay bar and club continues to be a south London institution. Drag shows are usually the order of the day, and it's always packed at weekends.

Village Soho
81 Wardour Street, Soho, W1V 3DG (7434 2124). Piccadilly Circus tube. **Open** 4pm-1am Mon-Sat; 4-11pm Sun. **Admission** £2 after 11pm Fri, Sat. **Credit** MC, V. **Map** p398 J6.
A busy boys' café-bar on two floors, Village Soho is popular with a young crowd. Still, it pales in comparison with some of the glitzier venues nearby.

The Yard
57 Rupert Street, Soho, W1V 7BJ (7437 2652/ www.yardbar.co.uk). Piccadilly Circus tube. **Open** *Summer* noon-11pm Mon-Sat; noon-10.30pm Sun. *Winter* 5-11pm Mon-Sat; 5-10.30pm Sun. **Credit** AmEx, MC, V. **Map** p401 K7.
Understandably popular in the summer, this gay men's bar has a coveted courtyard. An upstairs loft bar keeps the smarter, after-work crowd interested in colder weather.

Saunas

Chariots
1 Fairchild Street, Shoreditch, EC2A 3NS (7247 5333/www.gaysauna.co.uk). Shoreditch tube/ Liverpool Street tube/rail. **Open** noon-9am daily. **Admission** £13; £11 concessions. **Credit** AmEx, MC, V. **Map** p403 4R.
Decked out like a Roman bath, Chariots is London's biggest and busiest gay sauna. It comprises a swimming pool, two steam rooms, two saunas, a jacuzzi and a host of private cabins. The Waterloo branch (101 Lower Marsh, SE1, 7247 5333) boasts the largest sauna in the UK (with room for 50 guys) and a special baggage check for Eurostar customers – save a bundle on a hotel and get lucky at the same time! The new Chariots Limehouse branch (574 Commercial Road, E14, 7791 2808) is split into two sections: Heaven is filled with blue walls and soft music, whereas Hell sports sinister black walls and resonates with hard dance music.
Other locations: 57 Cowcross Street, Farringdon, EC1 (7251 5553); 292 Streatham High Road, Streatham, SW16 (8696 0929).

The Sauna Bar
29 Endell Street, Covent Garden, WC2H 9BA (7836 2236). Covent Garden tube. **Open** 11am-2am Mon-Thur; 24hrs from noon Fri-2am Mon. **Admission** £13; £10 concessions. **Credit** MC, V. **Map** p399 L6.
A comfy bar, steam room, splash pool, showers and private rooms have all been crammed into this small, men-only sauna.

Music

From purist to grime, London knows the score.

Bush Hall. *See p302.*

Classical & Opera

Clive Gillinson, chief executive of the London Symphony Orchestra, recently claimed that there was more happening in the classical music world in London than any other city. And the evidence speaks for itself: five orchestras and two opera houses compares favourably to New York (one orchestra); Paris (four orchestras, two opera houses); and Berlin (two, three).

The reason for London's success in these areas can be put down to two things: immigration and the BBC. Throughout the 20th century, other nations were busy kicking their musicians out, and London took them in. Views and techniques were swapped and music became a medium for the city's polyglot culture.

In the 1930s the BBC, still full of idealism, broadcast nightly concerts to which culture-starved citizens of mistrustful dictatorships secretly tuned in on crackly receivers. Major labels based themselves here. The EMI studios at Abbey Road became well known. Talented musicians and record companies flocked to town. The first concert hall to be built anywhere in the world after the war was

the **Royal Festival Hall** (*see p304*), and international orchestras lined up to perform there. Many of them were invited to play at the **Proms** (*see p306*) in the **Royal Albert Hall** (*see p302*) when they started in the 1950s, and London's annual summer music festival soon became a world event.

Meanwhile, Londoners who had once considered opera a continental and rather silly form of art came increasingly to love it. Today Covent Garden's **Royal Opera House** (*see p305*) ranks with La Scala in Milan and the Met in New York as one of the world's greatest opera houses. Its spectacular lottery-funded renovation in 2000 also made it one of the most luxurious nights out money can afford. The Coliseum, which houses the **English National Opera** (*see p305*), has also just completed a lengthy, expensive but overwhelmingly successful refurbishmen.

TICKETS AND INFORMATION

Tickets for most classical and opera events in London are available direct from the venues: book ahead for good seats. Many major venues have online booking systems in addition to the telephone box offices.

A number of venues, such as the Barbican and the South Bank, operate standby schemes, in which unsold tickets are sold off at cut-rate prices to students, seniors and others who are eligible for discounted rates hours before the show. Call the venues for full details.

Classical venues

As well as the following major venues, London's music schools, the **Royal Academy of Music** (7873 7300, www.ram.ac.uk), **Royal College of Music** (7589 3643, www.rcm.ac.uk), **Guildhall School of Music & Drama** (7628 2571, www.gsmd.ac.uk) and **Trinity College of Music** (8305 4444, www.tcm.ac.uk) also hold regular performances during term-time.

Barbican Centre

Silk Street, The City, EC2Y 8DS (7638 4141/box office 7638 8891/www.barbican.org.uk). Barbican tube/Moorgate tube/rail. **Box office** 9am-8pm daily. **Tickets** £6.50-£35. **Credit** AmEx, MC, V. **Map** p402 P5.

This arts complex is the home of the London Symphony Orchestra (LSO), the richest if not the best of the capital's international orchestras. It plays 90 concerts a year here, tours the world and records prolifically for both film and CD. Its rivals include the BBC Symphony Orchestra, which also performs here at subsidised rates. The venue has just been renovated at the cost of some £25m with the intention of attracting some of the Continent's most prestigious orchestras. Meanwhile, the modern music programming, taking in jazz, rock, world and country, continues to find ever larger audiences. There is occasional free music in the foyer.

Bush Hall

310 Uxbridge Road, Shepherd's Bush, W12 7LJ (8222 6955/box office 8222 6933/www.bushhall music.co.uk). Shepherd's Bush tube. **Box office** 10am-5pm Mon-Fri. **Tickets** £6-£25. **Credit** AmEx, MC, V.

Opened in 1904 as the Carlton Ballroom (the plasterwork is dotted with musical motifs) and then used as a snooker hall, Bush Hall was refurbished as a plush music venue in 2000. It stages an even spread of chamber music concerts and low-key, often acoustic, rock shows.

Cadogan Hall

5 Sloane Terrace, Chelsea, SW1X 9DH (7730 4500). Sloane Square tube. **Box office** 10am-7pm Mon-Sat. **Tickets** £10-£65. **Credit** Am, MC, V.

London's newest concert venue, Cadogan Hall, opened in June 2004. The 100-year-old building was formerly a Christian Scientist church, but has now been transformed into a light and airy auditorium with good acoustics. Seating around 900 people, the ground floor is raked so that sight lines are excellent and there is a horseshoe balcony running the entire circumference of the hall. The English

Chamber Orchestra intends to be a regular player and the Royal Philharmonic Orchestra will use it for rehearsal and recording, and for chamber pieces.

Royal Albert Hall

Kensington Gore, South Kensington, SW7 2AP (information 7589 3203/box office 7589 8212/ www.royalalberthall.com). South Kensington tube/ 9, 10, 52 bus. **Box office** 9am-9pm daily. **Tickets** £4-£50. **Credit** AmEx, MC, V. **Map** p397 D9.

This grand 6,000-seat rotunda is the home of the Proms (*see p306*), which occupy the building during the summer months each year. Otherwise, the hall, built as a memorial to Queen Victoria's husband, is a venue for all forms of public event including opera, rock, jazz, tennis, boxing, circus, fashion shows, business conventions and awards ceremonies. A recent programme of refurbishment has installed discreet air-conditioning, modernised the backstage area and moved the main entrance to the south side, right opposite the Royal College of Music.

St James's Church Piccadilly

197 Piccadilly, St James's, W1J 9LL (7381 0441/ www.sjpconcerts.org.uk). Green Park/Piccadilly Circus tube. **Open** 8am-6.30pm daily. **Admission** free-£20; tickets available at the door 30 mins before start of performances. **No credit cards**. **Map** p400 J7.

The only Wren church outside the City, this lovely, simply designed building hosts free lunchtime recitals (Mon, Wed, Fri) and a less regular programme of evening concerts. The church also hosts conventions and lectures by leading world figures. It has a decent café and a courtyard craft market around a spreading Indian Bean tree. It's worth dropping by to pick up a programme and see what upcoming events are scheduled.

St John's, Smith Square

Smith Square, Westminster, SW1P 3HA (7222 1061/www.sjss.org.uk). Westminster tube. **Box office** 10am-5pm Mon-Fri, or until start of performance on concert nights; from 1hr before start of performance Sat, Sun. **Tickets** £5-£45. **Credit** MC, V. **Map** p401 K10.

This elegant 18th-century ex-church hosts a nightly programme (except during summer) of orchestral and chamber concerts with occasional vibrant recitals on its magnificent Klais organ. There's also a wonderfully secluded restaurant in the crypt, open whether or not any musical events are scheduled. In an interesting historic note, the café is called 'the Footstool', which has been the building's nickname ever since Queen Anne was asked how she would like the new church to look when complete and, kicking hers over, said, 'Like that!'

St Martin-in-the-Fields

Trafalgar Square, Westminster, WC2N 4JJ (concert information 7839 8362/www.stmartin-in- the-fields.org). Charing Cross tube/rail. **Box office** 10am-5pm Mon-Sat, or until start of performance. **Admission** *Lunchtime concerts* donations requested. *Evening concerts* £6-£18. **Credit** MC, V. **Map** p401 L7.

Arts & Entertainment

London Coliseum

In its time, it's been a cinema, a music hall and a greyhound track, seen performances by the Marx Brothers, Lily Langtree, WC Fields and Sarah Bernhardt, and been home to the Kirov Ballet, *Annie Get Your Gun* and a boxing kangaroo; the London Coliseum has had myriad interesting uses during its unusual life. Recently refurbished, this beautiful venue on St Martin's Lane just off Trafalgar Square has been home to the English National Opera, the premier company for opera in English, since 1968. Along with the Royal Opera House, the Coliseum is the best place to see opera in this country.

Built in 1904 by renowned architect Frank Matcham, refurbishment was completed in September 2004 – the first major restoration for 100 years. Funded partly by the ENO and partly by the Arts Council (and drawing a veil over the numerous squabbles and scandals that broke out during this lengthy process), the £80 million restoration was a mammoth project intended to enlarge public spaces, improve acoustics, redecorate the auditorium in accordance with the original decor, create a dramatic new public gallery space, restore the exterior and tart things up backstage. It took three years, with the Coliseum opening for short seasons whenever building work allowed, but the results are magnificent. The building was always an impressive one, from the marble patterned floors to the revolving dome on the roof, but this sympathetic restoration has brought out the wonderful colours of the foyer – striking purple and scarlet set against cream and gold – and spruced up the immaculate auditorium so every ornate detail stands out.

That's not all. The public areas have been opened up; previously riff-raff and toffs were segregated, but dividing walls have been knocked through. The famous dome that crowns the building was originally glass, but this has been painted over and backlit – it's still hugely impressive. A new addition is the Trafalgar Bar, a glass-roofed conservatory-like public bar with views over Trafalgar Square. This will host talks and events. There is also a smaller performance space, fully kitted out with lights, which will be used for children's workshops and the like.

So, it might look the part, but will people turn up? Responsibility for that falls upon Sean Doran, the artistic director and chief executive, who is trying to tread that fine line between tradition and innovation (along with Alex Poots, he was behind the ENO's groundbreaking performance at the 2004 Glastonbury festival). The 2004-5 season includes Wagner and a Christmas Gilbert and Sullivan as well as *Don Giovanni*, Berlioz's epic *The Trojans*, a 1950s take on Handel's *Semele*, Tippett's powerful World War II oratorio *A Child of Our Time* and Bernstein's score for *On the Town*. There are also plans to get rock bands involved; already in production is an opera about Colonel Gaddaffi written by the innovative dance rock outfit Asian Dub Foundation. Interesting and unusual; isn't this where we came in?

Royal Albert Hall. *See p302.*

Overlooking Trafalgar Square, St Martin's hopelessly romantic candlelight concerts (Thur-Sat) are popular with both locals and visitors, while its frequently wonderful free lunchtime recitals (Mon, Tue) are one of the best bargains in town.

South Bank Centre

Belvedere Road, South Bank, SE1 8XX (0870 380 0400/www.rfh.org.uk). Embankment tube/Waterloo tube/rail. **Box office** *In person* 11am-8pm. *By phone* 9am-8pm Mon-Sun. **Tickets** £5-£75. **Credit** AmEx, MC, V. **Map** p401 M8.

The South Bank Centre has three concert halls: the 3,000-seat Royal Festival Hall for major orchestral concerts, the slightly smaller Queen Elizabeth Hall for piano recitals and the little Purcell Room for chamber groups and contemporary music concerts. It is home to six classical music ensembles – including the Philharmonia and the London Philharmonic Orchestras, the unique period instrument Orchestra of the Age of Enlightenment, the Alban Berg String Quartet and London Sinfonietta, the country's leading contemporary music ensemble. The Royal Festival Hall, the most advanced concert hall in the world back in the '50s, is feeling its age and closes in July 2005 for 18 months of refurbishment. During this time, the Philharmonia and LPO intend to stay at the South Bank, playing extra concerts at the Queen Elizabeth Hall and Purcell Room.

Wigmore Hall

36 Wigmore Street, Marylebone, W1U 2BP (7935 2141/www.wigmore-hall.org.uk). Bond Street tube. **Box office** *In person* mid Mar-Nov 10.30am-8pm daily; Nov-Mar 10am-8.30pm Mon-Sat; 10.30am-5pm Sun; *By phone* 10am-7pm Mon-Sat; 10am-6.30pm Sun (summer); 10.30am-4.30pm Sun (winter). **Tickets** £8-£35. **Credit** AmEx, DC, MC, V. **Map** p398 G6.

Built in 1901 as the display and recital hall for Bechstein Pianos, this is the jewel of London's music venues. With its perfect acoustic, discreet art nouveau decor and excellent basement restaurant, it remains one of the world's top concert venues for chamber music and song. A recent refurbishment has seen the hall receive a new roof and ventilation system, better sight lines, new seats, improved public spaces, sympathetic lighting and restored foyer. Also new is artistic director Paul Kildea, who replaces the much-loved William Lyne and has the tricky task of attracting a fresh audience to the hall without alienating the hard core.

Lunchtime concerts

A great tradition of midday performing mainly by talented music students and burgeoning young professionals has grown up in London's beautiful churches. Admission to most of these events is either free or by donation. Those listed below are all centrally located in the City but there are many more around town. See *Time Out* magazine for comprehensive coverage.

Regular organ recitals are held at **Temple Church** (off Fleet Street, The City, EC4, 7353 8559), **Grosvenor Chapel** (South Audley Street, Mayfair, W1, 7499 1684), **St James's** (Clerkenwell Close, EC1, 7251 1190) and **Southwark Cathedral**.

St Anne & St Agnes *Gresham Street, The City, EC2V 7BX (7606 4986). St Paul's tube.* **Performances** 1.10pm Mon, Fri. **Map** p404 P6.

St Bride's *Fleet Street, The City, EC4Y 8AU (7427 0133). Blackfriars tube/rail.* **Performances** 1.15pm Tue, Fri (except Aug, Advent, Lent). **Map** p404 N6.

St John's *Waterloo Road, Waterloo, SE1 8TY (7928 2003/www.stjohnswaterloo.co.uk). Waterloo tube/rail.* **Performances** 1.10pm Wed, call ahead to check. **Map** p404 N8.

St Lawrence Jewry *Guildhall, The City, EC2V 5AA (7600 9478). Mansion House or St Paul's tube/ Bank tube/DLR.* **Performances** 1pm Mon, Tue. **Map** p404 P6.

St Margaret Lothbury *Lothbury, The City, EC2R 7HH (7606 8330/www.stml.org.uk). Bank tube/DLR.* **Performances** 1.10pm Thur. **Map** p405 Q6.

St Martin within Ludgate *40 Ludgate Hill, The City, EC4M 7DE (7248 6054). Blackfriars/St Paul's tube.* **Performances** 1.15pm Wed. **Map** p404 O6.

St Mary-le-Bow *Cheapside, The City, EC2V 6AU (7248 5139/www.stmarylebow.co.uk). Bank/Mansion House tube.* **Performances** 1.05pm Thur. **Map** p404 P6.

Opera companies

As well as the following, there are also performances at **Sadler's Wells** (0870 737 7737, www.sadlerswells.com) and the **Peacock Theatre** (7863 8222, www.sadlerswells.com). The latter is possibly the only theatre in London that is haunted by a dolphin.

English National Opera

The Coliseum, St Martin's Lane, Covent Garden, WC2N 4ES (box office 7632 8300/fax 7379 1264/ www.eno.org). Leicester Square tube/Charing Cross tube/rail. **Box office** *By phone* 24hrs daily; day tickets can be purchased from 10am on day of performance or by phone from 12.30pm on day of performance. **Tickets** £5-£85. **Credit** AmEx, DC, MC, V. **Map** p401 L7.

The Coliseum, the traditional home of the English National Opera (ENO), reopened in September 2004. For more, *see p303* **London Coliseum**.

Royal Opera

Royal Opera House, Covent Garden, WC2E 9DD (7304 4000/www.royaloperahouse.org.uk). Covent Garden tube. **Box office** 10am-8pm Mon-Sat. **Tickets** £3-£175. **Credit** AmEx, DC, MC, V. **Map** p399 L6.

Covent Garden is one of the great opera houses of the world, and a hugely expensive refurbishment in 2000 only made it better. The conversion of Floral Hall, the old flower warehouse, into a restaurant and bars is one of London's wonders. The discreetly air-conditioned auditorium and comfy new seating make a night out at the opera a positive prospect whatever the production. In a nod to the proletariat, a new system allows passers-by in the piazza out-side to hear the music.

Festivals

In addition to the annual festivals listed below, the **Barbican** (*see p302*), the **South Bank** and **Wigmore Hall** (for both, *see p304*) all present events throughout the year. There are also open-air festivals of tried-and-tested favourites at Hampstead's **Kenwood House** (*see p154*) and **Marble Hill Park** (*see p180*) in July and August. For more information, call 8233 7435 or visit www.picnicconcerts.com.

City of London Festival
Venues in & around the City (information 7377 0540/box office 0845 120 7502/www.colf.org). **Date** 27 June-13 July 2005. **Box office** 9am-8pm daily. **Tickets** free-£40. **Credit** AmEx, MC, V.
This rich event continues to expand, but the core of its annual programme remains chamber music concerts in the beautiful halls of ancient livery companies, such as the Ironmongers' and Goldsmiths', which the public never otherwise see. Concerts, talks and exhibitions also take place in churches as well as the Barbican and great St Paul's Cathedral itself.

Hampton Court Palace Festival
Hampton Court, East Molesey, Surrey (Ticketmaster 0870 534 4444/www.hamptoncourtfestival.com). Hampton Court rail/riverboat from Westminster or Richmond to Hampton Court Pier (Apr-Oct). **Date** Mid June 2005 (tbc). **Tickets** £15-£85. **Credit** AmEx, MC, V.
Cardinal Wolsey built this vast luxury home for himself but later gave it to King Henry VIII who frolicked here with Anne Boleyn. The air of idle pleasure persists in the annual summer festival, where overtures and operatic arias have supper intervals during which audiences picnic on the grass or loiter in champagne tents while stilt-walkers, tumblers and jugglers wander among them.

Holland Park Theatre
Holland Park, Kensington High Street, Kensington, W8 6LU (7602 7856/www.operahollandpark.com). High Street Kensington or Holland Park tube. **Date** June-early Aug 2005. **Tickets** £20-£42. **Credit** AmEx, MC, V. **Map** p394 A8.
This open-air, canopied theatre hosts a summer season of opera where the experience can be magical whatever the weather. Although it is harder for the performers in the rain, the audience is correspondingly more appreciative. The cries of unseen peacocks beyond the wall add a surreal touch.

The Proms
Royal Albert Hall, Kensington Gore, South Kensington, SW7 2AP (information 7765 5575/ box office 7589 8212/www.bbc.co.uk/proms). South Kensington tube/9, 10, 52 bus. **Date** 15 July-10 Sept 2005. **Box office** 9am-9pm daily. **Tickets** £4-£35. **Credit** AmEx, MC, V. **Map** p397 D9.
The BBC Sir Henry Wood Promenade Concerts, or Proms for short, is arguably the world's finest orchestral music festival. Running annually from mid July until mid September, it features 70 concerts of both staple repertoire and newly commissioned works. The Proms began in 1895 with the aim of occupying idle musicians during the summer holidays and of informally educating those Londoners

who could not afford to take holidays. Audiences paid a minimal ticket price provided they were prepared to do without a seat. The tradition continues today, as you can buy reserved seats in advance, but many prefer to queue on the day for cheap tickets for the seatless promenade area in front of the stage.

It's best to buy a festival programme from a bookshop and plan ahead: the choice is wide. Tickets for the hilariously over-the-top Last Night, when normally well-behaved grown-ups act like schoolchildren, throwing paper darts and parping klaxons at inappropriate moments, are difficult to get hold of, but a secondary event is staged simultaneously in Hyde Park, where there's plenty of room.

Spitalfields Festival
Christ Church Spitalfields, E1 or Shoreditch Church, E1 (7377 1362/www.spitalfieldsfestival.org.uk). Liverpool Street tube/rail. **Dates** 6-24 June 2005. **Box office** 10am-5.30pm Mon-Fri. **Tickets** free-£30. **Credit** MC, V. **Map** p403 S5.
This enchanting, twice-yearly festival features new and old music, works by neglected composers, and walks and talks in and around the Spitalfields area. The festival returns to the splendid Christ Church after an absence due to impressive renovations.

Rock, Dance Roots & Jazz

Sure, it can be an expensive experience, involving bad sound and flat beer, and, granted, it can be almost impossible to keep track of what's cool and what's not in this inconsistent town, but London's music scene is still one of the best around. That's perhaps more to do with touring artists than any home-grown pool of talent – though there are rumblings of a scene in New Cross – but the truth is that anybody who is anybody will visit London some time on tour. Each night, the capital is crowded with an intoxicating selection of acts local and international, famous and unknown, who between them bring an impossibly diverse range of music to an equally impossibly diverse audience. There is so much on offer here that, put simply, if you don't find something you like, you're not looking.

TICKETS AND INFORMATION
Your first stop should be the weekly *Time Out* magazine, which details hundreds of gigs in London. Most venues have websites detailing future shows, and some have online booking.

Prices vary wildly: on any given night, you could pay £45 for the privilege of watching Justin Timberlake at Earl's Court or catch a perfectly serviceable jazz act free in a bar or restaurant. Look out, too, for the regular free signings in the **Virgin Megastore**, **HMV** and

Rough Trade (for all three, *see pp256-257*). Most pub venues – the **Water Rats** (see *p313*) and **Barfly** (*see p312*) and are the main exceptions – don't sell advance tickets, and for most roots and some jazz venues you can just pay on the night. For everywhere else, buy tickets in advance if possible. Whether heavy metal or jazz, headline acts come on at 9-10pm.

Buy tickets with cash direct from the venue's box office if you want to avoid insidious, needlessly inflated booking fees and charges, which can add as much as 30 per cent to the ticket price. If the venue has sold out, try a ticket agency: the big four are **Ticketmaster** (0870 534 4444, www.ticketmaster.co.uk), **Stargreen** (7734 8932, www.stargreen.com), **Ticketweb** (08700 600 100, www.ticketweb.co.uk) and **Way Ahead** (0870 120 1149, www.seetickets.com). Most important of all, though, is to avoid buying from the shady chancers otherwise known as ticket touts who hang around outside bigger venues: you'll pay a fortune, plus your ticket may be forged. And, as far as we know, they don't give refunds.

Asian explosion

British Asians have been making pop for as long as rock 'n' roll has existed. The first generation of immigrants from the Indian subcontinent included Cliff Richard, Engelbert Humperdinck, Peter Sarstedt and Freddie Mercury – although given the lack of any 'Indian' references in their music, you would be forgiven for not being aware of their provenance.

In the late 1970s and early '80s another generation of musicians from Southall and the Midlands was pioneering bhangra, a mix of Punjabi folk rhythms and Western dance music. And, by the mid '90s, a third wave of confident, musicianly British Asians emerged – including Talvin Singh, Nitin Sawhney, Cornershop, Najma Akhtar, State Of Bengal, Fun-Da-Mental and Asian Dub Foundation – who made complex, politicised music that allied North Indian classical and folk traditions to cutting-edge British electronica. London became a home from home for Indian music, performing the same role that Paris does for African music or New York with Latin and salsa.

Now London is witnessing another generation of British Asian musicians; the children or even grandchildren of immigrants who are indulging their love affair with black American music. These rappers, DJs, MCs and producers wear their ethnicity lightly: there are glimpses of bhangra, a few Bollywood breaks and some samples of dhol drums or sitars, but the basic pulse is the strut of London creole culture – hip hop, R&B and Jamaican dancehall.

Rishi Rich, a 25-year-old producer from Harrow, has been producing and remixing a host of clients – Madonna, Britney, Ricky Martin, Mis-Teeq, J-Lo, Craig David – from his small studio in Perivale. His protégés include

23-year-old Southall singer and rapper Jay Sean (pictured), who already has a couple of top ten hits under his belt, and rapper Juggy D. Watch out also for Panjabi Hit Squad and Trickbaby, along with rejuvenated old-timers like Apache Indian, Bally Sagoo and Panjabi MC, not to mention the Canadian-born R&B singer Raghav or big-name DJs like Bobby Friction and Nihal. And, with US hip hop and R&B increasingly picking up Asian beats, it looks like British Asians' love affair with US street culture has been reciprocated.

Grime time

For nearly four decades, a large part of pop has been about Brits falling in love with black American music and then selling it back to the Yanks with a uniquely British twist. But hip hop seemed to have halted this transatlantic dialogue. UK hip hop has been burdened by speaking the same language as the US culture it venerates, often lapsing into lame imitation and cod-American accents.

But that's beginning to change. The uniquely British twist comes via Jamaican MC culture – a gabbling, half-spoken, triumphalist narration delivered with a certain tightness in the throat and a crisp diction. 'Grime' is the term that's been given to the London-based underground rave scene. The dainty delivery of the grime MC is one part cockney market trader, one part Jamaican horse-racing commentator, one part Bronx sling-slang. And the music is often astonishing, taking the sonic energy of rave culture, the beats and rhythm of drum 'n' bass and the relentless verbiage of hip hop.

Hurriedly pressed on to white labels, the records are bought by a select band of DJs and aficionados at record shop Rhythm Division (391 Roman Road, Bow, E3 5QS, 8981 2203). Teenage Mercury Music Prize winner Dizzee Rascal (pictured) and his mentor Wiley are the two mavericks who've taken this genre overground – and Mike Skinner's the Streets are certainly in the same ball park – but there are hundreds of young MCs and musicians who you'll hear at so many grime raves or on inner London's myriad pirate radio stations like Rinse FM (100.3 FM).

The scene is predominantly black but there are plenty of white, Asian and Arabic MCs, along with females like the tiny, blonde Lady Sovereign. Most of the music is played by So Solid-style collectives with names like Meridian and Venom. Each of these tribes has its own particular star MC: Roll Deep's star player is Wiley; his old crew the Pay As You Go Cartel features MC Maxwell D; Black Ops are led by Jon E Cash; Ruff Squad has the hotly tipped Tinchy Stryder; Boyz In Da Hood features Durrty Doogz; while Nasty Crew have D Double, Kano, Sharkey Major, Ghetto, Hyper, Stormin and Marcus Nasty. Expect a few of these names to go mainstream sometime in the immediate future.

Rock & dance venues

Major venues

In addition to the venues listed below, the **South Bank Centre** (see p304), **Royal Albert Hall** (see p302) and **Barbican Centre** (see p302) all stage major gigs on a regular basis. In summer, **Hyde Park** (see p141) stages sizeable outdoor shows, while the beautiful courtyard at **Somerset House** (see p102) hosts shows from ineffably cool acts that draw up to 3,000 people. There are also occasional shows from acclaimed singer-songwriters and acoustic acts at **Bush Hall** (see p302) and **UCL Bloomsbury Theatre** (15 Gordon Street, Bloomsbury, WC1H OAH, 7388 8822). Elephant & Castle's **Coronet** (26-28 New Kent Road, Newington, SE1 6TJ, 7701 1500/0870 0601793) is primarily a club and cinema, but also hosts the occasional unusual live show. As we went to press, the legendary **Marquee Club** was about to open at a new 900-capacity site (1 Leicester Square, Soho, WC2H 7NA). This is the fourth incarnation of the venue, and should hopefully be more successful than the last one, which closed and became the Islington Academy months after opening. The new Marquee has the same bookers as **Water Rats** (see p313) and **Betsey Trotwood** (see p312) and will bring in emerging rock and indie acts. Finally, Camden's venerable **Electric Ballroom**, threatened by rebuilding work, struggles on. See www.electricballroom.co.uk for the latest.

Astoria

157 Charing Cross Road, Soho, WC2H OEL (information 8963 0940/box office 08701 500044/ www.meanfiddler.com). Tottenham Court Road tube. **Box office** *In person* 10am-6pm Mon-Sat. *By phone* 24hrs daily. **Tickets** £10-£20. **Credit** AmEx, MC, V. **Map** p399 K6.

Grubby decor, hopeless air-conditioning and atrocious sound have never stopped this 2,000-capacity hall from being London's pre-eminent alt-rock venue (Franz Ferdinand, MC5).

Blackheath Halls

23 Lee Road, Blackheath, SE3 9RQ (8463 0100). Blackheath rail/54, 89, 108, 202, N53 bus. **Box office** 10am-6pm Mon-Sat; 11am-3pm Sun. **Tickets** £2.50-£18.50. **Credit** AmEx, MC, V.

South-east London's premier music venue presents a variety of different styles, from classical to rock. Not hugely accessible but it still attracts top performers.

Brixton Academy

211 Stockwell Road, Brixton, SW9 9SL (information 7771 3000/box office 08707 712 000/www.brixton-academy.co.uk). Brixton tube/rail. **Box office** *By phone* 24hrs daily. **Tickets** £10-£40. **Credit** MC, V.

It's a little ragged around the edges, and if it's not full, the echo can be overwhelming. Still, this 4,700-capacity cod-Gothic south London venue is one of the best in town, thanks to excellent sight lines, decent sound and many well-staffed bars. Acts run the gamut from Bob Dylan to Prodigy.

Carling Apollo

Queen Caroline Street, Hammersmith, W6 9QH (information 8748 8660/box office 0870 606 3400/www.getlive.co.uk). Hammersmith tube. **Box office** *By phone* 24hrs daily. **Tickets** £10-£40. **Credit** AmEx, MC, V.

Now owned by global entertainment giant Clear Channel, the long-time Hammersmith Odeon was relaunched in October 2003 as an all-standing, 5,000-capacity venue. AC/DC headlined its re-opening night; Tom Waits and Kylie followed. Tom got seats.

Earl's Court Exhibition Centre

Warwick Road, Earl's Court, SW5 9TA (7385 1200/ box office 7370 8078/www.eco.co.uk). Earl's Court tube. **Box office** *In person* 9am-6pm Mon-Fri. *By phone* 24hrs daily. **Tickets** £17-£50. **Credit** MC, V. **Map** p396 A11.

An immense aircraft hangar of a venue (its capacity of 20,000 makes it London's largest), cursed by horrible acoustics and expensive concessions. That doesn't stop the likes of Radiohead and Justin Timberlake from playing here.

Forum

9-17 Highgate Road, Kentish Town, NW5 1JY (information 7284 1001/box office 0870 150 0044/ www.meanfiddler.com). Kentish Town tube/rail/N2 bus. **Box office** *In person* from the Astoria or the Jazz Café. *By phone* 24hrs daily. **Tickets** £10-£20. **Credit** MC, V (phone bookings only).

One of London's better venues, but much underused. A pity, really: its grey location aside, this once-grand theatre, blessed with fine sound and friendly staff, is much more inviting than the Astoria (see above). It still gets a few big shows, including the likes of the Flaming Lips and Dizzee Rascal.

Islington Academy

N1 Centre, 16 Parkfield Street, Islington, N1 0PS (information 7288 4400/box office 0870 771 2000/www.islington-academy.co.uk). Angel tube. **Box office** *In person* noon-4pm Mon-Sat. *By phone* 24hrs daily. **Tickets** £3-£20. **Credit** MC, V.

Ex-Eurythmic Dave Stewart's relaunch of the venerable Marquee club in this gleaming Islington shopping mall was a flop. Now under the Carling roster, it features the likes of Ash and the Zutons but remains a rather antiseptic environment.

Koko

1A Camden Road, Camden, NW1 OJH (0870 432 5527/www.koko.uk.com). Mornington Crescent tube. **Box office** phone ahead for details. **Tickets** £3-£15. **Credit** MC, V.

Formerly the Camden Palace, this grand old ballroom has reopened as Koko. The Clash and the Pistols played here, as did Madonna for her first UK

Arts & Entertainment

show. These days, expect to see decrepit '80s legends (Suggs, Shane McGowan) on Fridays or bright young things on Wednesdays for Club NME.

Ocean
270 Mare Street, Hackney, E8 1HE (switchboard 8986 5336/box office 8533 0111/24hr bookings 0845 070 1571/www.ocean.org.uk). Hackney Central or Hackney Downs rail. **Box office** noon-6pm Mon-Fri; later on performance nights. **Tickets** £3-£30. **Credit** MC, V.
This newish venue has staged a wide mix of shows, including lots of world music, but the quality of acts has declined recently and the future looks uncertain.

Shepherd's Bush Empire
Shepherd's Bush Green, W12 8TT (8354 3300/box office 0870 771 2000/www.shepherds-bush-empire.co.uk). Shepherd's Bush tube. **Box office** *In person* noon-2.30pm, 3-5pm Mon-Sat. *By phone* 24hrs daily. **Tickets** £10-£40. **Credit** MC, V.
This 2,000-capacity former BBC theatre is London's best mid-sized venue. The sound is usually splendid (with the exception of the alcove behind the stalls bar), the atmosphere is cosy, and the staff are among London's friendliest. An eclectic booking policy also adds to its appeal.

Union Chapel
Compton Terrace, Islington, N1 2XD (7226 1686/box office 0870 120 1349/www.unionchapel.org.uk). Highbury & Islington tube/rail/N19, N65, N92 bus. **Box office** 24hrs daily. **Tickets** £4-£20. **Credit** MC, V.
This Islington landmark leads an intriguing double existence as both church and concert venue. It's a gorgeous space – amid the atmospheric ruins of a historic sanctuary – but a muddying echo has the potential to ruin a show.

Wembley Arena
Empire Way, Wembley, Middx HA9 0DW (0870 739 0739/www.wembleyticket.com). Wembley Park tube/Wembley Central tube/rail. **Box office** *In person* 10.30am-4.30pm Mon-Sat. *By phone* 24hrs daily. **Tickets** £5-£100. **Credit**, MC, V.
Competition is stiff, but this might nevertheless qualify as the worst music venue in London. Still, with a 12,500 capacity there are few alternatives when such crowd-pullers as Busted, Elton John and Britney come to town.

Club venues

As well as the following, the clubs **Cargo** *(see p317)* and **93 Feet East** *(see p320)* are trendy places that host an interesting mix of shows. **Pleasure Unit** (359 Bethnal Green Road, Bethnal Green, E2 6LG, 7729 0167) has the odd gig and good club nights, and **Rhythm Factory** (16-18 Whitechapel Road, E1 1EW, Whitechapel, 7375 3774, www.rhythmfactory.co.uk) is a hip venue for anything from punk rock to acid jazz.

Borderline
Orange Yard, Manette Street, Soho, W1B 4JB (information 7734 5547/box office 7534 6970/www.meanfiddler.com). Tottenham Court Road tube. **Box office** (Astoria) 10am-6pm Mon-Sat. **Open** *Gigs* 7-11pm Mon-Sat, Sun; *Club* 11pm-3am Thur-Sat. **Admission** *Gigs* £6-£16. *Club* £2-£7. **Credit** MC, V. **Map** p399 K6.
A fine basement space, this, with great sound and an enthusiastic promoter who mixes the best in Americana with home-grown hopefuls. And despite having been bought by Vince Power's Mean Fiddler empire, Borderline remains a terrific place to either see a band or dance the night away (Alan McGee's Friday Queen Is Dead club dead is hugely popular). One of London's finest.

Garage
20-22 Highbury Corner, Islington, N5 1RD (information 8963 0940/box office 0870 150 0044/www.meanfiddler.com). Highbury & Islington tube/rail. **Box office** 24hrs daily. **Open** *Gigs* 8pm-midnight Mon-Thur, some Sun; 8pm-3am Fri, Sat. **Admission** £5-£15. **Credit** MC, V.
The Garage is home to indie-leaning acts too big to play the Barfly *(see p312)* but not famous enough for the Astoria *(see p309)*. The sound at this low-ceilinged venue is usually below average, and it can get unbearably hot in here if it's more than about two-thirds full, but there's often a good atmosphere. Loses points for a nasty policy of forcing customers to hand their bags over to the paying cloakroom. Smaller sister venue Upstairs at the Garage (guess where it is) is a similar affair.

Infinity
10 Old Burlington Street, Mayfair, W1S 3AG (7287 5255, www.infinityclub.co.uk). Oxford Circus or Piccadilly Circus tube. **Tickets** £3-£8. **Credit** MC, V.
This new, intimate Mayfair venue hosts a range of different club nights and live shows by young indie bands and is becoming increasingly hip thanks to patronage by music press faves the Libertines.

ICA
The Mall, SW1Y 5AH (box office 7930 3647/www.ica.org.uk). Embankment or Piccadilly Circus tube/Charing Cross tube/rail. **Box office** noon-9.30pm daily. **Tickets** £5-£15. **Credit** AmEx, DC, MC, V. **Map** p401 K8.
The Institute of Contemporary Arts hosts more and more live music these days (interesting, fashionable and alternative generally). Sound is good; the bar is one of the biggest scrums in London.

Lock 17
11 East Yard, Camden Lock, Chalk Farm Road, Camden, NW1 8AB (box office 7428 0010/Ticketmaster 7344 4040/www.dingwalls.com). Camden Town/Chalk Farm tube. **Box office** *In person* tickets from Rhythm Records, 281 Camden High Street (7267 0123). *By phone* 24hrs daily. **Open** *Gigs* 7.30pm-2am, nights vary. **Admission** £5-£15. **Credit** AmEx, MC, V.

Union Chapel. *See p310.*

Formerly known as Dingwalls, Lock 17 stages some good shows but, due to poor sight lines, works much better when they put back the tables and it becomes comedy venue Jongleurs (*see p276*) at weekends.

100 Club

100 Oxford Street, Fitzrovia, W1D 1LL (7636 0933/ www.the100club.co.uk). Oxford Circus or Tottenham Court Road tube. **Open** *Gigs* 7.30pm-midnight Mon-Thur; 8pm-1am Fri; 7.30pm-2am Sat; 7.30-11.30pm Sun. **Tickets** free-£12. **Credit** AmEx, MC, V. **Map** p399 K6.
Established 60 years ago, Glenn Miller was a regular. In the 1950s it became a leading trad-jazz joint, in the '60s a blues and R&B hangout, and in the '70s it was the home of punk. These days, a mix of indie wannabes and old-school jazz can be heard in the awkward room. Extra points for real ale at the bar.

Mean Fiddler

165 Charing Cross Road, Soho, WC2H 0EN (7434 9592/box office 0870 534 4444/www.meanfiddler. com). Leicester Square or Tottenham Court Road tube. **Box office** *In person* 10am-6pm Mon-Sat. *By phone* 24hrs daily. **Tickets** £10-£25. **Credit** MC, V. **Map** p399 K6.
Little brother to the adjacent Astoria (*see p309*), with a superior sound system and better sight lines. If the band's rubbish, head to the glassed-off bar to the left of the balcony. The Fiddler also puts on some pretty decent indie club nights.

Metro

19-23 Oxford Street, Soho, W1D 2DN (7437 0964). Tottenham Court Road tube. **Open** *Office* from 5pm Mon-Fri. *Club* 11pm-3am Tue-Thur; 11pm-4am Fri, Sat.* **Admission** £5-£10. **Map** p399 K6.

Mushy sound and terrible layout, but this basement fast cemented a reputation as *the* place to play during the recent garage rock boom. Not quite what it was, but things can still get enjoyably messy here; expect your shirt to be drenched with both sweat and beer by the time you leave, whenever that is.

Scala

275 Pentonville Road, King's Cross, N1 9NL (7833 2022/box office 0870 060 0100). King's Cross tube/rail. **Box Office** 24hrs daily. **Open** Call for details. **Tickets** £8-£15. **Credit** MC, V.
A King's Cross landmark. Primarily a club venue, but plenty of good live acts, often from America (Shellac, Interpol), still pass through its doors.

Spitz

Old Spitalfields Market, 109 Commercial Street, Spitalfields, E1 6BG (7392 9032/box office 0871 220 0260/www.spitz.co.uk). Liverpool Street tube/rail. **Open** 11am-midnight Mon-Sat; 10am-10.30pm Sun. **Box office** 24hrs daily. **Tickets** £4-£12. **Credit** MC, V. **Map** p403 R5.
On the edge of Spitalfields, the Spitz tries to be all things to all people: gallery, restaurant, café and (upstairs) live music venue. Expect anything from experimental electronica to gutsy country.

Underworld

174 Camden High Street, Camden, NW1 0NE (7482 1932/0870 060 0100/www.theunderworld camden.co.uk). Camden Town tube. **Open** *Gigs* 7-10.30pm. **Admission** £5-£20. **No credit cards**.
This is a maddening underground space, a maze of corridors and pillars and bars and, eventually, a decent live room deep below Camden Town that is very popular with the heavy rock and metal crowd.

Razorlight rock out at **Barfly**.

University of London Union (ULU)

Malet Street, Bloomsbury, WC1E 7HY (box 7664 2000/www.ulu.lon.ac.uk). Goodge Street tube. **Box office** 8.30am-11pm Mon-Fri; 9am-11pm Sat, Sun. **Open** *Gigs* 7.30-11pm, nights vary. **Admission** £8-£15. **No credit cards. Map** p399 K4.

This student venue has recently had a spruce-up and new £100,000 sound system installed, which will hopefully improve what has always been a cosy if anonymous spot. Acts are whoever is tipped in *NME* that week; bar prices are student-friendly.

Pub & bar venues

In addition to the venues listed below, the Hank Dogs' Wednesday-night **Easycome** acoustic club at the Ivy House (40 Stuart Road, Nunhead, SE15 3BE, 7732 0222) and Alan Tyler's country-rockin' shindig **Come Down and Meet the Folks**, held every Sunday at the Fiddlers Elbow (1 Malden Road, Kentish Town, NW5 3HS, www.comedownandmeetthefolks.co.uk) are worth investigating. More centrally, **Needles Wine Bar** (5-6 Clipstone Street, Fitzrovia, W1, 7436 0035) has started to put on shows featuring everything from garage rock to experimental jazz. The nascent New Cross scene, an emerging, enjoyably incoherant mash of friends in bands playing rock and electronica, is best experienced at **Paradise Bar** (460 New Cross Road, SE14, 8692 1530).

Barfly

49 Chalk Farm Road, Camden, NW1 8AN (7691 4244/box office 0870 907 0999/www.barfly club.com). Chalk Farm tube. **Open** 7.30-11pm Mon-Thur; 7.30pm-3am Fri, Sat; 7-10.30pm Sun. *Gigs* 8.15pm daily. **Admission** £4-£8. **Credit** *Box office only* AmEx, MC, V.

The Barfly club sure knows how to churn 'em out: around 20 indie acts – three a night – play here weekly. Coldplay, Stereophonics, the Strokes and the Darkness all clocked in on their way up.

Betsey Trotwood

56 Farringdon Road, Clerkenwell, EC1R 3BL(7253 4285). Farringdon tube. **Open** noon-11pm Mon-Fri; 11am-11pm Sat; noon-10.30pm Sun. *Gigs* 8pm Mon-Sat. **Admission** £4-£5. **Credit** MC, V.

For several years the chaps from the Water Rats (*see p313*) have promoted nights of indie-kid bliss in the 70-capacity upstairs room at this boozer, an ideal place for spotting lo-fi alt-rock microcelebs.

Boston Arms

178 Junction Road, Tufnell Park, N19 5QQ (7272 8153/www.dirtywaterclub.com). Tufnell Park tube. **Open** 11am-midnight Mon-Wed, Sun; 11am-1am Thur-Sat. *Gigs* 10pm, day varies. *Club* 9pm every other Fri. **Admission** £4-£6. **No credit cards.**

Briefly the trendiest venue in Britain when the White Stripes rolled into town in 2001 and claimed it as their home from home, it's still a great place to see emerging garage rock. On Fridays, the Dirty Water Club is legendary.

Buffalo Bar

259 Upper Street, Islington, N1 1RU (7359 6191/ www.thebuffalobar.co.uk). Highbury & Islington tube/rail. **Open** 8.30pm-2am Mon-Sat; 7pm-midnight Sun. **Admission** free-£6. **Credit** MC, V.

Music fanzines *Plan-B* and *Loose Lips* plus e-zine *Artrocker* all put on nights at this tiny basement bar, attracting some of the most interesting acts around.

Bull & Gate
389 Kentish Town Road, NW5 2TJ (7485 5358).
Kentish Town tube/rail. **Open** 11am-midnight
Mon-Sat; noon-10.30pm Sun. *Gigs* 8.30pm daily.
Admission £4-£5. **No credit cards**.
Once a dive, this has been smartened up, but still
entertains guitar-toting hopefuls in search of a big
break. Not in the same league as Barfly (*see p312*);
but better than Dublin Castle (*see below*).

Dublin Castle
94 Parkway, Camden, NW1 7AN (7485 1773/
www.bugbearbookings.com). Camden Town tube.
Open noon-1am Mon-Sat; noon-midnight Sun. *Gigs*
8.45pm Mon-Sat; 8.30pm Sun. **Admission** £4.50-£6.
No credit cards.
Though the refurbishment a couple of years ago
improved it, some think the Dublin Castle is still
better used as a pub than as a music venue. That
doesn't stop it hosting dozens of bands every week
– a tiny proportion of whom go on to make it big.

Hope & Anchor
207 Upper Street, Islington, N1 1RL (7354 1312).
Highbury & Islington tube/rail. **Open** noon-1am Mon-
Sat; noon-midnight Sun. *Gigs* 8pm daily. **Admission**
£4-£6. **Credit** MC, V. **Map** p402 O1.
This minuscule cellar was once a rock and punk legend. These days, the pub upstairs is smarter and the
acts are less noteworthy. Acoustic nights on Monday
and Wednesday; otherwise, it's indie and punk.

Notting Hill Arts Club
21 Notting Hill Gate, W11 3JQ (7460 4459/www.
nottinghillartsclub.com). Notting Hill Gate tube.
Open 6pm-Mon-Wed; 6pm-2am Thur, Fri;
4pm-2am Sat; 4pm-12.30am Sun. *Gigs* times vary.
Admission free-£8. **Credit** MC, V.
This painfully hip basement in the heart of Notting
Hill has all the charm of root canal work and its staff
are all too easily distracted. Still, Rota on Saturday
afternoons often throws up some decent live acts, as
does Alan McGee's Wednesday night, Death Disco.

Verge
147 Kentish Town Road, Camden, NW1 8PB
(7284 1178). Camden Town or Kentish Town
tube/rail. **Open** 8pm-midnight Mon-Wed, Sun; 8pm-
2am Thur-Sat. **Admission** £3-£15. **Credit** MC, V.
Its location isn't the only thing about the Verge
that's just ever so slightly removed from Camden.
The line-ups here tend to be a little edgier than the
standard NW1 pub circuit.

Water Rats
328 Gray's Inn Road, King's Cross, WC1X 8BZ
(7837 7269/www.plumpromotions.co.uk). King's
Cross tube/rail. **Open** *Gigs* 8.30-11pm Mon-Sat.
Admission £3-£6. **Credit** MC, V. **Map** p399 M3.
Bob Dylan played his first UK gig in the quietly
impressive back room of this King's Cross boozer
four decades ago. These days, the line-ups tend to
be a little noisier: alt-rock and metal types, sometimes on the edge of big things or secretly showcasing new material.

Windmill
22 Blenheim Gardens, Brixton, SW2 5BZ (8671
0700/www.windmillbrixton.com). Brixton tube/rail.
Open *Gigs* 7pm-11pm Mon-Sat; 7-10.30pm Sun.
Admission free-£3/£4. **No credit cards**.
At present, the best small venue in London, thanks
to an adventurous bookings policy (anything goes,
from techno to country to punk to folk to metal to
avant-garde electronica), cheap admission, friendly
staff and an endearingly shambolic but utterly honest attitude towards entertainment. Almost perfect.

Roots venues

Cecil Sharp House
2 Regent's Park Road, Camden, NW1 7AY (7485
2206/). Camden Town tube. **Open** *Gigs* times vary.
Admission £2.50-£8. **Credit** MC, V.
This is the centre of the English Folk Dance and
Song Society. Sharp's Folk Club on Tuesdays is fun
and totally untouched by the modern era, and is supplemented by regular barn dances, ceilidhs and folk
dance classes.

Hammersmith & Fulham Irish Centre
Blacks Road, Hammersmith, W6 9DT (8563
8232/www.lbhf.gov.uk/irishcentre). Hammersmith
tube. **Open** *Gigs* 8.15pm Fri, Sat. **Admission**
£4-£12. **No credit cards**.
You'll find all kinds of Irish music events, from free
ceilidhs to biggish-name Irish acts such as the
Popes, on offer at this small, friendly *craic* dealer.

12 Bar Club
22-23 Denmark Place, St Giles's, WC2H 8NL
(information 7916 6989/box office 7209 2248/
www.12barclub.com). Tottenham Court Road tube.
Open 7.30pm-1am Mon-Sat; 7.30pm-midnight Sun.
Admission £5-£10. **Credit** MC, V. **Map** p399 K6.
The tiny but classy 12 Bar is to acoustic music what
the Borderline is to rock. A popular haunt with visiting US singer-songwriters.

Jazz venues

As we went to press, the future of the **Vortex**,
a Stoke Newington legend, remained in doubt.
The club was closed and hoping to move to new
premises in Dalston in 2005. For more info, call
7254 6516 or visit www.vortexjazz.co.uk.

Bull's Head
373 Lonsdale Road, Barnes, SW13 9PY (8876
5241/www.thebullshead.com). Barnes Bridge rail.
Open 11am-11pm Mon-Sat; noon-10.30pm Sun.
Gigs 8.30pm Mon-Sat; 2-4.30pm, 8-10.30pm Sun.
Admission £3-£10. **Credit** AmEx, DC, MC, V.
This delightful riverside pub (and Thai bistro)
is something of a jazz landmark, staging gigs by
musicians from both here and the States. In true jazz
tradition, it also has a well-stocked bar; check out,
in particular, the selection of malt whiskies.

Arts & Entertainment

Jazz Café

*5 Parkway, Camden, NW1 7PG (information 7916
6060/box office 0870 150 0044/www.jazzcafe.co.uk).
Camden Town tube.* **Open** 7pm-1am Mon-Thur;
7pm-2am Fri, Sat; 7pm-midnight Sun. *Gigs* 9pm
daily. **Admission** £8-£25. **Credit** MC, V.
The name doesn't tell the whole story: jazz is a small
piece in the jigsaw of events here, which also takes
in funk, hip hop, soul, R&B, singer-songwriters and
more besides. Pray that the expense-accounters who
pack the balcony don't talk through the entire set.

Pizza Express Jazz Club

*10 Dean Street, Soho, W1V 5RL (restaurant 7437
9595/Jazz Club 7439 8722/www.pizzaexpress.co.uk).
Tottenham Court Road tube.* **Open** *Restaurant*
11.30am-midnight daily. *Jazz Club* 7.45pm-midnight
daily. *Gigs* 9pm daily. **Admission** £15-£20.
Credit AmEx, DC, MC, V. **Map** p399 K6.
The food takes second billing in the basement of this
eaterie: this is all about the largely contemporary
mainstream jazz. This is a proper venue and audiences are respectful: there's no talking through the
sets here. Other Pizza Express branches offer jazz,
albeit more as background noise than anything else.

Pizza on the Park

*11 Knightsbridge, Knightsbridge, SW1X 7LY
(7235 5273). Hyde Park Corner tube.* **Open** 8.30am-
midnight Mon-Fri; 9.30am-midnight Sat, Sun.
Gigs 9.15pm, 10.45pm daily. **Admission** £10-£20.
Credit AmEx, DC, MC, V. **Map** p400 G8.
Used to be owned by Pizza Express, but the music
here isn't quite as jazzy; acts lean towards cabaret
and show tunes around the piano.

Ronnie Scott's

*47 Frith Street, Soho, W1D 4HT (7439 0747/www.
ronniescotts.co.uk). Leicester Square or Tottenham
Court Road tube.* **Open** 8.30pm-3am Mon-Sat; 7.30-
11pm Sun. **Admission** (non-members) £15 Mon-
Thur; £25 Fri, Sat; £10 students/musician union
members Mon-Wed. **Credit** AmEx, DC, MC, V.
Map p399 K6.
Scott died in 1996 after running one of the world's
most famous jazz clubs for almost four decades. It
remains a hugely atmospheric Soho fixture but the
roster of acts, which play two sets a night for runs
of at least a week, is not as interesting or as jazzy as
it was, and the crowds are brasher than ever.
Original co-founder Pete King has bowed out to new
management (impresario and restaurateur Sally
Greene, possibly with the input of Kevin Spacey).
Change is inevitable, but at least the new team has
an evident love for the venu. Call to book a table.

606 Club

*90 Lots Road, Chelsea, SW10 0QD (7352 5953/
www.606club.co.uk). Earl's Court or Fulham
Broadway tube/11, 211 bus.* **Open** 7.30pm-1.30am
Mon-Wed; 8pm-1.30am Thur; 8pm-2am Fri, Sat; 8pm-
midnight Sun. *Gigs* 8pm-1am Mon-Wed; 9.30pm-
1.30am Thur-Sat; 9.30pm-midnight Sun. **Admission**
Music charge (non-members) £7 Mon-Thur; £9 Fri,
Sat; £8 Sun. **Credit** MC, V. **Map** p396 C13.

A restaurant, late-night club and popular musicians'
hangout, this Chelsea joint has the laudable policy
of placing an emphasis on booking British-based
jazz musicians. So this is mostly home-grown talent,
and it brings in the crowds. There's no entry fee: the
musicians are funded from a music charge that is
added to your bill at the end of the night. Alcohol is
only served with meals.

Festivals

As well as the following specifically music
related events, you can catch some music at
**Greenwich & Docklands International
Festival** (8305 1818) in July, the **Notting
Hill Carnival** (*see p264*); **Pride In The
Park** (*see p263*), **Fruitstock** (*see p264*) and the
Spitalfields Festival (*see p261*). The **South
Bank** (*see p304*) and **Barbican** (*see p302*) also
put on regular events such as Only Connect and
BITE that incorporate music with theatre, dance
and film. See the weekly *Time Out* for details.

Ealing Jazz Festival

*Walpole Park, Matlock Lane, Ealing, W5 (8825
6640/www.ealing.gov.uk/ealingsummer). Acton
Town tube.* **Date** Late July-early Aug 2005.
The largest free jazz event in Europe attracts around
50,000 people to listen to a multitude of top names.

Jazz On The Streets

*Venues around Soho & Covent Garden
(www.jazzonthestreets.co.uk).* **Date** July 2005.
This seven-day event draws talent from all over the
world for a series of performances in the West End.

London Jazz Festival

Various venues (7405 9900/www.serious.org.uk).
Date Nov 2005.
This creatively curated festival spans many genres
and attracts good artists. It's held at major concert
halls and small clubs around London.

Meltdown

*South Bank, SE1 (0870 380 0400/www.rfh.org.uk).
Waterloo tube/rail.* **Date** June/July 2005.
This annual music festival is curated by somebody
different each year – past curators include
Morrissey, Lee Perry, David Bowie and Scott
Walker – and can throw up some unexpected and
interesting performers.

Respect

Venue tbc (79836554/www.respectfestival.org.uk).
Date July 2005.
A free music and dance anti-racism festival supported by the mayor's office. Past performers have
included Run-DMC.

Rhythm Sticks

*South Bank, SE1 (0870 380 0400/www.rfh.org.uk).
Waterloo tube/rail.* **Date** July 2005.
This lively annual festival attracts drummers and
percussionists from all over the world.

Nightlife

Sleep is for the weak.

Right now, London's nightlife is the best in the world, bar none. You'll find more DJs playing more types of music in more quality clubs (and dingy basements, and trashed warehouses...) on more days of the week than anywhere else. There's a reason why jocks the world over are desperate to play London: the venues are superb, the crowds are clued up, and once a spinner's made it here, they've made it full stop. Of course, the flipside to that record is that it can also be brain-numbingly overwhelming. With so much choice, where do you go, what do you listen to, what do you wear, and how on earth do you wear it?

Even if you have a pretty good idea of what you're looking for, the trick is to match up your expectations with the reality. If you're a big fan of, say, hard dance or hardcore (enormously vibrant scenes, despite their 'uncool' reputation), hit the internet and find any of a number of websites and forums that service the communities. Of course, this is best done in advance; you don't want to discover that the ultimate party sold out the day before you show up. If there are DJs that you hold

close to your heart, again, hit their websites and find out their residencies. It's a whole other experience seeing DJs on their home turf – they tend to be far more experimental than they are when playing one-off gigs out of town. The usual trick of sourcing flyers in record shops is always worth doing, and keep an eye out when leaving clubs (especially the bigger ones) for kids handing out flyer bags. You'll find out about dozens of upcoming parties of all kinds, and with all the competition, the flyers are practically works of art in their own right. London's particularly well known for street posters – though you'll need to keep your eyes peeled since they're often taken down the same day they go up – and, of course, magazine listings are a great place to start (you'll find everything and more in the weekly Nightlife section of *Time Out* magazine).

London is nothing if not fashionable, but that's not to say that your expensive designer labels will cut it. Avant-garde personal style and customised pieces are where it's at, and when in doubt, *dress down* (this ain't New York or Paris). Most clubs allow trainers, unless

Every gardener's dream night out: **Herbal**. *See p319.*

Cargo.

you're going extremely upmarket or cheesy, and if they've got a dress code, their website, flyer or listing will state it.

Finally, if you can't walk home from the club, find out which night bus gets you home and where you get it from before you head out. The tube doesn't start until around 8am on Sundays, black cabs are expensive and rare, official minicabs are even more expensive at night, and only fans of Russian roulette would take notice of the illegal touts who drive around, seedily asking if you 'want a taxi'.

Clubs

Aquarium

256 Old Street, Hoxton, EC1V 9DD (7251 6136/ www.clubaquarium.co.uk). Old Street tube/rail. **Open** 10pm-3am Thur; 10pm-4am Fri, Sat; 10am-10pm Sun. **Admission** £8-£15. **Map** p403 R3.
The only nightclub in the UK with a swimming pool and a six-person jacuzzi, Aquarium is proud of its aquatic status. And, leaving aside the watersports gags, it certainly ups the fun element no end. Despite being in the ultra-hip Old Street area, nights are strictly tongue-in-cheek affairs, with the '70s funkfest Carwash still ruling the roost on Saturdays.

Bar Rumba

36 Shaftesbury Avenue, Soho, W1V 7DD (7287 6933/www.barrumba.co.uk). Piccadilly Circus tube. **Open** 9pm-3.30am Mon; 6pm-3am Tue-Wed; 6pm-3.30am Thur-Fri; 9pm-5am Sat; 8pm-2am Sun. **Admission** £3-£12; free before 9pm Tue, 10pm Wed, 8pm Thur, 9pm Fri. **Map** p401 K7.
Eleven years old and still going strong, this basement club is where to head for some of the most respected leftfield nights in town. Gilles Peterson's long-running Monday nighter THIS! (That's How It Is) mixes international sounds, while drum 'n' bass fans worship at Movement's altar every Thursday.

Canvas

King's Cross Goods Yard, off York Way, King's Cross, N1 0UZ (7833 8301/www.canvaslondon.net). King's Cross tube/rail. **Open** 8pm-midnight Thur; 10pm-6am Fri, Sat. **Admission** £10-£20.
Part of a cluster of venues in the area that's put King's Cross firmly on the clubbing map in the last year or so, Canvas (formerly Bagley's Studios) is a massive warehouse space that takes in three dancefloors and two bars. Thursdays are disco-tastic with Roller Disco (best fun on wheels), plus there are the free Hum Allnighters for breaks fans, the ultra high fashion of Drama and guitarfest Kill All Hippies.

Cargo

Kingsland Viaduct, 83 Rivington Street, Shoreditch, EC2A 3AY (7739 3440/www.cargo-london.com). Old Street tube/rail. **Open** noon-1am Mon-Thur; noon-3am Fri; 6pm-3am Sat; 1pm-midnight Sun. **Admission** free-£10. **Map** p403 R4.
Fans of music (any music, all music), tattoo Cargo's address on your forearm right now. Down a side street, under some arches, smack bang in the middle of 'trendy' Shoreditch, this bar-club-restaurant is *the* venue for exciting DJs, bands, and all those inbetween. If it's at Cargo, it's essential.

Cirque

Hippodrome Corner, Leicester Square, WC2H 7JH (7437 4311/www.cirquehippodrome.com). Leicester Square tube. **Open** 9pm-3am Thur-Sat. **Admission** £20 Thur, Sat; £12 Fri. **Map** p401 K7.
One for the, ahem, more mainstream clubber who doesn't find the West End at the weekend the nightmare that the more self-conscious hipsters insist it is. Famous in its former incarnation as the enormous Hippodrome (the huge neon sign remains high up on the exterior), it's now become the enormous Cirque instead. Apart from that, not much else has changed. Nights tend to lean towards R&B, and there are trapeze artists and plenty of plush drinking areas to keep you amused.

Arts & Entertainment

Mr Wobbly Man, **Pacha London**. See p320.

The Cross

Arches, 27-31 King's Cross Goods Yard, off York Way, King's Cross, N1 OUZ (7837 0828/www.the-cross.co.uk). King's Cross tube/rail. **Open** 11pm-5am Fri; 10pm-6am Sat; 11pm-5am Sun. **Admission** £12-£15. **Map** p399 L2.

A stylish brick-and-arches venue, this, but with an unexpected Alan Titchmarsh touch in its added bonus: a garden area full of lush plants all interspersed with comfy sofas that becomes another dancefloor in summer. Catering for the glam side of house with Danny Rampling's Union, Seb Fontaine's Type, Serious, X Press 2's Muzik Xpress and Prologue (on rotation Saturdays) as well as Italo-house Fiction on Fridays. The Ibizan spirit flows freely, thanks to the friendly, sussed crowd who together whip up a great atmosphere.

EGG

200 York Way, King's Cross, N7 9AX (7609 8364/ www.egglondon.net). King's Cross tube/rail. **Open** 10pm-6am Fri; 10pm Sat-noon Sun; phone for weekday openings. **Admission** £5-£15. **Map** p399 L2.

Yet another reason why the King's Cross area shines particularly brightly on the London nightlife map, EGG's Mediterranean-style three-floored interior is both labyrinthine and low-ceilinged with an intimate atmosphere. The upstairs bar in red ostrich leather is particularly elegant, while the main dancefloor downstairs aims at, and achieves, a warehouse rave feel. EGG also boasts a large terrace and covered courtyard. Clubs range from dark electro synth raves to proper house nights.

The End

18 West Central Street, Holborn, WC1A 1JJ (7419 9199/www.the-end.co.uk). Holborn or Tottenham Court Road tube. **Open** 10pm-3am Mon, Wed; 10pm-3am Mon, Wed; 10pm-4am Thur; 10pm-5am Fri; 10pm-7am Sat; phone for details Sun. **Admission** £4-£15. **Map** p399 L6.

Truly, the End ticks all the right boxes: from its ultra-minimal AKA bar (*see p321*) to the dark and moody lounge and the heady main room with its cheer-from-all-sides island DJ booth. The clubs on rotation ooze underground cool: indie Trash, Fabio's Swerve, Bugged Out!, Layo & Bushwacka All Night Long, Derrick Carter's Classic, DJ Sneak's Sneak Beats, Steve Lawler's Harlem, owner Mr C's Super Freak, Darren Emerson's Underwater... All of which attract an international (of course, this is London) and super-friendly crowd.

Fabric

77A Charterhouse Street, Farringdon, EC1M 3HN (7336 8898/advance tickets for Fri 7344 4444/www. fabriclondon.com). Farringdon tube/rail. **Open** 9.30pm-5am Fri; 10pm-7am Sat. **Admission** £12-£15. **Map** p402 O5.

Renowned around the world, thanks to adoring reviews from the punters and DJs alike, this club used to be a meat cellar but (thank goodness) didn't metamorphosise into a meat market. Fabric is all about the music, usually of the leftfield, extremely underground variety. Its three rooms get pretty ramma-jamma jam-jammed: the main is home to the stomach wobbling Bodysonic dancefloor; the second's a warehouse straight out of Ravesville (with a laser and everything); and the baby-sized third is where all the cool shit happens. The best club in the world? Definitely a contender.

The Fridge

1 Town Hall Parade, Brixton, SW2 1RJ (7326 5100/www.fridge.co.uk). Brixton tube/rail. **Open** 10pm-6am Fri, Sat. **Admission** £8-£20.

Hailed by many hard house and psy trance heads as their favourite venue in London, the refurbed Fridge is Brixton's biggest club. It's nigh on impossible to overstate the importance this place has for the hard dance scene in London; regular events like Fusion, Sunday Night Orange and Knowwhere revolve around irregular, monster parties.

Ghetto

5-6 Falconberg Court (behind the Astoria Theatre), Soho, W1D 3AB (7287 3726/www. ghetto-london.co.uk). Tottenham Court Road tube. **Open** 10.30pm-3am Mon-Thur; 10.30pm-4am Fri; 10.30pm-5am Sat; 10pm-3am Sun. **Admission** free-£8. **Map** p399 K6.

Done out in raving red, this fabulously louche basement venue has really come into its own. It hosts two of London's hippest electro fests, the Cock on Fridays and NagNagNag on Wednesdays. Both attract a gay/straight crowd of club characters and disco dollies, who work up a sweat on a dancefloor with minimal air-conditioning.

Herbal

10-14 Kingsland Road, Shoreditch, E2 8DA (7613 4462/www.herbaluk.com). Old Street tube/rail. **Open** 8pm-1am Tue; 9pm-2am Wed, Thur, Sun; 9pm-3am Fri, Sat. **Admission** free-£7. **Map** p403 R3.

The downstairs main room sure gets sweaty, especially when Grooverider's weekly Grace is in session (Sundays, naturally) and the superstar DJs and MCs step up to the plate to unleash drum 'n' bass mayhem. Upstairs has an NYC loft feel about it, which helps the house party vibe. Tuesday is hip hop Spitkingdom, while other nights feature soulful house, eclectic electro sounds, and even party hip hop. Hugely popular with a grounded clientele.

The ICA

ICA, The Mall, St James's, SW1Y 5AH (7930 3647/www.ica.org.uk). Piccadilly Circus tube/Charing Cross tube/rail. **Open** noon-1am Tue-Sat; noon-11pm Mon; noon-10.30pm Sun. **Admission** free-£6. **Map** p401 J8.

The classy, achingly contemporary and highly respected Institute of Contemporary Arts – a mecca for the avant garde in all its self absorbed finery – is not surprisingly a beacon to those vanguards of modernity, DJs, musicians, artists, performers and clubbers, too. This is due to a constant range of multimedia events such as Rob Da Bank's excellent and much-loved Sunday Best A-Z parties.

The Key

King's Cross Freight Depot, King's Cross, N1 9NW (7837 1027/www.thekeylondon.com). King's Cross tube/rail. **Open** 10.30pm-6am Fri, Sat. **Admission** £5-£10.

Set in a King's Cross industrial wasteland (it's a glow-stick's throw from the Cross; *see p318*, and in the same building as Canvas; *see p317*), this baby-sized venue is not only cool, it also has the best dancefloor in London – all glass and flashing lights. Leave any notions of strutting your John Travolta moves at the door, though; it's strictly hedonistic house, deep tech, battlin' breaks, electro-a-go-go and party hip hop.

KoKo

1A Camden High Street, Camden, NW1 7JE (0870 432 5527/www.koko.uk.com). Camden Town or Mornington Crescent tube. **Open** 10pm-3am Wed, Fri, Sat. **Admission** £4 before 11pm, £6 after 11pm Wed; £7 before 11pm, £10 after 11pm Fri, Sat.

This 19th-century building has worn numerous hats in its time: music hall, BBC radio studio, gig venue and nightclub, before being allowed to fall apart as the Camden Palace. Reopening in September 2004 with an incredible makeover, the multi-levelled venue has ditched the run-down '80s look for plush reds and purples reminiscent of its theatrical history. Regular nights range from Club NME every Wednesday (brand-new guitar-based noise) to the all-out fun of Kitsch Lounge Riot on Fridays. Now, if someone could just explain the name…

Madame Jo Jo's

8 Brewer Street, Soho, W1F 0SP (7734 3040/www.madamejojos.com). Leicester Square or Piccadilly Circus tube. **Open** 10pm-3am Wed-Sat. **Admission** £5-£8. **Map** p401 K6.

A great venue, enhanced by a touch of Soho cabaret sleaze. There are some promising midweek funk and hip hop nights, but the big draw is Keb Darge's Deep Funk, where blindingly funky chickens move furiously to obscure '60s and '70s cuts.

Jock in a box

Like what you hear? Take some home with you…

Major compilations are available in major record stores, but you'll get better deals if you hit the club's website. Note that Fabric (*see p318*) puts out monthly compilations via subscription (£6/mth) from its website: www.fabriclondon.com

Big Chill Classics at The Big Chill Bar
www.bigchill.net

The End: End Recordings 050
www.endclub.com

The Heavenly Social: The Social
www.thesocial.com

Layo & Bushwacka All Night Long!
www.endclub.com

NagNagNag at The Ghetto
www.nagnagnag.info

Saturday Sessions
Jon Carter and Marc Hughes at Ministry of Sound
www.ministryofsound.com

Street Beats/The Sound of Smoove
Smoove at Ministry of Sound
www.ministryofsound.com

Suck My Deck
Bugged Out! at The End
www.buggedout.net

Sunday Best
www.sundaybest.net

Ministry of Sound

103 Gaunt Street, Newington, SE1 6DP (7378 6528/ www.ministryofsound.com). Elephant & Castle tube/rail. **Open** 10pm-3am Wed (student night); 10.30pm-5am Fri; 11pm-7am Sat. **Admission** £12-£15. **Map** p404 O10.

With millions of compilations, tours and this famous London venue to its name, the MoS has to be the world's most recognised clubbing brand. As such, it's sneered at by more cutting-edge clubbers, but it is one of the few UK clubs that can actually afford to put on the likes of NYC house legends Masters At Work all night long. Apart from the money it's no wonder DJs flock to play here: the sound system is shockingly good. Always packed, Fridays are Smoove, the capital's biggest urban party, while Saturdays feature house music. And don't fret about trying to get into the over-designed VIP room – it has zero atmosphere, and that's on a good night.

Neighbourhood

12 Acklam Road, Ladbroke Grove, W10 5QZ (7524 7979/www.neighbourhoodclub.net). Ladbroke Grove or Westbourne Park tube. **Open** 8pm-2am Thur-Sat; 5pm-midnight Sun; check website for weeknight times & events. **Admission** £5-£10.

The brand-new 500-capacity Neighbourhood was built on the site of the once-sterling Subterania. Run by Ben Watt (Everything But the Girl) and Alan Grant, its varied repertoire includes live music, one-off weeknight events and house music on weekends.

93 Feet East

150 Brick Lane, Spitalfields, E1 6QN (7247 3293/www.93feeteast.co.uk). Aldgate East tube or Liverpool Street tube/rail. **Open** 5-11pm Mon-Thur; 5pm-1am Fri; noon-1am Sat; noon-10.30pm Sun. **Admission** free-£10. **Map** p403 S5.

Such a bugger that the licence only runs till 1am. Still, the sheer variety (and top-notch quality) of the live gigs and club nights mean that 93 Feet East doesn't struggle to attract a cool, knowledgeable crowd. The three-room venue sports a stylish downstairs bar, kitsch upstairs room and enormous main dancefloor, plus stacks of outdoor space for summer.

Notting Hill Arts Club

21 Notting Hill Gate, Notting Hill, W11 3JQ (7460 4459/www.nottinghillartsclub.com). Notting Hill Gate tube. **Open** 6pm-1am Mon-Wed; 6pm-2am Thur, Fri; 4pm-2am Sat; 4pm-1am Sun. **Admission** £5-£8; free before 8pm. **Map** p394 A7.

With oodles more diversity and creativity than most other clubs combined, the NHAC is where artists, musos and DJs get together and swap ideas, put on parties and get all arty. It's a sure-fire bet that whatever rocks your world, you'll find it here; from Brazilian Love Affair to the mayhem of Death Disco.

Pacha London

Terminus Place, Victoria, SW1V 1JR (7833 3139/ www.pachalondon.com). Victoria tube/rail. **Open** 10pm-4am Fri; 10pm-6am Sat. **Admission** £15-£20. **Map** p400 H10.

This lavish outpost of the global club giant that has dominated Ibiza for years was made for lording it: chandeliers, oak panels and a stained-glass ceiling ensure a chic clubbing experience. But who would have thought clubs would come the multi-national corporation on us? Still, the glammed-up clubbers dress in keeping with the sumptuous decor, shaking their booties to the rocking house beats.

Plan B

418 Brixton Road, Brixton, SW9 7AY (7733 0926/ www.plan-brixton.co.uk). Brixton tube/rail. **Open** 5pm-2am Wed, Thur; 5pm-4am Fri; 7pm-4am Sat; 7pm-2am Sun. **Admission** free before 9pm; £3 after 9pm; £5 after 10pm Fri, Sat; £7 after 11pm Fri, Sat.

A new addition to Brixton, this gleaming, spacious club-bar is modern rather than trendy in design. Similarly, it attracts a good-natured local crowd to its weekly hip hop, soul, funk and breaks nights. On Saturdays, the ace sound system pumps it out.

Plastic People

147-149 Curtain Road, Shoreditch, EC2A 3QE (7739 6471/www.plasticpeople.co.uk). Old Street tube/rail. **Open** 10pm-2am Mon-Thur; 10pm-3.30am Fri, Sat; 7.30pm-midnight Sun. **Admission** £3-£8. **Map** p403 R4.

This tiny downstairs club is a good place to come for after-hours drinks without breaking the bank, and it's also a music lover's paradise. Sounds range from Afro-jazz and hip hop to Latin and deep house: watch the little dancefloor get rammed with a chilled but funky crowd. The sound system is bliss.

The Telegraph

228 Brixton Hill, Brixton, SW2 1HE (8678 0777). Brixton tube/rail. **Open** noon-2am Mon-Thur; noon-4am Fri; noon-6am Sat; noon-1.30am Sun. **Admission** £5-£10.

Situated at the top of Brixton Hill, further up than some may care to venture, this spacious old Brixton pub was home to the infamous Rooty raves by south London's Basement Jaxx. You'll still find local DJs and promoters getting the run of things here, which is the best possible thing: from regular reggae and hip hop parties to big house and electro, the surprisingly big room through the back goes off like few clubs in London. Prepare to sweat.

333

333 Old Street, Hoxton, EC1V 9LE (7739 5949/ www.333mother.com). Old Street tube/rail. **Open** *Bar* 8pm-3am Mon-Wed, Fri; 8pm-4am Thur, 8pm-1am Sat. *Club* 10pm-5am Fri, Sat. **Admission** *Club* £5-£10. **Map** p403 Q4.

The dominant landmark on Old Street, this pivotal East End venue houses a no-frills three-storey interior. The lively punters (a whole lot of 'em, too: beware the queues) are there for the music, which is always excellent and varied. The basement usually bounces to techno, drum 'n' bass or crazy mash-ups, while the main room heaves to house, electro and even reggae. The top-floor bar, Mother, is plusher: a great hangout that runs good nights of its own.

Hands up if you're having fun, at **Turnmills**.

straddle the ground in-between – for you to
choose from, and with such variety, probability
suggests some of them will get it right. With so
many DJs around, don't be surprised to find A-
listers behind the decks at little bars like the
Social (*see p324*) or **Barfly** (*see below*),
revelling in the chance to play dusty 45s and
soul, or classic rock and Country & Western,
rather than pumping 4am house music. You'll
also find rising stars getting a go, cutting their
teeth in the big smoke. Who knows, you might
be witnessing a superstar in the making as you
nurse your pint (and incubate your hangover…).

Which segues nicely to the rise and rise of
Sunday recovery sessions, and that's when DJ
bars really come into their own. Dirty stop-outs
should feel right at home. Grab the Sunday
papers, fill your JD and coke with plenty of ice,
and enjoy the loungin' entertainment. And don't
be too surprised if Fatboy Slim comes to sit at
your table (happens surprisingly often at the
Lock Tavern, *see p322*). Fun and games, it's
what DJ bars were made for.

Turnmills

*63B Clerkenwell Road, Clerkenwell, EC1M 5PT
(7250 3409/www.turnmills.com). Farringdon
tube/rail.* **Open** 6.30pm-midnight Tue; 9pm-2am
Thur; 10.30pm-7.30am Fri; 10pm-6am Sat; 9pm-3am
Sun. **Admission** £5-£15. **Map** p402 N4.
Turnmills' neo-classical, acid-warehouse nooks and
crannies are a hedonist's playground; in fact, the
whole venue is something of a legend in its own lifetime. While it offers the full musical spectrum, the
club's long-running house and trance night, Gallery,
on Friday night is particularly well subscribed.
Hugely friendly (rather than achingly fashionable),
it's one of the most popular venues in town.

DJ bars

Such a hit and miss thing, DJ bars. Grab any old
man's boozer, shine the place up a bit, throw in
a sound system that has seen better days, get
your mate's younger brother and his dubious
record collection, and voilà, call yourself a DJ
bar. The flipside, of course, is that there are also
some genuinely low-key, excellent DJ bars out
there too. And we're not talking the over-styled
monstrosities that pride themselves on their
unusual (and impossible to figure out)
bathroom fittings. No, what we appreciate are
places that have well-thought-out menus, easily
accessible bars and ample loos, comfy seating,
perhaps some space around the DJ booth for
some casual shimmying, and a sound system
that doesn't blast away any chance of a natter
with your pals. If we wanted to go raving,
we'd find a warehouse.

The beauty of London is its sheer scope of
pubs, bars, clubs, nosheries – and those that

AKA

*18 West Central Street, Holborn, WC1A 1JJ (7836
0110/www.akalondon.com). Holborn or Tottenham
Court Road tube.* **Open** 6pm-3am Mon-Fri; 7pm-7am
Sat; 8pm-3am Sun. **Admission** £3 after 11pm Tue,
Wed; £5 after 11pm Thur; £7 after 10pm Fri; £10
after 9pm Sat. **Map** p399 L6.
Joined – physically as well as musically – to the End
next door (*see p318*), this popular hangout attracts
top international DJs, who entertain punters loos-
ened up by good food and cocktails. The venue is
incorporated into the End's club nights on Fridays
and Saturdays; be prepared to queue at weekends.

Barfly

*49 Chalk Farm Road, Camden, NW1 8AN (7691
4244/www.barflyclub.com). Camden Town or Chalk
Farm tube.* **Open** 7.30pm-midnight Mon-Thur; 7.30pm-
3am Fri, Sat; 7.30-10.30pm Sun. **Admission** £4-£7.
Part of the Barfly chain, this spit 'n' sawdust venue
has a spacious ground-floor bar and upstairs stage
area. It has done its time as a workaday live venue,
but its profile has been raised by the revival of rock
and live music. Now it's home to fashionable rock
club Queens of Noize and the brilliant Kill 'Em All,
Let God Sort It Out every fortnight.

Big Chill Bar

*91-95 Dray Walk, Spitalfields, E1 6PU (7392 9180/
www.bigchill.net). Aldgate East tube or Liverpool
Street tube/rail.* **Open** noon-midnight Mon-Sat; noon-
11.30pm Sun. **Admission** free. **Credit** MC, V.
A big box of a bar with a helpfully long bartop running down the left-hand side and plenty of comfy
sofa action to be had, this is the place to head when
the famous Big Chill festival seems just too long
away. Attracting all the DJs and characters you've
come to expect at the loveliest of festivals, and guess
what? The atmosphere's just as perfect too.

Arts & Entertainment

Bug Bar

The Crypt, St Matthew's Church, Brixton Hill, Brixton, SW2 1JF (7738 3366/www.bug brixton.co.uk). Brixton tube/rail. **Open** 7pm-2am Wed; 8pm-2am Thur, Sun; 8pm-3am Fri, Sat. **Admission** free before 9pm; £4 after 9pm; £6 after 11pm.

Housed in a converted crypt, the Bug Bar is dead good. Sorry. But there's no escaping the fact that the mix of live music, fine local DJs and cheapish drinks makes it a killer place to tear through an evening.

Cherry Jam

58 Porchester Road, Bayswater, W2 6ET (7727 9950/www.cherryjam.net). Royal Oak tube. **Open** 7pm-2am Wed-Sat; Sun (phone to check). **Admission** £5-£8 after 8pm, depending on nights; phone for details. **Map** p394 C5.

You could do far worse in west London than this great bar, easily the hippest for blocks and blocks. There's an elevated area for sitting and supping cocktails (or nursing a beer), and a proper dancefloor that doesn't get as much use as it used to (when it leaned more to the club side of things), but still, it's nice to know it's there. Ben Watts (Everything But The Girl) is one of the bods behind this joint, so the music is nothing if not quality.

Dogstar

389 Coldharbour Lane, Brixton, SW9 8LQ (7733 7515/www.thedogstar.com). Brixton tube/rail. **Open** noon-2.30am Mon-Thur; noon-4am Fri, Sat; noon-2.30am Sun. **Admission** £3 after 10pm Fri, Sat; £5 after 11pm Fri, Sat.

A Brixton institution, Dogstar is set in a large street-corner pub, and it exudes the urban authenticity beloved by clubbers. The atmosphere can be intense, but it is absolutely never less than vibrant. It's something of a training ground for the DJ stars of tomorrow, so it's worth visiting for that reason alone. While the music varies from night to night, the quality always stays at the same high level.

Elbow Room

89-91 Chapel Market, Angel, N1 9EX (7278 3244/ www.theelbowroom.co.uk). Angel tube. **Open** 5pm-2am Mon; noon-2am Tue, Wed; noon-3am Thur-Sat; noon-midnight Sun. **Admission** free-£5. **Credit** MC, V. **Map** p402 N2.

The biggest London location of this decidedly upmarket DJ bar/club/pool hall entertainment emporium, Elbow Room follows a well-established, slick, good-time formula that wins it many friends around these parts. It's particularly good at putting on hip hop, you don't stop parties. **Other locations**: 103 Westbourne Grove, Notting Hill, W2 4UW (7221 5211); 97-113 Curtain Road, Shoreditch, EC2A 3BF (7613 1316).

Ion

161-165 Ladbroke Grove, Ladbroke Grove, W10 6HJ (8960 1702/www.meanfiddler.com). Ladbroke Grove tube. **Open** 5pm-midnight Mon-Fri; noon-midnight Sat; 5pm-midnight Sun. **Admission** free; £4 after 9pm Fri-Sat; £5 after 9pm Sun. **Credit** MC, V.

The red and brown velvet sofas in this lounge bar make for a particularly relaxing settting. The music is varied and soulful, and the vibe is the purest west London cool. But be prepared to feel like a goldfish in a bowl if you're self-conscious – there's a big glass window in the front: see and be seen.

The Legion

348 Old Street, Shoreditch, EC1V 9NQ (7729 4441/ www.thelegionbar.com). Old Street tube/rail. **Open** 5pm-11pm/midnight Mon-Thur; 5pm-2am Fri; noon-2am Sat; noon-10.30pm Sun. **Admission** free-£5. **Credit** AmEx, MC, V. **Map** p402 P4.

A long wood and brick box that has become a must on the DJ bar circuit thanks to its inspired music programming. Everything from High Fidelity (big-name DJs play their all-time fave five records before being quickly kicked off) to live acts and Elliot Eastwick's World Famous Pub Quiz (complete with acid house gargling rounds).

The Lock Tavern

35 Chalk Farm Road, Chalk Farm, NW1 9BH (7482 7163). Camden Town tube. **Open** noon-11pm Mon-Sat; noon-10.30pm Sun. **Admission** free.

This tarted-up boozer is part owned by DJ Jon Carter, and, as you would expect, the music is to the fore. With a beer garden at the back, two floors full of sink-into-and-never-emerge sofas and ample bar space, and a terrace overlooking busy Chalk Farm Road, this is a great place to unwind or play out your recovery session. There are DJs most nights of the week, but Sundays are the musical staples, with Manchester's Friends & Family, the guitar noise of Sonic Mook, the soul/hip hop of Moulin-X, the Queens of Noize and others on rotation.

Market Place

11 Market Place, Marylebone, W1W 8AH (7079 2020). Oxford Circus tube. **Open** 11am-midnight Mon-Wed; 11am-1am Thur-Sat; 1-11pm Sun. **Admission** free Mon-Thur, Sun; £7 after 11pm Fri; £3 after 8pm, £7 after 11pm Sat (redeemable against food & drink). **Map** p398 J6.

Another new recruit to the ever-expanding DJ bar scene, Market Place's wooden chalet-style basement oozes warmth and cosiness, while the global cuisine and dynamic music line-ups make it an essential stopoff. As it's just off Oxford Circus, it tends to attract a post-work crowd in the week, but weekends have more of a party spirit.

Medicine Bar

89 Great Eastern Street, Shoreditch (7739 5173). Old Street tube/rail. **Open** 5pm-midnight Mon-Thur; 5pm-2am Fri; noon-2am Sat; noon-10.30pm Sun. **Admission** free. **Map** p403 R4.

Stylish but comfortable, this funky and popular Shoreditch hangout fills with pre-clubbers as the post-work City drinkers fade away. The main bar gets pretty busy, so head down to the basement, which doubles as a sweaty house party. **Other locations**: 181 Upper Street, Islington, N1 1RX (7704 9536).

Day is the new night

To really feel like you've experienced London's nightlife, forget any notions of only hitting the big places on a Friday or Saturday night. Some of the very best clubs in London happen on a weeknight and, in some cases, even during the day.

For most people, Monday night is a quiet time, reserved for sitting placidly on the sofa reading a good book, watching the box – that kind of thing. But if you did that in London, you'd be missing out, big time. For a start, there's Erol Alkan's Trash at the End (*see p318*), which, despite going through several phases of being hyped to the moon by trendsetters (usually the kiss of death), is still packed every week. The mix of indie guitars, bootlegs, electro and pop genius makes it nigh on impossible to leave the dancefloor. For a more chilled start to the week, Gilles Peterson's THIS! at Bar Rumba (*see p317*) is a less hectic, but no less inspirational, option on the same night.

Midweek blues? NagNagNag is one of the capital's most exciting electro synth parties, if only for the wild outfits that the punters wear, and it happens every Wednesday at the

Ghetto (*see p318*). To find out how the outrageous like to dress themselves, head to Siren Suite at Turnmills (*see p321*) on Sundays, or for some truly extreme fashion, get on board with Kashpoint one Thursday a month on a boat on the Thames (the *Tattershall Castle*, north side of Embankment, opposite London Eye, 7278 5486).

Drum 'n' bass fans have two of the world's most famous clubs to choose from, and they're on Thursdays (Movement at Bar Rumba, *see p317*) and Sundays (Grooverider's Grace at Herbal, *see p319*).

For sheer eclecticism, the Notting Hill Arts Club (*see p320*) has something every night of the week, and it's always top-notch quality, whether Japanese pop or Brazilian beats via Parisian flamenco.

Finally, Horse Meat Disco is a queer party that's for everyone (South Central, 349 Kennington Lane, Kennington Oval, SE11 5QY; 07971 971469), in a debauched, Sunday afternoon tea-dance kind of way.

So just think, next time you stroll down Oxford Street or sit on the South Bank: somewhere in London, it's going right off.

Trash at the End.

Redstar

319 Camberwell Road, Camberwell, SE5 0HQ (7326 0055/www.redstarbar.co.uk). Oval tube, then 36, 185 bus. **Open** 5pm-1am Mon-Thur; 5pm-4am Fri; noon-4am Sat; noon-midnight Sun. **Admission** free before 11pm; £4 after 11pm Fri, Sat.

With consistently great DJs, an easygoing loungey ambience, decent prices and views over Camberwell Green, it's not surprising this place is so popular.

Salmon & Compasses

58 Penton Street, Islington, N1 9PZ (7837 3891). Angel tube. **Open** 5pm-midnight Mon-Wed; 5pm-3am Thur-Sat; 2pm-midnight Sun. **Admission** free; £3 after 9pm Fri; £5 after 9pm Sat. **Map** p402 N2.

Islington's no-nonsense DJ bar packs in an up-for-it crowd on weekends with a rotating series of theme nights. Early in the week, it's chilled.

The Social

5 Little Portland Street, Marylebone, W1W 7JD (7636 4992/www.thesocial.com). Oxford Circus tube. **Open** noon-11pm Mon-Sat. **Admission** free; £3 acoustic nights. **Map** p398 J5.

Established by Heavenly Records in 1999, the Social is popular with music industry workers, minor alt-rock celebs and other sassy trendies.

Other locations: 33 Linton Street, Islington, N1 7DU (7354 5809).

Vibe Bar

Old Truman Brewery, 91-95 Brick Lane, Shoreditch, E1 6QL (7426 0491/www.vibe-bar.co.uk). Aldgate East tube or Liverpool Street tube/rail. **Open** 11am-11.30pm Mon-Thur, Sun; 11am-1am Fri, Sat. **Admission** £3.50 after 8pm Fri, Sat. **Map** p403 S5.

Rotating DJs and a full book of live acts play diverse styles (reggae to hip hop, proper songs to experimental leftfield). In the summer, folk hang in the fairy-lit courtyard, a convenient stumble across the road from 93 Feet East (*see p320*).

Casinos

Until 1999 British casinos were forbidden to advertise. Even now, advertisements are required by law to be 'informative' rather than 'promotional', an interesting distinction. However, the law does allow visitors to apply for membership of a casino in advance, rather than having to turn up in person. Legally speaking, all casinos have to be notified of your intention to play at least 24 hours in advance, and you must either be a member yourself, or be the guest of a member in order to enter.

While British law forbids us to list casinos in this guide, a flip through the *Yellow Pages* or a chat to the concierge of your hotel will help you find a gaming establishment near you. Most casinos are open from mid-afternoon through to around 4am every night, and the vast majority are in central London (not least in and around the traditional rich gents' playground that is Mayfair). Check with the casino directly if you're worried about a dress code. However, as a rule of thumb, while casual attire – though not jeans or trainers – may be acceptable for the afternoons, in the evenings gentlemen almost always have to don a jacket and tie.

Yeah, it's the Yeah Yeah Yeahs at Queens of Noize, **Barfly**. *See p321.*

Sport & Fitness

London's burning the calories.

Check the weekly Sport section of *Time Out* magazine for a comprehensive guide to the main action. For a more in-depth approach to keeping fit in the capital, choose the *Time Out Sport, Health & Fitness Guide* (£9.99).

For the latest on London's bid to host the 2012 Olympics, see www.london2012.org.

Major stadia

Crystal Palace National Sports Centre

Ledrington Road, Crystal Palace, SE19 2BB (8778 0131/www.crystalpalace.co.uk). Crystal Palace rail. This Grade II listed building is in desperate need of repair, and faces either closure or redevelopment. Money from Sport England has given it a stay of execution until 2006, which means that the popular summer Grand Prix athletics event will continue.

Wembley Arena & Conference Centre/Wembley Stadium

Elvin House, Stadium Way, Wembley, Middx HA9 0DW (8902 8833/box office 0800 600 0870/www.whatsonatwembley.com). Wembley Park tube/Wembley Stadium rail. International boxing bouts, snooker and basketball tournaments and showjumping take place infrequently at Wembley Arena. The lavish new Wembley Stadium is due for completion in 2006; for more information, see www.wembleystadium.com.

Spectator sports

Basketball

The **Towers** are in the British Basketball League. For more information – including a list of indoor and outdoor courts – contact the English Basketball Association (0870 7744 225, www.englandbasketball.co.uk).

Kinder London Towers

Crystal Palace National Sports Centre, Ledrington Road, Crystal Palace, SE19 2BB (8776 7755/www.london-towers.co.uk). Crystal Palace rail. **Admission** £8; £6 concessions.

Cricket

Test matches are not for those with busy schedules, so if you're pushed for time, catch a one-day match in the C&G Trophy or Totesport League or, even shorter still, the popular

Twenty20 matches (20 overs per side, played in the evening). **Lord's** (home to Middlesex) and the **Oval** (Surrey's home ground) also host Test matches and one-day internationals, for which you should book ahead (and even then you'd be lucky; best chance of getting in is on the last day of a test, for which tickets are not sold in advance as play isn't guaranteed depending on the progres of the match). 2005's tourists are Australia and Bangladesh. The season runs April to September.

Brit Oval

Kennington Oval, Kennington, SE11 5SS (7582 6660/7764/www.surreycricket.com). Oval tube. **Tickets** *County* £5-£10. *Test* £40-£50.

Lord's

St John's Wood Road, St John's Wood, NW8 8QN (MCC 7289 1611/tickets 7432 1000/www.lords. org.uk). St John's Wood tube. **Tickets** *County* £5-£10. *Test* £40-£50.

Football

Tickets for teams in the top Barclays Premiership league are all but impossible to come by, especially for glamour sides like Chelsea and Arsenal. But there are London clubs in the Coca-Cola Championship and both divisions of the Coca-Cola Football League, for which tickets are cheaper and easier to obtain. For more information, try www.thefa.com. Prices quoted are for adult non-members.

Arsenal

Arsenal Stadium, Avenell Road, Highbury, N5 1BU (7704 4040/www.arsenal.com). Arsenal tube. **Tickets** £28-£51. **Premiership**.

Brentford

Griffin Park, Braemar Road, Brentford, Middx (8847 2511/www.brentfordfc.co.uk). South Ealing tube/Brentford rail. **Tickets** *Standing* £13 adults; £7 OAPs; £3 under-15s. *Seated* £17 adults; £12 OAPs; £3 under-15s. **Division 1**.

Charlton Athletic

The Valley, Floyd Road, Charlton, SE7 8BL (8333 4010/www.cafc.co.uk). Charlton rail. **Tickets** £20-£30 adults. **Premiership**.

Chelsea

Stamford Bridge, Fulham Road, Chelsea, SW6 1HS (0870 300 1212/www.chelseafc.co.uk). Fulham Broadway tube. **Tickets** £38-£48. **Premiership**.

Crystal Palace

Selhurst Park, Whitehorse Lane, Selhurst, SE25 6PU (0871 200 0071/www.cpfc.co.uk). Selhurst rail/468 bus. **Tickets** £30-£40. **Premiership.**

Fulham

Craven Cottage, Stevenage Road, Fulham, SW6 6HH (0870 442 1234/www.fulhamfc.com). Putney Bridge tube. **Tickets** £26-£44. **Premiership.**

Leyton Orient

Matchroom Stadium, Brisbane Road, Leyton, E10 5NF. (8926 1111/tickets 8926 1010/ www.leytonorient.com). Leyton tube/Leyton Midland Road rail. **Tickets** £16. **Division 2.**

Millwall

The Den, Zampa Road, Bermondsey, SE16 3LN (7232 1222/tickets 7231 9999/www.millwallfc. co.uk). South Bermondsey rail. **Tickets** £17-£26. **Championship.**

Queens Park Rangers

Rangers Stadium, South Africa Road, Shepherd's Bush, W12 7PA (0870 112 1967/www.qpr.co.uk). White City tube. **Tickets** £19-£26. **Championship.**

The rise of the Roman empire

Jose Mourinho is not a man who lacks self-confidence. When he quit the manager's job at Champions' League winners Porto to take charge at Chelsea in the summer of 2004, he declared himself a 'special' coach. Mourinho will need that certainty in his own skills at Stamford Bridge, since he is now working for the most demanding owner in English football history. If Chelsea fail to improve on 2003/4's second place in the Premiership and Champions' League semi-final spot, then Russian oil tycoon Roman Abramovich will have no hesitation in axing Mourinho as he did his predecessor Claudio Ranieri.

Abramovich's willingness to pay what it takes – £150 million and counting on players alone – has made rivals' bouts of reckless spending look like mere trips to the bargain basement. However, money can never bring guarantees. While Chelsea have overtaken Manchester United in the domestic pecking order, both still lie some way behind Arsenal – whose coach Arsene Wenger has fashioned one of the most exciting teams ever seen in this country without constant recourse to the chequebook. When asked about bringing a first league title for 49 years to south-west London, Mourinho has proved more circumspect; it could take up to four seasons, he believes. Unfortunately, that'll probably be three too many for Abramovich.

Although the transformation of once-decrepit Stamford Bridge into flash Chelsea Village was almost complete under previous chairman Ken Bates, the effect of the Russian takeover in SW6 has been to alienate further all non-Chelsea supporting football fans. While Sir Alex Ferguson and Manchester United will always be popular hate figures, not least for the manner in which the Reds have brilliantly exploited global branding opportunities to turn kids from Tampa to Tokyo into consumers of Man U products, the Blues' charmless bid to buy success runs counter to the deep vein of tradition in the English game. It was no surprise when Peter Kenyon, one of the key figures behind United's commercial triumphs, was enticed down to London to fulfil the same role for Chelsea.

What, then, of the team that blends English talent with a dizzying array of international egos? Chelsea are sure to go close in every competition they enter – but, for Roman Abramovich, will it be close enough?

Tottenham Hotspur

White Hart Lane Stadium, 748 High Road, Tottenham, N17 0AP (0870 420 5000/www. spurs.co.uk). White Hart Lane rail. **Tickets** £25-£55. **Premiership.**

West Ham United

Boleyn Ground, Green Street, West Ham, E13 9AZ (0870 112 2700/www.whufc.com). Upton Park tube. **Tickets** £24-£35. **Championship.**

Greyhound racing

A night at the dogs almost guarantees fun: drink cheap beer, shout yourself hoarse and even make a few pounds in the process. For more information, visit www.thedogs.co.uk.

Walthamstow Stadium

Chingford Road, Walthamstow, E4 8SJ (8531 4255/www.wsgreyhound.co.uk). Walthamstow Central tube/rail, then 97, 215 bus. **Races** 7.45pm Tue, Thur; 7.30pm Sat. **Admission** £1-£6; free lunchtimes Mon, Fri.

Wimbledon Stadium

Plough Lane, Wimbledon, SW17 0BL (8946 8000/www.wimbledonstadium.co.uk). Tooting Broadway tube/Wimbledon tube/rail/Haydons Road rail. **Races** 7.30pm Tue, Fri, Sat. **Admission** £5.50.

Horse racing

The racing year is divided into the flat racing season, which runs from April to September, and the National Hunt season over jumps, going through the winter from October to April. For more information about the 'sport of kings', visit www.discover-racing.com.

The most famous racecourse of them all, **Ascot** (www.ascot.co.uk) will be closed until June 2006 as it undergoes a £180 million redevelopment. Its glamorous Royal Meeting will be held instead at York Racecourse in 2005.

Epsom

Epsom Downs, Epsom, Surrey KT18 5LQ (01372 726311/www.epsomderby.co.uk). Epsom Downs or Tattenham Corner rail. **Open** *Box office* 9am-5pm Mon-Fri. **Admission** £5-£35.

The annual Derby, held here in June, is one of the great events in Britain's social and sporting calendar, attracting around 15,000 spectators every year. The impressive Queen's Stand and grandstand both offer fine viewing and restaurants.

Kempton Park

Staines Road East, Sunbury-on-Thames, Middx TW16 5AQ (01932 782292/www.kempton.co.uk). Kempton Park rail (race days only). **Open** *Box office* 9am-5pm Mon-Fri. **Admission** £7-£19.

Far from glamorous, this course is the Londoner's local haunt. The year-round meetings are well attended, especially in summer.

Sandown Park

Portsmouth Road, Esher, Surrey KT10 9AJ (01372 463072/www.sandown.co.uk). Esher rail. **Open** *Box office* 9am-5pm Mon-Fri. **Admission** £6-£35.

Most famous for hosting the Whitbread Gold Cup in April and the Coral Eclipse Stakes in July, Sandown pushes horses to the limit with an infamous hill finish. Very family-friendly.

Windsor

Maidenhead Road, Windsor, Berks SL4 5JJ (01753 498400/tickets 0870 220 0024/www.windsor-racecourse.co.uk). Windsor & Eton Riverside rail. **Open** *Box office* 9.30am-5.30pm Mon-Fri. **Admission** £6-£18.

A pleasant Thames-side location in the shadow of Windsor Castle makes this a lovely spot for first-timers and families, especially during the three-day festival in May or on one of its summer Monday evening meetings.

Motorsport

Wimbledon Stadium (8946 8000/www.wimbledonstadium.co.uk) is the place to come for pedal-to-the-metal entertainment: Wednesday is speedway motorbike racing; every other Sunday bangers, hot rods and stock cars come together for family-oriented mayhem.

Rugby union

The popularity of the ruffians' sport is very hard to ignore – particularly in the wake of England's historic victory in the 2003 Rugby World Cup. Fans come out in full force to support the annual **Six Nations Championship** (January to March). Tickets for these games – which take place at Twickenham (Rugby Road, Twickenham, Middx, 8892 2000; *see also p181*), the home of **English Rugby Union** – are virtually impossible to get hold of, but those for other matches are readily available. The **Zurich Premiership** and the three-division **National League** run from August to May; most games are played on Saturday and Sunday afternoons.

Listed below are the Premiership clubs. However, for a more comprehensive list, call the **Rugby Football Union** (8892 2000) or visit its website, www.rfu.com.

London Irish

Madejski Stadium, Shooters Way, Reading, RG2 0SL (0118 968 1000/www.london-irish.com). Reading rail; shuttle bus to ground £2. **Admission** £5-£25.

London Wasps

Causeway Stadium, Hillbottom Road, High Wycombe HP12 4HJ (8993 8298/tickets 0870 414 1515/www.wasps.co.uk). High Wycombe rail. **Admission** £15-£25.

Arts & Entertainment

NEC Harlequins
Stoop Memorial Ground, Langhorn Drive, Twickenham, Middx TW2 7SX (8410 6000/tickets 0871 871 8877/www.quins.co.uk). Twickenham rail. **Open** *Box office* 9am-5pm Mon-Fri. **Admission** £12-£30.

Saracens
Vicarage Road Stadium, Watford, Herts WD18 0EP (01923 475222/www.saracens.com). Watford High Street rail. **Open** *Box office* 9am-5.30pm Mon-Fri. **Admission** £11-£22.

Tennis

Getting to see the main action at **Wimbledon**'s All England Lawn Tennis Club (20 June-3 July 2005) requires forethought, as seats on Centre and Number One courts must be applied for by ballot the previous year, although enthusiasts who queue on the day may gain entry to the outer courts. You can also turn up later in the day and pay a reasonable rate to occupy seats vacated by spectators who have left early. Wimbledon is preceded by the Stella Artois tournament, where stars from the men's circuit can be seen warming up for the main event: the 2005 tournament will be held 6-12 June at **Queen's Club** (*see below*).

All England Lawn Tennis Club
PO Box 98, Church Road, Wimbledon, SW19 5AE (8944 1066/tickets 8971 2700/information 8946 2244/www. wimbledon.org). Southfields tube.

Queen's Club
Palliser Road, West Kensington, W14 9EQ (7385 3421/ticket information 0870 890 0518/www.queensclub.co.uk). Barons Court tube.

Participation sports & fitness

Cycling

Speed merchants can pedal round the following bike circuits. For those wanting to hire a bike and zip around town, *see p365.*

Herne Hill Velodrome
Burbage Road, Herne Hill, SE24 9HE (7737 4647/www.hernehillvelodrome.org.uk). Herne Hill or North Dulwich rail. **Open** *Summer* 10am-6pm Mon-Fri; 9am-12.30pm Sat. *Winter* 10am-4pm Mon-Fri; 9am-1pm Sat. **Cost** *With bike hire* £8. *With own bike* £5.50.
Refurbishment plans are afoot at the oldest cycle circuit in the world.

Lee Valley Cycle Circuit
Quartermile Lane, Stratford, E10 5PD (8534 6085/www.leevalleypark.com). Leyton tube/Leyton Midland Road rail. **Open** *Summer* 8am-8pm daily.

Winter 8am-4pm daily. **Cost** *With bike hire* £5; £9 (whole day); £4 under-16s. *With own bike* £2.50; £1.35 under-16s.
BMX, road-racing, mountain biking, time trials and cyclo-cross are all on the menu.

Golf

You don't have to be a member to tee off at any of the public courses below – but book in advance. For a list of clubs in the London area, go to www.englishgolfunion.org.

Dulwich & Sydenham Hill
Grange Lane, College Road, Dulwich, SE21 7LH (8693 8491/www.dulwichgolf.co.uk). Sydenham Hill rail. **Open** 8am-dusk daily. **Green fee** £35 adults; £17.50 member's guest Mon-Fri.
A lovely-looking course with fantastic views over London. Note that it's members-only at weekends.

North Middlesex
Manor House, Friern Barnet Lane, Arnos Grove, N20 0NL (8445 3060/www.northmiddlesexgc.co.uk). Arnos Grove or Totteridge & Whetstone tube. **Open** 8am-4pm Mon-Fri; 1pm-dusk Sat, Sun. **Green fee** £15-£25 Mon-Fri; £25-£30 Sat, Sun.
An undulating course set in 74 acres and dating back to 1905. Not one for beginners.

Health clubs & sports centres

Many clubs and centres in central London allow non-members to use their facilities and even to participate in classes on a drop-in basis. Some of the main contenders are listed below, but for an exhaustive list of venues in Camden and Westminster, call 7974 4456 and 7641 1846, respectively. For more independent spirits, Hyde Park, Kensington Gardens and Batttersea Park have particularly good jogging trails.

Catalyst
The Economist Building, 30 Bury Street, St James's, SW1Y 6AU (7930 0742/www.catalysthealth.com). Green Park or Piccadilly Circus tube. **Open** *By appointment* 6am-9pm daily.
An immaculate little gym manned by expert staff, Catalyst tailors training programmes to the needs of its (mainly executive) clientele. The mobile service, which dispatches a trainer right to the door of your hotel room, is particularly handy for visitors.

Central YMCA
112 Great Russell Street, Bloomsbury, WC1B 3NQ (7343 1700/www.centralymca.org.uk). Tottenham Court Road tube. **Open** 7am-10pm Mon-Fri; 10am-8.30pm Sat, Sun.
Conveniently located and user-friendly, the Y has a good range of cardiovascular and weight-training equipment, as well as a pool, a squash court and a full timetable of excellently taught classes. Recent refurbishments have added a Pilates studio and modernised the main hall.

The icing on the wall

In recent years, the books of hardcore mountaineer-turned-adventure writer Joe Simpson (he of *Touching the Void* fame) have allowed Joe Public to decide exactly where he/she stands in relation to extreme alpine ascents. The answer tends to be 'as far away as humanly possible'. Fingers lost to frostbite; cheeks punctured by errant ice-axes. For Londoners, it makes the rush-hour Circle line look like a luxury cruise.

Despite all this, ice climbing is enjoying something of a renaissance at mountain resorts across Europe. In response, Covent Garden's outdoor specialists Ellis Brigham has opened this country's first indoor ice-climbing wall, Vertical Chill. Enclosed in a temperature-controlled, glass-fronted cubicle running between two floors, it gives would-be ice-climbers an 26-foot (eight-metre) induction into one of sport's most compelling pursuits.

A pickaxe in each hand, you repeatedly pitch yourself higher by stabbing at the ice and raising yourself up, digging spike shoe-irons (crampons) into the face as you ascend. 'It's about weight distribution, learning to use your legs and getting to grips with the equipment,' says Barry Horton, who runs introductory sessions at the wall.

Indeed, the wall is best suited to beginners: tall enough to be challenging without being off-putting, it's top-roped from an elevated

platform, so first-timers are secured from the moment their feet leave the floor. And yet, somehow, even insulated against all danger, you're given an occasional glimpse of the abyss that faces more serious mountaineers. A foot slips free, or the ice under your axe comes away in a small sheet, dropping silently into what seems like infinity below. Despite being kitted out in protective gear, it's possible to come away with small cuts from flying shards of ice.

'Many people feel intimidated by the thought of diving into the big ice-climbing areas like Chamonix,' adds Barry. 'All we're doing is providing them with a hassle-free environment, where they can get a feel for things, and see whether or not they like it.'

And if it turns out that you do like it, be warned: the Eiger is closer to Covent Garden than you might think.

Vertical Chill

Ellis Brigham, Tower House, 3-11 Southampton Street, Covent Garden, WC2E 7HA (7395 1010/www.ellis-brigham.com). Covent Garden tube. **Open** *10.30am-6.30pm Tue, Wed, Fri; 10.30am-7pm Thur; 10am-6pm Sat; noon-5pm Sun.* **Admission** *Fully supervised with equipment incl £40/hr. Fully supervised with own equipment £30/hr. Supervised £20/hr.* **Credit** *AmEx, MC, V.*

Arts & Entertainment

Triyoga. *See p331.*

Jubilee Hall Leisure Centre

30 The Piazza, Covent Garden, WC2E 8BE (7836 4835/www.jubileehallclubs.co.uk). Covent Garden tube. **Open** 7am-10pm Mon-Fri; 9am-9pm Sat; 10am-5pm Sun. Last entry 45mins before closing. **Map** p401 L7.

For cardiovascular workouts in calm surroundings, this central centre is a reliable bet.

Queen Mother Sports Centre

223 Vauxhall Bridge Road, Victoria, SW1V 1EL (7630 5522/www.courtneys.co.uk). Victoria tube/rail. **Open** 6.30am-10pm Mon-Fri; 8am-8pm Sat, Sun. **Map** p400 J10.

A busy venue with a pool, the QM has plenty of decent sweating and lifting facilities.

Seymour Leisure Centre

Seymour Place, Marylebone, W1H 5TJ (7723 8019/ www.courtneys.co.uk). Edgware Road tube. **Open** 6.30am-10pm Mon-Fri; 7am-8pm Sat; 8am-8pm Sun. **Map** p395 F5.

Unglamorous but central, the Seymour has a pool and enough weights to get the job done.

Soho Gym

12 Macklin Street, Holborn, WC2B 5NF (7242 1290/www.sohogyms.com). Holborn tube. **Open** 7am-10pm Mon-Fri; 8am-8pm Sat; noon-6pm Sun.

Busy and well-equipped, Soho Gym is particularly notable for its gay-friendly atmosphere.

Westway Sports Centre

1 Crowthorne Road, Ladbroke Grove, W10 6RP (8969 0992/www.westway.org). Ladbroke Grove or Latimer Road tube. **Open** 8am-10pm Mon-Fri; 8am-8pm Sat; 10am-10pm Sun.

A smart, diverse activity centre, with all-weather pitches, tennis courts and the largest indoor climbing facility in the country.

Ice skating

Broadgate is London's only permanent outdoor rink, but beautiful **Somerset House** has an outdoor rink over the Christmas period (*see p102*), as do **Marble Arch** (*see p112*) and the spectacular **Hampton Court Palace** (*see p180*). Most indoor arenas offer skating classes and discos.

Alexandra Palace Ice Rink

Alexandra Palace Way, Muswell Hill, N22 7AY (8365 4386/www.alexandrapalace.com). Wood Green tube/W3 bus. **Open** 11am-1.30pm, 2-5.30pm Mon-Fri; 10.30am-12.30pm, 2-4.30pm, 8.30-11pm Sat, Sun. **Admission** £4.50-£6; £4-£5 children.

Broadgate Ice Rink

Broadgate Circle, The City, EC2A 2QS (7505 4068/ www.broadgateestates.co.uk). Liverpool Street tube/ rail. **Open** *Nov-mid Apr* noon-2.30pm, 3.30-6pm

Mon-Thur; noon-2.30pm, 3.30-6pm, 7-10pm Fri;
11am-1pm, 2-4pm, 5-8.30pm Sat; 11am-1pm, 2-4pm,
5-7pm Sun. **Admission** (incl skate hire) £7; £4
children. **Map** p403 Q5.

Riding

There are a number of riding stables in and
around the city; for a list of those approved by
the British Horse Society, see www.bhs.org.uk.
Those listed below offer outdoor classes for all
ages and abilities.

Hyde Park & Kensington Stables

*63 Bathurst Mews, Lancaster Gate, W2 2SB (7723
2813/www.hydeparkstables.com). Lancaster Gate
tube.* **Open** *Summer* 7.15am-4pm daily. *Winter*
7.15am-3pm daily. **Fees** *Lessons* £32-£70/hr.
Map p395 D6.

Wimbledon Village Stables

*24 High Street, Wimbledon, SW19 5DX (8946
8579/www.wimbledonvillagestables.co.uk).
Wimbledon tube/rail.* **Open** 10am-5pm Tue-Sun.
Fees £35-£40/hr.

Street sports

PlayStation Skate Park and Stockwell Skate
Park are the city's most popular skateboarding
venues, although many prefer the unofficial
spaces, such as under the Royal Festival Hall
and the expanse beside the *Cutty Sark* in
Greenwich. Skaters collect at the **Sprite
Urban Games** (*see p264*) held on Clapham
Common every July, and **Board-X** at
Alexandra Palace (*see p156*) in November
(for both, see www.board-x.com).

Inline skaters and BMXers tend to use the
same skateparks (BMXers may be required to
wear helmets). Rollerbladers should keep one
eye on www.londonskaters.com for a diary of
inline events across the city.

Swimming

To find your nearest pool check the *Yellow Pages*.
Listed below are three of the best (*see also p328*
Health clubs & sports centres). For pools particularly suited to children, check www.british-
swimming.co.uk. Or if alfresco swimming is your
thing, check out www.londonpoolscampaign.com
for a comprehensive list of outdoor pools and lidos.

Highbury Pool

*Highbury Crescent, Highbury, N5 1RR (7704 2312/
www.aquaterra.org). Highbury & Islington tube/rail.*
Open 6.30am-10pm Mon-Fri; 7.30am-7.30pm Sat;
7.30am-10pm Sun. **Admission** £3.10; £1.40 5-16s; free under-4s.
Hidden away at the bottom of Highbury Fields, this
compact pool building is light, airy and has laud-
ably clean facilities. A pleasure to visit.

Ironmonger Row Baths

*Ironmonger Row, Finsbury, EC1V 3QN (7253 4011/
www.aquaterra.org). Old Street tube/rail.* **Open**
6.30am-9pm Mon; 6.30am-8pm Tue-Thur; 6.30am-
7pm Fri; 9am-5.30pm Sat; noon-5pm Sun.
Admission £3.10; £1.40 4-16s; free under-3s.
Map p402 P4.
A 31m pool with excellent lane swimming; the site
also features good-value Turkish baths.

Oasis Sports Centre

*32 Endell Street, Covent Garden, WC2H 9AG (7831
1804). Holborn tube.* **Open** *Indoor pool* 6.30am-
6.30pm Mon, Wed; 6.30am-7.15pm Tue, Thur, Fri;
9.30am-5.30pm Sat, Sun. *Outdoor pool* 7.30am-9pm
Mon-Fri; 9.30am-5.30pm Sat, Sun. **Admission** £3.20;
£1.25 5-16s; free under-5s. **Map** p399 L6.
A central London gem renowned for its sun terrace
and outdoor pool; adjacent is an indoor version.

Tennis

Many parks around the city have council-run
courts that cost little or nothing to use. For
lessons, try the **Regent's Park Golf &
Tennis School** (7724 0643, www.rpgts.co.uk).
For grass courts, phone the Lawn Tennis
Association's Information Department (7381
7000/www.lta.org.uk). The **Islington Tennis
Centre** (7700 1370/www.aquaterra.org) has
indoor as well as outdoor courts, as does the
Westway Sports Centre (*see p330*).

Ten-pin bowling

A useful first stop when looking for lanes is
the **British Ten-pin Bowling Association**
(8478 1745, www.btba.org.uk).

Rowans Bowl

*10 Stroud Green Road, Finsbury Park, N4 2DF
(8800 1950/www.rowans.co.uk). Finsbury Park
tube/rai or Crouch Hill rail.* **Open** 10.30am-12.30am
Mon-Thur, Sun; 10.30am-2.30am Fri, Sat. **Cost**
Per game £2-£3.25. **Lanes** 24.

Streatham MegaBowl

*142 Streatham Hill, Streatham, SW2 4RU (8678
6007/www.megabowl.co.uk). Streatham Hill rail.*
Open noon-midnight Mon; noon-1am Tue-Fri; 10am-
1am Sat; 10am-midnight Sun. **Cost** *Per game* £4.75;
£3.75 children. **Lanes** 36.

Yoga & Pilates

For something more than just a quick stretch
in your hotel room, check out one of the many
special yoga activities and classes (and the fully
equipped Pilates studio) at Triyoga.

Triyoga

*6 Erskine Road, NW3 3DJ (7483 3344/
www.triyoga.co.uk). Chalk Farm tube.* **Open** 6am-
10pm Mon-Fri; 8am-8.30pm Sat; 9am-9.30pm Sun.

Arts & Entertainment

Theatre

From improv nights to men in tights.

Speaking on Radio 4's *Front Row* arts programme in September 2004, actor Kevin Spacey, the new director of the **Old Vic** (*see p333*), gave London theatre-goers a stern warning. Audience members who fidget with sweet papers or forget to switch off mobiles, he said, should not come to the theatre: they should stay at home. Which would be a harsh confinement indeed, considering the current good health of London's stages.

In the West End, an ambitious superbreed of musicals is preparing to hatch in 2005, undaunted by a sector where over half the productions lose money. Sir Cameron Mackintosh and Disney have teamed up for *Mary Poppins* (from Dec 2004); Elton John has scored *Billy Elliot* (from May 2005); and later in the year will come the all-singing, all-dancing *Lord of the Rings*. Until a few years ago, musicals were not the done thing for a theatre that took itself seriously, but now, buoyed by the success of shows such as the **National**'s *Anything Goes* (*see p335*), the genre is fashionable again, and worth investigating beyond smash-hit territory.

The increasing political bite of London theatre has been another talking point. The small north London **Tricycle Theatre** (*see p340*) made a piercing but unsensationalised critique of post-9/11 politics with its staging of *Guantanamo* – a docudrama that transferred to both the West End and Broadway. David Hare's *Stuff Happens* at the National, a Blair-Bush docudrama, sold out almost before it opened.

Renewals haven't been limited to content, either. The glorious old **Hackney Empire** (*see p162* **Age of Empire**) music hall has been restored to its original Victorian plushness and will build up to a grand opening with a trickle of theatre and comedy. The avant-gardist Théâtre de Complicité, meanwhile, wants to turn the Victorian chocolate-box **Alexandra Palace Theatre** into its temporary home, but so far lacks the necessary funds. Further out, in Kingston-upon-Thames, another ambitious project, the **Rose of Kingston**, is awaiting fruition. The brainchild of veteran director Sir Peter Hall, the theatre is modelled on the 16th-century Rose theatre that stood on Bankside. A scattering of productions will preface the opening proper (24-26 High Street, Kingston-upon-Thames, Surrey KT1 1EY, 8546 6983).

For all the latest developments, reviews and practical information, check the theatre section of the weekly *Time Out* magazine. It offers a brief critique of every West End show running, and has useful 'book ahead' listings.

WHERE TO GO AND WHAT TO SEE

Although the West End, strictly speaking, is not a geographical term, for most Londoners it is synonymous with the traditional theatre quarter clustered around Shaftesbury Avenue. West End venues in this area tend to be faded Edwardian glories, hosting transfers of successful smaller-scale productions, plus the usual blockbusting fare. More polished and more innovative are West End venues such as the Royal National Theatre, aka the National (*see p335*), on the South Bank, or the Old Vic (*see p333*) in Waterloo.

Off-West End denotes smaller budgets and smaller capacity. These theatres – many of which are sponsored or subsidised – challenge creative boundaries with new, experimental writing, often brought to life by the cream of acting and directing talent. The **Soho Theatre** (*see p340*) and the **Bush** (*see p339*) are good for up-and-coming playwrights, while the **Almeida** and **Donmar Warehouse** (for both, *see p339*) are safe bets for classy production values.

Lurking under the 'Fringe' moniker are dozens of smaller theatres, not always guaranteed to deliver quality, but nevertheless mobbed by hopefuls looking for their London stage debut. The **Menier Chocolate Factory** (51-53 Southwark Street, Southwark, SE1 1TE, 7907 7060) is an attractive new fringe venue with reliable, mainstream fare and a restaurant attached – great for a glass of wine and pudding post-play. The small but accomplished **Arcola Theatre** (27 Arcola Street, E8 2DJ, 7503 1646) in Dalston is worth the trek to hear fresh writing voices.

TICKETS AND INFORMATION

The first rule to observe when buying tickets for London performances is to book ahead. The second rule is to bypass agents and go direct to the theatre's box office. Booking agencies such as **Ticketmaster** (7344 4444, www.ticketmaster.co.uk) and **First Call** (7420 0000, www.firstcalltickets.com) sell tickets to many shows, but you'll get hit with booking fees that could top a whopping 20 per cent.

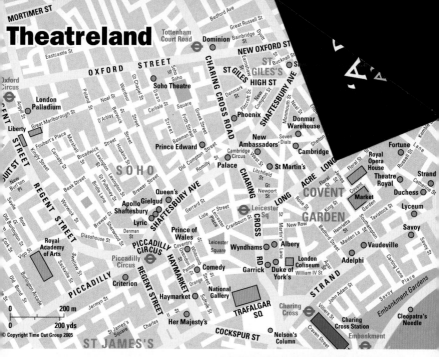

Theatreland

In a late bid to fill their venues, many West End theatres offer reduced-price tickets for shows that have not sold out. These seats, available only on the night, are known as 'standby' tickets, and usually sell for about half what a top-priced ticket would normally cost. Always call to check both the availability and the conditions: some standby deals are limited to those with student ID, and it varies as to when tickets go on sale.

Alternatively, try **tkts**, a non-profit-making organisation run from the Clock Tower building in Leicester Square by the Society of London Theatres that sells tickets for West End shows on a first-come, first-served basis on the day of the performance. Each ticket is subject to a fee of £2.50 and a maximum of four are allowed per customer, but it's worth fighting your way through it all, as tickets for many shows can be snapped up for as much as 50 per cent off face value. Be aware that the other gaudy booths advertising cheap seats around Leicester Square are unofficial and can be expensive.

tkts

Leicester Square, WC2 7NA (www.officiallondon theatre.co.uk). Leicester Square tube. **Open** 10am-7pm Mon-Sat; noon-3pm Sun. **Credit** AmEx, DC, MC, V. **Map** p401 K7.
There's a second tkts location in Docklands (Platforms 4/5, Canary Wharf DLR; open 11.30am-6pm Mon-Sat).

West End

Repertory companies

Barbican Centre

Silk Street, City, EC2Y 8DS (0845 120 7550/www. barbican.org.uk). Barbican tube/Moorgate tube/rail. **Box office** 9am-8pm daily. **Tickets** Barbican £7-£50. Pit £15. **Credit** AmEx, DC, MC, V. **Map** p402 P5.
The RSC made a messy departure from the Barbican Centre in 2002, leaving the stage door open for an eclectic mix of touring regional and foreign companies, grouped together under the BITE season (Barbican International Theatre Events). The Bard-shaped hole has been filled by acclaimed troupes such as Bristol's Shakespeare at the Tobacco Factory.

Old Vic

Waterloo Road, Waterloo, SE1 8NB (0870 060 6628/ www.oldvictheatre.com). Waterloo tube/rail. **Box office** 9am-9pm Mon-Sat; 10am-6pm Sun. **Tickets** £10-£40. **Credit** AmEx, MC, V. **Map** p404 N9.
All eyes turned to Waterloo Road when the Old Vic bagged Kevin Spacey as artistic director in 2004. Among his first moves with top producer David Liddiment has been to woo funding from Morgan Stanley, which should ensure 100 £12 tickets for under-25s at every show. Artistically, his first season promises unlikely casting (Ian McKellen as Widow Twanky in a pantomime *Cinderella*) and slick new writing, with Spacey busy on stage (he's set to star in 2005 in *The Philadelphia Story*) as well as off.

Arts & Entertainment

Open Air Theatre

Regent's Park, NW1 4NR (7935 5756/box office 0870 060 1811/www.openairtheatre.org). Baker Street tube. **Repertory season** June-Sept; phone for details. **Tickets** £9.50-£26. Standby £9 (approx). **Credit** AmEx, DC, MC, V. **Map** p398 G3.

The lovely verdant setting of this alfresco theatre lends itself perfectly to summery Shakespeare romps. Standards are far above village green dramatics, with productions of the Bard particularly imaginative. Book well ahead and take an extra layer for chills in Act Three. Buy good-value, tasty grub on site or bring a picnic.

Riverside Studios

Crisp Road, Hammersmith, W6 9RL (8237 1111/ www.riversidestudios.co.uk). Hammersmith tube. **Box office** noon-9pm daily. **Tickets** £10-£25. **Credit** MC, V.

A chameleon overlooking the Thames, this multi-purpose venue started as the Triumph Film Studios in 1933, morphing in the 1970s and '80s into a platform for new and international theatre. Its drama programming continues to be fresh, featuring innovative troupes such as Forced Entertainment. In addition to dance, film, music and TV sidelines, there's a great riverside bar for interval sipping.

Royal Court

Sloane Square, Chelsea, SW1W 8AS (7565 5000/ www.royalcourttheatre.com). Sloane Square tube. **Box office** 10am-6pm Mon-Sat. **Tickets** 10p-£27.50; all tickets £7.50 Mon. **Credit** AmEx, MC, V. **Map** p400 G11.

The emphasis at the RC is always on new, uncompromising voices in British theatre – from John Osborne's *Look Back in Anger* in the inaugural year, 1956, to numerous discoveries over the past decade: Sarah Kane, Joe Penhall and Conor McPherson among them. There are two stages: Upstairs (a studio theatre) and Downstairs (the main stage).

Royal National Theatre

South Bank, SE1 9PX (information 7452 3400/ box office 7452 3000/www.nationaltheatre.org.uk). Embankment or Southwark tube/Waterloo tube/rail. **Box office** 10am-8pm Mon-Sat. **Tickets** Olivier & Lyttelton £10-£35. Cottesloe £10-£27. Standby £19. **Credit** AmEx, DC, MC, V. **Map** p401 M8.

Its concrete buildings are, arguably, not getting any prettier, but behind the scenes at the traditionally difficult-to-manage National, things could be a lot uglier. Nicholas Hytner's first two years as artistic director have been flush with critical and popular successes: an infectiously energetic and witty take on *Anything Goes*; a superb new Alan Bennett play, *The History Boys*; and much new work besides, particularly from ethnic minority writers. The Travelex season, where two-thirds of the seats are offered for £10, included the hot-ticket Sondheim musical, *A Funny Thing Happened on the Way to the Forum*, and is set to continue. Hytner also wants to make the National 'sceptical of authority'; three plays about the Iraq conflict have already been staged here.

Royal Shakespeare Company

Albery Theatre, St Martin's Lane, Soho, WC2N 5AU (0870 060 6621/www.rsc.org.uk). Leicester Square tube. **Box office** *In person* 10am-7.30pm Mon-Sun. *By phone* 9am-9pm Mon-Sat; 10am-6pm Sun. **Tickets** £10-£39. **Credit** AmEx, MC, V. **Map** p401 L7.

The dust has settled on the Royal Shakespeare Company's frantic search for a new home, following its controversial exit from the Barbican in 2002. RSC productions will, until March 2005 at least, be staged at the Albery Theatre, in the full glare of the West End. Artistic director Michael Boyd has chosen four heavyweight tragedies – *Hamlet, Romeo & Juliet, King Lear* and *Macbeth* – to cover the period.

Shakespeare's Globe

21 New Globe Walk, Bankside, SE1 9DT (7401 9919/ www.shakespeares-globe.org). Mansion House tube/ London Bridge tube/rail. **Box office** *Off season* 10am-5pm Mon-Fri. *Theatre* 10am-8pm daily. **Tickets** £5-£29. **Credit** AmEx, MC, V. **Map** p404 O7.

Although it has hit poor ticket sales when trying to look beyond the Complete Works (for example, with other playwrights such as Marlowe), the reconstructed Globe is still an undeniable success story, underwritten in part by its popular exhibition centre (*see p83*). Artistic director Mark Rylance, who often takes leading roles, has turned out some interesting productions in a difficult space, although his experiments with Elizabethan-style single-sex casts (including a ladies-only *Much Ado*) have had mixed results. The pit audiences are never as garrulous as they might be, but during a bad production their restlessness is infectious.

Long-runners & musicals

Most theatres have evening shows Monday to Saturday (starting 7.30pm-8pm) and matinées on one weekday (usually Wednesday) and Saturday. Check *Time Out* magazine for details.

Blood Brothers

Phoenix Theatre, Charing Cross Road, Soho, WC2H 0JP (0870 060 6629/www.theambassadors.com). Tottenham Court Road tube. **Box office** *In person* 10am-7.45pm Mon-Sat. *By phone* 9am-9pm Mon-Sat; 10am-6pm Sun. *Ticketmaster* 24hrs daily. **Tickets** £17.50-£42.50. Standby £15 (concessions only). **Credit** AmEx, MC, V. **Map** p399 K6.

Scouse sentiment and toe-tapping songs in Willy Russell's likeable, long-running melodrama about two brothers separated at birth and exiled to opposite ends of the social ladder.

Chicago

Adelphi Theatre, Strand, Covent Garden, WC2E 7NA (Ticketmaster 08704 030303). Charing Cross tube/rail. **Box office** *In person* 10am-8pm Mon-Sat. *By phone* 24hrs daily. **Tickets** £16-£43.50. **Credit** AmEx, MC, V. **Map** p401 L7.

The jailbird roles are passed at regular intervals from one blonde TV star to the next, but this production still razzle dazzles 'em with high spirits.

A pint and a play

The barman rings the bell and a dozen or so people pick up their drinks, shuffle through a back door and take their seats for an evening of theatre. At the **King's Head** pub in Islington, this happens almost every night. And at pubs all over London too. Of course, the audience reappears at the interval to refresh their glasses: just one of the many cheap and convivial advantages to pub theatre-going. The King's Head Theatre was the original London pub theatre, founded by the still-resident artistic director Dan Brown 35 years ago. Like most of the others set up in the years that followed, it has a small stage shoehorned into the pub premises, and an even smaller, more awkward budget (the theatre lost its Arts Council funding five years ago). But what history. A young Hugh Grant appeared here in *The Jockeys of Norfolk*, and the A-list of past performers goes on till the present day. The pub itself is a Victorian charmer, always with a crowd in ramshackle high spirits (there's live music here too).

The nearby **Hen & Chickens**, whose young artistic team favours new British and international writing, receives hundreds of hopeful scripts every year. Quality is high and variety is immense. Its black box theatre is so small that almost every seat is the best in the house, wonderfully close to every twitch and nuance on the actors' faces. Also in Islington is the **Old Red Lion Theatre**, which finds a home in an old-man-and-his-dog, dusty velvet seat pub. It shows a good pick of new and old plays, plus some comedy.

One of the most innovative of the bunch is the **Gate Theatre**, above the Prince Albert pub in Notting Hill, a posh young Hillbillies' hangout. Its emphasis is on new or under-championed international writing, usually performed in translation by the excellent in-house company. And rising young artistic director Thea Sharrock looks set to raise its profile even further. The performing space feels like a doll's house theatre, with rows of rickety wooden chairs (choose wisely) set before a tiny stage, curtained off with red velvet. Its former sister theatre at the cosy Latchmere pub in Battersea has been reorganised and rechristened **Theatre 503**. Housed in an old Victorian hotel, it stages the work of new playwrights.

At the 42-seater **Etcetera** in Camden, co-artistic director Zina Barrie admits that five people 'feels like you've got a decent audience'. The theatre is supportive of young actors and writers and it has also bagged some big-name premieres such as Alan Ayckbourn's *Between the Lines*. The host pub is the Oxford Arms, a boozy local where on match nights you have to squeeze through a crush of football fans to reach the theatre.

Etcetera

Oxford Arms, 265 Camden High Street, Camden, NW1 7BU (7482 4857). Camden Town tube. **Tickets** £5-£10.

Arts & Entertainment

Chitty Chitty Bang Bang

London Palladium, Argyll Street, Soho, W1F 7TF (0870 890 1108/www.chittythemusical.co.uk). Oxford Circus tube. **Box office** *In person* 10am-8pm Tue-Sat. *Seetickets* 24-hrs daily. **Tickets** £12-£45. **Credit** AmEx, MC, V. **Map** p398 J6.
There's life in the old banger yet. This adaptation boasts excellent stage sets and jokes for all ages. Beware the Child Catcher though. We remember many sleepless childhood nights, convinced he was waiting at the door with his net at the ready.

Jerry Springer – The Opera

Cambridge Theatre, Earlham Street, Covent Garden, WC2H 9HU (7494 5399/Seetickets 0870 890 1102 /www.jerryspringertheopera.com). Covent Garden tube. **Box office** *In person* 10am-8pm Mon-Sat. *Seetickets* 24hrs daily. **Tickets** £25-£50. **Credit** AmEx, MC, V. **Map** p399 L6.
The freak show-talk show world is transformed into a spoof opera, and lampooned for all it's worth. Bitingly funny.

Les Misérables

Queen's Theatre, Shaftesbury Avenue, Soho, W1D 8AS (7494 5040/www.lesmis.com). Leicester Square or Piccadilly Circus tube. **Box office** *In person* 10am-7.30pm Mon-Sat. *Seetickets* 24hrs daily. **Tickets** £15-£45. **Credit** AmEx, MC, V. **Map** p401 K7.
The RSC's version of Boubil and Schonberg's musical, 18 years-old and still raking in the cash and the crowds, continues to idealise the struggles of the poor in Victor Hugo's revolutionary Paris.

The Lion King

Lyceum Theatre, Wellington Street, Covent Garden, WC2E 7DA (7420 8112/box office 0870 243 9000). Covent Garden tube/Charing Cross tube/rail. **Box office** 10am-6pm Mon-Sat. *Ticketmaster* 24hrs daily. **Tickets** £14.40-£49.50. **Credit** AmEx, MC, V. **Map** p401 L7.
This Disney extravaganza about an orphaned young lion cub struggling to grow up and find his place on the savannah has been widely acclaimed, particularly by those who have small children.

King's Head Theatre.

Hen & Chickens
109 St Paul's Road, Islington, N1 2NA (7704 2001). Highbury & Islington tube/rail. **Tickets** *£12; £9 concessions.*

King's Head Theatre
115 Upper Street, Islington, N1 1QN (7226 1916/www.kingsheadtheatre.org). Angel tube. **Tickets** *£12-£19.* **Map** *p402 N2.*

Old Red Lion Theatre
St John Street, Farringdon, EC1V 4NJ (7833 3053). Angel tube. **Tickets** *£12; £10 concessions.* **Map** *p402 O3.*

Theatre 503
In the Latchmere pub, 503 Battersea Park Road, Battersea, SW11 3BW (7978 7040). Clapham Junction rail/44, 49, 319, 344, 345, N19 bus. **Tickets** *£8; £6 concessions.*

The Gate
Above the Prince Albert pub, 11 Pembridge Road, Notting Hill, W11 3HQ (7229 0706). Notting Hill Gate, Queensway or Bayswater tube. **Tickets** *£14; £7 concessions.* **Map** *p394 A7.*

Mamma Mia!
Prince of Wales Theatre, 31 Coventry Street, Soho, W1D 6AS (0870 850 0393/www.mamma-mia.com). Leicester Square tube. **Box office** *In person* 10am-8pm Mon-Sat. *By phone* 24-hrs daily. **Tickets** £25-£49. **Credit** AmEx, MC, V. **Map** p401 K7.
This feel-good musical links Abba's hits into a continuous but spurious story. Endlessly popular.

The Mousetrap
St Martin's Theatre, West Street, Covent Garden, WC2H 9NZ (0870 162 8787). Leicester Square tube. **Box office** 10am-8pm Mon-Sat. **Tickets** £11.50-£33. **Credit** AmEx, MC, V.
It's looking unlikely the mouse will ever be caught.

Phantom of the Opera
Her Majesty's Theatre, Haymarket, St James's, SW1Y 4QR (0870 160 2878/www.thephantomoftheopera. com). Piccadilly Circus tube. **Box office** *In person* 10am-8pm Mon-Sat. *By phone* 24hrs daily. **Tickets** £15-£45. **Credit** AmEx, MC, V. **Map** p401 K7.

Lloyd Webber's best musical, a must-see for its '80s spectacle and a score packed with great songs.

The Producers
Theatre Royal, Drury Lane, Catherine Street, Covent Garden, WC2B 5JF (0870 890 1109). Covent Garden tube. **Box office** *In person* 10am-8pm Mon-Sat. *By phone* 24 hrs daily. **Tickets** £10-£49. **Credit** AmEx, MC, V. **Map** p401 M6.
Showered with Tony awards on Broadway, this is Mel Brooks's hilarious story of two producers whose insurance fraud is bungled when their deliberately awful show, *Springtime for Hitler*, becomes a hit. Nathan Lane and Lee Evans star.

We Will Rock You
Dominion Theatre, Tottenham Court Road, Fitzrovia, W1P 0AG (7413 1713/www.london-dominion.co.uk). Tottenham Court Road tube. **Box office** *In person* 9am-7.45pm Mon-Sat. *Ticketmaster* 24hrs daily. **Tickets** £12.50-£55. **Credit** AmEx, MC, V. **Map** p399 K5.

Arts & Entertainment

ALF PRICE TICKETS FO
OP WEST END SHOWS

e OFFICIAL outlets for on-the-day bargain ticke

Leicester Square

Mon - Sat 10.00am - 7.00pm
Sun 12.00pm - 3.00pm

Docklands

at Canary Wharf DLR station
platforms 4/5
Mon - Sat 11.30am - 6.00pm

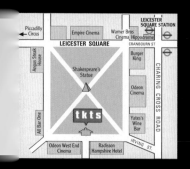

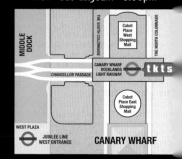

tkts Canary Wharf is operated by the Society of London Theatre in association with Docklands Light Railway

tkts is a trademark owned by and used under licence from Theatre Development Inc.

All your favourite Queen hits, unconvincingly rendered and stitched together by a deeply feeble Ben Elton plot. Freddie would've hated it.

The Woman in White

Palace Theatre, Shaftesbury Avenue, Soho, W1D 5AY (0870 895 5579). Leicester Square tube. **Box office** *In person* 10am-8pm Mon-Sat. *Seetickets* 24 hrs daily. **Tickets** £12.50-£50. **Credit** AmEx, MC, V. **Map** p399 K6.

Lloyd Webber's downturned career in musicals gets a jolt with this mostly likeable adaptation of Wilkie Collins's enigmatic Victorian thriller. Woozy stage projections accompany some awkward melodies, refreshed by flashes of wit and a fine cast.

Off-West End

Almeida

Almeida Street, Islington, N1 1TA (7359 4404/www. almeida.co.uk). Angel tube. **Box office** *In person* 10am-7.30pm Mon-Sat. *By phone* 24hrs daily. **Tickets** £6-£27.50. **Credit** AmEx, MC, V. **Map** p399 L2.

In the past two years the Almeida has received a fresh coat of paint and a new artistic director, Michael Attenborough. He has upheld its image as a high-minded theatre, while the refurbishment has improved facilities. London's best stage actors can often be seen here – in January 2005 Simon Russell Beale and Emma Fielding will play the fearsome duo in *Macbeth*. There's a great Conran restaurant.

BAC (Battersea Arts Centre)

Lavender Hill, Battersea, SW11 5TN (7223 2223/ www.bac.org.uk). Clapham Common tube/Clapham Junction rail/77, 77A, 345 bus. **Box office** *In person* 10am-6pm Mon; 10am-9pm Tue-Fri; 4-8pm Sat, Sun. *By phone* 10.30am-6pm Mon-Fri; 4.30-7pm Sat, Sun. **Tickets** £5.50-£12.75; 'pay what you can' Tue (phone ahead). **Credit** MC, V.

The forward-thinking BAC, which inhabits the old Battersea Town Hall, plays alma mater to new writers and companies. With Tom Morris departed as artistic director (he's now associate director at the National), the hot seat has been taken up by longtime BAC collaborator David Jubb. His track record includes starting up the now-infamous Scratch programme, which shows a work in progress to progressively larger audiences until it's finished and polished (this is how *Jerry Springer – The Opera* first started).

The Bush

Shepherd's Bush Green, Shepherd's Bush, W12 8QD (7610 4224/www.bushtheatre.co.uk). Goldhawk Road or Shepherd's Bush tube. **Box office** *In person* 5-8pm Mon-Sat (performance nights only). *By phone* 10am-7pm Mon-Sat. **Tickets** £8-£13.50. **Credit** AmEx, MC, V.

A small, cash-poor champion of new writers and performers, the Bush has over 30 years' experience under its belt. Alumni include Stephen Poliakoff, Mike Leigh and Jim Broadbent, so watch that space.

Donmar Warehouse

41 Earlham Street, Covent Garden, WC2H 9LX (0870 060 6624/www.donmarwarehouse.com). Covent Garden or Leicester Square tube. **Box office** *In person* 10am-7.30pm Mon-Sat. *By phone* 9am-9pm Mon-Sat; 10am-6pm Sun. *Ticketmaster* 24hrs daily. **Tickets** £15-£26. **Credit** AmEx, MC, V. **Map** p399 L6.

Less warehouse, more intimate chamber, the Donmar is another favourite crossover spot for actors more often seen on screen cutting their theatrical chops. Artistic director Michael Grandage's first few seasons have been independent-minded, featuring new work by the likes of Patrick Marber and some foreign revivals, but inevitably still draw comparisons with Sam Mendes's award-laden '90s reign. Grandage's big project for 2005 is a West End adaptation of *Guys and Dolls*.

Drill Hall

16 Chenies Street, Fitzrovia, WC1E 7EX (7307 5060/www.drillhall.co.uk). Goodge Street tube. **Box office** 10am-9.30pm Mon-Sat; 10am-6pm Sun. **Tickets** £2-£10. **Credit** AmEx, MC, V. **Map** p399 K5.

Polyfunctional (it's a theatre, cabaret, gig venue and photo studio) and polysexual, Drill Hall is London's biggest gay and lesbian theatre, and often premieres exciting new work and writers.

Hampstead Theatre

Eton Avenue, Swiss Cottage, NW3 3EU (7722 9301/www.hampsteadtheatre.com). Swiss Cottage tube. **Box office** 9am-8pm Mon-Sat. **Tickets** £13-£22. **Credit** MC, V.

The Hampstead's portacabin days are officially a distant memory now that it's installed in this polished, purpose-built space, the first new London theatre to open its doors to the public since 1976 – proving that there's still plenty of life in theatre.

The Producers.
See p337.

An old dog with new tricks: **Hampstead Theatre**. *See p339*.

Its programme of fresh British and international playwrights is astute but accessible. The theatre has also just launched its Start Nights, offering nervous fledgling artists 15 minutes each to perform a slice of rehearsed material in its small, 80-seater Space theatre. It's a great introduction to performance.

Lyric Hammersmith

Lyric Square, King Street, Hammersmith, W6 0QL (0870 050 0511/www.lyric.co.uk). Hammersmith tube. **Box office** 10am-6pm or 8pm (performance nights) Mon-Sat. **Tickets** £9-£25. **Credit** DC, MC, V.

The Lyric has a knack for vibrant, offbeat scheduling, and it also offers good kids' theatre. The frankly hideous façade, built when reinforced concrete was still regarded as an architectural panacea to all building ills, hides a 19th-century gem of an auditorium designed by the Victorian theatre design supremo Frank Matcham. A smaller space, the Lyric Studio, houses short-run shows. As we went to press, the well-respected Neil Bartlett had just resigned as artistic director, leaving a tough legacy for his successor to live up to.

Soho Theatre

21 Dean Street, Soho, W1D 3NE (7478 0100/ box office 0870 429 6883/www.sohotheatre.com). Tottenham Court Road tube. **Box office** *In person* 10am-6pm or 7.30pm (performance nights) Mon-Sat. *By phone* 24 hrs daily. **Tickets** £5-£15. **Credit** AmEx, MC, V. **Map** p399 K6.

Its cool blue neon lights and front-of-house café may seem to blend it into the Soho landscape, but since taking up its lottery-funded residence on Dean Street in 2000, the Soho Theatre has firmly made a name for itself. The keystone of its approach is the nurturing of new writing talent: it encourages playwrights to submit their work by offering a free script-reading service, runs numerous workshops and also offers computer facilities to writers looking for some peace and quiet to finish their masterpiece.

Theatre Royal Stratford East

Gerry Raffles Square, Stratford, E15 1BN (8534 0310/www.stratfordeast.com). Stratford tube/ rail/DLR. **Box office** 10am-7pm Mon-Sat. **Tickets** £8-£20. **Credit** MC, V.

This theatre is an important part of the local community, with a high proportion of the shows on offer written, directed and performed by black or Asian artists. Musicals have been big news here – whether they are about hip hop culture or the *Windrush* generation of immigrants. Money is very tight, but 2005 should see an adaptation of Benjamin Zephaniah's new novel *Gangster Rap*.

Tricycle

269 Kilburn High Road, Kilburn, NW6 7JR (7328 1000/www.tricycle.co.uk). Kilburn tube. **Box office** 10am-9pm Mon-Sat; 2-9pm Sun. **Tickets** £8-£22. **Credit** MC, V.

The Tricycle has been free-wheeling over the past few years with wide acclaim for its most recent 'tribunal' docudramas, which have have followed a theatrical pursuit of the dark political truths in the Stephen Lawrence case, the Hutton Inquiry and Guantanamo Bay. Other shows are aimed at the local Irish, Asian, black and Jewish audiences.

Young Vic

Temporary office: *Kennington Park, 2nd Floor, Chester House, 1-3 Brixton Road, SW9 6DE (box office 7928 6363/www.youngvic.org).* **Box office** 10am-6pm Mon-Fri. **Tickets** £10-£36. **Credit** MC, V.

The Young Vic theatre, erected in 1969 as a temporary space, has finally exited, stage left, pursued by memories: it's started to crumble, and will be closed for rebuilding until 2006. Until then, when we might finally get to see head honcho David Lan's long-awaited *Hamlet* with Jude Law as the Dane, the theatre will go out on a 'Walkabout' programme, revisiting some of its greatest production hits from the past few years. See website for details.

Trips Out of Town

Getting there   342
Bath   345
Brighton   347
Cambridge   349
Canterbury   350
Oxford   351
Stratford-upon-Avon   353
Winchester   353
Seaside towns   357

Features

Rambling free   346
Grand designs   354

Map

Trips Out of Town   343

Trips Out of Town

More than a breath of fresh air.

A useful first stop for the visitor planning a trip away from London is the **Britain & London Visitor Centre** (*see below*). We've also listed the local tourist information centres, which can provide further information about specific areas. For the main entries, we've included details of opening times, admission and transport, but be aware that these can change without notice: always phone to check. Major sights are open all through the year, but many minor attractions close from November to March.

Britain & London Visitor Centre

1 Regent Street (south of Piccadilly Circus), SW1Y 4XT (no phone/www.visitbritain.com). Piccadilly Circus tube. **Open** *Oct-May* 9.30am-6.30pm Mon; 9am-6.30pm Tue-Fri; 10am-4pm Sat, Sun. *June-Sept* 9.30am-6.30pm Mon; 9am-6.30pm Tue-Fri; 9am-5pm Sat; 10am-4pm Sun. **Credit** AmEx, MC, V. **Map** p401 K7.
Come in person to pick up free leaflets and advice on destinations in the UK and Ireland. You can also book rail, road or air travel, reserve tours, theatre tickets and hotels. There's a bureau de change too.

Getting there

By train

For information on train times and ticket prices, call **08457 484950**. Ask about the cheapest ticket for the journey you are planning, and be aware that for long journeys, the earlier you book, the cheaper the ticket. If you need extra help, there are **rail travel centres** in London's main-line stations, as well as in Heathrow and Gatwick airports. These can give you guidance for things like timetables and booking. The journey times we give are the fastest available.

The website www.virgintrains.co.uk gives online timetable information for any British train company; buy tickets online for any train operator in the UK via www.thetrainline.com.

London main-line rail stations

Charing Cross *Strand, Covent Garden, WC2.* **Map** p401 L7.
For trains to and from south-east England (including Dover, Folkestone and Ramsgate).
Euston *Euston Road, Euston, NW1.* **Map** p399 K3.
For trains to and from north and north-west England and Scotland, and a north London suburban line.
King's Cross *Euston Road, King's Cross, N1.* **Map** p399 L2.
For trains to and from north and north-east England and Scotland; lines to north London and Herts.
Liverpool Street *Liverpool Street, the City, EC2.* **Map** p403 R5.
For trains to and from the east coast and Stansted airport; also for trains to East Anglia and suburban services to north and east London.
London Bridge *London Bridge Street, London Bridge, SE1.* **Map** p405 Q8.
For trains to and from south-east England and Kent; also suburban services to south London.
Paddington *Praed Street, Paddington, W2.* **Map** p395 D5.
For trains to and from south-west and west England, south Wales and the Midlands.

River Avon. See p345.

Trips Out of Town

Trips Out of Town

Victoria *Terminus Place, Victoria, SW1.*
Map p400 H10.
For fast trains to and from the Channel ports (Dover, Folkestone, Newhaven); also for trains to and from Gatwick, plus services to south London.
Waterloo *York Road, Waterloo, SE1.* **Map** p401 M8.
For fast trains to and from the south and south-west of England (Portsmouth, Southampton, Dorset, Devon), the Eurostar to Paris and Brussels, and suburban services to south London.

By coach

National Express (0870 580 8080) coaches travel throughout the country and depart from Victoria Coach Station on Buckingham Palace Road, five minutes' walk from Victoria rail and tube stations. **Green Line Travel** (0870 608 7261) runs coaches as well.

Victoria Coach Station
164 Buckingham Palace Road, Victoria, SW1W 9TP (7730 3466). Victoria tube/rail. **Map** p400 H11.
Britain's most comprehensive coach company **National Express** and **Eurolines** (01582 404511), which travels to the Continent, are based here. There are many other companies operating to and from London (some departing from Marble Arch).

By car

If you're in a group of three or four, it may be cheaper to hire a car (*see p361*) Directory: Getting Around), especially if you plan to take in several sights within an area. The road directions given in the listings below should be used in conjunction with a map. (We've used a little shorthand, though, so for example, 'J13 off M11' means 'exit the M11 motorway at Junction 13'.)

Bicycle tours

Capital Sport (01296 631671, www.capital-sport.co.uk) offers gentle cycling tours along the River Thames from London. Leisurely itineraries include plenty of time to explore royal palaces, parks and historic attractions.
Or you could try **Country Lanes** (01425 655022, www.countrylanes.co.uk), which has representatives who meet you off the train from London and lead you on cycling tours of the New Forest in Hampshire (01590 622627) and the Cotswolds (01608 650065).

Bath

An ancient spa town surrounded like Rome by seven hills, Bath's ability to restore and revive officially dates from Roman times but, according to Celtic legend, as far back as 863 BC a swine-herd bathed his leprous pigs in the naturally hot waters and they were cured. From there, Bath's

reputation for healing extended beyond mere livestock, until the 18th century, when a housing boom signalled the rise of Georgian Bath. The visionary architect John Wood the Elder (1704-54) was, together with his son, responsible for the extraordinary unity of the architecture, which is elegant English Palladianism.
Bath's heyday lasted almost a century, until Jane Austen's time (she lived here from 1800 to 1805), after which it declined until after World War II when the current revival began. The city is as beautiful as ever now, although it can be stiflingly crowded in the summer when it often seems as if all of its three million annual visitors descend at once.
Most head first for the wonderful, steam-enshrouded **Roman Baths Museum**. Once a temple to Sulis Minerva, this is the city's most famous attraction. The hot water bubbles up at a rate of 250,000 gallons (over a million litres) a day, filling the pool, surrounded by classical statues. You can taste sulphuric water in the adjoining **Pump Room**, if you're so inclined. Although its opening is behind schedule, **Thermae Bath Spa** on Hot Bath Street (01225 477051, www.thermaebath.com, open daily) is due to open in 2005 – the website has regularly updated information.
Adjacent to the Roman baths are the noble towers of **Bath Abbey** (Abbey Churchyard, 01225 422462). It was built on the site of the Saxon church where Edgar, first king of a united England, was crowned back in 973. If the crypt is open, you can trace the building's history through the centuries in its stones and artefacts.
Bath has close to 20 museums, including the **Building of Bath Museum** and the **Museum of East Asian Art**, which contains a fine collection of Chinese jade carvings. Opposite, in the Assembly Rooms (the social focus of high society in Georgian times), there's the renowned **Museum of Costume**, where the oldest posh togs displayed date back to the 1660s. On Bridge Street, the **Victoria Art Gallery** (01225 477233) houses a collection of British and European art from the 15th century to the present. The **American Museum in Britain** contains reconstructed US domestic interiors from the 17th, 18th and 19th centuries.
The grandest street in Bath is the much-photographed **Royal Crescent**, a curl of 30 grand white houses designed by John Wood the Younger between 1767 and 1775. The house at **No.1** is furnished in period style with a restored Georgian garden (closed Dec-mid Feb). Nearby is the **Circus**, designed by the elder John Wood and completed by his son in 1767.
The **River Avon**, spanned by the Italianate shop-lined **Pulteney Bridge**, adds to the city's appeal. There are walks beside the river and the

Kennet and Avon Canal; in summer boats can be hired from the Victorian **Bath Boating Station** (Forester Road, 01225 312900).

American Museum in Britain
Claverton Manor, BA2 7BD (01225 460503/www.americanmuseum.org). **Open** *Late Mar-end Oct, mid Nov-mid Dec* noon-5pm Tue-Sun. Closed early Nov, mid Dec-late Mar. **Admission** £6.50; £5 concessions; free under-5s. **Credit** AmEx, MC, V.

Building of Bath Museum
The Countess of Huntingdon's Chapel, The Vineyards, BA1 5NA (01225 333895/www.bath-preservation-trust.org.uk). **Open** *Mid Feb-Nov* 10.30am-5pm Tue-Sun. Closed Dec-mid Feb. **Admission** £4; £3 concessions; £1.50 6-16s; free under-6s. **Credit** AmEx, MC, V.

Museum of Costume
The Assembly Rooms, Bennett Street, BA1 2QH (01225 477789/www.museumofcostume.co.uk). **Open** 11am-5pm daily. **Admission** £6; £4-£5 concessions; free under-6s. **Credit** MC, V.

No.1 Royal Crescent
1 Royal Crescent, BA1 2LR (01225 428126/ www.bath-preservation-trust.org.uk). **Open** *Mid Feb-Oct* 10.30am-5pm Tue-Sun. *Nov* 10.30am-4pm

Rambling free

One of the best ways to explore the countryside around London is to go on one of the many easily accessible walks. The new edition of *Time Out Country Walks* lists 30 walks close to London, which all start and end at a train station and give lunch and tea options for those who want a breather. Nicholas Albery created the first issue of this book in which he publicised the self-organising Saturday Walkers' Club (SWC), which, six years later, is still thriving and has contributed to the writing of Volume II. Members meet each week to do a walk from this book. They may choose a short or circular walk along the Thames Valley, a coastal walk or a ramble in the South Downs. The walks are organised way ahead and are listed in *Country Walks* right up until the end of 2007 – for instance, if you joined a walk on 18 June 2005 it would be an 18.1km (11.3-mile) walk from Lewes via West Firle Circular, in the South Downs – and all those who buy this book are invited to join the SWC on walks.
Time Out Country Walks can be bought from all good bookshops, for £12.99.

Tue-Sun. *1st 2wks Dec* 10.30am-4pm Sat, Sun. Last entry 30mins before closing. Closed mid Dec-mid Feb. **Admission** £4; £3.50 concessions; free under-5s; family £12. **Credit** MC, V.

Roman Baths
Abbey Churchyard, BA1 1LZ (01225 477785/ www.romanbaths.co.uk). **Open** *Nov-Feb* 9.30am-5.30pm daily. *Mar-June, Sept, Oct* 9am-6pm daily. *July, Aug* 9am-10pm daily. Last entry 1hr before closing. **Admission** £8.50; £4.80-£7.50 concessions; free under-6s. **Credit** MC, V.

Where to eat & drink

Bath has a formidable gourmet reputation. Four of the best restaurants are the classic and Mediterranean **Pimpernel's** (Royal Crescent Hotel, 16 Royal Crescent, 01225 823333, set lunch £18 2 courses, £25 3 courses), classy Modern British **Moody Goose** (7A Kingsmead Square, 01225 466688, main courses £16-£19.50), recently refurbished **Olive Tree** (Queensbury Hotel, Russell Street, 01225 447928; main courses £18-£19.50; set lunch £17.50, set dinner £25), and the **Priory** (Bath Priory Hotel, Weston Road, 01225 331 922, main courses £26), where you'll find the kind of country house dining that dreams are made of.

At **Sally Lunn's Refreshment House & Museum** (4 North Parade Passage, 01225 461634, main courses £8-£9) you can sample the buns made fashionable in the 1680s.

Popular pubs include the **Bell Inn** in Walcot Street, the **Old Green Tree** on Green Street, and the 300-year-old **Crystal Palace** on Abbey Green with its walled garden.

Where to stay

Harington's Hotel (8-10 Queen Street, 01225 461728, www.haringtonshotel.co.uk, doubles £88-£128) is the best-value central hotel. **Holly Lodge** (8 Upper Oldfield Park, 01225 424042, doubles £79-£97) is a classy B&B perched high above the city. The **Queensberry Hotel** (Russell Street, 01225 447928, www.the queensberry.co.uk, doubles £100-£285) provides Regency elegance in the centre of town. **Royal Crescent** (16 Royal Crescent, 01225 823333, www.royalcrescent.co.uk, doubles £210-£380) is the place to come if money is no object.

Getting there

By train
Trains to Bath Spa leave hourly from Paddington most days (1hr 25mins).

By coach
National Express coaches to Bath leave from Victoria Coach Station (3hrs 20mins).

Sea-fresh snacks on Brighton beach.

By car

Take Junction 18 off the M4, then follow the A46 to Bath. Use park & rides to get into the centre.

Tourist information

Tourist Information Centre

Abbey Chambers, Abbey Churchyard, BA1 1LY (0906 711 2000/www.visitbath.co.uk). **Open** *May-Sept* 9.30am-6pm Mon-Sat; 10am-4pm Sun. *Oct-Apr* 9.30am-5pm Mon-Sat; 10am-4pm Sun.

Brighton

Pretty Victorian Brighton seems to trip down the hill upon which it is built, and dash toward the sea on a perpetual holiday. Its creamy gold and white architecture has long been a draw for coachloads of tourists and day-trippers from London, just over an hour away by train.

The presence of universities and language schools make this one of the youngest and most multicultural cities outside London. With more than 60 per cent of the population under the age of 45, the 'vegetarian capital of Europe' also has a large and thriving gay and lesbian scene.

Brighton began life as Bristmestune, a small fishing village, and so it remained until 1783, when Prince George (later George IV) rented a farmhouse here. He became the centre of a kind of hip court in waiting, and he kept the architect John Nash busy converting a modest abode into a faux-oriental pleasure palace. That building is now the elaborate-to-the-point-of-gaudy **Royal Pavilion**, where guided tours are full of quirky facts. Next door, the **Brighton Museum & Art Gallery** (Royal Pavilion Gardens, 01273 290900) has entertaining displays and a good permanent art collection.

Only two of Brighton's three Victorian piers are (barely) still standing. Lacy, delicate **Brighton Pier** is a clutter of hotdog stands,

karaoke, candyfloss and fairground rides, filled with customers in the summertime. But sadly, the **West Pier** is now a spooky, twisted ruin. It had been closed since 1975, while the city dithered over what to do about it. As it did nothing, time did its work, weakening the pier's foundations. Finally, in 2003 a violent storm and fire damage delivered the *coup de grâce*. The pier's future is undecided but the West Pier Trust hopes that reconstruction will go ahead.

With seven miles of coastline, Brighton has all the seaside resort trappings, hence the free **Brighton Fishing Museum** (201 King's Road Arches, on the lower prom between the piers, 01273 723064) and the **Sea-Life Centre**, the world's oldest functioning aquarium.

Perhaps reflecting its singular character, the town has a huge number of independent shops, boutiques and art stores. The best shopping for clothes, records and gift shops is found in and around **North Laine** and in the charming network of narrow cobbled streets known as the **Lanes**, which contain dozens of jewellers, clothiers and antiques shops.

After dark, Brighton rocks. Pick up club flyers on Gardner Street and Kensington Gardens on Saturday afternoons, or check listings mags such as *The Latest* or *The Brighton Source*.

The Royal Pavilion

Brighton, BN1 1EE (01273 292820/www.royal pavilion.org.uk). **Open** *Apr-Sept* 9.30am-5.45pm daily. *Oct-Mar* 10am-5.15pm daily. Last admission 45mins before closing. **Admission** £5.95; £3.50-£4.20 concessions. **Guided tours** (£1.50 extra) 11.30am, 2.30pm daily. **Credit** AmEx, MC, V.

Sea-Life Centre

Marine Parade, BN2 1TB (01273 604234). **Open** *Mar-Oct* 10am-6pm daily. Last entry 5pm. *Nov-Feb* 10am-5pm. Last entry 4pm. **Admission** £9.50; £5.50-£7.50 concessions; free under-2s. **Credit** AmEx, DC, MC, V.

Canterbury's **Goods Shed**. *See p350*.

Where to eat & drink

There's a menu of beautifully presented, wholly authentic French fare at **La Fourchette** (105 Western Road, 01273 722556, set lunch £10-£13, set dinner £22-£28).

One of England's most celebrated vegetarian restaurants is here: **Terre à Terre** (71 East Street, 01273 729051, main courses £11.50-£12.50) is known for its innovative menu. The newly opened **Real Eating Company** (86-87 Western Road, Hove, 01273 221444, main courses £7.50-£15.95) is a great place for lunch, and fantastic food and considerate staff make **Seven Dials** (1-3 Buckingham Place, 01273 885555, set lunch £10-£15, set dinner £10-£25) an excellent choice for dinner.

This city's laid-back attitude makes it ideal for café culture, and its excellent coffeeshops include **Nia Café Bar** (87-88 Trafalgar Street, 01273 671371) and **Alfresco** (Milkmaid Pavilion, King's Road Arches, 01273 206523).

Of the traditional pubs, the **Cricketers** (15 Black Lion Street), the **Druid's Head** (9 Brighton Place) and the **Battle of Trafalgar** (34 Guildford Road) all have the most charm.

Classic Brighton boozer the **Prince Albert** (48 Trafalgar Street) has theme nights. The **St James** (16 Madeira Place) is a pre-club bar with DJs. **Sidewinder** (65 Upper St James Street) and the **Hampton** (57 Upper North Street) and **Riki-Tik** (18A Bond Street) are also reliable bets for a good night out.

Of the gay bars, the most fun is to be had at the **Amsterdam Hotel** (11-12 Marine Parade). **Doctor Brighton's** (16 King's Road) on the seafront is also worth a punt, with DJs playing house and techno. And for the ladeeez… the **Candy Bar** (33 St James Street) is a strictly women-only lesbian hangout.

Where to stay

Given Brighton's popularity, it's perhaps not surprising that hotel prices here can be high. An interesting choice is one of the newest: **Seattle** (01273 679799, www.aliasseattle.com, doubles £95-£115), which is situated on the newly developed Brighton Marina and feels much like a state-of-the-art liner. For another good quality stop, try **Hotel du Vin** (2-6 Ship Street, 01273 718588, www.hotelduvin. com, doubles £140-£355), or **Blanch House** (17 Atlingworth Street, 01273 603504, www.blanchhouse.co.uk, doubles £125-£220), which is unassuming from the outside, but highly chic. **Nineteen** (19 Broad Street, 01273 675529, www.hotelnineteen.co.uk, doubles £95-£160) has just seven rooms in a stylish townhouse. **Hotel Pelirocco** (10 Regency Square, 01273 327055,www.hotelpelirocco.co.uk, doubles £90-£130) is funky, with themed decor in the bedrooms. **Hotel Twenty One** (21 Charlotte Street, 01273 686450, doubles £60-£95) is a well-run B&B a few minutes' walk from the Palace Pier and town centre. **Oriental Hotel** (9 Oriental Place, 01273 205050, doubles £70-£140) is laid-back and centrally located. For a clean, cheap, central but otherwise rather bland chain try **Brighton Premier Lodge** (144 North Street, 0870 990 6340, www.premier lodge.com, doubles £54).

Getting there

By train

Trains for Brighton leave from Victoria (50mins) or King's Cross (1hr 10mins).

By coach

National Express coaches for Brighton leave from Victoria Coach Station (1hr 50mins).

By car

Take the M23, then the A23 to Brighton.

Tourist information

Tourist Information Centre

10 Bartholomew Square (0906 711 2255/ www.visitbrighton.com). **Open** *July, Aug* 9am-5.30pm Mon-Fri; 10am-6pm Sat; 10am-4pm Sun. *Jan-June, Sept, Oct* 9am-5pm Mon-Fri; 10am-5pm Sat; 10am-4pm Sun. *Nov, Dec* 9am-5pm Mon-Fri; 10am-5pm Sat.

Cambridge

Gorgeous, intimidating Cambridge has the feel of an enclosed city. With its narrow streets and tall old buildings blocking out the sun in the town centre, it has a way of conveying disapproval to visitors. But it's worth persevering as behind the façade is a pretty little town of green parks and streams where time seems to have stopped back in the 18th century.

Cambridge first became an academic centre when a fracas at Oxford – apparently involving a dead woman, an arrow and a scholar holding a bow – led to some of the learned monks bidding a hasty farewell to Oxford and a hearty how do you do to Cambridge.

Once the dust settled, the monks needed somewhere to peddle their knowledge. The first college, **Peterhouse**, was established in 1284. The original hall survives, though most of the present buildings are 19th century. Up the road is **Corpus Christi College**, founded in 1352. Its Old Court dates from that time and is linked by a gallery to its original chapel, the 11th-century **St Bene't's Church** (Bene't Street, 01223 353903), the oldest surviving building in Cambridge.

Down Silver Street is 15th-century **Queens' College**; most of its original buildings remain, including the timbered president's lodge. The inner courts are wonderfully picturesque.

Further up on King's Parade, grand **King's College** was founded by Henry VI in 1441 and is renowned for its **chapel** (01223 331155), built between 1446 and 1515. It has a breathtaking interior with the original stained glass. Attend a service in term-time to hear its choirboys.

Further north, pretty **Trinity College** was founded in 1336 by Edward III and then refounded by Henry VIII in 1546. A fine crowd of Tudor buildings surrounds the Great Court where, legend has it, Lord Byron was known to bathe naked in the fountain with his pet bear. Wittgenstein studied and taught here, and the library (designed by Wren) is open to visitors at certain times (noon-2pm Mon-Fri all year, 10.30am-12.30pm Sat term-time, 01223 338400).

Further on, at the corner of Bridge and St John's Streets, is the 12th-century **Round Church** (Church of the Holy Sepulchre, Bridge Street, 01223 311602), the oldest of only four remaining round churches in the country.

Behind the main colleges, the beautiful meadows bordering the willow-shaded River Cam are known as the **Backs**. This is idyllic for summer strolling, or 'punting' (pushing flat boats with long poles). Punts can be hired; **Scudamore's Boatyard** (01223 359750) is the largest operator. If you get handy at the surprisingly difficult skill of punting, you could

boat down to the **Orchard Tea Rooms** (Mill Way, Grantchester, 01223 845788) where Rupert Brooke lodged when he was a student. There's a small museum dedicated to the poet (rather prosaically) in the car park outside.

Among Cambridge's relatively few non-collegiate attractions, the **Fitzwilliam Museum** on Trumpington Street (01223 332900) has an outstanding collection of antiquities and Old Masters; **Kettle's Yard** (Castle Street, 01223 352124) has fine displays of 20th-century art; and the **Botanic Gardens** (01223 336265) on Bateman Street offer a relaxing place to watch the grass grow.

Where to eat & drink

Graffiti (Hotel Felix, White House Lane, Huntingdon Road, 01223 277977, main courses £11.95-£23.95) has a beautiful terrace for summer dining, and a fine Mediterranean menu. **Midsummer House** (Midsummer Common, 01223 369299, set lunch £20-£26, set dinner £48.50-£60) is where chef-patron Daniel Clifford creates posh and inventive French dishes in a bid to earn a second Michelin star.

For superlative (but pricey) Chinese food, try **Peking** (21 Burleigh Street, 01223 354755, main courses £7-£14).

Cambridge has many creaky old inns in which to enjoy the city's decent local ales. The **Eagle** on Bene't Street (01223 505020) is the

King's College.

most famous, but there are many, including the **Pickerel Inn** (30 Magdalene Street, 01223 355068), **Fort St George** by the river on Midsummer Common (01223 354327), the **Mill** (14 Mill Lane, 01223 357026) and the **Anchor** (Silver Street, 01223 353554) on the river.

A stroll along the Cam from Midsummer Common will take you to the picturesque **Green Dragon** (5 Water Street, 01223 505035), with its beer garden by the river.

Where to stay

Because of the university, there are plenty of guesthouses in town, and the **Meadowcroft Hotel** (16 Trumpington Road, 01223 346120, www.meadowcrofthotel.co.uk, doubles £130-£150) is one of the best. Also lovely is the **Cambridge Garden House Moat House** (Granta Place, Mill Lane, 01223 259988, www.moathousehotels.com, doubles £200-£254) on the banks of the Cam. A mile out of town, the new **Hotel Felix** has a great restaurant, landscaped gardens and stylishly elegant rooms (Whitehouse Lane, Huntingdon Road, 01223 277977, www.hotelfelix.co.uk, doubles £155-£260). For budget travellers, the simple modern cells of the **Sleeperz Hotel** betray minimalist Scandinavian and Japanese influences (Station Road, 01223 304050, doubles £55).

Getting there

By train

Trains to Cambridge leave from King's Cross (50mins) or Liverpool Street (1hr 15mins).

By coach

National Express coaches to Cambridge leave from Victoria Coach Station (1hr 50mins).

By car

Take Junction 11 or Junction 12 off the M11.

Tourist information

Tourist Information Centre

Old Library, Wheeler Street (0906 586 2526/www.tourismcambridge.com). **Open** *Apr-Oct* 10am-6.30pm Mon-Fri; 10am-5pm Sat; 11am-4pm Sun. *Nov-Mar* 10am-5.30pm Mon-Fri; 10am-5pm Sat.

Canterbury

The soaring towers of the cathedral, and the swirl of medieval streets around it, never let you forget where you are when you're wandering through this lovely, historic town. The home of the Church of England since St Augustine was based here in 597, the ancient city of Canterbury is rich in atmosphere.

Its busy tourist trade and large university provide a colourful counterweight to the brooding mass of history present in its old buildings and, of course, the glorious **Canterbury Cathedral**. Be warned, this is one of the most egregious of England's charging cathedrals – you have to pay even to get into the walled-off cathedral close. But it is, quite simply, worth it. It has superb stained glass, stone vaulting and a vast Norman crypt. A plaque near the altar marks what is believed to be the exact spot where Archbishop Thomas à Becket was murdered. **Trinity Chapel** contains the site of the original shrine, plus the tombs of Henry IV and the Black Prince.

The pilgrimage to Becket's tomb was the focus of Chaucer's *Canterbury Tales*. At the exhibition named after the book, visitors are given a device that they point at tableaux inspired by Chaucer's tales of a knight, a miller and others, to hear the stories.

Eastbridge Hospital (High Street, 01227 471688), founded to provide shelter for pilgrims, retains the smell of ages past. The **Roman Museum** has the remains of a townhouse and mosaic floor among its treasures.

The city centre nestling up to the cathedral is a pleasure to explore.

Canterbury Cathedral

The Precincts, CT1 2EH (01227 762862/www. canterbury-cathedral.org). **Open** *Easter-Sept* 9am-5pm Mon-Sat; 12.30-2.30pm, 4.30-5.30pm Sun. *Oct-Easter* 9am-4.30pm Mon-Sat; 12.30-2.30pm, 4.30-5.30pm Sun. During evensong certain parts of cathedral are closed. **Admission** £4; £3 concessions; free under-5s. **Credit** MC, V.

Canterbury Tales

St Margaret's Street, CT1 2TG (01227 454888/479227/www.canterburytales.org.uk). **Open** *Mid Feb-June, Sept, Oct* 10am-5pm daily. *July, Aug* 9.30am-5pm daily. *Nov-mid Feb* 10am-4.30pm daily. **Admission** £6.95; £5.25-£5.95 concessions; free under-4s. **Credit** MC, V.

Roman Museum

Butchery Lane, CT1 2JR (01227 785575/www. canterbury-museums.co.uk). **Open** *Nov-May* 10am-5pm Mon-Sat. *June-Oct* 10am-5pm Mon-Sat; 1.30-5pm Sun. Last entry 1hr before closing. **Admission** £2.80; £1.75 concessions; free under-5s. **No credit cards**.

Where to eat & drink

The **Goods Shed** (Station Road West, 01227 459153, main courses £8-£16) is just perfect for a leisurely lunch or dinner. **Café des Amis du Mexique** (93-95 St Dunstan's Street, 01227 464390, main courses £6.95-£14.95) is upbeat and popular, while the refined atmosphere and Modern European cuisine at **Augustine's** (102 Longport, 01227 453063, main courses £9.50-

£15.90) make it a perfect treat. Stop for a drink in the peaceful **Unicorn** with its kitsch garden (61 St Dunstan's Street, 01227 463187).

Where to stay

Prices are good at the 19th-century **Acacia Lodge & Tanglewood** B&B (39-40 London Road, 01227 769955/www.acacialodge.com, doubles £46-£55). Mid range is the **Coach House**, a recently refurbished B&B (34 Watling Steet, 01227 784324, doubles £60-£70). At the other end of the scale, the **Falstaff** is a lovely historic hotel (8-10 St Dunstan's Street, www.corushotels.co.uk, 01227 462138, doubles £112).

Getting there

By train
From Victoria Station to Canterbury East (1hr 20mins), or from Charing Cross to Canterbury West (1hr 30mins).

By coach
National Express from Victoria (1hr 50mins).

By car
Take the A2 then the M2 then the A2 again.

Tourist information

Tourist Information Centre
12-13 Sun Street, The Buttermarket, CT1 2HX (01227 378100/www.canterbury.co.uk). **Open** *Jan-Mar, Nov, Dec* 9.30am-5pm Mon-Sat, 10am-4pm Sun. *Apr-Oct* 9.30am-5.30pm Mon-Sat; 10am-4pm Sun.

Oxford

With its soaring spires, domed library and narrow old streets, Oxford has a noble, ancient beauty that is not undone by the packs of French schoolchildren roaming its streets and giggling at its robed students glumly trudging off to take their formal exams.

The myriad colleges that make up **Oxford University** have defined this town since the middle of the 12th century. Nearly everything else in town – the galleries and museums, the good restaurants, the expansive green parks – stems from the schools.

This wasn't always the way. Oxford arose as a Saxon burg built to defend Wessex from the dastardly Danes (the 11th-century **St Michael's Tower** in Cornmarket Street is the only survivor of this period). The dissolution of the monasteries under Henry VIII meant that much of Oxford's land and money passed from the Church to the colleges, setting the town's course.

Most of Oxford's many colleges are open to the public and the chapel at **Christ Church College** also serves as Oxford's cathedral. **Magdalen College** (pronounced 'maudlin') has a lovely meadow and deer park. Nearby **Merton College**, founded in 1264, has a medieval library and garden.

Other centres of academia include the grand **Bodleian**, the university's huge, reference-only library in a spectacular building, with the oldest part dating back to 1488. It contains every book published in the United Kingdom and Ireland.

The **Real Eating Company**. *See p348.*

Trips Out of Town

The **University Botanic Gardens** (Rose Lane, 01865 286690) are the oldest in Great Britain and have occupied this spot by the River Cherwell for more than 375 years.

Oxford's non-university sights include **Carfax Tower** (01865 792653), the only surviving part of the 14th-century church of St Martin, with its two 'quarter-boy' clocks (they chime every quarter-hour). Climb the 99 steps to the top for fantastic views.

A wealth of museums ranges from the quirky (and free) **Pitt Rivers** (Parks Road, 01865 270927), with its voodoo dolls, shrunken heads and other ethnological delights, to the all-embracing (also free) **Ashmolean** (Beaumont Street, 01865 278000), the country's oldest museum housing the university's collection of art and antiquities. There's also **Modern Art Oxford** (30 Pembroke Street, 01865 722733), which has established an international reputation for pioneering exhibitions of contemporary work.

Central Oxford, with its sweet **Covered Market** (opened in 1774) linking Market Street to the High, its car-unfriendly streets and bicycling youth, is a wonderful place to wander. It can get uncomfortably clogged with tourists, but there are always the neighbourhoods of Jericho, Summertown and Cowley to explore. Beyond Jericho, wild horses roam on the vast expanse of lovely **Port Meadow**.

Bodleian Library

Broad Street, OX1 3BG (01865 277000/www.bodley. ox.ac.uk). **Open** 9am-4.45pm Mon-Fri; 9am-1pm Sat. **Guided tours** (01865 277224) *Mid Mar-Oct* 10.30am, 11.30am, 2pm, 3pm Mon-Fri; 10.30am, 11.30am Sat. *Nov-mid Mar* 2pm, 3pm Mon-Fri; 10.30am, 11.30am Sat. **Admission** *Guided tour £4. Audio tour £2. Ages 14 & over only.* **No credit cards**.

Where to eat & drink

Enjoy excellent lunchtime dim sum at **Liaison** (29 Castle Street, 01865 242944, main courses £6.50-£28). **Branca** (111 Walton Street, 01865 556111, main courses £8.25-£16.95) is perfect for those seeking a zippy atmosphere with their pasta. Popular diner **Joe's** (21 Cowley Road, 01865 201120, main courses £7.95-£11.95) is renowned for its excellent brunches. **Cherwell Boat House** (Bardwell Road, 01865 552746, set lunch £12.50-£21.50, set dinner £23.50) is a riverside favourite.

Oxford has loads of pubs, but few are cheap or quiet – the 16th-century **King's Arms** in Holywell Street (01865 242369) is studenty with good beer; the **Turf Tavern** (01865 243235) between Hertford and New Colleges is Oxford's oldest inn. The **Perch** (01865 728891) on Binsey Lane has a garden with children's play area.

The **Ashmolean**.

Where to stay

Burlington House is an outstanding small hotel with B&B prices, but a little way out of town (374 Banbury Road, 01865 513513, doubles £80-£95). The **Old Parsonage** (1 Banbury Road, 01865 310210, doubles £155-£200) is classy and ancient, and the **Old Bank Hotel** is sleek, modernist and arty (92-94 High Street, 01865 799599, doubles £160-£320). Next to the station is the prosaic **Royal Oxford Hotel** (Park End Street, 01865 248432, doubles £129).

Getting there

By train

There are regular trains from Paddington (1hr); your rail ticket qualifies you for a free ride into the centre on an electric bus (every 10mins).

By coach

There are frequent, cheap, fast services from several London departure points; details from **National Express** (1hr 40mins), **Stagecoach** (01865 772250) and **Oxford Bus Company** (01865 785410).

By car

Take Junction 8 off the M40, and then the A40 into town. Park at the edge and use the park & rides.

Tourist information

Oxford Information Centre

15-16 Broad Street, OX1 3AS (01865 726871/www.vis-itoxford.org). **Open** *Easter-Oct* 9.30am-5pm Mon-Sat; 10am-3.30pm Sun. *Nov-Easter* 9.30am-5pm Mon-Sat.

Stratford-upon-Avon

This chocolate-box of a town is England's second biggest tourist draw (after London), and for good reason. It's charming, historic and filled with interesting little sights, but unless you visit in the off-season you won't get much chance to appreciate any of that. The problem with Stratford is that it gets almost unbearably crowded in the summertime, which can make it hard to enjoy its beauty. Don't be put off by the aggressive marketing of 'Shakespeare Country' – half-timbered architecture overkill, over-zealous cobbling and teashops everywhere. It can all be forgiven if you're one of Will's fans.

There's never a shortage of his works to see, and the **Royal Shakespeare Theatre** is the place to see them. If you can't get a ticket, take a backstage tour and visit the **RSC Collection** museum of props and costumes.

Stratford has been a **market** town since 1169 and, in a way, that's still what it does best. See it on a Friday, when locals flock in from outlying villages to the colourful stalls at the top of Wood Street.

In the town centre, with its medieval grid pattern, many fine old buildings survive, among them **Harvard House** (High Street, 01789 204507, open June-Oct), which dates from 1596. It was home to Katharine Rogers, mother of John Harvard, founder of Harvard University, and now houses a pewter collection.

In the town centre are **Shakespeare's Birthplace** (01789 204016) on Henley Street; **Hall's Croft** (01789 292107) on Old Town, named after Dr John Hall, who married the Bard's daughter Susanna; and **Nash's House** (01789 292325) on Chapel Street, which once belonged to the first husband of Shakespeare's granddaughter, Elizabeth. In the garden of the latter are the foundations of **New Place**, the writer's last home, demolished in 1759. Shakespeare was educated at **Stratford Grammar School**, on Church Street, and buried in **Holy Trinity** church.

A mile and a half away at **Shottery**, and accessible from Stratford by public footpath, is **Anne Hathaway's Cottage** (01789 292100), where Shakespeare's wife lived before she married him. The girlhood home of his mother, **Mary Arden's House** (01789 293455), is at **Wilmcote**, a pleasant four-mile stroll along the Stratford Canal. Both may also be reached by bus; there are also trains to Wilmcote.

Stratford's charms are enhanced by the **River Avon** and the **Stratford Canal** and the walks alongside. Spend some time on the water by hiring a boat at **Stratford Marina**. The long-established **Avon Boating** (01789 267073) has punts and rowing boats for hire.

Royal Shakespeare Company
Waterside, CV37 6BB (box office 0870 6091110/tours 01789 403405/www.rsc.org.uk). **Backstage tours** times vary; phone to check. **Tickets** *Tour* £5; £4 concessions. *Performances* prices vary. **Credit** MC, V.

Where to eat & drink

Callands (13-14 Meer Street, 01789 269304, set lunch £6.50-£8.95, set dinner £19.95-£23.95) offers eclectic modern cooking. For British ingredients with a French flair, try **Restaurant Margaux** (6 Union Street, 01789 269106, main courses £8.95-£18), while the **Fox & Goose Inn** (Armscote, off A3400, 01608 682293, main courses £8.95-£14.95) may be off the beaten track but is well worth the journey for its boudoir-style dining room and home-cooked food.

Drink with thesps at the **Dirty Duck** (aka the **Black Swan**, Waterside, 01789 297312).

Where to stay

Caterham House Hotel (58-59 Rother Street, 01789 267309, doubles £80-£85) is close to the Royal Shakespeare Theatre and popular with both audience and actors. The **Falcon Hotel** (Chapel Street, 0870 609 6122, doubles £80-£140) is well olde worlde: at least 20 of the 84 en suite rooms are in a 16th-century inn. Another good choice, **Victoria Spa Lodge** (Bishopton Lane, 01789 267985, doubles £65) has the feel of a grand country house; Princess Victoria stayed here in 1837.

Tourist information

Tourist Information Centre
Bridgefoot, CV37 6GW (01789 293127/www. shakespeare-country.co.uk). **Open** *Apr-Sept* 9.30am-5.30pm Mon-Sat; 10.30am-4.30pm Sun. *Oct-Mar* 9.30am-5pm Mon-Sat.

Getting there

By train
Regular service from Paddington (2hrs 10mins).

By coach
National Express (2hrs 45mins).

By car
Take Junction 15 off the M40, then A46 into town.

Winchester

Lovely, regal Winchester, the ancient capital of Wessex is often overlooked by international travellers, and more's the pity. It dates back to 450 BC, when an Iron Age settlement was

Grand designs

England's castles and stately homes are a quintessential feature of its landscape, and they often provide some of the countryside's loveliest settings for walks and picnics (surrounded by the handiwork of some of history's more creative gardeners). Not listed among those below is **Althorp**, the burial place of Diana, Princess of Wales, which is in Northamptonshire, a 90-minute drive from London (contact 01604 770107, www.althorp.com for details). The house is only open during July, August and September.

Arundel Castle

Arundel, West Sussex BN18 9AB (01903 882173/www.arundelcastle.org). **Getting there** *By train* from Victoria (1hr 30mins). *By car* A24 then A280 and A27. **Open** *Apr-Oct* noon-5pm Mon-Fri, Sun (last entry 4pm). **Admission** £11; £9 concessions; £7.50 5-16s; £31 family. **Credit** MC, V.
The original castle, built in the 11th century, was damaged during the Civil War, then remodelled in the 18th and 19th centuries. Inside is a collection of 16th-century furniture, and paintings by Van Dyck, Gainsborough and Reynolds, among others. Don't miss the 14th-century Fitzalan Chapel, a Roman Catholic chapel inside an Anglican church so that the dukes and their families could worship according to Catholic rites. Home to a clutch of tombs of Dukes of Norfolk past, it shows no signs of the time when Oliver Cromwell used it as a stable.

Audley End

Saffron Walden, Essex CB11 4JF (01799 522399/www.english-heritage.org.uk). **Getting there** *By train* Liverpool Street to Audley End (1hr) then 1-mile walk or 2min taxi ride. *By car* J8 off M11 then B1383. **Open** *Apr-Sept* 10am-6pm Mon, Wed-Sun; tours by appointment. **Admission** £8.50; £6.40 concessions; £4.30 5-16s; £22 family. **Credit** MC, V.
This unmissable Jacobean mansion was the largest house in the country when it was built for Thomas Howard, first Earl of Suffolk, in 1614. It was later owned by Charles II, but was given back to the Howards in the 18th century. The latter demolished two-thirds of it in order to make the place more manageable. Many of the rooms, brimming with the accumulated wealth of its aristocratic owners, have been restored to Robert Adam's 1760s designs. 'Capability' Brown landscaped the gardens.

Blenheim Palace

Woodstock, Oxfordshire OX20 1PX (0870 060 2080/www.blenheimpalace.com). **Getting there** *By train* Paddington to Oxford (1hr) then 30-40min bus ride. *By car* J9 off M40 then A34 and A44. **Open** *Palace & gardens* mid Feb-Oct 10.30am-4.45pm (last entry) daily; *Nov-Dec* 10.30am-4.45pm Wed-Sun. *Park* 9am-4.45pm daily. **Admission** *Palace, park & gardens* £11; £8.50 concessions; £5.50 5-15s; £28 family. *Park & gardens* £6; £4 concessions; £2 5-15s; £14 family. **Credit** AmEx, MC, V.

established on St Catherine's Hill, just to the east. The Romans moved it to create the city of Venta Belgarum west of the River Itchen in around AD 70. The first cathedral was begun after the arrival of the Saxons, in 648.

The town is on the long list of possible locations for King Arthur's Camelot. In homage, a round table is hung in the **Great Hall** (Great Hall Castle Avenue, 01962 846476), the last remaining part of what was for 500 years one of England's principal royal palaces.

Winchester's medieval core is still very much the heart of town, with winding lanes of typically English charm – neat, compact and easy to wander. The **cathedral**, a majestic Norman edifice begun in 1079, dominates it all. Inside, there are too many treasures to detail, among them 12th-century wall paintings and the grave of Jane Austen. The Triforium gives

you a spectacular view of the transepts. In the 17th-century library the centrepiece is the Winchester Bible, a gorgeous illuminated manuscript begun in 1160.

Winchester College was founded in 1382. The oldest continuously running public school in England, it remains prominent in the life of the town. On College Street, the now-ruined **Wolvesey Castle** (01962 854766) was the main residence of the Bishops of Winchester in the 12th century.

South of town the **Hospital of St Cross** (St Cross Road, 01962 851375), founded in 1136 as an almshouse, is the oldest still-functioning house of charity in the country.

Seven miles south, **Marwell Zoological Park** has some 1,000 animals living in 100 acres of parkland, with picnic areas, World of Lemurs and Penguin World.

After defeating the French at the Battle of Blenheim in 1704, John Churchill, first Duke of Marlborough, was so handsomely rewarded that he could afford to build this fabulous palace. Designed by Sir John Vanbrugh and set in huge grounds landscaped by (guess who?) 'Capability' Brown, Blenheim is the only non-royal residence in the country grand enough to be given the title 'palace'. The grounds include a butterfly house, a miniature railway, a lake for boating and fishing, and what has the dubious honour of being the world's biggest symbolic hedge maze.

Hatfield House

Hatfield, Hertfordshire AL9 5NQ (01707 287010/www.hatfield-house.co.uk). **Getting there** *By train* King's Cross to Hatfield (25mins). *By car* J4 off A1(M). **Open** Easter-Sept only. *House* noon-4pm Sat-Wed. *West Gardens* 11am-5.30pm Sat-Wed. *East Gardens* 11am-5.30pm Mon (except Bank Holidays). **Admission** *House, park & gardens* £8; £4 5-15s. *Park & gardens* £4.50; £3.50 5-15s. *Park only* £2; £1 5-15s. *Mon only* £6.50; £5 (house tour). **Credit** MC, V.
Built by Robert Cecil, Earl of Salisbury, in 1611, this superb Jacobean mansion oozes history. In the grounds stands the remaining wing of the Royal Palace of Hatfield, the childhood home of Queen Elizabeth I: she held her first Council of State here in 1558. The gardens include herb terraces, orchards and fountains restored to their former glory,

as well as a lovely woodland timber playground for children. A number of special events, such as craft fairs, run throughout the year.

Hever Castle

Hever, nr Edenbridge, Kent TN8 7NG (01732 865224/www.hevercastle.co.uk). **Getting there** *By train* Victoria to Edenbridge (1hr), then 5min taxi journey, or Victoria to Hever (1hr), then 1-mile walk. *By car* J5 off M25 then B2042 and B269, or J6 off M25 then A22, A25 and B269. **Open** *Mar-Oct* 11am-6pm daily. *Nov* 11am-dusk daily. **Admission** *House & gardens* £8.80; £7.40 concessions; £4.80 5-14s; free under-5s; £22.40 family. *Garden only* £7; £6 concessions; £4.60 5-14s; £18.60 family. **Credit** MC, V.
The childhood home of Anne Boleyn, and scene of Henry VIII's wooing of her, Hever is a 13th-century castle and 15th-century manor house. The buildings, gardens and lake were restored in the early 20th century by American millionaire Waldorf Astor (of posh hotel fame), who also built the 'Tudor' village behind it. Among other excellent exhibits, the castle contains precious paintings, a gruesome (and appropriate) exhibition of instruments of execution and two rare Books of Hours – illuminated manuscripts inscribed by Anne Boleyn. The grounds are glorious with a yew maze, secret grottoes and classic statuary. The water maze is inundated with dripping children in sunny weather. Check the website for seasonal events.

▶

Winchester is located at a junction of many long-distance footpaths across the **South Downs** and coastward. The tourist office has maps and guidance.

Marwell Zoological Park

Colden Common, Winchester, SO21 1JH (07626 943163/01962 777407/www.marwell.org.uk). **Open** *Apr-Oct* 10am-6pm daily. Last entry 4.30pm. *Nov-Mar* 10am-4pm daily. Last entry 2.30pm. **Admission** £11.50; £8-£9.50 concessions. **Credit** MC, V.

Winchester Cathedral & Close

The Close, SO23 9LS (01962 857200/www.winchester-cathedral.org.uk). **Open** *Cathedral* 8.30am-6pm Mon-Sat; 8.30am-5pm Sun. *Triforium & library* Mon; 11am-4.30pm Tue-Fri; 10.30am-4.30pm Sat. *Visitors' centre* 9.30am-5.30pm daily. **Admission** *Cathedral* free; recommended donation £3.50. *Triforium & library* £1; 50p concessions. **Credit** AmEx, MC, V.

Where to eat & drink

The kooky **Wykeham Arms** (75 Kingsgate Street, 01962 853834, main courses £10.75-£15.50) dates to 1755 and is more institution than pub. It's particularly popular with the upper echelons of Winchester society, so there'll be no dancing on the tables. There's a posh dining room and an inn (doubles £90-£120). Little has changed at **Chesil Rectory** (1 Chesil Street, 01962 851555, set lunch £35, set dinner £45 3 courses) even though it has a new owner and chef. A stylishly modern set-up is at **Loch Fyne** (18 Jewry Street, 01962 872930, main courses £10-£15) includes a menu dominated by fish with a Scottish heritage.

Of the many pubs, the tiny **Eclipse Inn** (25 The Square, 01962 865676, main courses £6.50-£6.75), once the rectory of St Lawrence's

Leeds Castle

*Broomfield, nr Maidstone, Kent ME17 1PL
(01622 765400/www.leeds-castle.com).*
Getting there *By train* Victoria to Bearsted
(1hr), then 10min bus transfer. *By car* J8 off
M20. **Open** *Mar-Oct* 10am-7pm daily (last entry
5pm). *Nov-mid Mar* 10am-5pm daily (last entry
3pm). **Admission** *Castle & park (peak season)*
£12.50; £11 concessions; £9 4-15s; £39
family. **Credit** MC, V.

The castle of queens (many a king gave it to
the wife), Leeds Castle was built by Normans
shortly after 1066, and fortified by various
royal householders, including Henrys V and VIII.
The last private owner was Lady Baillie, an
Anglo-American heiress, who bequeathed the
place to the Leeds Castle Foundation in 1974.
The old castle takes in the 12th-century cellar
and the 13th-century chapel, the gloriette or
keep, the bedrooms of various queens and the
heraldry room. The New Castle, rebuilt in
1822, has conference rooms and halls. A Dog
Collar Museum is in the gatehouse. Outside,
the woodland is fabulous in spring and the
gardens include glasshouses, vineyards and
an aviary. Black swans glide in the moat. The
yew maze has at its centre a shell and stone
grotto. The Culpeper Garden, the castle's
kitchen garden, is fragrant with herbs, including
the national collection of bergamot. It's also
worth consulting the website to check the
timetable of special events at the castle
(such as the peerless open-air concerts).

Windsor Castle

*High Street, Windsor, Berkshire SL4 1NJ
(01753 831118/www.royal.gov.uk).* **Getting
there** *By train* Paddington to Slough then
change for Windsor Central (45mins); Waterloo
to Eton & Windsor Riverside (1hr). *By car* J6 off
M4. **Open** *Mar-Sept* 9.45am-5.15pm (4pm last
entry) daily. *Oct-Feb* 9.45am-4.15pm (3pm last
entry) daily. *Changing of the Guard* (weather
permitting) Apr-June 11am daily; July-Mar every
other day, call ahead. **Admission** £12; £10
concessions; £6 4-15s; £30 family. **Credit**
AmEx, MC, V.

One of the Queen's official residences, Windsor
was the scene of many a red face back in June
2003, when comedian Aaron Barshak
gatecrashed Prince William's 21st birthday
party. Usually, however, the many visitors to
this, the oldest occupied castle in the world,
are well behaved. The 15th-century St George's
Chapel is the burial place of ten monarchs,
including Henry VIII and Queen Elizabeth the
Queen Mother, who died in 2002. The chapel
is closed to visitors on Sunday, although
worshippers are welcome. Queues are longest
for the Queen Mary's Dolls' House, designed
by Edward Lutyens. The miniature home has
flushing loos, real wine in tiny casks and
electric lights. State apartments include the
Waterloo Chamber, built to celebrate the
victory over the French in 1815. The Long
Walk crosses Windsor Great Park, a 5,000-acre
hunting ground dating back to the 13th century.

church, serves up reliable pub nosh, although
the **Old Vine**, also on the Square (01962
854616, main courses £4.50-£7), is bigger and
has a wider choice. Near the river, the **Mash
Tun** on Eastgate Street (01962 861440) is a
favourite among students unwinding after
a hard week hitting the books.

Where to stay

First choice for nostalgia junkies would be the
Wykeham Arms (*see p355*), but **Hotel du
Vin & Bistro** offers sober luxury and the bistro
bit is a lovely place for a meal (14 Southgate
Street, 01962 841414, www.hotel duvin.com, doubles £115-£230, main courses £14.50). A top end
B&B, **Enmill Barn** is in a huge converted barn
just two miles outside Winchester (Pitt, 01962
856740, doubles £60).

Getting there

By train

There's a regular train service to Winchester from
Waterloo (1hr).

By coach

National Express coaches leave for Winchester from
Victoria Coach Station (2hrs).

By car

Take Junction 9 off the M3, then use park & ride.

Tourist information

Tourist Information Centre

*The Guildhall, The Broadway, SO23 9LJ (01962
840500/www.winchester.gov.uk).* **Open** *May-Sept*
9.30am-5.30pm Mon-Sat; 11am-4pm Sun. *Oct-Apr*
10am-5pm Mon-Sat.

Waddesdon Manor

Waddesdon, nr Aylesbury, Buckinghamshire HP18 0JH (01296 653226/www.waddesdon. org.uk). **Getting there** *By train* Marylebone to Aylesbury (53mins) then bus. *By car* J9 off M40 then A41. **Open** *House* end Mar-Oct 11am-4pm Wed-Sun. *Grounds* Mar-Dec 10am-5pm Wed-Sun. **Admission** *House & grounds* £11; £8 5-16s; free under-5s. *Grounds only* £4; £2 5-16s; free under-5s. **No credit cards**. Ferdinand de Rothschild's French Renaissance-style château was constructed in the 1870s and houses one of the world's best collections of 18th-century French decorative art, sadly depleted after a burglary in June 2003. The wine cellars are famous worldwide – keep an eye out for tastings and events.

Windsor Castle.

Seaside towns

See also p347 **Brighton**.

Broadstairs & Margate

The **Isle of Thanet**, with its 24-mile coastal path, sandy coves and bucket-and-spade seaside towns, is like the land that time forgot. It's still 1954 here, and probably always will be.

Broadstairs is where Charles Dickens spent several years; the town enjoys an annual Dickens Festival (18-20 June 2005; phone 01843 861827 for details). The **Dickens House Museum** closes from mid October to Easter (2 Victoria Parade, 01843 861232).

Elsewhere, the popularity of Broadstairs derives from its seven beaches, the largest of which, **Viking Bay**, combines a crescent shoreline with a picturesque harbour and shops, amusements and ice-cream stalls. Several beaches are more secluded – hence their popularity with 18th-century smugglers.

The town's many small and winding streets are lined with fishermen's cottages converted into pubs, cafés and gift shops. The oldest working lighthouse in England overlooks the North Foreland, and is best seen from Joss Bay.

Margate was Britain's first ever seaside resort. Back in the 1730s, visitors witnessed the newfangled deckchair, the unheard-of employment of donkeys as ride givers and the first bathing machine, which allowed for naked sea-dipping with modesty intact. It remains the quintessential family beach resort for one very good reason: the **Main Sands Bay**, with kids' amenities, from donkeys to swings and slides. It still packs them in every summer.

Don't miss the subterranean **Shell Grotto** (01843 220008) dug into the chalk and covered with strange markings of unknown age or origin. Even if you wanted to miss it, the sheer number of brochures and signs about town would see to it that you didn't.

Other spots of interest include the **Margate Caves** (01843 220139), once a hangout for smugglers and unsavoury types.

RESOURCES

Broadstairs: Getting there *By train* Broadstairs rail. *By car* J5 off M2. **Tourist information** 6B High Street, Broadstairs, Kent CT10 1LH (01843 583334/www.tourism.thanet.gov.uk). **Open** *Easter-Sept* 9.15am-4.45pm Mon-Fri; 10am-4pm Sat, Sun. *Oct-Easter* 9.15am-4.45pm Mon-Fri; 10am-4.45pm Sat.

Margate: Getting there *By train* Margate rail. *By car* M2 then A2. **Tourist information** 12-13 The Parade, Margate, Kent CT9 1EY (01843 583334/www.tourism.thanet.gov.uk). **Open** as for Broadstairs.

Hastings & Battle

Hastings is an odd combination of fading resort, still-active fishing port and bohemian outpost (fittingly, the **Hastings Museum & Art Gallery** is on Bohemia Road). The barely discernible ruins of William the Conqueror's Norman **castle** sit atop a cliff above the seaside town's rock shops and crazy golf course. It houses the **1066 Story** (01424 781112), but the **Smugglers' Adventure** (01424 422964) in St Clement's Caves is more grisly and more exciting. Smuggling was one of Hastings' major industries until the early 19th century, although the more virtuous industry of tourism keeps the locals busy these days.

Five miles inland, **Battle** is where William and Harold slugged it out for the English crown. To thank God for his victory, William built **Battle Abbey** (01424 773792) on the spot where Harold was killed. The abbey is now reduced to evocative ruins, but an audio-visual display fills in the details. The town is rather touristy, but the 14th-century **Almonry** on the High Street is worth a look if only for the 300-year-old Guy Fawkes effigy in the hallway. The **Battle Museum of Local History** (01424 775 9555) opened in 2003; it costs £1 for adults, 20p for children (free when they are accompanied by an adult). The museum is closed November to March.

RESOURCES

Getting there *By train* Charing Cross to Hastings, Kent (1hr 50mins). *By car* M25 then A21. **Tourist information** Queens Square, Priory Meadow, Hastings, TN34 1TL (01424 781111/www.hastings.gov.uk). **Open** 8.30am-6.15pm Mon-Fri; 9am-5pm Sat; 10.30am-4.30pm Sun.

Rye

Rye was one of the original Cinque Ports, but its river silted up, the sea retreated and the town found itself two miles inland. Nowadays its narrow cobbled streets and skew-whiff little houses draw hordes of snap-happy visitors (it's best to visit out of season). Novelist Henry James lived here at **Lamb House** (01892 890651). **Rye Castle** (01797 226728) and **Rye Art Gallery** (01797 222433) are worth a peek.

A few miles east of Rye, **Dungeness** is gloriously desolate. The promontory on which it sits is the world's biggest accumulation of shingle, built up over 1,000 years. Investigate the area's ecology at the Dungeness **RSPB Nature Reserve** (01797 320588), enjoy the views from the **Old Lighthouse** (01797 321300) or watch the miniature railway, built in 1927 by racing driver Captain Howey, puff across the bleak landscape. Eat the best fish and chips at the **Britannia** (01797 321959), which can also provide a bed for the night.

RESOURCES

Getting there *By train* Charing Cross to Ashford then change for Rye (1hr 40mins). *By car* J10 off M20 then A2070 and A259. **Tourist information** The Heritage Centre, Strand Quay, Rye, Kent, TN31 7AY (01797 226696/www.rye.org.uk/heritage). **Open** 9.30am-5pm Mon-Sat; 10am-5pm Sun.

Whitstable

This rickety old fishing town in Kent is quite fashionable; many an ex-Londoner has been lured to live by its pebbly shoreline. The small harbour provides plenty to see and enjoy, especially at the end of July, when the **Oyster Festival** brings a party atmosphere. The best places for oysters are the well-run **Whitstable Oyster Fishery Company** (01227 276856), an upmarket choice offering unfussy dishes, or the more basic **Wheeler's** (01227 273311), the town's oldest oyster bar; be sure to book in advance. **Crab & Winkle** (01227 779377) on Whitstable Harbour has seafood, fish and chips and great breakfasts. You can learn more about the oysters than how to eat them at the **Whitstable Museum & Gallery** (01227 276998). Want to stay? Book one of the restored 1860s **Fishermen's Huts** (01227 280280, doubles £100-£130). **Copeland House** (01227 266207, doubles from £50-£90) has simple rooms and fine sea views.

RESOURCES

Getting there *By train* Victoria to Whitstable, Kent (1hr 15mins). *By car* J7 off M2 then A99. **Tourist information** 7 Oxford Street, Whitstable (01227 275482). **Open** *July, Aug* 10am-5pm Mon-Sat. *Sept-June* 10am-4pm Mon-Sat.

Directory

Getting Around   360
Resources A-Z   366
Further Reference   379
Index   381
Advertisers' Index   390

Features

Travel advice   369
Weather report   378

Directory

Getting Around

For London's domestic rail and coach stations, *see p342*.

By air

Gatwick Airport

0870 000 2468/www.baa.co.uk/ gatwick. About 30 miles (50km) south of central London, off the M23.
Of the three rail services that link Gatwick to London, the quickest is the **Gatwick Express** (0845 850 1530, www.gatwickexpress.co.uk) to Victoria Station, which takes about 30 minutes and runs from 5.20am to 1.35am daily: the second train is at 5.50am, then there are trains every 15 minutes until 12.50am. Tickets cost £12 for a single, £12.20 for a day return (after 9.30am) and £23.50 for a period return (valid for 30 days). Under-15s get half-price tickets; under-5s travel free.

Southern (08457 484950, www.southernrailway.com) also runs a rail service between Gatwick and Victoria, with trains around every 15 minutes (or around hourly 1-4am). It takes about eight minutes longer than the Gatwick Express but tickets are slightly cheaper: £10 for a single, £10.50 for a day return (after 9.30am) and £20 for a period return (valid for one month). Under-15s get half-price tickets, and under-5s go for free.

If you're staying in Bloomsbury, take the **Thameslink** service (08457 484950, www.thameslink.co.uk) through London Bridge, Blackfriars, City Thameslink, Farringdon and King's Cross; journey times vary. Tickets to King's Cross cost £9.80 single (after 9.30am), £9.90 for an off-peak day return and £20 for a 30-day period return.

If you want your hand held from airport to hotel and have £22 to spare (each way), try **Hotelink** (01293 532244, www.hotelink.co.uk). A taxi will cost about £100 and take forever.

Heathrow Airport

0870 000 0123/www.baa.co.uk/ heathrow. About 15 miles (24km) west of central London, off the M4.
The **Heathrow Express** (0845 600 1515, www.heathrowexpress.co.uk), which runs to Paddington every 15 minutes between 5.10am and 12.30am daily, takes 15-20 minutes. The train can be boarded at either of the airport's two tube stations. Tickets cost £13 each way or £25 return; under-16s go half-price. Many airlines have check-in desks at Paddington.

A longer but considerably cheaper journey is by tube on the **Piccadilly line**. Tickets for the 50- to 60-minute ride into central London cost £3.80 one way (£1.50 under-16s). Trains run every few minutes from about 5am-11.45pm daily except Sunday, when they run 6am-11pm.

National Express (08705 808080, www.nationalexpress.com) runs daily coach services to London Victoria between 5.15am and 10.15pm daily, leaving Heathrow Central bus terminal around every 30 minutes. For a 90-minute journey to London, you'll pay £6 for a single (£3 under-16s) or £11 (£5.50 under-16s) for a return.

As at Gatwick, **Hotelink** (*see above*) offers a hand-holding service for £15 per person each way. A taxi into town will cost roughly £100 and take an hour on average – which the traffic seldom is.

London City Airport

7646 0000/www.londoncityairport.com. About 9 miles (14km) east of central London, Docklands.
Silvertown rail station, on the Silverlink line, offers a service that runs around every 20 minutes to Stratford for the tube.

Most people head to London on the blue **Shuttlebus** (7646 0088), whose 25-minute ride to Liverpool Street Station goes via Canary Wharf. It leaves every ten minutes (6.50am-9.20pm during the week; 6.50am-1.15pm on Saturdays; and 12.30-9.20pm on Sundays). Tickets to Liverpool Street Station cost £6 one-way, or £3.50 to Canary Wharf. A taxi costs around £20; less to the City.

Luton Airport

01582 405100/www.london-luton. com. About 30 miles (50km) north of central London, J10 off the M1.
Luton Airport Parkway Station is close to the airport, but not in it: there's still a short shuttle-bus ride. The **Thameslink** service (*see above*) calls at many stations (King's Cross St Pancras among them) and has a journey time of 35-45 minutes. Trains leave every 15 minutes or so, and cost £10.60 single and £19.20 return, or £10.40 for a cheap day return (after 9.30am Monday to Friday).

The journey from Luton to Victoria takes 60-90 minutes by coach. **Green Line** (0870 608 7261, www.greenline.co.uk) runs a 24-hour service every 30 minutes or so at peak times. A single is £8.50, £5 for under-16s, while returns cost £12.50 and £9. A taxi costs upwards of £50.

Stansted Airport

0870 0000 0303/www.baa. co.uk/stansted. About 35 miles (60km) north-east of central London, J8 off the M11.
The quickest way to get to London from Stansted is on the Stansted Express train (08457 484950) to Liverpool Street Station; the journey time is 40-45 minutes. Trains leave every 15-45 minutes depending on the time of day, and tickets cost £13.80 for a single and £24 for a period return, under-15s travel half-price, under-5s go free.

The **Airbus** (08705 808080, www.nationalexpress.com) coach service from Stansted to Victoria takes at least an hour and 40 minutes and runs 24 hours. Coaches run roughly every 30 minutes, more frequently during peak times. An adult single costs £10 (£5 for under-16s), a return is £15 (£7.50 for under-16s). A taxi is about £80.

By rail

Eurostar

Waterloo International Terminal, SE1 (08705 186186/www.eurostar.com). Waterloo tube/rail. Map p401 M8.
Eurostar trains arrive into the central Waterloo Station (*see p342*).

Information

Details on public transport in London can be found online at www.thetube.com and/or www.tfl.gov.uk, or on 7222 1234. The TfL website has a journey planner to help you find the quickest route.

Travel Information Centres

TfL's Travel Information Centres provide maps and information about the tube, buses and Docklands Light Railway (DLR; *see below*). You can find them in the stations listed below. Call 7222 5600 for more information.

Heathrow Airport *Terminals 1, 2 & 3 Underground station* 6.30am-10pm daily.
Liverpool Street 7.15am-9pm Mon-Sat; 8.15am-8pm Sun.
Victoria 7.15am-9pm Mon-Sat; 8.15am-8pm Sun.

Travelcards

A flat cash fare per journey applies across the entire London bus and tram network. Tube and DLR fares are based on a zonal system. There are six zones stretching 12 miles out from the centre of London. Beware of on-the-spot penalty fares for anyone caught without a ticket. For most visitors, the Travelcard (*see below*) is the cheapest way of getting around. These can be bought at tube and rail stations, London Travel Information Centres or shops such as newsagents that display the relevant sign.

One-day LT Cards

One-day LT Cards will only be of interest if you intend to travel before 9.30am on weekdays using zones 1-6 and make several journeys during the day. They're valid for travel throughout Greater London on tube, Tramlink and DLR services. They are also valid for travel across the London bus network, but not on special bus services or excursions. A one-day LT card costs £11 and £5.50 for children (5-15s), and is valid from midnight on the date of validity and for any journey that starts before 4.30am the following day.

Day Travelcards

Day Travelcards (peak) can be used all day Mondays to Fridays (except public holidays). They cost from £6 (£3 for under-16s) for zones 1-2, with prices rising to £12 (£6 for under-16s) for zones 1-6. All tickets are valid for journeys started before 4.30am the next day. Most people are happy with the off-peak day Travelcard, which allows you to travel from 9.30am (Mon-Fri) and all day Saturday, Sunday and public holidays. They cost from £4.70 for zones 1-2, rising to £6 for zones 1-6.

One-day Family Travelcards

Anyone travelling with children can take advantage of this Travelcard. It offers unlimited travel for up to two adults and up to four children. During the week each adult pays £3.10, and each child 80p, in Zones 1-2, rising to £4 per adult and 80p per child for zones 1-6. Each child in the Family Travelcard group travels free in all zones on weekends and public holidays.

Three-day Travelcards

If you plan to spend a few days charging around town, you can buy a three-day Travelcard. The peak version can be used all day Monday to Friday (except public holidays) on the start date and for any journey that starts before 4.30am on the day following the expiry date, and is available for £15 (zones 1-2) or £36 (zones 1-6). The off-peak version can be used from 9.30am Monday to Friday and all day on Saturday, Sunday and public holidays on the start date and for any journey that starts before 4.30am on the day following the expiry date. It is available for £18 zones 1-6. If the three days you chose to travel on include a Saturday, Sunday or public holiday, it may be cheaper to buy a combination of day Travelcards.

Oyster card

The Oyster card is a travel smart-card, which can be charged with Pre Pay and/or seven-day, monthly and longer period (including annual) Travelcards and bus passes. Oyster cards are currently available to adults and student photocard holders when buying a ticket. They can be bought from www.oystercard.com, by phone on 0870 849 9999 and at tube station ticket offices, London Travel Information Centres, some National Rail station ticket offices and newsagents. Oyster cards speed up passage through tube station ticket gates as they need only be touched on a special yellow card reader. They can also be used on bus and tram services, the DLR and National Rail.

Oyster Pre Pay allows you to travel on tube, bus, DLR, Tramlink and participating National Rail services at a cheaper rate than the standard single fare. The fare varies according to the time of day and mode of travel. Pre Pay (at whatever value you choose to purchase, the maximum is £90) is charged on to an Oyster card. Fares are deducted from the value on your card as you travel. In mid 2005, these fares will be capped at a daily rate applicable to the time and mode of travel used.

Children

Child fares are available to under-16s on tube, bus, DLR, tram and National Rail services. Under-11s can travel free on buses and trams.

Children aged 14 or 15 need a Child- or 11-15-photocard to travel at child rate on the tube, buses, DLR and trams. Children travelling with adult-rate 7-day, monthly or longer period Travelcard holders can buy a day Travelcard for just £1.

Photocards

Photocards are not required for adult rate seven-day Travelcards, bus passes or for any adult rate Travelcard or bus pass charged on an Oyster card. Photocards for children can be obtained from any tube or National Rail station, Oyster Ticket stop or London Travel Information Centre. Proof of ID (eg passport) and a photograph are required.

London Underground

Delays are common. Escalators are often out of action. Some lines close at weekends for engineering. It's hot and crowded in rush hour (8-9.30am and 4.30-7pm Mon-Fri). Still, the underground rail system, or tube, is still the quickest way to get around.

Using the system

Tube tickets can be purchased from a ticket office or from self-service machines. You can buy most tickets, including carnets and one-day LT Cards, from self-service machines. Ticket offices in some stations close early (around 7.30pm), but it's best to keep change with you at all times: using a ticket machine is quicker than queuing at a ticket office.

To enter the tube, insert your ticket in the automatic checking gates with the black magnetic strip facing downward, then pull it out of the top to open the gates. Exiting the system at your destination is done in much the same way, though if you have a single journey ticket, it will be retained by the gate as you leave. Oyster card (*see above*) holders touch their card on the yellow reader on top of the ticket gate.

There are 12 Underground lines, colour-coded on the tube map for ease of use. There's a full map of the London Underground on page 414 of this book.

Underground timetable

Tube trains run daily from around 5.30am (except Sunday, when they start an hour or two later, depending on the line). The only exception is Christmas Day, when there is no service. Generally, you won't have to wait more than ten minutes for a train, and during peak times the

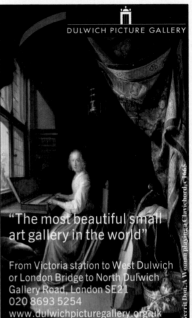

service should run every two or three minutes. Times of last trains vary, though they're usually around 11.30pm-1am daily except Sunday, when they finish 30 minutes to an hour earlier. The only all-night public transport is by night bus (*see p359*).

Fares

The single fare for adults within zone 1 is £2 (Pre Pay £1.70). For zones 1-2 it's £2.30 (Pre Pay £2.10 or £2.00). The zones 1-6 single fare is £3.80 (Pre Pay £3.50 or £2.00). The single fare for children in zone 1 is 60p, 80p for zones 1-2, rising to £1.40 for zones 1-6.

Carnet

If you're planning on making a lot of short-hop journeys within zone 1 over a period of several days, it makes sense to buy a carnet of ten tickets for £15 (£5 for children). Note that if you exit a station outside of zone 1 and are caught with only a carnet ticket, you'll be liable to a £10 penalty fare.

Docklands Light Railway (DLR)

7363 9700/dlr.co.uk.
DLR trains run from Bank (Central or Waterloo & City lines) or Tower Gateway, close to Tower Hill tube (Circle and District lines), to Stratford, Beckton and the Isle of Dogs to Island Gardens, then south of the river to Greenwich, Deptford and Lewisham. Trains run 5.30am to 12.30am Monday to Saturday and 7am to 11.30pm Sunday.

Fares

Docklands Shuttle South (Lewisham to Canary Wharf) one-day tickets cost £2.30; Docklands Shuttle East (valid between Beckton/Stratford and Island Gardens via Westferry) tickets are £2.60; City Flyer South (valid between Bank and Lewisham) tickets are £3.90; and City Flyer East (valid between Beckton/Stratford and Bank) tickets are £4.60. Child tickets cost from 90p to £2.20.

The DLR also offers one day 'Rail & River Rover' tickets that combine unlimited DLR travel with a riverboat trip between Greenwich, Tower and Westminster piers (boats run 10am-6pm; call City Cruises on 7740 0400 for round-trip times). Starting at Tower Gateway, trains leave on the hour (from 10am), with a DLR guide giving a commentary as the train glides along. Tickets cost £9 for adults, £4.50 for kids and £25 for a family pass (two adults and up to three kids); under-5s go free. These prices may change from 1 April 2005.

Note that family tickets can only be bought in person from the piers.

Buses

In the past year, hundreds of new buses have been introduced to London's network. These are all low-floor and more easily accessible to wheelchair-users and passengers with buggies. The introduction of 'bendy buses' with multiple-door entry and the 'Pay Before You Board' scheme have also contributed to speeding up boarding times at bus stops. Many buses, particularly in central London, now require you to buy a ticket before boarding. Do so: there are inspectors about. Where you do not already have a ticket you can buy one (or a one-day Bus Pass) from pavement ticket machines. Yellow signs on bus stops show where this is a requirement.

Fares

Single bus fares are £1.20 (Pre Pay £1 or 80p) and 40p for children. A one-day Bus Pass gives unlimited bus and tram travel at £3.00 adult (£1 children). Children under 11 travel free on buses and trams.

Savers

Saver tickets are in a book of six and cost £6 (£2.10 for children). Savers can be bought at newsagents and at tube station ticket offices.

Night buses

Many night buses run 24 hours a day, seven days a week. There are also some special night buses with an 'N' prefix to the route number, which operate from about 11pm to 6am. Most services run every 15 to 30 minutes, but many busier routes have a bus around every ten minutes. Fares for night buses are the same as for daytime buses. Travelcards and Bus Passes can be used on night buses at no additional charge – and until 4.30am on the day after they expire. Oyster Pre Pay and bus Saver tickets are also valid on night buses.

Green Line buses

Green Line buses (0870 608 7261,/ www.greenline.co.uk) serve the suburbs and towns within a 40-mile (64km) radius of London. Their main departure point is Eccleston Bridge, SW1 (Colonnades Coach Station, behind Victoria).

Routes 205 & 705

Bus routes 205 and 705 (7222 1234) connect all the main London rail termini (except Charing Cross) on circular trips. These express services are convenient for the disabled, the elderly, people laden with luggage or those with small children. Bus 205

runs from Whitechapel station to Euston Square station via Aldgate, Aldgate East, Liverpool Street, Moorgate, Old Street, Angel, King's Cross, St Pancras and Euston. Starting at around 5am (6am on Sunday) to just after midnight every day, they run around every 10-15 minutes; check the timetable. Route 705 starts at Paddington around 7.50am (8.15am from Liverpool Street) and runs around every 30 minutes until 7.50pm (8.15pm from Liverpool Street), stopping at Victoria, Waterloo, London Bridge and Fenchurch Street.

Rail services

Independently run commuter services leave from the city's main rail stations (*see p338*). Travelcards are valid on these services within the right zones. Perhaps the most useful is **Silverlink** (0845 601 4867, www.silverlink-trains.com; or National Rail Enquiries on 08457 484950), which runs from Richmond in the south-west to North Woolwich in the east, via London City Airport. Trains run about every 20 minutes daily except Sunday, when they run every half-hour.

Tramlink

A tram service runs between Beckenham, Croydon, Addington and Wimbledon in south London. Travelcards that include zones 3, 4, 5 or 6 and all Bus Passes can be used on trams. Single tram fares are £1.20 (Pre Pay £1 or 80p) and 40p for children. A one-day Bus Pass gives unlimited tram and bus travel at £3 for adults (£1 children). Under-11s travel free on buses and trams.

Water transport

The times of London's assortment of river services vary, but most operate every 20 minutes to one hour between 10.30am and 5pm. Services may be more frequent and run later in summer. Journey times are longer than by tube, but it's a nicer way to travel. Call the operators listed below for schedules and fares, or see www.tfl.gov.uk. Travelcard holders can expect one-third off scheduled Riverboat fares. **Thames Clippers** (www.thames clippers.com) runs a fast, reliable commuter boat service. Piers to board the Clippers from are: Savoy (near Embankment tube), Blackfriars, Bankside (for the Globe), London Bridge and St Katharine's (Tower Bridge). The names in bold below are the names of piers.

Embankment–Tower (30mins)–**Greenwich** (40mins); Catamaran Cruises 7987 1185/www.bateaux london.com.

Greenland Dock–Canary Wharf (8mins)–**St Katharine's** (7mins)–**London Bridge City** (4mins)–**Bankside** (3mins)–**Blackfriars** (3mins)–**Savoy** (4mins); Collins River Enterprises 7977 6892/ www.thamesclippers.com.

Savoy–Cadogan (20mins)–**Chelsea** (2mins); Connoisseur Charters 7376 3344.

Westminster–(Thames) Barrier Gardens (1hr 30mins); Thames Cruises 7930 3373/www.thames cruises.com.

Westminster–Festival (5mins)–**London Bridge City** (20mins)–**St Katharine's** (5mins); Crown River 7936 2033/www.crownriver.com.

Westminster–Greenwich (1hr); Thames River Services 7930 4097/www.westminsterpier.co.uk.

Westminster–Kew (1hr 30mins)–**Richmond** (30mins)–**Hampton Court** (1hr 30mins); Westminster Passenger Service Association 7930 2062/www.wpsa.co.uk.

Westminster–Tower (40mins); City Cruises 7740 0400/ www.citycruises.com.

Taxis

Black cabs

Licensed London taxis are known as black cabs – even though they now come in a variety of colours – and are a quintessential feature of London life. Drivers of black cabs must pass a test called the Knowledge to prove they know every street in central London and the shortest route to it.

If a taxi's yellow 'For Hire' sign is switched on, it can be hailed. If a taxi stops, the cabbie must take you to your destination, provided it's within seven miles. Expect to pay slightly higher rates after 8pm on weekdays and all weekend.

You can book black cabs in advance. Both **Radio Taxis** (7272 0272; credit cards only) and **Dial-a-Cab** (7253 5000) run 24-hour services for black cabs (there'll be a booking fee in addition to the regular fare). Enquiries or complaints about black cabs should be made to the Public Carriage Office. Note the badge number of the offending cab, which should be displayed in the rear of the cab as well as on its back bumper. For lost property, *see p371*.

Public Carriage Office

200 Baker Street, Marylebone, NW1 5RZ (7918 2000). Baker Street tube. **Open** *By phone* 8.30am-4pm Mon-Fri. *In person* 9am-2pm Mon-Fri.

Minicabs

Minicabs (saloon cars) are generally cheaper than black cabs, but be sure to use only licensed firms and avoid minicab drivers who tout for business on the street (common at Victoria Station, in Soho and outside many nightclubs). They'll be unlicensed and uninsured, almost certainly won't know how to get around, and charge extortionate fares.

There are, happily, plenty of trustworthy and licensed local minicab firms. Among Londonwide firms are **Lady Cabs** (7272 3300), which employs only women drivers (great for women travelling alone), and **Addison Lee** (7387 8888). Whoever you use, ask the price when you book and confirm it with the driver when the car arrives.

Driving

Congestion charge

Every driver driving in central London – an area defined as within King's Cross (N), Old Street roundabout (NE), Aldgate (E), Old Kent Road (SE), Elephant & Castle (S), Vauxhall (SW), Hyde Park Corner (W) and Edgware Road tube (NW) – between 7am and 6.30pm Monday to Friday has to pay a £5 fee. Expect a fine of £50 if you fail to do so (rising to £155, if you delay payment). Passes can be bought from newsagents, garages and NCP car parks; the scheme is enforced by countless CCTV cameras. You can pay any time during the day of entry, even afterward, but it's an extra £5 after 10pm. For more information call 0845 900 1234 or go to www.cc london.com. See also the **Central London by Area** map, *pp412-3*.

Breakdown services

If you're a member of a motoring organisation in another country, check to see if it has a reciprocal agreement with a British organisation. Both the AA and the RAC offer schemes that cover Europe in addition to the UK.

AA (Automobile Association)
Information 08705 500600/ breakdown 0800 887766/members 0800 444999/www.theaa.co.uk. **Open** 24hrs daily. **Membership** £45-£231/yr. **Credit** MC, V.
ETA (Environmental Transport Association) *68 High Street, Weybridge, Surrey KT13 8RS (01932 828882/www.eta.co.uk).* **Open** *Office* 8am-6pm Mon-Fri; 9am-4pm Sat. *Breakdown service* 24hrs daily. **Membership** £25/yr. **Credit** MC, V.
RAC (Royal Automobile Club) *RAC House, 1 Forest Road, Feltham, Middx TW13 7RR (breakdown 0800 828282/office & membership 08705 722722/www.rac.co.uk).* **Open** *Office* 8am-8pm Mon-Fri; 8.30am-5pm Sat. *Breakdown service* 24hrs daily. **Membership** £39-£164/yr. **Credit** AmEx, DC, MC, V.

Parking

Central London is scattered with parking meters, but finding a free one could take ages, and when you do it'll cost you up to £1 for every 15 minutes to park there, and you'll be limited to two hours on the meter. Parking on a single or double yellow line, a a red line or in residents' parking areas during the day is illegal, and you may end up being fined, clamped or towed.

However, in the evening (from 6pm or 7pm in much of central London) and at various times at weekends, parking on single yellow lines is legal and free. If you find a clear spot on a single yellow line during the evening, look for a sign giving the regulations for that area. Meters also become free at certain times during evenings and weekends. Parking on double yellow lines and red routes is, by and large, illegal at all times.

NCP 24-hour car parks (0870 606 7050, www.ncp. co.uk) in and around central London are numerous but expensive. Prices vary with location, but expect to pay £6-£10 for two hours. Among its central car parks are those at Arlington House, Arlington Street, St James's, W1; Upper Ground, Southwark, SE1; and 2 Lexington Street, Soho, W1.

Most NCPs in central London are underground, and a few – such as the car park on Adeline Place behind Tottenham Court Road – are frequented by drug users looking for somewhere quiet to indulge. Take care.

Clamping

The immobilising of illegally parked vehicles by attaching a clamp to one wheel is commonplace in London. There will be a label attached to the car telling you which payment centre to phone or visit. You'll have to stump up an £80 clamp release fee and show a valid licence.

Staff at the payment centre will de-clamp your car some time within the next four hours, but they won't say exactly when. If you don't remove your car immediately, they might clamp it again, so you may have to spend some time waiting by your car.

If you feel you've been clamped unfairly, you can look for the appeals procedure and contact number on the back of your ticket for redress.

Vehicle removal

If your car has mysteriously disappeared, chances are that, if it was legally parked, it's been nicked; if not, it's probably been taken to a car pound, and you're facing a stiff penalty: a fee of £150 is levied for removal, plus £25 per day from the first midnight after removal. To add insult to injury, you'll probably get a parking ticket of £60-£100 when you collect the car (there's a 50% discount if you pay within 14 days). To find out where your car has been taken and how to retrieve it, call the Trace Service hotline (7747 4747).

Vehicle hire

To hire a car, you must have at least one year's driving experience with a full current driving licence; in addition, many car hire firms refuse to hire vehicles out to people under 23. If you're an overseas visitor, your driving licence is valid in Britain for a year.

Prices vary wildly; always ring several competitors for a quote. **Easycar's** online-only service, at www.easycar.com, offers competitive rates, just so long as you don't mind driving a branded car around town.

Alamo 0870 400 4508/www.alamo. com. Open 8am-7pm Mon-Fri; 8am-6pm Sat; 9am-4pm Sun. Credit AmEx, MC, V.
Avis 08705 900500/www.avis. co.uk. Open 24hrs daily. Credit AmEx, DC, MC, V.
Budget 0870 156 5656/www. gobudget.com. Open 8am-8pm daily. Credit AmEx, DC, MC, V.
Enterprise 0870 607 7757/ www.enterprise.com. Open 8am-6pm Mon-Fri; 8am-noon Sat. Credit AmEx, MC, V.
Europcar 0870 607 5000/www. europcar.co.uk. Open 24hrs daily. Credit AmEx, DC, MC, V.
Hertz 0870 599 6699/www. hertz.co.uk. Open 24hrs daily. Credit AmEx, MC, V.

Motorbike hire

HGB Motorcycles 69-71 Park Way, Ruislip Manor, Middx HA4 8NS (01895 676451/www. hgbmotorcycles.co.uk). Ruislip Manor tube. Open 9am-6pm Mon-Fri; 9am-6pm Sat. Credit MC, V. Map p399 M3.
It costs £75 a day or £385 a week to hire an ST1100 Pan European. All rental prices include 250 miles (402km) a day, with excess mileage at 10p a mile, AA cover, insurance

and VAT. Bikes can only be hired with a credit card and a deposit (£350-£850, depending on bike size). There's no crash helmet hire; you'll need your own.

Cycling

The traffic being what it is, London is an unfriendly town for cyclists, but the **London Cycle Network** (7974 2016, www.londoncyclenetwork.org) and **London Cycling Campaign** (7928 7220, www.lcc.org.uk) help make it better. A helmet and mask are advisable.

Cycle hire

OY Bike (www.oybike.com) has 27 bike stations in Hammersmith and Fulham where you can pick up a bike for a reasonable rental 24/7 by calling in on a mobile phone (the lock is electronically released). The scheme may extend to other areas.

London Bicycle Tour Company
1A Gabriel's Wharf, 56 Upper Ground, South Bank, SE1 9PP (7928 6838/www.londonbicycle.com). Southwark tube, Blackfriars or Waterloo tube/rail. Open 10am-6pm daily. Hire £2.50/hr; £14/1st day; £7/day thereafter. Deposit £100 (by credit card). Credit AmEx, DC, MC, V. Map p404 N7.
Bikes, tandems and rickshaw hire; and bicycle tours.

Walking

The best way to see London is on foot. However, this sprawling city is extremely complicated in terms of its street layout – even locals carry maps around with them. We've included street maps of central London in the back of this book (starting on *p394*), but we recommend that you also buy a separate map of the city: both the standard Geographers' *A-Z* and Collins' *London Street Atlas* versions come in a variety of sizes and are very easy to use. And expect to get lost on a semi-regular basis.

Resources A-Z

Addresses

London postcodes are less helpful than they could be for locating addresses. The first element starts with a compass point – out of N, E, SE, SW, W and NW, plus the smaller EC (East Central) and WC (West Central) – which at least gives you a basic idea. However, the number that follows bears no relation to geography (unless it's a 1, which indicates that the address is central). So N2, for example, is way out in the boondocks, while W2 includes the very central Bayswater. The remaining characters are meaningless to pretty much everyone (including, judging by London's increasingly erratic mail delivery, the Post Office; *see p374*).

Age restrictions

You must be 17 or older to drive in the United Kingdom, and 18 to buy cigarettes or buy or be served alcohol (to be safe, carry photo ID if you look as if you could be younger than this). The age of heterosexual and homosexual consent is 16.

Business

Conventions & conferences

London Tourist Board & Convention Bureau

7234 5800/www.londontown.com.
The LTB runs a venue enquiry service for conventions and exhibitions. Call or email for an information pack that lists the facilities offered by various venues.

Queen Elizabeth II Conference Centre

Broad Sanctuary, Westminster, SW1P 3EE (7222 5000/www.qeiicc. co.uk). Westminster tube. **Open** 8am-6pm Mon-Fri. *Conference facilities* 24hrs daily. **Map** p401 K9.

This purpose-built centre has some of the best conference facilities in the capital. Rooms have capacities ranging from 40 to 1,100, all with wireless LAN technology installed.

Couriers & shippers

DHL and FedEx offer local and international courier services; Excess Baggage is the UK's largest shipper of luggage.

DHL *St Alphage House, 2 Fore Street, The City, EC2Y 5DA (0870 110 0300/www.dhl.co.uk). Moorgate tube/rail.* **Open** 9am-6pm Mon-Fri. **Credit** AmEx, DC, MC, V. **Map** p401 L7.
Excess Baggage *168 Earl's Court Road, Earl's Court, SW5 9QQ (7373 1977/www.excess-baggage.com). Earl's Court tube.* **Open** 8am-6pm Mon-Fri; 9am-5pm Sat; noon-5pm Sun. **Credit** AmEx, MC, V. **Map** p396 B10.
FedEx *0800 123800/www.fedex. com.* **Open** 7.30am-7.30pm Mon-Fri. **Credit** AmEx, DC, MC, V.

Office hire & business centres

ABC rents office equipment, while British Monomarks offers communications services.

ABC Business Machines *59 Chiltern Street, Marylebone, W1U 6NF (7486 5634/www.abc business.co.uk). Baker Street tube.* **Open** 9am-5.30pm Mon-Fri; 9.30am-12.30pm Sat. **Credit** MC, V. **Map** p398 G5.
British Monomarks *Monomarks House, 27 Old Gloucester Street, Holborn, WC1N 3XX (7419 5000/ www.britishmonomarks.co.uk). Holborn tube.* **Open** *Mail forwarding* 9.30am-5.30pm Mon-Fri. *Telephone answering* 9am-6pm Mon-Fri. **Credit** AmEx, MC, V. **Map** p399 L5.

Customs

See www.hmce.gov.uk for more details.

From inside the EU

You may bring in the following quantities of tax-paid goods, as long as they are for your own consumption.

● 3,200 cigarettes or 400 cigarillos or 200 cigars or 3kg (6.6lb) tobacco;
● 90 litres wine plus either 10 litres of spirits or liqueurs (more than 22% alcohol by volume) or 20 litres of fortified wine (under 22% ABV), sparkling wine or other liqueurs.

From outside the EU

These are total allowances, whether or not the goods were purchased duty-free.

● 200 cigarettes or 100 cigarillos or 50 cigars or 250g of tobacco;
● 2 litres of still table wine plus either 1 litre of spirits or strong liqueurs over 22% volume or 2 litres of fortified wine, sparkling wine or other liqueurs;
● £145 worth of all other goods including gifts and souvenirs.

Disabled

As a city that evolved long before the needs of disabled people were considered, London is a difficult city for disabled visitors, though legislation is gradually improving access and general facilities. In October 2004 anyone who provides a service to the public was required to make 'reasonable adjustments' to their properties, and the bus fleet is now becoming more wheelchair accessible. The tube, however, is so escalator-dependent as to be of limited use. The *Access to the Underground* booklet is available free from ticket offices, or call the Travel and Information line (7222 1234).

Most major visitor attractions and hotels offer good accessibility, though facilities for the hearing- and sight-disabled are patchier. Call businesses in advance to enquire about facilities, and use your judgement in interpreting their response. *Access in London* is an invaluable reference, available for a £10 donation (a sterling cheque, or dollars in cash) from Access Project (PHSP), 39 Bradley Gardens, West Ealing, W13 8HE.

Artsline
54 Chalton Street, Somers Town, NW1 1HS (tel/textphone 7388 2227/www.artsline.org.uk). Euston tube/rail. **Open** 9.30am-5.30pm Mon-Fri. **Map** p399 K3.
Information on disabled access to arts and entertainment events.

Can Be Done
11 Woodcock Hill, Harrow, Middx HA1 2RZ (8907 2400/www.canbe done.co.uk). Kenton tube/rail. **Open** 9am-5.30pm Mon-Fri. **Map** p396 A9.
Disabled-adapted holidays and tours in London and around the UK.

DAIL (Disability Arts in London)
Diorama Arts Centre, 34 Osnaburgh Street, Fitzrovia, NW1 3ND (7916 6351/www.ldaf.org). Great Portland Street tube. **Enquiries** 11am-4pm Mon-Fri. **Map** p398 H4.
DAIL produces a bi-monthly magazine with reviews and articles on the arts and the disabled (£15/yr, £40 for overseas subscribers). DAIL is part of **LDAF** (London Disability Arts Forum; 7916 5484), which organises events for disabled people in London.

Greater London Action on Disability
336 Brixton Road, Brixton, SW9 7AA (7346 5800/textphone 7326 4554/www.glad.org.uk). Brixton tube/rail. **Open** *Phone enquiries* 9am-5pm Mon-Fri.
A valuable source of information for disabled visitors and residents.

Holiday Care Service
0845 124 9971/www.holidaycare. org.uk. **Open** *Helpline* 9am-5pm Mon, Tue; 9am-1pm Wed-Fri.
An advisory service specialising in disabled holiday accommodation.

Royal Association for Disability & Rehabilitation
12 City Forum, 250 City Road, Islington, EC1V 2PU (7250 3222/ textphone 7250 4119/www.radar.org .uk). Old Street tube/rail. **Open** 9am-4pm Mon-Fri. **Map** p402 P3.
A national campaigning organisation for disabled voluntary groups that also publishes books on disabled access in the UK and the bi-monthly magazine *New Bulletin* (£35/yr).

Wheelchair Travel & Access Mini Buses
1 Johnston Green, Guildford, Surrey GU2 9XS (01483 233640/

www.wheelchair-travel.co.uk). **Open** 9am-5.30pm Mon-Fri; 9am-noon Sat.
Hires out converted vehicles including minibuses (driver optional), plus cars with hand controls and 'Chairman' cars.

Electricity
The United Kingdom uses the standard European 220-240V, 50-cycle AC voltage. British plugs use three pins rather than the standard two, so travellers with appliances from mainland Europe should bring an adaptor, as should anyone using US appliances, which run off a 110-120V, 60-cycle.

Embassies & consulates
American Embassy *24 Grosvenor Square, Mayfair, W1A 1AE (7499 9000/www.us embassy.org.uk). Bond Street or Marble Arch tube.* **Open** 8.30am-5.30pm Mon-Fri. **Map** p400 G7.
Australian High Commission *Australia House, Strand, Holborn, WC2B 4LA (7379 4334/www. australia.org.uk). Holborn or Temple tube.* **Open** 9.30am-3.30pm Mon-Fri. **Map** p401 M6.
Canadian High Commission *38 Grosvenor Street, Mayfair, W1K 4AA (7258 6600/www.canada.org. uk). Bond Street or Oxford Circus tube.* **Open** 8-11am Mon-Fri. **Map** p400 H7.
Irish Embassy *17 Grosvenor Place, Belgravia, SW1X 7HR (7235 2171/passports & visas 7225 7700). Hyde Park Corner tube.* **Open** 9.30am-1pm, 2.30-5.30pm Mon-Fri. **Map** p400 G9.
New Zealand High Commission *New Zealand House, 80 Haymarket, St James's, SW1Y 4YQ (7930 8422/www.nzembassy. com). Piccadilly Circus tube.* **Open** 9am-5pm Mon-Fri. **Map** p401 K7.
South African High Commission *South Africa House, Trafalgar Square, St James's, WC2N 5DP (7451 7299/www.southafrica house.com). Charing Cross tube/rail.* **Open** 8.45am-12.45pm Mon-Fri. **Enquiries** 8.30am-5pm Mon-Fri. **Map** p401 K7.

Emergencies
In the event of a serious accident, fire or incident, call **999** – free from any phone,

including payphones – and specify whether you require ambulance, fire service or police. For addresses of Accident & Emergency departments in central London hospitals, *see p369*; for helplines, *see p370*; and for city police stations, *see p374*.

Gay & lesbian
For a complete gay guide to the capital, purchase *Time Out Gay & Lesbian London*, £9.99. The phonelines below offer help and information.
London Friend *7837 3337/ www.londonfriend.org.uk.* **Open** 7.30-10pm daily.
London Lesbian & Gay Switchboard *7837 7324/ www.queery.org.uk.* **Open** 24hrs daily.

Health
Free emergency medical treatment under the National Health Service (NHS) is available to the following:
● European Union nationals, plus those of Iceland, Norway and Liechtenstein. They may also be entitled to treatment for a non-emergency condition on production of form E112 or E128.
● Nationals of Bulgaria, the Czech and Slovak Republics, Gibraltar, Hungary, Malta, New Zealand, Russia, most former Soviet Union states and the former Yugoslavia.
● Residents, irrespective of nationality, of Anguilla, Australia, Barbados, British Virgin Islands, Channel Islands, Falkland Islands, Iceland, Isle of Man, Montserrat, Poland, Romania, St Helena and Turks & Caicos Islands.
● Anyone who has been in the UK for the previous 12 months.
● Anyone who has come to the UK to take up permanent residence.
● Students and trainees whose courses require more than 12 weeks in employment during the first year.
● Refugees and others who have sought refuge in the UK.
● People with HIV/AIDS at a special clinic for the treatment of STDs. The treatment covered is limited to a diagnostic test and counselling associated with that test.

There are no NHS charges for services including:

Directory

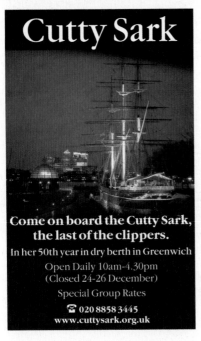

● Treatment in Accident & Emergency departments.
● Emergency ambulance transport to a hospital.
● Diagnosis and treatment of certain communicable diseases, including STDs.
● Family planning services.
● Compulsory psychiatric treatment.

Accident & emergency

Below are listed most of the central London hospitals that have 24-hour Accident & Emergency departments.

Charing Cross Hospital *Fulham Palace Road, Hammersmith, W6 8RF (8846 1234). Barons Court or Hammersmith tube.*
Chelsea & Westminster Hospital *369 Fulham Road, Chelsea, SW10 9NH (8746 8000). South Kensington tube.* **Map p396 C12.**
Guy's Hospital *St Thomas Street (entrance Snowsfields), Bankside, SE1 9RT (7188 7188). London Bridge tube/rail.* **Map p404 P8.**
Homerton Hospital *Homerton Row, Homerton, E9 6SR (8510 5555). Homerton rail/bus 242.*
Royal Free Hospital *Pond Street, Hampstead, NW3 2QG (7794 0500). Belsize Park tube/Hampstead Heath rail.*
Royal London Hospital *Whitechapel Road, Whitechapel, E1 1BB (7377 7000). Whitechapel tube.*
St Mary's Hospital *Praed Street, Paddington, W2 1NY (7886 6666). Paddington tube/rail.* **Map p395 D5.**
St Thomas's Hospital *Lambeth Palace Road, Lambeth, SE1 7EH (7188 7188). Westminster tube/Waterloo tube/rail.* **Map p401 M9.**
University College Hospital *Grafton Way, Fitzrovia, WC1E 3BG (7387 9300). Euston Square or Warren Street tube.* **Map p398 J4.**
Whittington Hospital *Highgate Hill, Archway, N19 5NF (7272 3070). Archway tube.*

Complementary medicine

For a full list of alternative health centres, see the *Time Out Sport, Health & Fitness* guide (£9.99).

British Homeopathic Association

0870 444 3950/www.trust homeopathy.org. **Open** *Phone enquiries* 9am-5pm Mon-Fri.
The BHA will refer you to the nearest homeopathic chemist/doctor.

Contraception & abortion

Family planning advice, contraceptive supplies and abortions are free to British citizens on the NHS; also to EU residents and foreign nationals living in Britain. Phone the Contraception Helpline on 0845 310 1334 for your local **Family Planning Association**. The 'morning after' pill (£25), effective up to 72 hours after intercourse, is available over the counter.

British Pregnancy Advisory Service

08457 304030/www.bpas.org.
Callers are referred to their nearest clinic for treatment. Contraceptives are available, as is pregnancy testing.

Brook Advisory Centre

7284 6040/helpline 0800 018 5023/www.brook.org.uk). **Open** *Helpline* 9am-5pm Mon-Fri.
Advice and referrals on sexual health, contraception and abortion, plus free pregnancy tests for under-25s. Call for your nearest clinic.

Marie Stopes House

Family Planning Clinic/Well Woman Centre *108 Whitfield Street, Fitzrovia, W1P 6BE (0845 300 8090/www.mariestopes.org.uk). Warren Street tube.* **Open** *Clinic* 9am-5pm Mon-Fri. *Termination helpline* 7am-10pm Mon-Fri. **Map p398 J5.**
For contraceptive advice, emergency contraception, pregnancy testing, an abortion service, cervical and health screening or gynaecological services. Fees may apply.

Dentists

Dental care is free for resident students, under-18s and people on benefits. All other patients must pay. NHS-eligible patients pay on a subsidised scale. To find an NHS dentist, get in touch with the local Health Authority or a Citizens' Advice Bureau (*see p370*), or the following:

Dental Emergency Care Service

Guy's Hospital, St Thomas Street, Bankside, SE1 9RT (7188 0511). London Bridge tube/rail. **Open** 9am-5pm Mon-Fri. **Map p405 Q8.**
Queues start forming at 8am; arrive before noon if you're to be seen at all.

Doctors

If you're a British citizen or working in the United Kingdom, you can go to any general practitioner (GP). If you're not visiting your usual GP, you'll need to give their details so your records can be updated. People ordinarily resident in the UK, including overseas students, are also permitted to register with an

Travel advice

For up-to-date information on travelling to a specific country – including the latest news on safety and security, health issues, local laws and customs – contact your home country government's department of foreign affairs. Most have websites packed with useful advice for would-be travellers.

Australia
www.smartraveller.gov.au

Canada
www.voyage.gc.ca

New Zealand
www.mft.govt.nz/travel

Republic of Ireland
http://foreignaffairs.gov.ie

UK
www.fco.gov.uk/travel

USA
www.state.gov/travel

Directory

NHS doctor. If you fall outside these categories, you can still see a GP but will need to pay. Your hotel should be able to recommend one.

Great Chapel Street Medical Centre

13 Great Chapel Street, Soho, W1F 8FL (7437 9360). Leicester Square, Oxford Circus or Tottenham Court Road tube. **Open** *Drop in* 11am-12.30pm, 2-4pm Mon, Tue, Thur; 2-4pm Wed, Fri.* **Map** p399 K6.
A walk-in NHS surgery for anyone without a doctor. Phone first, as it operates different clinics each day.

Hospitals

For a list of hospitals with A&E departments, *see p369*; for other hospitals, see the *Yellow Pages*.

Pharmacies

Also called 'chemists' in the UK. Larger supermarkets and all branches of Boots (*see p252*) have a pharmacy, and there are many high-street independents. Staff are qualified to advise on over-the-counter medicines. Most pharmacies keep shop hours (9am-6pm, closed Sun). A few open later; *see p252*.

Prescriptions

A pharmacist will dispense medicines on receipt of a prescription from a GP. NHS prescriptions cost £6.40, but under-16s and over-60s are exempt, and contraception is free for all. If you're not eligible to see an NHS doctor, you'll be charged cost price for medicines prescribed by a private doctor.

STDs, HIV & AIDS

NHS Genito-Urinary Clinics (such as the Centre for Sexual Health; *see below*) are affiliated to major hospitals. They provide free, confidential treatment of STDs and other problems, such as thrush and

cystitis; offer counselling about HIV and other STDs; and can conduct blood tests to determine HIV status.

The 24-hour **Sexual Healthline** (0800 567123, textphone 0800 521361, www.playingsafely.co.uk) is free and confidential. For other helplines, *see below*; for abortion and contraception services, *see p369*.

Ambrose King Centre

Royal London Hospital, Whitechapel Road, Whitechapel, E1 1BB (7377 7306). Whitechapel tube. **Open** 9.30am-4pm Mon, Tue; noon-4pm Wed, Thur; 9.30am-noon Fri.
The centre provides a specific gay health clinic, East One, Thursday 6.30-8.30pm, by appointment only – call 7377 7313.

Centre for Sexual Health

Genito-Urinary Clinic, Jefferiss Wing, St Mary's Hospital, Praed Street, Paddington, W2 1NY (7886 1697). Paddington tube/rail. **Open** *Walk-in clinic* 8.45am-6.15pm Mon, Tue, Thur; 11.45am-6.15pm Wed; 8.45am-1.15pm Fri.* **Map** p395 D5.
A free and confidential walk-in clinic. New patients must arrive at least 30 minutes before closing.

Mortimer Market Centre for Sexual Health

Mortimer Market Centre, Mortimer Market, off Capper Street, Bloomsbury, WC1E 6JD (appointments 7530 5050). Goodge Street or Warren Street tube. **Open** 9am-6pm Mon, Tue, Thur; 1-7pm Wed; 9am-3pm Fri.* **Map** p398 J4.
Axis 22 is a clinic for gay and bisexual men aged 22 and under (Thur 6-8pm). Make an appointment if you can. There is also a walk-in clinic for women aged under 22 (Mon 3.45-6pm.

Terrence Higgins Trust Lighthouse

52-54 Gray's Inn Road, Holborn, WC1X 8JU (office 7831 0330/ helpline 0845 122 1200/www.tht. org.uk). Chancery Lane tube. **Open** *Office* 9.30am-5.30pm Mon-Fri. *Helpline* 10am-10pm Mon-Fri; noon-6pm Sat, Sun.* **Map** p399 M5.
This charity advises and counsels those with HIV/AIDS, their relatives, lovers and friends. It also offers free leaflets about AIDS and safer sex.

Helplines

See also above **STDs, HIV & AIDS**.

Alcoholics Anonymous

0845 769 7555, www.alcoholics-anonymous.org.uk

Citizens' Advice Bureaux

The council-run CABs offer free legal, financial and personal advice. Check the phone book for your nearest.

NHS Direct

0845 4647/www.nhsdirect.nhs.uk. **Open** 24hrs daily.
NHS Direct is a free, first-stop service for medical advice on all subjects.

National Missing Persons Helpline

0500 700 700/www.missingpersons. org. **Open** 24hrs daily.
The volunteer-run NMPH publicises information on anyone reported missing, helping to find missing persons through a network of contacts. Its 'Message Home' freephone service (0800 700 740) allows runaways to reassure friends or family of their wellbeing without revealing their whereabouts.

Rape & Sexual Abuse Support Centre

8683 3300. **Open** noon-2.30pm, 7-9.30pm Mon-Fri; 2.30-5pm Sat, Sun.
Provides support and information for victims and families.

Samaritans

08457 909090/www.samaritans. org.uk. **Open** 24hrs daily.
The Samaritans listen to anyone with emotional problems. It's a busy service, so persevere when phoning.

Victim Support

National Office, Cranmer House, 39 Brixton Road, Brixton, SW9 6DZ (0845 303 0900/www.victimsupport. com). **Open** *Support line* 9am-9pm Mon-Fri; 9am-7pm Sat, Sun.
Victims of crime are put in touch with a volunteer who provides emotional and practical support, including information and advice on legal procedures. Interpreters can be arranged where necessary.

Insurance

Insuring personal belongings is highly advisable. It can be difficult to arrange once you've arrived in London, so do so before you leave.

Medical insurance is usually included in travel insurance packages. Unless your country has a reciprocal medical treatment arrangement with Britain (see p367), it's very important to check that you do have adequate health cover.

Internet

Most hotels in London now have modem plug-in points (dataports) in each room; those that don't usually offer some other form of surfing. Wireless and high-speed access have boomed in hotels too.

There are lots of cybercafés around town. The biggest are in the **easyEverything** chain (see below). Big stores such as **Virgin** (see p256) offer internet terminals, as do public libraries (see p371). For more, check www.cybercafes.com.

Wireless access is just taking off here, slightly more slowly than in the US (perhaps because of higher charges). Some major railway stations, including London Bridge and Charing Cross, parts of the major airports and most Starbucks locations offer it, as well as the increasing number of hotels. For locations, check with your wireless provider or visit www.wi-fihotspotlist.com/

Internet access

easyInternetCafé
160-166 Kensington High Street, W8 7RG (www.easyeverything.com).
High Street Kensington tube. **Open** 7.30am-11.30pm daily. **Net access** from 50p. **Terminals** 394. **Map** p396 B9.
Other locations: throughout the city.

Left luggage

Airports

Gatwick Airport *South Terminal 01293 502014/North Terminal 01293 502013.*
Heathrow Airport *Terminal 1 8745 5301/Terminals 2-3 8759 3344/Terminal 4 8897 6874.*
London City Airport *7646 0162.*
Stansted Airport *01279 663213.*

Rail & bus stations

The threat of terrorism has meant that London stations tend to have left-luggage desks rather than lockers; to find out whether a train station offers this facility, call 08457 484950.

Legal help

Those in difficulties can visit a Citizens' Advice Bureau (see p370) or contact the groups below. Try the Legal Services Commission (7759 0000, www. legalservices.gov.uk) for information. If you are arrested, your first call should be to your embassy (see p367).

Community Legal Services Directory

0845 608 1122/www.clsdirect.org.uk. **Open** 9am-5.30pm daily.
This free telephone service guides those with legal problems to government agencies and law firms that may be able to help.

Joint Council for the Welfare of Immigrants

115 Old Street, Hoxton, EC1V 9RT (7251 8706). Old Street tube/rail. **Open** Phone enquiries 2-5pm Tue, Thur.
JCWI's telephone-only legal advice line offers guidance and referrals.

Law Centres Federation

Duchess House, 18-19 Warren Street, Fitzrovia, W1T 5LR (7387 8570/www.lawcentres.org.uk).
Warren Street tube/rail. **Open** Phone enquiries 10am-5pm Mon-Fri.
Free legal help for people who can't afford a lawyer. Local centres only offer advice to those living or working in their immediate area; this central office connects you with the nearest.

Libraries

Unless you're a London resident, you won't be able to join a lending library. Only the exhibition areas of the British Library are open to non-members; other libraries listed can be used for reference.

Barbican Library
Barbican Centre, Silk Street, City, EC2Y 8DS (7638 0569/www.cityof london.gov.uk/barbicanlibrary).

Barbican tube/Moorgate tube/ rail. **Open** 9.30am-5.30pm Mon, Wed; 9.30am-7.30pm Tue, Thur; 9.30am-2pm Fri; 9.30am-4pm Sat. **Map** p402 P5.
British Library *96 Euston Road, Somers Town, NW1 2DB (7412 7000/www.bl.uk).* King's Cross tube/rail. **Open** 9.30am-6pm Mon, Wed-Fri; 9.30am-8pm Tue; 9.30am-5pm Sat; 11am-5pm Sun. **Map** p399 K3.
Holborn Library *32-38 Theobald's Road, Bloomsbury, WC1X 8PA (7974 6345). Chancery Lane tube.* **Open** 10am-7pm Mon, Thur; 10am-6pm Tue, Wed, Fri; 10am-5pm Sat. **Map** p399 M5.
Kensington Central Library *12 Philimore Walk, Kensington, W8 7RX (7937 2542). High Street Kensington tube.* **Open** 9.30am-8pm Mon, Tue, Thur; 9.30am-5pm Wed, Fri, Sat.
Marylebone Library *109-117 Marylebone Road, Marylebone, NW1 (7641 1041). Baker Street tube/Marylebone tube/rail.* **Open** 9.30am-8pm Mon, Tue, Thur, Fri; 10am-8pm Wed; 9.30am-5pm Sat; 1.30-5pm Sun. **Map** p396 A9.
Victoria Library *160 Buckingham Palace Road, Belgravia, SW1W 9UD (7641 4287). Victoria tube/rail.* **Open** 9.30am-7pm Mon, Tue, Thur; 10am-7pm Wed; 9.30am-8pm Fri; 9.30am-5pm Sat. *Music library* 11am-7pm Mon-Fri; 10am-5pm Sat. **Map** p400 H10.
Westminster Reference Library *35 St Martin's Street, Westminster, WC2H 7HP (7641 4636). Leicester Square tube.* **Open** 10am-8pm Mon-Fri; 10am-5pm Sat. **Map** p401 K7.

Lost property

Always inform the police if you lose anything, if only to validate insurance claims. See p374 or the *Yellow Pages* for your nearest police station. Only dial 999 if violence has occurred. Report lost passports both to the police and to your embassy (see p367).

Airports

For property lost on the plane, contact the relevant airline; for items lost in a particular airport, contact the following:
Gatwick Airport *01293 503162.*
Heathrow Airport *8745 7727.*
London City Airport *7646 0000.*
Luton Airport *01582 395219.*
Stansted Airport *01279 663293.*

Public transport

If you've lost property in an overground station or on a train, call 08700 005151; an operator will connect you to the appropriate station.

Transport for London

Lost Property Office, 200 Baker Street, Marylebone, NW1 5RZ (7918 2000/www.tfl.gov.uk). Baker Street tube. **Open** 9am-2pm Mon-Fri. **Map** p398 G4.

Allow three working days from the time of loss. If you lose something on a bus, call 7222 1234 and ask for the phone numbers of the depots at either end of the route. If you lose something on a tube, pick up a lost property form from any station.

Taxis

Taxi Lost Property

200 Baker Street, Marylebone, NW1 5RZ (7918 2000/www.tfl.gov.uk). Baker Street tube. **Open** 9am-2pm Mon-Fri. *Phone enquiries* 9am-4pm Mon-Fri. **Map** p398 G4.

This office deals only with property found in registered black cabs. For items lost in a minicab, contact the office from which you hired the cab.

Media

Magazines

Rumours of the renaissance of the *London Illustrated News* having so far not borne fruit, *Time Out* remains London's only quality magazine. It's widely available every Tuesday in central London, giving listings for the week from the Wednesday. If you really want to know what's going on and how good it is, this is where you look. An esoteric complement is the Talk of the Town section in the *Independent on Sunday*'s *ABC* supplement.

Nationally, *Loaded, FHM* and *Maxim* are big men's titles, while women have taken to handbag-sized *Glamour*, alongside *Vogue, Marie Claire* and *Elle*. The appetite for celebrity magazines like *Heat* and *OK* doesn't seem to have abated, and style mags like *i-D*

and *Dazed and Confused* have found a profitable niche.

The *Spectator*, the *New Statesman, Prospect* and *The Economist* are about as good as it gets at the serious end of the market, while the satirical fortnightly *Private Eye* adds a little levity. It helps if you buy the *Big Issue*, sold on the streets by homeless people.

Newspapers

London's main daily paper is the dull, right-wing *Evening Standard*, which comes out in several editions during the day (Mon-Fri). The free morning paper *Metro* is picked up and discarded at tube stations.

National newspapers include, from right to left, the *Daily Telegraph* and *The Times* (which is best for sport), the *Independent* and the *Guardian* (best for arts). All have bulging Sunday equivalents bar the *Guardian*, which has a sister Sunday paper, the *Observer*. The pink *Financial Times* (daily except Sunday) is the best for business facts and figures. In the middle market, the leader is the right-wing *Daily Mail* (and *Mail on Sunday*); the *Daily Express* (and *Sunday Express*) tries to compete. Tabloids remain strong, with the *Sun* (and Sunday's *News of the World*) the undisputed leader. The *Daily Star* and *Mirror* are the main lowbrow contenders.

Radio

The stations listed are broadcast on standard wavebands as well as digital, where they are joined by some interesting new channels, particularly from the BBC. The format is not yet widespread, but you may be lucky enough to have digital in your hotel room or hire car (worth asking about when you book – digital was designed for listening on the move so quality is high).

BBC Radio 1 *97-99 FM.* Youth-oriented pop, indie, metal and dance.
BBC Radio 2 *88-91 FM.* Still bland during the day, but good after dark.
BBC Radio 3 *90-93 FM.* Classical music dominates, but there's also discussion, world music and arts.
BBC Radio 4 *92-95 FM, 198 LW.* The BBC's main speech station. News agenda-setter *Today* (6-9am Mon-Fri) bristles with self-importance.
BBC Radio 5 Live *693, 909 AM.* Rolling news and sport. Avoid the morning phone-ins, but *Up All Night* (1-5am nightly) is terrific.
BBC London *94.9 FM.* A shadow of its former (GLR) self, but Robert Elms (noon-3pm Mon-Fri) is OK.
BBC World Service *648 AM.* A distillation of the best of all the other BBC stations; transmitted worldwide.
Capital FM *95.8 FM.* London's best-known station.
Classic FM *100.9 FM.* Easy-listening classical.
Heart FM *106.2 FM.* Capital for grown-ups.
Jazz FM *102.2 FM.* Smooth jazz (aka elevator music) now dominates.
LBC *97.3 FM.* Phone-ins and features. The cabbies' favourite.
Liberty *963 & 972 AM.* Cheesy hits from the 1970s and '80s.
Resonance *104.4 FM.* Arts radio.
Xfm *104.9 FM.* Alternative rock.

Television

With a multiplicity of formats, there are plenty of pay-TV options. However, the relative quality of free TV (most notably the BBC's new digital channels) keeps subscriptions from attaining US levels.

Network channels

BBC1 The Corporation's mass-market station. Depends perhaps too much on soaps, game shows and reality and lifestyle TV, but has quality offerings, too, particularly in nature, drama and travel. Daytime programming isn't great. As with all BBC radio and TV stations, there are no commercials.
BBC2 A reasonably intelligent cultural cross-section and plenty of documentaries, but upstaged by the BBC's digital arts channel, BBC4, on fresh cultural programming.
ITV1 Carlton provides weekday monotonous, mass-appeal shows, with oft-repeated successes for ITV. LWT (London Weekend Television) takes over at the weekend with more of the same. ITV2 is on digital.
Channel 4 C4's output includes a variety of extremely successful US imports (*Six Feet Under, ER, The OC, The Sopranos* and so on), but it

still comes up with some gems of its own, particularly documentaries.
Five Plenty of sex, US TV movies, a lot of rubbish comedy, US sport and the occasional good documentary.

Selected satellite, digital & cable
BBC3 *EastEnders* reruns and other light fare.
BBC4 Highbrow stuff, including earnest documentaries and dramas.
BBC News 24 The Beeb's rolling news network.
Bravo B-movies and cult TV.
CNN News and current affairs.
Discovery Channel Science and nature documentaries.
FilmFour Channel 4's movie outlet.
Performance Dance, theatre and opera, plus interviews with the stars.
Sky News Rolling news.
Sky One Sky's version of ITV.
Sky Sports Sports. There are also Sky Sports 2 and Sky Sports 3.

Money

Britain's currency is the pound sterling (£). One pound equals 100 pence (p). Coins are copper (1p, 2p), silver (round: 5p, 10p; seven-sided: 20p, 50p), yellowy-gold (£1) or silver in the centre with a yellowy-gold edge (£2). Paper notes are blue (£5), orange (£10), purple (£20) or red (£50). You can exchange foreign currency at banks, bureaux de change and post offices; there's no commission charge at the latter. Many large stores also accept euros.

Western Union
0800 833833/www.westernunion.com. The old standby for bailing out cash-challenged travellers. Chequepoint (*see below*) also offers this service.

ATMs

As well as inside and outside banks, cash machines can be found in some supermarkets and in larger tube and rail stations. You will also find 'pay-ATMs' on commercial premises. If you are visiting from outside the UK, your cash card should work via one of the debit networks, but check charges in advance. ATMs also allow you to make withdrawals on your credit card if you know

your PIN number; you will be charged interest plus, usually, a currency exchange fee (1% for Visa and Mastercard at press time). Generally getting cash with a card is the cheapest form of currency exchange but increasingly there are hidden charges, so do your research. Bank of America customers can use Barclays ATMs free.

Increasingly, shops prefer you to enter your PIN rather than sign off debit and credit card payments. Learn it.

Banks

No commission is charged for cashing sterling travellers' cheques if you go to one of the banks affiliated with the issuing company. You do have to pay to cash travellers' cheques in foreign currencies, and to change cash. You always need ID, such as a passport, to cash travellers' cheques.

Bureaux de change

You'll be charged for cashing travellers' cheques or buying and selling foreign currency at bureaux de change. Commission rates, which should be clearly displayed, vary. Major rail and tube stations have bureaux, and there are many in tourist areas and on well-known shopping streets. Most open 8am-10pm, but Chequepoint opens 24 hours daily.

Chequepoint *548-550 Oxford Street, Marylebone, W1N 9HJ (0800 699799). Marble Arch tube.* **Open** 24hrs daily. **Map** p398 G6.
Other locations: throughout town.
Garden Bureau *30A Jubilee Market Hall, Covent Garden, WC2 8BE (7240 9921). Covent Garden tube.* **Open** 9.30am-6pm daily. **Map** p401 L7.
This independent bureau has decent rates and a good reputation.

Credit cards

Credit cards are accepted pretty much ubiquitously in shops (except small corner shops) and restaurants (except

caffs), particularly Visa and MasterCard. American Express and Diners Club tend to be accepted at more expensive outlets and multiples.

Report **lost/stolen credit cards** immediately to both the police and the 24-hour services below.

American Express *01273 696933.*
Diners Club *01252 513500.*
JCB *7499 3000.*
MasterCard/Eurocard *0800 964767.*
Switch *08706 000459.*
Visa/Connect *0800 895082.*

Tax

With the exception of food, books, newspapers, children's clothing and a few other items, UK purchases are subject to VAT – Value Added Tax, aka sales tax – of 17.5 per cent. Unlike in the US, this is included in prices quoted in shops. In hotels, always check that the room rate quoted includes tax.

Opening hours

The following are general guidelines: there will be variations. Government offices all close on every bank (public) holiday (*see p377);* shops are increasingly remaining open. Only Christmas Day seems sacrosanct. Most visitor attractions remain open on the other public holidays but always call before visiting.

Banks 9am-4.30pm (some close at 3.30pm, some 5.30pm) Mon-Fri; sometimes also Saturday mornings.
Bars 11am-11pm Mon-Sat; noon-10.30pm Sun.
Businesses 9am-5pm Mon-Fri.
Post offices 9am-5.30pm Mon-Fri; 9am-noon Sat.
Shops 10am-6pm Mon-Sat; increasingly to 8pm.

Police stations

The police are a good source of information about the area and are used to helping visitors. If you've been robbed, assaulted

Directory

or involved in an infringement of the law, go to your nearest police station. (We've listed a handful in central London; look under 'Police' in the book or call Directory Enquiries on 118 118/500/888 for more). If you have a complaint, ensure that you take the offending police officer's identifying number (it should be displayed on his or her epaulette). You can then register a complaint with the **Independent Police Complaints Commission** (90 High Holborn, WC1V 6BH, 0845 300 2002).

Belgravia Police Station
202-206 Buckingham Palace Road, Pimlico, SW1W 9SX (7730 1212). Victoria tube/rail. **Map** p400 H10.
Charing Cross Police Station
Agar Street, Covent Garden, WC2N 4JP (7240 1212). Charing Cross tube/rail. **Map** p401 L7.
Chelsea Police Station
2 Lucan Place, Chelsea, SW3 3PB (7589 1212). Sloane Square tube. **Map** p397 E10.
Islington Police Station
2 Tolpuddle Street, Islington, N1 0YY (7704 1212). Angel tube. **Map** p402 N2.
Kensington Police Station
72-74 Earl's Court Road, Kensington, W8 6EQ (7376 1212). High Street Kensington tube. **Map** p396 B11.
King's Cross Police Station
76 King's Cross Road, Bloomsbury, WC1X 9QG (7713 1212). King's Cross tube/rail. **Map** p399 M3.
Marylebone Police Station
1-9 Seymour Street, Marylebone, W1H 7BA (7486 1212). Baker Street tube/Marylebone tube/rail. **Map** p395 F6.
Paddington Green Police Station *2-4 Harrow Road, Paddington, W2 1XJ (7402 1212). Edgware Road tube.* **Map** p396 E5.
West End Central Police Station *27 Savile Row, Mayfair, W1X 2DU (7437 1212). Piccadilly Circus tube.* **Map** p400 J7.

Postal services

You can buy stamps at all post offices and many newsagents and supermarkets. Current prices are 28p for first-class letters and 21p for second-class letters and 40p for letters to EU countries. Postcards cost 40p to send within Europe and 43p to countries outside Europe. Rates for other letters and parcels vary with weight and destination.

Post offices

Post offices are usually open 9am to 5.30pm Monday-Friday and 9am to noon Saturday, with the exception of **Trafalgar Square Post Office** (24-8 William IV Street, WC2N 4DL, 08457 223344, Charing Cross tube/rail), which is open 8.30am to 6.30pm Monday to Friday and 9am to 5.30pm on Saturday. The busiest time of day is usually 1pm to 2pm. Listed below are the other main central London offices. For general post office enquiries, call the central information line on 08457 223344 or consult www.postoffice.co.uk.

43-44 Albemarle Street *Mayfair, W1S 4DS (08456 223344). Green Park tube.* **Map** p400 J7.
111 Baker Street *Marylebone, W1U 6SG (08456 223344). Baker Street tube.* **Map** p398 G5.
54-56 Great Portland Street *Fitzrovia, W1W 7NE (08456 223344). Great Portland Street tube.* **Map** p398 H4.
1-5 Poland Street *Soho, W1F 8AA (08456 223344). Oxford Circus tube.* **Map** p398 J6.

Poste restante

If you want to receive mail while you're away, you can have it sent to Trafalgar Square Post Office (*see above*), where it will be kept at the enquiry desk for a month. Your name and 'Poste Restante' must be clearly marked on the letter. You'll need ID to collect it.

Religion

Anglican

St Paul's Cathedral *For listings details, see p92.* **Services** 7.30am, 8am, 12.30pm, 5pm Mon-Fri; 8am, 8.30am, 12.30pm, 5pm Sat; 8am, 10.15am, 11.30am, 3.15pm, 6pm Sun. **Map** p404 O6.
Times may vary; phone to check.

Westminster Abbey *For listings details, see p138.* **Services** 7.30am, 8am, 12.30pm, 5pm Mon-Fri; 8am, 9am, 12.30pm, 3pm Sat; 8am, 10am, 11.15am, 3pm, 5.45pm Sun. **Map** p401 K9.

Baptist

Bloomsbury Central Baptist Church *235 Shaftesbury Avenue, Covent Garden, WC2H 8EP (7240 0544/www.bloomsbury.org.uk). Tottenham Court Road tube.* **Open** 10am-4pm Mon-Fri. *Friendship Centre Oct-June* noon-2.30pm Tue. **Services & meetings** 11am, 6.30pm Sun. **Map** p399 L6.

Buddhist

Buddhapadipa Thai Temple *14 Calonne Road, Wimbledon, SW19 5HJ (8946 1357/www.buddhapadipa.org). Wimbledon tube/rail, then 93 bus.* **Open** *Temple* 1-6pm Sat, Sun. *Meditation retreat* 7-9pm Tue, Thur; 4-6pm Sat, Sun.

Catholic

Oratory Catholic Church *For listings, see p144.* **Services** 7am, 8am (Latin mass), 10am, 12.30am, 6pm Mon-Fri; 7am, 8.30am, 10am, 6pm Sat; 7am, 8.30am, 10am (tridentine), 11am (sung Latin), 12.30pm, 3.30pm, 4.30pm, 7pm Sun. **Map** p397 E10.
Westminster Cathedral *For listings, see p139.* **Services** 7am, 8am, 9am, 10.30am, 12.30pm, 5pm Mon-Fri; 8am, 9am, 12.30pm, 6pm Sat; 7am, 8am, 9am, 10.30am, noon, 5.30pm, 7pm Sun. **Map** p400 J10.

Islamic

London Central Mosque *146 Park Road, St John's Wood, NW8 7RG (7724 3363). Baker Street tube/74 bus.* **Open** dawn-dusk daily. **Services** 5.30am, 1pm, 4pm, 7pm, 8.30pm daily.
East London Mosque *82-92 Whitechapel Road, E1 1JQ (7247 1357. Aldgate East or Whitechapel tube.* **Open** 10am-10pm daily. **Services** *Friday prayer* 1.30pm (1.15pm in winter). **Map** p405 S6.

Jewish

Liberal Jewish Synagogue *28 St John's Wood Road, St John's Wood, NW8 7HA (7286 5181/www.ljs.org). St John's Wood tube.* **Open** 9am-5pm Mon-Thur; 9am-1pm Fri. **Services** 6.45pm Fri; 11am Sat.
West Central Liberal Synagogue *21 Maple Street, Fitzrovia, W1T 4BE (7636 7627/www.wcls.org.uk). Warren Street tube.* **Services** 3pm Sat. **Map** p398 J4.

Methodist

Methodist Central Hall *Central Hall, Storey's Gate, Westminster,*

SW1H 9NH (7222 8010). St James's Park tube. **Open** *Chapel* 8am-6pm daily. **Services** 12.45pm Wed; 11am, 6.30pm Sun. **Map** p401 K9.

Quaker

Religious Society of Friends (Quakers) *Friends House, 173-177 Euston Road, Bloomsbury, NW1 2BJ (7663 1000/www.quaker.org.uk). Euston tube/rail.* **Open** 8.30am-9.30pm Mon-Fri; 8.30am-4.30pm Sat. **Meetings** 11am Sun. **Map** p399 K3.

Safety & security

There are no 'no-go' areas as such, but thieves haunt busy shopping areas and transport nodes as they do in all cities. Use common sense and follow these basic rules.

● **Keep** wallets and purses out of sight, and handbags securely closed.
● **Don't** leave briefcases, bags or coats unattended.
● **Don't** leave bags or coats beside, under or on the back of a chair.
● **Don't** put bags on the floor near the door of a public toilet.
● **Don't** take short cuts through dark alleys and car parks.
● **Don't** keep your passport, money, credit cards, etc together.
● **Don't** carry a wallet in your back pocket.

Smoking

Smoking is permitted in almost all pubs and bars – though an increasing number have no-smoking areas – and in many restaurants. Specify when you book if you'd like a table in the smoking section. Smoking is forbidden in shops and on public transport. There is pressure for a change in the law; *see p29* **No butts**.

Study

Being a student in London is as expensive as it is exciting; *Time Out's Student Guide*, available from September each year, provides the lowdown on how to enjoy and survive the experience. In this guide, entry prices for students are usually designated 'concessions'. You'll have to show ID (an NUS or ISIC card) to qualify for these rates.

Language classes

Aspect Covent Garden Language Centre

3-4 Southampton Place, Covent Garden, WC1A 2DA (7404 3080/ www.aspectworld.com). Holborn tube. **Map** p399 L5.

Central School of English

1 Tottenham Court Road, Bloomsbury, W1T 1BB (7580 2863/ www.centralschool.co.uk). Tottenham Court Road tube. **Map** p397 K5.

Frances King School of English

77 Gloucester Road, South Kensington, SW7 4SS (7870 6533/ www.francesking.co.uk). Gloucester Road tube. **Map** p395 F9.

London Study Centre

Munster House, 676 Fulham Road, Fulham, SW6 5SA (7731 3549/ www.londonstudycentre.com). Parsons Green tube.

Sels College

64-65 Long Acre, Covent Garden, WC2E 9SX (7240 2581/www.sels.co.uk). Covent Garden tube. **Map** p399 L6.

Shane English School

59 South Molton Street, Mayfair, W1K 5SN (7499 8533/www. sgvenglish.com). Bond Street tube. **Map** p398 H6.

Students' unions

Many unions will only let in students with ID, so always carry your NUS or ISIC card with you. We've listed those with the best bars, all of which offer a good night out. Call for opening times, which vary with the academic year and events.

Imperial College *Beit Quad, Prince Consort Road, South Kensington, SW7 2BB (7594 8060). South Kensington tube.* **Map** p397 D9.

International Students House *229 Great Portland Street, Marylebone, W1W 5PN (7631 8300). Great Portland Street tube.* **Map** p398 H4.

King's College *Macadam Building, Surrey Street, Covent Garden, WC2R 2NS (7836 7132). Temple tube.* **Map** p401 M7.

London Metropolitan University *166-220 Holloway Road, Holloway, N7 8DB (7607 2789). Holloway Road tube.*

University of London Union (ULU) *Malet Street, Bloomsbury, WC1E 7HY (7664 2000). Goodge Street tube.* **Map** p399 K4.

Universities

Brunel University *Cleveland Road, Uxbridge, Middx UB8 3PH (01895*

274000/students' union 01895 462200). Uxbridge tube.

City University *Northampton Square, Clerkenwell, EC1V 0HB (7040 5060/students' union 7040 5600). Angel tube.* **Map** p402 O3.

London Metropolitan University *166-220 Holloway Road, Holloway, N7 8DB (7607 2789/students' union 7133 2769). Holloway Road tube.*

South Bank University *Borough Road, Borough, SE1 0AA (7928 8989/students' union 7815 6060). Elephant & Castle tube/rail.* **Map** p404 O9.

University of Greenwich *Old Royal Naval College, Park Row, Greenwich, SE10 9LS (8331 8000/students' union 8331 7629). Greenwich DLR.*

University of Middlesex *Trent Park, Bramley Road, Cockfosters, N14 4YZ (8411 5000/students' union 8411 6450). Cockfosters or Oakwood tube.*

University of Westminster *309 Regent Street, Mayfair, W1B 2UW (7911 5000/students' union 7915 5454). Oxford Circus tube.* **Map** p398 H4.

University of London

The university consists of 34 colleges, spread across the city; the seven largest are listed below. All London universities (except Imperial College) are affiliated to the National Union of Students (NUS; 7272 8900, www.nusonline.co.uk).

Goldsmiths' College *Lewisham Way, New Cross, SE14 6NW (7919 7171/students' union 8692 1406). New Cross/New Cross Gate tube/rail.*

Imperial College *Exhibition Road, Kensington, SW7 2AZ (7589 5111/students' union 7594 8060). South Kensington tube.* **Map** p397 D9.

King's College *Strand, Covent Garden WC2R 2NS (7836 5454/students' union 7836 7132). Temple tube.* **Map** p401 M7.

Kingston University *Penrhyn Road, Kingston, Surrey KT1 2EE (8547 2000/students' union 8547 8868). Kingston rail.*

London School of Economics (LSE) *Houghton Street, Holborn, WC2A 2AE (7405 7686/students' union 7955 7158). Holborn tube.* **Map** p399 M6.

Queen Mary University of London *327 Mile End Road, Stepney, E1 4NS (7882 5555/ students' union 7882 5390). Mile End or Stepney Green tube.*

University College London (UCL) *Gower Street, Bloomsbury, WC1E 6BT (7679 2000/students' union 7387 3611). Euston Square, Goodge Street or Warren Street tube.* **Map** p399 K4.

Directory

Useful organisations

More useful organisations for students in this country, including BUNAC and the Council on International Educational Exchange, can be found on *p378*.

National Bureau for Students with Disabilities *Chapter House, 18-20 Crucifix Lane, SE1 3JW (7450 0620/www.skill.org.uk).* **Open** *Phone enquiries* 11.30am-1.30pm Tue; 1.30-3.30pm Thur.

Telephones

London's dialling code is 020; standard landlines have eight digits after that. You don't need to dial the 020 from within the area, so we have not given it in this book. If you're calling from outside the UK, dial your international access code, then the UK code, 44, then the full London number, omitting the first 0 from the code. For example, to make a call to 020 7813 3000 from the US, dial 011 44 20 7813 3000. To dial abroad from the UK, first dial 00, then the relevant country code from the list below. For more international dialling codes, check the phonebook or www.kropla.com/dialcode.htm.

Australia 61; **Canada** 1; **Ireland** 353; **New Zealand** 64; **South Africa** 27; **USA** 1.

Public phones

Public payphones take coins or credit cards (sometimes both). The minimum cost is 20p, which buys you a 110-second local call. Some payphones, such as the counter-top ones found in many pubs, require more. International calling cards offering bargain minutes via a freephone number are widely available.

Operator services

Operator

Call **100** for the operator if you have difficulty in dialling; for an alarm call; to make a credit card call; for information about the cost of a call; and for help with international person-to-person calls. Dial **155** for the international operator if you need to reverse the charges (call collect) or if you can't dial direct, but be warned that this service is very expensive.

Directory enquiries

This service is now provided by various six-digit 118 numbers. They're pretty pricey to call: dial (free) 0800 953 0720 for a rundown of options and prices. The best known is 118 118, which charges 49p per call, then 9p per minute thereafter. 118 888 charges 39p per call, then 9p per minute. 118 180 charges 25p per call, then 30p per minute. Online, use the free www.ukphonebook.co.uk.

Yellow Pages

This 24-hour service lists the numbers of thousands of businesses in the UK. Dial **118 247** (40p/min) and say what type of business you require, and in what area of London.

Telephone directories

There are three telephone directories for London (two for private numbers, one for companies), available at post offices and libraries. These hefty tomes are issued free to all residents, as is the invaluable *Yellow Pages* directory (also accessible online at www.yell.com), which lists businesses and services.

Mobile phones

Mobile phones in the UK work on either the 900 or 1800 GSM system. The situation is complex for US travellers. If your service provider in the US uses the GSM system, your phone probably runs on the 1900 band, so you'll need a tri-band handset.

The simplest option may be to buy a 'pay as you go' phone (about £50-£200); there's no monthly fee, you top up talk time using a card. Check before buying whether it can make and receive international calls.

Alternatively, you can rent a mobile phone from the AmEx offices at Terminals 3 and 4 at Heathrow Airport.

Telegrams

To send telegrams abroad, call 0800 190190. This is also the number to call to send an international telemessage: phone in your message and it will be delivered by post the next day.

Time

London operates on Greenwich Mean Time (GMT), which is five hours ahead of the US's Eastern Standard time. In spring (27 March 2005) the UK puts its clocks forward by one hour to British Summer Time. In autumn (30 October 2005) the clocks go back to GMT.

Tipping

In Britain it's accepted that you tip in taxis, minicabs, restaurants (some waiting staff rely heavily on tips), hotels, hairdressers and some bars (not pubs). Ten per cent is normal, with some restaurants adding as much as 15 per cent. Always check if service has been included in your bill: some restaurants include service, then leave the space for a gratuity on your credit card slip blank.

Toilets

Public toilets are few and far between in London, and pubs and restaurants reserve their toilets for customers only. However, all main-line rail stations and a few tube stations – Piccadilly Circus, for one – have public toilets (you may be charged a small fee). It's also usually possible to sneak into a department store.

Tourist information

Visit London (7234 5800, www.visitlondon.com) is the city's official tourist information company. There are also tourist offices in

Greenwich and next to St Paul's (**Map** p404 O6).

Britain & London Visitor Centre
1 Lower Regent Street, Piccadilly Circus, SW1Y 4XT (8846 9000/www.visitbritain.com). Piccadilly Circus tube. **Open** *Oct-May* 9.30am-6.30pm Mon; 9am-6.30pm Tue-Fri; 10am-4pm Sat, Sun. *June-Sept* 9.30am-6.30pm Mon; 9am-6.30pm Tue-Fri; 9am-5pm Sat; 10am-4pm Sun. **Map** p401 K7.

London Information Centre
Leicester Square, WC2H 7BP (7292 2333/www.londontown.com). Leicester Square tube. **Open** 8am-11pm daily.
Information and booking services.

London Visitor Centre *Arrivals Hall, Waterloo International Terminal, SE1 7LT.* **Open** 8.30am-10.30pm Mon-Sat; 9.30am-10.30pm Sun. **Map** p405 M9.

Visas & immigration

EU citizens do not require a visa to visit the UK; citizens of the USA, Canada, Austrlia, South Africa and New Zealand can also enter with only a passport for tourist visits of up to six months as long as they can show they can support themselves during their visit and plan to return. If you're visiting for any other purpose or not a national of one of the above countries, use www.uk visas.gov.uk to check your visa status well before you travel, or contact the British embassy, consulate or high commission in your own country. You can arrange visas online at www.vis4UK. fco.gov.uk. For work permits, *see p378.*

Home Office *Immigration & Nationality Bureau, Lunar House, 40 Wellesley Road, Croydon, Surrey CR9 1AT (0870 606 7766/ application forms 0870 241 0645/www.homeoffice.gov.uk).* **Open** *Phone enquiries* 9am-4.45pm Mon-Thur; 9am-4.30pm Fri.

Weights & measures

The United Kingdom is slowly but surely moving towards full metrication. Distances are still measured in miles but all goods are now officially sold in metric quantities, with no legal requirement for the imperial equivalent to be given.

Some useful conversions:

1 centimetre (cm) = 0.39 inches (in)
1 inch (in) = 2.54 centimetres (cm)
1 yard (yd) = 0.91 metres (m)
1 metre (m) = 1.094 yards (yd)
1 mile = 1.6 kilometres (km)
1 kilometre (km) = 0.62 miles
1 ounce (oz) = 28.35 grammes (g)
1 gramme (g) = 0.035 ounces (oz)
1 pound (lb) = 0.45 kilogrammes (kg)
1 kilogramme (kg) = 2.2 pounds (lb)
1 pint (US) = 0.8 pints (UK)
1 pint (UK) = 0.55 litres (l)
1 litre (l) = 1.75 pints (UK)

When to go

Climate

The British climate is famously unpredictable, but Weathercall on 09003 444 900 (60p per min) can offer some guidance. *See also p378* **Weather report**. The best websites for weather news and features include www.metoffice.com; www.weather.com; and www.bbc.co.uk/london/ weather, which all offer good detailed long-term international forecasts and are easily searchable.

Spring extends approximately from March to May, though frosts can last into April. March winds and April showers may be a month early or a month late, but May is often very pleasant.
Summer (June, July and August) can be unpredictable, with searing heat one day followed by sultry greyness and violent thunderstorms the next. There are plenty of sunny days, too, though. High temperatures, humidity and pollution can create problems for those with hayfever or breathing difficulties, especially later on. Temperatures down in the tube can reach dangerous levels, particularly during rush hour.
Autumn starts in September, although the weather can still have a mild, summery feel. Real autumn comes with October, when the leaves start to fall. When the November cold, grey and wet sets in, you'll be reminded that London is situated on a fairly northerly latitude.
Winter can have some delightful crisp, cold days, but don't bank on them. The usual scenario is for a disappointingly grey, wet Christmas, followed by a cold snap in January and February, when we may even see a sprinkling of snow, and public transport chaos ensues.

Public holidays

On public holidays (bank holidays), many shops remain open, but public transport services generally run to a Sunday timetable. The exception is Christmas Day, when almost everything shuts.

New Year's Day Mon 3 Jan 2005; Mon 2 Jan 2006.
Good Friday Fri 25 Mar 2005; Fri 14 Apr 2006.
Easter Monday Mon 28 Mar 2005; Mon 17 Apr 2006.
May Day Holiday Mon 2 May 2005; Mon 1 May 2006.
Spring Bank Holiday Mon 30 May 2005; Mon 29 May 2006.
Summer Bank Holiday Mon 29 Aug 2005; Mon 28 Aug 2006.
Christmas Day Sun 25 Dec 2005; Mon 25 Dec 2006.
Boxing Day Mon 26 Dec 2005; Tue 26 Dec 2006.

Women

London is home to dozens of women's groups and networks, from day centres to rights campaigners; www.gn.apc.org and www.wrc.org.uk provide information and many links.

Visiting women are unlikely to be harassed. Bar the very occasional sexually motivated attack, London's streets are no more dangerous for women than for men, if you follow the usual precautions (*see p375*).

The Women's Library
25 Old Castle Street, Whitechapel, E1 7NT (7320 2222/www.thewomens library.ac.uk). Aldgate or Aldgate East tube. **Open** *Reading room* 9.30am-5pm Tue, Wed, Fri; 9.30am-8pm Thur; 10am-4pm Sat.
Europe's largest women's studies archive, with changing exhibitions.

Working in London

Finding temporary work in London can be a full-time job in itself. Those with a reasonable level of English who are EU citizens or have

Directory

work permits should be able to find work in catering, labouring, bars/pubs, coffee bars or shops. Graduates with an English or foreign-language degree could try teaching. Ideas can be found in *Summer Jobs in Britain*, published by Vacation Work, 9 Park End Street, Oxford, OX1 1HJ (£10.99 plus £1.75 p&p).

Good sources of job information are the *Evening Standard*, local/national newspapers and newsagents' windows. Vacancies for temporary and unskilled work are often displayed on Jobcentre noticeboards; your nearest Jobcentre can be found under 'Employment Agencies' in the *Yellow Pages*. If you have good typing (over 40 wpm) or word processing skills, you could sign on with some of the temp agencies. Many of them have specialist areas beyond the obvious administrative or secretarial roles, such as translation.

For shop, bar and restaurant work, just go in and inquire.

Work permits

With few exceptions, citizens of non-European Economic Area (EEA) countries have to have a work permit before they can legally work in the United Kingdom. Employers who are unable to fill particular vacancies with a resident or EEA national must apply for a permit to the Department for Education and Employment (DfEE; *see below*). Permits are issued only for high-level jobs.

Au Pair Scheme

Citizens aged 17 to 27 from the following non-EEA countries are permitted to become au pairs (along, of course, with EEA nationals): Andorra, Faroe Islands, Romania, Bosnia-Herzegovina, Greenland, San Marino, Bulgaria, Macedonia, Turkey, Croatia. A visa is sometimes required.

Sandwich students

Approval for course-compulsory sandwich placements at recognised UK colleges must be obtained for potential students by their college from the DfEE's **Overseas Labour Service** (*see below* **Department for Education & Employment**).

Students

Visiting students from the US, Canada, Australia or Jamaica can get a sign up for the BUNAC programme, which lets them work in the UK for up to six months. Contact the Work in Britain Department of the **Council on International Educational Exchange** or call **BUNAC**. Students should get an application form OSS1 (BUNAC) from BUNAC, and submit it to a Jobcentre to obtain permission to work.

Working holidaymakers

Citizens of Commonwealth countries aged 17 to 27 may apply to come to the UK as a working holidaymaker by contacting their nearest British Diplomatic Post in advance. They are then allowed to take part-time work without a DfEE permit.

Useful addresses

BUNAC

16 Bowling Green Lane, Clerkenwell, EC1R 0QH (7251 3472/www. bunac.org.uk). Farringdon tube/rail. **Open** 9.30am-5.30pm Mon-Thur; 9.30am-5pm Fri. **Map** p402 N4.

Council on International Educational Exchange

3rd Floor, 7 Custom House Street, Portland, Maine, ME 04101, USA (00 1 207 553 7600/www.ciee.org). **Open** 9am-5pm Mon-Fri.
The Council on International Educational Exchange aids young people to study, work and travel abroad. It's divided into international study programmes and exchanges.

Department for Education & Employment

Work Permits UK helpline 0114 259 4074/www.workpermits. gov.uk. **Open** *Phone* enquiries 9am-5pm Mon-Fri.
Employers seeking work permit application forms should phone 08705 210224 or visit the website.

Home Office

Immigration & Nationality Directorate, Lunar House, 40 Wellesley Road, Croydon, Surrey CR9 2BY (0870 606 7766/www.ind.homeoffice.gov.uk). **Open** *Phone* enquiries 9am-4.45pm Mon-Thur; 9am-4.30pm Fri.
The Home Office is able to provide advice on whether or not a work permit is required.

Overseas Visitors Records Office

180 Borough High Street, Borough, SE1 1LH (7230 1208). Borough tube/Elephant & Castle or London Bridge tube/rail. **Open** 9am-4pm Mon-Fri. **Map** p404 P9.
In a former incarnation, this was the Aliens Registration Office run by the Metropolitan Police. These days, though, it's known as the vastly less scary Overseas Visitors Records Office, and it charges £34 to register a person if they already have a work permit.

Weather report

Average daytime temperatures, rainfall and hours of sunshine in London

	Temp (°C/°F)	Rainfall (mm/in)	Sunshine (hrs/dy)
Jan	6/43	54/2.1	1.5
Feb	7/44	40/1.6	2.3
Mar	10/50	37/1.5	3.6
Apr	13/55	37/1.5	5.3
May	17/63	46/1.8	6.4
June	20/68	45/1.8	7.1
July	22/72	57/2.2	6.4
Aug	21/70	59/2.3	6.1
Sept	19/66	49/1.9	4.7
Oct	14/57	57/2.2	3.2
Nov	10/50	64/2.5	1.8
Dec	7/44	48/1.9	1.3

Directory

Further Reference

Fiction

Peter Ackroyd *Hawksmoor; The House of Doctor Dee; Great Fire of London; The Lambs of London*
Intricate studies of arcane London.
Monica Ali *Brick Lane* Arranged marriage in Tower Hamlets.
Debi Alper *Nirvana Bites*
Peckham-based writer's debut.
Martin Amis *London Fields* Darts and drinking way out east.
Paul Bryers *The Used Women's Book Club* Murder most torrid in contemporary Spitalfields.
Jonathan Coe *The Dwarves of Death* Mystery, music, mirth, malevolence.
Norman Collins *London Belongs to Me* A witty saga of '30s Kennington.
Joseph Conrad *The Secret Agent* Anarchism in seedy Soho.
Charles Dickens *Oliver Twist; David Copperfield; Bleak House; Our Mutual Friend*
Four of the master's most London-centric novels.
Sir Arthur Conan Doyle *The Complete Sherlock Holmes*
Reassuring sleuthing shenanigans.
Maureen Duffy *Capital*
The bones beneath our feet and the stories they tell.
Christopher Fowler *Soho Black*
Walking dead in Soho.
Anthony Frewin *London Blues*
One-time Kubrick assistant explores '60s porn movie industry.
Neil Gaiman *Neverwhere*
A new world above and below the streets by *Sandman* creator.
Graham Greene *The End of the Affair* Adultery and Catholicism.
Alan Hollinghurst
The Swimming Pool Library
Gay life around Russell Square.
The Line of Beauty
Beautiful, ruthless look at metropolitan debauchery. 2004 Booker Prize winner.
Hanif Kureishi *The Buddha of Suburbia* 1970s sexual confusion and identity crisis.
Colin MacInnes *City of Spades; Absolute Beginners* Coffee 'n' jazz, Soho 'n' Notting Hill.
Tour of rock history's blue plaque sites.
Derek Marlowe *A Dandy in Aspic* A capital-set Cold War classic.
Michael Moorcock *Mother London*
A love letter to London.
Ferdinand Mount *Heads You Win* Tale of East End headhunting scam.
George Orwell *Keep the Aspidistra Flying* Saga of a struggling writer.

Antony Powell *A Dance to the Music of Time*
Epic interwar novel cycle.
Derek Raymond *I Was Dora Suarez* The blackest London noir.
Nicholas Royle *The Matter of the Heart; The Director's Cut*
Abandoned buildings and secrets.
Edward Rutherfurd *London*
A city's history given a novel voice.
Will Self *Grey Area* Short stories.
Iain Sinclair *Downriver; Radon Daughters; White Chappell, Scarlet Tracings*
The Thames's *Heart of Darkness*;
William Hope Hodgson; Ripper murders and book dealers.
Evelyn Waugh *Vile Bodies*
Shameful antics in 1920s Mayfair.
Virginia Woolf *Mrs Dalloway*
A kind of London *Ulysses*.

Non-fiction

Peter Ackroyd *London: The Biography*
Wilfully obscurantist city history.
Marc Atkins & Iain Sinclair *Liquid City*
Sinclair haunts photographed.
Nicholas Barton *The Lost Rivers of London* Fascinating studies of old watercourses and their legacy.
James Boswell *Boswell's London Journal 1762-1763*
Rich account of ribald literary life.
Anthony Burgess *A Dead Man in Deptford*
The life and murder of Elizabethan playwright Christopher Marlowe.
Daniel Farson *Soho in the Fifties*
An affectionate portrait.
Geoffrey Fletcher *The London Nobody Knows*
By an opinionated expert.
Peter Guillery *The Small House in 18th Century London*
Social and architectural history
Derek Hanson
The Dreadful Judgement
The embers of the Great Fire re-raked.
Sarah Hartley *Mrs P's Journey* Biography of Phyllis Pearsall, the woman who created the *A–Z*.
Stephen Inwood *A History of London* A recent, readable history.
Ian Jack (ed) *Granta, London: the Lives of the City*
Fiction, reportage and travel writing.
Edward Jones & Christopher Woodward *A Guide to the Architecture of London* What it says. A brilliant work.
Jack London *The People of the Abyss* Poverty in the East End.
Malcolm Mclaren *Rock 'n' Roll London* A tour thereof.
Nick Merriman (ed) *The Peopling of London* 2,000 years of settlement.

Tim Moore *Do Not Pass Go*
A hysterically funny Monopoly addict's London.
Gilda O'Neill *Pull No More Bines; My East End*
A social histories of east London.
George Orwell *Down and Out in Paris and London*
Waitering and starving.
Samuel Pepys *Diaries*
Fires, plagues, bordellos and more.
Liza Picard *Dr Johnson's London; Restoration London.*
London past, engagingly revisited.
Patricia Pierce *Old London Bridge* The story of the world's longest inhabited bridge.
Roy Porter *London: A Social History* An all-encompassing history.
Jonathan Raban *Soft City*
The city as state of mind; a classic.
Iain Sinclair *Lights Out for the Territory; London Orbital.*
Time-warp visionary crosses London; and circles it on the M25.
Stephen Smith
Underground London: Travels Beneath the City Streets
Absorbing writing on the subterranean city.
Judith Summers
Soho: A History of London's Most Colourful Neighbourhood.
So-Ho! Great local history.
Richard Tames
Feeding London Eating history from coffee houses onwards; *East End Past* A close look at the area.
William Taylor *This Bright Field* Spitalfields in enjoyable detail.
Adrian Tinniswood *His Invention So Fertile* Illuminating biography of Christopher Wren.
Richard Trench *London Under London* Beneath the city.
Ben Weinreb & Christopher Hibbert (eds) *The London Encyclopaedia*
Fascinating, thorough, indispensable.
Andrew White (ed)
Time Out Book of London Walks Volumes 1 & 2.
Writers, cartoonists, comedians and historians take a walk through town.
Jerry White *London in the 20th Century: A City and Its People.*

Films

Alfie *dir.* Lewis Gilbert (1966)
What's it all about, Michael?
Beautiful Thing *dir.* Hettie MacDonald (1996)
A tender, amusing coming-of-age flick.
A Clockwork Orange *dir.* Stanley Kubrick (1971)
Kubrick's vision still shocks.
Blow-Up *dir.* Michelangelo Antonioni (1966)

Directory

Blog jam

A weblog gives intimacy through anonymity, bringing a city's thoughts and secrets to your desktop. Check out www.aggregators.weblogs.co.uk for links to more blogs in London and nationwide.

Belle de Jour
Elegant diary of a London call girl.
www.belledejour-uk.blogspot.com

The Big Smoker
London gossip and goings-on.
www.thebigsmoker.co.uk

Blogadoon
Out and about gay life in London.
www.iansie.com/nonsense/blog.html

Hackney Lookout
Keeping tabs on local eccentrics.
www.hackneylookout.blogspot.com

In the Aquarium
Poetic observations and life drawings.
www.intheaquarium.blogspot.com

London geezer
Lists, guides and photos of out-of-the-way London landmarks.
www.lndn.blogspot.com

Londonmark
Off-the-wall take on Camden life.
www.londonmark.blogspot.com

Route 79
A second-generation Indian on London life and aloo gobi. www.route79.com/journal/

Sashinka
Sharp stories from a Jewish girl-about-town.
www.sashinka.blogspot.com

This isn't London
Delightfully misleading miscellany.
www.thisisntlondon.blogspot.com

Swingin' London captured in unintentionally hysterical fashion.
Death Line *dir. Gary Sherman* (1972) Cannibalism on the tube. Yikes.
Dirty Pretty Things *dir. Stephen Frears* (2002) Drama centred on immigrant hotel workers.
Jubilee *dir. Derek Jarman* (1978) A horribly dated but still interesting romp through the punk era.
The Krays *dir. Peter Medak* (1990) The Kemps as East End gangsters.
Life is Sweet; **Naked**; **Secrets & Lies**; **Career Girls**; **All or Nothing**; **Vera Drake** *dir. Mike Leigh* (1990; 1993; 1996; 1997; 2002; 2004) An affectionate look at Metroland; a character study; familiar tensions; old friends meet; family falls apart; postwar austerity.

Lock, Stock & Two Smoking Barrels; **Snatch** *dir. Guy Ritchie* (1998; 2000) Mr Madonna's pair of East End faux-gangster flicks.
London; **Robinson in Space** *dir. Patrick Keiller* (1994; 1997) Fiction meets documentary.
The Long Good Friday *dir. John MacKenzie* (1989) Bob Hoskins stars in the classic London gangster flick.
Mona Lisa; **The Crying Game** *dir. Neil Jordan* (1986; 1992) Prostitution, terrorism, transvestism.
Mrs Dalloway *dir. Marleen Goris* (1997) Vanessa Redgrave stars in this adaptation of the Woolf novel.
Nil by Mouth *dir. Gary Oldman* (1997) A violent tale of working-class life.

Notting Hill *dir. Roger Michell* (1999) Hugh Grant and Julia Roberts get it on in west London.
Peeping Tom *dir. Michael Powell* (1960) Powell's creepy murder flick.
Performance *dir. Nicolas Roeg, Donald Cammell* (1970) The cult movie to end all cult movies made west London cool for life.
28 Days *dir. Danny Boyle* (2002) Post-apocalyptic London.
Wimbledon *dir. Richard Loncraine* (2004) Paul Bettany plays up an idyllic, postcard England.
Wonderland *dir. Michael Winterbottom* (1999) Love, loss and deprivation.

Music

Bad Manners *Vive La Ska Revolution* Jangly ska rampage through '80s London.
Blur *Modern Life is Rubbish* (1993); *Park Life* (1994) Modern classics by the Essex exiles.
The Clash *London Calling* (1979) Epoch-making punk classic.
The Jam *This is the Modern World* (1977) Weller at his splenetic finest.
Madness *Rise & Fall* (1982) The nutty boys wax lyrical.
Morrissey *Vauxhall & I* (1994) His finest solo album.
The Rolling Stones *December's Children (and Everybody's)* (1965) Moodily cool evocation of the city.
Squeeze *Greatest Hits* (1994) Lovable south London geezer pop.

Websites

BBC London *www.bbc.co.uk/london* Online news, travel, weather, entertainment and sport.
Classic Cafés *www.classiccafes.co.uk* London's '50s and '60s caffs.
Greater London Authority *www.london.gov.uk*
Hidden London *www.hiddenlondon.com*
London Active Map *www.uktravel.com* Click on a tube station and find out which attractions are nearby.
London Footprints *www.london-footprints.co.uk* Free walks to print out.
Pubs.com *www.pubs.com* London's traditional boozers.
The River Thames Guide *www.riverthames.co.uk* Places along the riverbank.
Street Map *www.streetmap.co.uk* Grid references and postcodes.
This is London *www.thisislondon.co.uk* The *Evening Standard* online.
Time Out *www.timeout.com* An essential source, of course. From here you can access our invaluable eating and drinking guides.

Directory

Index

Note: Page numbers in **bold**
  indicate section(s) giving key
  information on a topic; *italics*
  indicate photographs.

a

Abbey Mill 162
Abbey Road 23, 73, **150**
Abney Park Cemetery 156
abortion 369
Abramovich, Roman 326
Abu Hamza 29
accident & emergency 369
accommodation **45-70**
  by price:
    cheap 46-47, 53, 57, 62,
      65, 66, 69
    deluxe 47, 49, 53-55, 57-58,
      59-61, 62, 66
    expensive 47, 49-50, 55-57,
      59, 61, 63-65, 66
    moderate 49, 50, 53, 62,
      65, 66-69
  the best hotels 47
  hotels with views 54
Act of Settlement of 1701 19
Adam, Robert 32, **35**, 116, 147,
  154, 188, 190
Adamsdale, Will 276
addresses 366
Adelphi, the 35
Admiralty Arch 72, **133**
age restrictions 366
Ahmed-Ahmed 276
AIDS 370
air, arriving & leaving by 360
airports 360
Albert, Prince **20**, 140, 144
Albert Bridge 175
Albert Memorial *21*, 36, **144**
Aldgate 10
Aldwych 11
Alexander Fleming Laboratory
  Museum 182
Alexandra Palace Theatre 332
Alexandra Park & Palace 21,
  73, **155**
Alfie's Antiques Market
  113, **235**
Alfred, King **11**, *13*, 25
All England Lawn Tennis Club
  179, 328
All Hallows by the Tower 97, **98**
All Saints 111
All Souls 111
Alma-Tadema, Lawrence 150
Almeida, the 155, 332, **339**
Alsop, Will 38
Alston Dance Company,
  Richard 279
Althorp 354
Anderson shelters 22
Anglican churches 374
Anne, Queen 19
Anne of Denmark, Queen 170
antiquarian book shops 236
antiques shops 235
apartment rental 69
Apothecaries' Hall 91
Apple Day 152
Apple Market 127
Apsley House: The Wellington
  Museum 115, **116**
Archer, Thomas 167
Architectural Association 293
architecture **31-38**
Architecture Week 263
Archway 154
Archway Bridge 154

Argyll Street 125
Arnold, Benedict 175
Arnos Grove Station 36
Arsenal FC 155, **325**
art
  festivals 261, 264
  see also galleries *and*
    museums & galleries
'art squatters' 291
Arthur, King 354
Arundel Castle 354
ASBOs 27
Ascot Racecourse 327
Ashton, Frederick 279
Asian Dub Foundation 165
Astoria, The 309
Aterman, Peter 276
ATMs 373
Attlee, Clement 22
audio-visual shops 239
Audley End 354
Augustine 10
Austen, Jane 344, 354
Australia House 101
Australians in London 187
Avon, River *342*, 345

b

BAC (Battersea Arts Centre) 339
Bacon, Francis 121
Baden-Powell, Robert 179
Baird, John Logie 124
Baker, Sir Herbert 95
Baker Street 113
bakeries 247
Baldwin, Stanley 21
ballet 279
balloon tours 74
Baltic Exchange 25
Bank 95
Bank of England 19, 25, 35, **95**
Bank of England Museum 95
banks 373
Bankside 14, 75, **79-83**
  for children 268
  hotels 46-47
  pubs & bars 221
  restaurants & cafés 193-195
Bankside Gallery 81
Bankside Power Station 38, **81**
Bannister, Roger 183
Banqueting House 17, 33,
  134, **136**
Baptist churches 374
Barbican Art Gallery 100
Barbican Centre, the 88, **100**,
  268, **278**, 302, 305, 309,
  314, **333**
Barbican International Theatre
  Event (BITE) 278, 333
Barclays Premiership 325
Barker's 124
Barnado, Dr 162
Barnes 177-178
Barnes Common 177
Barrett, Elizabeth 112
Barry, Charles **35**, 132, 137
bars *see* pubs & bars
Barter, Richard 183
basketball 325
Bath 345-347
Battersea 175
Battersea Bridge 175
Battersea Dogs' Home 175
Battersea Park **175**, 273
Battersea Power Station 31, **175**
Battle 358
Baynard's Castle 11
Bayswater 46, **182**

Bazalgette, Joseph **18**, 20, 162, 175
BBC 21, 101, 111, 112, 155, 187
BBC Sir Henry Wood Promenade
  Concerts 301, 264, **306**
BBC Television Centre
  & Tours 187
Beating Retreat 263
Beatles, the 111, 115, 150
Beauchamp Place 144
Beaufort House 145
Beck's Futures 134
Becket, Thomas à 350
bed & breakfasts 70
Bedford, Dukes and Earls of
  106, 126
Bedford Square 106
Bedlam 19
Beefeaters *88*, 99
Belgravia 144
  hotels 62-65
  pubs & bars 227
Bell, Clive & Vanessa 106
Bennett, Alan 148
Bentley, John Francis 113, 139
Berkeley Square 115
Bermondsey 86-87
Bermondsey Antiques Market 86
Berwick Street 124
Berwick Street Market 256
Bethnal Green 160-161
Bethnal Green Museum of
  Childhood **160**, 273
Betjeman, John 98
Bevis Marks Synagogue 34, 73, **98**
Bexleyheath 173
BFI London IMAX Cinema 79,
  268, **285**
BFM International Film
  Festival 286
Biba 23
bicycle tours **74**, 344
Big Ben *132*, 136
Billingsgate Fish Market
  11, 13, 166
Bishop of Ely **104**, 105
Bishop's Park 187
Bishopsgate 25
Black Death of 1348-49, the
  13, 25
Blackfriars Bridge 19, 25
Blackheath 149
Blackheath Halls 309
Blair, Tony 24
Blake, William 100, 117, 124, 175
Bleak House 103
Bleeding Heart Yard 104
Blenheim Palace 354
Bligh, Captain 78, 164
Blitz, the **21**, 23, 25, 165
Blood, 'Colonel' Thomas 139, 164
'Bloody Mary' 14
Bloomsbury 19, 72, 73, **106-119**
  hotels 45, **49-53**
  pubs & bars 223
Bloomsbury Central Baptist
  Church 374
Bloomsbury Group 3, **106**
Bloomsbury Square 106
Blore, Edward 117
BMX riding 331
Boat Race, the 176, **261**
boat tours 74
Bolan, Marc 156, 177
Boleyn, Anne 355
Bollywood cinemas 281, **285**
Bombay Saree House 158
Bonfire Night 14, **267**
Bonnington Square 174
book shops 107, 131, **235-236**
books on London 379

Booth, William 156, 161
Borderline, The 310
Borough 83-86
Borough High Street 83
Borough Market 83, **256**
Boswell, James 126
Bosworth, Battle of 14
Boudicca **10**, 25, 136
boutiques, fashion 239
Bow 161-162
Bow Street Magistrates Court 129
Bow Street Runners **19**, 129
Bowie, David 130
Boy George 111
Boyle, Richard, Earl of
  Burlington 188
Bramah Museum of Tea
  & Coffee 81
Brawne, Fanny 154
breakdown services 364
Brentford FC 325
Brick Lane 159
Brick Lane Festival 264
Brick Lane Market 254
Bridgeman, Charles 188
Brighton 347-348, *347*
Brit Oval 171, **325**
Britain, Battle of 21
Britain & London Visitor Centre
  342, **377**
British Airways London Eye 25,
  73, 75, *75*, **77**, 268
British Library 110
British Museum 38, 72, *106*, **107**,
  250, 272
Brixton 175
Brixton Academy 309
Brixton Market 175, **254**
Brixton Prison 175
Brixton riots of 1981 **24**, 25, 175
Broadcasting House 36, 111, **112**
Broadgate Circle **266**, 330
Broadstairs 357
Broadway Market 160, *161*
Brompton 144
Brompton Cemetery 187
Brown, Lancelot 'Capability'
  177, 355
Browning, Robert 112, 138, 146
Brunel, Isambard Kingdom 167,
  182, 184
Brunel, Marc Isambard 167
Brunel Engine House & Tunnel
  Exhibition 167
Brunel University 375
Brunswick Centre 107
Bryanston Square 112
BT Tower 114
Buckingham Palace 31, 35, 73,
  116, **117**, *117*, 130, 133
Buddhapadipa Thai Temple 374
Buddhist temples 374
Bunhill Fields 100
Bunyan, John 100
Burbage, James 160
bureaux de change 373
Burgess Park 172
Burgh House 151
Burghers of Calais 138
Burke, Edmund 111
Burlington, Lord 188
Burlington Arcade 117
Burlington House 117
Burton, Decimus 118
buses 20, 25, 72, **363**
  Routemaster 72, **118-119**,
    118-119
  tours 74
Bush Hall *301*, **302**, 309

Bush House 101
Bush Theatre, the 187, 332, **339**
business centres 366
Business Design Centre 155
business services 366
Butler's Wharf 86
Butterfield, William 111
Buxton Drinking Fountain 138

C

Cabinet War Rooms 135, **136**, *137*
Cable Street, 'Battle' of 165
Cabmen's Shelters 101
Cade, Jack 94
Cadogan family 145
Cadogan Hall 302
Café Royal 20
cafés *see* restaurants & cafés
caffs 204
cake shops 248-249
Calvert, Edward 156
Camberwell 171-172
Cambridge 349-350
Camden **148-150**, 233
Camden Arts Centre 73, **151**, 287
Camden Market 148, **149**, *149*
Camley Street Natural Park *148*,
149, 153, 272
Campden House 184
camping 70
canal trips 153
Canary Wharf 25, 36, 166
Canary Wharf IRA bomb 164
Canary Wharf Tower **36**, 166
Candoco 279
Canonbury Square 155
Canterbury *348*, 350-351
Canterbury Tales 13
Capital City Academy 31
capoeira classes 280
car
   getting around by 364
   rental 365
   caravanning 70
Carling Apollo Hammersmith
   187, **309**
Carlton House Terrace 120, **134**
Carlyle, Thomas 120, **146**
Carlyle's House 146
Carnaby Street 23, **125**
Cartoon Art Trust 107
Cartwright Gardens 107
Casanova 124
casinos 324
castles 354-356
Catherine of Aragon 14
Catholic churches 374
Cavendish Square 112
Caxton Hall 139
Caxton, William 25, 138
CD shops 256-257
Cecil Sharp House English Folk
   Dance & Song Society 280
Cenotaph, the 135
Central Criminal Court 91
Centre Court shopping centre 179
Centrepoint 72, **130**, *131*
Ceremony of the Keys 262
Chamberlain, Neville 21
Chambers, Sir William 102
Changing of the Guard 134, **262**
Channel Tunnel Rail Link 109
Chapel Market 155
Chapel Royal 120
Charing Cross 131
Charing Cross Road **131**, 233
Charing Cross Station 342
Charles, Prince 32, 120
Charles I, King **17**, 25, 120
Charles II, King 17
Charlton 170-171
Charlton Athletic FC 325
Charlton House 170
Charlton Park 325
Charterhouse 104
Charterhouse Street 104

Chartism 111
Chaucer, Geoffrey **13**, 350
Cheapside 13
Chelsea 73, **145-147**
   pubs & bars 226
   restaurants & cafés 212-213
Chelsea FC 325, **326**
Chelsea Flower Show 145,
   146, **261**
Chelsea Harbour 146
Chelsea Old Church 146
Chelsea Pensioners 145, **147**, *147*
Chelsea Physic Garden 145, **146**
Chessington World of
   Adventures 274
Chevalier, Albert 15
Cheyne Row 146
Cheyne Walk 145
children **268-274**
   childcare & advice 269
   clothes shops 242
Children's Friendly Society 160
Chinatown 125
   hotels 57
Chinese London 42, 125, 156
Chinese New Year Festival 260
Ching Court 129
Chisenhale Dance Space 279
Chiswick 188-189
Chiswick Mall 188
Chiswick House 188
cholera epidemic of 1848-49 25
Cholmondeleys, the *278*, 279
Christ Church Spitalfields 35, **159**
Christchurch Gardens 139
Christmas Lights & Tree 267
Churchill, Duke of Marlborough,
   John 355
Churchill, Winston **21-22**, 35, 41,
   86, 115, 135, 136, *137*
Churchill Museum 135, 136
cinemas 283-285
Cinque Ports, the 358
Circus Space, The 280
Citigroup Centre 166
City, the 13, 72, **88-100**
   for children 268
   hotels 47
   pubs & bars 221
   restaurants & cafés 195-196
city farms 269
City Hall 24, 86
City Information Centre 89
City Livery Companies 13
City of London Festival **263**, 306
City of London Flower Show 265
City University 375
Civil War **17**, 25
Clapham 175-176
Clapham Common **175**, 294
Clapham Junction 175
Clapham Old Town 175
Clarence House 120
classical music *see* music,
   classical & opera
Claudius, Emperor 10
Cleopatra's Needle 131
Clerk's Well 103
Clerkenwell 72, **103-105**
   hotels 47-49
   pubs & bars 221-222
   restaurants & cafés 196-199
climate 377, 378
climbing wall 329
Clink Prison Museum 81
Clissold Park 156
Clockmakers' Museum 95
clothes shops *see* fashion shops
clubs 317-324
   gay 295-298
Cnut, King 11
Coca-Cola Championship &
   Football League 325
cockneys 15
cocktails, London's coolest 223
Cocteau, Jean 125

coffee houses 126
Coin Street Community Builders
   79
Coin Street Festival **262**, 268
Coliseum *see* London Coliseum
College of Arms 91, **92**
Colliers Wood 179
Collins, Wilkie 168
Columbia Road 160
Columbia Road Flower Market
   160, **256**
comedy 275-277
   festivals 261
Commonwealth, the **17**, 25
complementary medicine 369
computer shops 237-239
concerts, lunchtime 304
Conduit Street 115
confectioners 247
congestion charge 27, **364**
Conran Shop 253
Conservative Party 23, 24
Constable, John 124, 151
consulates 367
contraception 369
Convent of St Peter 126
conventions & conferences 366
Conway Hall 103
Cook, Captain 175
Cook, Peter 151
Cooney, Selwyn 42
Coram, Thomas 19, 107, **270**
Coram's Fields 107, **273**
Cork Street 115
Cornell, George 42, 158
Cornwall House 104
cosmetics shops 251
County Hall **77**, 87
couriers 366
Courtauld Gallery 173
Courtauld, Stephen and
   Virginia 173
Covent Garden 34, 72, **126-130**
   for children 268
   hotels 57-59
   pubs & bars 224
   restaurants & cafés 209-211
Covent Garden Piazza 127
Crafts Council 293
Craven Street 131
credit cards 373
cricket 150, **325**
crime 27-29, **39-42**
Crocker, Frank 183
Cromwell, Oliver **17**, 25, 100
Cromwell, Thomas 176
Cross, the 32
Crossrail 24, 27, 31, **104**
Crouch End 154
Crystal Palace 173
Crystal Palace, the 20
Crystal Palace FC 326
Crystal Palace National Sports
   Centre 173, **325**
Crystal Palace Park **173**, 273, *273*
Crystal Palace Park Museum 173
Cubitt, Sir William 175
Cubitt, Thomas 139
Custom House 7
customs allowances 366
Cutty Sark 168, **169**, 269
cycling & cycle hire 328, **365**

D

D'Oyly Carte, Richard 131
Da Vinci Code, The 101
Daily Express building **36**, 89
Daily Telegraph building 89
Dali Universe 77
Dalston 156
dance 278-280
   classes 280
   companies 279
   festivals 261, 267, **286**
Dance, George 98, 190
Dance Umbrella 278, 279

Danish Embassy building 144
Danson Mansion 173
Darwin, Charles 146
Daunt Books 113
Deakin, John 121
Dean Street 124
Dee, John 94
Defoe, Daniel 98, 100
delicatessens 247-250
Denmark Street 130
Dennis Severs' House 73, **159**
dentists 369
department stores 236-237
Deptford 14, 25, **167-168**
Derby Day 263
Design Museum **86**, 254, 293
diamond trade 104
Diana, Princess of Wales 25, 120,
   142, **143**, 273, 274, 354
Diana, Princess of Wales
   Memorial Playground 73, 142,
   143, 273, **274**
Dickens, Charles 20, 83, 86, 97,
   101, 103, 105, 106, 107, **109**,
   110, 112, 115, 130, 146, 148,
   164, 165, 168, 226, 357
Dickens' House 73, **109**, *111*
directory 360-380
disabled visitors 366
Disraeli, Benjamin 18, 115
Diwali 267
Dixon Jones 38
DJ bars 321-324
Docklands 164-166
Docklands Light Railway 363
Dr Johnson's House 73, **89**
doctors 369
Donmar Warehouse 332, **339**
Donne, John 93, 102
Downing Street 19, **135**
'Drain, the' 104
Drake, Sir Francis 14, 81
Drill Hall 280, 339
drink *see* food & drink
driving *see* cars
Drury Lane 129
dry cleaning 245
Dryden, John 138
duck tours 74
Duke of York Square 266
Dulwich 173
Dulwich Park 273
Dulwich Picture Gallery 35,
   167, 173
Dungeness 358
DV8 Physical Theatre 279

e

Ealing 189-190
Ealing Jazz Festival 314
Ealing Studios 189
Earl's Court 45, **186-187**
Earl's Court Exhibition Centre
   186, **309**
Earlham Street 129
East 17 162
East End *see* East London
East India Dock 165
East London 19, **157-166**
   galleries 290-292
   pubs & bars 228
   restaurants & cafés 215-216
East London Mosque 371
East London Muslim Centre *30*
Eastcheap 13
Edgware Road 182
Edward the Confessor, King
   11, 25, 132, 138
Edward I, King 11
Edward III, King 179
Edward VII, King 20
Eisenhower, Dwight 115
Eleanor of Castile 131
Electric Cinema 184, **284**, 286
electricity 367
electronics shops 237-239

Elephant & Castle 171
Elephant Man, the 158
Eliot, George 145, 150, 155
Eliot, TS 156
Elizabeth I, Queen **14**, 101, 105, 120, 163, 180, 355
Elizabeth II, Queen **23**, 25
Ellis, Ruth 151
Eltham 173
Eltham Palace 73, **173**
Ely Place 104
Embankment 131
Embankment Gardens 131
embassies 367
emergencies 367
EMI Studios 150
Emin, Tracey **96**, 169
Endell Street 129
Engels, Friedrich 142
English National Ballet 279
English National Opera (ENO) 301, **303**, **305**
Epping Forest 163
Epsom Racecourse 327
Eros 119
Estorick Collection of Modern Italian Art 155, *155*, **156**
Ethelbert, King **10**, 25
Ethical Society, the 103
ethnic diversity 30
Eurostar 109, 110, **360**
Euston Station **110**, 342
events *see* festivals & events
Execution Dock 164

f

Fabric 93, 103, **318**
Fame, Georgie 121
Fan Museum 169
Faraday, Michael 115, **116**, 155
Faraday Museum 115
Farmers' Market 256
farms, city 269
Farringdon 103-105
Fashion & Textile Museum 86, **87**
fashion
    accessories & services 245-247
    shops 239-245
Father Fowl 42
Father Thames 97
Fawkes, Guy **14**, 25, 99
Fayed, Mohammed Al 144
Featherstonehaughs, the *278*, 279
Fenton House 151, **152**
ferries 164
Festival of Britain of 1951 **23**, 25, 36, 75, 79, 175
festivals & events 260-267
    art 261, 264
    comedy 261
    dance 262, 264
    film 261, 267, **286**
    gay 263
    music, classical & opera 263, 264, **305-306**
    music, rock, dance, roots & jazz 262, 263, 264, 265, **314**
    sport 261, 263, 264, 267
    theatre 261, 263, 264, 265
Fiat Bravo gang 42
Fielding, Henry 19, 126, 129
film 281-286
    about London 379
    for children 272
    festivals 261, 267, **286**
Finchley 156
Fire of 1666 *see* Great Fire of 1666
Firepower 170, **171**
Fitz Stephen, William 11
Fitzalwin, Henry 25
Fitzrovia 72, **110-111**
    hotels 49-53
    pubs & bars 223
    restaurants & cafés 199-201

Fitzroy, Henry 110
Flamsteed, John 170
Fleet, River 89, 104, 136
Fleet Street 89
Fleming, Alexander 182
Fleming, Ian 154, 184
Floral Street 129
Florence Nightingale Museum 77
flower markets 256
food & drink
    markets 256
    shops 247-250
football 325-327
Foreign Office 36
Forest Hill 172
Forster, EM 106
Fortnum & Mason 116, **236**
Forum, The 309
Foster, Norman 31, 38, 86, 107, 159
Foundling Hospital 19, 107, **270**
Foundling Museum 73, 107, **270**
Fournier Street 159
Foyles 131, **235**
Franklin, Benjamin 95, 131
Fraser, 'Mad' Frankie 168-169
Freemason's Hall 36, **129**
Freightliners City Farm 269
Freud, Sigmund & Anna 153
Freud Museum 153
Frieze Art Fair 287
Frith Street 124
Fruitstock **264**, 314
Fu Manchu 165
Fulham 186-187
Fulham FC 326
Fulham Palace 187
Full Metal Jacket 166
Fuller's Griffin Brewery 188
Future Systems 38

g

Gabriel's Wharf 79
galleries 287-293 *see also* museums & galleries
games shops 258
Garlick Hill 91
Garrick, David 126, 127
Gatti, Carlo 150
Gatwick Airport 360
de Gaulle, Charles 124
gay & lesbian London 184, 187, **294-300**, 367
    apartment rental 69
    best venues 295
    festivals 263, 286
Geffrye Museum 73, **160**, 293
General Strike of 1926 21
Geoffrey of Monmouth 10
George I, King 19
George II, King 181
George III, King 117
George IV, King 117, 120
Gerrard Street 125
Gherkin, the *see* Swiss Re tower
Giaconda Café 130
Gibbons, Grinling 98
Gibbs, James **34**, 101, 132, 181
gift shops 250
Gilbert, Arthur 102
Gilbert Collection 102
Gill, Eric 139
gin palaces 227
GLC (Greater London Council) **24**, 25
Globe, The *see* Shakespeare's Globe
'Glorious Revolution' of 1688, the 19
Godwin, Mary 73
Godwin, William 110
Golborne Road 184
Golden Hinde **81**, 268
Golden Square 125
Golders Green 156
Golders Green Crematorium 156
Goldfinger, Ernö 151, 154, 184

Goldsmiths' College 375
golf 328
Goodwin's Court 129
Gordon Riots of 1780 **19**, 25
Gosford Park 188
Gospel Oak lido 151
Gower Street 106, 107
Grand Union Canal 152
Grant, Duncan 106
Gray, Dorian 165
Gray's Inn 101, **103**
Great British Beer Festival 264
Great Exhibition of 1851, the **20**, 25, 140, 173
Great Fire of 1666, the **17**, *17*, 19, 25, 32, 88, 89, 98, 100
Great Plague of 1665, the **17**, 25, 88, 100
Great Spitalfields Pancake Day Race 261
'Great Stink' of 1858, the **18**, 20
Great Windmill Street 125
Greater London Assembly (GLA) 24
Greek London 124, 156
Greek Street 124
Green Lanes 156
Green Park 116
Greenwich **167-170**, 269
Greenwich Dance Agency 280
Greenwich & Docklands International Festival **264**, 314
Greenwich Market 168, 235, **255**
Greenwich Mean Time 75
Greenwich Park 14, **168**, 269
Greenwich Tourist Information Centre 168
Gresham, Sir Thomas **14**, 25
Greville Street 104
greyhound racing 327
Grimshaw, Nicholas 37, 79, 148
Grosvenor Chapel 304
Grosvenor Square 115
Groucho Club 124
Guards' Museum 134
Guildhall 88, 95, **96**
Guildhall Art Gallery 95, **96**
Guildhall School of Music & Drama 302
Guinness, Edward 154
gun salutes 262
Gunpowder Plot **14**, 25, 99
Gurdwara Sri Guru Singh Sabha Southall 190
Gustafson, Kathryn 143
Guy's Hospital 19

h

Hackney 160-161
Hackney Empire 160, **162**, *163*, 332
Hadrian, Emperor 25
hairdressers 252-253
Hall Place 173
Halloween Short Film Festival 286
Ham House 180
Hamilton, Lady 154
Hamleys 119, **258**
Hammersmith 187
Hammersmith Bridge 187
Hampstead 73, **151-154**
Hampstead Heath **151**, 273, 294
Hampstead Scientific Society Observatory 151
Hampstead Theatre 339, *340*
Hampton Court Palace 14, 73, **180**, 266, 330
Hampton Court Palace Festival 306
Handel, George Frideric 115, **116**, 127, 188, **270**
Hanover Square 115
Hardwick, Philip 110
Hardy, Thomas 107
Haringey 156

Harlequins 328
Harley Street 112
Harold, King **11**, 358
Harrods 25, 73, 144, **236**, *236*, 244
Harvard, John 83
Harvey Nichols 144, **237**, 244
Hastings 358
Hastings, 1066, Battle of 11
Hatfield House 355
Hatton, Lady 105
Hatton, Sir Christopher 105
Hatton Garden **104**, 105
Hawksmoor, Nicholas 33, **34-35**, 95, 107, 138, 159, 165
Hay's Galleria 83
Haymarket Theatre 35
Hayward Gallery 36, **79**
Hazlitt, William 124
health 367-370
    & beauty shops & services 251-253
    clubs 328
Heathrow Airport 38, **360**
Hefeld, Paul 41
Heine, Heinrich 131
helicopter tours 74
helplines 370
Hendon 156
Hendrix, Jimi 111, 115
Heneage Street 159
Henley Royal Regatta 263
Henry VII Chapel 14, 33, **138**
Henry VII, King 14, 179
Henry VIII, King **14**, 25, 137, 141, 155, 163, 168, 173, 180, 188
Henry, Prince 101
Henslowe, Philip 82
Hepworth, Barbara 151
Hermitage Rooms 102
Herne Hill 173
Herne Hill Velodrome 328
Herzog and de Meuron 38
Hever Castle 355
Highbury 155
Highbury Fields **155**, 273
Highbury Stadium 155
Highgate 154-155
Highgate Cemetery 73, 154, **155**
Highgate Woods 154
hip hop 308
Hirst, Damien 159
history 10-25
Hitler, Adolf 21
HIV 370
HMS Belfast **82**, 85, 268
Hodgkinson, Patrick 107
Hodgson, Will 276
Hogarth, William 130, **188**, 270
Hogarth's House 188
Holborn 72, **101-103**
    hotels 47-49
    pubs & bars 221-222
    restaurants & cafés 196-199
Holborn Viaduct 105
Holden, Charles 36
holidays, public 377
Holland House 184
Holland Park **184**, 186, *190*
Holland Park Theatre 306
Holly Village 154
Holmes, Sherlock 113, 131
Holy Trinity 175
homewares shops 253-254
Honor Oak 172
Hooke, Robert 98
Horn Fair 170
Hornby, Nick 155
Horner, Thomas 152
Horniman Museum **172**, 273
Hornsey Town Hall 154
Horse Guards building 134
horse racing 327
horse riding 331
hospitals **369**, 370
hostels, youth 70
hotels *see* accommodation

Houndsditch 13
House of Commons 11
House of Lords 11
Houses of Parliament **35**,
135, **136**
housing 29-30
Housing Act of 1890 25
Howard, Catherine 180, 188
Howard, Earl of Suffolk,
Thomas 354
Howard, Henrietta 181
Hoxton 15, 72, **159-160**, 233
Hoxton Square 160
HSBC Tower 166
Huguenots in London 104, 121,
157, 159, 182
Human Rights Watch
International Film Festival 286
Hungerford footbridges 75, *78*
Huxley, TH 172
Hyde Park 14, 73, **141**, 182, 309
Hyde Park Corner 116
Hytner, Nicholas 335

ICA **134**, 280, 281, **283**, 310
ICA Gallery 134
ice skating 266, **330**
IMAX cinemas 285
immigration 23, 377
Imperial College 375
Imperial War Museum **171**,
172, 272
India House 101
Indians in London 190
inline skating 331
Inner Temple 101
Inns of Court 101
Institute of Contemporary Arts
see ICA
insurance 370
internet 371
IRA bombings in London
23-24, 25, 98
Iraq War 24
Isabella Plantation **180**, 273
Island Gardens 166
Isle of Thanet 357
Islington 155-156
Islington Academy 309
Iveagh Bequest *see*
Kenwood House

Jack the Ripper **25**, 158
Jacksons Lane 280
Jacob's Island 86
Jacobsen, Arne 144
James, Henry 358
James I, King **14**, 17, 25, 136, 168
James II, King 19
Jamme Masjid mosque 159
Japanese London 156
Jay Sean 307, *307*
jazz 23, **313-314**
festivals 263, **314**
Jazz On The Streets 314
Jeffreys, Judge George 164
Jewel Tower 136, 137, **138**
jewellery shops 245
Jewish London 25, 34, 98, 104,
149, 156, 157, 159
Jewish Museum Finchley 156
Jewish Museum, Camden
148, **149**
John, King 11, 13
John Lewis 237
Johnson, Samuel **89**, 138
Jones, Christopher 167
Jones, Horace 86, 93, 95, 99
Jones, Inigo 17, **33**, 34, 120, 126,
127, 131, 136, 168, 188
Jonson, Ben 160
Jubilee Bridge 83
Jubilee Market 127

Kahn, Keith 165
Kean, Edmund 127
Keats House 73, 151; **154**
Keats, John **151**, 174
Kempton Park Racecourse 327
Kennington 171
Kennington Park 171
Kensal Green Cemetery 184
Kensington 184-185
Kensington Gardens 73,
141-142, 273
Kensington High Street 184
Kensington Palace 73, **142**
Kensington Square 184
Kent, William 188
Kentish Town 149
Kenwood House/Iveagh Bequest
35, *150-151*, 151, **154**
Kenwood House concerts 306
Kew 177
Kew Bridge Steam Museum 188
Kew Gardens *see* Royal
Botanic Gardens
Kew Summer Festival 262
Keynes, John Maynard 106
Kidd, Captain William 164
Kilburn 182-183
Kilburn High Road 183
Kinder London Towers 325
King's College **101**, 375
King's Cross 30, **109**, 110
King's Cross Station 32, 109, 342
King's Road 23, **145**, 233
Kingston University 375
Knights Templar 101
Knightsbridge 73, **144**, 233
hotels 59-62
pubs & bars 225
restaurants & cafés 211-212
'Knowledge, the' 155
Koko 309
Krays, the, 39, 42, 158, 160

Laban Centre 32, **280**
Labour Party 21, 22, 24
Lambeth Bridge 77
Lambeth Palace 77
Lancaster House 120
Landseer, Edwin 132
Lang, David 97
Langham Hotel 112
Langham Place 112
language classes 375
Lauderdale House 154
laundry services 245
Lawrence, Andrew 276
Leadenhall Market 95
Leather Lane Market 104
Lee Valley Park 164
Leeds Castle 357
left luggage 371
legal help 371
Legoland 274
Leicester Square **125**, 130
pubs & bars 223-224
Leigh, Vivien 113
Leighton, Frederic, Lord 186
Leighton House 184, **186**
Lenin, Vladimir Ilyich 104,
107, 142, 158
Lepidus, Jacob 41
lesbians *see* gay & lesbian
Lewis, CS 151
Leyton 164
Leyton Orient FC 326
Liberal Democrat Party 21
Liberal Party 21
Liberty 36, 119, *233*, **237**
Liberty, Arthur 176, 179, 237
libraries 158, **371**
Limehouse 165
Lincoln's Inn 101, **103**

Lincoln's Inn Fields 103
Linley Sambourne House 184, **186**
Lisson Gallery 113, **289**
Little Portugal 174
Little Venice 182
Liverpool Street Station 342
Livery Companies 13
Livesey Museum for Children 273
Livingstone, Ken 24, 25, 26-30,
37, **87**
Lloyd, Marie 160, 162
Lloyd George, David 21
Lloyd Park 163
Lloyd's Building **36**, 95
Lollards, the 104
Londinium **10**, 25
London Aquarium **77**, 268
London Art Fair 261
London Bridge 13
London Bridge Station 342
London Bridge Tower 37
London to Brighton Veteran
Car Run 267
London Butterfly House 188
London Canal Museum 149,
150, 153
London Central Mosque **113**, 374
London City Airport 360
London Coliseum 38, 129,
303, 305
London County Council **20**,
21, 25
London Dungeon 73, **83**, **85**, 268
London Eye *see* British Airways
London Eye
London Film Festival **267**, **286**
London Fire Brigade 25
London Fire Brigade Museum 85
London Garden Squares
Weekend 263
London Harness Horse Parade 261
London Hospital 19
London Information Centre 377
London International Boat
Show 260
London International Horse
Show 267
London International Mime
Festival 260
London Irish 327
London Jazz Festival 314
London Lesbian & Gay Film
Festival **286**, **294**
London Library 120
London Marathon *260*, **261**
London Metropolitan University
375
London Muslim Centre 158
London Necropolis Station 79
London Palladium 125
London Pass 73
London Philharmonic Orchestra,
the 304
London Planetarium 113
London School of Economics
(LSE) 375
London Silver Vaults 103
London Stone 94
London Symphony Orchestra 302
London Towers 325
London Underground *see*
Underground, the
London Visitor Centre 377
London Wall 100
London Wasps 327
London Wildlife Trust Centre for
Wildlife Gardening 272
London Zoo 25, 36, 113, **114**,
268, 273
London's Transport Museum
127, 269
Lord Mayor's Show 267
Lord's Cricket Ground 38, 73,
150, **325**
Lord's Tour & MCC Museum
73, **150**
lost property 371

Lots Road Power Station 146
Lower Marsh 79
Lubetkin, Bertold **36**, 114
Lud, King 10
Ludgate 10
Luton Airport 360
Lutyens, Edwin 132, 135
Lyons Tea Shops & Corner
Houses 20
Lyric Hammersmith 187, **340**

MacColl, Kirsty 124
MacDonald, Ramsay 21
Macmillan, Harold 23
Madame Tussaud's 25, 73, 113,
114, *114*, 129
magazines 372
Magna Carta 11, 13, 25
Maida Vale 182-183
Major, John 24, 175
Manchester Square 112
Mansfield, Earl of 154
Mansion House 89, **95**
Marble Arch 73, 112, **114**, 330
Marble Hill House 180, *181*
Marble Hill House concerts 306
Marconi House 21
Mare Street 160
Margate 357
markets 83, 86, 104, 113, 127, 155,
158, 163, 166, 168, 175, 187,
235, **254-256**
Marks & Spencer 237
Marks Barfield 75
Marlborough House 120
Marlowe, Christopher 168
Marquee Club 121, **309**
Marshalsea Prison 83
Martin, Leslie 79
Marwell Zoological Park 354, 355
Marx, Karl 73, 107, **111**, 142,
154, 155
Marx Memorial Library 104
Mary, Queen **14**, 120
Marylebone 19, 72, **112-114**
hotels 53
pubs & bars 224
restaurants & cafés 201-203
Marylebone Farmers' Market 256
Marylebone High Street 73,
112, 233
Marylebone Lane 113
Marylebone Library 114
Marylebone Road 113
Maryon Wilson Park 170
Matcham, Frank 162, 303
May Fair 25, 115
May Fayre & Puppet
Festival 261
Mayfair 19, 72, **115-116**
hotels 45, **53-57**
pubs & bars 224
restaurants & cafés 203-206
Mayflower, the 167
Mayor's Thames Festival 265
Maze Hill 169
McAslan, John 32
measures 371
Mecklenburgh Square 107
media 372
Mellitus, Bishop 11
Meltdown **263**, 314
Memorial Garden of Rest 112
Mercury, Freddie 187
Merrick, Joseph 158
Merton Abbey Mills 177, **179**
Methodist Central Hall 374
Methodist churches 374
Metroland 21
Metropolitan Board of Works 20
Metropolitan Police 25, 40
Middle Temple 101
Middle Temple Hall 101
Middlesex Guildhall 135
Middlesex Hospital 19

Midland Grand Hotel, the 36, 110
Mile End 161-162
Mile End Park **161**, 273
Mill, John Stuart 184
Millbank 138-139
Millbank Penitentiary 139
Millbank Tower 139
Millennium Bridge 31, **38**, **75**, *78*
Millennium Dome, the 24, 32, **168**
Milliner, Mary 39
Millwall FC 326
Milton, John 100, 138
Minerva 37, *37*
MI6 Building 139, **174**
mobile phones 376
Model Parliament of 1295, the 11
Mohocks, the 104
Mona Lisa 110
money 373
Monmouth Street 129
Montague Square 112
Montevetro 175
Monument 32, 73, *97*, **98**
Moore, Henry 95, 151
Morden 177
More, Sir Thomas 14, 145, 146
Morris, William 163, **164**, 173, 176, 179
Mortimer, John 94
Mosaïques Festival 261
Mosley, Sir Oswald 165
mosques 374
motorbike hire 365
motorsport 327
Mountford, Edward 91
Mourinho, Jose 326
Moxon Street 113
Mozart, Wolfgang Amadeus 124
Mudchute City Farm 269
Muldoon, Roland 162
Murdoch, Rupert 164
Museum in Docklands 166, *166*
Museum of Garden History
77, **78**, *81*
Museum & Library of the Order
of St John 104, **105**
Museum of London 97, **100**, 268
Museum of Methodism & John
Wesley's House 100
Museum of Richmond 180
museums & galleries
    archaeology: British Museum
    38, 72, *106*, **107**, 250, 272;
    Petrie Museum of
    Archaeology 109
    art: Bankside Gallery 81;
    Barbican Art Gallery 100;
    Cartoon Art Trust 107;
    Courtauld Gallery 103;
    Dali Universe 77; Dulwich
    Picture Gallery 35, *167*,
    173; Estorick Collection
    of Modern Italian Art 155,
    155, **156**; Guildhall Art
    Gallery 95, **96**; Hayward
    Gallery 36, **79**; Hogarth's
    House 188; ICA Gallery 134;
    Kenwood House/Iveagh
    Bequest 34, *150-151*, 151,
    154; Leighton House 184,
    186; National Gallery 25,
    38, 72, **132**, 269; National
    Portrait Gallery 38, 72, **133**,
    269; Orleans House Gallery
    181; PM (Pitzhanger Manor)
    Gallery & House 190; Royal
    Academy of Arts 116, **117**;
    Saatchi Gallery 73, 77, **78**,
    82, 96; Serpentine Gallery
    141, *142*, **144**, 266; Sir John
    Soane's Museum 35, **103**;
    Somerset House museums
    102; South London Gallery
    172; Tate Britain 38, 138,
    139, 272; Tate Modern 38,
    25, 73, 81, **83**, 96, 250, 272;
    Wallace Collection 38, 112,

112, **113**; Whitechapel
    Art Gallery 73, **158**, 287;
    William Morris Gallery 73,
    163, **164**
    canals: London Canal Museum
    149, **150**, 153
    children: Bethnal Green
    Museum of Childhood **160**,
    273; Foundling Museum
    73, 107, **270**, *270*; Livesey
    Museum for Children 273;
    Pollock's Toy Museum 111;
    Ragged School Museum
    161, **162**, 273
    clocks: Clockmakers' Museum
    95
    decorative arts: Gilbert
    Collection 102; Hermitage
    Rooms 102; Victoria &
    Albert Museum 140, **141**,
    269, 293; Percival David
    Foundation of Chinese
    Art 107
    design: Design Museum **86**,
    254, 293
    everything: British Museum
    38, 72, *106*, **107**, 250, 272
    fans: Fan Museum 169
    fashion: Fashion & Textile
    Museum 86, **87**
    finance: Bank of England
    Museum 95
    fire brigade: London Fire
    Brigade Museum 85
    gardens: Museum of Garden
    History 77, **78**, *81*
    historic buildings: Apsley
    House: The Wellington
    Museum 115, **116**;
    Banqueting House 17, 33,
    134, **136**; Buckingham
    Palace 31, 35, 73, 116, **117**,
    117, 130; Burgh House
    151; Charlton House 170;
    Chiswick House 188;
    Clarence House 120;
    Danson Mansion 173;
    Dennis Severs' House 73,
    159; Eltham Palace 73,
    173; Fenton House 151,
    152; Fulham Palace 187;
    Guildhall 88, 95, **96**; Hall
    Place 173; Ham House 180;
    Hampton Court Palace 14,
    73, **180**, 266, 330; Hogarth's
    House 188; Kensington
    Palace 73, **142**; Kenwood
    House 35, *150-151*, 151,
    154; Leighton House 184,
    186; Linley Sambourne
    House 184, **186**; Marble
    Hill House 180, *181*; 19
    Princelet Street 73, *157*,
    159; Old Royal Naval
    College 168, **170**; Osterley
    House 35, 73, **190**;
    Pitzhanger Manor 190;
    Prince Henry's Room 101;
    Queen's House 17, 34, 168,
    170; Ranger's House 168,
    170; Red House 173, **173**;
    Spencer House 120; Sutton
    House 161; Syon House 35,
    73, **188**, 273; Tower of
    London 11, 25, 32, *34*, 88,
    96, *97*, **99**, 268; 2 Willow
    Road 151, **154**
    horror: London Dungeon
    73, 83, **85**, 268
    *industrial history &
    technology:* Kew Bridge
    Steam Museum 188;
    Three Mills Island 162;
    Tower Bridge Experience
    73, 86, **99**
    interior design: Geffrye
    Museum 73, **160**, 293

literary: Carlyle's House 146;
    Dickens' House 73, **109**,
    111; Dr Johnson's House
    73, **89**; Freud Museum
    153; Keats House 73, 151;
    154; Sherlock Holmes
    Museum 113
    local history: Crystal Palace
    Park Museum 173; Museum
    in Docklands 166, *166*;
    North Woolwich Old Station
    Museum **166**, 170; Museum
    of Richmond 180; Vestry
    House Museum 163
    London: Museum of London
    97, **100**, 268
    maritime: Cutty Sark 168,
    169, 269; Golden Hinde **81**,
    268; HMS Belfast **82**, 85,
    268; National Maritime
    Museum 38, 168, **169**, 269
    medical: Alexander Fleming
    Laboratory Museum 182;
    Faraday Museum 115;
    Florence Nightingale
    Museum 77; Freud Museum
    153; Old Operating Theatre,
    Museum & Herb Garret 73,
    85; Royal London Hospital
    Archives & Museum 158;
    St Bartholomew's Hospital
    Museum 93
    miscellaneous: Horniman
    Museum **172**, 273
    music: Fenton House 151, **152**;
    Horniman Museum 172;
    Musical Museum 188
    natural history: Natural
    History Museum 36,
    140, **141**, 269
    prison: Clink Prison
    Museum 81
    religion & religious orders:
    Jewish Museum, Camden
    148, **149**; Jewish Museum,
    Finchley 156; Museum &
    Library of the Order of St
    John 104, **105**; Museum
    of Methodism & John
    Wesley's House 100
    science: London Planetarium
    113; Royal Observatory &
    Planetarium 169, **170**;
    Science Museum 73, 140,
    140, **141**, 250, 269
    sport: Lord's Tour & MCC
    Museum 73, **150**; Rugby
    Museum/Twickenham
    Stadium 73, **181**;
    Wimbledon Lawn Tennis
    Museum 73, **179**, 273
    tea & coffee: Bramah Museum
    of Tea & Coffee 81
    theatre: Theatre Museum
    73, **127**, 268
    toys: Pollock's Toy Museum 111
    transport: London's Transport
    Museum **127**, 269
    wine: Vinopolis, City of Wine
    81, **83**
    war & military: Cabinet War
    Rooms 135, **136**, *137*;
    Churchill Museum 135,
    136; Firepower 170, **171**;
    Guards' Museum 134;
    Imperial War Museum **171**,
    172, 272; National Army
    Museum 145, **146**, 272;
    Royal Air Force Museum
    Hendon 73, **156**, 273;
    Winston Churchill's Britain
    at War Experience 83, **86**
    waxworks: Madame Tussauds
    73, 113, **114**, *114*, 129
    zoos, aquariums & wildlife:
    London Aquarium **77**, 268;
    London Zoo 36, 113, **114**,

268, 273; WWT Wetland
    Centre 177
mushrooms 253
music, classical & opera 301-306
    festivals 263, 264, **305-306**
music, rock, dance, roots & jazz
306-314
    festivals 262, 263, 264, 265, **314**
    London-centric 380
music shops 256-257
Musical Museum 188
musicals 335-339

n

Narrow Street 165
Nash, John **35**, 112, 113, 114,
116, 117, 118, 119, 120, 121,
132, 134, 152, 347
National Army Museum 145,
146, 272
National Film Theatre 79, 281,
285, **335**
National Gallery 25, 38, 72,
132, 269
National Health Service 22
National Maritime Museum
38, 168, **169**, 269
National Portrait Gallery 38,
72, **133**, 269
National Science Week 261
National Theatre *see* Royal
National Theatre 332
Natural History Museum 36,
140, **141**, 269
Neal Street 129
Neal's Yard 129
Neasden 190
NEC Harlequins 328
Neckinger, River 86
Nelson, Horatio 73, 93, 115,
132, 151, 169, 170
Nelson's Column 132
New Adventures 279
New Bond Street 115
New River 155
New Scotland Yard 139
New Year's Eve 267
Newburgh Street 125
Newgate Prison 10, 25, 40, 91
Newington 171
Newman, Albert 41
newspapers 372
Nightingale, Florence **77**, 115
nightlife 315-324
    gay 295-298
19 Princelet Street 73, *157*, **159**
Norman London 11, 25
North London 148-156
    hotels 65
    pubs & bars 227-228
    restaurants & cafés 214-215
North Woolwich 170
North Woolwich Old Station
Museum **166**, 170
Northcote Road Market 256
Norwegian Church & Seaman's
Mission 167
Notre Dame de France 125
Notting Hill 184
Notting Hill Carnival 184, *186*,
264, 314
Notting Hill Farmers' Market 256
Notting Hill Gate 184
Notting Hill race riots 23
Le Nôtre, André 168

o

Oasis 124
Ocean 160, **310**
office hire 366
Oguike, Henry 279
Old Bailey 91
Old Compton Street *121*, 122
Old Operating Theatre, Museum
& Herb Garret 73, **85**

Old Royal Naval College 168, **170**
Old Vic theatre 79, 332, **333**
100 Club 111, **311**
onedotzero 286
Open Air Theatre 335
Open House London 77, **265**
opening hours 373
opera 301, **305**
opticians 253
Oratory Catholic Church **144**, 374
Orleans House Gallery 181
Orwell, George 111, 142, 155
Osterley House 35, 73, **190**
Our Mutual Friend 165
Outer Circle 113
Oval, the 171, **325**
Oxford 351-352, *352*
Oxford Street 20, 72, **114**, 130, 233
Oxo Tower Wharf 79

P

Paddington 46, **182**
Paddington Recreation Ground 183
Paddington Station 342
Paddington Waterside project 182
Paine, Thomas 111
Palace of Westminster 11, 25
Pankhurst, Christabel 296
Pankhurst, Emmeline 138, 142, 187
Park Lane 73
parking 364
Parliament Hill 151
Parliament *see* Houses of Parliament
Parliament Square 135
Parson's Green 187
Paternoster Square 32, *33*, **91**
pâtisseries 247
Pavlova, Anna 156
Paxton, Joseph 20, 173
Peabody, George **20**
Peabody buildings 25
Pearly Kings & Queens Harvest Festival 265
Peasants' Revolt of 1381 **13**, 25, 98
Peckham 171-172
Peckham Library 38, **172**
Peckham Rye Common 172
Peel, Sir Robert 115
Pelli, Cesar **36**, 166
Pembroke Lodge 180
Pennybank Chambers 104
Pepys, Samuel 97, 135, 164, 174
Perceval, Spencer 25, 190
Percival David Foundation of Chinese Art 107
Performing London 105
Perrier Awards 276
Peter Jones 32
Peter Pan statue 142
Peter's Hill 91
Petrie Museum of Archaeology 109
Petticoat Lane Market 158, **254**
pharmacies **257**, 370
Philharmonia, the 304
Phoenix Garden 129
phones, public 376
Phoney War, the 21
photography
  galleries 293
  shops 239
Piano, Renzo 37
Piccadilly 72, **116**
Piccadilly Circus 72, 116, **118**
pilates 331
Pimlico 139
  hotels 65
Pimlico Farmers' Market 256

Pitzhanger Manor 190
Place, The 278
Plague of 1665 *see* Great Plague of 1665, the
playgrounds 273-274
Playtex Moonwalk 262
PM (Pitzhanger Manor) Gallery & House 190
Poe, Edgar Allan 106
police 19, 25
police stations 373
Poll Tax riot 24
Pollock's Toy Museum 111
Pope, Alexander 126
Porchester Spa 183
Port of London Authority 97
Portland Place 112
Portobello Film Festival 286
Portobello Road 184
Portobello Road Market 184, 235, **255**
Portuguese London 174, 184
Post Office Tower *see* BT Tower
post offices 374
postal services 374
Postman's Park 93
Potters Fields 31
du Pré, Jacqueline 156
Prescott, John 37
prescriptions 370
Pride In The Park **263**, 314
Pride London **263**, 285, 294
Primrose Hill 73, **149**
Prince Charles Cinema 125, **285**
Prince Henry's Room 101
Prince Regent, the 132, 152
Princess Diana Memorial Fountain 143, *143*
Proms, the 301, **264**, **306**
Prospect of Whitby 164, **228**
pub crawl 104-105
public holidays 377
pubs & bars 220-232
  the best drinking holes 220
  DJ bars 321-324
  gay 298-300
  late-opening 230-231
  music venues 312-313
  theatres 336-337
Pudding Lane 17
Pugin, Augustus **35**, 137
Punch & Judy Festival 265
Punch 89
puppet theatres 272
Putney 176-177
Pyle, Joey 42

Q

Quant, Mary 23
Queen Elizabeth Hall 36
Queen Mary University of London 375
Queen Mother 25, 120
Queen's Chapel 120
Queen's Club 187, **328**
Queen's House 17, 34, 168, **170**
Queenhithe 11
Queens Park Rangers FC 326
Queensway 182
de Quincey, Thomas 124

R

racial mix 30
radio 372
Ragged School Museum 161, **162**, 273
rail
  arriving & leaving by 360
  services 363
Railton, William 132
Raindance 286
Raleigh, Walter 138
Rambert Dance Company 279
Ranelagh Gardens 145
Ranger's House 168, **170**

Ranieri, Claudio 326
Raymond, Paul 122-123
Raymond's Revuebar 122
Read, Herbert 134
Red House 73, **173**
Red Lion Square 103
Reformation, the 14
Regent Street 35, 72, 112, **119**
Regent Street Festival 265
Regent's Canal 25, 149, **152**, 155
Regent's Park 14, **112**, 273
Regent's Park Zoo *see* London Zoo
religion 374
Religious Society of Friends (Quakers) 375
Remembrance Sunday Ceremony 267
Renoir Cinema 107, **283**
repertory cinemas 285
repertory companies 333-334
Repton, Humphrey 154
Resfest 286
Resolution! 278
resources A-Z 366-378
Respect Week & Festival **264**, 314
restaurants 192-219
  the best 193
  for children 271
  by cuisine:
    American 199, 203, 210, 218
    Belgian 209
    British 196, 203, 206, 210
    cafés & brasseries 193, 195, 196, 203, 206, 210, 211, 215, 217, 218
    Chinese 195, 206-207
    fish 193, 195, 210, 218
    fish & chips 201, 210, 217
    French 195, 196, 205, 207, 210, 212, 214, 217, 218
    gastropubs 193, 196, 212, 214, 218
    global 193, 199, 201, 211, 214, 215, 217, 219
    Indian 199, 205, 208, 211, 212, 216, 219
    Italian 200, 201, 205, 208, 216, 217, 219
    Japanese 195-196, 212
    Mediterranean 196, 214
    Middle Eastern 203, 205, 216
    Modern European 195, 196, 199, 200, 203, 205, 208-209, 210, 211-212, 217, 218
    North African 205
    oriental 200, 202, 206, 209, 211, 212, 214, 218, 219
    Spanish 199, 212
    Turkish 214
    vegetarian & organic 196, 209, 210, 215, 219
    Vietnamese 216
Rhodes, Zandra 86, 87
Rhythm Sticks **264**, 314
Rich Mix 165
Richard Alston Dance Company 279
Richard II, King 13
Richard III, King 14
Richmond 179-180
Richmond Green 179
Richmond Park 14, **180**, 273
Richmond Theatre 179
Rishi Rich 307
Ritzy Cinema 175, **284**
river cruises & transport 72, 74, **363**
Riverside Studios 187, 281, 280, **285**, **335**
Rodin, Auguste 138
Rodway, Simon 296
Rogers, Richard 32, 36, 37, 38, 95, 139, 175
Rohmer, Sax 165

Rolling Stones 111, 130
'Roman' bath 101
Roman London **10**, 25, 97, 100
Romney, George 151
Ronnie Scott's 23
Roosevelt, Franklin D 115
Roosevelt, Theodore 115
Rose of Kingston 332
Rose theatre, the 14, **82**
Rossetti, Christina 155
Rossetti, DG 145
Rotherhithe 167
Roundhouse, the 148
Routemaster buses 72, **118-119**
Royal Academy of Arts 116, **117**
Royal Academy of Music **112**, 302
Royal Air Force Museum Hendon 73, **156**, 273
Royal Albert Hall 301, **302**, 309
Royal Artillery Barracks 170
Royal Ballet 279
Royal Botanic Gardens 20, 73, **177**, 266
Royal College of Music **140**, 302
Royal College of Surgeons 103
Royal Court theatre 145, **335**
Royal Courts of Justice 31, 36, 101, **102**
Royal Dockyards **14**, 25
Royal Exchange 19, 25, **95**
Royal Festival Hall 36, **79**, 301, **304**
Royal Geographical Society 20, **140**
Royal Greenwich Park *see* Greenwich Park
Royal Hospital Chelsea 145, **147**
Royal Institute of British Architects 112
Royal London Hospital Archives & Museum 158
Royal Mews 117
Royal National Theatre **79**, 85, 266, 268, **335**
Royal National Theatre Summer Festival 263
Royal Naval College *see* Old Royal Naval College
Royal Observatory & Planetarium 169, **170**
Royal Opera House 38, 127, **279**, 301, *304-305*, **305**
Royal Parks 14
Royal Shakespeare Company 335, 353
Royal Society for the Arts 35
Royal Victoria Patriotic Building 176
Rubens, Peter Paul 33, 136
Rugby Museum/Twickenham Stadium 73, **181**
rugby union 181, **327**
Rupert Street 124
Rushes Soho Shorts Festival 286
Russell, Bertrand 180
Russell, William 32
Russell family 126
Russell Square 106
Rye 358

S

Saatchi Gallery 73, 77, **78**, *82*, 96
Sadleir, Sir Ralph 161
Sadler's Wells Theatre **279**, 305
safety 375
Sailor's Society Mission 165
St Alphage Garden 100
St Andrew-by-the-Wardrobe 91
St Andrew Undershaft 14
St Anne & St Agnes 305
St Anne's 124
St Anne's Limehouse 34, **165**
St Bartholomew's Hospital 25, **93**
St Bartholomew's Hospital Museum 93
St Bartholomew-the-Great 93

St Benet Welsh Church 91
St Botolph-Without-Aldgate 98
St Bride's 34, **89**, 305
St Clement Danes 34, 101, **102**
St Dunstan-in-the-East 98
St Ethelburga Centre for
  Reconciliation & Peace 98
St Ethelburga-the-Virgin 32, **98**
St Ethelreda 104, **105**
St George-the-Martyr 83
St George's Bloomsbury 34, **107**
St George's Hanover Square 115
St George's Hospital 19
St George's Wharf 174
St Giles Camberwell 172
St Giles Cripplegate 100
St Giles in the Fields *129*, 130
St Giles's 130-131
  hotels 57-59
  pubs & bars 224
  restaurants & cafés 209-211
St Helen's Bishopsgate 98
St James Garlickhythe 91
St James Square 120
St James's 72, **119-120**
  hotels 53-57
  pubs & bars 224
  restaurants & cafés 203-206
St James's (EC1) 304
St James's (W1) 113
St James's Palace 14, **120**
St James's Park 116
St James's Piccadilly 116,
  117, 302
St John at Hampstead 151
St John of Jerusalem 103-105
St John Smith Square **138**, 302
St John's 305
St John's Wood 150
St Katharine's 164
St Lawrence Jewry **95**, 305
St Magnus-the-Martyr 98
St Margaret Lothbury 305
St Margaret Pattens 98
St Margaret's 135, **138**
St Martin-in-the-Fields 34, 132,
  133, 268, 302
St Martin-within-Ludgate
  91, 305
St Martin's Lane 129
St Mary Abbots 184
St Mary Abchurch 95
St Mary Aldermary 91
St Mary Magdalene 179
St Mary Overie 81
St Mary Woolnoth 95
St Mary's Battersea 175
St Mary's Rotherhithe 167
St Mary's Walthamstow 163
St Mary's Wyndham Place 113
St Mary-at-Hill 98
St Mary-le-Bow **91**, 93, 305
St Mary-le-Strand 34, **101**
St Nicholas 188
St Nicholas Cole Abbey 91
St Nicholas's Deptford 168
St Olave Hart Street 97
St Pancras Chambers 31, 36, **110**
St Pancras New Church 110
St Pancras Old Church &
  St Pancras Gardens 110
St Pancras Station 32, 36,
  109, **110**
St Patrick's Day Parade &
  Festival 261
St Paul's Cathedral 11, 19, 25, 34,
  73, 88, 89, **92**, *92-93*, 374
St Paul's Covent Garden 73,
  126, **127**
St Paul's Deptford 167
St Paul's Knightsbridge 144
St Saviour's Dock 86
St Stephen Walbrook 95
St Thomas's Hospital 25, 85
St Vedast-alias-Foster 93
Salvation Army 161
Sambourne, Linley 186

Sandown Park Racecourse 327
Sanitation Act of 1866 25
Saracens 328
saunas, gay 300
Savile Row 115, **246**
Savoy Palace 13
Savoy Theatre 131
Saward, James 40
Saxon London **10-11**, 25
Science Museum 73, 140, *140*,
  141, 250, 269
Science Museum IMAX
  Theatre 285
Scott, George Gilbert **35**, 36,
  110, 144, 172, 184
Scott, Giles Gilbert **38**, 81,
  110, 175
Sebert, King 11
security 375
Seeing Late Gardens 97
Selfridges 20, **237**, 244
Senate House 107
Serpentine Gallery 141, *142*,
  144, 266
services *see* shops & services
Seven Dials 129
Severs, Dennis 159
sewers **18**, 20
sex industry 121-124
Sex Pistols 111, 130, 145
Shaftesbury, Earl 118
Shaftesbury Avenue 125
Shakespeare, William 14, *14*, 81,
  82, 83, 180, **353**
Shakespeare's Globe 14, 25, 73,
  79, 81, **82**, 160, 335
Shaw, George Bernard 127, 158
Shelley, Mary 110
Shelley, Percy Bysshe 73
Shepherd, Edward 115
Shepherd Market 115
Shepherd's Bush 187
Shepherd's Bush Empire
  187, **310**
Shepherd's Bush Green 187
Shepherd's Bush Market 187
Sheppard, Jack 40
Sherlock Holmes Museum 113
shoe shops 246
shops & services 233-258
  gay 295
Shoreditch 72, **159-160**
Shri Swaminarayan Mandir 190
Sicilian Place 107
Sidney Street siege of 1911
  39, **41**, 158
sightseeing tours 74
Sir John Soane's Museum 35,
  103, *103*
Six Nations Championships 327
Sixteen-String Jack 187
skateboarding 331
Sloane, Sir Hans **145**, 146
Sloane Square 145
Sloane Street 144
Small Faces 130
Smirke, Robert 98, 101,
  107, 113
Smith Square 138
Smithfield 13, **93**, 105
Smithfield Meat Market 93, *99*
smoking 29, **375**
Snow, John 124
Soane, Sir John **35**, 95, **103**,
  110, 147, 190
Soho 19, 23, 72, **121-125**, 233
  hotels 57
  pubs & bars 223-224
  restaurants & cafés 206-209
Soho Festival 264
Soho Square 124, *125*
Soho Theatre 124, 332, **340**
Somers Town 110
Somerset House 101, **102**,
  309, 330
Somerset House concerts 266
Somerset House museums 102

South Bank 75-87
  for children 268
  hotels 46-47
  pubs & bars 221
  restaurants & cafés 193-195
South Bank Centre 23, **31**, 75,
  78, **279**, 304, 305, 309, 314
South Bank University 375
South Downs 355
South Kensington 73, **140-141**
  for children 269
  hotels 46, **59-62**
  pubs & bars 225
  restaurants & cafés 211-212
South London Gallery 172
South-east London 167-173
  galleries 292-293
  pubs & bars 229
  restaurants & cafés 217
Southall 190
Southampton, Earl of 106
Southwark Cathedral 81, **82**, 304
Southwark Park 167
South-west London 174-181
  hotels 65-66
  pubs & bars 230-232
  restaurants & cafés 217-218
Spacey, Kevin 79, 332, 333
Spanish Armada 14
spas 183
Speakeasy 111
Speakers' Corner 142
Spencer House 120
Spitalfields 73, **157-159**, 233
Spitalfields Festival **306**, 314
Spitalfields Festival Fringe 261
Spitalfields Market 96, 158, **256**
sport & fitness 324-331
  events 261, 263, 264, 267
  shops 257
  sports centres 328
Sprite Urban Games 264
Stables Market 254
Stalin, Joseph 158
Stamford Bridge 326
Stanley, Bob
Stansted Airport 360
Staple Inn 103
State Opening of Parliament 267
stationery shops 250
Stella Artois tennis tournament
  187, 328
Stock Exchange 25
Stockwell 174
Stoke Newington 156
Stow, John 14
Strachey, Lytton 106
Strand 131
Stratford-upon-Avon 353
Straw, Jack 13
Strawberry Hill 180
street fashion shops 242-243
street sports 331
Strutton Ground 139
students' unions 375
studying in London 375
Suffragettes 139
  guided walk 296
Summer in the Square 132,
  263, **266**
Summer Pavilion programme 266
Sun, Nick 276
Survey of London 14
Sutton House 161
swimming 331
'Swinging '60s' 23
Swiss Cottage 156
Swiss Re tower *31*, **32**, **95**, 159
Sydenham 20, **173**
synagogues 374
Syon House 35, 73, **188**, 273

t

tailors 246-247
Tango Al Fresco 264
Tate Britain 38, 138, **139**, 272

Tate Modern 38, 25, 73, 81,
  83, 96, 250, 272
tax 373
taxis 264
tours 74
Taylor, Robert 95
telegrams 376
telephones 376
television 372
Temple Bar 91, 101
Temple Church **101**, 304
Temple of Mithras 95, **97**
Temple Place 101
tennis 179, **328**, **331**
Tennyson, Alfred Lord 138, 146
ten-pin bowling 331
terrorism 29
Thackeray, William Makepeace
  107, 168, 174, 184
Thames Barrier 25, 166, 170, **171**
Thames Barrier Park 166
Thames Barrier Visitors'
  Centre 171
Thames Gateway 29
Thatcher, Margaret **23-24**, 100
theatre 14, **332-340**
  for children 272
  festivals 261, 263, 264, 265
Theatre Museum 73, **127**, 268
Theatre Royal Stratford East 340
theme parks 274
Thomas, Dylan 111, 124
Thorney Island 11, 132
Thornhill, Sir James 170
Thorpe Park 274
Three Mills Island 162
time 376
Time Out 23, **372**
tipping 376
Tisbury Court 124
Tite Street 145
tkts booth 125, **333**
Todd, Sweeney 102
toilets 376
Tooting 179
Tooting Common 179
Tottenham 156
Tottenham Court Road 237
Tottenham Hotspur FC 327
'Tottenham Outrage', the 41
Tottenham riots of 1985 24
tourist information 342, **376**
tours 74
Tower Bridge 36, 86, *91*, **99**
Tower Bridge Experience 73,
  86, **99**
Tower Environs scheme 266
Tower House 158
Tower of London 11, 25, 32, *34*,
  88, 96, 97, **98**, 268
Town of Ramsgate 164
toy shops 258
Trades Union Congress (TUC) 21
Tradescant, John 77, **78**
Trafalgar Day Parade 265
Trafalgar Great River Race 264
Trafalgar Square 25, 72, **132-133**,
  134-135, 266, 269
Traids 42
train
  getting around by 342
  stations 342
tramlink 363
trams 20
transport 26-27
transport, public 360-364
travel advice 369
travel information centres 361
travelcards 361
Trellick Tower 184, *185*
Tricycle Theatre 183, 332, **340**
Trinity Almshouses 161
Trinity College of Music 302
Trinity Hospital 168
Trinity Square 97
trips out of town 342-358
Trollope, Anthony 106, 146, 184

Trooping the Colour 263
Truman Brewery 159
Tube, the *see* Underground, the
Turkish baths 183
Turkish London 156
Turner, JMW 139, 146, 164, 175
Turnham Green 17
12 Bar Club 130, **313**
28 Days Later 281
Twickenham Stadium 181
2 Willow Road 151, **154**
Tyburn 19, 25, **112**, 130
Tyler, Wat **13**, 98
Tyler, William 41

Underground, the 25, 26-27, 104, **361-362**
underwear shops 243
Union Chapel 155, **310**, *311*
universities and colleges 375
University College London (UCL) **107**, 375
University of Greenwich **170**, 375
University of London **107**, **375**
University of London Union (ULU) 312
University of Middlesex 375
university residences 70
University of Westminster 375
Urquhart, David 183
US Embassy 115

V&A *see* Victoria & Albert Museum
van Gogh, Vincent 174
Vanbrugh, John 169, 355
Vauxhall 174
Vauxhall City Farm 269
Vauxhall Pleasure Gardens 174
Venerable Bede 11
Vertical Chill 329
Vestry House Museum 163
Victoria, Queen **20**, 95, 117, 139
Victoria & Albert Museum 140, **141**, 269, 293
Victoria Coach Station 344
Victoria Park **161**, 273
Victoria Station 344
Victoria Tower Gardens 138
Vietnamese London 160
views, hotels with 54
Viking London **11**, 25
Villiers Street 131
Vinopolis, City of Wine 81, **83**
vintage clothes shops 243-245
Virgin Megastore 256
visas 377
Visit London 46

Waddesdon Manor 357
Walkers Court 124
walking 104-105, **365**
    country 346
    tours 74
Wallace, Sir Richard 113
Wallace, William 93
Wallace Collection 38, 112, *112*, **113**
Walpole Park 190
Walpole, Horace 120, 180, 181
Walpole, Sir Robert 19
Walthamstow 162-164
Walthamstow Market 163
Walthamstow Stadium 163, **327**
Walthamstow Town Hall 163
Walworth, William **13**, 98
Wanamaker, Sam 82, 83
Wandle, River 176
Wandle Meadow Nature Meadow 177

Wandle Trail 176
Wandsworth 175-176
Wandsworth Common 176
Wapping 164
Wapping High Street 164
Wapping Project 164, **292**
Wardour Street 124
Wars of the Roses 14
Warwick Road 186
Wasps 327
water transport 363
Waterloo 79
    pubs & bars 226
Waterloo Bridge 73, **79**
Waterloo Station **79**, 344
Waterlow Park 154
Waterlow, Sir Sydney 154
WaterWorks Nature Reserve 164
Waugh, Evelyn 155
weather 377, 378
Webb, Aston 133
Webb, Philip 173
weblogs 380
websites 380
weights 377
Wellington 73
Wellington Arch 73, 116, **118**
Wellington Barracks 134
Wellington, Duke of 93, 115, **116**, 118
Wellington Museum, The *see* Apsley House
Welsey, John 171
Wembley 190
Wembley Stadium, Arena & Conference Centre 32, 190, 310, **325**
Wernher, Julius 170
Wesley, John 100
West Central Liberal Synagogue 374
West Ham Park 273
West Ham United FC 327
West India Dock 165
West Indian London 175
West London 182-190
    hotels 66-69
    pubs & bars 232
    restaurants & cafés 218-219
West London Tram Project 187
'West Minster', the **11**, 25
West Soho 125
Westbourne Grove 182
Westbourne Park **184**, 233
Westcheap 11
Westminster 25, 72, **132-139**
    pubs & bars 224-225
    restaurants & cafés 211
Westminster Abbey 11, 14, 25, 33, 135, **138**, 374
Westminster Bridge 19, 25, **77**
Westminster Cathedral **139**, 374
Westminster Hall 11, 135, **137**
Westminster Hospital 19
Westwood, Vivienne 23
Whistler, JM 145
White City 187
White Cube 92, 160, **292**
White Tower, the 11
Whitechapel 157-159
Whitechapel Art Gallery 73, **158**, 287
Whitechapel Bell Foundry 158
Whitehall 134
Whitehall Palace 14, 134, 136
Whitehall Theatre 134
Whitstable 358
Whittington Stone 154
Whittington, Dick 15, 25, 88, **154**
Wigmore Hall 114, **304**, 305
Wild, Jonathan 39-40
Wilde, Oscar 129, 145, 165, 296
Wilkins, William 107
William I the Conqueror, King **11**, 25, 358
William III (of Orange), King **19**, 95, 142

William IV, King 120
William Morris Gallery 73, 163, **164**
Wimbledon 179
Wimbledon Lawn Tennis Championships **263**, 328
Wimbledon Lawn Tennis Museum 73, **179**, 273
Wimbledon Stadium 327
Wimbledon Theatre 179
Wimpole Street 112
Winchester 353-356
'Winchester Geese' 81
Winchester, Palace of 81
Windmill Theatre 125
Windsor Castle 356, *357*
Windsor Racecourse 327
wine & spirits shops 250
Winston Churchill's Britain at War Experience 83, **86**
Woburn Walk 107
Wollstonecraft, Mary 106, 110
Wolsey, Cardinal 180
Wombles, the 179
women in London 377
Women's Library 158
Wood the Elder, John 344
Woolf, Virginia & Leonard 106
Woolwich 14, 25, **170-171**
Woolwich Arsenal 170
Woolwich Ferry 170
de Worde, Wynkyn 89
working in London 377
World Cup 1966 25
World War I 20
World War II **21-23**, 36
Wormwood Scrubs 187
Wren, Sir Christopher **19**, 32, 34, 73, 81, 91, 92, 93, 98, 102, 116, 117, 147, 168, 170, 180
WWT Wetland Centre 177
Wyatt, Benjamin Dean 120

yardies 42
Yeats, William Butler 106, 107
Yeoman Warders **88**, 99
YMCAs 70
yoga 331
Young Vic 79, **340**
youth hostels 70

Zembla 189
Zeppelin raids **21**, 25
Zoo Art Fair 287
Zurich Premiership 327

Where to Stay

Academy Hotel 50
Arosfa 53
Ashlee House 53
Aster House 62
Baglioni, The 47, *58-59*, **59**
Bentley, The 61
Blakes 47, **61**
Charlotte Street Hotel **49**, 286
City Inn Westminster 54, **63**, *63*
Claridge's **53**, 115
Colonnade Town House 66
Covent Garden Hotel **57**, 286
Dolphin Square Hotel 54, **63**
Dorchester, The 47, **55**
easyhotel 45
Five Sumner Place 62
Garden Court Hotel 69
Generator, The 53
Gore, The 61
Great Eastern Hotel 47
Guesthouse West 45, **66**
Hampstead Village Guesthouse 65
Harlingford Hotel 50
Hazlitt's 57
Hempel, The 54, **66**

Jenkins Hotel 50
Landmark Hotel 113
Lanesborough, The 62
Langham Hotel 112
London County Hall Travel Inn Capital **46**, 47
London Marriott County Hall 54
Mad Hatter, The 47
Malmaison 45, **49**
Mayflower Hotel 47, **69**
Metropolitan, The 54, **55**
Milestone Hotel & Apartments 54, **61**
Miller's Residence 66, *67*
Montague on the Gardens 50
Morgan Hotel 50
Morgan House 65
myhotel Bloomsbury 50
myhotel Chelsea 61
No.5 Maddox Street 55
Number Sixteen 61
One Aldwych **59**, 286
Pavilion, The *45*, 69
Pembridge Court 68
Piccadilly Backpackers 57
Portobello Hotel 47, **68**
Ritz, The 20, **55**, 116
Riverside Hotel 47, **66**
Rookery, The 47
Rushmore Hotel 47, **69**
Saint Gregory 54, **47**
St Margaret's Hotel 53
St Martin's Lane Hotel 58
Sanderson, The 49
Savoy, The 54, **58**
Sherlock Holmes 53
Soho Hotel 57
Swiss House Hotel 62
Trafalgar, The 54, **57**
Travelodge Covent Garden 45
Twenty Nevern Square 47, **68**
Vancouver Studios 47, **69**
Vicarage Hotel 167
Windermere Hotel 65
Windmill on the Common 47, **65**
Zetter Restaurant & Rooms 45, *46*, 47, **49**, 54

Restaurants & Cafés

Admiralty, The 210
Afghan Kitchen 214
Al Sultan 205
Alastair Little 208
Anchor & Hope **193**, 220
Andrew Edmunds 208
Andrews 204
Arkansas Café 193, **215**
Armadillo 215
Assaggi 219
Balans *294*, 295
Baltic 193
Bamboula 193, **217**
Bank Aldwych 199
Bar Italia 124, **206**
Belgo Centraal 193, **209**
Bibendum 212
Blue Kangaroo 271
Boiled Egg & Soldiers 271
Bonds 196
Boxwood Café 212
Brick Lane Beigel Bake 215
Busaba Eathai 200
Bush Garden Café 271
Café Corfu 214
Café in the Crypt 211
Café Spice Namaste 216
Caldesi 213
Cambio de Tercio 212
Canyon 217
Caprice, Le 205
Carluccio's Caffè 200
Cecconi's 205
Chez Bruce 217
Christopher's 193, **210**
Chutney Mary 212

Cigala 193, **199**
Cinnamon Club 211
City Miyama 195
Club Gascon 193, **196**
Coach & Horses **196**, 207, 220
Cow Dining Room 218
De Gustibus 195
Dexter's Grill 271
Dorchester Grill Room 203
Drunken Monkey 193, **195**, *195*
E&O 219
Eagle, the 103
Eagle Bar Diner **199**, 223, 230
ECapital 206
Embassy 205
Enoteca Turi 217
L'Escargot 207
Eyre Brothers 196
Fifteen 192, **216**
First Out 295
Fish Hoek 218
Flâneur Food Hall 193, **196**
Food for Thought 211
Fook Sing 207
1492 *208-209*, **218**
Frizzante@City Farm 207, **271**
Gate, The 193, **219**
Gaucho Grill 193, **199**
Gay Hussar 124, **209**
Giraffe 271
Glasshouse, The 218
Golden Eagle 113
Golden Hind 201
Gordon Ramsay 192, **213**
Gordon Ramsay at Claridge's 55, 192, **213**
Gourmet Burger Kitchen 176, 193, **217**
Hakkasan 192, **201**, 207, 220, 223, 230
Han Kang 201
Hard Rock Café 116, 193, **203**
Harlem 193, *216*, **218**
Heartstone 193, **215**
Hookah Lounge 216
Hunan 213
Imperial China 206
Inn the Park *201*, 203
Inside 217
Ivy, The 192, **210**
Jakob's 211
Jones Dairy Café 215
Kastoori 179
Kaya 206
Kiku 206
Konditor & Cook 193
Kulu Kulu 209
Lavender, The 217
Levant 203
Lindsay House 206
Lisboa Patisserie 184, **218**
Livebait 193
Locanda Locatelli 201
Lots Road Pub & Dining Room **212**, 220
Louis Hungarian Pâtisserie 150
Lucky 7 193, **218**
Maison Bertaux 193, **206**
Mandalay 219
Mandarin Kitchen 219
Mango Room 214
Manna 193, 207, **215**
Marine Ices 149
Maroush 203
Masala Zone 208
Mazgal 154
Medcalf *192*, **196**, 207
Mildred's 209
Momo 205
Morgan M 193, **214**, *215*
Moro 199
Mr Kong 207
Nahm 192, **211**
New World 207
19 Numara Bos Cirrik 214
Nobu 206
1 Lombard Street 195

Original Tagines 201
Orrery 203
Oxo Tower Restaurant, Bar & Brasserie 195
Pàtisserie Valerie 122, **206**
Pellicci's 204
Perseverance 199
Pied á Terre 200
Place Below, The 193, **196**
Providores & Tapa Room 201
Quilon 211
Quo Vadis 208
Racine 212
Radha Krishna Bhavan 179
Rainforest Café 271
Ramen Seto 193, **209**
Rasa 156
Rasa Samudra 199
Real Greek, The 215
Red Fort 208
Ritz, The 205
Rock & Soul Plaice 129, 193, **210**
Rodizio Rico 193, **219**
Rosmarino 219
Royal China 203
Sardo 200
Sariyer Balik 214
Savoy Grill, The 210
Sea Cow 217
Sheekey, J 210
Simpson's-in-the-Strand 210
Six-13 201
Smiths of Smithfield 193, **199**, 220, 222, 230
Smollenksy's on the Strand 211
Sông Quê 216
St John 96, 103, 193, **196**
Sweetings 195
Tamarind 205
Tas 193
Tate Modern Café: Level 2 193
TGI Friday's 271
Trompette, La 218
Trouvaille, La 207
Tsunami 218
Victory Café 203
Vijaya Krishna 179
Vincent Rooms, The 207, **211**
Wagamama 193, **214**
Wells 214
Wolseley, The **205**, 207
World Food Café 211
Yauatcha 207
Yming 207
Yokoso Sushi 193, **196**
Zaika 219
Zeta 213, *213*
Zoomslide Café 210
Zuma 212

Pubs & Bars

Admiral Duncan 298
Ain't Nothin' But? The Blues Bar **223**, 230
Akbar 230
Albert 227
American Bar 230, *231*
Anchor & Hope **193**, 220
Angel 130
Apartment 195 226
Archduke 221
Argyll Arms 227
Ashburnham Arms 229
Baltic 220, **226**
Barcode 298
BJ's White Swan 294, **298**
Black Cap 294, **298**
Black Friar 221
Bleeding Heart Tavern 220, **221**
Blind Beggar *40-41*, **42**, 158
Blue Bar 220, **227**, 230
Boisdale 220, **224**, 230
Box, The 298
Bradley's Spanish Bar 223
Bread & Roses 230
Bromptons 299
Café Bohème 230

Café Kick 222
Candy Bar 294, 295, **299**
City Barge 220, **232**
Clifton 227
Coach & Horses, EC1 **196**, 220
Coach & Horses, W1 220, **223**
Compton's of Soho 299
Cork & Bottle 220, **223**
Court 111
Crocker's Folly 183
Crown & Two Chairman 124
Cutty Sark Tavern 168
Dogstar 230
Dove 232
Drawing Room & Sofa Bar 230
Duke's Head 231
Dusk 224
Eagle Bar Diner 193, 199, **223**
Edge, The 299
Effra 231
Elgin 232
Embassy Bar 220, **227**, 230
Engineer 149
Escape Bar 299
Fire Stables 231
Fitzroy Tavern 110
Florist 228
Fox & Anchor 93
Fox & Grapes 179
French House 124, 220, **223**
G.A.Y. Bar 299
George 83
Glass Bar 299
Golden Heart 96
Golden Lion 121
Gordon's 224
Grand Union 232
Grapes 228
Grenadier 144
Guinea 224
Hakkasan 192, 201, 207, 220, **223**, 230
Hand in Hand 179
Hill **227**, 230
Hoist, The 295, **299**
Holly Bush 151, **227**
Home **228**, 230
International 231
Island Queen 227
Jack Horner 111
Jamaica Wine House 221
Jerusalem 231
Jerusalem Tavern 220, **222**
John Oldcastle 104
Keston Lodge 227
King William IV 299
Kudos 299
Lab 231
Lamb & Flag 224
Lamb 223
Langley 231
Lock Tavern 227
Long Bar 230, **231**
Lonsdale *229*, 230, **232**
Lots Road Pub & Dining Room **212**, 220
Loungelover 207, **228**, 230
Lowlander 220, **224**
Magdala 151
Market Porter 220, **221**
Match EC1 **222**, 230
Mayflower, the 167
Milk & Honey 207, **224**
Mitre, the 105
Monkey Chews **228**, 230
Mortimer Arms 111
Mother Bar 220, **228**, 230
Nag's Head 144, **225**
Nordic 223
North Pole 229
Oak Bar 299
One Tun, the 104
Paxton's Head 226
Player **224**, 230
Point 101 231
Pride of Spitalfields *225*, 228

Princess Louise 226
Prospect of Whitby 164, **228**
Red Lion, W1 224
Red Lion, SW1 225
Retro Bar 300
Rising Sun 111
Royal Oak 220, **221**
Royal Vauxhall Tavern 174, **296**
Ruby Lounge 231
Rupert Street 300
Salt Whisky Bar 220, **224**, 230
Sanctuary Soho 294, 295, **300**
Sand 230, 231
Seven Stars 220, *221*, **222**
Shadow Lounge, The 295, **300**
Shakespeare 228
Shaun & Joe 294, **300**
Shepherd's Tavern 115
Ships 231
Smersh **228**, 230
Smiths of Smithfield 193, 199, 220, **222**, 230
Sosho 220, **228**, 230
South London Pacific 230, **232**
Star Tavern 220, **225**
Sultan 207, **232**
Thirst 231
Tom & Dick's 230, **232**
Tongue & Groove 220, 230, **232**
Too 2 Much 122, 294, **300**
Townhouse 220, **225**, 230
Trafalgar Tavern 168, **229**
Trailer Happiness 232
Two Brewers 294, **300**
Vertigo 42/Twentyfour 220, **221**
Viaduct Tavern 105, **227**
Village Soho 300
Wenlock Arms 220, **228**
White Cross 179
White Horse 220, **232**
White Swan 220, **232**
William Morris 179
Yard, The 300
Ye Grapes 115
Ye Olde Cheshire Cheese 89, **221**

Advertisers' Index

Please refer to relevant sections for addresses and/or telephone numbers

Where to Stay

57 Pont Street	60
Abbey Court Hotel	64
Astons Apartments	44
Cardiff Hotel	48
City University	44
Elegant English Hotels	64
Falcon Hotel	60
Garden Court Hotel	64
Hart House Hotel	56
Host & Guest Service	60
Hotel Connect	48
Lancaster Court Hotel	52
Lincoln House Hotel	56
Londontown.com	IBC
Oxford London Hotel	64
Ramsees Hotel	56
Stylotel	44
Swiss House Hotel	56
Tudor Court Hotel	368
Wake Up! London	44

Sightseeing

British Library	178
Catamaran Cruisers	128
Churchill's Britain at War Experience	108
Cutty Sark	368
Dulwich Picture Gallery	362
English Heritage / Apsley House	8
Geffrye Museum	90
Hatfield House	344
Horniman Museum	362
Keats House	178
Kew Gardens	28
Legoland Windsor	344
London Aquarium	76
London Eye	80
Museum of Childhood	90
Museum of Docklands	12
Museum of London	12
Museum of the Order of St. John	108
Painshill Park	344
Tower Bridge Exhibition	90
Wallace Collection	28
Wimbledon Lawn Tennis Museum	178

Eating & Drinking

Bateaux London	194
Café Naz	198
Eco	198
Gaylord	362
Golden Palace	202
Medieval Banquet	202
Sagar	202
Sông Quê Café	202
Thai Origin	368
Thai Pin	368
Wagamama	16

Shops & Services

Alfies Antiques Market	234
Camden Lock	234
Carhartt	282
Intoxica!	362
Merton Abbey Mills	234
Spitalfields Market	238

Arts & Entertainment

Les Misérables	IFC
Lion King	IFC
Mary Poppins	IFC
Phantom of the Opera	IFC
Royal Academy of Arts	108
Shakespeare's Globe	84
Society of London Theatre	388
Tate Britain	288
Tate Modern	288
Women in White	334

Places of interest or entertainment	▢
Railway stations	▪
Underground stations	⊖
Parks	▢
Hospitals	▢
Casualty units	✚
Churches	✚
Synagogues	✡
Congestion Charge Zone	ⒸG
Districts	MAYFAIR
Theatre	●

Maps

London Overview	392
Street Maps	394
Street Index	406
Central London by Area	412
London Underground	414

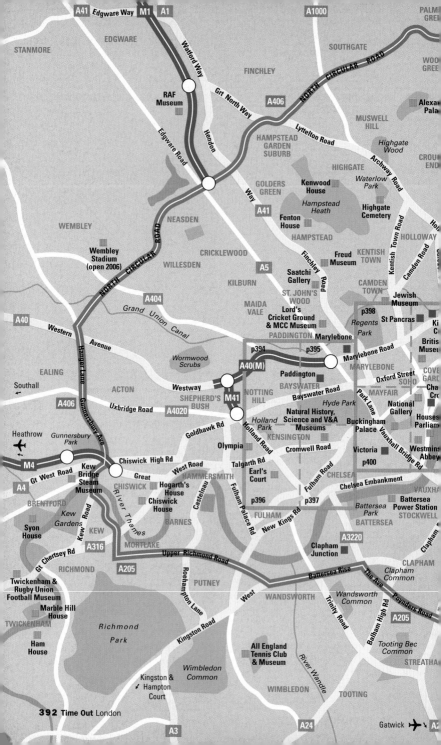

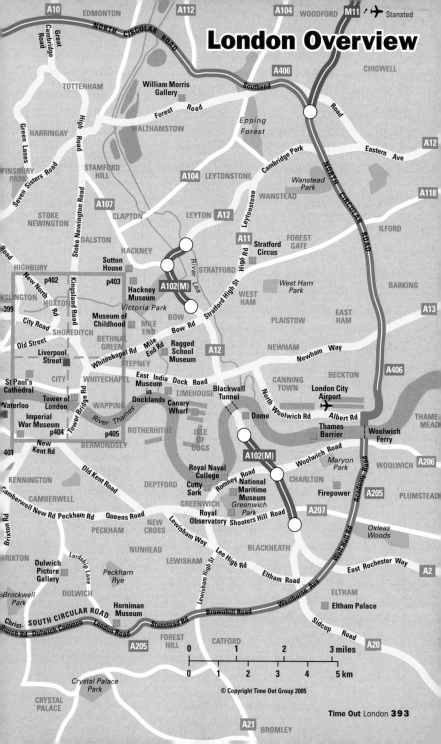

London Overview

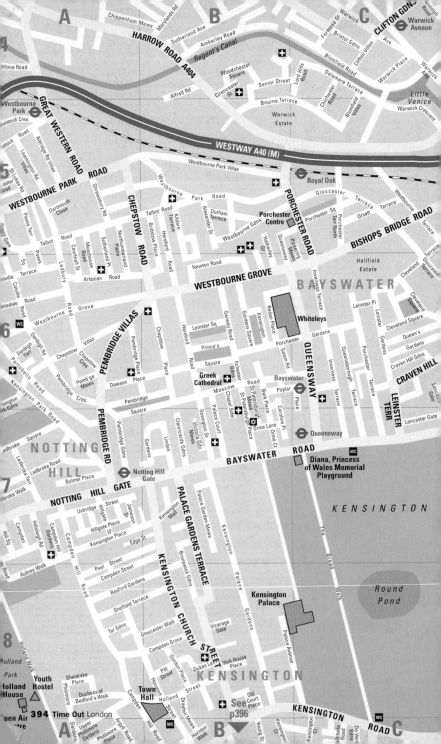

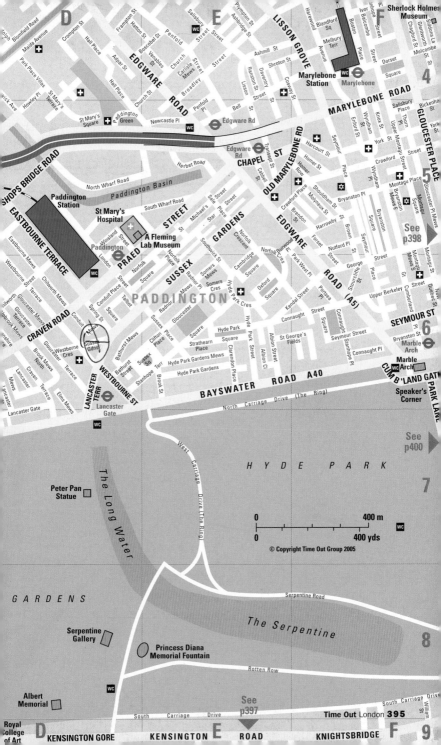

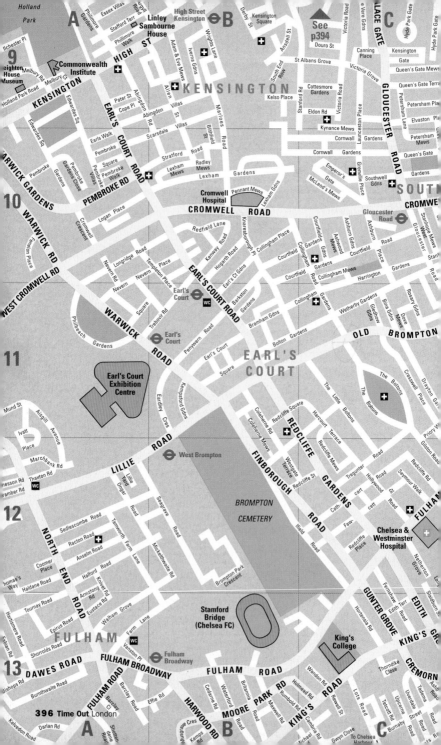

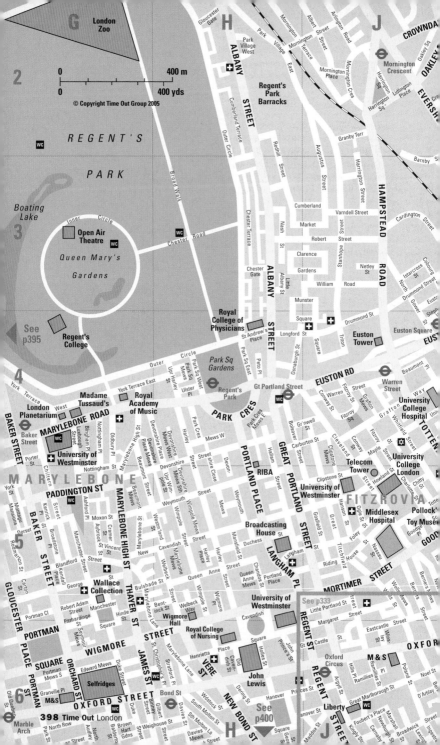

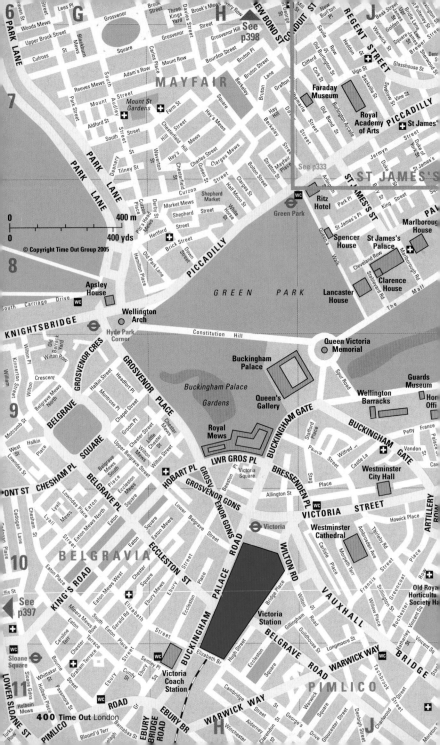

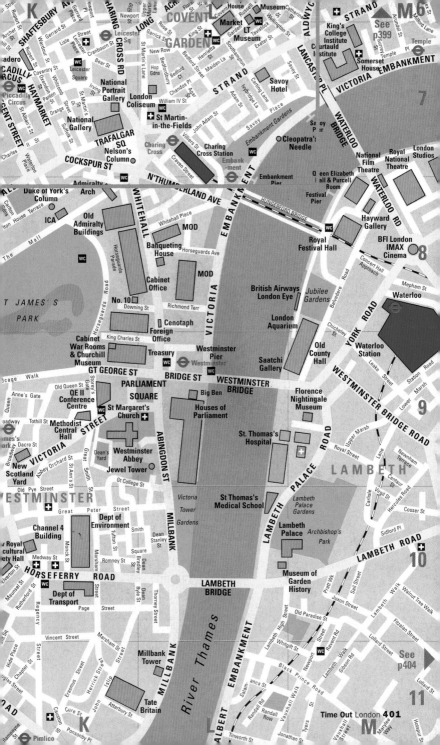

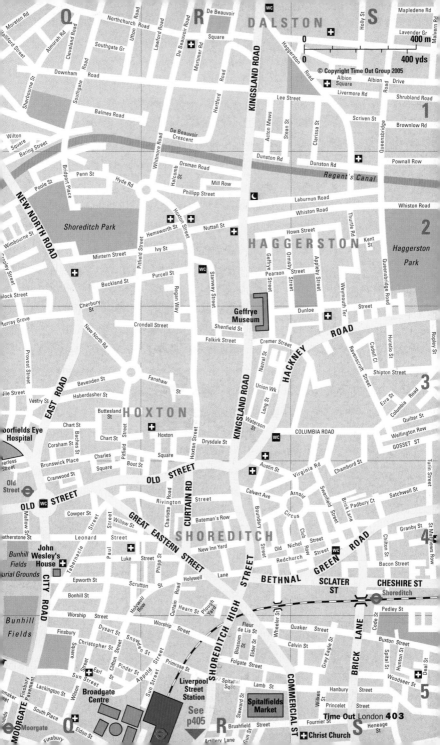

Street Index

Abbey Orchard Street - p401 K9
Abbey Street - p405 R10/S10
Abchurch Lane - p405 Q7
Abingdon Road - p396 A9/B10
Abingdon Street - p401 L9
Abingdon Villas - p396 A9/B9
Acton Mews - p403 R1
Acton Street - p399 M3
Adam & Eve Mews - p396 B9
Adam Street - p401 L7
Adam's Row - p400 G7
Agar Street - p401 L7
Agdon Street - p402 O4
Aisgill Avenue - p396 A11/12
Albany Street - p398 H2/3
Albemarle Street - p400 H7/J7
Albert Bridge - p397 E13
Albert Bridge Road - p397 E13
Albert Court - p397 D9
Albert Embankment - p401 L10/11
Albert Street - p398 J2
Albion Close - p395 E6
Albion Drive - p403 S1
Albion Square - p403 S1
Albion Street - p395 E6
Aldenham Street - p399 K2
Alder Square - p404 P6
Alder Street - p405 S6
Aldermanbury - p404 P6
Alderney Street - p400 H11
Aldersgate Street - p404 O6/P5/6
Aldford Street - p400 G7
Aldgate - p405 R6
Aldridge Road Villas - p394 A5
Aldwych - p399 M6
Alexander Square - p397 E10
Alexander Street - p394 B5
Alfred Place - p399 K5
Alfred Road - p394 B4
Alice Street - p405 Q10
Alie Street - p405 S6
Ali Saints Street - p399 M2
Allen Street - p396 B9/10
Allington Street - p400 H10
Almeida Street - p402 O1
Almorah Road - p403 Q1
Amberley Road - p394 B4
Ambrosden Avenue - p400 J10
Ampton Street - p399 M3
Amwell Street - p402 N3
Andrew Borde Street - p399 K6
Angel Street - p404 O6
Anhalt Road - p397 E13
Ann Lane - p397 D13
Ansdell Street - p396 B9
Anselm Road - p396 A12
Appleby Street - p403 S2
Appold Street - p403 Q5/R5
Aquinas Street - p404 N8
Archer Street - p401 K7
Argyle Square - p399 L3
Argyle Street - p399 L3
Argyll Road - p394 A9, p396 A9/B9
Arlington Avenue - p402 P2
Arlington Road - p398 J2
Arlington Street - p400 J8
Armstrong Road - p396 A12
Arne Street - p399 L6
Arnold Circus - p403 R4/S4
Artesian Road - p394 A6
Arthur Street - p405 Q7
Artillery Lane - p403 R5
Artington Way - p402 N3
Arundel Street - p401 M6/7
Aryll Street - p398 J6
Ashbridge Street - p395 E4
Ashburn Gardens - p396 C10
Ashburn Place - p396 C10
Ashburnham Road - p396 C13, p397 D13
Ashby Street - p402 O3
Ashmill Street - p395 E4
Ashwood Mews - p396 C10
Astell Street - p397 E11
Atterbury Street - p401 K11
Aubrey Road - p394 A7/8
Aubrey Walk - p394 A7/8
Augustus Street - p398 J2/3
Austin Friars - p405 Q6
Avery Row - p400 H6
Aybrook Street - p398 G5
Ayers Street - p404 P8/9
Aylesbury Road - p402 O4

Babmaes Street - p401 K7
Baches Street - p403 Q3
Back Church Lane - p405 S6/7

Back Hill - p402 N4
Bacon Street - p403 S4
Bainbridge Street - p399 K5
Baker Street - p398 G4/5
Balcombe Street - p395 F4
Balderton Street - p398 G6
Baldwin Terrace - p402 P2
Baldwin's Gardens - p402 N5
Balfe Street - p399 L2
Balmes Road - p403 Q1
Baltic Street - p402 P4
Bankside - p404 P7
Banner Street - p402 P4
Barclay Close - p396 A13
Barclay Road - p396 A13
Barford Street - p402 N2
Baring Street - p403 Q1/2
Bark Place - p394 B6/7
Barkston Gardens - p396 B11
Barnabas Street - p400 G11
Barnby Street - p398 J3
Barnham Street - p405 Q9
Barnsbury Road - p402 N1/2
Barnsbury Street - p402 N1/O1
Baron Street - p402 N2
Barons Place - p404 N9
Barter Street - p399 L5
Bartholomew Square - p402 P4
Basil Street - p397 F9
Basinghall Avenue - p404 P6
Basinghall Street - p404 P6
Basire Street - p402 P1
Bastwick Street - p402 O4/P4
Bateman Street - p399 K6
Bateman's Row - p403 R4
Bath Street - p402 P3/4
Bath Terrace - p404 P10
Bathurst Mews - p395 D6
Bathurst Street - p395 D6
Battersea Bridge - p397 E13
Battersea Bridge Road - p397 E13
Battersea Church Road - p397 E13
Battle Bridge Lane - p405 Q8
Battle Bridge Road - p399 L2
Bayley Street - p399 K5
Baylis Road - p404 N9
Bayswater Road - p394 B7/C7, p395 E6/F6
Beak Street - p400 J6
Bear Gardens - p404 P7/8
Bear Lane - p404 O8
Bear Street - p401 K7
Beauchamp Place - p397 F9/10
Beaufort Street - p397 D12
Beaumont Mews - p398 G5
Beaumont Place - p398 J4
Beaumont Street - p398 G5
Bedford Avenue - p399 K5
Bedford Court - p401 L7
Bedford Gardens - p394 A8/B8
Bedford Place - p399 L5
Bedford Row - p399 M5
Bedford Square - p399 K5
Bedford Street - p401 L7
Bedford Way - p399 K4
Bedfordbury - p401 L7
Beech Street - p402 P5
Beeston Place - p400 H9
Belgrave Mews North - p400 G9
Belgrave Mews South - p400 G9
Belgrave Place - p400 G10
Belgrave Road - p400 H10/J11
Belgrave Square - p400 G9
Belgrave Street - p399 L3
Bell Lane - p405 R6
Bell Street - p395 E4/5
Bell Yard - p399 M6
Belvedere Road - p401 M8/9
Bentinck Street - p398 H5
Berkeley Square - p400 H7
Berkeley Street - p400 H7/8
Bermondsey Street - p405 Q8/9/10
Bermondsey Wall West - p405 S9
Bernard Street - p399 L4
Berners Mews - p398 J5
Berners Street - p398 J5/6
Berry Street - p402 O4
Berwick Street - p398 J6, p399 K6
Bethnal Green Road - p403 R4/S4
Betterton Street - p399 L6
Bevenden Street - p403 Q3
Bevis Marks - p405 R6
Bickenhall Street - p395 F5
Bidborough Street - p399 L3
Billiter Street - p405 R6/7
Bina Gardens - p396 C11
Bingham Place - p398 G4

Binney Street - p398 G6
Birchin Lane - p405 Q6
Birdcage Walk - p401 K9
Birkenhead Street - p399 L3
Bishops Bridge Road - p394 C5, p395 D5
Bishops Road - p396 A13
Bishopsgate - p405 Q6/R5/6
Black Prince Street - p401 L11/M11
Blackburn Mews - p400 G7
Blackfriars Bridge - p404 O7
Blackfriars Lane - p404 O6
Blackfriars Road - p404 N8, p405 O8
Blackland Terrace - p397 F11
Blandford Square - p395 F4
Blandford Street - p398 G5
Blantyre Street - p397 D13
Bleeding Heart Yard - p402 N5
Bletchley Street - p402 P3
Blithfield Street - p396 B10
Blomfield Road - p394 C4, p395 D4
Blomfield Street - p405 Q5/6
Blomfield Villas - p394 C5
Bloomfield Terrace - p400 G11
Bloomsbury Square - p399 L5
Bloomsbury Street - p399 K5
Bloomsbury Way - p399 L5
Blossom Street - p403 R5
Blue Anchor Yard - p405 S7
Bolsover Street - p398 H4/J5
Bolton Gardens - p396 B11/C11
Bolton Street - p400 H7/8
Bonhill Street - p403 Q4
Borough High Street - p404 P8/9
Borough Road - p404 O9
Boscobel Street - p395 E4
Boston Place - p395 F4
Boswell Street - p399 L5
Boundary Street - p403 R4
Bourchier Street - p399 K6
Bourdon Street - p400 H7
Bourne Street - p400 G11
Bourne Terrace - p394 B5/C5
Bouverie Street - p404 N6
Bow Lane - p404 P6
Bow Street - p399 L6
Bowling Green Lane - p402 N4
Brad Street - p404 N8
Braes Street - p402 O1
Braham Street - p405 S6
Bramber Road - p396 A12
Bramerton Street - p397 E12
Bramham Gardens - p396 B11
Bray Place - p397 F11
Bread Street - p404 P6
Bream's Building - p404 N6
Bressenden Place - p400 H9/J10
Brewer Street - p400 J7, p401 K6
Brick Lane - p403 S4/5, p405 S5/6
Brick Street - p400 H8
Bride Lane - p404 N6
Bridewell Place - p404 N6
Bridge Place - p400 H11
Bridge Street - p401 L9
Bridgeway Street - p399 K2
Bridle Lane - p400 J6/7
Bridstow Place - p394 B5
Brill Place - p399 K2
Bristol Gardens - p394 C4
Britannia Road - p396 B13
Britannia Row - p402 P1
Britannia Street - p399 M3
Britten Street - p397 E11
Britton Street - p402 O4/5
Broad Street - p395 E4
Broad Walk - p398 H2/3
Broadley Street - p395 E4
Broadstone Place - p398 G5
Broadway - p401 K9
Broadwall - p404 N7/8
Broadwick Street - p398 J6
Brompton Gardens - p397 F9
Brompton Park Crescent - p396 B12
Brompton Place - p397 F9
Brompton Road - p397 E9/10/F9
Brompton Square - p397 E9
Brook Drive - p404 N10
Brook Mews North - p395 D6
Brook Street W1 - p398 H6, p400 H6
Brook Street W2 - p395 E6
Brooke Street - p402 N5
Brook's Mews - p400 H6
Brown Hart Gardens - p398 G6
Brown Street - p395 F5
Brownlow Mews - p399 M4
Brownlow Road - p403 S1

Brownlow Street - p399 M5
Brunswick Gardens - p394 B7/8
Brunswick Place - p403 Q3/4
Brunswick Square - p399 L4
Brushfield Street - p403 R5
Bruton Lane - p400 H7
Bruton Place - p400 H7
Bruton Street - p400 H7
Bryanston Mews East - p395 F5
Bryanston Place - p395 F5
Bryanston Square - p395 F5
Bryanston Street - p395 F6
Buckingham Gate - p400 H9/J9
Buckingham Palace Road - p400 H10
Buckland Street - p403 Q2
Bucknall Street - p399 K6/L6
Bulmer Place - p394 A7
Bunhill Row - p402 P4, p403 Q4
Burbage Close - p404 P10
Burdett Street - p404 N9
Burgh Street - p402 O2
Burlington Arcade - p400 J7
Burnaby Street - p396 C13
Burnthwaite Road - p396 A13
Burrell Street - p404 O8
Burton Street - p399 K3/4
Burwood Place - p395 E5
Bury Place - p399 L5
Bury Street EC3 - p405 R6
Bury Street SW1 - p400 J7/8
Bury Walk - p397 E11
Bute Street - p397 D10
Buttesland Street - p403 Q3
Buxton Street - p403 S5
Byward Street - p405 Q7/R7
Bywater Street - p397 F11

Cabbell Street - p395 E5
Cadell Close - p403 S3
Cadogan Gardens - p397 F10/11
Cadogan Lane - p400 G10
Cadogan Place - p400 G10
Cadogan Square - p397 F10
Cadogan Street - p397 F10/11
Cale Street - p397 E11
Caledonia Street - p399 L2
Caledonian Road - p399 L2/M2
Callendar Road - p397 D9
Callow Street - p397 D12
Calshot Street - p399 M2
Calthorpe Street - p399 M4
Calvert Avenue - p403 R4
Calvin Street - p403 R5/S5
Cambria Road - p396 C13
Cambridge Circus - p399 K6
Cambridge Square - p395 E6
Cambridge Street - p400 H11
Camden Passage - p402 O2
Camley Street - p399 K2/L2
Camomile Street - p405 R6
Campden Grove - p394 B8
Campden Hill Gardens - p394 A7
Campden Hill Road - p394 A8/B9
Campden Hill Square - p394 A7
Campden Street - p394 A8/B7
Canning Place - p396 C9
Cannon Street - p404 P6/7
Canonbury Villas - p402 O1
Capper Street - p398 J4, p399 K4
Carburton Street - p398 H4/J4
Cardington Street - p398 J3
Carey Street - p399 M6
Carlisle Lane - p401 M9/10
Carlisle Mews - p395 E4
Carlisle Place - p400 J10
Carlisle Street - p399 K6
Carlton Gardens - p401 K8
Carlton House Terrace - p401 K8
Carlyle Square - p397 E12
Carmelite Street - p404 N7
Carnaby Street - p398 J6
Carnegie Street - p399 M2
Caroline Terrace - p400 G10
Carriage Drive North - p397 F13
Carriage Drive West - p397 F13
Carter Lane - p404 O6
Carting Lane - p401 L7
Carton Street - p398 G5
Cartwright Gardens - p399 L3
Cartwright Street - p405 S7
Castle Baynard Street - p404 O7
Castle Lane - p400 J9
Cathcart Road - p396 C12
Catherine Place - p400 J9
Catherine Street - p401 M6
Catton Street - p399 L5/M5
Causton Street - p401 K11

Cavendish Square - p398 H5/6
Caversham Street - p397 F12
Caxton Street - p400 J9, p401 K9
Cedarne Road - p396 B13
Centaur Street - p401 M9
Central Avenue - p397 F13
Central Street - p402 P3/4
Chadwell Street - p402 N3
Chagford Street - p395 F4
Chalton Street - p399 K2/3
Chamber Street - p405 S7
Chambers Street - p405 S9
Chancel Street - p404 O8
Chancery Lane - p399 M5, p404 N6
Chandos Place - p401 L7
Chandos Street - p398 H5
Chantry Street - p402 O2
Chapel Market - p402 N2
Chapel Side - p394 B6/7
Chapel Street NW1 - p395 E5
Chapel Street SW1 - p400 G9
Chaplin Close - p404 N9
Chapter Street - p401 K11
Charing Cross Road - p399 K6, p401 K7
Charles II Street - p401 K7
Charles Square - p403 Q3/4
Charles Street - p400 H7
Charlotte Road - p403 R4
Charlotte Street - p398 J5, p399 K5
Charlotte Terrace - p399 M2
Charlton Place - p402 O2
Charlwood Street - p400 J11
Charrington Street - p399 K2
Chart Street - p403 Q3
Charterhouse Square - p402 O5
Charterhouse Street - p402 O5
Cheapside - p404 P6
Chelsea Embankment - p397 F12
Chelsea Manor Street - p397 E11/12
Chelsea Park Gardens - p397 D12
Chelsea Square - p397 D11/E11
Cheltenham Terrace - p397 F11
Cheney Road - p399 L2
Chenies Mews - p399 K4
Chenies Street - p399 K5
Chepstow Crescent - p394 A6
Chepstow Place - p394 B6
Chepstow Road - p394 A5/B6
Chepstow Villas - p394 A6
Chequer Street - p402 P4
Cherbury Street - p403 Q2
Chesham Place - p400 G9
Chesham Street - p400 G10
Cheshire Street - p403 S4
Chesson Road - p396 A12
Chester Gate - p398 H3
Chester Mews - p400 H9
Chester Road - p398 H3
Chester Row - p400 G10/11
Chester Square - p400 G10
Chester Street - p400 G9/H9
Chester Terrace - p398 H3
Chesterfield Hill - p400 H7
Chesterfield Street - p400 H7/8
Cheval Place - p397 E9
Cheyne Mews - p397 E12
Cheyne Row - p397 E12
Cheyne Walk - p397 D13/E12/13
Chicheley Street - p401 M8
Chichester Road - p394 B5
Chicksand Street - p405 S5
Chiltern Street - p398 G5
Chilton Street - p403 S4
Chilworth Mews - p395 D6
Chilworth Street - p395 D6
Chippenham Mews - p394 A4/5
Chiswell Street - p402 P5, p403 Q5
Chitty Street - p398 J5
Christchurch Street - p397 F12
Christopher Street - p403 Q5
Church Square - p404 P9
Church Street - p395 D5/E4
Churchway - p399 K3
Cirencester Street - p394 B4
City Garden Row - p402 O3
City Road - p402 O3/P3, p403 Q4/5
Clabon Mews - p397 F10
Clanricarde Gardens - p394 B7
Claremont Square - p402 N3
Clarence Gardens - p398 H3/J3
Clarendon Place - p395 E6
Clarendon Street - p400 H11
Clareville Grove - p397 D10
Clareville Street - p397 D10
Clarges Mews - p400 H7/8
Clarges Street - p400 H7/8
Clarissa Street - p403 S1
Clement's Inn - p399 M6
Clements Lane - p405 Q7
Clerkenwell Close - p402 N4
Clerkenwell Green - p402 N4
Clerkenwell Road - p402 N4/O4
Cleveland Road - p403 Q1
Cleveland Row - p400 J8
Cleveland Square - p394 C6

Cleveland Street - p398 J4/5
Cleveland Terrace - p394 C5/6, p395 D5
Clifford Street - p400 J7
Clifton Gardens - p394 C4
Clifton Place - p395 E6
Clifton Street - p403 Q5
Clifton Villas - p394 C4
Clink Street - p404 P8
Clipstone Mews - p398 J4
Clipstone Street - p398 J5
Cloth Fair - p402 O5
Cloudesley Road - p402 N1/2
Cloudesley Square - p402 N1/2
Cloudesley Street - p402 N1/2
Club Row - p403 S4
Cobb Street - p405 R6
Cobourg Street - p398 J3
Cock Lane - p404 O5
Cockspur Street - p401 K7
Code Street - p403 S4/5
Coin Street - p404 N8
Cole Street - p404 P9
Colebrook Row - p402 O2
Coleherne Mews - p396 B11/12
Coleherne Road - p396 B11/12
Coleman Fields - p402 P1/2
Coleman Street - p404 P6
College Hill - p404 P7
College Street - p404 P7
Collier Street - p399 M2
Collingham Mews - p396 C10
Collingham Place - p396 B10
Collingham Road - p396 C10/11
Colombo Street - p404 N8
Colonnade - p399 L4
Columbia Road - p403 S3
Colville Road - p394 A6
Colville Terrace - p394 A6
Commercial Road - p405 S6
Commercial Street - p403 R5/S5, p405 S5/6
Compton Street - p402 O4
Concert Hall Approach - p401 M8
Conduit Mews - p395 D6
Conduit Place - p395 D6
Conduit Street - p400 H7/J6
Connaught Place - p395 F6
Connaught Square - p395 F6
Connaught Street - p395 E6/F6
Construction Hill - p400 H8/9
Conway Street - p398 J4
Coombs Street - p402 O3
Coomer Place - p396 A12
Coopers Lane - p399 K2
Coopers Row - p405 R7
Cope Place - p396 A9
Copenhagen Street - p402 N2
Copperfield Street - p404 O8
Copthall Avenue - p405 Q6
Coptic Street - p399 L5
Coral Street - p404 N9
Coram Street - p399 L4
Cork Street - p400 J7
Cornhill - p405 Q6
Cornwall Gardens - p396 C10
Cornwall Road - p404 N8
Corporation Row - p402 N4
Corsham Street - p403 Q3
Cosser Street - p401 M10
Cosway Street - p395 E4/F5
Cottesmore Gardens - p396 C9
Coulson Street - p397 F11
Courtfield Gardens - p396 B10/11
Courtfield Road - p396 C10
Courtnell Street - p394 A5/6
Covent Garden - p401 L6/7
Coventry Street - p401 K7
Cowcross Street - p402 O5
Cowper Street - p403 Q4
Cramer Street - p398 G5
Cranbourn Street - p401 K7
Cranleigh Street - p398 J2
Cranley Gardens - p397 D11
Cranley Mews - p397 D11
Cranley Place - p397 D11
Cranwood Street - p403 Q4
Craven Hill - p394 C6
Craven Hill Gardens - p394 C6
Craven Road - p395 D6
Craven Street - p401 L7
Craven Terrace - p395 D6
Crawford Passage - p402 N4
Crawford Place - p395 E5/F5
Crawford Street - p395 F5
Creechurch Lane - p405 R6
Cremer Street - p403 R3
Cremorne Road - p396 C13, p397 D13
Cresswell Place - p396 C11
Crestfield Street - p399 L3
Crinian Street - p399 L2
Croft Street - p405 S7
Cromer Street - p399 L3
Crompton Street - p395 D4
Cromwell Mews - p397 D10
Cromwell Place - p397 D10

Cromwell Road - p396 B10/C10/D10
Crondall Street - p403 Q3/R3
Cropley Street - p403 Q2
Crosby Row - p405 Q9
Cross Street - p402 O1
Crosswall - p405 R7
Crown Office Row - p404 N6
Crowndale Road - p398 J2, p399 K2
Crucifix Lane - p405 Q9/R9
Cruden Street - p402 O1/2
Crutched Friars - p405 R7
Cubitt Street - p399 M3
Culford Gardens - p397 F11
Cullum Street - p405 Q7/R7
Culross Street - p400 G7
Cumberland Gate - p395 F6
Cumberland Market - p398 H3/J3
Cumberland Terrace - p398 H2/3
Cumming Street - p399 M2
Cundy Street - p400 G11
Cure Street - p401 K11
Curlew Street - p405 R9/S9
Cursitor Street - p404 N6
Curtain Road - p403 R4
Curzon Place - p400 G8
Curzon Street - p400 H7/8
Cutler Street - p405 R6
Cynthia Street - p399 M2
Cyrus Street - p402 O4

Dacre Street - p401 K9
Dagmar Street - p402 O1
Dallington Street - p402 O4
Danbury Street - p402 O2
Danube Street - p397 E11
Danvers Street - p397 D12/E12
D'Arblay Street - p398 J6
Darlan Road - p396 A13
Dartmouth Close - p394 A5
Daventry Street - p395 E4/5
Davies Mews - p398 H6
Davies Street - p398 H6, p400 H6/7
Dawes Road - p396 A13
Dawson Place - p394 B6
De Beauvoir Crescent - p403 Q1
De Beauvoir Road - p403 R1
De Beauvoir Square - p403 R1
De Vere Gardens - p394 C9, p396 C9
Deal Street - p403 S5
Dean Bradley Street - p401 K10/L10
Dean Ryle Street - p401 K10/L10
Dean Stanley Street - p401 L10
Dean Street - p399 K6
Deanery Street - p400 G7
Dean's Yard - p401 K9
Decima Street - p405 Q10
Delamere Terrace - p394 C4
Denbigh Road - p394 A6
Denbigh Street - p400 J11
Denbigh Terrace - p394 A6
Denman Street - p400 J7
Denmark Street - p399 K6
Denyer Street - p397 F10
Derby Street - p400 H8
Dering Street - p398 H6
Derry Street - p396 B9
Deverell Street - p405 Q10
Devonia Road - p402 O2
Devonshire Close - p398 H4/5
Devonshire Mews South - p398 H5
Devonshire Mews West - p398 H4
Devonshire Place - p398 G4/H4
Devonshire Place Mews - p398 G4
Devonshire Row - p405 R6
Devonshire Square - p405 R6
Devonshire Street - p398 H4
Devonshire Terrace - p395 D6
Dewey Road - p402 N2
Dibden Street - p402 P1
Dilke Street - p397 F12
Dingley Road - p402 P3
Dock Street - p405 S7
Dodson Street - p404 N9
Dombey Street - p399 M5
Donegal Street - p399 M2, p402 N2
Doric Way - p399 K3
Dorset Rise - p404 N6
Dorset Square - p395 F4
Dorset Street - p398 G5
Doughty Mews - p399 M4
Doughty Street - p399 M4
Douglas Street - p401 K11
Douro Street - p396 C9
Dove Mews - p396 C11
Dovehouse Street - p397 E11/12
Dover Street - p400 H7/J7
Down Street - p400 G8/H8
Downham Road - p403 Q1
Downing Street - p401 K8/L8
Doyle Street - p404 O10
Drake Street - p399 M5
Draycott Avenue - p397 E10/F12
Draycott Place - p397 F10
Draycott Terrace - p397 F10
Drayton Gardens - p396 C11, p397 D11/12

Drayton Mews - p394 B8
Druid Street - p405 R9/S10
Drummond Crescent - p399 K3
Drummond Street - p398 J3/4
Drury Lane - p399 L6/M6
Drysdale Street - p403 R3
Duchess of Bedford's Walk 1 A8
Duchess Street - p398 H5
Duchy Street - p404 N8
Dufferin Street - p402 P4
Duke of York Street - p400 J7
Duke Street - p398 G6
Duke Street, St James's - p400 J7/8
Duke's Hill - p405 Q8
Dukes Lane - p394 B8
Duke's Place - p405 R6
Duke's Road - p399 K3
Duncan Street - p402 O2
Duncan Terrace - p402 O2
Dunloe Street - p403 S3
Dunraven Street - p400 G6
Dunston Road - p403 R2/S2
Durham Terrace - p394 B5
Dyott Street - p399 L6
Dysart Street - p403 Q5

Eagle Court - p402 O4/5
Eagle Street - p399 M5
Eagle Wharf Road - p402 P2, p403 Q2
Eardley Crescent - p396 B11
Earl Street - p403 Q5
Earlham Street - p399 K6/L6
Earl's Court Square - p396 B11
Earl's Court Gardens - p396 B10
Earl's Court Road - p396 A9/10, B10/11
Earls Walk - p396 E10
Earnshaw Street - p399 K6
East Lane - p405 S9
East Road - p403 Q3
East Smithfield - p405 S7
Eastbourne Mews - p395 D5/6
Eastbourne Terrace - p395 D5/6
Eastcastle Street - p398 J5/6
Eastcheap - p405 Q7
Eaton Mews - p400 H10
Eaton Place - p400 G9/10
Eaton Square - p400 G10/H10
Eaton Terrace - p400 G10/12
Ebury Bridge - p400 H11
Ebury Bridge Road - p400 G11
Ebury Mews - p400 H10
Ebury Square - p400 G11
Ebury Street - p400 G10/11/H10
Ecclesbourne Road - p402 P1
Eccleston Mews - p400 G9
Eccleston Place - p400 H10
Eccleston Square - p400 H11
Eccleston Street - p400 G10/H10
Edge Street - p394 A7
Edgware Road - p395 D4/E4/5
Edith Grove - p396 C12/13
Edith Terrace - p396 C13
Edward Mews - p398 G6
Edwardes Square - p396 A9/10
Effie Road - p396 A13/B13
Egerton Crescent - p397 E10
Egerton Gardens - p397 E10
Egerton Terrace - p397 E10
Elcho Street - p397 E13
Elder Street - p403 R5
Eldon Road - p396 C9
Eldon Street - p403 Q5
Elia Street - p402 O2
Elizabeth Avenue - p402 P1, p403 Q1
Elizabeth Bridge - p400 H11
Elizabeth Street - p400 G10/H10
Elkstone Road - p394 A4
Elliot's Row - p404 O10
Elm Park Gardens - p397 D11/12
Elm Park Lane - p397 D12
Elm Park Road - p397 D12
Elm Place - p397 D11
Elm Street - p399 M4
Elms Mews - p395 D6
Elvaston Place - p396 C9, p397 D9
Elverton Street - p401 K10
Ely Place - p402 N5
Elystan Place - p397 F11
Elystan Street - p397 E11
Emerald Street - p399 M5
Emerson Street - p404 O8
Endell Street - p399 L6
Endsleigh Gardens - p399 K3/4
Endsleigh Street - p399 K4
Enford Street - p395 F5
Enid Street - p405 S10
Ennismore Gardens - p397 E9
Ennismore Mews - p397 E9
Ensign Street - p405 S7
Epirus Road - p396 A13
Epworth Street - p403 Q4
Erasmus Street - p401 K11
Errol Street - p402 P4
Essex Road - p402 O1/P1

Essex Street - p401 M6
Essex Villas - p396 A9
Eustace Road - p396 A13
Euston Road - p398 J4, p399 K3/4/L3/4
Euston Street - p398 J3
Evelyn Gardens - p397 D11
Eversholt Street - p398 J2, p399 K3
Ewer Street - p404 O8
Exeter Street - p401 L7
Exhibition Road - p397 D9/10
Exmouth Market - p402 N4
Exton Street - p404 N8

Fabian Road - p396 A13
Falkirk Street - p403 R3
Falmouth Road - p404 P10
Fann Street - p402 P5
Fanshaw Street - p403 R3
Farm Lane - p396 A13/B13
Farm Street - p400 H7
Farringdon Lane - p402 N4
Farringdon Road - p402 N4/5
Farringdon Street - p404 N6/O6
Fashion Street - p405 S5
Fawcett Street - p396 C12
Featherstone Street - p403 Q4
Fenchurch Avenue - p405 R7
Fenchurch Street - p405 Q7/R7
Fendall Street - p405 R10
Fenelon Place - p396 A10
Fernshaw Road - p396 C12/13
Fetter Lane - p404 N6
Finborough Road - p396 B12/C12
Finsbury Circus - p403 Q5, p405 Q5
Finsbury Pavement - p403 Q5
Finsbury Square - p403 Q5
First Street - p397 E10
Fisher Street - p399 L5
Fitzalan Street - p401 M10
Fitzhardinge Street - p398 G6
Fitzroy Square - p398 J4
Fitzroy Street - p398 J4
Flaxman Terrace - p399 K3
Fleet Lane - p404 O6
Fleet Street - p404 N6
Fleur de Lis Street - p403 R5
Flitcroft Street - p399 K6
Flood Street - p397 E12/F12
Flood Walk - p397 E12
Floral Street - p399 L6, p401 L6
Florence Street - p402 O1
Foley Street - p398 J5
Folgate Street - p403 R5
Fore Street - p402 P5
Formosa Street - p394 C4
Forset Street - p395 F5/6
Fortune Street - p402 P4
Foster Lane - p404 P6
Foubert's Place - p398 J6
Foulis Terrace - p397 D11
Fournier Street - p403 S5
Frampton Street - p395 D4
Francis Street - p400 J10
Franklin's Row - p397 F11
Frazier Street - p404 N9
Frederick Street - p399 M3
Friend Street - p402 O3
Frith Street - p399 K6
Frome Street - p402 P2
Fulham Broadway - p396 A13/B13
Fulham Road - p396 A13/B13/C12/13/D12, p397 D11/12/E11
Furnival Street - p404 N5

Gainsford Street - p405 R9/S9
Galway Street - p402 P3/4
Gambia Street - p404 O8
Garden Row - p404 O10
Garlichythe - p404 P7
Garrick Street - p401 L7
Garway Road - p394 B6
Gaskin Street - p402 O1
Gate Place - p397 D10
Gaunt Street - p404 O10
Gee Street - p402 O4/P4
Geffrye Street - p403 R2
George Row - p405 S9
George Street - p395 F5/6, p398 G5
Gerald Road - p400 G10
Gerrard Road - p402 O2
Gerrard Street - p401 K6/7
Gerridge Street - p404 N9
Gertrude Street - p397 D12
Gibson Road - p401 M11
Gibson Square - p402 N1
Gilbert Place - p399 L5
Gilbert Street - p398 H6
Gillingham Street - p400 H10/J10
Gilston Road - p396 C12
Giltspur Street - p404 O5
Gladstone Street - p404 N10/O10
Glasshill Street - p404 O9
Glasshouse Street - p400 J7
Glebe Place - p397 E12
Gledhow Gardens - p396 C11

Glendower Place - p397 D10
Glentworth Street - p395 F4
Gloucester Gate - p398 H2
Gloucester Mews - p395 D6
Gloucester Place - p395 F5, p398 G5/6
Gloucester Place Mews - p395 F5
Gloucester Road - p396 C9/10
Gloucester Square - p395 E6
Gloucester Street - p400 J11
Gloucester Terrace - p394 C5, p395 D6
Gloucester Walk - p394 B8
Gloucester Way - p402 N3
Godfrey Street - p397 E11
Godliman Street - p404 O6
Golden Lane - p402 P4/5
Golden Square - p400 J7
Goldington Crescent - p399 K2
Goldington Street - p399 K2
Goodge Place - p398 J5
Goodge Street - p398 J5, p399 K5
Goodman's Yard - p405 R7/S7
Goods Way - p399 L2
Gordon Place - p394 B8
Gordon Square - p399 K4
Gordon Street - p399 K4
Gore Street - p397 D9
Gosfield Street - p398 J5
Goslett Yard - p399 K6
Gosset Street - p403 S3
Goswell Road - p402 O3/4/5/P5
Gough Square - p404 N6
Gough Street - p399 M4
Goulston Street - p405 R6/S6
Gower Mews - p399 K5
Gower Place - p399 K4
Gower Street - p399 K4/5
Gower's Walk - p405 S6/7
Gracechurch Street - p405 Q6/7
Grafton Mews - p398 J4
Grafton Place - p399 K3
Grafton Street - p400 H7
Grafton Way - p398 J4
Graham Street - p402 O2/P3
Graham Terrace - p400 G11
Granby Street - p403 S4
Granby Terrace - p398 J2
Grange Court - p399 M6
Grange Road - p405 R10
Grange Walk - p405 R10
Grantbridge Street - p402 O2
Granville Place - p398 G6
Granville Square - p399 M3
Gravel Lane - p405 R6
Gray Street - p404 N9
Gray's Inn Road - p399 L3/M3/4/5
Great Castle Street - p398 J6
Great Chapel Street - p399 K6
Great College Street - p401 K9/10
Great Cumberland Place - p395 F6
Great Dover Street - p404 P9/10, p405 Q10
Great Eastern Street - p403 Q4/R4
Great George Street - p401 K9
Great Guildford Street - p404 O8
Great James Street - p399 M5
Great Marlborough Street - p398 J6
Great Maze Pond - p405 Q8/9
Great Newport Street - p401 K6
Great Ormond Street - p399 L5/M4
Great Percy Street - p399 M3/p402 N3
Great Peter Street - p401 K10
Great Portland Street - p398 H5/J5
Great Pulteney Street - p400 J6
Great Queen Street - p399 L6
Great Russell Street - p399 K5/L5
Great Smith Street - p401 K9/10
Great Suffolk Street - p404 O8/9
Great Sutton Street - p402 O4
Great Titchfield Street - p398 J5/6
Great Tower Street - p405 Q7/R7
Great Western Road - p394 A4/5
Great Winchester Street - p405 Q6
Great Windmill Street - p401 K7
Greek Street - p399 K6
Green Street - p398 G6
Greencoat Place - p400 J10
Greenman Street - p402 P1
Greenwell Street - p398 H4/J4
Greet Street - p404 N8
Grenville Place - p396 C10
Grenville Street - p399 L4
Gresham Street - p404 P6
Gresse Street - p399 K5
Greville Street - p402 N5
Grey Eagle Street - p403 S5
Greycoat Street - p400 J10, p401 K10
Groom Place - p400 G9
Grosvenor Crescent - p400 G9
Grosvenor Gardens - p400 H9/10
Grosvenor Hill - p400 H7
Grosvenor Place - p400 G9/H9
Grosvenor Road - p400 G6/7
Grosvenor Street - p400 H6/7
Great Swan Alley - p405 Q6
Guildhouse Street - p400 J10/11

Guilford Street - p399 L4/M4
Gun Street - p403 R5
Gunter Grove - p396 C13
Gunthorpe Street - p405 S6
Gutter Lane - p404 P6
Guy Street - p405 Q9
Gwyn Close - p396 C13

Haberdasher Street - p403 Q3
Hackney Road - p403 R3/S3
Haggerston Road - p403 R1/S1
Haldane Road - p396 A13
Half Moon Street - p400 H8
Halford Road - p396 A12
Halkin Place - p400 G9
Halkin Street - p400 G9
Hall Place - p395 D4/5
Hall Street - p402 O3
Hallam Street - p398 H4/5
Halliford Street - p402 P1, p403 Q1
Halsey Street - p397 F10
Halton Road - p402 O1
Hamilton Park Road - p402 O1
Hamilton Place - p400 G8
Hampstead Road - p398 J3
Hanbury Street - p403 S5
Handel Street - p399 L4
Hankey Place - p405 Q9
Hanover Square - p398 H6
Hanover Street - p398 H6/J6
Hans Crescent - p397 F9
Hans Place - p397 F9
Hans Road - p397 F9
Hans Street - p397 F9
Hanson Street - p398 J5
Hanway Place - p399 K6
Hanway Street - p399 K5
Harbet Road - p395 E5
Harcourt Street - p395 F5
Harcourt Terrace - p396 C11/12
Hardwick Street - p402 N3
Harewood Avenue - p395 F4
Harley Place - p398 H5
Harley Street - p398 H4/5
Harper Street - p404 P10
Harpur Street - p399 M5
Harriet Walk - p397 F9
Harrington Gardens - p396 C10
Harrington Road - p397 D10
Harrington Square - p398 J2
Harrington Street - p398 J2/3
Harrison Street - p399 L3
Harrow Place - p405 R6
Harrow Road - p394 A4/B4/5
Harrowby Street - p395 F5
Hartismere Road - p396 A13
Harwood Road - p396 B13
Hasker Street - p397 F10
Hastings Street - p399 L3
Hatfields - p404 N8
Hatherley Grove - p394 B5/6
Hatherley Street - p400 J10
Hatton Garden - p402 N5
Hatton Street - p395 D4/E4
Hatton Wall - p402 N5
Haverstock Street - p402 O3
Hay Hill - p400 H7
Haydon Street - p405 R7/S7
Hayles Street - p404 O10
Haymarket - p401 K7
Hay's Mews - p400 H7
Headfort Place - p400 G9
Hearn Street - p403 R4
Heathcote Street - p399 M4
Heddon Street - p400 J7
Helmet Row - p402 P4
Hemsworth Street - p403 R2
Heneage Street - p403 S5
Henrietta Place - p398 H6
Henrietta Street - p401 L7
Herbal Hill - p402 N4
Herbrand Street - p399 L4
Hercules Road - p401 M9/10
Hereford Road - p394 B5/6
Herrick Street - p401 K11
Hertford Road - p403 R1
Hertford Street - p400 H8
Hester Road - p397 E13
Hide Place - p401 K11
High Holborn - p399 L5/6/M5
High Timber Street - p404 O7/P7
Hill Street - p400 H7
Hillgate Place - p394 A7
Hillgate Street - p394 A7
Hills Place - p398 J6
Hillsleigh Road - p394 A7
Hobart Place - p400 H9
Hobury Street - p397 D12
Hogarth Road - p396 B10
Holbein Mews - p400 G11
Holbein Place - p400 G11
Holborn - p402 N5
Holborn Viaduct - p404 N5/O5/6
Holland Park Road - p396 A9
Holland Street SE1 - p404 O7/8
Holland Street W8 - p394 B8

Holland Walk - p394 A8
Holles Street - p398 H6
Holly Street - p403 S1
Hollywood Road - p396 C12
Holmead Road - p396 C13
Holywell Lane - p403 R4
Holywell Row - p403 Q4/R4
Homer Row - p395 F5
Homer Street - p395 F5
Hooper Street - p405 S7
Hop Gardens - p401 L7
Hopkins Street - p398 J6
Hopton Street - p404 O7/8
Horatio Street - p403 S3
Hornton Street - p394 B8
Horseferry Road - p401 K10
Horseguards Avenue - p401 L8
Horseguards Parade - p401 K8
Horseguards Road - p401 K8
Horselydown Lane - p405 R8/9
Hortensia Road - p396 C13
Hosier Lane - p402 O5
Hotspur Street - p401 M11
Houndsditch - p405 R6
Howick Place - p400 J10
Howie Street - p397 E13
Howland Street - p398 J4/5
Howley Place - p395 D4/5
Hows Street - p403 R2/S2
Hoxton Square - p403 R3
Hoxton Street - p403 R2
Hudson's Place - p400 H10
Hugh Street - p400 H10/11
Hungerford Bridge - p401 L8/M8
Hunter Street - p399 L4
Huntley Street - p399 K4/5
Hunton Street - p403 S5
Hyde Park Crescent - p395 E6
Hyde Park Gardens - p395 E6
Hyde Park Gardens Mews - p395 E6
Hyde Park Gate - p396 C9
Hyde Park Square - p395 E6
Hyde Park Street - p395 E6
Hyde Road - p403 Q2

Ifield Road - p396 B12/C12
Ilchester Gardens - p394 B6
Ilchester Place - p396 A9
Imperial College Road - p397 D9
Ingestre Place - p398 J6
Inglebert Street - p402 N3
Inner Circle - p398 G3
Inner Temple Lane - p404 N6
Inverness Terrace - p394 C6/7
Ironmonger Lane - p404 P6
Ironmonger Row - p402 P3/4
Irving Street - p401 K7
Islington Green - p402 O2
Islington High Street - p402 O2
Istarcross Street - p398 J3
Ivatt Place - p396 A11/12
Iverna Gardens - p396 B9
Ives Street - p397 E10
Ivor Place - p395 F4
Ivy Street - p403 R2
Ivybridge Lane - p401 L7
Ixworth Place - p397 E11

Jacob Street - p405 S9
Jamaica Road - p405 S9/10
James Street W1 - p398 G6
James Street WC2 - p401 L6
Jay Mews - p397 D9
Jermyn Street - p400 J7
Jewry Street - p405 R6/7
Joan Street - p404 N8
Jockey's Field - p399 M5
John Adam Street - p401 L7
John Carpenter Street - p404 N7
John Fisher Street - p405 S7
John Islip Street - p401 K10/11
John Prince's Street - p398 H6
John Street - p399 M4/5
John's Mews - p399 M4/5
Jonathan Street - p401 L11/M11
Jubilee Place - p397 E11
Judd Street - p399 L3
Juer Street - p397 E13
Juxon Street - p401 M10

Kean Street - p399 M6
Keeley Street - p399 M6
Kelso Place - p396 B9
Kelvedon Road - p396 A13
Kemble Street - p399 L6/M6
Kemps Road - p396 B13
Kempsford Gardens - p396 B11
Kendal Street - p395 E6/F6
Kendall Place - p398 G5
Kennington Road - p404 N9/10
Kenrick Place - p398 G5
Kensington Church Street - p394 B7/8
Kensington Court - p394 B9, p396 B9
Kensington Gardens Square - p394 B6
Kensington Gate - p396 C9
Kensington Gore - p395 D9

Kensington High Street - p396 A9/B9
Kensington Mall - p394 B7
Kensington Palace Gardens 1 B7/8
Kensington Park Gardens - p394 A6
Kensington Park Road - p394 A6/7
Kensington Place - p394 A7
Kensington Road - p394 B9/C9, p395 E9/F9
Kensington Square - p396 B9
Kent Street - p403 S2
Kenton Street - p399 L4
Kenway Road - p396 B10
Keppel Row - p404 O8/P8
Keppel Street - p399 K5
Keystone Crescent - p399 M2
Keyworth Street - p404 O9/10
Kildare Terrace - p394 B5
Killick Street - p399 M2
King Charles Street - p401 K9/L9
King Edward Walk - p404 N10
King James Street - p404 O9
King Street EC2 - p404 P6
King Street SW1 - p400 J8
King Street WC2 - p401 L7
King William Street - p405 Q6/7
Kingly Street - p398 J6
King's Cross Road - p399 M3
King's Mews - p399 M4
King's Road - p396 C13, p397 D12/13/E11/12/F11
King's Road - p400 G10
Kingsland Road - p403 R1/2/3
Kingsway - p399 M6
Kinnerton Street - p400 G9
Kipling Street - p405 Q9
Kirby Street - p402 N5
Knightsbridge - p400 G8
Knivet Road - p396 A12
Knox Street - p395 F5
Kynance Mews - p405 C9

Laurence Pountney Lane - p405 Q7
Laburnum Road - p403 R2/S2
Lackington Street - p403 Q5
Ladbroke Road - p394 A7
Ladbroke Square - p394 A7
Ladbroke Terrace - p394 A7
Ladbroke Walk - p394 A7
Lafone Street - p405 R9
Lamb Street - p403 R5
Lamb Walk - p405 Q9
Lambeth Bridge - p401 L10
Lambeth High Street - p401 L10
Lambeth Palace Road - p401 L10/M9
Lambeth Road - p401 M10, p404 N10
Lambeth Walk - p401 M10/11
Lamb's Conduit Street - p399 M4/5
Lamb's Pass - p402 P5
Lamont Road - p397 D12
Lancaster Gate - p394 C6/7, p395 D6/7
Lancaster Mews - p395 D6
Lancaster Place - p401 M7
Lancaster Road - p394 O9
Lancaster Terrace - p395 D6
Langham Place - p398 H5
Langham Street - p398 H5/J5
Langley Street - p399 L6
Langton Street - p396 C12/13
Lansdowne Terrace - p399 L4
Lant Street - p404 O9/P9
Launceston Place - p396 C9/10
Lavender Grove - p403 S1
Lavington Street - p404 O8
Law Street - p405 Q10
Lawford Road - p403 R1
Lawrence Street - p397 E12
Leadenhall Street - p405 Q6/R6
Leake Street - p401 M9
Leamington Road Villas - p394 A5
Leather Lane - p402 N5/11 N5
Leathermarket Street - p405 Q9
Ledbury Road - p394 A6
Lee Street - p403 R1/S1
Leeke Street - p399 M3
Lees Place - p400 G6
Leicester Place - p401 K7
Leicester Square - p401 K7
Leigh Street - p399 L3
Leinster Gardens - p394 C6
Leinster Square - p394 B6
Leinster Terrace - p394 C6/7
Leman Street - p405 S6/7
Lennox Gardens - p397 F10
Lennox Gardens Mews - p397 F10
Leonard Street - p403 Q4
Lever Street - p402 P3
Lexham Gardens - p396 B10
Lexham Mews - p396 B10
Lexington Street - p398 J6, p400 J6
Lidlington Place - p398 J2
Lile Road - p396 A12/B11
Lillie Yard - p396 A12
Lime Street - p405 Q7/R6
Limerston Street - p397 D12
Lincoln Street - p397 F11

Lincoln's Inn Fields - p399 M5/6
Linden Gardens - p394 B7
Linhope Street - p395 F4
Linton Street - p402 P2
Lisle Street - p401 K7
Lisson Grove - p395 E4/F4
Lisson Street - p395 E4/5
Litchfield Street - p401 K6
Little Albany Street - p398 H3
Little Britain - p402 O5, p404 O5
Little Chester Street - p400 H9
Little Dorrit Court - p404 P9
Little Portland Street - p398 J5
Little Russell Street - p399 L5
Livermore Road - p403 S1
Liverpool Road - p402 N1/2
Liverpool Street - p405 Q5/6
Lloyd Baker Street - p402 N3
Lloyd Square - p402 N3
Lloyds Avenue - p405 R7
Lofting Road - p402 N1
Logan Place - p396 A10
Lollard Street - p401 M10/11
Loman Street - p404 O8
Lombard Street - p405 Q6/7
London Bridge - p405 Q7/8
London Bridge Street - p405 Q8
London Road - p404 O10
London Street - p395 D5/6
London Wall - p404 P5/Q6
Long Acre - p399 L6, p401 L6/7
Long Lane EC1 - p402 O5
Long Lane SE1 - p404 P9/Q9
Long Street - p403 R3
Longford Street - p398 H4/J4
Longmoore Street - p400 J10/11
Longridge Road - p396 A10
Lonsdale Road - p394 A6
Lonsdale Square - p402 N1
Lord Hills Road - p394 C4
Lorenzo Street - p399 M3
Lots Road - p396 C13, p397 D13
Love Lane - p404 P6
Lower Belgrave Street - p400 H10
Lower Grosvenor Place - p400 H9
Lower James Street - p400 J7
Lower Marsh - p401 M9
Lower Sloane Street - p400 G11
Lower Thames Street - p405 Q7/R7
Lowndes Square - p397 F9
Lowndes Street - p400 G9
Lucan Place - p397 E10/11
Ludgate Hill - p404 O6
Luke Street - p403 Q4/R4
Lumley Street - p398 G6
Luxbough Street - p398 G4/5
Lyall Mews - p400 G10
Lyall Street - p400 G10

Macclesfield Street - p402 P3
Macklin Street - p399 L6
Maddox Street - p398 J6
Maguire Street - p405 S9
Maida Avenue - p395 D4
Maiden Lane WC2 - p401 L7
Maiden Lane SE1 - p404 P8
Malet Street - p399 K4/5
Mallow Street - p403 Q4
Maltby Street - p405 R9/10
Malvern Road - p403 S1
Manchester Square - p398 G5/6
Manchester Street - p398 G5
Manciple Street - p405 Q9
Manette Street - p399 K6
Manresa Road - p397 E11/12
Mansell Street - p405 S6/7
Mansfield Street - p398 H5
Manson Mews - p397 D10
Manson Place - p397 D10
Maple Street - p398 J4
Mapledene Road - p403 S1
Marble Quay - p405 S8
Marchbank Road - p396 A12
Marchmont Street - p399 L4
Margaret Street - p398 J5/6
Margaretta Terrace - p397 E12
Margery Street - p402 N3
Mark Lane - p405 R7
Market Mews - p400 H8
Markham Square - p397 F11
Markham Street - p397 F11
Marlborough Road - p400 J8
Marloes Road - p396 B9/10
Marshall Street - p398 J6
Marshalsea Road - p404 P9
Marsham Street - p401 K10/11
Marylands Road - p394 B4
Marylebone High Street - p398 G4/5
Marylebone Lane - p398 G5/H6
Marylebone Mews - p398 H5
Marylebone Road - p395 F4/5, p398 G4
Marylebone Street - p398 G5
Marylee Way - p401 M11
Maunsel Street - p401 K10
Maxwell Road - p396 B13

Mayfair Place - p400 H7
Mcleod's Mews - p396 C10
Meadow Row - p404 P10
Meard Street - p399 K6
Mecklenburgh Square - p399 M4
Medburn Street - p399 K2
Medway Street - p401 K10
Melbury Court - p396 A9
Melbury Road - p396 A9
Melbury Terrace - p395 F4
Melcombe Street - p395 F4
Melton Court - p397 D10
Melton Street - p399 K3
Mepham Street - p401 M8
Mercer Street - p399 L6
Merlin Street - p402 N3
Mermaid Court - p404 P9
Merrick Square - p404 P10
Mews Street - p405 S8
Meymott Street - p404 N8
Micawber Street - p402 P3
Michael Road - p396 B13/C13
Mickelthwaite Road - p396 B12
Middle Temple Lane - p404 N6/7
Middlesex Street - p405 R5/6
Middleton Road - p403 S1
Midland Road - p399 L2/3
Milford Lane - p401 M6/7
Milford Street - p402 P5
Milk Street - p404 P6
Mill Street W1 - p400 H6/J6
Mill Street SE1 - p405 S9
Millbank - p401 L10/11
Millman Street - p399 M4
Milman's Street - p397 D12/13
Milner Place - p402 N1/01
Milner Square - p402 N1/01
Milner Street - p397 F10
Mincing Lane - p405 R7
Minera Mews - p400 G10
Minories - p405 R6/7
Mintern Street - p403 Q2
Mitchell Street - p402 P4
Mitre Road - p404 N9
Molyneux Street - p395 F5
Monck Street - p401 K10
Monmouth Street - p399 L6
Montagu Mansions - p398 G5
Montagu Mews South - p395 F6
Montagu Place - p395 F5
Montagu Square - p395 F5
Montagu Street - p395 F6
Montague Place - p399 K5
Montague Street - p399 L5
Montpelier Place - p397 E9
Montpelier Street - p397 E9
Montpelier Terrace - p397 E9
Montpelier Walk - p397 E9
Montrose Place - p400 G9
Monument Street - p405 Q7
Moor Lane - p402 P5
Moor Street - p399 K6
Moore Park Road - p396 B13
Moore Street - p397 F10
Moorfields - p403 Q5
Moorgate - p403 Q5, p405 Q5/6
Moorhouse Road - p394 A5/6
Mora Street - p402 P3
Moreland Street - p402 O3/P3
Moreton Road - p402 P1
Moreton Street - p400 J11
Morgan's Lane - p405 Q8
Morley Street - p404 N9
Mornington Crescent - p398 J2
Mornington Place - p398 J2
Mornington Street - p398 H2/J2
Mornington Terrace - p398 H2/J2
Morocco Street - p405 Q9
Morpeth Terrace - p400 J10
Mortimer Road - p403 R1
Mortimer Street - p398 J5
Morwell Street - p399 K5
Moscow Road - p394 B6
Mossop Street - p397 E10
Motcomb Street - p400 G9
Mount Pleasant - p399 M4
Mount Row - p400 H7
Mount Street - p400 G7
Moxon Street - p398 G5
Mund Street - p396 A11
Munster Square - p398 H3/4/J3/4
Muriel Street - p399 M2
Murray Grove - p402 P3/10 Q3
Museum Street - p399 L5/6
Musgrave Crescent - p396 B13
Myddelton Square - p402 N3
Myddelton Street - p402 N3/O3
Mylne Street - p402 N3

Napier Grove - p402 P2
Nash Street - p398 H3
Nassau Street - p398 J5
Nazral Street - p403 R3
Neal Street - p399 L6
Nebraska Street - p404 P9
Neckinger - p405 S10

Nelson Terrace - p402 O3
Nesham Street - p405 S8
Netherton Grove - p396 C12
Netley Street - p398 J3
Nevern Place - p396 A10/B10
Nevern Square - p396 A11
Neville Street - p397 D11
New Bond Street - p398 H6, p400 H6/7
New Change - p404 O6
New Compton Street - p399 K6
New Fetter Lane - p404 N5
New Globe Walk - p404 O8/P7
New Inn Yard - p403 R4
New North Road - p402 P1, p403 Q2/3
New North Street - p399 L5
New Oxford Street - p399 K6/L5
New Quebec Street - p395 F6
New Row - p401 L7
New Square - p399 M6
New Street - p404 N5/6, p405 R5/6
New Wharf Road - p399 M2
Newburgh Street - p398 J6
Newcastle Place - p395 E5
Newcomen Street - p404 P9/Q9
Newgate Street - p404 O6
Newington Causeway - p404 O9/10
Newman Street - p398 J5
Newnham Terrace - p401 M9
Newport Place - p401 K6/7
Newport Street - p401 L11/M10/11
Newton Road - p394 B6
Newton Street - p399 L5/6
Nicholas Lane - p405 Q7
Nile Street - p402 P3, p403 Q3
Noble Street - p404 P5/6
Noel Road - p402 O2
Noel Street - p398 J6
Norfolk Crescent - p395 E5
Norfolk Place - p395 E5/6
Norfolk Square - p395 D6/E6
North Audley Street - p398 G6
North Carriage Drive - p395 E6/F6
North Crescent - p399 K5
North End Road - p396 A12/13
North Gower Street - p398 J3/4
North Mews - p399 M4
North Row - p398 G6
North Wharf Road - p395 D5
Northampton Road - p402 N4
Northampton Square - p402 O3
Northburgh Street - p402 O4
Northchurch Road - p403 Q1/R1
Northdown Street - p399 M2
Northington Street - p399 M4
Northumberland Avenue - p401 L8
Northumberland Place - p394 A5/6
Notting Hill Gate - p394 A7
Nottingham Place - p398 G4
Nottingham Street - p398 G4/5
Nutford Place - p395 F5
Nuttal Street - p403 R2

Oakey Lane - p404 N9/10
Oakley Gardens - p397 E12
Oakley Square - p398 J2
Oakley Street - p397 E12
Ogle Street - p398 J5
Old Bailey - p404 O6
Old Barrack Yard - p400 G9
Old Bond Street - p400 J7
Old Broad Street - p405 Q6
Old Brompton Road - p396 C11, p397 D11
Old Burlington Street - p400 J7
Old Castle Street - p405 S6
Old Cavendish Street - p398 H6
Old Church Street - p397 D11/12/E12
Old Compton Street - p399 K6
Old Court Place - p394 B8
Old Gloucester Street - p399 L5
Old Jamaica Road - p405 S10
Old Jewry - p404 P6
Old Marylebone Road - p395 E5/F5
Old Mitre Court - p404 N6
Old Montagu Street - p405 S5/6
Old Nichol Street - p403 R4/S4
Old Paradise Street - p401 M10
Old Park Lane - p400 G8
Old Pye Street - p401 K10
Old Quebec Street - p398 G6
Old Queen Street - p401 K9
Old Street - p402 P4, p403 Q4/R4
Oldbury Place - p398 G4
Ongar Road - p396 A12/B12
Onslow Gardens - p397 D11
Onslow Square - p397 D10/11/E10/11
Orange Street - p401 K7
Orchard Street - p398 G6
Orde Hall Street - p399 M5
Orme Court - p394 B7
Orme Lane - p394 B7

Ormonde West Road - p397 F12
Ormsby Street - p403 R2
Orsett Terrace - p394 C5
Osborn Street - p405 S6
Osnaburgh Street - p398 H4
Ossington Street - p394 B7
Ossulston Street - p399 K3
Outer Circle - p398 G4/H2/3/4
Ovington Gardens - p397 E9/10
Ovington Street - p397 F10
Oxendon Street - p401 K7
Oxford Square - p395 E6
Oxford Street - p398 G6/H6/J6, p399 K6

Packington Square - p402 P2
Packington Street - p402 O1/P1
Paddington Green - p395 D5
Paddington Street - p398 G5
Page Street - p401 K10
Pakenham Street - p399 M4
Palace Avenue - p394 B8/C8
Palace Court - p394 B6/7
Palace Garden Mews - p394 B7
Palace Gardens Terrace - p394 B7/8
Palace Gate - p396 C9
Palace Street - p400 J9
Pall Mall - p400 J8, p401 K8
Panton Street - p401 K7
Paradise Walk - p397 F12
Paris Garden - p404 N8
Park Crescent - p398 H4
Park Crescent Mews East - p398 H4
Park Crescent Mews West - p398 H4
Park Lane - p395 F6, p400 G7/8
Park Place - p400 J8
Park Place Villas - p395 D4
Park Square East - p398 H4
Park Square Mews - p398 H4
Park Square West - p398 H4
Park Street SE1 - p404 P8
Park Street W1 - p400 G7
Park Village East - p398 H2
Park Village West - p398 H2
Park Walk - p397 D12
Park West Place - p395 F6
Parker Street - p399 L6
Parkfield Street - p402 N2
Parkgate Road - p397 E13
Parliament Square - p401 K9
Passmore Street - p400 G11
Pater Street - p396 A9
Paternoster Row - p404 O6
Paternoster Square - p404 O6
Paul Street - p403 Q4
Paultons Square - p397 D12
Paultons Street - p397 E12
Pavilion Road - p397 F9/10
Pear Tree Court - p402 N4
Pear Tree Street - p402 O4/P4
Pearman Street - p404 N9
Pearson Street - p403 R2
Pedley Street - p403 S4
Peel Street - p394 A7/8
Pelham Crescent - p397 E10
Pelham Place - p397 E10
Pelham Street - p397 E10
Pembridge Crescent - p394 A6
Pembridge Gardens - p394 A7
Pembridge Mews - p394 A6
Pembridge Place - p394 A6
Pembridge Road - p394 A7
Pembridge Square - p394 A5/B6
Pembridge Villas - p394 A6
Pembroke Gardens - p396 A10
Pembroke Gardens Close - p396 A10
Pembroke Road - p396 A10
Pembroke Villas - p396 A10
Pembroke Walk - p396 A10
Penfold Place - p395 E4/5
Penfold Street - p395 E4
Penn Street - p403 Q2
Pennant Mews - p396 B10
Penton Rise - p399 M3
Penton Street - p402 N2
Pentonville Road - p399 L3/M3, p402 N2
Penywern Road - p396 B11
Pepper Street - p404 O8
Pepys Street - p405 R7
Percey Circus - p399 M3
Percival Street - p402 O4
Percy Street - p399 K5
Peter Street - p399 K6
Petersham Lane - p396 C9
Petersham Place - p396 C9
Petit Place - p398 H4
Petty France - p400 J9
Phene Street - p397 E12
Philbeach Gardens - p396 A11
Phillimore Gardens - p394 A8/9, p396 A9
Phillimore Walk - p394 B9, p396 A9
Phillimore Place - p394 A9
Phillip Street - p403 R2
Philpott Lane - p405 Q7

Phoenix Place - p399 M4
Phoenix Road - p399 K2/3
Phoenix Street - p399 K6
Piccadilly - p400 H8/J7
Piccadilly Circus - p401 K7
Pickard Street - p402 O3
Pickering Mews - p394 C5/6
Pilgrim Street - p404 O6
Pilgrimage Street - p404 P9/Q9
Pimlico Road - p400 G11
Pindar Street - p403 Q5
Pinder Street - p403 Q5/R5
Pitfield Street - p403 Q2/3/4/R2
Pitt Street - p394 B8
Platt Street - p399 K2
Plough Yard - p403 R4
Plumbers Row - p405 S6
Plympton Street - p395 E4
Pocock Street - p404 O8/9
Poland Street - p398 J6
Polygon Road - p399 K2
Pond Place - p397 E11
Ponsonby Place - p401 K11
Pont Street - p397 F10, p400 G10
Poole Street - p403 Q2
Popham Road - p402 P1
Popham Street - p402 P1
Poplar Place - p394 B6/C6
Porchester Gardens - p394 B6/C6
Porchester Road - p394 C5
Porchester Square - p394 C5
Porchester Terrace - p394 C6/7
Porchester Terrace North - p394 C5
Porlock Street - p405 Q9
Porter Street SE1 - p404 P8
Porter Street W1 - p398 G4
Portland Place - p398 H4/5
Portman Close - p398 G5
Portman Mews South - p398 G6
Portman Square - p398 G6
Portman Street - p398 G6
Portobello Road - p394 A6
Portpool Lane - p402 N5
Portsea Place - p395 F6
Portsoken Street - p405 R7/S7
Portugal Street - p399 M6
Potier Street - p405 Q10
Powis Gardens - p394 A5
Powis Square - p394 A6
Powis Terrace - p394 A5
Pownall Row - p403 S2
Praed Street - p395 D6/E5
Pratt Walk - p401 M10
Prebend Street - p402 P1/2
Prescot Street - p405 S7
Primrose Street - p403 Q5/R5
Prince Consort Road - p397 D9
Princelet Street - p403 S5
Princes Gardens - p397 D9/E9
Prince's Square - p394 B6
Princes Street EC2 - p404 P6/Q6
Princes Street W1 - p398 H6
Princeton Street - p399 M5
Prioress Street - p405 Q10
Priory Green - p399 M2
Priory Walk - p396 C11
Procter Street - p399 M5
Provost Street - p403 Q3
Pudding Lane - p405 Q7
Purbrook Street - p405 R10
Purcell Street - p403 R2
Purchese Street - p399 K2

Quaker Street - p403 S5
Queen Anne Mews - p398 H5
Queen Anne Street - p398 H5
Queen Anne's Gate - p401 K9
Queen Elizabeth Street - p405 R9
Queen Square - p399 L4
Queen Street EC4 - p404 P6/7
Queen Street W1 - p400 H7
Queen Victoria Street - p404 O7/P6/7
Queen's Gardens - p394 C6
Queens Gate - p397 D9/10
Queen's Gate Gardens - p396 C10
Queens Gate Mews - p396 C9
Queen's Gate Place Mews - p397 D10
Queen's Gate Terrace - p396 C9, p397 D9
Queen's Walk - p400 J8
Queensborough Terrace - p394 C6/7
Queensbridge Road - p403 S1/2
Queensbury Place - p397 D10
Queensway - p394 B5/6/C6/7
Quilter Street - p403 S3

Racton Road - p396 A12
Radley Mews - p396 B10
Radnor Mews - p395 E6
Radnor Place - p395 E6
Radnor Street - p402 P4
Radnor Walk - p397 F11/12
Railway Approach - p405 Q8
Railway Street - p399 L2
Raleigh Street - p402 O2
Ramillies Place - p398 J6

Ramillies Street - p398 J6
Rampayne Street - p401 K11
Randall Road - p401 L11
Randall Row - p401 L11
Randolph Road - p394 C4, p395 D4
Ranelagh Grove - p400 G11
Ranston Street - p395 E4
Raphael Street - p397 F9
Rathbone Place - p399 K5
Rathbone Street - p398 J5
Ravenscroft Street - p403 S3
Ravent Road - p401 M10/11
Rawlings Street - p397 F10
Rawstone Street - p402 O3
Raymond Buildings - p399 M5
Red Lion Square - p399 M5
Red Lion Street - p399 M5
Redan Place - p394 B6
Redburn Street - p397 F12
Redchurch Street - p403 R4/S4
Redcliffe Gardens - p396 B11/C12
Redcliffe Mews - p396 C12
Redcliffe Place - p396 C12
Redcliffe Road - p396 C12
Redcliffe Square - p396 B11/C11
Redcliffe Street - p396 C12
Redcross Way - p404 P8/9
Redesdale Street - p397 F12
Redfield Lane - p396 B10
Redhill Street - p398 H2/3
Reece Mews - p397 D10
Reeves Mews - p400 G7
Regan Way - p403 R2/3
Regency Street - p401 K10/11
Regent Square - p399 L3
Regent Street - p398 J6, p400 J6/7, p401 K7
Remnant Street - p399 M6
Rennie Street - p404 N7
Rewell Street - p396 C13
Rheidol Terrace - p402 P2
Richmond Avenue - p402 N1
Richmond Crescent - p402 N1
Richmond Terrace - p401 L8
Ridgmount Gardens - p399 K4/5
Ridgmount Street - p399 K5
Riding House Street - p398 J5
Riley Road - p405 R9/10
Riley Street - p397 D13
Ripplevale Grove - p402 N1
Risbor Street - p404 O8
Ritchie Street - p402 N2
River Street - p402 N3
Rivington Street - p403 R4
Robert Adam Street - p398 G5
Robert Street - p398 H3/J3
Rochester Row - p400 J10
Rockingham Street - p404 O10/P10
Rodmarton Street - p398 G5
Rodney Street - p399 M2
Roger Street - p399 M4
Roland Gardens - p396 C11, p397 D11
Romilly Street - p399 K6
Romney Street - p401 K10
Rood Lane - p405 Q7
Ropemaker Street - p403 Q5
Ropley Street - p403 S3
Rosary Gardens - p396 C11
Rose Street - p401 L7
Rosebery Avenue - p402 N3/4
Rosemoor Street - p397 F10
Rotary Street - p404 O9
Rotherfield Street - p402 P1, p403 Q1
Rothesay Street - p405 Q10
Rotten Row - p395 E8/F8
Roupell Street - p404 N8
Royal Avenue - p397 F11
Royal Hospital Road - p397 F11/12
Royal Mint Street - p405 S7
Royal Street - p401 M9
Rugby Street - p399 M4
Rumbold Road - p396 B13
Rupert Street - p401 K6/7
Rushworth Street - p404 O9
Russell Square - p399 L4/5
Russell Street - p399 L6, p401 L6
Russia Row - p404 P6
Rutherford Street - p401 K10
Rutland Gate - p397 E9
Rutland Street - p397 E9

Sackville Street - p400 J7
Saffron Hill - p402 N5
Sail Street - p401 M10
St Albans Grove - p396 B9/C9
St Alban's Street - p401 K7
St Alphage Gardens - p402 P9
St Andrews Hill - p404 O6
St Andrew's Place - p398 H4
St Anne's Court - p399 K6
St Anne's Street - p401 K9/10
St Botolph Street - p405 R6
St Bride Street - p404 N6
St Chad's Place - p399 L3/M3
St Chad's Street - p399 L3
St Christopher's Place - p398 H6

St Clement's Lane - p399 M6
St Cross Street - p402 N5
St Dunstens Hill - p405 Q7
St George Street - p398 H6, p400 H6
St George's Circus - p404 N9
St George's Drive - p400 H11/J11
St George's Fields - p395 E6/F6
St George's Road - p404 N10/O10
St Giles High Street - p399 K6
St Helen's Place - p405 R6
St James's Place - p400 J8
St James's Square - p400 J7/8
St James's Street - p400 J8
St John Street - p402 O3/4/5
St John's Lane - p402 O4/5
St John's Square - p402 O4/5
St Katherine's Way - p405 S8
St Leonard's Terrace - p397 F11
St Loo Avenue - p397 F12
St Lukes Road - p394 A5
St Luke's Street - p397 E11
St Mark Street - p405 S7
St Martin's Lane - p401 L7
St Mary At Hill - p405 Q7
St Mary Axe - p405 R6
St Mary's Square - p395 D5
St Mary's Terrace - p395 D4
St Matthews Row - p403 S4
St Michael's Street - p395 E5
St Pancras Road - p399 K2
St Paul Street - p402 P1/2
St Paul's Churchyard - p404 O6
St Peters Street - p402 O2
St Petersburgh Mews - p394 B6/7
St Petersburgh Place - p394 B6/7
St Swithins Lane - p405 Q6/7
St Thomas Street - p405 Q8/9
St Vincent Street - p398 G5
Salamanca Street - p401 L11
Sale Place - p395 E5
Salem Road - p394 B6
Salisbury Place - p395 F5
Salisbury Street - p395 E4
Sandell Street - p404 N8
Sandland Street - p399 M5
Sandwich Street - p399 L3
Sans Walk - p402 N4
Savile Row - p400 J7
Savoy Place - p401 L7/M7
Savoy Street - p401 M7
Sawyer Street - p404 O8/9
Scala Street - p398 J5
Scarsdale Villas - p396 A10/B9
Sclater Street - p403 S4
Scores Street - p404 O8
Scott Lidgett Crescent - p405 S10
Scriven Street - p403 S3
Scrutton Street - p403 Q4/R4
Seacoal Lane - p404 O6
Seaford Street - p399 L3
Seagrave Road - p396 B12
Searles Close - p397 E13
Sebastian Street - p402 O3
Sebbon Street - p402 O1
Sedlescombe Road - p396 A12
Seething Lane - p405 R7
Sekforde Street - p402 O4
Selwood Terrace - p397 D11
Semley Place - p400 G11/H11
Senior Street - p394 B4
Serle Street - p399 M6
Serpentine Road - p395 E8/F8
Seven Dials - p399 L6
Seward Street - p402 O4/P4
Seymour Place - p395 F5/6
Seymour Street - p398 F6
Seymour Walk - p396 C12
Shad Thames - p405 R8/S9
Shaftesbury Avenue - p401 K6/7/L6
Shaftesbury Street - p402 P2
Shalcomb Street - p397 D12
Shand Street - p405 Q9/R8
Shanfield Street - p397 E11/F12
Sheffield Terrace - p394 A8/B8
Sheldrake Place - p394 A8
Shelton Street - p399 L6
Shenfield Street - p403 R3
Shepherd Street - p400 H8
Shepherdess Walk - p402 P2/3
Shepherds Market - p400 H8
Shepperton Road - p402 P1, p403 Q1
Sherborne Street - p403 Q1
Sherwood Street - p400 J7
Shipton Street - p403 S3
Shoe Lane - p404 N5/6
Shoreditch High Street - p403 R4/5
Shorrolds Road - p396 A13
Shorter Street - p405 R7/S7
Shorts Gardens - p399 L6
Shottendene Road - p396 A13
Shouldham Street - p395 F5
Shrewsbury Road - p394 A5
Shroton Street - p395 E4
Shrubland Road - p403 S1
Sicilian Avenue - p399 L5
Siddons Lane - p395 F4
Sidford Place - p401 M10

Sidmouth Street - p399 L3/M3
Silex Street - p404 O9
Silk Street - p402 P5
Skinner Street - p402 N4/O4
Skinners Lane - p404 P7
Slaidburn Street - p396 C12/13
Sloane Avenue - p397 E10/F11
Sloane Gardens - p400 G11
Sloane Street - p397 F9/10
Smith Square - p401 K10/L10
Smith Street - p397 F11/12
Smith Terrace - p397 F11
Snowden Street - p403 R5
Snowsfields - p405 Q9
Soho Square - p399 K6
Soho Street - p399 K6
Somers Crescent - p395 E6
Soton Place - p399 L5
South Audley Street - p400 G7
South Carriage Drive - p395 E8/F8/G8
South Crescent - p399 K5
South Eaton Place - p400 G10
South End Row - p396 B9
South Molton Lane - p398 H6
South Molton Street - p398 H6
South Parade - p397 D11
South Place - p403 Q5
South Street - p400 G7
South Terrace - p397 E10
South Wharf Road - p395 D5/E5
Southampton Row - p399 L5
Southampton Street - p401 L7
Southgate Grove - p403 Q1
Southgate Road - p403 Q1
Southwark Bridge - p404 P7
Southwark Bridge Road - p404 O9/10/P7/8
Southwick Street - p395 E5/6
Spa Road - p405 S10
Spencer Street - p402 O3
Spital Square - p403 R5
Spital Street - p403 S5
Sprimont Place - p397 F11
Spring Street - p395 D6
Spur Road - p400 J9
Spurgeon Street - p404 P10
Stableyard Road - p400 J8
Stacey Street - p399 K6
Stafford Place - p400 J9
Stafford Terrace - p396 A9
Stag Place - p400 J9
Stamford Street - p404 N8
Stanford Road - p396 B9
Stanford Street - p400 J11
Stanhope Gardens - p396 C10, p397 D10
Stanhope Mews East - p397 D10
Stanhope Mews West - p396 C10
Stanhope Place - p395 F6
Stanhope Street - p398 J3
Stanhope Terrace - p395 E6
Stanway Street - p403 R2/3
Staple Street - p405 Q9
Star Street - p395 E5
Station Road - p401 M9
Stean Street - p403 R1
Stephen Street - p399 K5
Stephenson Way - p398 J3/4
Steward Street - p403 R5
Stewart's Grove - p397 E11
Stillington Street - p400 J10
Stone Buildings - p399 M6
Stone Street - p404 N6
Stones End Street - p404 O9
Stoney Lane - p405 R6
Stoney Street - p404 P8
Store Street - p399 K5
Storey's Gate - p401 K9
Stourcliffe Street - p395 F6
Strand - p401 L7/M6/7
Stratford Place - p398 H6
Stratford Road - p396 B10
Strathearn Place - p395 E6
Stratton Street - p400 H7/8
Streatham Street - p399 K5/L5
Stukeley Street - p399 L6
Sturge Street - p404 O9
Sturt Street - p402 P2
Suffolk Street - p401 K7
Sumner Place - p397 D10/11
Sumner Street - p404 O8/P8
Sun Street - p403 Q5
Surrey Row - p404 O8/9
Surrey Street - p401 M6/7
Sussex Gardens - p395 E5/6
Sussex Place - p395 E6
Sussex Square - p395 D6/E6
Sutherland Avenue - p394 B4
Sutherland Place - p394 A5/6
Sutton Row - p399 K6
Swallow Street - p400 J7
Swan Street - p404 P9
Swan Walk - p397 F12
Swanfield Street - p403 S4
Sweeney Court - p405 S10

Swinton Street - p399 M3
Sydney Close - p397 E11
Sydney Place - p397 E11
Sydney Street - p397 E11
Symons Street - p397 F11

Tabard Street - p404 P9/Q10
Tabernacle Street - p403 Q4
Tachbrook Street - p400 J11
Tadema Road - p396 C13
Talbot Road - p394 A5/B5
Talbot Square - p395 D6
Tamworth Farm Lane - p396 A12
Tanner Street - p405 R9
Taplow Street - p402 P3
Tavistock Crescent - p394 A5
Tavistock Place - p399 L4
Tavistock Road - p394 A5
Tavistock Square - p399 K4
Tavistock Street - p401 L6/7
Taviton Street - p399 K4
Tedworth Square - p397 F12
Temple Avenue - p404 N7
Temple Place - p401 M7
Tennis Street - p404 P9
Tetcott Road - p396 C13
Thanet Street - p399 L3
Thaxton Road - p396 A12
Thayer Street - p398 G5
The Boltons - p396 C11
The Broad Walk - p394 C7/8
The Cut - p404 N8
The Grange - p405 R10
The Little Boltons - p396 C11
The Mall - p401 J8/K8
The Vale - p397 D12
Theberton Street - p402 N1/O1
Theed Street - p404 N8
Theobald's Road - p399 L5/M5
Thirleby Road - p400 J10
Thomas More Street - p405 S8
Thorn Place - p395 F5
Thorndike Close - p396 C13
Thorney Crescent - p397 E13
Thorney Street - p401 L10
Thornhill Road - p402 N1
Thrale Street - p404 P8
Threadneedle Street - p405 Q6
Three Kings Yard - p400 H6
Throgmorton Avenue - p405 Q6
Throgmorton Street - p405 Q6
Thurloe Place - p397 E10
Thurloe Square - p397 E10
Thurtle Road - p403 S2
Tilney Street - p400 G7
Tinworth Street - p401 L11
Tite Street - p397 F12
Tiverton Street - p404 O10
Tolpuddle Street - p402 N2
Tonbridge Street - p399 L3
Tooley Street - p405 Q8/R8/9
Tor Gardens - p394 A8
Torrington Place - p399 K4
Torrington Square - p399 K4
Tothill Street - p401 K9
Tottenham Court Road - p398 J4, p399 K5
Tottenham Street - p398 J5
Tower Bridge - p405 R8
Tower Bridge Approach - p405 R8/S7
Tower Bridge Road - p405 Q10/R8/9/10
Tower Hill - p405 R7
Tower Street - p399 K6
Toynbee Street - p405 S5/6
Trafalgar Square - p401 K7
Transept Street - p395 E5
Trebovir Road - p396 B11
Tregunter Road - p396 C12
Trevor Place - p397 E9
Trinity Square - p405 R7
Trinity Street - p404 P9/10
Triton Square - p398 J4
Trump Street - p404 P6
Tryon Street - p397 F11
Tudor Street - p404 N6
Tufton Street - p401 K10
Turks Row - p397 F11, p400 G11
Turnmill Street - p402 N5/O5
Tyers Street - p401 M10
Tysoe Street - p402 N3

Ufford Street - p404 N9
Ufton Road - p403 Q1
Ulster Place - p398 H4
Undershaft - p405 Q6/R6
Underwood Street - p402 P3
Union Street - p404 O8/P8
Union Walk - p403 R3
University Street - p398 J4, p399 K4
Upcerne Road - p396 C13
Upper Belgrave Street - p400 G9
Upper Berkeley Street - p395 F6
Upper Brook Street - p400 G7
Upper Cheyne Row - p397 E12

Upper Ground - p404 N7/8
Upper Harley Street - p398 H4
Upper James Street - p400 J6
Upper Marsh - p401 M9
Upper Montagu Street - p395 F5
Upper Phillimore Gardens - p394 A8/9
Upper St Martin's Lane - p401 L6
Upper Street - p402 N2/O1/2
Upper Thames Street - p404 O7/P7
Upper Wimpole Street - p398 H5
Upper Woburn Place - p399 K3/4
Uverdale Road - p396 C13
Uxbridge Street - p394 A7

Vandon Street - p400 J9
Vanston Place - p396 A13
Varndell Street - p398 J3
Vaughan Way - p405 S7
Vauxhall Bridge Road - p400 J10/11, p401 K11
Vauxhall Street - p401 M11
Vauxhall Walk - p401 L11/M11
Venables Street - p395 E4
Vere Street - p398 H6
Vernon Rise - p399 M3
Verulam Street - p402 N5
Vicarage Gate - p394 B8
Victoria Embankment - p401 L7/8/M7, p404 N7
Victoria Garden Mews - p394 B7
Victoria Grove - p396 C9
Victoria Road - p394 C9/3 C9
Victoria Square - p400 H9
Victoria Street - p400 H10/J10/K9
Vigo Street - p400 J7
Villiers Street - p401 L7/8
Vincent Square - p400 J10/11, p401 K10/11
Vincent Street - p401 K10
Vincent Terrace - p402 O2
Vine Street - p400 J7
Virgil Street - p401 M10
Virginia Road - p403 R4/S3/4

Wakefield Street - p399 L3/4
Wakley Street - p402 O3
Walbrook - p404 P6/7
Walham Grove - p396 A13/B12
Walnut Tree Walk - p401 M10
Walpole Street - p397 F11
Walton Street - p397 E10/F10
Wandon Road - p396 C13
Wardour Street - p398 J6, p399 K6, p401 K7
Warner Street - p402 N4
Warren Street - p398 J4
Warwick Avenue - p394 C4, p395 D4/5
Warwick Crescent - p394 C5
Warwick Gardens - p396 A10
Warwick Lane - p404 O6
Warwick Place - p394 C4
Warwick Road - p396 A10/11/B11
Warwick Square - p400 J11
Warwick Street - p400 J7
Warwick Way - p400 H11/J11
Waterford Road - p396 B13
Waterloo Bridge - p401 M7
Waterloo Place - p401 K7/8
Waterloo Road - p401 M8, p404 N8/9
Waterloo Terrace - p402 O1
Watling Street - p404 P6
Watton Place - p397 F9
Waverton Street - p400 H7
Webb Street - p405 Q10
Webber Row - p404 N9
Webber Street - p404 N9/O9
Weighhouse Street - p398 G6/H6
Welbeck Street - p398 H5
Welbeck Way - p398 H5
Wellington Row - p403 S3
Wellington Square - p397 F11
Wellington Street - p401 L6/7
Wells Mews - p398 J5
Wells Street - p398 J5/6
Wenlock Road - p402 P2/3
Wenlock Street - p402 P2, p403 Q2
Wentworth Street - p405 R6/S6
Werrington Street - p399 K2/3
West Carriage Drive - p395 E7
West Central Street - p399 L6
West Cromwell Road - p396 A11
West Halkin Street - p400 G9
West Smithfield - p402 O5
West Square - p404 N10
West Street - p399 K6
West Tenter Street - p405 S7
Westbourne Crescent - p395 D6
Westbourne Park Road - p394 A5/B5
Westbourne Gardens - p394 B5
Westbourne Grove - p394 A6/B6
Westbourne Park Villas - p394 B5
Westbourne Street - p395 D6
Westbourne Terrace - p394 C5, p395 D6
Westgate Terrace - p396 B12

Westminster Bridge - p401 L9
Westminster Bridge Road - p401 M9, p404 N9
Westmoreland Street - p398 H5
Weston Rise - p399 M3
Weston Street - p405 Q9/10
Weston Street - p405 Q9
Westway A40 (M) - p394 A4/B5/C5
Wetherby Gardens - p396 C11
Weymouth Mews - p398 H5
Weymouth Street - p398 G5/H5
Weymouth Terrace - p403 S2/3
Wharf Road - p402 P2/3
Wharfedale Road - p399 L2/M2
Wharton Street - p399 M3
Wheeler Street - p403 R4/5
Whetstone Park - p399 M5
Whidborne Street - p399 L3
Whiskin Street - p402 O3
Whistlers Avenue - p397 D13/E13
Whiston Road - p403 R2/S2
Whitcomb Street - p401 K7
White Church Lane - p405 S6
White Horse Street - p400 H8
White Lion Hill - p404 O7
White Lion Street - p402 N2
Whitechapel High Street - p405 S6
Whitechapel Road - p405 S6
Whitecross Street - p402 P4/5
Whitefriars Street - p404 N6
Whitehall - p401 L8/9
Whitehall Place - p401 L8
Whiteheads Grove - p397 F11
White's Gardens - p405 Q9/R9
White's Row - p405 R5
Whitfield Street - p398 J4/5, p399 K5
Whitgift Street - p401 L11/M11
Whitmore Road - p403 R2
Whittlesey Street - p404 N8
Wicklow Street - p399 M3
Wigmore Place - p398 H5
Wigmore Street - p398 G6
Wild Court - p399 L6
Wild Street - p399 L6
Wild's Rent - p405 Q10
Wilfred Street - p400 J9
Wilkes Street - p403 S5
William IV Street - p401 L7
William Mews - p400 G9
William Road - p398 J3
William Street - p395 F8/9
Willow Place - p400 J10
Willow Street - p403 Q4
Wilmington Square - p402 N3/4
Wilson Street - p403 Q5
Wilton Crescent - p400 G9
Wilton Mews - p400 G9
Wilton Place - p400 G9
Wilton Road - p400 H10/J10
Wilton Row - p400 G9
Wilton Square - p403 Q1
Wilton Street - p400 H9
Wimbourne Street - p403 Q2
Wimpole Mews - p398 H5
Wimpole Street - p398 H5
Winchester Street - p400 H11
Windmill Street - p399 K5
Windsor Terrace - p402 P3
Winsland Street - p395 D5
Winsley Street - p398 J6
Woburn Place - p399 L4
Woburn Square - p399 K4
Woburn Walk - p399 K3
Wolseley Street - p405 S9
Wood Street - p404 P6
Woodbridge Street - p402 O4
Woodchester Square - p394 B4
Woodfall Street - p397 F11
Woods Mews - p400 G6/7
Woodseer Street - p403 S5
Woodstock Street - p398 H6
Wootton Street - p404 N8
Worfield Street - p397 E13
Worship Street - p403 Q4/5/R5
Wren Street - p399 M4
Wrights Lane - p396 B9
Wyclif Street - p402 O3
Wyndham Place - p395 F5
Wyndham Street - p395 F5
Wynford Road - p399 M2

Yardley Street - p402 N4
Yeoman's Row - p397 E10
York House Place - p394 B8
York Road - p401 M8/9
York Street - p395 F5, p398 G5
York Terrace East - p398 G4/H4
York Terrace West - p398 G4
York Way - p399 L2
Young Street - p394 B9, p396 B9

Zoar Street - p404 O8

Central London
by Area

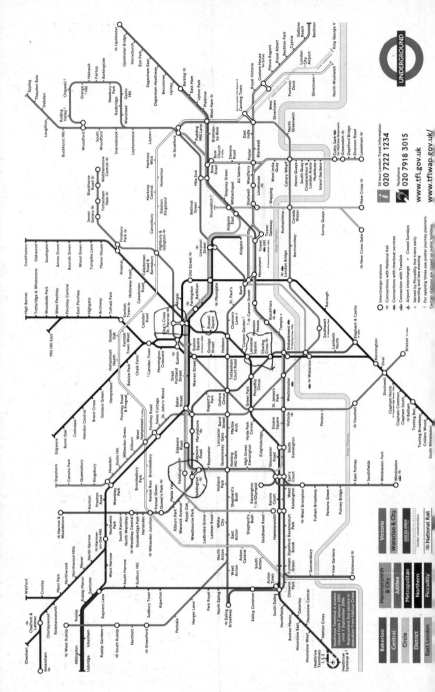